CAMBRIDGE LIBRAR

Books of enduring sch

C000060420

Classics

From the Renaissance to the nineteenth century, Latin and Greek were
compulsory subjects in almost all European universities, and most early
modern scholars published their research and conducted international
correspondence in Latin. Latin had continued in use in Western Europe long
after the fall of the Roman empire as the lingua franca of the educated classes
and of law, diplomacy, religion and university teaching. The flight of Greek
scholars to the West after the fall of Constantinople in 1453 gave impetus
to the study of ancient Greek literature and the Greek New Testament.
Eventually, just as nineteenth-century reforms of university curricula were
beginning to erode this ascendancy, developments in textual criticism and
linguistic analysis, and new ways of studying ancient societies, especially
archaeology, led to renewed enthusiasm for the Classics. This collection
offers works of criticism, interpretation and synthesis by the outstanding
scholars of the nineteenth century.

The Golden Bough: The Third Edition

This work by Sir James Frazer (1854–1941) is widely considered to be one of
the most important early texts in the fields of psychology and anthropology.
At the same time, by applying modern methods of comparative ethnography
to the classical world, and revealing the superstition and irrationality beneath
the surface of the classical culture which had for so long been a model for
Western civilisation, it was extremely controversial. Frazer was greatly
influenced by E.B. Tylor's *Primitive Culture* (also reissued in this series), and
by the work of the biblical scholar William Robertson Smith, to whom the
first edition is dedicated. The twelve-volume third edition, reissued here, was
greatly revised and enlarged, and published between 1911 and 1915; the two-
volume first edition (1890) is also available in this series. Volume 3 (1911) is
concerned with the concept of taboo, and its presence in all religious systems.

Cambridge University Press has long been a pioneer in the reissuing of out-of-print titles from its own backlist, producing digital reprints of books that are still sought after by scholars and students but could not be reprinted economically using traditional technology. The Cambridge Library Collection extends this activity to a wider range of books which are still of importance to researchers and professionals, either for the source material they contain, or as landmarks in the history of their academic discipline.

Drawing from the world-renowned collections in the Cambridge University Library and other partner libraries, and guided by the advice of experts in each subject area, Cambridge University Press is using state-of-the-art scanning machines in its own Printing House to capture the content of each book selected for inclusion. The files are processed to give a consistently clear, crisp image, and the books finished to the high quality standard for which the Press is recognised around the world. The latest print-on-demand technology ensures that the books will remain available indefinitely, and that orders for single or multiple copies can quickly be supplied.

The Cambridge Library Collection brings back to life books of enduring scholarly value (including out-of-copyright works originally issued by other publishers) across a wide range of disciplines in the humanities and social sciences and in science and technology.

The Golden Bough
The Third Edition

VOLUME 3:
TABOO AND THE PERILS OF THE SOUL

J.G. FRAZER

CAMBRIDGE
UNIVERSITY PRESS

CAMBRIDGE UNIVERSITY PRESS

Cambridge, New York, Melbourne, Madrid, Cape Town,
Singapore, São Paolo, Delhi, Mexico City

Published in the United States of America by Cambridge University Press, New York

www.cambridge.org
Information on this title: www.cambridge.org/9781108047326

© in this compilation Cambridge University Press 2012

This edition first published 1911
This digitally printed version 2012

ISBN 978-1-108-04732-6 Paperback

THE GOLDEN BOUGH

A STUDY IN MAGIC AND RELIGION

THIRD EDITION

PART II

TABOO

AND THE PERILS OF THE SOUL

MACMILLAN AND CO., Limited
LONDON · BOMBAY · CALCUTTA
MELBOURNE

THE MACMILLAN COMPANY
NEW YORK · BOSTON · CHICAGO
ATLANTA · SAN FRANCISCO

THE MACMILLAN CO. OF CANADA, Ltd.
TORONTO

TABOO

AND THE PERILS OF THE SOUL

BY

J. G. FRAZER, D.C.L., LL.D., Litt.D.

FELLOW OF TRINITY COLLEGE, CAMBRIDGE
PROFESSOR OF SOCIAL ANTHROPOLOGY IN THE UNIVERSITY OF LIVERPOOL

MACMILLAN AND CO., LIMITED
ST. MARTIN'S STREET, LONDON

1911

PREFACE

THE term Taboo is one of the very few words which the English language has borrowed from the speech of savages. In the Polynesian tongue, from which we have adopted it, the word designates a remarkable system which has deeply influenced the religious, social, and political life of the Oceanic islanders, both Polynesians and Melanesians, particularly by inculcating a superstitious veneration for the persons of nobles and the rights of private property. When about the year 1886 my ever-lamented friend William Robertson Smith asked me to write an article on Taboo for the Ninth Edition of the *Encyclopaedia Britannica*, I shared what I believe to have been at the time the current view of anthropologists, that the institution in question was confined to the brown and black races of the Pacific. But an attentive study of the accounts given of Taboo by observers who wrote while it still flourished in Polynesia soon led me to modify that view. The analogies which the system presents to the superstitions, not only of savages elsewhere, but of the civilised races of antiquity, were too numerous and too striking to be overlooked ; and I came to the conclusion that Taboo is only one of a number of similar systems of superstition which among many, perhaps among all races of men have contributed in large measure, under many different names and with many variations of detail, to build up the complex fabric of society in all the various sides or elements of it which we describe as religious, social, political, moral and economic. This conclusion I briefly indicated in my article. My general views on the subject were accepted by my friend Robertson Smith and applied by him in his celebrated *Lectures* to the elucidation of some aspects of Semitic religion. Since then the importance of Taboo and of systems like it in the evolution of religion and morality, of government and property, has been generally recognised and has indeed become a commonplace of anthropology.

The present volume is merely an expansion of the corresponding chapter in the first edition of *The Golden Bough*. It treats of the principles of taboo in their special application to sacred personages, such as kings and priests, who are the proper theme of the book. It does not profess to handle the subject as a whole, to pursue it into all its ramifications, to trace the manifold influences which systems of this sort have exerted in moulding the multitudinous forms of human society. A treatise which should adequately discuss these topics would far exceed the limits which I have prescribed for myself in *The Golden Bough*. For example, I have barely touched in passing on the part which these superstitions have played in shaping the moral ideas and directing the moral practice of mankind, a profound subject fraught perhaps with momentous issues for the time when men shall seriously set themselves to revise their ethical code in the light of its origin. For that the ethical like the legal code of a people stands in need of constant revision will hardly be disputed by any attentive and dispassionate observer. The old view that the principles of right and wrong are immutable and eternal is no longer tenable. The moral world is as little exempt as the physical world from the law of ceaseless change, of perpetual flux. Contemplate the diversities, the inconsistencies, the contradictions of the ethical ideas and the ethical practice, not merely of different peoples in different countries, but of the same people in the same country in different ages, then say whether the foundations of morality are eternally fixed and unchanging. If they seem so to us, as they have probably seemed to men in all ages who did not extend their views beyond the narrow limits of their time and country, it is in all likelihood merely because the rate of change is commonly so slow that it is imperceptible at any moment and can only be detected by a comparison of accurate observations extending over long periods of time. Such a comparison, could we make it, would probably convince us that if we speak of the moral law as immutable and eternal, it can only be in the relative or figurative sense in which we apply the same words to the outlines of the great mountains, by comparison with the short-lived generations of men. The mountains, too, are passing away, though we do not see it ; nothing is stable and abiding under or above the sun. We can as little arrest the process of moral evolution as we can stay the sweep of the tides or the courses of the stars.

Therefore, whether we like it or not, the moral code by which we regulate our conduct is being constantly revised and altered : old rules are being silently expunged and new rules silently inscribed in the palimpsest by the busy, the unresting hand of an invisible scribe. For unlike the public and formal revision of a legal code, the revision of the moral code is always private, tacit, and informal. The legislators who make and the judges who administer it are not clad in ermine and scarlet, their edicts are not proclaimed with the blare of trumpets and the pomp of heraldry. We ourselves are the lawgivers and the judges : it is the whole people who make and alter the ethical standard and judge every case by reference to it. We sit in the highest court of appeal, judging offenders daily, and we cannot if we would rid ourselves of the responsibility. All that we can do is to take as clear and comprehensive a view as possible of the evidence, lest from too narrow and partial a view we should do injustice, perhaps gross and irreparable injustice, to the prisoners at the bar. Few things, perhaps, can better guard us from narrowness and illiberality in our moral judgments than a survey of the amazing diversities of ethical theory and practice which have been recorded among the various races of mankind in different ages ; and accordingly the Comparative Method applied to the study of ethical phenomena may be expected to do for morality what the same method applied to religious phenomena is now doing for religion, by enlarging our mental horizon, extending the boundaries of knowledge, throwing light on the origin of current beliefs and practices, and thereby directly assisting us to replace what is effete by what is vigorous, and what is false by what is true. The facts which I have put together in this volume as well as in some of my other writings may perhaps serve as materials for a future science of Comparative Ethics. They are rough stones which await the master-builder, rude sketches which more cunning hands than mine may hereafter work up into a finished picture.

J. G. FRAZER.

CAMBRIDGE,
1st February 1911.

CONTENTS

CHAPTER V.—TABOOED THINGS   .   . Pp. 224-317

Chapter VI.—Tabooed Words . . Pp. 318-418

CHAPTER VII.—OUR DEBT TO THE SAVAGE

CHAPTER I

THE BURDEN OF ROYALTY

§ 1. *Royal and Priestly Taboos*

AT a certain stage of early society the king or priest is often thought to be endowed with supernatural powers or to be an incarnation of a deity, and consistently with this belief the course of nature is supposed to be more or less under his control, and he is held responsible for bad weather, failure of the crops, and similar calamities.[1] To some extent it appears to be assumed that the king's power over nature, like that over his subjects and slaves, is exerted through definite acts of will; and therefore if drought, famine, pestilence, or storms arise, the people attribute the misfortune to the negligence or guilt of their king, and punish him accordingly with stripes and bonds, or, if he remains obdurate, with deposition and death.[2] Sometimes, however, the course of nature, while regarded as dependent on the king, is supposed to be partly independent of his will. His person is considered, if we may express it so, as the dynamical centre of the universe, from which lines of force radiate to all quarters of the heaven; so that any motion of his—the turning of his head, the lifting of his hand—instantaneously affects and may seriously disturb some part of nature. He is the point of support on which hangs the balance of the world, and the slightest irregularity on his part may overthrow the delicate equipoise. The greatest care must, therefore, be taken both by and of him;

Life of divine kings and priests regulated by minute rules.

[1] See *The Magic Art and the Evolution of Kings*, vol. i. pp. 332 *sqq.*, 373 *sqq.*

[2] *The Magic Art and the Evolution of Kings*, vol. i. pp. 352 *sqq.*

and his whole life, down to its minutest details, must be so regulated that no act of his, voluntary or involuntary, may disarrange or upset the established order of nature. Of this class of monarchs the Mikado or Dairi, the spiritual emperor of Japan, is or rather used to be a typical example. He is an incarnation of the sun goddess, the deity who rules the universe, gods and men included; once a year all the gods wait upon him and spend a month at his court. During that month, the name of which means "without gods," no one frequents the temples, for they are believed to be deserted.[1] The Mikado receives from his people and assumes in his official proclamations and decrees the title of "manifest or incarnate deity" (*Akitsu Kami*) and he claims a general authority over the gods of Japan.[2] For example, in an

The Mikado or Dairi of Japan.

[1] *Manners and Customs of the Japanese in the Nineteenth Century: from recent Dutch Visitors to Japan, and the German of Dr. Ph. Fr. von Siebold* (London, 1841), pp. 141 *sqq.*

[2] W. G. Aston, *Shinto (the Way of the Gods)* (London, 1905), p. 41; Michel Revon, *Le Shintoïsme*, i. (Paris, 1907), pp. 189 *sqq.* The Japanese word for god or deity is *kami.* It is thus explained by the native scholar Motoöri, one of the chief authorities on Japanese religion: "The term *Kami* is applied in the first place to the various deities of Heaven and Earth who are mentioned in the ancient records as well as their spirits (*mi-tama*) which reside in the shrines where they are worshipped. Moreover, not only human beings, but birds, beasts, plants and trees, seas and mountains, and all other things whatsoever which deserve to be dreaded and revered for the extraordinary and pre-eminent powers which they possess, are called *Kami.* They need not be eminent for surpassing nobleness, goodness, or serviceableness alone. Malignant and uncanny beings are also called *Kami* if only they are the objects of general dread. Among *Kami* who are human beings I need hardly mention first of all the successive Mikados—with reverence be it spoken. . . . Then there have been numerous examples of divine human beings both in ancient and modern times, who, although not accepted by the nation generally, are treated as gods, each of his several dignity, in a single province, village, or family." Hirata, another native authority on Japanese religion, defines *kami* as a term which comprises all things strange, wondrous, and possessing *isao* or virtue. And a recent dictionary gives the following definitions : "*Kami.* 1. Something which has no form but is only spirit, has unlimited supernatural power, dispenses calamity and good fortune, punishes crime and rewards virtue. 2. Sovereigns of all times, wise and virtuous men, valorous and heroic persons whose spirits are prayed to after their death. 3. Divine things which transcend human intellect. 4. The Christian God, Creator, Supreme Lord." See W. G. Aston, *Shinto (the Way of the Gods)*, pp. 8-10, from which the foregoing quotations are made. Mr. Aston himself considers that "the deification of living Mikados was titular rather than real," and he adds: "I am not aware that any specific so-called miraculous powers were authoritatively claimed for them" (*op. cit.* p. 41). No doubt it is very difficult for the Western mind to put itself at the point of view of the Oriental and to seize the precise point (if it can be said to exist) where the divine fades into the human or the human brightens into the divine. In translating, as we must

official decree of the year 646 the emperor is described as
" the incarnate god who governs the universe." [1]

The following description of the Mikado's mode of life was written about two hundred years ago :—[2]

" Even to this day the princes descended of this family, more particularly those who sit on the throne, are looked upon as persons most holy in themselves, and as Popes by birth. And, in order to preserve these advantageous notions in the minds of their subjects, they are obliged to take an uncommon care of their sacred persons, and to do such things, which, examined according to the customs of other nations, would be thought ridiculous and impertinent. It will not be improper to give a few instances of it. He thinks that it would be very prejudicial to his dignity and holiness to touch the ground with his feet ; for this reason, when he intends to go anywhere, he must be carried thither on men's shoulders. Much less will they suffer that he should expose his sacred person to the open air, and the sun is not thought worthy to shine on his head. There is such a holiness ascribed to all the parts of his body that he dares to cut off neither his hair, nor his beard, nor his nails. However, lest he should grow too dirty, they may clean him in the night when he is asleep ; because, they say, that which is taken from his body at that time, hath been stolen from him, and that such a theft doth not prejudice his holiness or dignity. In ancient times, he was obliged to sit on the throne for some hours every morning, with the imperial crown on his head, but to sit altogether like a

Rules of life formerly observed by the Mikado.

---

do, the vague thought of a crude theology into the comparatively exact language of civilised Europe we must allow for a considerable want of correspondence between the two : we must leave between them, as it were, a margin of cloudland to which in the last resort the deity may retreat from the too searching light of philosophy and science.

[1] M. Revon, *op. cit.* i. 190 n.[2]

[2] Kaempfer, " History of Japan," in Pinkerton's *Voyages and Travels,* vii. 716 *sq.* However, Mr. W. G. Aston tells us that Kaempfer's statements regarding the sacred character of

the Mikado's person cannot be depended on (*Shinto, the Way of the Gods*, p. 41, note†). M. Revon quotes Kaempfer's account with the observation that, "*les naïvetés recèlent plus d'une idée juste*" (*Le Shintoïsme*, vol. i. p. 191, note [2]). To me it seems that Kaempfer's description is very strongly confirmed by its close correspondence in detail with the similar customs and superstitions which have prevailed in regard to sacred personages in many other parts of the world and with which it is most unlikely that Kaempfer was acquainted. This correspondence will be brought out in the following pages.

Rules
of life
formerly
observed
by the
Mikado.

statue, without stirring either hands or feet, head or eyes, nor indeed any part of his body, because, by this means, it was thought that he could preserve peace and tranquillity in his empire ; for if, unfortunately, he turned himself on one side or the other, or if he looked a good while towards any part of his dominions, it was apprehended that war, famine, fire, or some other great misfortune was near at hand to desolate the country. But it having been afterwards discovered, that the imperial crown was the palladium, which by its immobility [1] could preserve peace in the empire, it was thought expedient to deliver his imperial person, consecrated only to idleness and pleasures, from this burthensome duty, and therefore the crown is at present placed on the throne for some hours every morning. His victuals must be dressed every time in new pots, and served at table in new dishes : both are very clean and neat, but made only of common clay ; that without any considerable expense they may be laid aside, or broke, after they have served once. They are generally broke, for fear they should come into the hands of laymen, for they believe religiously, that if any layman should presume to eat his food out of these sacred dishes, it would swell and inflame his mouth and throat. The like ill effect is dreaded from the Dairi's sacred habits ; for they believe that if a layman should wear them, without the Emperor's express leave or command, they would occasion swellings and pains in all parts of his body." To the same effect an earlier account of the Mikado says : "It was considered as a shameful degradation for him even to touch the ground with his foot. The sun and moon were not even permitted to shine upon his head. None of the superfluities of the body were ever taken from him, neither his hair, his beard, nor his nails were cut. Whatever he eat was dressed in new vessels." [2]

---

[1] In Pinkerton's reprint this word appears as "mobility." I have made the correction from a comparison with the original (Kaempfer, *History of Japan*, translated from the original Dutch manuscript by J. G. Scheuchzer, London, 1728, vol. i. p. 150).

[2] Caron, "Account of Japan," in Pinkerton's *Voyages and Travels*, vii.

613. Compare B. Varenius, *Descriptio regni Japoniae et Siam* (Cambridge, 1673), p. 11 : "*Nunquam attingebant (quemadmodum et hodie id observat) pedes ipsius terram : radiis Solis caput nunquam illustrabatur : in apertum aërem non procedebat,*" etc. The first edition of this book was published by Elzevir at Amsterdam in 1649. The

Similar priestly or rather divine kings are found, at a Rules
of life
observed
by kings
and priests
in Africa
and
America. lower level of barbarism, on the west coast of Africa. At Shark Point near Cape Padron, in Lower Guinea, lives the priestly king Kukulu, alone in a wood. He may not touch a woman nor leave his house; indeed he may not even quit his chair, in which he is obliged to sleep sitting, for if he lay down no wind would arise and navigation would be stopped. He regulates storms, and in general maintains a wholesome and equable state of the atmosphere.[1]   On Mount Agu in Togo, a German possession in West Africa, there lives a fetish or spirit called Bagba, who is of great importance for the whole of the surrounding country. The power of giving or withholding rain is ascribed to him, and he is lord of the winds, including the Harmattan, the dry, hot wind which blows from the interior. His priest dwells in a house on the highest peak of the mountain, where he keeps the winds bottled up in huge jars. Applications for rain, too, are made to him, and he does a good business in amulets, which consist of the teeth and claws of leopards. Yet though his power is great and he is indeed the real chief of the land, the rule of the fetish forbids him ever to leave the mountain, and he must spend the whole of his life on its summit. Only once a year may he come down to make purchases in the market; but even then he may not set foot in the hut of any mortal man, and must return to his place of exile the same day. The business of government in the villages is conducted by subordinate chiefs, who are appointed by him.[2] In the West African kingdom of Congo there was a supreme pontiff called Chitomé or Chitombé, whom the negroes regarded as a god on earth and all-powerful in heaven. Hence before they would taste the new crops they offered him the first-fruits, fearing that manifold misfortunes would befall them if they broke this rule. When he left his residence to visit other places within his jurisdiction, all married people had to observe strict continence the whole time he was out;

Geographia Generalis of the same writer had the honour of appearing in an edition revised and corrected by Isaac Newton (Cambridge, at the University Press, 1672).
[1] A. Bastian, Die deutsche Expedi-
tion an der Loango-Küste (Jena, 1874-75), i. 287 sq., compare pp. 353 sq.
[2] H. Klose, Togo unter deutscher Flagge (Berlin, 1899), pp. 189, 268.

Rules of
life ob-
served by
kings and
priests in
Africa and
America. for it was supposed that any act of incontinence would prove fatal to him. And if he were to die a natural death, they thought that the world would perish, and the earth, which he alone sustained by his power and merit, would immediately be annihilated.[1] Similarly in Humbe, a kingdom of Angola, the incontinence of young people under the age of puberty used to be a capital crime, because it was believed to entail the death of the king within the year. Of late the death penalty has been commuted for a fine of ten oxen inflicted on each of the culprits. This commutation has attracted thousands of dissolute youth to Humbe from the neighbouring tribes, among whom the old penalty is still rigorously exacted.[2] Amongst the semi-barbarous nations of the New World, at the date of the Spanish conquest, there were found hierarchies or theocracies like those of Japan ;[3] in particular, the high pontiff of the Zapotecs in Southern Mexico appears to have presented a close parallel to the Mikado. A powerful rival to the king him-self, this spiritual lord governed Yopaa, one of the chief cities of the kingdom, with absolute dominion. It is impossible, we are told, to overrate the reverence in which he was held. He was looked on as a god whom the earth was not worthy to hold nor the sun to shine upon. He profaned his sanctity if he even touched the ground with his foot. The officers who bore his palanquin on their shoulders were members of the highest families ; he hardly deigned to look on anything around him ; and all who met him fell with their faces to the earth, fearing that death would over-take them if they saw even his shadow. A rule of continence was regularly imposed on the Zapotec priests, especially upon the high pontiff ; but " on certain days in each year, which were generally celebrated with feasts and dances, it was customary for the high priest to become drunk. While in this state, seeming to belong neither to heaven nor to earth, one of the most beautiful of the virgins consecrated to the service of the gods was brought to him." If the child

[1] J. B. Lahat, *Relation historique de l'Éthiopie occidentale* (Paris, 1732), i. 254 *sqq.*

[2] Ch. Wunenberger, "La Mission et le royaume de Humbé, sur les bords du Cunène," *Missions Catholiques,* xx. (1888) p. 262.

[3] See *The Magic Art and the Evolution of Kings,* vol. i. pp. 415 *sq.*

she bore him was a son, he was brought up as a prince of
the blood, and the eldest son succeeded his father on the
pontifical throne.[1] The supernatural powers attributed to
this pontiff are not specified, but probably they resembled
those of the Mikado and Chitomé.

Wherever, as in Japan and West Africa, it is supposed *The rules*
that the order of nature, and even the existence of the world, *of life*
is bound up with the life of the king or priest, it is clear *imposed*
that he must be regarded by his subjects as a source both of *on kings in*
infinite blessing and of infinite danger. On the one hand, *early*
the people have to thank him for the rain and sunshine *society are*
which foster the fruits of the earth, for the wind which *intended*
brings ships to their coasts, and even for the solid ground *to preserve*
beneath their feet. But what he gives he can refuse ; *their lives*
and so close is the dependence of nature on his person, so *for the*
delicate the balance of the system of forces whereof he is the *good of*
centre, that the least irregularity on his part may set up a *their*
tremor which shall shake the earth to its foundations. And *people.*
if nature may be disturbed by the slightest involuntary act of
the king, it is easy to conceive the convulsion which his death
might provoke. The natural death of the Chitomé, as we
have seen, was thought to entail the destruction of all things.
Clearly, therefore, out of a regard for their own safety, which
might be imperilled by any rash act of the king, and still more
by his death, the people will exact of their king or priest
a strict conformity to those rules, the observance of which is
deemed necessary for his own preservation, and consequently
for the preservation of his people and the world. The idea
that early kingdoms are despotisms in which the people
exist only for the sovereign, is wholly inapplicable to the
monarchies we are considering. On the contrary, the
sovereign in them exists only for his subjects ; his life is
only valuable so long as he discharges the duties of his
position by ordering the course of nature for his people's
benefit. So soon as he fails to do so, the care, the devotion,
the religious homage which they had hitherto lavished on
him cease and are changed into hatred and contempt ; he is

---

[1] Brasseur de Bourbourg, *Histoire des*   Bancroft, *Native Races of the Pacific*
nations civilisées du Mexique et de   *States,* ii. 142 *sq.*
l'Amérique-centrale, iii. 29 *sq.*; H. H.

dismissed ignominiously, and may be thankful if he escapes with his life. Worshipped as a god one day, he is killed as a criminal the next. But in this changed behaviour of the people there is nothing capricious or inconsistent. On the contrary, their conduct is entirely of a piece. If their king is their god, he is or should be also their preserver; and if he will not preserve them, he must make room for another who will. So long, however, as he answers their expectations, there is no limit to the care which they take of him, and which they compel him to take of himself. A king of this sort lives hedged in by a ceremonious etiquette, a network of prohibitions and observances, of which the intention is not to contribute to his dignity, much less to his comfort, but to restrain him from conduct which, by disturbing the harmony of nature, might involve himself, his people, and the universe in one common catastrophe. Far from adding to his comfort, these observances, by trammelling his every act, annihilate his freedom and often render the very life, which it is their object to preserve, a burden and sorrow to him.

Taboos observed by African kings.

Of the supernaturally endowed kings of Loango it is said that the more powerful a king is, the more taboos is he bound to observe; they regulate all his actions, his walking and his standing, his eating and drinking, his sleeping and waking.[1] To these restraints the heir to the throne is subject from infancy; but as he advances in life the number of abstinences and ceremonies which he must observe increases, "until at the moment that he ascends the throne he is lost in the ocean of rites and taboos."[2] In the crater of an extinct volcano, enclosed on all sides by grassy slopes, lie the scattered huts and yam-fields of Riabba, the capital of the native king of Fernando Po. This mysterious being lives in the lowest depths of the crater, surrounded by a harem of forty women, and covered, it is said, with old silver coins. Naked savage as he is, he yet exercises far more influence in the island than the Spanish governor at Santa Isabel. In him the conservative spirit of the Boobies or aboriginal inhabitants of the island is, as it were, incor-

---

[1] A. Bastian, *Die deutsche Expedition an der Loango-Küste*, i. 355.

[2] O. Dapper, *Description de l'Afrique* (Amsterdam, 1686), p. 336.

porate. He has never seen a white man and, according to the firm conviction of all the Boobies, the sight of a pale face would cause his instant death. He cannot bear to look upon the sea ; indeed it is said that he may never see it even in the distance, and that therefore he wears away his life with shackles on his legs in the dim twilight of his hut. Certain it is that he has never set foot on the beach. With the exception of his musket and knife, he uses nothing that comes from the whites ; European cloth never touches his person, and he scorns tobacco, rum, and even salt.[1]

Among the Ewe-speaking peoples of the Slave Coast, in West Africa, "the king is at the same time high priest. In this quality he was, particularly in former times, unapproachable by his subjects. Only by night was he allowed to quit his dwelling in order to bathe and so forth. None but his representative, the so-called 'visible king,' with three chosen elders might converse with him, and even they had to sit on an ox-hide with their backs turned to him. He might not see any European nor any horse, nor might he look upon the sea, for which reason he was not allowed to quit his capital even for a few moments. These rules have been disregarded in recent times."[2]   The king of Dahomey himself is subject to the prohibition of beholding the sea,[3] and so are the kings of Loango[4] and Great Ardra in Guinea.[5]   The sea is the fetish of the Eyeos, to the north-west of Dahomey, and they and their king are threatened with death by their priests if ever they dare to look on it.[6]   It is believed that the king of Cayor in Senegal would infallibly die within the year if he were to cross a river or an arm of the sea.[7]   In Mashonaland down to recent times the chiefs would not cross certain rivers, particularly the Rurikwi and the Nyadiri ; and the

[margin notes:] Taboos observed by African kings.

Prohibition to see the sea.

[1] O. Baumann, *Eine afrikanische Tropen-Insel, Fernando Póo und die Bube* (Wien und Olmütz, 1888), pp. 103 *sq.*

[2] G. Zündel, "Land und Volk der Eweer auf der Sclavenküste in Westafrika," *Zeitschrift der Gesellschaft für Erdkunde zu Berlin*, xii. (1877) p. 402.

[3] Béraud, "Note sur le Dahomé," *Bulletin de la Société de Géographie* (Paris), Vme Série, xii. (1866) p. 377.

[4] A. Bastian, *Die deutsche Expedition an der Loango-Küste*, i. 263.

[5] Bosman's "Guinea," in Pinkerton's *Voyages and Travels*, xvi. 500.

[6] A. Dalzell, *History of Dahomey* (London, 1793), p. 15 ; Th. Winterbottom, *An Account of the Native Africans in the Neighbourhood of Sierra Leone* (London, 1803), pp. 229 *sq.*

[7] J. B. L. Durand, *Voyage au Sénégal* (Paris, 1802), p. 55.

custom was still strictly observed by at least one chief within the last few years. "On no account will the chief cross the river. If it is absolutely necessary for him to do so, he is blindfolded and carried across with shouting and singing. Should he walk across, he will go blind or die and certainly lose the chieftainship."[1] So among the Mahafalys and Sakalavas in the south of Madagascar some kings are

Horror of the sea.

forbidden to sail on the sea or to cross certain rivers.[2] The horror of the sea is not peculiar to kings. The Basutos are said to share it instinctively, though they have never seen salt water, and live hundreds of miles from the Indian Ocean.[3] The Egyptian priests loathed the sea, and called it the foam of Typhon ; they were forbidden to set salt on their table, and they would not speak to pilots because they got their living by the sea ; hence too they would not eat fish, and the hieroglyphic symbol for hatred was a fish.[4] When the Indians of the Peruvian Andes were sent by the Spaniards to work in the hot valleys of the coast, the vast ocean which they saw before them as they descended the Cordillera was dreaded by them as a cause of disease ; hence they prayed to it that they might not fall ill. This they all did without exception, even the little children.[5] Similarly the inland people of Lampong in Sumatra are said to pay a kind of adoration to the sea, and to make it an offering of cakes and sweetmeats when they behold it for the first time, deprecating its power of doing them mischief.[6]

Taboos observed by chiefs among the Sakalavas and the hill tribes of Assam.

Among the Sakalavas of southern Madagascar the chief is regarded as a sacred being, but "he is held in leash by a crowd of restrictions, which regulate his behaviour like that of the emperor of China. He can undertake nothing whatever unless the sorcerers have declared the omens favourable : he may not eat warm food : on certain days he may not quit

[1] W. S. Taberer (Chief Native Commissioner for Mashonaland), "Mashonaland Natives," *Journal of the African Society*, No. 15 (April 1905), p. 320.

[2] A. van Gennep, *Tabou et totémisme à Madagascar* (Paris, 1904), p. 113.

[3] Father Porte, "Les Réminiscences d'un missionnaire du Basutoland," *Missions Catholiques*, xxviii. (1896) p. 235.

[4] Plutarch, *Isis et Osiris*, 32.

[5] P. J. de Arriaga, *Extirpacion de la idolatria del Piru* (Lima, 1621), pp. 11, 132.

[6] W. Marsden, *History of Sumatra* (London, 1811), p. 301.

his hut; and so on."[1]   Among some of the hill tribes of Assam both the headman and his wife have to observe many taboos in respect of food; thus they may not eat buffalo, pork, dog, fowl, or tomatoes.   The headman must be chaste, the husband of one wife, and he must separate himself from her on the eve of a general or public observance of taboo. In one group of tribes the headman is forbidden to eat in a strange village, and under no provocation whatever may he utter a word of abuse.   Apparently the people imagine that the violation of any of these taboos by a headman would bring down misfortune on the whole village.[2]

The ancient kings of Ireland, as well as the kings of the four provinces of Leinster, Munster, Connaught, and Ulster, were subject to certain quaint prohibitions or taboos, on the due observance of which the prosperity of the people and the country, as well as their own, was supposed to depend. Thus, for example, the sun might not rise on the king of Ireland in his bed at Tara, the old capital of Erin; he was forbidden to alight on Wednesday at Magh Breagh, to traverse Magh Cuillinn after sunset, to incite his horse at Fan-Chomair, to go in a ship upon the water the Monday after Bealltaine (May day), and to leave the track of his army upon Ath Maighne the Tuesday after All-Hallows. The king of Leinster might not go round Tuath Laighean left-hand-wise on Wednesday, nor sleep between the Dothair (Dodder) and the Duibhlinn[3] with his head inclining to one side, nor encamp for nine days on the plains of Cualann, nor travel the road of Duibhlinn on Monday, nor ride a dirty black-heeled horse across Magh Maistean.   The king of Munster was prohibited from enjoying the feast of Loch Lein from one Monday to another; from banqueting by night in the beginning of harvest before Geim at Leitreacha; from encamping for nine days upon the Siuir; and from holding a border meeting at Gabhran.   The king of

Taboos observed by Irish kings.

---

[1] A. van Gennep, *Tabou et toté-misme à Madagascar*, p. 113, quoting De Thuy, *Étude historique, géographi-que et ethnographique sur la province de Tuléar*, Notes, Rec., Expl., 1899, p. 104.

[2] T. C. Hodson, "The *genna* amongst the Tribes of Assam," *Journal of the Anthropological Institute*, xxxvi. (1906) p. 98.   The word for taboo among these tribes is *genna*.

[3] The Duibhlinn is the part of the Liffey on which Dublin now stands.

Connaught might not conclude a treaty respecting his ancient palace of Cruachan [1] after making peace on All-Hallows Day, nor go in a speckled garment on a grey speckled steed to the heath of Dal Chais, nor repair to an assembly of women at Seaghais, nor sit in autumn on the sepulchral mounds of the wife of Maine, nor contend in running with the rider of a grey one-eyed horse at Ath Gallta between two posts. The king of Ulster was forbidden to attend the horse fair at Rath Line among the youths of Dal Araidhe, to listen to the fluttering of the flocks of birds of Linn Saileach after sunset, to celebrate the feast of the bull of Daire-mic-Daire, to go into Magh Cobha in the month of March, and to drink of the water of Bo Neimhidh between two darknesses. If the kings of Ireland strictly observed these and many other customs, which were enjoined by immemorial usage, it was believed that they would never meet with mischance or misfortune, and would live for ninety years without experiencing the decay of old age; that no epidemic or mortality would occur during their reigns; and that the seasons would be favourable and the earth yield its fruit in abundance; whereas, if they set the ancient usages at naught, the country would be visited with plague, famine, and bad weather.[2]

The kings of Egypt were worshipped as gods,[3] and the routine of their daily life was regulated in every detail by precise and unvarying rules. "The life of the kings of Egypt," says Diodorus, "was not like that of other monarchs who are irresponsible and may do just what they choose; on the contrary, everything was fixed for them by law, not only their official duties, but even the details of their daily life. . . . The hours both of day and night were

---

[1] The site, marked by the remains of some earthen forts, is now known as Rathcroghan, near Belanagare in the county of Roscommon.

[2] *The Book of Rights*, edited with translation and notes by John O'Donovan (Dublin, 1847), pp. 3-8. This work, comprising a list both of the prohibitions (*urgharta* or *geasa*) and the prerogatives (*buadha*) of the Irish kings, is preserved in a number of manuscripts, of which the two oldest

date from 1390 and about 1418 respectively. The list is repeated twice, first in prose and then in verse. I have to thank my friend Professor Sir J. Rhys for kindly calling my attention to this interesting record of a long-vanished past in Ireland. As to these taboos, see P. W. Joyce, *Social History of Ancient Ireland*, i. 310 *sqq.*

[3] See *The Magic Art and the Evolution of Kings*, vol. i. pp. 418 *sqq.*

arranged at which the king had to do, not what he pleased, but what was prescribed for him. . . . For not only were the times appointed at which he should transact public business or sit in judgment; but the very hours for his walking and bathing and sleeping with his wife, and, in short, performing every act of life were all settled. Custom enjoined a simple diet; the only flesh he might eat was veal and goose, and he might only drink a prescribed quantity of wine."[1] However, there is reason to think that these rules were observed, not by the ancient Pharaohs, but by the priestly kings who reigned at Thebes and in Ethiopia at the close of the twentieth dynasty.[2] Among the Karen-nis of Upper Burma a chief attains his position, not by hereditary right, but on account of his habit of abstaining from rice and liquor. The mother, too, of a candidate for the chieftainship must have eschewed these things and lived solely on yams and potatoes so long as she was with child. During that time she may not eat any meat nor drink water from a common well. And if her son is to be qualified for the office of chief he must continue to observe these habits.[3]

Of the taboos imposed on priests we may see a striking example in the rules of life prescribed for the Flamen Dialis at Rome, who has been interpreted as a living image of Jupiter, or a human embodiment of the sky-spirit.[4] They were such as the following:—The Flamen Dialis might not ride or even touch a horse, nor see an army under arms,[5] nor wear a ring which was not broken, nor have a knot on any part of his garments; no fire except a sacred fire might be taken out of his house; he might not touch wheaten flour or leavened bread; he might not touch or even name a goat, a dog,[6] raw meat,

Taboos observed by the Flamen Dialis at Rome.

---

[1] Diodorus Siculus, i. 70.

[2] G. Maspero, *Histoire ancienne des peuples de l'Orient classique*, ii. 759, note 3; A. Moret, *Du caractère religieux de la royauté Pharaonique* (Paris, 1902), pp. 314-318.

[3] (Sir) J. G. Scott, *Gazetteer of Upper Burma and the Shan States*, part ii. vol. i. (Rangoon, 1901) p. 308.

[4] See *The Magic Art and the Evolution of Kings*, vol. ii. pp. 191 *sq.*

[5] Among the Gallas the king, who also acts as priest by performing sacrifices, is the only man who is not allowed to fight with weapons; he may not even ward off a blow. See Ph. Paulitschke, *Ethnographie Nordost-Afrikas: die geistige Cultur der Danâkil, Galla und Somâl*, p. 136.

[6] Among the Kafirs of the Hindoo Koosh men who are preparing to be headmen are considered ceremonially

Taboos observed by the Flamen Dialis.

beans,[1] and ivy ; he might not walk under a vine ; the feet of his bed had to be daubed with mud ; his hair could be cut only by a free man and with a bronze knife, and his hair and nails when cut had to be buried under a lucky tree ; he might not touch a dead body nor enter a place where one was burned ;[2] he might not see work being done on holy days ; he might not be uncovered in the open air ; if a man in bonds were taken into his house, the captive had to be unbound and the cords had to be drawn up through a hole in the roof and so let down into the street. His wife, the Flaminica, had to observe nearly the same rules, and others of her own besides. She might not ascend more than three steps of the kind of staircase called Greek ; at a certain festival she might not comb her hair ; the leather of her shoes might not be made from a beast that had died a natural death, but only from one that had been slain or sacrificed ; if she heard thunder she was tabooed till she had offered an expiatory sacrifice.[3]

Taboos observed by the Bodia of Sierra Leone.

Among the Grebo people of Sierra Leone there is a pontiff who bears the title of Bodia and has been compared, on somewhat slender grounds, to the high priest of the Jews. He is appointed in accordance with the behest of an oracle. At an elaborate ceremony of installation he is anointed, a

pure, and wear a semi-sacred uniform which must not be defiled by coming into contact with dogs. "The Kaneash [persons in this state of ceremonial purity] were nervously afraid of my dogs, which had to be fastened up whenever one of these august personages was seen to approach. The dressing has to be performed with the greatest care, in a place which cannot be defiled with dogs. Utah and another had convenient dressing-rooms on the top of their houses which happened to be high and isolated, but another of the four Kaneash had been compelled to erect a curious-looking square pen made of poles in front of his house, his own roof being a common thoroughfare " (Sir George Scott Robertson, *The Kafirs of the Hindu Kush* (London, 1898), p. 466).

[1] Similarly the Egyptian priests abstained from beans and would not even look at them. See Herodotus, ii. 37, with A. Wiedemann's note ; Plutarch, *Isis et Osiris*, 5.

[2] Similarly among the Kafirs of the Hindoo Koosh the high priest "may not traverse certain paths which go near the receptacles for the dead, nor may he visit the cemeteries. He may not go into the actual room where a death has occurred until after an effigy has been erected for the deceased. Slaves may cross his threshold, but must not approach the hearth " (Sir George Scott Robertson, *op. cit.* p. 416).

[3] Aulus Gellius, x. 15 ; Plutarch, *Quaest. Rom.* 109-112 ; Pliny, *Nat. Hist.* xxviii. 146 ; Servius on Virgil, *Aen.* i. 179, 448, iv. 518 ; Macrobius, *Saturn.* i. 16. 8 *sq.* ; Festus, p. 161 A, ed. C. O. Müller. For more details see J. Marquardt, *Römische Staatsverwaltung*, iii.[2] 326 *sqq.*

ring is put on his ankle as a badge of office, and the doorposts of his house are sprinkled with the blood of a sacrificed goat. He has charge of the public talismans and idols, which he feeds with rice and oil every new moon ; and he sacrifices on behalf of the town to the dead and to demons. Nominally his power is very great, but in practice it is very limited; for he dare not defy public opinion, and he is held responsible, even with his life, for any adversity that befalls the country. It is expected of him that he should cause the earth to bring forth abundantly, the people to be healthy, war to be driven far away, and witchcraft to be kept in abeyance. His life is trammelled by the observance of certain restrictions or taboos. Thus he may not sleep in any house but his own official residence, which is called the " anointed house " with reference to the ceremony of anointing him at inauguration. He may not drink water on the highway. He may not eat while a corpse is in the town, and he may not mourn for the dead. If he dies while in office, he must be buried at dead of night ; few may hear of his burial, and none may mourn for him when his death is made public. Should he have fallen a victim to the poison ordeal by drinking a decoction of sassywood, as it is called, he must be buried under a running stream of water.[1]

Among the Todas of Southern India the holy milkman (*palol*), who acts as priest of the sacred dairy, is subject to a variety of irksome and burdensome restrictions during the whole time of his incumbency, which may last many years. Thus he must live at the sacred dairy and may never visit his home or any ordinary village. He must be celibate ; if he is married he must leave his wife. On no account may any ordinary person touch the holy milkman or the holy dairy ; such a touch would so defile his holiness that he

Taboos observed by sacred milkmen among the Todas of South India.

---

[1] Sir Harry Johnston, *Liberia* (London, 1906), ii. 1076 *sq.*, quoting from Bishop Payne, who wrote " some fifty years ago." The Bodia described by Bishop Payne is clearly identical with the Bodio of the Grain Coast who is described by the Rev. J. L. Wilson (*Western Africa*, pp. 129 *sqq.*). See below, p. 23 ; and *The Magic Art and the Evolution of Kings*, vol. i. p. 353.

As to the iron ring which the pontiff wears on his ankle as the badge of his office we are told that it " is regarded with as much veneration as the most ancient crown in Europe, and the incumbent suffers as deep disgrace by its removal as any monarch in Europe would by being deprived of his crown" (J. L. Wilson, *op. cit.* pp. 129 *sq.*).

Taboos
observed
by sacred
milkmen
among the
Todas of
South
India.
would forfeit his office. It is only on two days a week, namely Mondays and Thursdays, that a mere layman may even approach the milkman ; on other days if he has any business with him, he must stand at a distance (some say a quarter of a mile) and shout his message across the intervening space. Further, the holy milkman never cuts his hair or pares his nails so long as he holds office ; he never crosses a river by a bridge, but wades through a ford and only certain fords ; if a death occurs in his clan, he may not attend any of the funeral ceremonies, unless he first resigns his office and descends from the exalted rank of milkman to that of a mere common mortal. Indeed it appears that in old days he had to resign the seals, or rather the pails, of office whenever any member of his clan departed this life. However, these heavy restraints are laid in their entirety only on milkmen of the very highest class.[1] Among the Todas there are milkmen and milkmen ; and some of them get off more lightly in consideration of their humbler station in life.[2] Still, apart from the dignity they enjoy, the lot even of these other milkmen is not altogether a happy one. Thus, for example, at a place called Kanodrs there is a dairy-temple of a conical form. The milkman who has charge of it must be celibate during the tenure of his office : he must sleep in the calves' house, a very flimsy structure with an open door and a fire-place that gives little heat : he may wear only one very scanty garment : he must take his meals sitting on the outer wall which surrounds the dairy : in eating he may not put his hand to his lips, but must throw the food into his mouth ; and in drinking he may not put to his lips the leaf which serves as a cup, he must tilt his head back and pour the liquid into his mouth in a jet from above. With the exception of a single layman, who is allowed to bear the milkman company, but who is also bound to celibacy and has a bed rigged up for him in the calves' house, no other person is allowed to go near this very sacred dairy under any pretext whatever. No wonder that some years ago the dairy was unoccupied and the office of milkman

---

[1] W. H. R. Rivers, *The Todas* (London, 1906), pp. 98-103.

[2] For restrictions imposed on these lesser milkmen see W. H. R. Rivers, *op. cit.* pp. 62, 66, 67 *sq.*, 72, 73, 79-81.

stood vacant. "At the present time," says Dr. Rivers, "a dairyman is appointed about once a year and holds office for thirty or forty days only. So far as I could ascertain, the failure to occupy the dairy constantly is due to the very considerable hardships and restrictions which have to be endured by the holder of the office of dairyman, and the time is probably not far distant when this dairy, one of the most sacred among the Todas, will cease altogether to be used." [1]

§ 2. *Divorce of the Spiritual from the Temporal Power*

The burdensome observances attached to the royal or priestly office produced their natural effect. Either men refused to accept the office, which hence tended to fall into abeyance ; or accepting it, they sank under its weight into spiritless creatures, cloistered recluses, from whose nerveless fingers the reins of government slipped into the firmer grasp of men who were often content to wield the reality of sovereignty without its name. In some countries this rift in the supreme power deepened into a total and permanent separation of the spiritual and temporal powers, the old royal house retaining their purely religious functions, while the civil government passed into the hands of a younger and more vigorous race. *The effect of these burdensome rules was to divorce the temporal from the spiritual authority.*

To take examples. In a previous part of this work we saw that in Cambodia it is often necessary to force the kingships of Fire and Water upon the reluctant successors,[2] and that in Savage Island the monarchy actually came to an end because at last no one could be induced to accept the dangerous distinction.[3] In some parts of West Africa, when the king dies, a family council is secretly held to determine his successor. He on whom the choice falls is suddenly seized, bound, and thrown into the fetish-house, where he is kept in durance till he consents to accept the crown. Sometimes the heir finds means of evading the honour which it is sought to thrust upon him ; a ferocious chief has been known to go about *Reluctance to accept sovereignty with its vexatious restrictions.*

[1] W. H. R. Rivers, *The Todas*, pp. 79-81.

[2] *The Magic Art*, vol. ii. p. 4.
[3] *Id.* vol. i. pp. 354 *sq.*

constantly armed, resolute to resist by force any attempt to set him on the throne.[1] The savage Timmes of Sierra Leone, who elect their king, reserve to themselves the right of beating him on the eve of his coronation ; and they avail themselves of this constitutional privilege with such hearty goodwill that sometimes the unhappy monarch does not long survive his elevation to the throne. Hence when the leading chiefs have a spite at a man and wish to rid themselves of him, they elect him king.[2] Formerly, before a man was proclaimed king of Sierra Leone, it used to be the custom to load him with chains and thrash him. Then the fetters were knocked off, the kingly robe was placed on him, and he received in his hands the symbol of royal dignity, which was nothing but the axe of the executioner.[3] It is not therefore surprising to read that in Sierra Leone, where such customs have prevailed, " except among the Mandingoes and Suzees, few kings are natives of the countries they govern. So different are their ideas from ours, that very few are solicitous of the honour, and competition is very seldom heard of."[4] Another writer on Sierra Leone tells us that " the honour of reigning, so much coveted in Europe, is very frequently rejected in Africa, on account of the expense attached to it, which sometimes greatly exceeds the revenues of the crown."[5] A reluctance to accept the sovereignty in the Ethiopian kingdom of Gingiro was simulated, if not really felt, as we learn from the old Jesuit missionaries. " They wrap up the dead king's body in costly garments, and killing a cow, put it into the hide ; then all those who hope to succeed him, being his sons or others of the royal blood, flying from the honour they covet, abscond and hide themselves in the woods. This done, the electors, who are all great sorcerers, agree among themselves who shall be king, and go out to seek him, when entering the woods by means of their enchantments, they say, a large

---

[1] A. Bastian, *Die deutsche Expedition an der Loango-Küste,* i. 354 *sq.*, ii. 9, 11.

[2] Zweifel et Moustier, "Voyage aux sources du Niger," *Bulletin de la Société de Géographie* (Paris), VIme Série, xx. (1880) p. 111.

[3] O. Dapper, *Description de l'Afrique* (Amsterdam, 1686), p. 250.

[4] J. Matthews, *Voyage to Sierra-Leone* (London, 1791), p. 75.

[5] T. Winterbottom, *Account of the Native Africans in the Neighbourhood of Sierra Leone* (London, 1803), p. 124.

bird called *liber*, as big as an eagle, comes down with mighty cries over the place where he is hid, and they find him encompass'd by lyons, tygers, snakes, and other creatures gather'd about him by witchcraft. The elect, as fierce as those beasts, rushes out upon those who seek him, wounding and sometimes killing some of them, to prevent being seiz'd. They take all in good part, defending themselves the best they can, till they have seiz'd him. Thus they carry him away by force, he still struggling and seeming to refuse taking upon him the burthen of government, all which is mere cheat and hypocrisy."[1]

The Mikados of Japan seem early to have resorted to the expedient of transferring the honours and burdens of supreme power to their infant children; and the rise of the Tycoons, long the temporal sovereigns of the country, is traced to the abdication of a certain Mikado in favour of his three-year-old son. The sovereignty having been wrested by a usurper from the infant prince, the cause of the Mikado was championed by Yoritomo, a man of spirit and conduct, who overthrew the usurper and restored to the Mikado the shadow, while he retained for himself the substance, of power. He bequeathed to his descendants the dignity he had won, and thus became the founder of the line of Tycoons. Down to the latter half of the sixteenth century the Tycoons were active and efficient rulers; but the same fate overtook them which had befallen the Mikados. Immeshed in the same inextricable web of custom and law, they degenerated into mere puppets, hardly stirring from their palaces and occupied in a perpetual round of empty ceremonies, while the real business of government was managed by the council of state.[2] In Tonquin the monarchy ran a similar course. Living like his predecessors in effeminacy and sloth, the king was driven from the throne by an ambitious adventurer named Mack, who from a fisherman had risen to be Grand Mandarin. But the king's brother Tring put down the usurper and restored the king, retaining, however, for himself and his descendants the

Sovereign powers divided between a temporal and a spiritual head.

---

[1] *The Travels of the Jesuits in Ethiopia*, collected and historically digested by F. Balthazar Tellez (London, 1710), pp. 197 *sq.*

[2] *Manners and Customs of the Japanese*, pp. 199 *sqq.*, 355 *sqq.*

Sovereign
powers
divided
between a
temporal
and a
spiritual
head.
dignity of general of all the forces. Thenceforward the kings or *dovas*, though invested with the title and pomp of sovereignty, ceased to govern. While they lived secluded in their palaces, all real political power was wielded by the hereditary generals or *chovas*.[1] The present king of Sikhim, "like most of his predecessors in the kingship, is a mere puppet in the hands of his crafty priests, who have made a sort of priest-king of him. They encourage him by every means in their power to leave the government to them, whilst he devotes all his time to the degrading rites of devil-worship, and the ceaseless muttering of meaningless jargon, of which the Tibetan form of Buddhism chiefly consists. They declare that he is a saint by birth; that he is the direct descendant of the greatest king of Tibet, the canonised Srongtsan Gampo, who was a contemporary of Mahomed in the seventh century A.D. and who first introduced Buddhism to Tibet." "This saintly lineage, which secures for the king's person popular homage amounting to worship, is probably, however, a mere invention of the priests to glorify their puppet-prince for their own sordid ends. Such devices are common in the East."[2] The custom regularly observed by the Tahitian kings of abdicating on the birth of a son, who was immediately proclaimed sovereign and received his father's homage, may perhaps have originated, like the similar custom occasionally practised by the Mikados, in a wish to shift to other shoulders the irksome burden of royalty; for in Tahiti as elsewhere the sovereign was subjected to a system of vexatious restrictions.[3] In Mangaia, another Polynesian island, religious and civil authority were lodged in separate hands, spiritual functions being discharged by a line of hereditary kings, while the temporal government was entrusted from time to time to a victorious war-chief, whose investiture, however, had to be completed by the king. To the latter were assigned the best lands, and he received daily offerings of the choicest food.[4] The Mikado and

[1] Richard, "History of Tonquin," in Pinkerton's *Voyages and Travels*, ix. 744 *sqq.*

[2] L. A. Waddell, *Among the Himalayas* (Westminster, 1899), pp. 146 *sq.*

[3] W. Ellis, *Polynesian Researches*, Second Edition (London, 1832-1836), iii. 99 *sqq.*

[4] W. W. Gill, *Myths and Songs of the South Pacific*, pp. 293 *sqq.*

Tycoon of Japan had their counterparts in the Roko Tui
and Vunivalu of Fiji. The Roko Tui was the Reverend
or Sacred King. The Vunivalu was the Root of War or
War King. In one kingdom a certain Thakambau, who
was the War King, kept all power in his own hands, but in
a neighbouring kingdom the real ruler was the Sacred
King.[1] Similarly in Tonga, besides the civil king or *How*,
whose right to the throne was partly hereditary and partly
derived from his warlike reputation and the number of his
fighting men, there was a great divine chief called *Tooitonga*
or "Chief of Tonga," who ranked above the king and the
other chiefs in virtue of his supposed descent from one of the
chief gods.   Once a year the first-fruits of the ground were
offered to him at a solemn ceremony, and it was believed
that if these offerings were not made the vengeance of the
gods would fall in a signal manner on the people.   Peculiar
forms of speech, such as were applied to no one else, were
used in speaking of him, and everything that he chanced to
touch became sacred or tabooed.   When he and the king
met, the monarch had to sit down on the ground in token
of respect until his holiness had passed by.   Yet though he
enjoyed the highest veneration by reason of his divine
origin, this sacred personage possessed no political
authority, and if he ventured to meddle with affairs of
state it was at the risk of receiving a rebuff from the
king, to whom the real power belonged, and who finally
succeeded in ridding himself of his spiritual rival.[2]   The
king of the Getae regularly shared his power with a
priest, whom his subjects called a god.   This divine man
led a solitary life in a cave on a holy mountain, seeing
few people but the king and his attendants.   His counsels
added much to the king's influence with his subjects, who
believed that he was thereby enabled to impart to them the
commands and admonitions of the gods.[3]   At Athens the
kings degenerated into little more than sacred functionaries,
and it is said that the institution of the new office of

Sovereign powers divided between a temporal and a spiritual head.

---

[1] The late Rev. Lorimer Fison, in a
letter to the author, dated August 26,
1898.

[2] W. Mariner, *An Account of the
Natives of the Tonga Islands*, Second
Edition (London, 1818), ii. 75-79,
132-136.

[3] Strabo, vii. 3. 5, pp. 297 *sq.*
Compare *id.* vii. 3. 11, p. 304.

Polemarch or War Lord was rendered necessary by their growing effeminacy.[1]   American examples of the partition of authority between a king and a pope have already been cited from the early history of Mexico and Colombia.[2]

Fetish
kings and
civil kings
in West
Africa.   In some parts of western Africa two kings reign side by side, a fetish or religious king and a civil king, but the fetish king is really supreme.   He controls the weather and so forth, and can put a stop to everything.   When he lays his red staff on the ground, no one may pass that way.   This division of power between a sacred and a secular ruler is to be met with wherever the true negro culture has been left unmolested, but where the negro form of society has been disturbed, as in Dahomey and Ashantee, there is a tendency to consolidate the two powers in a single king.[3]   Thus, for example, there used to be a fetish king at New Calabar who ranked above the ordinary king in all native matters, whether religious or civil, and always walked in front of him on public occasions, attended by a slave who held an umbrella over his head.   His opinion carried great weight.[4]   The office and the causes which led to its extinction are thus described by a missionary who spent many years in Calabar : " The worship of the people is now given especially to their various *idems*, one of which, called Ndem Efik, is a sort of tutelary deity of the country. An individual was appointed to take charge of this object of worship, who bore the name of King Calabar ; and likely, in bypast times, possessed the power indicated by the title, being both king and priest.   He had as a tribute the skins of all leopards killed, and should a slave take refuge in his shrine he belonged to Ndem Efik.   The office, how- ever, imposed certain restrictions on its occupant.   He, for instance, could not partake of food in the presence of

[1] Aristotle, *Constitution of Athens*, iii. 2.   My friend Professor Henry Jackson kindly called my attention to this passage.

[2] See *The Magic Art and the Evolution of Kings*, vol. i. p. 416, and above, p. 6.

[3] Miss Mary H. Kingsley in *Journal of the Anthropological Institute*, xxix. (1899) pp. 61 *sqq.*   I had some con- versation on this subject with Miss Kingsley (1st June 1897) and have embodied the results in the text.   Miss Kingsley did not know the rule of succession among the fetish kings.

[4] T. J. Hutchinson, *Impressions of Western Africa* (London, 1858), pp. 101 *sq.* ;   Le Comte C. N. de Cardi, "Ju-ju Laws and Customs in the Niger Delta," *Journal of the Anthropological Institute*, xxix. (1899) p. 51.

any one, and he was prohibited from engaging in traffic. Fetish kings and civil kings in West Africa. On account of these and other disabilities, when the last holder of the office died, a poor old man of the Cobham family, no successor was found for him, and the priesthood has become extinct." [1] One of the practical inconveniences of such an office is that the house of the fetish king enjoys the right of sanctuary, and so tends to become little better than a rookery of bad characters. Thus on the Grain Coast of West Africa the fetish king or Bodio, as he is called, " exercises the functions of a high - priest, and is regarded as protector of the whole nation. He lives in a house provided for him by the people, and takes care of the national fetiches. He enjoys some immunities in virtue of his office, but is subject to certain restrictions which more than counterbalance his privileges. His house is a sanctum to which culprits may betake themselves without the danger of being removed by any one except by the Bodio himself." [2] One of these Bodios resigned office because of the sort of people who quartered themselves on him, the cost of feeding them, and the squabbles they had among themselves. He led a cat-and-dog life with them for three years. Then there came a man with homicidal mania varied by epileptic fits ; and soon afterwards the spiritual shepherd retired into private life, but not before he had lost an ear and sustained other bodily injury in a personal conflict with this very black sheep.[3]

At Porto Novo there used to be, in addition to the The King of the Night. ordinary monarch, a King of the Night, who reigned during the hours of darkness from sunset to sunrise. He might not shew himself in the street after the sun was up. His duty was to patrol the streets with his satellites and to arrest all whom he found abroad after a certain hour. Each band of his catchpoles was led by a man who went about concealed from head to foot under a conical casing of straw and blew blasts on a shell which caused every one that heard it to shudder. The King of the Night never met the ordinary

---

[1] H. Goldie, *Calabar and its Mission*, New Edition (London, 1901), p. 43.

[2] J. L. Wilson, *Western Africa* (London, 1856), p. 129. As to the taboos observed by the Bodio or Bodia see above, p. 15.

[3] Miss Mary H. Kingsley, in *Journal of the Anthropological Institute*, xxix. (1899) p. 62.

king except on the first and last days of their respective
reign ; for each of them invested the other with office and
paid him the last honours at death.[1] With this King of
the Night at Porto Novo we may compare a certain king of
Hawaii who was so very sacred that no man might see
him, even accidentally, by day under pain of death ; he
only shewed himself by night.[2]

Civil rajahs
and taboo
rajahs in
the East
Indies.

In some parts of the East Indian island of Timor we
meet with a partition of power like that which is represented by the civil king and the fetish king of western
Africa. Some of the Timorese tribes recognise two rajahs,
the ordinary or civil rajah, who governs the people, and
the fetish or taboo rajah (*radja pomali*), who is charged
with the control of everything that concerns the earth
and its products. This latter ruler has the right of
declaring anything taboo ; his permission must be obtained
before new land may be brought under cultivation, and he
must perform certain necessary ceremonies when the work
is being carried out. If drought or blight threatens the
crops, his help is invoked to save them. Though he ranks
below the civil rajah, he exercises a momentous influence on
the course of events, for his secular colleague is bound to
consult him in all important matters. In some of the
neighbouring islands, such as Rotti and eastern Flores, a
spiritual ruler of the same sort is recognised under various
native names, which all mean "lord of the ground."[3]
Similarly in the Mekeo district of British New Guinea
there is a double chieftainship. The people are divided
into two groups according to families, and each of the
groups has its chief. One of the two is the war chief, the
other is the taboo (*afu*) chief. The office of the latter is
hereditary ; his duty is to impose a taboo on any of the

---

[1] Marchoux, "Ethnographie, Porto-
Novo," *Revue Scientifique*, Quatrième
Série, iii. (1895) pp. 595 *sq.* This
passage was pointed out to me by
Mr. N. W. Thomas.

[2] O. von Kotzebue, *Entdeckungs-
Reise in die Süd-See und nach der
Berings-Strasse* (Weimar, 1821), iii.
149.

[3] J. J. de Hollander, *Handleiding*

*bij de Beofening der Land- en Volken-
kunde van Nederlandsch Oost-Indië*,
ii. 606 *sq.* In other parts of Timor
the spiritual ruler is called *Anaha paha*
or "conjuror of the land." Compare
H. Zondervan, "Timor en de Timoreezen," *Tijdschrift van het Nederlandsch Aardrijkskundig Genootschap*,
Tweede Serie, v. (1888) Afdeeling, mehr
uitgebreide artikelen, pp. 400-402.

crops, such as the coco-nuts and areca nuts, whenever he thinks it desirable to prohibit their use. In his office we may perhaps detect the beginning of a priestly dynasty, but as yet his functions appear to be more magical than religious, being concerned with the control of the harvests rather than with the propitiation of higher powers. The members of another family are bound to see to it that the taboo imposed by the chief is strictly observed. For this purpose some fourteen or fifteen men of the family form a sort of constabulary. Every evening they go round the village armed with clubs and disguised with masks or leaves. All the time they are in office they are forbidden to live with their wives and even to look at a woman. Hence women may not quit their houses while the men are going their rounds. Further, the constables on duty are prohibited from chewing betel nut and drinking coco-nut water, lest the areca and coco-nuts should not grow. When there is a good show of nuts, the taboo chief proclaims that on a certain day the restriction will come to an end.[1] In Ponape, one of the Caroline Islands, the kingship is elective within the limits of the blood royal, which runs in the female line, so that the sovereignty passes backwards and forwards between families which we, reckoning descent in the male line, should regard as distinct. The chosen monarch must be in possession of certain secrets. He must know the places where the sacred stones are kept, on which he has to seat himself. He must understand the holy words and prayers of the liturgy, and after his election he must recite them at the place of the sacred stones. But he enjoys only the honours of his office ; the real powers of government are in the hands of his prime-minister or vizier.[2]

[1] A. C. Haddon, *Head-hunters, Black, White, and Brown* (London, 1901), pp. 270-272.

[2] Dr. Hahl, "Mittheilungen über Sitten und rechtliche Verhältnisse auf Ponape," *Ethnologisches Notizblatt*, ii. Heft 2 (Berlin, 1901), pp. 5 *sq.*, 7. The title of the prime-minister is *Nanekin*.

CHAPTER II

THE PERILS OF THE SOUL

§ 1. *The Soul as a Mannikin*

What is the primitive conception of death?

THE foregoing examples have taught us that the office of a sacred king or priest is often hedged in by a series of burdensome restrictions or taboos, of which a principal purpose appears to be to preserve the life of the divine man for the good of his people. But if the object of the taboos is to save his life, the question arises, How is their observance supposed to effect this end? To understand this we must know the nature of the danger which threatens the king's life, and which it is the intention of these curious restrictions to guard against. We must, therefore, ask: What does early man understand by death? To what causes does he attribute it? And how does he think it may be guarded against?

Savages conceive the human soul as a mannikin, the prolonged absence of which from the body causes death.

As the savage commonly explains the processes of inanimate nature by supposing that they are produced by living beings working in or behind the phenomena, so he explains the phenomena of life itself. If an animal lives and moves, it can only be, he thinks, because there is a little animal inside which moves it: if a man lives and moves, it can only be because he has a little man or animal inside who moves him. The animal inside the animal, the man inside the man, is the soul. And as the activity of an animal or man is explained by the presence of the soul, so the repose of sleep or death is explained by its absence; sleep or trance being the temporary, death being the permanent absence of the soul. Hence if death be the permanent absence of the soul, the way to guard against it is either to prevent the soul from leaving the body, or, if it does depart, to ensure that it shall return. The precautions adopted by savages to secure one or other of these ends take the form of certain prohibitions or taboos, which are nothing but rules intended to ensure either the continued presence or the return of the soul. In short, they are life-preservers or life-guards. These general statements will now be illustrated by examples.

Addressing some Australian blacks, a European missionary said, " I am not one, as you think, but two." Upon this they laughed. "You may laugh as much as you like," continued the missionary, " I tell you that I am two in one; this great body that you see is one; within that there is another little one which is not visible. The great body dies, and is buried, but the little body flies away when the great one dies." To this some of the blacks replied, "Yes, yes. We also are two, we also have a little body within the breast." On being asked where the little body went after death, some said it went behind the bush, others said it went into the sea, and some said they did not know.[1] The Hurons thought that the soul had a head and body, arms and legs; in short, that it was a complete little model of the man himself.[2] The Esquimaux believe that " the soul exhibits the same shape as the body it belongs to, but is of a more subtle and ethereal nature."[3] According to the Nootkas of British Columbia the soul has the shape of a tiny man; its seat is the crown of the head. So long as it stands erect, its owner is hale and hearty; but when from any cause it loses its upright position, he loses his senses.[4] Among the Indian tribes of the Lower Fraser River, man is held to have four souls, of which the principal one has the form of a mannikin, while the other

The soul as a mannikin in Australia, America, and among the Malays.

[1] R. Salvado, *Mémoires historiques sur l'Australie* (Paris, 1854), p. 162 ; *Journal of the Anthropological Institute*, vii. (1878) p. 282. In this edifying catechism there is little to choose between the savagery of the white man and the savagery of the black.

[2] *Relations des Jésuites*, 1634, p. 17 ; *id.*, 1636, p. 104 ; *id.*, 1639, p. 43 (Canadian reprint, Quebec, 1858).

[3] H. Rink, *Tales and Traditions of the Eskimo*, p. 36. The Esquimaux

of Bering Strait believe that every man has several souls, and that two of these souls are shaped exactly like the body. See E. W. Nelson, " The Eskimo about Bering Strait," *Eighteenth Annual Report of the Bureau of American Ethnology*, part i. (Washington, 1899) p. 422.

[4] Fr. Boas, in *Sixth Report on the North-Western Tribes of Canada*, p. 44 (separate reprint from the *Report of the British Association for 1890*).

three are shadows of it.[1]   The Malays conceive the human soul (*semangat*) as a little man, mostly invisible and of the bigness of a thumb, who corresponds exactly in shape, proportion, and even in complexion to the man in whose body he resides.   This mannikin is of a thin unsubstantial nature, though not so impalpable but that it may cause displacement on entering a physical object, and it can flit quickly from place to place; it is temporarily absent from the body in sleep, trance, and disease, and permanently absent after death.[2]

The soul as a mannikin in ancient Egypt.   The ancient Egyptians believed that every man has a soul (*ka*) which is his exact counterpart or double, with the same features, the same gait, even the same dress as the man himself.   Many of the monuments dating from the eighteenth century onwards represent various kings appearing before divinities, while behind the king stands his soul or double, portrayed as a little man with the king's features.   Some of the reliefs in the temple at Luxor illustrate the birth of King Amenophis III.   While the queen-mother is being tended by two goddesses acting as midwives, two other goddesses are bringing away two figures of new-born children, only one of which is supposed to be a child of flesh and blood: the inscriptions engraved above their heads shew that, while the first is Amenophis, the second is his soul or double.   And as with kings and queens, so it was with common men and women.   Whenever a child was born, there was born with him a double which followed him through the various stages of life; young while he was young, it grew to maturity and declined along with him.   And not only human beings, but gods and animals, stones and trees, natural and artificial objects, everybody and everything had its own soul or double. The doubles of oxen and sheep were the duplicates of the original oxen or sheep; the doubles of linen or beds, of chairs or knives, had the same form as the real linen, beds, chairs, and knives.   So thin and subtle was the stuff, so fine and delicate the texture of these doubles, that they made no impression on ordinary eyes.   Only certain classes of priests

---

[1] Fr. Boas, in *Ninth Report on the North-Western Tribes of Canada*, p. 461 (*Report of the British Association* for *1894*).

[2] W. W. Skeat, *Malay Magic* (London, 1900), p. 47.

or seers were enabled by natural gifts or special training to perceive the doubles of the gods, and to win from them a knowledge of the past and the future. The doubles of men and things were hidden from sight in the ordinary course of life ; still, they sometimes flew out of the body endowed with colour and voice, left it in a kind of trance, and departed to manifest themselves at a distance.[1]

So exact is the resemblance of the mannikin to the man, in other words, of the soul to the body, that, as there are fat bodies and thin bodies, so there are fat souls and thin souls ; [2] as there are heavy bodies and light bodies, long bodies and short bodies, so there are heavy souls and light souls, long souls and short souls. The people of Nias (an island to the west of Sumatra) think that every man, before he is born, is asked how long or how heavy a soul he would like, and a soul of the desired weight or length is measured out to him. The heaviest soul ever given out weighs about ten grammes. The length of a man's life is proportioned to the length of his soul ; children who die young had short souls.[3] The Fijian conception of the soul as a tiny human being comes clearly out in the customs observed at the death of a chief among the Nakelo tribe. When a chief dies, certain men, who are the hereditary undertakers, call him, as he lies, oiled and ornamented, on fine mats, saying, " Rise, sir, the chief, and let us be going. The day has come over the land." Then they conduct him to the river side, where the ghostly ferryman comes to ferry Nakelo ghosts across the stream.

The soul as a mannikin in Nias, Fiji, and India.

---

[1] G. Maspero, *Études de mythologie et d'archéologie égyptiennes* (Paris, 1893), i. 388 *sq.* ; A. Wiedemann, *The ancient Egyptian Doctrine of the Immortality of the Soul* (London, 1895), pp. 10 *sqq.* In Greek works of art, especially vase - paintings, the human soul is sometimes represented as a tiny being in human form, generally winged, sometimes clothed and armed, sometimes naked. See O. Jahn, *Archäologische Beiträge* (Berlin, 1847), pp. 128 *sqq.* ; E. Pottier, *Étude sur les lécythes blancs attiques* (Paris, 1883), pp. 75-79 ; *American Journal of Archaeology*, ii. (1886) pll. xii., xiii. ; O. Kern, in *Aus der Anomia, Archäologische Beiträge Carl Robert zur Erinnerung an*

Berlin dargebracht (Berlin, 1890), pp. 89-95. Greek artists of a later period sometimes portrayed the human soul in the form of a butterfly (O. Jahn, *op. cit.* pp. 138 *sqq.*). There was a particular sort of butterfly to which the Greeks gave the name of soul (ψυχή). See Aristotle, *Hist. anim.* v. 19, p. 550 b 26, p. 551 b 13 *sq.* ; Plutarch, *Quaest. conviv.* ii. 3. 2.

[2] W. W. Gill, *Myths and Songs of the South Pacific* (London, 1876), p. 171.

[3] H. Sundermann, " Die Insel Nias und die Mission daselbst," *Allgemeine Missions - Zeitschrift*, Bd. xi. October 1884, p. 453.

As they thus attend the chief on his last journey, they hold their great fans close to the ground to shelter him, because, as one of them explained to a missionary, " His soul is only a little child." [1] People in the Punjaub who tattoo themselves believe that at death the soul, "the little entire man or woman" inside the mortal frame, will go to heaven blazoned with the same tattoo patterns which adorned the body in life.[2] Sometimes, however, as we shall see, the human soul is conceived not in human but in animal form.

§ 2. Absence and Recall of the Soul

Attempts to prevent the soul from escaping from the body.

The soul is commonly supposed to escape by the natural openings of the body, especially the mouth and nostrils. Hence in Celebes they sometimes fasten fish-hooks to a sick man's nose, navel, and feet, so that if his soul should try to escape it may be hooked and held fast.[3] A Turik on the Baram River, in Borneo, refused to part with some hook-like stones, because they, as it were, hooked his soul to his body, and so prevented the spiritual portion of him from becoming detached from the material.[4] When a Sea Dyak sorcerer or medicine-man is initiated, his fingers are supposed to be furnished with fish-hooks, with which he will thereafter clutch the human soul in the act of flying away, and restore it to the body of the sufferer.[5] But hooks, it is plain, may be used to catch the souls of enemies as well as of friends. Acting on this principle head-hunters in Borneo hang wooden hooks beside the skulls of their slain enemies in the belief that this helps them on their forays to hook in fresh heads.[6] When an epidemic is raging, the Goajiro Indians of Colombia attribute it to an evil spirit, it may be the prowling ghost of an enemy.

---

[1] The late Rev. Lorimer Fison, in a letter to the author, dated November 3, 1898.

[2] H. A. Rose, "Note on Female Tattooing in the Panjâb," *Indian Antiquary*, xxxi. (1902) p. 298.

[3] B. F. Matthes, *Over de Bissoes of heidensche priesters en priesteressen der Boeginezen* (Amsterdam, 1872), p. 24 (reprinted from the *Verhandelingen der*

Koninklijke Akademie van Wetenschappen, Afdeeling Letterkunde, Deel vii.).

[4] A. C. Haddon, *Head-hunters*, p. 439.

[5] H. Ling Roth, "Low's Natives of Borneo," *Journal of the Anthropological Institute*, xxi. (1892) p. 115.

[6] A. C. Haddon, *Head-hunters*, pp. 371, 396.

So they hang strings furnished with hooks from the roofs of their huts and from all the trees in the neighbourhood, in order that the demon or ghost may be caught on a hook and thus rendered powerless to harm them.[1] Similarly the Calchaquis Indians to the west of Paraguay used to plant arrows in the ground about a sick man to keep death from getting at him.[2] One of the implements of a Haida medicine-man is a hollow bone, in which he bottles up departing souls, and so restores them to their owners.[3] When any one yawns in their presence the Hindoos always snap their thumbs, believing that this will hinder the soul from issuing through the open mouth.[4] The Marquesans used to hold the mouth and nose of a dying man, in order to keep him in life by preventing his soul from escaping ;[5] the same custom is reported of the New Caledonians ;[6] and with the like intention the Bagobos of the Philippine Islands put rings of brass wire on the wrists or ankles of their sick.[7] On the other hand, the Itonamas in South America seal up the eyes, nose, and mouth of a dying person, in case his ghost should get out and carry off others ;[8] and for a similar reason the people of Nias, who fear the spirits of the recently deceased and identify them with the breath, seek to confine the vagrant soul in its earthly tabernacle by bunging up the nose or tying up the jaws of the corpse.[9] Before leaving a corpse the Wakelbura in Australia used to place hot coals in its ears in order to keep the ghost in the body, until they had got such a good start that he could not

Attempts to prevent the soul from escaping from the body.

[1] H. Candelier, *Rio-Hacha et les Indiens Goajires* (Paris, 1893), pp. 258 sq.

[2] R. Southey, *History of Brazil*, iii. 396.

[3] G. M. Dawson, "On the Haida Indians of the Queen Charlotte Islands," *Geological Survey of Canada, Report of Progress for 1878-1879* (Montreal, 1880), pp. 123 B, 139 B.

[4] *Panjab Notes and Queries*, ii. p. 114, § 665.

[5] M. Radiguet, *Les Derniers Sauvages* (Paris, 1882), p. 245 ; Matthias G***, *Lettres sur Îles les Marquises* (Paris, 1843), p. 115 ; Clavel, *Les Marquisiens*, p. 42 note.

[6] Gagnière, in *Annales de la Propagation de la Foi*, xxxii. (1860) p. 439.

[7] F. Blumentritt, "Das Stromgebiet des Rio Grande de Mindano," *Petermanns Mitteilungen*, xxxvii. (1891) p. 111.

[8] A. d'Orbigny, *L'Homme américain*, ii. 241 ; T. J. Hutchinson, "The Chaco Indians," *Transactions of the Ethnological Society of London*, N.S., iii. (1865) pp. 322 sq. ; A. Bastian, *Culturländer des alten Amerika*, i. 476. A similar custom is observed by the Cayuvava Indians (A. d'Orbigny, *op. cit.* ii. 257).

[9] E. Modigliani, *Un Viaggio a Nias* (Milan, 1890), p. 283.

overtake them.[1]   Esquimaux mourners plug their nostrils with deerskin, hair, or hay for several days,[2] probably to prevent their souls from following that of their departed friend ; the custom is especially incumbent on the persons who dress the corpse.[3]   In southern Celebes, to hinder the escape of a woman's soul at childbirth, the nurse ties a band as tightly as possible round the body of the expectant mother.[4]   The Minangkabauers of Sumatra observe a similar custom ; a skein of thread or a string is sometimes fastened round the wrist or loins of a woman in childbed, so that when her soul seeks to depart in her hour of travail it may find the egress barred.[5] Among the Kayans of Borneo illness is attributed to the absence of the soul ; so when a man has been ill and is well again, he attempts to prevent his soul from departing afresh.   For this purpose he ties the truant into his body by fastening round his wrist a piece of string on which a *lukut*, or antique bead, is threaded ; for a magical virtue appears to be ascribed to such beads.   But lest the string and the bead should be broken and lost, he will sometimes tattoo the pattern of the bead on his wrist, and this is found to answer the purpose of tethering his soul quite as well.[6] Again, the Koryak of North-Eastern Asia fancy that if

Tying the soul in the body.

[1] A. W. Howitt, *Native Tribes of South-East Australia* (London, 1904), p. 473.

[2] Fr. Boas, "The Central Eskimo," *Sixth Annual Report of the Bureau of Ethnology* (Washington, 1888), pp. 613 sq.   Among the Esquimaux of Smith Sound male mourners plug up the right nostril and female mourners the left (E. Bessels in *American Naturalist*, xviii. (1884) p. 877 ; cp. J. Murdoch, "Ethnological Results of the Point Barrow Expedition," *Ninth Annual Report of the Bureau of Ethnology* (Washington, 1892), p. 425).   This seems to point to a belief that the soul enters by one nostril and goes out by the other, and that the functions assigned to the right and left nostrils in this respect are reversed in men and women.   Among the Esquimaux of Baffin Land " the person who prepares a body for burial puts rabbit's fur into his nostrils to prevent the exhalations from entering his own lungs" (Fr. Boas, "The Eskimo of Baffin Land and Hudson Bay," *Bulletin of the American Museum of Natural History*, xv. part i. (1901) p. 144).   But this would hardly explain the custom of stopping one nostril only.

[3] G. F. Lyon, *Private Journal* (London, 1824), p. 370.

[4] B. F. Matthes, *Bijdragen tot de Ethnologie van Zuid-Celebes* (The Hague, 1875), p. 54.

[5] J. L. van der Toorn, " Het animisme bij den Minangkabauer der Padangsche Bovenlanden," *Bijdragen tot de Taal- Land- en Volkenkunde van Nederlandsch-Indië*, xxxix. (1890) p. 56.

[6] C. Hose and R. Shelford, "Materials for a Study of Tatu in Borneo," *Journal of the Anthropological Institute*, xxxvi. (1906) p. 65.

there are two sick people in a house and one of them is at Tying the soul in the body.
the last extremity, the soul of the other is apt to be lured
away by the soul of the dying man ; hence in order to
hinder its departure they tie the patient's neck by a string
to the bands of the sleeping-tent and recite a charm over
the string so that it may be sure to detain the soul.[1] And
lest the soul of a babe should escape and be lost as
soon as it is born, the Alfoors of Celebes, when a birth is
about to take place, are careful to close every opening in the
house, even the keyhole ; and they stop up every chink and
cranny in the walls. Also they tie up the mouths of all
animals inside and outside the house, for fear one of them
might swallow the child's soul. For a similar reason all
persons present in the house, even the mother herself, are
obliged to keep their mouths shut the whole time the birth
is taking place. When the question was put, Why they did
not hold their noses also, lest the child's soul should get into
one of them? the answer was that breath being exhaled
as well as inhaled through the nostrils, the soul would
be expelled before it could have time to settle down.[2]
Popular expressions in the language of civilised peoples,
such as to have one's heart in one's mouth, or the soul on
the lips or in the nose, shew how natural is the idea that the
life or soul may escape by the mouth or nostrils.[3]

Often the soul is conceived as a bird ready to take The soul as a bird.
flight. This conception has probably left traces in most

---

[1] W. Jochelson, "The Koryak, Religion and Myths" (Leyden and New York, 1905), p. 103 (*Memoir of the American Museum of Natural History, The Jesup North Pacific Expedition*, vol. vi. part i.).

[2] W. F. A. Zimmermann, *Die Inseln des Indischen und Stillen Meeres* (Berlin, 1864-65), ii. 386 *sq.*

[3] Compare τοῦτον κατ' ὤμου δεῖρον, ἄχρις ἡ ψυχὴ | αὐτοῦ ἐπὶ χειλέων μοῦνον ἡ κακὴ λειφθῇ, Herodas, *Mimiambi*, iii. 3 *sq.* ; μόνον οὐκ ἐπὶ τοῖς χείλεσι τὰς ψυχὰς ἔχοντας, Dio Chrysostom, *Orat.* xxxii. vol. i. p. 417, ed. Dindorf ; modern Greek μὲ τὴ ψυχὴ 's τὰ δόντια, G. F. Abbott, *Macedonian Folklore*, p. 193 note ; "*mihi anima*

in naso esse, stabam tanquam mortuus," Petronius, *Sat.* 62 ; "*in primis labris animam habere,*" Seneca, *Natur. quaest.* iii. praef. 16 ; "*Voilà un pauvre malade qui a le feu dans le corps, et l'âme sur le bout des lèvres,*" J. de Brebeuf, in *Relations des Jésuites*, 1636, p. 113 (Canadian reprint) ; "This posture keeps the weary soul hanging upon the lip ; ready to leave the carcass, and yet not suffered to take its wing," R. Bentley, "Sermon on Popery," quoted in Monk's *Life of Bentley*,[2] i. 382. In Czech they say of a dying person that his soul is on his tongue (Br. Jelínek, in *Mittheilungen der anthropolog. Gesellschaft in Wien*, xxi. (1891) p. 22).

languages,[1] and it lingers as a metaphor in poetry. But what is metaphor to a modern European poet was sober earnest to his savage ancestor, and is still so to many people. The Bororos of Brazil fancy that the human soul has the shape of a bird, and passes in that shape out of the body in dreams.[2] According to the Bilqula or Bella Coola Indians of British Columbia the soul dwells in the nape of the neck and resembles a bird enclosed in an egg. If the shell breaks and the soul flies away, the man must die. If he swoons or becomes crazed, it is because his soul has flown away without breaking its shell. The shaman can hear the buzzing of its wings, like the buzz of a mosquito, as the soul flits past ; and he may catch and replace it in the nape of its owner's neck.[3] A Melanesian wizard in Lepers' Island has been known to send out his soul in the form of an eagle to pursue a ship and learn the fortunes of some natives who were being carried off in it.[4] The soul of Aristeas of Proconnesus was seen to issue from his mouth in the shape of a raven.[5] There is a popular opinion in Bohemia that the parting soul comes forth from the mouth like a white bird.[6] The Malays carry out the conception of the bird-soul in a number of odd ways. If the soul is a bird on the wing, it may be attracted by rice, and so either prevented from taking wing or lured back again from its perilous flight. Thus in Java when a child is placed on the ground for the first time (a moment which uncultured people seem to regard as especially dangerous), it is put in a hen-coop and the mother makes a clucking sound, as if she were calling hens.[7] Amongst the Battas of Sumatra, when a man returns from a dangerous enterprise, grains of rice are placed on his head, and these

[1] Compare the Greek ποτάομαι, ἀναπτερόω, etc.

[2] K. von den Steinen, *Unter den Naturvölkern Zentral-Brasiliens* (Berlin, 1894), pp. 511, 512.

[3] Fr. Boas, in *Seventh Report on the North-Western Tribes of Canada*, pp. 14 sq. (separate reprint of the *Report of the British Association for 1891*).

[4] R. H. Codrington, *The Melanesians*, pp. 207 sq.

[5] Pliny, *Nat. Hist.* vii. 174. Compare Herodotus, iv. 14 sq. ; Maximus Tyrius, *Dissert.* xvi. 2.

[6] Br. Jelínek, "Materialien zur Vorgeschichte und Volkskunde Böhmens," *Mittheilungen der anthropologischen Gesellschaft in Wien*, xxi. (1891) p. 22.

[7] G. A. Wilken, "Het animisme bij de volken van den Indischen Archipel," *De Indische Gids*, June 1884, p. 944.

grains are called *padiruma tondi,* that is, " means to make the soul *(tondi)* stay at home." In Java also rice is placed on the head of persons who have escaped a great danger or have returned home unexpectedly after it had been supposed that they were lost.[1] Similarly in the district of Sintang in West Borneo, if any one has had a great fright, or escaped a serious peril, or comes back after a long and dangerous journey, or has taken a solemn oath, the first thing that his relations or friends do is to strew yellow rice on his head, mumbling, " Cluck! cluck! soul!" *(koer, koer semangat).*

And when a person, whether man, woman, or child, has fallen out of a house or off a tree, and has been brought home, his wife or other kinswoman goes as speedily as possible to the spot where the accident happened, and there strews rice, which has been coloured yellow, while she utters the words, " Cluck! cluck! soul! So-and-so is in his house again. Cluck! cluck! soul!" Then she gathers up the rice in a basket, carries it to the sufferer, and drops the grains from her hand on his head, saying again, " Cluck! cluck! soul!"[2] Here the intention clearly is to decoy back the loitering bird-soul and replace it in the head of its owner. In southern Celebes they think that a bridegroom's soul is apt to fly away at marriage, so coloured rice is scattered over him to induce it to stay. And, in general, at festivals in South Celebes rice is strewed on the head of the person in whose honour the festival is held, with the object of detaining his soul, which at such times is in especial danger of being lured away by envious demons.[3] For example, after a successful war the welcome to the victorious prince takes the form of strewing him with roasted and coloured rice " to

The soul conceived as a bird ready to fly away.

---

[1] G. A. Wilken, *l.c.*

[2] E. L. M. Kühr, " Schetsen uit Borneo's Westerafdeeling," *Bijdragen tot de Taal- Land- en Volkenkunde van Nederlandsch-Indië,* xlvii. (1897) p. 57.

[3] B. F. Matthes, *Bijdragen tot de Ethnologie van Zuid-Celebes,* p. 33; *id., Over de Bissoes of heidensche priesters en priesteressen der Boeginezen,* pp. 9 *sq.; id., Makassaarsch-Hollandsch Woordenboek, s.vv. Kôèrrôe* and *soe-*

mångå, pp. 41, 569. Of these two words, the former means the sound made in calling fowls, and the latter means the soul. The expression for the ceremonies described in the text is *ápakôèrrôe soemångå.* So common is the recall of the bird-soul among the Malays that the words *koer (kur) semangat* (" cluck! cluck! soul!") often amount to little more than an expression of astonishment, like our " Good gracious me!" See W. W. Skeat, *Malay Magic,* p. 47, note 2.

prevent his life-spirit, as if it were a bird, from flying out of his body in consequence of the envy of evil spirits."[1] In Central Celebes, when a party of head-hunters returns from a successful expedition, a woman scatters rice on their heads for a similar purpose.[2] Among the Minangkabauers of Sumatra the old rude notions of the soul seem to be dying out. Nowadays most of the people hold that the soul, being immaterial, has no shape or form. But some of the sorcerers assert that the soul goes and comes in the shape of a tiny man. Others are of opinion that it does so in the form of a fly ; hence they make food ready to induce the absent soul to come back, and the first fly that settles on the food is regarded as the returning truant. But in native poetry and popular expressions there are traces of the belief that the soul quits the body in the form of a bird.[3]

The soul is supposed to be absent in sleep.

The soul of a sleeper is supposed to wander away from his body and actually to visit the places, to see the persons, and to perform the acts of which he dreams. For example, when an Indian of Brazil or Guiana wakes up from a sound sleep, he is firmly convinced that his soul has really been away hunting, fishing, felling trees, or whatever else he has dreamed of doing, while all the time his body has been lying motionless in his hammock. A whole Bororo village has been thrown into a panic and nearly deserted because somebody had dreamed that he saw enemies stealthily approaching it. A Macusi Indian in weak health, who dreamed that his employer had made him haul the canoe up a series of difficult cataracts, bitterly reproached his master next

[1] B. F. Matthes, "Over de *ádá's* of gewoonten der Makassaren en Boegineezen," *Verslagen en Mededeelingen der koninklijke Akademie van Wetenschappen* (Amsterdam), Afdeeling Letterkunde, Reeks iii. Deel ii. (1885) pp. 174 *sq.* ; J. K. Niemann, "De Boegineezen en Makassaren," *Bijdragen tot de Taal- Land- en Volkenkunde van Nederlandsch-Indië*, xxxviii. (1889) p. 281.

[2] A. C. Kruyt, "Het koppensnellen der Toradja's," *Verslagen en Mededeelingen der koninklijke Akademie van Wetenschappen* (Amsterdam), Afdeel-

ing Letterkunde, Reeks iv. Deel iii. (1899) p. 162.

[3] J. L. van der Toorn, "Het animisme bij den Minangkabauer der Padangsche Bovenlanden," *Bijdragen tot de Taal- Land- en Volkenkunde van Nederlandsch - Indië*, xxxix. (1890) pp. 56-58. On traces of the bird-soul in Mohammedan popular belief, see I. Goldziher, "Der Seelenvogel im islamischen Volksglauben," *Globus*, lxxxiii. (1903) pp. 301-304 ; and on the soul in bird-form generally, see J. von Negelein, "Seele als Vogel," *Globus*, lxxix. (1901) pp. 357-361, 381-384.

morning for his want of consideration in thus making a poor invalid go out and toil during the night.[1]   The Indians of the Gran Chaco are often heard to relate the most incredible stories as things which they have themselves seen and heard ; hence strangers who do not know them intimately say in their haste that these Indians are liars.   In point of fact the Indians are firmly convinced of the truth of what they relate ; for these wonderful adventures are simply their dreams, which they do not distinguish from waking realities.[2]

Now the absence of the soul in sleep has its dangers, for if from any cause the soul should be permanently detained away from the body, the person thus deprived of the vital principle must die.[3]   There is a German belief that the soul escapes from a sleeper's mouth in the form of a white mouse or a little bird, and that to prevent the return of the bird or animal would be fatal to the sleeper.[4]   Hence in Transylvania they say that you should not let a child sleep with its mouth open, or its soul will slip out in the shape of a mouse, and the child will never wake.[5] Many causes may detain the sleeper's soul.   Thus, his soul may meet the soul of another sleeper and the two souls may fight ; if a Guinea negro wakens with sore bones in the morning, he thinks that his soul has been thrashed by another soul in sleep.[6]   Or it may meet the soul of a person just deceased and be carried off by it ; hence in the Aru Islands the inmates of a house will not sleep the night after a death has taken place in it, because the soul of the deceased is supposed to be still in the house and they fear to meet it in a dream.[7]   Similarly among the Upper Thompson Indians of British Columbia, the friends and neighbours

The soul absent in sleep may be prevented from returning to the body.

---

[1] K. von den Steinen, *Unter den Naturvölkern Zentral-Brasiliens*, p. 340; E. F. im Thurn, *Among the Indians of Guiana*, pp. 344 *sqq.*

[2] V. Frič, "Eine Pilcomayo-Reise in den Chaco Central," *Globus*, lxxxix. (1906) p. 233.

[3] Shway Yoe, *The Burman, his Life and Notions* (London, 1882), ii. 100.

[4] R. Andree, *Braunschweiger Volkskunde* (Brunswick, 1896), p. 266.

[5] H. von Wlislocki, *Volksglaube und Volksbrauch der Siebenbürger Sachsen* (Berlin, 1893), p. 167.

[6] J. L. Wilson, *Western Africa* (London, 1856), p. 220 ; A. B. Ellis, *The Ewe-speaking Peoples of the Slave Coast*, p. 20.

[7] J. G. F. Riedel, *De sluik- en kroesharige rassen tusschen Selebes en Papua*, p. 267.   For detention of a sleeper's soul by spirits and consequent illness, see also Mason, quoted in A. Bastian's *Die Völker des östlichen Asien*, ii. 387 note.

The soul absent in sleep may be prevented from returning to the body.

who gathered in a house after a death and remained there till the burial was over were not allowed to sleep, lest their souls should be drawn away by the ghost of the deceased or by his guardian spirit.[1] The Lengua Indians of the Gran Chaco hold that the vagrant spirits of the dead may come to life again if only they can take possession of a sleeper's body during the absence of his soul in dreams. Hence, when the shades of night have fallen, the ghosts of the departed gather round the villages, watching for a chance to pounce on the bodies of dreamers and to enter into them through the gateway of the breast.[2] Again, the soul of the sleeper may be prevented by an accident or by physical force from returning to his body. When a Dyak dreams of falling into the water, he supposes that this accident has really befallen his spirit, and he sends for a wizard, who fishes for the spirit with a hand-net in a basin of water till he catches it and restores it to its owner.[3] The Santals tell how a man fell asleep, and growing very thirsty, his soul, in the form of a lizard, left his body and entered a pitcher of water to drink. Just then the owner of the pitcher happened to cover it ; so the soul could not return to the body and the man died. While his friends were preparing to burn the body some one uncovered the pitcher to get water. The lizard thus escaped and returned to the body, which immediately revived ; so the man rose up and asked his friends why they were weeping. They told him they thought he was dead and were about to burn his body. He said he had been down a well to get water, but had found it hard to get out and had just returned. So they saw it all.[4] A similar story is reported from Transylvania

---

[1] J. Teit, "The Thompson Indians of British Columbia," *Memoir of the American Museum of Natural History, The Jesup North Pacific Expedition,* vol. i. part iv. (April 1900) p. 327. The Koryak of North-Eastern Asia also keep awake so long as there is a corpse in the house. See W. Jochelson, "The Koryak, Religion and Myths," *Memoir of the American Museum for Natural History, The Jesup North Pacific Expedition,* vol. vi. part i. (Leyden and New York, 1905) p. 110.

[2] G. Kurze, "Sitten und Gebräuche der Lengua - Indianer," *Mitteilungen der Geographischen Gesellschaft zu Jena,* xxiii. (1905) p. 18.

[3] H. Ling Roth, "Low's Natives of Borneo," *Journal of the Anthropological Institute,* xxi. (1892) p. 112.

[4] *Indian Antiquary,* vii. (1878) p. 273 ; A. Bastian, *Völkerstämme am Brahmaputra,* p. 127. A similar story is told by the Hindoos and Malays, though the lizard form of the soul is not mentioned. See *Panjab*

as follows. In the account of a witch's trial at Mühlbach in
the eighteenth century it is said that a woman had engaged
two men to work in her vineyard. After noon they all lay
down to rest as usual. An hour later the men got up and
tried to waken the woman, but could not. She lay motionless with her mouth wide open. They came back at sunset
and still she lay like a corpse. Just at that moment a big
fly came buzzing past, which one of the men caught and
shut up in his leathern pouch. Then they tried again to
waken the woman, but could not. Afterwards they let out
the fly ; it flew straight into the woman's mouth and she
awoke. On seeing this the men had no further doubt that
she was a witch.[1]

It is a common rule with primitive people not to waken **Danger of**
a sleeper, because his soul is away and might not have time **awaking a sleeper**
to get back ; so if the man wakened without his soul, he **suddenly**
would fall sick. If it is absolutely necessary to rouse a **before his soul has**
sleeper, it must be done very gradually, to allow the soul **time to**
time to return.[2] A Fijian in Matuku, suddenly wakened **return.**
from a nap by somebody treading on his foot, has been

Notes and Queries, iii. p. 166, § 679 ;
N. Annandale, " Primitive Beliefs and
Customs of the Patani Fishermen,"
Fasciculi Malayenses, Anthropology,
part i. (April 1903) pp. 94 *sq.*

[1] E. Gerard, *The Land beyond the
Forest,* ii. 27 *sq.* A similar story is told
in Holland (J. W. Wolf, *Nederlandsche Sagen,* No. 250, pp. 343 *sq.*). The
story of King Gunthram belongs to the
same class ;- the king's soul comes out
of his mouth as a snake (Paulus
Diaconus, *Hist. Langobardorum,* iii. 34).
In an East Indian story of the same
type the sleeper's soul issues from his
nose in the form of a cricket (G. A.
Wilken, in *De Indische Gids,* June 1884,
p. 940). In a Swabian story a girl's
soul creeps out of her mouth in the form
of a white mouse (A. Birlinger, *Volksthümliches aus Schwaben,* i. 303). In
a Saxon story the soul comes out of the
sleeper's mouth in the shape of a red
mouse. See E. Mogk, in R. Wuttke's
Sächsische Volkskunde[2] (Dresden, 1901),
p. 318.

[2] Shway Yoe, *The Burman,* ii. 103 ;

M. and B. Ferrars, *Burma* (London,
1900), p. 77 ; R. G. Woodthorpe, in
Journal of the Anthropological Institute,
xxvi. (1897) p. 23 ; A. Bastian, *Die
Völker des östlichen Asien,* ii. 389 ; F.
Blumentritt, " Der Ahnencultus und
die religiösen Anschauungen der
Malaien des Philippinen-Archipels,"
*Mittheilungen der Wiener Geogr. Gesell-
schaft,* 1882, p. 209 ; J. G. F. Riedel,
*De sluik- en kroesharige rassen tusschen
Selebes en Papua,* p. 440 ; *id.,* " Die
Landschaft Dawan oder West-Timor,"
Deutsche geographische Blätter, x. 280 ;
A. C. Kruijt, " Een en ander aangaande het geestelijk en maatschapelijk
leven van den Poso-Alfoer," *Mededeelingen van wege het Nederlandsche Zendelinggenootschap,* xxxix. (1895) p. 4 ;
K. von den Steinen, *Unter den Naturvölkern Zentral-Brasiliens,* pp. 340,
510 ; L. F. Gowing, *Five Thousand
Miles in a Sledge* (London, 1889),
p. 226 ; A. C. Hollis, *The Masai*
(Oxford, 1905), p. 308. The rule is
mentioned and a mystic reason assigned
for it in the *Satapatha Brâhmana* (part
v. p. 371, J. Eggeling's translation).

heard bawling after his soul and imploring it to return.
He had just been dreaming that he was far away in Tonga,
and great was his alarm on suddenly wakening to find his
body in Matuku. Death stared him in the face unless his
soul could be induced to speed at once across the sea and
reanimate its deserted tenement. The man would probably
have died of fright if a missionary had not been at hand to
allay his terror.[1] Some Brazilian Indians explain the headache from which a man sometimes suffers after a broken
sleep by saying that his soul is tired with the exertions it
made to return quickly to the body.[2] A Highland story,
told to Hugh Miller on the picturesque shores of Loch Shin,
well illustrates the haste made by the soul to regain its body
when the sleeper has been prematurely roused by an indiscreet friend. Two young men had been spending the early
part of a warm summer day in the open air, and sat down
on a mossy bank to rest. Hard by was an ancient ruin
separated from the bank on which they sat only by a
slender runnel, across which there lay, immediately over a
miniature cascade, a few withered stalks of grass. "Overcome by the heat of the day, one of the young men fell
asleep ; his companion watched drowsily beside him ; when
all at once the watcher was aroused to attention by seeing a
little indistinct form, scarce larger than a humble-bee, issue
from the mouth of the sleeping man, and, leaping upon the
moss, move downwards to the runnel, which it crossed along
the withered grass stalks, and then disappeared among the
interstices of the ruin. Alarmed by what he saw, the
watcher hastily shook his companion by the shoulder, and
awoke him ; though, with all his haste, the little cloud-like
creature, still more rapid in its movements, issued from the
interstice into which it had gone, and, flying across the
runnel, instead of creeping along the grass stalks and over
the sward, as before, it re-entered the mouth of the sleeper,
just as he was in the act of awakening. ' What is the
matter with you ? ' said the watcher, greatly alarmed, ' what
ails you ? ' ' Nothing ails me,' replied the other ; ' but you

---

[1] Rev. Lorimer Fison, in a letter
to the author dated August 26,
1898.

[2] K. von den Steinen, *Unter den
Naturvölkern Zentral-Brasiliens*, p.
340.

have robbed me of a most delightful dream. I dreamed I was walking through a fine rich country, and came at length to the shores of a noble river ; and, just where the clear water went thundering down a precipice, there was a bridge all of silver, which I crossed ; and then, entering a noble palace on the opposite side, I saw great heaps of gold and jewels ; and I was just going to load myself with treasure, when you rudely awoke me, and I lost all.'"[1]

Still more dangerous is it in the opinion of primitive man to move a sleeper or alter his appearance, for if this were done the soul on its return might not be able to find or recognise its body, and so the person would die. The Minangkabauers of Sumatra deem it highly improper to blacken or dirty the face of a sleeper, lest the absent soul should shrink from re-entering a body thus disfigured.[2] Patani Malays fancy that if a person's face be painted while he sleeps, the soul which has gone out of him will not recognise him, and he will sleep on till his face is washed.[3] In Bombay it is thought equivalent to murder to change the aspect of a sleeper, as by painting his face in fantastic colours or giving moustaches to a sleeping woman. For when the soul returns it will not know its own body and the person will die.[4] The Coreans are of opinion that in sleep "the soul goes out of the body, and that if a piece of paper is put over the face of the sleeper he will surely die, for his soul cannot find its way back into him again."[5] The Servians believe that the soul of a sleeping witch often leaves her body in the form of a butterfly. If during its absence her body be turned round, so that her feet are placed where her head was before, the butterfly soul will not find its way back into her body through the mouth, and the witch will die.[6] The Esthonians

Danger of moving a sleeper or altering his appearance.

---

[1] Hugh Miller, *My Schools and Schoolmasters* (Edinburgh, 1854), ch. vi. pp. 106 *sq.*

[2] J. L. van der Toorn, "Het animisme bij den Minangkabauer der Padangsche Bovenlanden," *Bijdragen tot de Taal- Land- en Volkenkunde van Nederlandsch-Indië*, xxxix. (1890) p. 50.

[3] N. Annandale, in *Fasciculi Ma-*

layenses, *Anthropology*, part i. (April 1903) p. 94.

[4] *Panjab Notes and Queries*, iii. p. 116, § 530.

[5] W. W. Rockhill, "Notes on some of the Laws, Customs, and Superstitions of Korea," *American Anthropologist*, iv. (1891) p. 183.

[6] W. R. S. Ralston, *Songs of the Russian People*, pp. 117 *sq.* ; F. S.

of the island of Oesel think that the gusts which sweep up
all kinds of trifles from the ground and whirl them along
are the souls of old women, who have gone out in this shape
to seek what they can find. Meantime the beldame's body
lies as still as a stone, and if you turn it round her soul will
never be able to enter it again, until you have replaced the
body in its original position. You can hear the soul
whining and whimpering till it has found the right aperture.[1]
Similarly in Livonia they think that when the soul of a
were-wolf is out on his hateful business, his body lies like
dead ; and if meanwhile the body were accidentally moved,
the soul would never more find its way into it, but would
remain in the body of a wolf till death.[2] In the picturesque
but little known Black Mountain of southern France, which
forms a sort of link between the Pyrenees and the Cevennes,
they tell how a woman, who had long been suspected of
being a witch, one day fell asleep at noon among the
reapers in the field. Resolved to put her to the test, the
reapers carried her, while she slept, to another part of the
field, leaving a large pitcher on the spot from which they
had moved her. When her soul returned, it entered the
pitcher and cunningly rolled it over and over till the vessel
lay beside her body, of which the soul thereupon took
possession.[3]

The soul
may quit
the body
in waking
hours,
thereby
causing
sickness,
insanity
or death.
But in order that a man's soul should quit his body, it
is not necessary that he should be asleep. It may quit him
in his waking hours, and then sickness, insanity, or death
will be the result. Thus a man of the Wurunjeri tribe in
Victoria lay at his last gasp because his spirit (*murup*) had
departed from him. A medicine-man went in pursuit and
caught the spirit by the middle just as it was about to
plunge into the sunset glow, which is the light cast by the
souls of the dead as they pass in and out of the under-

Krauss, *Volksglaube und religiöser
Brauch der Südslaven* (Münster i. W.,
1890), p. 112. The latter writer tells
us that the witch's spirit is also supposed
to assume the form of a fly, a hen,
a turkey, a crow, and especially a
toad.

[1] Holzmayer, " Osiliana," *Verhandlungen der gelehrten Estnischen Gesell-*
schaft zu Dorpat, vii. (1872) No. 2,
p. 53.

[2] P. Einhorn, "Wiederlegunge der
Abgötterey," etc., reprinted in *Scriptores rerum Livonicarun*, ii. 645 (Riga
and Leipsic, 1848).

[3] A. de Nore, *Coutumes, mythes et
traditions des provinces de France*
(Paris and Lyons, 1846), p. 88.

world, where the sun goes to rest.   Having captured the Recalling
vagrant spirit, the doctor brought it back under his opossum truant souls in
rug, laid himself down on the dying man, and put the Australia,
soul back into him, so that after a time he revived.[1] Burma, China, and
The Karens of Burma are perpetually anxious about their Sarawak.
souls, lest these should go roving from their bodies, leaving
the owners to die.   When a man has reason to fear that
his soul is about to take this fatal step, a ceremony is
performed to retain or recall it, in which the whole family
must take part.   A meal is prepared consisting of a cock
and hen, a special kind of rice, and a bunch of bananas.
Then the head of the family takes the bowl which is used to
skim rice, and knocking with it thrice on the top of the house-
ladder says: " *Prrrroo!*   Come back, soul, do not tarry
outside!   If it rains, you will be wet.   If the sun shines,
you will be hot.   The gnats will sting you, the leeches will
bite you, the tigers will devour you, the thunder will crush
you.   *Prrrroo!*   Come back, soul!   Here it will be well
with you.   You shall want for nothing.   Come and eat
under shelter from the wind and the storm."   After that the
family partakes of the meal, and the ceremony ends with
everybody tying their right wrist with a string which has
been charmed by a sorcerer.[2]   Similarly the Lolos, an
aboriginal tribe of western China, believe that the soul
leaves the body in chronic illness.   In that case they read
a sort of elaborate litany, calling on the soul by name and
beseeching it to return from the hills, the vales, the rivers,
the forests, the fields, or from wherever it may be straying.
At the same time cups of water, wine, and rice are set at the
door for the refreshment of the weary wandering spirit.   When
the ceremony is over, they tie a red cord round the arm of
the sick man to tether the soul, and this cord is worn by him
until it decays and drops off.[3]   So among the Kenyahs of
Sarawak a medicine-man has been known to recall the stray
soul of a child, and to fasten it firmly in its body by
tying a string round the child's right wrist, and smearing

---

[1] A. W. Howitt, *Native Tribes of South-East Australia*, p. 387.

[2] Bringaud, "Les Karens de la Birmanie," *Missions Catholiques*, xx. (1888) pp. 297 *sq.*

[3] A. Henry, "The Lolos and other tribes of Western China," *Journal of the Anthropological Institute*, xxxiii. (1903) p. 102.

its little arm with the blood of a fowl.[1] The Ilocanes of Luzon think that a man may lose his soul in the woods or gardens, and that he who has thus lost his soul loses also his senses. Hence before they quit the woods or the fields they call to their soul, " Let us go ! let us go !" lest it should loiter behind or go astray. And when a man becomes crazed or mad, they take him to the place where he is supposed to have lost his soul and invite the truant spirit to return to his body.[2] The Mongols sometimes explain sickness by supposing that the patient's soul is absent, and either does not care to return to its body or cannot find the way back. To secure the return of the soul it is therefore necessary on the one hand to make its body as attractive as possible, and on the other hand to shew the soul the way home. To make the body attractive all the sick man's best clothes and most valued possessions are placed beside him ; he is washed, incensed, and made as comfortable as may be ; and all his friends march thrice round the hut calling out the sick man's name and coaxing his soul to return. To help the wanderer to find its way back a coloured cord is stretched from the patient's head to the door of the hut. The priest in his robes reads a list of the horrors of hell and the dangers incurred by souls which wilfully absent themselves from their bodies. Then turning to the assembled friends and the patient he asks, " Is it come ?" All answer "Yes," and bowing to the returning soul throw seed over the sick man. The cord which guided the soul back is then rolled up and placed round the patient's neck, who must wear it for seven days without taking it off. No one may frighten or hurt him, lest his soul, not yet familiar with its body, should again take flight.[3]

Some of the Congo tribes believe that when a man is ill, his soul has left his body and is wandering at large. The aid of the sorcerer is then called in to capture the

[1] C. Hose and W. M'Dougall, "The Relations between Men and Animals in Sarawak," *Journal of the Anthropological Institute*, xxxi. (1901) pp. 183 *sq.*

[2] De los Reyes y Florentino, " Die religiöse Anschauungen der Ilocanen (Luzon)," *Mittheilungen der k. k. Geograph. Gesellschaft in Wien*, xxxi. (1888) pp. 569 *sq.*

[3] A. Bastian, *Die Seele und ihre Erscheinungswesen in der Ethnographie*, p. 36.

vagrant spirit and restore it to the invalid. Generally the physician declares that he has successfully chased the soul into the branch of a tree. The whole town thereupon turns out and accompanies the doctor to the tree, where the strongest men are deputed to break off the branch in which the soul of the sick man is supposed to be lodged. This they do and carry the branch back to the town, insinuating by their gestures that the burden is heavy and hard to bear. When the branch has been brought to the sick man's hut, he is placed in an upright position by its side, and the sorcerer performs the enchantments by which the soul is believed to be restored to its owner.[1] The soul or shade of a Déné or Tinneh Indian in the old days generally remained invisible, but appeared wandering about in one form or another whenever disease or death was imminent. All the efforts of the sufferer's friends were therefore concentrated on catching the roving shade. The method adopted was simple. They stuffed the patient's moccasins with down and hung them up. If next morning the down was warm, they made sure that the lost soul was in the boots, with which accordingly they carefully and silently shod their suffering friend. Nothing more could reasonably be demanded for a perfect cure.[2] An Ottawa medicine-man has been known to catch a stray soul in a little box, which he brought back and inserted in the patient's mouth.[3]

Pining, sickness, great fright, and death are ascribed by the Battas or Bataks of Sumatra to the absence of the soul (*tendi*) from the body. At first they try to beckon the wanderer back, and to lure him, like a fowl, by strewing rice. Then the following form of words is commonly repeated: " Come back, O soul, whether thou art lingering in the wood, or on the hills, or in the dale. See, I call thee with a *toemba bras*, with an egg of the fowl Rajah *moelija*, with the eleven healing leaves. Detain it not, let it come straight here,

Recalling truant souls in Sumatra.

[1] H. Ward, *Five Years with the Congo Cannibals* (London, 1890), pp. 53 *sq.*

[2] A. G. Morice, "The Western Dénés, their Manners and Customs," *Proceedings of the Canadian Institute, Toronto*, Third Series, vii. (1888-1889)

pp. 158 *sq.* ; *id.*, *Au pays de l'ours noir, chez les sauvages de la Colombie Britannique* (Paris and Lyons, 1897), p. 75.

[3] Clicteur, in *Annales de l'Associa-tion de la Propagation de la Foi*, iv (1830) p. 479.

detain it not, neither in the wood, nor on the hill, nor in
the dale.   That may not be.   O come straight home!"[1]
Sometimes the means adopted by the Battas to procure
the return of a sick person's soul are more elaborate.   A
procession sets out from the village to the tuck of drum to
find and bring home the strayed soul.   First goes a person
bearing a basket which contains cakes of rice-meal, rice
dyed yellow, and a boiled fowl's egg.   The sorcerer follows
carrying a chicken, and behind him walks a man with a
black, red, and white flag.   A crowd of sympathisers brings
up the rear.   On reaching the spot where the lost soul is
supposed to tarry, they set up a small bamboo altar, and
the sorcerer offers on it the chicken to the spirit of the place,
the drums beating all the time.   Then, waving his shawl to
attract the soul of the sick man, he says: "Come hither,
thou soul of So-and-So, whether thou sittest among the
stones or in the mud.   In the house is thy place.   We
have besought the spirit to let thee go."   After that the
procession reforms and marches back to the village to the
roll of drums and the clash of cymbals.   On reaching the
door of the house the sorcerer calls out to the inmates,
"Has it come?" and a voice from within answers, "It is
here, good sorcerer."   At evening the drums beat again.[2]
A number of plants, including rice, a species of fig, and
garlic, are supposed by the Battas to possess soul-compelling
virtue and are accordingly made use of by them in rites
for the recovery of lost souls.   When a child is sick, the
mother commonly waves a cloth to beckon home its wandering spirit, and when a cock crows or a hen cackles in the
yard, she knows that the prodigal has returned.   If the
little sufferer persists in being ill in spite of these favourable
omens, the mother will hang a bag of rice at the head of
her bed when she goes to sleep, and next morning on
getting up she measures the rice.   If the rice has increased
in volume during the night, as it may do in a moisture-

---

[1] M. Joustra, "Het leven, de zeden
en gewoonten der Bataks," *Mededeelingen van wege het Nederlandsche
Zendelinggenootschap*, xlvi. (1902) p.
408.

[2] J. H. Meerwaldt, "Gebruiken
der Bataks in het maatschappelijk
leven," *Mededeelingen van wege het
Nederlandsche Zendelinggenootschap*,
li. (1907) pp. 98 *sq.*   The writer
gives *tondi* as the form of the Batak
word for "soul."

laden atmosphere, she is confident that the lost soul has
indeed come home to stay.[1]   The Kayans of Borneo
fasten packets of rice, flesh, and fish to the window in
the roof through which the wandering soul of a sick
man is expected to return home.   The doctor sits cross-
legged on a mat under the open window with a display
of pretty things spread out temptingly before him as baits
to entice the spirit back to its deserted tabernacle.   From
the window hangs a string of precious corals or pearls to serve
the returning prodigal as a ladder and so facilitate his descent
into the house.   The lower end of the string is attached to
a bundle composed of wooden hooks, a fowl's feather, little
packets of rice, and so forth.   Chanting his spells, the doctor
strokes the soul down the string into the bundle, which he
then deposits in a basket and hides in a corner till the dusk
of the evening.   When darkness has fallen, he blows the
captured soul back into the patient's head and strokes the
sufferer's arm downwards with the point of an old spear in
order to settle the soul firmly in his body.[2]   Once when a
popular traveller was leaving a Kayan village, the mothers,
fearing that their children's souls might follow him on his
journey, brought him the boards on which they carry
their infants and begged him to pray that the souls of
the little ones would return to the familiar boards and
not go away with him into the far country.   To each
board was fastened a looped string for the purpose of
tethering the vagrant spirits, and through the loop
each baby was made to pass a chubby finger to make sure
that its tiny soul would not wander away.[3]   When a Dyak
is dangerously ill, the medicine-men may say that his soul
has escaped far away, perhaps to the river; then they will
wave a garment or cloth about to imitate the casting of a
net, signifying thereby that they are catching the soul like a
fish in a net.   Or they may give out that the soul has
escaped into the jungle; and then they will rush out of the
house to circumvent and secure it there.   Or again they

[1] Dr. R. Römer, "Bijdrage tot de Geneeskunst der Karo-Batak's," *Tijdschrift voor Indische Taal- Land- en Volkenkunde*, l. (1908) pp. 212 *sq.*
[2] A. W. Nieuwenhuis, *In Centraal Borneo* (Leyden, 1900), i. 148, 152 *sq.*, 164 *sq.*; *id., Quer durch Borneo* (Leyden, 1904-1907), i. 112 *sq.*, 125.
[3] A. W. Nieuwenhuis, *Quer durch Borneo*, ii. 481.

Recalling
truant
souls in
Borneo
and
Celebes.
may allege that it has been carried away over seas to some
unknown land; and then they will play at paddling a boat
to follow it across the great water. But more commonly
their mode of treatment is as follows. A spear is set up in
the middle of the verandah with a few leaves tied to it and
the medicine-boxes of the medicine-men laid at its foot.
Round this the doctors run at full speed, chanting the while,
till one of them falls down and lies motionless. The
bystanders cover him with a blanket, and wait while his
spirit hies away after the errant soul and brings it back.
Presently he comes to himself, stares vacantly about like a
man awaking from sleep, and then rises, holding the soul in
his clenched right hand. He then returns it to the patient
through the crown of his head, while he mutters a spell.[1]
Among the Dyaks of the Kayan and Lower Melawie
districts you will often see, in houses where there are children,
a basket of a peculiar shape with shells and dried fruits
attached to it. These shells contain the remains of the
children's navel-strings, and the basket to which they are
fastened is commonly hung beside the place where the
children sleep. When a child is frightened, for example by
being bathed or by the bursting of a thunderstorm, its soul
flees from its body and nestles beside its old familiar friend
the navel-string in the basket, from which the mother easily
induces it to return by shaking the basket and pressing it to
the child's body.[2] The Toboongkoos of Central Celebes
believe that sickness in general is caused by the departure of
the soul. To recover the wanderer a priest will set out food
in the courtyard of the sufferer's house and then invoke the
soul, promising it many fine things if it will only come back.
When he thinks it has complied with his request, he catches
it in a cloth which he keeps ready for the purpose. This
cloth he afterwards claps on the sick man's head, thereby
restoring to him his lost soul.[3]

[1] J. Perham, "Manangism in
Borneo," *Journal of the Straits Branch
of the Royal Asiatic Society*, No. 19
(Singapore, 1887), p. 91, compare pp.
89, 90; H. Ling Roth, *The Natives
of Sarawak and British North Borneo*,
i. 274, compare pp. 272 *sq.*

[2] E. L. M. Kühr, "Schetsen uit
Borneo's Westerafdeeling," *Bijdragen
tot de Taal- Land- en Volkenkunde van
Nederlandsch-Indië*, xlvii. (1897) pp.
60 *sq.*

[3] A. C. Kruijt, "Eenige ethnografische aanteekeningen omtrent de

In an Indian story a king conveys his soul into the Wandering
dead body of a Brahman, and a hunchback conveys his soul souls in
popular
into the deserted body of the king. The hunchback is now tales.
king and the king is a Brahman. However, the hunchback
is induced to shew his skill by transferring his soul to the
dead body of a parrot, and the king seizes the opportunity
to regain possession of his own body.[1] A tale of the same
type, with variations of detail, reappears among the Malays.
A king has incautiously transferred his soul to an ape, upon
which the vizier adroitly inserts his own soul into the king's
body and so takes possession of the queen and the kingdom,
while the true king languishes at court in the outward
semblance of an ape. But one day the false king, who
played for high stakes, was watching a combat of rams,
and it happened that the animal on which he had laid his
money fell · down dead. All efforts to restore animation
proved unavailing till the false king, with the instinct of a
true sportsman, transferred his own soul to the body of the
deceased ram, and thus renewed the fray. The real king in
the body of the ape saw his chance, and with great presence
of mind darted back into his own body, which the vizier
had rashly vacated. So he came to his own again, and the
usurper in the ram's body met with the fate he richly
deserved.[2] In another Indian story a Brahman reanimates
the dead body of a king by conveying his own soul into it.
Meantime the Brahman's body has been burnt, and his soul
is obliged to remain in the body of the king.[3] In a Chinese
story we read of a monk in a Buddhist monastery who used
from time to time to send his soul away out of himself.
Whenever he was thus absent from the body, he took the
precaution of locking the door of his cell. On one of these
occasions an envoy from the north arrived and put up at

Toboengkoe en de Tomori," *Mede-*
deelingen van wege het Nederlandsche
Zendelinggenootschap, xliv. (1900) p.
225.

[1] *Pantschatantra*, übersetzt von Th.
Benfey (Leipsic, 1859), ii. 124 *sqq.*

[2] J. Brandes, "Iets over het Pape-
gaai-boek, zooals het bij de Maleiers
voorkomt," *Tijdschrift voor Indische*
Taal- Land- en Volkenkunde, xli.
(1899) pp. 480-483. A story of this

sort is quoted from the *Persian Tales*
in the *Spectator* (No. 578, Aug. 9,
1714).

[3] *Katha Sarit Ságara*, translated by
C. H. Tawney (Calcutta, 1880), i. 21
sq. For other Indian tales of the same
general type, with variations in detail,
see *Lettres édifiantes et curieuses*,
Nouvelle Édition, xii. 183 *sq.*; *North*
Indian Notes and Queries, iv. p. 28,
§ 54.

E

the monastery, but there was no cell for him to pass the night in. Then he looked into the cell of the brother whose soul was not at home, and seeing his body lying there motionless, he battered the door in and said, "I will lodge here. The man is dead. Take the body and burn it." His servants obeyed his orders, the monks being powerless to interfere. That very night the soul came back, only to find its body reduced to ashes. Every night it could be heard crying, "Where shall I settle?" Those who knew him then opened their windows, saying, "Here I am." So the soul came in and united itself with their body, and the result was that they became much cleverer than before.[1] Similarly the Greeks told how the soul of Hermotimus of Clazomenae used to quit his body and roam far and wide, bringing back intelligence of what he had seen on his rambles to his friends at home; until one day, when his spirit was abroad, his enemies contrived to seize his deserted body and committed it to the flames.[2] It is said that during the last seven years of his life Sultan Bayazid ate nothing that had life and blood in it. One day, being seized with a great longing for sheep's trotters, he struggled long in this glorious contest with his soul, until at last, a savoury dish of trotters being set before him, he said unto his soul, "My soul, the trotters are before thee; if thou wishest to enjoy them, leave the body and feed on them." Hardly had he uttered these words when a living creature was seen to issue from his mouth and drink of the juice in the dish, after which it endeavoured to return whence it came. But the austere sultan, determined to mortify his carnal appetite, prevented it with his hand from entering his mouth, and when it fell to the ground commanded that it should be beaten. The pages kicked it to death, and after this murder of his soul the sultan remained in gloomy seclusion, taking no part or interest in the affairs of government.[3]

[1] J. J. M. de Groot, *The Religious System of China*, iv. 104.

[2] Pliny, *Nat. Hist.* vii. 174; Plutarch, *De genio Socratis*, 22; Lucian, *Muscae encomium*, 7. Plutarch calls the man Hermodorus. Epimenides, the Cretan seer, had also the power of sending his soul out of his body and keeping it out as long as he pleased. See Hesychius Milesius, in *Fragmenta historicorum Graecorum*, ed. C. Müller, v. 162; Suidas, *s.v.* Ἐπιμενίδης. On such reported cases in antiquity see further E. Rohde, *Psyche*,[3] ii. 91 *sqq.*

[3] *Narrative of Travels in Europe, Asia, and Africa in the Seventeenth*

The departure of the soul is not always voluntary. It may be extracted from the body against its will by ghosts, demons, or sorcerers. Hence, when a funeral is passing the house, the Karens of Burma tie their children with a special kind of string to a particular part of the house, lest the souls of the children should leave their bodies and go into the corpse which is passing. The children are kept tied in this way until the corpse is out of sight.[1] And after the corpse has been laid in the grave, but before the earth has been shovelled in, the mourners and friends range themselves round the grave, each with a bamboo split lengthwise in one hand and a little stick in the other; each man thrusts his bamboo into the grave, and drawing the stick along the groove of the bamboo points out to his soul that in this way it may easily climb up out of the tomb. While the earth is being shovelled in, the bamboos are kept out of the way, lest the souls should be in them, and so should be inadvertently buried with the earth as it is being thrown into the grave; and when the people leave the spot they carry away the bamboos, begging their souls to come with them.[2] Further, on returning from the grave each Karen provides himself with three little hooks made of branches of trees, and calling his spirit to follow him, at short intervals, as he returns, he makes a motion as if hooking it, and then thrusts the hook into the ground. This is done to prevent the soul of the living from staying behind with the soul of the dead.[3] On the return of a Burmese or Shan family from a burial, old men tie up the wrists of each member of the family with string, to prevent his or her "butterfly" or soul from escaping; and this string remains till it is worn out and falls off.[4] When a mother dies leaving a young baby, the

The wandering soul may be detained by ghosts.

Century by *Evliyā Efendī*, translated from the Turkish by the Ritter Joseph von Hammer (Oriental Translation Fund), vol. i. pt. ii. p. 3. I have not seen this work. An extract from it, containing the above narrative, was kindly sent me by Colonel F. Tyrrel, and the exact title and reference were supplied to me by Mr. R. A. Nicholson, who was so good as to consult the book for me in the British Museum.

[1] E. B. Cross, "On the Karens,"

Journal of the American Oriental Society, iv. (1854) p. 311.

[2] A. R. McMahon, *The Karens of the Golden Chersonese* (London, 1876), p. 318.

[3] F. Mason, "Physical Character of the Karens," *Journal of the Asiatic Society of Bengal*, 1866, pt. ii. pp. 28 *sq.*

[4] R. G. Woodthorpe, in *Journal of the Anthropological Institute*, xxvi. (1897) p. 23.

The wandering soul may be detained by ghosts. Burmese think that the "butterfly" or soul of the baby follows that of the mother, and that if it is not recovered the child must die. So a wise woman is called in to get back the baby's soul. She places a mirror near the corpse, and on the mirror a piece of feathery cotton down. Holding a cloth in her open hands at the foot of the mirror, she with wild words entreats the mother not to take with her the "butterfly" or soul of her child, but to send it back. As the gossamer down slips from the face of the mirror she catches it in the cloth and tenderly places it on the baby's breast. The same ceremony is sometimes observed when one of two children that have played together dies, and is thought to be luring away the soul of its playmate to the spirit-land. It is sometimes performed also for a bereaved husband or wife.[1] The Bahnars of eastern Cochin-China think that when a man is sick of a fever his soul has gone away with the ghosts to the tombs. At sunset a sorcerer attempts to lure the soul back by offering it sugar-cane, bananas, and other fruits, while he sings an incantation inviting the wanderer to return from among the dead to the land of the living. He pretends to catch the truant soul in a piece of cotton, which he then lays on the patient's head.[2] When the Karo-Bataks of Sumatra have buried somebody and are filling in the grave, a sorceress runs about beating the air with a stick. This she does in order to drive away the souls of the survivors, for if one of these souls happened to slip into the grave and to be covered up with earth, its owner would die.[3] Among some of the Dyak tribes of south-eastern Borneo, as soon as the coffin is carried to the place of burial, the house in which the death occurred is sprinkled with water, and the father of the family calls out the names of all his children and the other members of his household. For they think that the ghost loves to decoy away the souls of his kinsfolk, but that

---

[1] C. J. S. F. Forbes, *British Burma* (London, 1878), pp. 99 *sq.*; Shway Yoe, *The Burman* (London, 1882), ii. 102; A. Bastian, *Die Völker des östlichen Asien*, ii. 389.

[2] Guerlach, "Mœurs et superstitions des sauvages Ba-hnars," *Mis-sions Catholiques*, xix. (1887) pp. 525 *sq.*

[3] J. H. Neumann, "De *begoe* in de godsdienstige begrippen der Karo-Bataks in de Doesoen," *Mededeelingen van wege het Nederlandsche Zende-linggenootschap*, xlvi. (1902) p. 27.

his designs upon them can be defeated by calling out their names, which has the effect of bringing back the souls to their owners. The same ceremony is repeated on the return from the burial.[1] It is a rule with the Kwakiutl Indians of British Columbia that a corpse must not be coffined in the house, or the souls of the other inmates would enter the coffin, and they, too, would die. The body is taken out either through the roof or through a hole made in one of the walls, and is then coffined outside the house.[2] In the East Indian island of Keisar it is deemed imprudent to go near a grave at night, lest the ghosts should catch and keep the soul of the passer-by.[3] The Kei Islanders believe that the spirits of their forefathers, angry at not receiving food, make people sick by detaining their souls. So they lay offerings of food on the grave and beg their ancestors to allow the soul of the sick to return, or to drive it home speedily if it should be lingering by the way.[4]

In Bolang Mongondo, a district in the west of Celebes, all sickness is ascribed to the ancestral spirits who have carried off the patient's soul. The object therefore is to bring back the soul of the sufferer and restore it to him. An eye-witness has thus described the attempted cure of a sick boy. The priestesses, who acted as physicians, made a doll of cloth and fastened it to the point of a spear, which an old woman held upright. Round this doll the priestesses danced, uttering charms, and chirruping as when one calls a .dog. Then the old woman lowered the point of the spear a little, so that the priestesses could reach the doll. By this time the soul of the sick boy was supposed to be in the doll, having been brought into it by the incantations. So the priestesses approached it cautiously on tiptoe and caught the soul in the many-coloured cloths which they had been waving in the air. Then they laid the soul on the boy's head, that is, they wrapped his head in the cloth in which the soul was

Attempts to rescue the lost soul from the spirits of the dead who are detaining it.

[1] F. Grabowsky, in *Internationales Archiv für Ethnographie*, ii. (1889) p. 182.
[2] Fr. Boas, in *Eleventh Report on the North-Western Tribes of Canada*, p. 6 (separate reprint from the *Report* of the British Association for 1896).
[3] J. G. F. Riedel, *De sluik- en kroesharige rassen tusschen Selebes en Papua*, p. 414.
[4] J. G. F. Riedel, *op. cit.* pp. 221 *sq.*

Attempts
to rescue
the lost
soul from
the spirits
of the dead
who are
detaining
it.
supposed to be, and stood still for some moments with great
gravity, holding their hands on the patient's head. Suddenly
there was a jerk, the priestesses whispered and shook their
heads, and the cloth was taken off—the soul had escaped.
The priestesses gave chase to it, running round and round
the house, clucking and gesticulating as if they were driving
hens into a poultry-yard. At last they recaptured the soul
at the foot of the stair and restored it to its owner as before.[1]
Much in the same way an Australian medicine-man will
sometimes bring the lost soul of a sick man into a puppet
and restore it to the patient by pressing the puppet to his
breast.[2] In Uea, one of the Loyalty Islands, the souls of
the dead seem to have been credited with the power of
stealing the souls of the living. For when a man was sick
the soul-doctor would go with a large troop of men and
women to the graveyard. Here the men played on flutes
and the women whistled softly to lure the soul home. After
this had gone on for some time they formed in procession and
moved homewards, the flutes playing and the women whistling
all the way, while they led back the wandering soul and drove
it gently along with open palms. On entering the patient's
dwelling they commanded the soul in a loud voice to enter
his body.[3] In Madagascar when a man was sick or lunatic in
consequence of the loss of his soul, his friends despatched a
wizard in haste to fetch him a soul from the graveyard.
The emissary repaired by night to the spot, and having made
a hole in the wooden house which served as a tomb, begged
the spirit of the patient's father to bestow a soul on his son
or daughter, who had none. So saying he applied a bonnet
to the hole, then folded it up and rushed back to the house
of the sufferer, saying he had a soul for him. With that he
clapped the bonnet on the head of the invalid, who at once
said he felt much better and had recovered the soul which he
had lost.[4]

[1] N. Ph. Wilken en J. A. Schwarz,
"Het heidendom en de Islam in
Bolaang Mongondou," *Mededeelingen
van wege het Nederlandsche Zendelinggenootschap*, xi. (1867) pp. 263 *sq.*
[2] James Dawson, *Australian Aborigines* (Melbourne, Sydney, and Adelaide, 1881), pp. 57 *sq.*
[3] W. W. Gill, *Myths and Songs of
the South Pacific* (London, 1876), pp.
171 *sq.*
[4] De Flacourt, *Histoire de la grande
Isle Madagascar* (Paris, 1658), pp.
101 *sq.*

When a Dyak or Malay of some of the western tribes
or districts of Borneo is taken ill, with vomiting and profuse
sweating as the only symptoms, he thinks that one of his
deceased kinsfolk or ancestors is at the bottom of it. To
discover which of them is the culprit, a wise man or woman
pulls a lock of hair on the crown of the sufferer's head, calling
out the names of all his dead relations. The name at which
the lock gives forth a sound is the name of the guilty party.
If the patient's hair is too short to be tugged with effect,
he knocks his forehead seven times against the forehead
of a kinsman who has long hair. The hair of the latter
is then tugged instead of that of the patient and answers
to the test quite as well. When the blame has thus
been satisfactorily laid at the door of the ghost who is
responsible for the sickness, the physician, who, as in other
countries, is often an old woman, remonstrates with him on
his ill behaviour. "Go back," says she, "to your grave;
what do you come here for? The soul of the sick man
does not choose to be called by you, and will remain yet a
long time in its body." Then she puts some ashes from the
hearth in a winnowing fan and moulds out of them a small
figure or image in human likeness. Seven times she moves
the basket with the little ashen figure up and down before
the patient, taking care not to obliterate the figure, while at
the same time she says, "Sickness, settle in the head, belly,
hands, etc.; then quickly pass into the corresponding part
of the image," whereupon the patient spits on the ashen
image and pushes it from him with his left hand. Next the
beldame lights a candle and goes to the grave of the person
whose ghost is doing all the mischief. On the grave she
throws the figure of ashes, calling out, "Ghost, plague the
sick man no longer, and stay in your grave, that he may see
you no more." On her return she asks the anxious relations
in the house, "Has his soul come back?" and they must
answer quickly, "Yes, the soul of the sick man has come
back." Then she stands beside the patient, blows out the
candle which had lighted the returning soul on its way, and
strews yellow-coloured rice on the head of the convalescent,
saying, "Cluck, soul! cluck, soul! cluck, soul!" Last of
all she fastens on his right wrist a bracelet or ring which he

Rescuing
lost souls
from
ghosts in
Melanesia.

must wear for three days.[1] In this case we see that the
saving of the soul is combined with a vicarious sacrifice to
the ghost, who receives a puppet on which to work his will
instead of on the poor soul. In San Cristoval, one of the
Melanesian islands, the vicarious sacrifice takes the form of
a pig or a fish. A malignant ghost of the name of Tapia
is supposed to have seized on the sick man's soul and tied it
up to a banyan-tree. Accordingly a man who has influence
with Tapia takes a pig or fish to the holy place where the
ghost resides and offers it to him, saying, " This is for you to
eat in place of that man ; eat this, don't kill him." This
satisfies the ghost ; the soul is loosed from the tree and
carried back to the sufferer, who naturally recovers.[2] A
regular part of the stock-in-trade of a Dyak medicine-man is
a crystal into which he gazes to detect the hiding-place of a
lost soul or to identify the demon who is causing the
sickness.[3] In one of the New Hebrides a ghost will sometimes impound the souls of trespassers within a magic fence
in his garden, and will only consent to pull up the fence and
let the souls out on receiving an unqualified apology and a
satisfactory assurance that no personal disrespect was
intended.[4] In Motlav, another Melanesian island, it is
enough to call out the sick man's name in the sacred place
where he rashly intruded, and then, when the cry of the
kingfisher or some other bird is heard, to shout " Come
back " to the soul of the sick man and run back with it to
the house.[5]

Buryat
mode of
recovering
a lost soul
from the
nether
world.

It is a comparatively easy matter to save a soul which
is merely tied up to a tree or detained as a vagrant in a
pound ; but it is a far harder task to fetch it up from the
nether world, if it once gets down there. When a Buryat
shaman is called in to attend a patient, the first thing he
does is to ascertain where exactly the soul of the invalid
is ; for it may have strayed, or been stolen, or be languish-

---

[1] E. L. M. Kühr, "Schetsen uit
Borneo's Westerafdeeling," *Bijdragen
tot de Taal- Land- en Volkenkunde van
Nederlandsch-Indië*, xlvii. (1897) pp.
61 *sq.*

[2] R. H. Codrington, *The Melanesians*, pp. 138 *sq.*

[3] Bishop Hose, "The Contents of a
Dyak Medicine Chest," *Journal of the
Straits Branch of the Royal Asiatic
Society*, No. 39, June 1903, p. 69.

[4] R. H. Codrington, *op. cit.* p. 208.

[5] R. H. Codrington, *op. cit.* pp.
146 *sq.*

ing in the prison of the gloomy Erlik, lord of the world below. If it is anywhere in the neighbourhood, the shaman soon catches and replaces it in the patient's body. If it is far away, he searches the wide world till he finds it, ransacking the deep woods, the lonely steppes, and the bottom of the sea, not to be thrown off the scent even though the cunning soul runs to the sheep-walks in the hope that its footprints will be lost among the tracks of the sheep. But when the whole world has been searched in vain for the errant soul, the shaman knows that there is nothing for it but to go down to hell and seek the lost one among the spirits in prison. At the stern call of duty he does not flinch, though he knows that the journey is toilsome, and that the travelling expenses, which are naturally defrayed by the patient, are very heavy. Sometimes the lord of the infernal regions will only agree to release the soul on condition of receiving another in its stead, and that one the soul of the sick man's dearest friend. If the patient consents to the substitution, the shaman turns himself into a hawk, pounces upon the soul of the friend as it soars from his slumbering body in the form of a lark, and hands over the fluttering, struggling thing to the grim warden of the dead, who thereupon sets the soul of the sick man at liberty. So the sick man recovers and his friend dies.[1]

When a shaman declares that the soul of a sick Thompson Indian has been carried off by the dead, the good physician, who is the shaman himself, puts on a conical mask and sets off in pursuit. He now acts as if on a journey, jumping rivers and such like obstacles, searching, talking, and sometimes engaging in a tussle for the possession of the soul. His first step is to repair to the old trail by which the souls of heathen Thompsons went to the spirit-land ; for nowadays the souls of Christian Thompsons travel by a new road. If he fails to find the tracks of the lost soul there, he searches all the graveyards, one after the other, and almost always discovers it in one of them. Sometimes he succeeds in heading off the departing soul by taking a short cut to the other world. A shaman can only

American Indian modes of recovering a lost soul from the land of the dead.

[1] V. M. Mikhailovskii, "Shamanism in Siberia and European Russia," *Journal of the Anthropological Institute*, xxiv. (1895) pp. 69 *sq.*

stay a short time there. So as soon as he lays hands on
the soul he is after, he bolts with it. The other souls
give chase, but he stamps with his foot, on which he wears
a rattle made of deer's hoofs. At the rattle of the hoofs
the ghosts retreat and he hurries on. A bolder shaman
will sometimes ask the ghosts for the soul, and if they refuse
to give it, he will wrest it from them. They attack him, but
he clubs them and brings away the soul by force. When
he comes back to the world, he takes off his mask and shews
his club all bloody. Then the people know he had a
desperate struggle. If he foresees that the harrowing of
hell is likely to prove a tough job, he increases the number
of wooden pins in his mask. The rescued soul is placed by
him on the patient's head and so returned to his body.[1]
Among the Twana Indians of Washington State the descent
of the medicine-men into the nether world to rescue lost
souls is represented in pantomime before the eyes of the
spectators, who include women and children as well as men.
The surface of the ground is often broken to facilitate the
descent of the rescue party. When the adventurous band
is supposed to have reached the bottom, they journey along,
cross at least one stream, and travel till they come to the
abode of the spirits. These they surprise, and after a
desperate struggle, sustained with great ardour and a
prodigious noise, they succeed in rescuing the poor souls,
and so, wrapping them up in cloth, they make the best of
their way back to the upper world and restore the recovered
souls to their owners, who have been seen to cry heartily for
joy at receiving them back.[2]

Often the abduction of a man's soul is set down to
demons. The Annamites believe that when a man meets a
demon and speaks to him, the demon inhales the man's
breath and soul.[3] The souls of the Bahnars of eastern
Cochin-China are apt to be carried off by evil spirits, and

[1] J. Teit, "The Thompson Indians
of British Columbia," *Memoir of the
American Museum of Natural History,
The Jesup North Pacific Expedition*,
vol. i. part iv. (April 1900) pp.
363 *sq.*

[2] Rev. Myron Eels, "The Twana,
Chemakum, and Klallam Indians of
Washington Territory," *Annual Report
of the Smithsonian Institution for
1887*, pt. i. pp. 677 *sq.*

[3] A. Landes, "Contes et légendes
annamites," No. 76 in *Cochinchine
Française: excursions et reconnais-
sances*, No. 23 (Saigon, 1885), p.
80.

the modes of recovering them are various.   If a man suffers
from a colic, the sorcerer may say that in planting sugar-
cane, maize or what-not, he has pierced the stomach of a
certain god who lives like a mole in the ground, and that
the injured deity has punished him by abstracting his soul
and burying it under a plant.   Hence the cure for the colic
is to pull up the plant and water the hole with millet wine
and the blood of a fowl, a goat, or a pig.   Again, if a child
falls ill in the forest or the fields, it is because some devil
has made off with its soul.   To retrieve this spiritual loss
the sorcerer constructs an apparatus which comprises an egg-
shell in an egg-holder, a little waxen image of the sick
child, and a small bamboo full of millet wine.   This
apparatus he sets up at a cross-road, praying the devil to
drink the wine and surrender the stolen soul by depositing
it in the egg-shell.   Then he returns to the house, and
putting a little cotton to the child's head restores the soul
to its owner.   Sometimes the sorcerer lays a trap for the
thievish demon, the bait consisting of the liver of a pig or a
fowl and the blood-smeared handle of a little mattock.   At
nightfall he sets the trap at a cross-road and lies in wait
hard by.   While the devil is licking the blood and munching
the liver, the artful sorcerer pounces out on him, and after a
severe struggle wrests the soul from his clutches, returning to the village victorious, but breathless and bleeding
from his terrific encounter with the enemy of souls.[1]
Fits and convulsions are generally set down by the
Chinese to the agency of certain mischievous spirits who
love to draw men's souls out of their bodies.   At Amoy
the spirits who serve babies and children in this way
rejoice in the high-sounding titles of " celestial agencies
bestriding galloping horses " and " literary graduates residing
halfway up in the sky."   When an infant is writhing in
convulsions, the frightened mother hastens to the roof of the
house, and, waving about a bamboo pole to which one of
the child's garments is attached, cries out several times, " My
child So-and-so, come back, return home ! "   Meantime,
another inmate of the house bangs away at a gong in the

[1] Guerlach, "Chez les sauvages   (1884) p. 436, xix. (1887) p. 453,
Ba-hnars," *Missions Catholiques*, xvi.   xxvi. (1894) pp. 142 *sq.*

hope of attracting the attention of the strayed soul, which is supposed to recognise the familiar garment and to slip into it. The garment containing the soul is then placed on or beside the child, and if the child does not die recovery is sure to follow sooner or later.[1] Similarly we saw that some Indians catch a man's lost soul in his boots and restore it to his body by putting his feet into them.[2]

Abduction of souls by demons in the East Indies. If Galelareese mariners are sailing past certain rocks or come to a river where they never were before, they must wash their faces, for otherwise the spirits of the rocks or the river would snatch away their souls.[3] When a Dyak is about to leave a forest through which he has been walking alone, he never forgets to ask the demons to give him back his soul, for it may be that some forest-devil has carried it off. For the abduction of a soul may take place without its owner being aware of his loss, and it may happen either while he is awake or asleep.[4] The Papuans of Geelvink Bay in New Guinea are apt to think that the mists which sometimes hang about the tops of tall trees in their tropical forests envelop a spirit or god called Narbrooi, who draws away the breath or soul of those whom he loves, thus causing them to languish and die. Accordingly, when a man lies sick, a friend or relation will go to one of these mist-capped trees and endeavour to recover the lost soul. At the foot of the tree he makes a peculiar sound to attract the attention of the spirit, and lights a cigar. In its curling smoke his fancy discerns the fair and youthful form of Narbrooi himself, who, decked with flowers, appears and informs the anxious enquirer whether the soul of his sick friend is with him or not. If it is, the man asks, " Has he done any wrong?" "Oh no!" the spirit answers, " I love him, and therefore I have taken him to myself." So the man lays down an offering at the foot of the tree, and goes home with the soul of the sufferer in a straw bag. Arrived at the house, he empties the bag with its precious contents

---

[1] J. J. M. de Groot, *The Religious System of China*, i. 243 *sq.*

[2] See above, p. 45.

[3] M. J. van Baarda, "Fabelen, Verhalen en Overleveringen der Gale-

lareezen," *Bijdragen tot de Taal- Land- en Volkenkunde van Nederlandsch-Indië*, xlv. (1895) p. 509.

[4] M. T. H. Perelaer, *Ethnographische Beschrijving der Dajaks* (Zalt-Bommel, 1870), pp. 26 *sq.*

over the sick man's head, rubs his arms and hands with ginger-root, which he had first chewed small, and then ties a bandage round one of the patient's wrists. If the bandage bursts, it is a sign that Narbrooi has repented of his bargain, and is drawing away the sufferer once more to himself.[1]

In the Moluccas when a man is unwell it is thought that some devil has carried away his soul to the tree, mountain, or hill where he (the devil) resides. A sorcerer having pointed out the devil's abode, the friends of the patient carry thither cooked rice, fruit, fish, raw eggs, a hen, a chicken, a silken robe, gold, armlets, and so forth. Having set out the food in order they pray, saying : " We come to offer to you, O devil, this offering of food, clothes, gold, and so on ; take it and release the soul of the patient for whom we pray. Let it return to his body, and he who now is sick shall be made whole." Then they eat a little and let the hen loose as a ransom for the soul of the patient ; also they put down the raw eggs ; but the silken robe, the gold, and the armlets they take home with them. As soon as they are come to the house they place a flat bowl containing the offerings which have been brought back at the sick man's head, and say to him : " Now is your soul released, and you shall fare well and live to grey hairs on the earth." [2]   A more modern account from the same region describes how the friend of the patient, after depositing his offerings on the spot where the missing soul is supposed to be, calls out thrice the name of the sick person, adding, " Come with me, come with me." Then he returns, making a motion with a cloth as if he had caught the soul in it. He must not look to right or left or speak a word to any one he meets, but must go straight to the patient's house. At the door he stands, and calling out the sick person's name, asks whether he is returned. Being

---

[1] "Eenige bijzonderheden betreffende de Papoeas van de Geelvinksbaai van Nieuw-Guinea," *Bijdragen tot de Taal- Land- en Volkenkunde van Neêrlandsch- Indië*, ii. (1854) pp. 375 *sq.* It is especially the souls of children that the spirit loves to take to himself. See J. L. van Hasselt, "Die Papua- stämme an der Geelvinkbai," *Mittei- lungen der Geographischen Gesellschaft*

zu Jena, ix. (1891) p. 103 ; compare *ib.* iv. (1886) pp. 118 *sq.* The mists seen to hang about tree-tops are due to the power of trees to condense vapour, as to which see Gilbert White, *Natural History of Selborne*, part ii. letter 29.

[2] Fr. Valentyn, *Oud- en nieuw Oost- Indiën*, iii. 13 *sq.*

answered from within that he is returned, he enters and lays the cloth in which he has caught the soul on the patient's throat, saying, " Now you are returned to the house." Sometimes a substitute is provided ; a doll, dressed up in gay clothing and tinsel, is offered to the demon in exchange for the patient's soul, with these words, " Give us back the ugly one which you have taken away and receive this pretty one instead." [1]

Abduction of souls by demons in Celebes and Siberia. Among the Alfoors or Toradjas of Poso, in Central Celebes, a wooden puppet is offered to the demon as a substitute for the soul which he has abstracted, and the patient must touch the puppet in order to identify himself with it. The effigy is then hung on a bamboo pole, which is planted at the place of sacrifice outside of the house. Here too are deposited offerings of rice, an egg, a little wood (which is afterwards kindled), a sherd of a broken cooking-pot, and so forth. A long rattan extends from the place of sacrifice to the sufferer, who grasps one end of it firmly, for along it his lost soul will return when the devil has kindly released it. All being ready, the priestess informs the demon that he has come to the wrong place, and that there are no doubt much better quarters where he could reside. Then the father of the patient, standing beside the offerings, takes up his parable as follows : " O demon, we forgot to sacrifice to you. You have visited us with this sickness ; will you now go away from us to some other place ? We have made ready provisions for you on the journey. See, here is a cooking-pot, here are rice, fire, and a fowl. O demon, go away from us." With that the priestess strews rice towards the bamboo-pole to lure back the wandering soul ; and the fowl promised to the devil is thrown in the same direction, but is instantly jerked back again by a string which, in a spirit of intelligent economy, has been previously attached to its leg. The demon is now supposed to accept the puppet, which hangs from the pole, and to release the soul, which, sliding down the pole and along the rattan, returns to its proper owner. And lest the

---

[1] Van Schmidt, "Aanteekeningen nopens de zeden, gewoonten en gebruiken, benevens de vooroordeelen en bijgeloovigheden der bevolking van de eilanden Saparoea, Haroekoe, Noessa Laut, en van een gedeelte van de zuidkust van Ceram," in *Tijdschrift voor Neêrlands Indië*, 1843, dl. ii. 511 *sqq.*

evil spirit should repent of the barter which has just been effected, all communication with him is broken off by cutting down the pole.[1] Similarly the Mongols make up a horse of birch-bark and a doll, and invite the demon to take the doll instead of the patient and to ride away on the horse.[2] A Yakut shaman, rigged out in his professional costume, with his drum in his hand, will boldly descend into the lower world and haggle with the demon who has carried off a sick man's soul. Not uncommonly the demon proves amenable to reason, and in consideration of the narrow circumstances of the patient's family will accept a more moderate ransom than he at first demanded. For instance, he may be brought to put up with the skin of an Arctic hare or Arctic fox instead of a foal or a steer. The bargain being struck, the shaman hurries back to the sufferer's bedside, from which to the merely carnal eye he has never stirred, and informs the anxious relatives of the success of his mission. They in turn gladly hasten to provide the ransom.[3]

Demons are especially feared by persons who have just entered a new house. Hence at a house-warming among the Alfoors of Minahassa in Celebes the priest performs a ceremony for the purpose of restoring their souls to the inmates. He hangs up a bag at the place of sacrifice and then goes through a list of the gods. There are so many of them that this takes him the whole night through without stopping. In the morning he offers the gods an egg and some rice. By this time the souls of the household are supposed to be

Souls rescued from demons at a house-warming in Minahassa.

---

[1] A. C. Kruijt, "Een en ander aangaande het geestelijk en maatschappelijk leven van den Poso-Alfoer," *Mededeelingen van wege het Nederlandsche Zendelinggenootschap,* xxxix. (1895) pp. 5-8.

[2] A. Bastian, *Die Seele und ihre Erscheinungswesen in der Ethnographie* (Berlin, 1868), pp. 36 *sq.* ; J. G. Gmelin, *Reise durch Sibirien,* ii. 359 *sq.* This mode of curing sickness, by inducing the demon to swap the soul of the patient for an effigy, is practised also by the Dyaks and by some tribes on the northern coast of New Guinea. See H. Ling Roth, "Low's Natives of Borneo," *Journal of the Anthropological*

Institute, xxi. (1892) p. 117 ; E. L. M. Kühr, "Schetsen uit Borneo's Wester-afdeeling," *Bijdragen tot de Taal- Land- en Volkenkunde van Nederlandsch-Indië,* xlvii. (1897) pp. 62 *sq.* ; F. S. A. de Clercq, "De West- en Noordkust van Nederlandsch Nieuw - Guinea," *Tijdschrift van het kon. Nederlandsch Aardrijkskundig Genootschap,* Tweede Serie, x. (1893) pp. 633 *sq.*

[3] V. Priklonski, "Todtengebräuche der Jakuten," *Globus,* lix. (1891) pp. 81 *sq.* Compare *id.,* "Über das Schamenthum bei den Jakuten," in A. Bastian's *Allerlei aus Volks- und Menschenkunde,* i. 218 *sq.*

gathered in the bag. So the priest takes the bag, and holding it on the head of the master of the house, says, " Here you have your soul ; go (soul) to-morrow away again." He then does the same, saying the same words, to the housewife and all the other members of the family.[1] Amongst the same Alfoors one way of recovering a sick man's soul is to let down a bowl by a belt out of a window and fish for the soul till it is caught in the bowl and hauled up.[2] And among the same people, when a priest is bringing back a sick man's soul which he has caught in a cloth, he is preceded by a girl holding the large leaf of a certain palm over his head as an umbrella to keep him and the soul from getting wet, in case it should rain ; and he is followed by a man brandishing a sword to deter other souls from any attempt at rescuing the captured spirit.[3]

Souls carried off by the sun and other gods.

In Nias, when a man dreams that a pig is fastened under a neighbour's house, it is a sign that some one in that house will die. They think that the sun-god is drawing away the shadows or souls of that household from this world of shadows to his own bright world of radiant light, and a ceremony must needs be performed to win back these passing souls to earth. Accordingly, while it is still night, the priest begins to drum and pray, and he continues his orisons till about nine o'clock next morning. Then he takes his stand at an opening in the roof through which he can behold the sun, and spreading out a cloth waits till the beams of the morning sun fall full upon it. In the sunbeams he thinks the wandering souls have come back again ; so he wraps the cloth up tightly, and quitting the opening in the roof, hastens with his precious charge to the expectant household. Before each member of it he stops, and dipping his fingers into the cloth takes out his or her soul and restores it to the owner by touching the person on the forehead.[4]

---

[1] P. N. Wilken, " Bijdragen tot de kennis van de zeden en gewoonten der Alfoeren in de Minahassa," *Mededeelingen van wege het Nederlandsche Zendelinggenootschap*, vii. (1863) pp. 146 *sq.* Why the priest, after restoring the soul, tells it to go away again, is not clear.

[2] J. G. F. Riedel, " De Minahasa in 1825," *Tijdschrift voor Indische Taal- Land- en Volkenkunde*, xviii. 523.

[3] N. Graafland, *De Minahassa* (Rotterdam, 1869), i. 327 *sq.*

[4] Fr. Kramer, "Der Götzendienst der Niasser," *Tijdschrift voor Indische Taal- Land- en Volkenkunde*, xxxiii. (1890) pp. 490 *sq.*

The Thompson Indians of British Columbia think that the setting sun draws the souls of men away towards it; hence they will never sleep with their heads to the sunset.[1] The Samoans tell how two young wizards, passing a house where a chief lay very sick, saw a company of gods from the mountain sitting in the doorway. They were handing from one to another the soul of the dying chief. It was wrapt in a leaf, and had been passed from the gods inside the house to those sitting in the doorway. One of the gods handed the soul to one of the wizards, taking him for a god in the dark, for it was night. Then all the gods rose up and went away; but the wizard kept the chief's soul. In the morning some women went with a present of fine mats to fetch a famous physician. The wizards were sitting on the shore as the women passed, and they said to the women, "Give us the mats and we will heal him." So they went to the chief's house. He was very ill, his jaw hung down, and his end seemed near. But the wizards undid the leaf and let the soul into him again, and forthwith he brightened up and lived.[2]

The Battas or Bataks of Sumatra believe that the soul of a living man may transmigrate into the body of an animal. Hence, for example, the doctor is sometimes desired to extract the patient's soul from the body of a fowl, in which it has been hidden away by an evil spirit.[3] *Lost souls extracted from a fowl.*

Sometimes the lost soul is brought back in a visible shape. In Melanesia a woman, knowing that a neighbour was at the point of death, heard a rustling in her house, as of a moth fluttering, just at the moment when a noise of weeping and lamentation told her that the soul was flown. She caught the fluttering thing between her hands and ran with it, crying out that she had caught the soul. But though she opened her hands above the mouth of the corpse, it did not revive.[4] In Lepers' Island, one of the New *Lost souls brought back in a visible form.*

[1] J. Teit, "The Thompson Indians of British Columbia," *Memoir of the American Museum of Natural History, The Jesup North Pacific Expedition,* vol. i. part iv. (April 1900) p. 357.
[2] G. Turner, *Samoa,* pp. 142 *sq.*
[3] J. B. Neumann, "Het Pane- en Bila - stroomgebied op het eiland Sumatra," *Tijdschrift van het Nederlandsch Aardrijkskundig Genootschap,* Tweede Serie, dl. iii., Afdeeling, meer uitgebreide artikelen, No. 2 (1886), p. 302.
[4] R. H. Codrington, "Religious

Lost souls brought back in a visible form.

Hebrides, for ten days after a birth the father is careful not to exert himself or the baby would suffer for it. If during this time he goes away to any distance, he will bring back with him on his return a little stone representing the infant's soul. Arrived at home he cries, " Come hither," and puts down the stone in the house. Then he waits till the child sneezes, at which he cries, " Here it is " ; for now he knows that the little soul has not been lost after all.[1] The Salish or Flathead Indians of Oregon believe that a man's soul may be separated for a time from his body without causing death and without the man being aware of his loss. It is necessary, however, that the lost soul should be soon found and restored to its owner or he will die. The name of the man who has lost his soul is revealed in a dream to the medicine-man, who hastens to inform the sufferer of his loss. Generally a number of men have sustained a like loss at the same time ; all their names are revealed to the medicine-man, and all employ him to recover their souls. The whole night long these soulless men go about the village from lodge to lodge, dancing and singing. Towards daybreak they go into a separate lodge, which is closed up so as to be totally dark. A small hole is then made in the roof, through which the medicine-man, with a bunch of feathers, brushes in the souls, in the shape of bits of bone and the like, which he receives on a piece of matting. A fire is next kindled, by the light of which the medicine-man sorts out the souls. First he puts aside the souls of dead people, of which there are usually several ; for if he were to give the soul of a dead person to a living man, the man would die instantly. Next he picks out the souls of all the persons present, and making them all to sit down before him, he takes the soul of each, in the shape of a splinter of bone, wood, or shell, and placing it on the owner's head, pats it with many prayers and contortions till it descends into the heart and so resumes its proper place.[2] In Amboyna the sorcerer, to recover a soul detained

Beliefs and Practices in Melanesia," *Journal of the Anthropological Institute*, x. (1881) p. 281 ; *id.*, *The Melanesians*, p. 267.

[1] R. H. Codrington, *The Melanesians*, p. 229.

[2] Horatio Hale, *United States Exploring Expedition, Ethnography and Philology* (Philadelphia, 1846), pp. 208 *sq.* Compare Ch. Wilkes, *Narrative of the United States Exploring Expedition* (London, 1845),

by demons, plucks a branch from a tree, and waving it to and fro as if to catch something, calls out the sick man's name. Returning he strikes the patient over the head and body with the branch, into which the lost soul is supposed to have passed, and from which it returns to the patient.[1] In the Babar Islands offerings for evil spirits are laid at the root of a great tree (*wokiorai*), from which a leaf is plucked and pressed on the patient's forehead and breast ; the lost soul, which is in the leaf, is thus restored to its owner.[2] In some other islands of the same seas, when a man returns ill and speechless from the forest, it is inferred that the evil spirits which dwell in the great trees have caught and kept his soul. Offerings of food are therefore left under a tree and the soul is brought home in a piece of wax.[3] Amongst the Dyaks of Sarawak the priest conjures the lost soul into a cup, where it is seen by the uninitiated as a lock of hair, but by the initiated as a miniature human being. This the priest pokes back into the patient's body through an invisible hole in his skull.[4] In Nias the sick man's soul is restored to him in the shape of a firefly, visible only to the sorcerer, who catches it in a cloth and places it on the forehead of the patient.[5] Amongst the Indians of Santiago Tepehuacan, if a child has fallen from the arms of its bearer and an illness has resulted from the fall, the parents will take the child's shirt, stretch it out on the spot where the little one fell, and say, " Come, come, come back to the infant."

Soul lost by a fall and recovered from the earth.

iv. 448 *sq.* Similar methods of recovering lost souls are practised by the Haidas, Nootkas, Shuswap, and other Indian tribes of British Columbia. See Fr. Boas, in *Fifth Report on the North-Western Tribes of Canada*, pp. 58 *sq.* (separate reprint from the *Report of the British Association for 1889*) ; *id.* in *Sixth Report*, etc., pp. 30, 44, 59 *sq.*, 94 (separate reprint of the *Report of the Brit. Assoc. for 1890*) ; *id.* in *Ninth Report*, etc., p. 462 (in *Report of the Brit. Assoc. for 1894*). Kwakiutl medicine-men exhibit captured souls in the shape of little balls of eagle down. See Fr. Boas, in *Report of the U.S. National Museum for 1895*, pp. 561, 575.

[1] J. G. F. Riedel, *De sluik- en kroesharige rassen tusschen Selebes en Papua*, pp. 77 *sq.*

[2] J. G. F. Riedel, *op. cit.* pp. 356 *sq.*

[3] J. G. F. Riedel, *op. cit.* p. 376.

[4] Spenser St. John, *Life in the Forests of the Far East*,[2] i. 189 ; H. Ling Roth, *The Natives of Sarawak and British North Borneo*, i. 261. Sometimes the souls resemble cotton seeds (Spenser St. John, *l.c.*). Compare *id.* i. 183.

[5] Nieuwenhuisen en Rosenberg, "Verslag omtrent het Eiland Nias," *Verhandel. van het Batav. Genootsch. van Kunsten en Wetenschappen*, xxx. (Batavia, 1863) p. 116 ; H. von Rosenberg, *Der Malayische Archipel*, p. 174 ; E. Modigliani, *Viaggio a Nías* (Milan, 1890), p. 192.

Soul lost by a fall and re-covered from the earth.

Then they bring back a little of the earth wrapped up in the shirt, and put the shirt on the child. They say that in this manner the spirit is replaced in the child's body and that he will recover.[1] With this we may compare an Irish custom reported by Camden. When any one happens to fall, he springs up again, and turning round thrice to the right, digs the earth with a sword or knife, and takes up a turf, because they say the earth restores his shade to him. But if he falls sick within two or three days thereafter, a woman skilled in these matters is sent to the spot, and there says: "I call thee, So-and-so, from the East and West, from the South and North, from the groves, woods, rivers, marshes, fairies white, red, and black," and so forth. After uttering certain short prayers, she returns home to the sick person, and whispering in his ear another prayer, along with a *Pater Noster*, puts some burning coals into a cup of clean water, and so decides whether the distemper has been inflicted by the fairies.[2] Here, though Camden is not very explicit, and he probably did not quite understand the custom he describes, it seems plain that the shade or soul of a man who has fallen is conceived as adhering to the ground where he fell. Accordingly he seeks to regain possession of it by digging up the earth; but if he fails to recover it, he sends a wise woman to the spot to win back his soul from the fairies who are detaining it.

Recovery of the soul in ancient Egypt.

The ancient Egyptians held that a dead man is not in a state to enter on the life hereafter until his soul has been found and restored to his mummified body. The vital spark had been commonly devoured by the malignant god Sit, who concealed his true form in the likeness of a horned beast, such as an ox or a gazelle. So the priests went in quest of the missing spirit, slaughtered the animal which had devoured it, and cutting open the carcase found the soul still undigested in its stomach. Afterwards the son of the deceased embraced the mummy or the image of his father in order to restore his soul to him. Formerly it was

---

1 "Lettre du curé de Santiago Tepehuacan à son évêque sur les mœurs et coutumes des Indiens soumis à ses soins," *Bulletin de la Société de Géographie* (Paris), IIme Série, ii.

(1834) p. 178.

2 W. Camden, *Britannia* (London, 1607), p. 792. The passage has not always been understood by Camden's translators.

customary to place the skin of the slain beast on the dead man for the purpose of recruiting his strength with that of the animal.[1]

Again, souls may be extracted from their bodies or detained on their wanderings not only by ghosts and demons but also by men, especially by sorcerers. In Fiji, if a criminal refused to confess, the chief sent for a scarf with which " to catch away the soul of the rogue." At the sight or even at the mention of the scarf the culprit generally made a clean breast. For if he did not, the scarf would be waved over his head till his soul was caught in it, when it would be carefully folded up and nailed to the end of a chief's canoe ; and for want of his soul the criminal would pine and die.[2] The sorcerers of Danger Island used to set snares for souls. The snares were made of stout cinet, about fifteen to thirty feet long, with loops on either side of different sizes, to suit the different sizes of souls ; for fat souls there were large loops, for thin souls there were small ones. When a man was sick against whom the sorcerers had a grudge, they set up these soul-snares near his house and watched for the flight of his soul. If in the shape of a bird or an insect it was caught in the snare the man would infallibly die.[3] When a Polynesian mother desired that the child in her womb should grow up to be a great warrior or a great thief, she repaired to the temple of the war-god Oro or of the thief-god Hiro. There the priest obligingly caught the spirit of the god in a snare made of coco-nut fibre, and then infused it into the woman. When the child was born, the mother took it to the temple and dedicated it to the god with whose divine spirit the infant was already possessed.[4] The Algonquin Indians also used nets to catch souls, but only as

Souls stolen or detained by sorcerers in Fiji and Polynesia.

<hr>

[1] A. Moret, Le Rituel du culte divin journalier en Égypte (Paris, 1902), pp. 32-35, 83 sq.

[2] Th. Williams, Fiji and the Fijians[2] (London, 1860), i. 250.

[3] W. W. Gill, Myths and Songs of the South Pacific, p. 171 ; id., Life in the Southern Isles, pp. 181 sqq. Cinet, sinnet, or sennit is cordage made from the dried fibre of the coco-nut husk. Large quantities of it are used in Fiji.

See Th. Williams, Fiji and the Fijians,[2] i. 69.

[4] J. Williams, Narrative of Missionary Enterprises in the South Sea Islands (London, 1838), pp. 93, 466 sq. A traveller in Zombo-land found traps commonly set at the entrances of villages and huts for the purpose of catching the devil. See Rev. Th. Lewis, " The Ancient Kingdom of Kongo," The Geographical Journal, xix. (1902) p. 554.

a measure of defence. They feared lest passing souls, which had just quitted the bodies of dying people, should enter their huts and carry off the souls of the inmates to deadland. So they spread nets about their houses to catch and entangle these ghostly intruders in the meshes.[1]

Detention of souls by sorcerers in Africa.

Among the Sereres of Senegambia, when a man wishes to revenge himself on his enemy he goes to the *Fitaure* (chief and priest in one), and prevails on him by presents to conjure the soul of his enemy into a large jar of red earthenware, which is then deposited under a consecrated tree. The man whose soul is shut up in the jar soon dies.[2] Among the Baoules of the Ivory Coast it happened once that a chief's soul was extracted by the magic of an enemy, who succeeded in shutting it up in a box. To recover it, two men held a garment of the sick man, while a witch performed certain enchantments. After a time she declared that the soul was now in the garment, which was accordingly rolled up and hastily wrapped about the invalid for the purpose of restoring his spirit to him.[3] Some of the Congo negroes think that enchanters can get possession of human souls, and enclosing them in tusks of ivory, sell them to the white man, who makes them work for him in his country under the sea. It is believed that very many of the coast labourers are men thus obtained; so when these people go to trade they often look anxiously about for their dead relations. The man whose soul is thus sold into slavery will die "in due course, if not at the time."[4] In some parts of West Africa, indeed, wizards are continually setting traps to catch souls that wander from their bodies in sleep; and when they have caught one, they tie it up over the fire, and as it shrivels in the heat the owner sickens. This is done, not out of any grudge towards the sufferer, but purely as a matter of business. The wizard does not care whose soul he has captured, and will readily restore it to its owner if only he is paid for doing so. Some sorcerers keep regular asylums for strayed souls, and any-

[1] *Relations des Jésuites*, 1639, p. 44 (Canadian reprint, Quebec, 1858).

[2] L. J. B. Bérenger-Féraud, *Les Peuplades de la Sénégambie* (Paris, 1879), p. 277.

[3] Delafosse, in *L'Anthropologie*, xi. (1895) p. 558.

[4] W. H. Bentley, *Life on the Congo* (London, 1887), p. 71.

body who has lost or mislaid his own soul can always have another one from the asylum on payment of the usual fee. No blame whatever attaches to men who keep these private asylums or set traps for passing souls ; it is their profession, and in the exercise of it they are actuated by no harsh or unkindly feelings.   But there are also wretches who from pure spite or for the sake of lucre set and bait traps with the deliberate purpose of catching the soul of a particular man ; and in the bottom of the pot, hidden by the bait, are knives and sharp hooks which tear and rend the poor soul, either killing it outright or mauling it so as to impair the health of its owner when it succeeds in escaping and returning to him. Miss Kingsley knew a Kruman who became very anxious about his soul, because for several nights he had smelt in his dreams the savoury smell of smoked crawfish seasoned with red pepper.   Clearly some ill-wisher had set a trap baited with this dainty for his dream-soul, intending to do him grievous bodily, or rather spiritual, harm ; and for the next few nights great pains were taken to keep his soul from straying abroad in his sleep.   In the sweltering heat of the tropical night he lay sweating and snorting under a blanket, his nose and mouth tied up with a handkerchief to prevent the escape of his precious soul.[1]

When Dyaks of the Upper Melawie are about to go out head-hunting they take the precaution of securing the souls of their enemies before they attempt to kill their bodies, calculating apparently that mere bodily death will soon follow the spiritual death, or capture, of the soul.   With this intention they clear a small space in the underwood of the forest, and set up in the clearing one of those miniature houses in which it is customary to deposit the ashes of the dead.   Food is placed in the little house, which, though raised on four posts, is connected with the ground by a tiny inverted ladder of the sort up which spirits are believed to swarm.   When these preparations have been completed, the leader of the expedition comes and sits down a little way from the miniature house, and addressing the spirits of kinsmen who had the misfortune to be beheaded by their enemies, he says, " O ghosts of So-and-so, come speedily back

Taking the souls of enemies first and their heads afterwards.

---

[1] Mary H. Kingsley, *Travels in West Africa* (London, 1897), pp. 461 *sq.*

Taking
the souls
of enemies
first and
their heads
afterwards.

to our village. We have rice in abundance. Our trees all bear ripe fruit. Our baskets are full to the brim. O ghosts, come swiftly back and forget not to bring your new friends and acquaintances with you." But by the new friends and acquaintances of the ghosts he means the souls of the enemies against whom he is about to lead the expedition. Meantime the other warriors have hidden themselves close by behind trees and bushes, and are listening with all their ears. When the cry of an animal is heard in the forest, or a humming sound seems to issue from the little house, it is a sign that the ghosts of their friends have come, bringing with them the souls of their enemies, which are accordingly at their mercy. At that the lurking warriors leap forth from their ambush, and with brandished blades hew and slash at the souls of their foemen swarming unseen in the air. Taken completely by surprise, the panic-stricken souls flee in all directions, and are fain to hide under every leaf and stone on the ground. But even here their retreat is cut off. For now the leader of the expedition is hard at work, grubbing up with his hands every stone and leaf to right and left, and thrusting them with feverish haste into the basket, which he at once ties up securely. He now flatters himself that he has the souls of the enemy safe in his possession ; and when in the course of the expedition the heads of the foe are severed from their bodies, he will pack them into the same basket in which their souls are already languishing in captivity.[1]

In Hawaii there were sorcerers who caught souls of living people, shut them up in calabashes, and gave them to people

---

[1] E. L. M. Kühr, in *Internationales Archiv für Ethnographie*, ii. (1889) p. 163 ; *id.*, "Schetsen uit Borneo's Westerafdeeling,"*Bijdragen tot de Taal-Land- en Volkenkunde van Nederlandsch-Indië*, xlvii. (1897) pp. 59 *sq.* Among the Haida Indians of Queen Charlotte Islands "every war-party must be accompanied by a shaman, whose duty it was to find a propitious time for making an attack, etc., but especially to war with and kill the souls of the enemy. Then the death of their natural bodies was certain." See J. R. Swanton, "Contributions to the Ethnology of the Haida" (Leyden and New York, 1905), p. 40 (*Memoir of the American Museum of Natural History, The Jesup North Pacific Expedition*, vol. v. part i.). Some of the Dyaks of south-eastern Borneo perform a ceremony for the purpose of extracting the souls from the bodies of prisoners whom they are about to torture to death. See F. Grabowsky, "Der Tod, das Begräbnis, etc., bei den Dajaken," *Internationales Archiv für Ethnographie*, ii. (1889) p. 199.

to eat. By squeezing a captured soul in their hands they discovered the place where people had been secretly buried.[1] Amongst the Canadian Indians, when a wizard wished to kill a man, he sent out his familiar spirits, who brought him the victim's soul in the shape of a stone or the like. The wizard struck the soul with a sword or an axe till it bled profusely, and as it bled the man to whom it belonged fell ill and died.[2] In Amboyna if a doctor is convinced that a patient's soul has been carried away by a demon beyond recovery, he seeks to supply its place with a soul abstracted from another man. For this purpose he goes by night to a house and asks, " Who's there ? " If an inmate is incautious enough to answer, the doctor takes up from before the door a clod of earth, into which the soul of the person who replied is thought to have passed. This clod the doctor lays under the sick man's pillow, and performs certain ceremonies by which the stolen soul is conveyed into the patient's body. Then as he goes home the doctor fires two shots to frighten the soul from returning to its proper owner.[3] A Karen wizard will catch the wandering soul of a sleeper and transfer it to the body of a dead man. The latter, therefore, comes to life as the former dies. But the friends of the sleeper in turn engage a wizard to steal the soul of another sleeper, who dies as the first sleeper comes to life. In this way an indefinite succession of deaths and resurrections is supposed to take place.[4]

Nowhere perhaps is the art of abducting human souls more carefully cultivated or carried to higher perfection than in the Malay Peninsula. Here the methods by which the wizard works his will are various, and so too are his motives. Sometimes he desires to destroy an enemy, sometimes to win the love of a cold or bashful beauty. Some of the charms operate entirely without contact ; in others, the receptacle into which the soul is to be lured has formed part of, or at least touched, the person of the victim. Thus, to take an

[1] A. Bastian, *Allerlei aus Volks- und Menschenkunde* (Berlin, 1888), i. 119.
[2] *Relations des Jésuites*, 1637, p. 50 (Canadian reprint, Quebec, 1858).
[3] J. G. F. Riedel, *De sluik- en kroesharige rassen tusschen Selebes en Papua* (the Hague, 1886), pp. 78 sq.
[4] E. B. Cross, " On the Karens," *Journal of the American Oriental Society*, iv. (1854) p. 307.

instance of the latter sort of charm, the following are the directions given for securing the soul of one whom you wish to render distraught. Take soil from the middle of his footprint; wrap it up in pieces of red, black, and yellow cloth, taking care to keep the yellow outside; and hang it from the centre of your mosquito curtain with parti-coloured thread. It will then become your victim's soul. To complete the transubstantiation, however, it is needful to switch the packet with a birch composed of seven leaf-ribs from a "green" coco-nut. Do this seven times at sunset, at midnight, and at sunrise, saying, "It is not earth that I switch, but the heart of So-and-so." Then bury it in the middle of a path where your victim is sure to step over it, and he will unquestionably become distraught.[1] Another way is to scrape the wood of the floor where your intended victim has been sitting, mix the scrapings with earth from his or her footprint, and knead the whole with wax from a deserted bees' comb into a likeness of him or her. Then fumigate the figure with incense and beckon to the soul every night for three nights successively by waving a cloth, while you recite the appropriate spell.[2] In the following cases the charm takes effect without any contact whatever, whether direct or indirect, with the victim. When the moon, just risen, looks red above the eastern horizon, go out, and standing in the moonlight, with the big toe of your right foot on the big toe of your left, make a speaking-trumpet of your right hand and recite through it the following words:

" *OM.   I loose my shaft, I loose it and the moon clouds over,*
I loose it, and the sun is extinguished.
I loose it, and the stars burn dim.
But it is not the sun, moon, and stars that I shoot at,
It is the stalk of the heart of that child of the congregation,
                        So-and-so.

Cluck! cluck! soul of So-and-so, come and walk with me,
Come and sit with me,
Come and sleep and share my pillow.
Cluck! cluck! soul."

Repeat this thrice and after every repetition blow through

---

[1] W. W. Skeat, *Malay Magic* (London, 1900), pp. 568 *sq.*
[2] W. W. Skeat, *op. cit.* pp. 569 *sq.*

your hollow fist.[1]   Or you may catch the soul in your turban,
thus.   Go out on the night of the full moon and the two
succeeding nights ; sit down on an ant-hill facing the moon,
burn incense, and recite the following incantation :

> *" I bring you a betel leaf to chew,*
> *Dab the lime on to it, Prince Ferocious,*
> *For Somebody, Prince Distraction's daughter, to chew.*
> *Somebody at sunrise be distraught for love of me,*
> *Somebody at sunset be distraught for love of me.*
> *As you remember your parents, remember me ;*
> *As you remember your house and house-ladder, remember me.*
> *When thunder rumbles, remember me ;*
> *When wind whistles, remember me ;*
> *When the heavens rain, remember me ;*
> *When cocks crow, remember me ;*
> *When the dial-bird tells its tales, remember me ;*
> *When you look up at the sun, remember me ;*
> *When you look up at the moon, remember me,*
> *For in that self-same moon I am there.*
> *Cluck ! cluck ! soul of Somebody come hither to me.*
> *I do not mean to let you have my soul,*
> *Let your soul come hither to mine."*

Now wave the end of your turban towards the moon
seven times each night.   Go home and put it under your
pillow, and if you want to wear it in the daytime, burn
incense and say, " It is not a turban that I carry in my girdle,
but the soul of Somebody." [2]

Perhaps the magical ceremonies just described may help
to explain a curious rite, of immemorial antiquity, which
was performed on a very solemn occasion at Athens.   On
the eve of the sailing of the fleet for Syracuse, when all
hearts beat high with hope, and visions of empire dazzled
all eyes, consternation suddenly fell on the people one May
morning when they rose and found that most of the images
of Hermes in the city had been mysteriously mutilated in
the night.   The impious perpetrators of the sacrilege were
unknown, but whoever they were, the priests and priestesses
solemnly cursed them according to the ancient ritual, standing with their faces to the west and shaking red cloths up
and down.[3]   Perhaps in these cloths they were catching the

*Athenian
curse ac-
companied
by the
shaking of
red cloths.*

---

[1] W. W. Skeat, *op. cit.* pp. 574 *sq.*
[2] W. W. Skeat, *op. cit.* pp. 576 *sq.*
[3] Lysias, *Or.* vi. 51, p. 51 ed. C.
Scheibe.   The passage was pointed

souls of those at whom their curses were levelled, just as we have seen that Fijian chiefs used to catch the souls of criminals in scarves and nail them to canoes.[1]

Extracting a patient's soul from the stomach of his doctor. The Indians of the Nass River, in British Columbia, are impressed with a belief that a physician may swallow his patient's soul by mistake. A doctor who is believed to have done so is made by the other members of the faculty to stand over the patient, while one of them thrusts his fingers down the doctor's throat, another kneads him in the stomach with his knuckles, and a third slaps him on the back. If the soul is not in him after all, and if the same process has been repeated upon all the medical men without success, it is concluded that the soul must be in the head-doctor's box. A party of doctors, therefore, waits upon him at his house and requests him to produce his box. When he has done so and arranged its contents on a new mat, they take the votary of Aesculapius and hold him up by the heels with his head in a hole in the floor. In this position they wash his head, and " any water remaining from the ablution is taken and poured upon the sick man's head." [2] Among the Kwakiutl Indians of British Columbia it is forbidden to pass behind the back of a shaman while he is eating, lest the shaman should inadvertently swallow the soul of the passer-by. When that happens, both the shaman and the person whose soul he has swallowed fall down in a swoon. Blood flows from the shaman's mouth, because the soul is too large for him and is tearing his inside. Then the clan of the person whose soul is doing this mischief must assemble and sing the song of the shaman. In time the suffering sorcerer

out to me by my friend Mr. W. Wyse. As to the mutilation of the Hermae, see Thucydides, vi. 27 - 29, 60 *sq.* ; Andocides, *Or.* i. 37 *sqq.* ; Plutarch, *Alcibiades*, 18.

[1] Above, p. 69.

[2] J. B. McCullagh, in *The Church Missionary Gleaner*, xiv. No. 164 (August 1887), p. 91. The same account is copied from the " North Star " (Sitka, Alaska, December 1888) in *Journal of American Folk-lore*, ii. (1889) pp. 74 *sq.* Mr. McCullagh's account (which is closely followed in the text) of the latter part of the custom is not quite clear. It would seem that failing to find the soul in the head-doctor's box it occurs to them that he may have swallowed it, as the other doctors were at first supposed to have done. With a view of testing this hypothesis they hold him up by the heels to empty out the soul ; and as the water with which his head is washed may possibly contain the missing soul, it is poured on the patient's head to restore the soul to him. We have already seen that the recovered soul is often conveyed into the sick person's head.

vomits out the soul, which he exhibits in the shape of a small bloody ball in the open palms of his hands. He restores it to its owner, who is lying prostrate on a mat, by throwing it at him and then blowing on his head. The man whose soul was swallowed has very naturally to pay for the damage he did to the shaman as well as for his own cure.[1]

§ 3. The Soul as a Shadow and a Reflection

But the spiritual dangers I have enumerated are not the only ones which beset the savage. Often he regards his

[1] Fr. Boas in *Eleventh Report on the North-Western Tribes of Canada*, p. 571 (*Report of the British Association for 1896*). For other examples of the recapture or recovery of lost, stolen, and strayed souls, in addition to those which have been cited in the preceding pages, see J. N. Vosmaer, *Korte Beschrijving van het Zuid-oostelijk Schiereiland van Celebes*, pp. 119-123 (this work, of which I possess a copy, forms part of a Dutch journal which I have not identified; it is dated Batavia, 1835); J. G. F. Riedel, "De Topantunuasu of oorspronkelijke volksstammen van Central Selebes," *Bijdragen tot de Taal- Land- en Volkenkunde van Nederlandsch-Indië*, xxxv. (1886) p. 93; J. B. Neumann, "Het Pane- en Bilastroom-gebeid," *Tijdschrift van het Nederlandsch Aardrijkskundig Genootschap*, Tweede Serie, dl. iii., Afdeeling, meer uitgebreide artikelen, No. 2 (1886), pp. 300 *sq.*; J. L. van der Toorn, "Het animisme bei den Minangkabauer," *Bijdragen tot de Taal- Land- en Volkenkunde van Nederlandsch-Indië*, xxxix. (1890) pp. 51 *sq.*; H. Ris, "De onderafdeeling Klein Mandailing Oeloe en Pahantan," *Bijdragen tot de Taal- Land- en Volkenkunde van Nederlandsch-Indië*, xlvi. (1896) p. 529; C. Snouck Hurgronje, *De Atjéhers* (Batavia and Leyden, 1893-4), i. 426 *sq.*; W. W. Skeat, *Malay Magic*, pp. 49-51, 452-455, 570 *sqq.*; *Journal of the Anthropological Institute*, xxiv. (1895) pp. 128, 287; Chimkievitch, "Chez les Bouriates de l'Amoor," *Tour du monde*, N.S. iii. (1897) pp. 622 *sq.*; Father Ambrosoli, "Notice sur l'île de Rook," *Annales de la Propagation de la Foi*, xxvii. (1855) p. 364; A. Bastian, *Die Völker des östlichen Asien*, ii. 388, iii. 236; *id.*, *Völkerstämme am Brahmaputra*, p. 23; *id.*, "Hügelstämme Assam's," *Verhandlungen der Berlin. Gesell. für Anthropol., Ethnol. und Urgeschichte*, 1881, p. 156; Shway Yoe, *The Burman*, i. 283 *sq.*, ii. 101 *sq.*; G. M. Sproat, *Scenes and Studies of Savage Life*, p. 214; J. Doolittle, *Social Life of the Chinese*, pp. 110 *sq.* (ed. Paxton Hood); T. Williams, *Fiji and the Fijians*,[2] i. 242; E. B. Cross, "On the Karens," *Journal of the American Oriental Society*, iv. (1854) pp. 309 *sq.*; A. W. Howitt, "On some Australian Beliefs," *Journal of the Anthropological Institute*, xiii. (1884) pp. 187 *sq.*; *id.*, "On Australian Medicine Men," *Journ. Anthrop. Inst.* xvi. (1887) p. 41; E. P. Houghton, "On the Land Dayaks of Upper Sarawak," *Memoirs of the Anthropological Society of London*, iii. (1870) pp. 196 *sq.*; L. Dahle, "Sikidy and Vintana," *Antananarivo Annual and Madagascar Annual*, xi. (1887) pp. 320 *sq.*; C. Leemius, *De Lapponibus Finmarchiae eorumque lingua, vita et religione pristina commentatio* (Copenhagen, 1767), pp. 416 *sq.*; A. E. Jenks, *The Bontoc Igorot* (Manilla, 1905), pp. 199 *sq.*; C. G. Seligmann, *The Melanesians of British New Guinea* (Cambridge, 1910), pp. 185 *sq.* My friend W. Robertson Smith suggested to me that the practice of hunting souls, which is denounced in Ezekiel xiii. 17 *sqq.*, may have been akin to those described in the text.

A man's
soul con-
ceived as
his shadow,
so that to
injure the
shadow is
to injure
the man.
shadow or reflection as his soul, or at all events as a vital part of himself, and as such it is necessarily a source of danger to him. For if it is trampled upon, struck, or stabbed, he will feel the injury as if it were done to his person ; and if it is detached from him entirely (as he believes that it may be) he will die. In the island of Wetar there are magicians who can make a man ill by stabbing his shadow with a pike or hacking it with a sword.[1] After Sankara had destroyed the Buddhists in India, it is said that he journeyed to Nepaul, where he had some difference of opinion with the Grand Lama. To prove his super- natural powers, he soared into the air. But as he mounted up, the Grand Lama, perceiving his shadow swaying and wavering on the ground, struck his knife into it and down fell Sankara and broke his neck.[2] In the Babar Islands the demons get power over a man's soul by holding fast his shadow, or by striking and wounding it.[3] Among the Tolindoos of central Celebes to tread on a man's shadow is an offence, because it is supposed to make the owner sick ;[4] and for the same reason the Toboongkoos of that region forbid their children to play with their shadows.[5] The Ottawa Indians thought they could kill a man by making certain figures on his shadow.[6] The Baganda of central Africa regarded a man's shadow as his ghost ; hence they used to kill or injure their enemies by stabbing or treading on their shadows.[7] Among the Bavili of West Africa it used to be considered a crime to trample on or even to cross the shadow of another, especially if the shadow were that of a married woman.[8] Some Caffres are very unwilling to let anybody stand on their shadow, believing that they can be

[1] J. G. F. Riedel, *De sluik- en kroesharige rassen tusschen Selebes en Papua*, p. 440.

[2] A. Bastian, *Die Völker des östlichen Asien*, v. 455.

[3] J. G. F. Riedel, *op. cit.* p. 340.

[4] N. Adriani en A. C. Kruijt, "Van Posso naar Parigi, Sigi en Lindoe," *Mededeelingen van wege het Neder- landsche Zendelinggenootschap*, xlii. (1898) p. 511 ; compare A. C. Kruijt, *ib.* xliv. (1900) p. 247.

[5] A. C. Kruijt, "Eenige ethno-

grafische aanteekeningen omtrent de Toboengkoe en de Tomori," *op. cit.* xliv. (1900) p. 226.

[6] *Annales de l'Association de la Propagation de la Foi*, iv. (1830) p. 481.

[7] Rev. J. Roscoe, in a letter to me dated Mengo, Uganda, May 26, 1904.

[8] R. E. Dennett, "Bavili Notes," *Folk-lore*, xvi. (1905) p. 372 ; *id.*, *At the Back of the Black Man's Mind* (London, 1906), p. 79.

influenced for evil through it.[1]   They think that "a sick
man's shadow dwindles in intensity when he is about to
die; for it has such an intimate relation to the man
that it suffers with him."[2]   The Ja-Luo tribes of Kavirondo,
to the east of Lake Victoria Nyanza, tell of the ancestor
of all men, Apodtho by name, who descended to earth
from above, bringing with him cattle, fowls, and seeds.
When he was old, the Ja-Luo plotted to kill him, but for a
long time they did not dare to attack him.   At last, hearing
that he was sick, they thought their chance had come, and
sent a girl to see how he was.   She took a small horn, used
for cupping blood, in her hand, and while she talked with
him she placed the cupping-horn on his shadow.   To her
surprise it drew blood.   So she returned and told her
friends that, if they wished to kill Apodtho, they must not
touch his body, but spear his shadow.   They did so, and he
died and turned into a rock, which has ever since possessed
the property of sharpening spears unusually well.[3]   In a
Chinese book we read of a sage who examined human
shadows by lamplight in order to discover the fate of their
owners.   "A man's shadow," he said, "ought to be deep,
for, if so, he will attain honourable positions, and a great
age.   Shadows are averse to being reflected in water, or in
wells, or in washing-basins.   It was on such grounds that
the ancients avoided shadows, and that in old days *Khü-seu*,
twan-hu, and other shadow-treading vermin caused injury by
hitting the shadows of men.   In recent times there have
been men versed in the art of cauterizing the shadows of their
patients."   Another sapient Chinese writer observes : " I have
heard that, if the shadow of a bird is hit with a piece of wood
that was struck by thunder, the bird falls to the ground immediately.   I never tried it, but on account of the matter
stated above I consider the thing certain."[4]   The natives of
Nias tremble at the sight of a rainbow, because they think it
is a net spread by a powerful spirit to catch their shadows.[5]

A person's soul conceived as the shadow, so that to injure the shadow is to injure him or her.

---

[1] Dudley Kidd, *The Essential Kafir*, p. 84.

[2] Dudley Kidd, *Savage Childhood*, p. 68.

[3] C. W. Hobley, "British East Africa," *Journal of the Anthropologi-*

cal Institute, xxxiii. (1903) pp. 327 *sq.*

[4] J. J. M. de Groot, *The Religious System of China*, iv. 84 *sq.*

[5] E. Modigliani, *Viaggio a Nias*, p. 620, compare p. 624.

Danger to a person of letting his shadow fall on certain things.

In the Banks Islands, Melanesia, there are certain stones of a remarkably long shape which go by the name of *tamate gangan* or "eating ghosts," because certain powerful and dangerous ghosts are believed to lodge in them. If a man's shadow falls on one of these stones, the ghost will draw his soul out from him, so that he will die. Such stones, therefore, are set in a house to guard it; and a messenger sent to a house by the absent owner will call out the name of the sender, lest the watchful ghost in the stone should fancy that he came with evil intent and should do him a mischief.[1] In Florida, one of the Solomon Islands, there are places sacred to ghosts, some in the village, some in the gardens, and some in the bush. No man would pass one of these places when the sun was so low as to cast his shadow into it, for then the ghost would draw it from him.[2] The Indian tribes of the Lower Fraser River believe that man has four souls, of which the shadow is one, though not the principal, and that sickness is caused by the absence of one of the souls. Hence no one will let his shadow fall on a sick shaman, lest the latter should purloin it to replace his own lost soul.[3] At a funeral in China, when the lid is about to be placed on the coffin, most of the bystanders, with the exception of the nearest kin, retire a few steps or even retreat to another room, for a person's health is believed to be endangered by allowing his shadow to be enclosed in a coffin. And when the coffin is about to be lowered into the grave most of the spectators recoil to a little distance lest their shadows should fall into the grave and harm should thus be done to their persons. The geomancer and his assistants stand on the side of the grave which is turned away from the sun; and the grave-diggers and coffin-bearers attach their shadows firmly to their persons by tying a strip of cloth tightly round their waists.[4] In the Nicobar Islands burial usually takes place at sundown, before midnight, or at early dawn. In no case can an interment be carried out at noon or within an hour of it, lest the shadows of the bearers who lower the

---

[1] R. H. Codrington, *The Melanesians*, p. 184.

[2] R. H. Codrington, *op. cit.* p. 176.

[3] Fr. Boas, in *Ninth Report on the North-Western Tribes of Canada*, pp. 461 *sq.* (*Report of the British Association for 1894*).

[4] J. J. M. de Groot, *The Religious System of China*, i. 94, 210 *sq.*

body into the earth, or of the mourners taking their last look at the shrouded figure, should fall into the grave; for that would cause them to be sick or die. And when the dead has been laid in his last home, but before the earth is shovelled in upon him, the leaves of a certain jungle tree are waved over the grave, and a lighted torch is brandished inside it, to disperse any souls of the sorrowing bystanders that may be lingering with their departed friend in his narrow bed. Then the signal is given, and the earth or sand is rapidly shovelled in by a party of young men who have been standing in readiness to perform the duty.[1] When the Malays are building a house, and the central post is being set up, the greatest precautions are taken to prevent the shadow of any of the workers from falling either on the post or on the hole dug to receive it; for otherwise they think that sickness and trouble will be sure to follow.[2] When members of some Victorian tribes were performing magical ceremonies for the purpose of bringing disease and misfortune on their enemies, they took care not to let their shadows fall on the object by which the evil influence was supposed to be wafted to the foe.[3] In Darfur people think that they can do an enemy to death by burying a certain root in the earth on the spot where the shadow of his head happens to fall. The man whose shadow is thus tampered with loses consciousness at once and will die if the proper antidote be not administered. In like manner they can paralyse any limb, as a hand or leg, by planting a particular root in the earth in the shadow of the limb they desire to maim.[4] Nor is it human beings alone who are thus liable to be injured by means of their shadows. Animals are to some extent in the same predicament. A small snail, which frequents the neighbourhood of the limestone hills in Perak, is believed to suck the blood of cattle through their shadows; hence the beasts grow lean and sometimes die from loss of

Animals also may be injured through their shadows.

---

[1] E. H. Man, "Notes on the Nicobarese," *Indian Antiquary*, xxviii. (1899) pp. 257-259. Compare Sir R. C. Temple, in *Census of India, 1901*, iii. 209.

[2] W. W. Skeat, *Malay Magic*, p. 143.

[3] J. Dawson, *Australian Aborigines*, p. 54.

[4] Mohammed Ebn - Omar El-Tounsy, *Voyage au Darfour*, traduit de l'Arabe par le Dr. Perron (Paris, 1845), p. 347.

Animals and trees may be injured through their shadows.

blood.[1] The ancients supposed that in Arabia, if a hyæna trod on a man's shadow, it deprived him of the power of speech and motion ; and that if a dog, standing on a roof in the moonlight, cast a shadow on the ground and a hyæna trod on it, the dog would fall down as if dragged with a rope.[2] Clearly in these cases the shadow, if not equivalent to the soul, is at least regarded as a living part of the man or the animal, so that injury done to the shadow is felt by the person or animal as if it were done to his body. Even the shadows of trees are supposed by the Caffres to be sensitive. Hence when a Caffre doctor seeks to pluck the leaves of a tree for medicinal purposes, he " takes care to run up quickly, and to avoid touching the shadow lest it should inform the tree of the danger, and so give the tree time to withdraw the medicinal properties from its extremities into the safety of the inaccessible trunk. The shadow of the tree is said to feel the touch of the man's feet." [3]

Danger of being over-shadowed by certain birds or people.

Conversely, if the shadow is a vital part of a man or an animal, it may under certain circumstances be as hazardous to be touched by it as it would be to come into contact with the person or animal. Thus in the North-West Provinces of India people believe that if the shadow of the goat-sucker bird falls on an ox or a cow, but especially on a cow buffalo, the beast will soon die. The remedy is for some one to kill the bird, rub his hands or a stick in the blood, and then wave the stick over the animal. There are certain men who are noted for their powers in this respect all over the district.[4] The Kaitish of central Australia hold that if the shadow of a brown hawk falls on the breast of a woman who is suckling a child, the breast will swell up and burst. Hence if a woman sees one of these birds in these circumstances, she runs away in fear.[5] In the Central Provinces of India a

---

[1] W. W. Skeat, *Malay Magic*, p. 306.

[2] [Aristotle] *Mirab. Auscult.* 145 (157) ; *Geoponica*, xv. 1. In the latter passage, for καταγει ἑαυτην we must read καταγει αὑτον, an emendation necessitated by the context, and confirmed by the passage of Damīrī quoted and translated by Bochart, *Hierozoicon*, i. col. 833, "*cum ad lunam calcat umbram canis, qui supra tectum est, canis ad*

eam [scil. hyaenam] *decidit, et ea illum devorat.*" Compare W. Robertson Smith, *The Religion of the Semites*,[2] p. 129.

[3] Dudley Kidd, *Savage Childhood*, p. 71.

[4] W. Crooke, in *Indian Antiquary*, xix. (1890) p. 254.

[5] Spencer and Gillen, *Northern Tribes of Central Australia*, p. 612.

pregnant woman avoids the shadow of a man, believing that if it fell on her, the child would take after him in features, though not in character.[1]   In Shoa any obstinate disorder, for which no remedy is known, such as insanity, epilepsy, delirium, hysteria, and St. Vitus's dance, is traced either to possession by a demon or to the shadow of an enemy which has fallen on the sufferer.[2]   The Bushman is most careful not to let his shadow fall on the dead game, as he thinks this would bring bad luck.[3]   Amongst the Caffres to overshadow the king by standing in his presence was an offence worthy of instant death.[4]   And it is a Caffre superstition that if the shadow of a man who is protected by a certain charm falls on the shadow of a man who is not so protected, the unprotected person will fall down, overcome by the power of the charm which is transmitted through the shadow.[5]   In the Punjaub some people believe that if the shadow of a pregnant woman fell on a snake, it would blind the creature instantly.[6]

Hence the savage makes it a rule to shun the shadow of certain persons whom for various reasons he regards as sources of dangerous influence.   Amongst the dangerous classes he commonly ranks mourners and women in general, but especially his mother-in-law.   The Shuswap Indians of British Columbia think that the shadow of a mourner falling upon a person would make him sick.[7]   Amongst the Kurnai tribe of Victoria novices at initiation were cautioned not to let a woman's shadow fall across them, as this would make them thin, lazy, and stupid.[8]   An Australian native is said to have once nearly died of fright because the shadow of his mother-in-law fell on his legs as he lay asleep under a tree.[9]

The shadows of certain persons are regarded as peculiarly dangerous.

The savage's dread of his mother-in-law.

[1] M. R. Pedlow, in *Indian Antiquary*, xxix. (1900) p. 60.

[2] W. Cornwallis Harris, *The Highlands of Aethiopia* (London, 1844), i. 158.

[3] Dudley Kidd, *The Essential Kafir*, p. 313.

[4] D. Kidd, *op. cit.* p. 356.

[5] Dudley Kidd, *Savage Childhood*, p. 70.

[6] *Panjab Notes and Queries*, i. p. 15, § 122.

[7] Fr. Boas, in *Sixth Report on the North-Western Tribes of Canada*, pp. 92, 94 (separate reprint from the *Report of the British Association for 1890*); compare *id.* in *Seventh Report*, etc., p. 13 (separate reprint from the *Rep. Brit. Assoc. for 1891*).

[8] A. W. Howitt, "The Jeraeil, or Initiation Ceremonies of the Kurnai Tribe," *Journal of the Anthropological Institute*, xiv. (1885) p. 316.

[9] Miss Mary E. B. Howitt, *Folklore and Legends of some Victorian Tribes* (in manuscript).

The awe and dread with which the untutored savage contemplates his mother-in-law are amongst the most familiar facts of anthropology. In the Yuin tribes of New South Wales the rule which forbade a man to hold any communication with his wife's mother was very strict. He might not look at her or even in her direction. It was a ground of divorce if his shadow happened to fall on his mother-in-law : in that case he had to leave his wife, and she returned to her parents.[1] In the Hunter River tribes of New South Wales it was formerly death for a man to speak to his mother-in-law ; however, in later times the wretch who had committed this heinous crime was suffered to live, but he was severely reprimanded and banished for a time from the camp.[2] In the Kulin tribe it was thought that if a woman looked at or spoke to her son-in-law or even his brother, her hair would turn white. The same result, it was supposed, would follow if she ate of game which had been presented to her husband by her son-in-law ; but she could obviate this ill consequence by blackening her face, and especially her mouth, with charcoal, for then her hair would not turn white.[3] Similarly in the Kurnai tribe of Victoria a woman is not permitted to see her daughter's husband in camp or elsewhere. When he is present, she keeps her head covered with an opossum rug. The camp of the mother-in-law faces in a different direction to that of her son-in-law. A screen of high bushes is erected between both huts, so that no one can see over from either. When the mother-in-law goes for firewood, she crouches down as she goes out or in, with her head covered.[4] In Uganda a man may not see his mother-in-law nor speak to her face to face. Should they meet by accident, she must turn aside and cover her head with her clothes ; or if her garments are too scanty for that, she may squat on her haunches and hide her face in her hands. If he wishes to hold any communication with her, it must be done through a third person, or through a wall or closed door. Were he to break these

[1] A. W. Howitt, *Native Tribes of South-East Australia*, p. 266.

[2] A. W. Howitt, *op. cit.* p. 267.

[3] A. W. Howitt, *op. cit.* pp. 256 *sq.*

[4] A. W. Howitt, *op. cit.* pp. 280 *sq.* Compare J. Dawson, *Australian Aborigines*, pp. 32 *sq.*

rules, he would certainly be seized with a shaking of the
hands and general debility.[1] Among some tribes of eastern
Africa which formerly acknowledged the suzerainty of the
sultan of Zanzibar, before a young couple had children they
might meet neither their father-in-law nor their mother-in-
law. To avoid them they must take a long roundabout.
But if they could not do that, they must throw themselves
on the ground and hide their faces till the father-in-law or
mother-in-law had passed by.[2] Among the Basutos a man
may never meet his wife's mother, nor speak to her, nor see
her. If his wife is ill and her mother comes to nurse her,
he must flee the house so long as she is in it; sentinels are
posted to warn him of her departure.[3] In New Britain the
native imagination fails to conceive the extent and nature of
the calamities which would result from a man's accidentally
speaking to his wife's mother ; suicide of one or both would
probably be the only course open to them. The most
solemn form of oath a New Briton can take is, " Sir, if I
am not telling the truth, I hope I may shake hands with
my mother-in-law." [4] At Vanua Lava in the Banks Islands,
a man would not so much as follow his mother-in-law along
the beach until the rising tide had washed out her footprints
in the sand.[5] To avoid meeting his mother-in-law face to
face a very desperate Apache Indian, one of the bravest of
the brave, has been seen to clamber along the brink of a
precipice at the risk of his life, hanging on to rocks from
which had he fallen he would have been dashed to pieces or
at least have broken several of his limbs.[6] Still more curious

[1] Partly from notes sent me by my
friend the Rev. J. Roscoe, partly from
Sir H. Johnston's account (*The Uganda
Protectorate*, ii. 688). In his printed
notes (*Journal of the Anthropological
Institute*, xxxii. (1902) p. 39) Mr.
Roscoe says that the mother-in-law
"may be in another room out of sight
and speak to him through the wall or
open door."

[2] Father Picarda, "Autour du
Mandera, Notes sur l'Ouzigoua,
l'Oukwéré et l'Oudoé (Zanguebar),"
Missions Catholiques, xviii. (1886) p.
286.

[3] Father Porte, "Les Réminiscences

d'un missionnaire du Basutoland,"
Missions Catholiques, xxviii. (1896)
p 318.

[4] H. H. Romily and Rev. George
Brown, in *Proceedings of the Royal
Geographical Society*, N.S. ix. (1887)
pp. 9, 17.

[5] R. H. Codrington, *The Melanesians*, p. 43.

[6] J. G. Bourke, *On the Border with
Crook*, p. 132. More evidence of the
mutual avoidance of mother-in-law and
son-in-law among savages is collected
in my *Totemism and Exogamy* ; see
the Index, *s.v.* "Mother-in-law."
The custom is probably based on a fear

and difficult to explain is the rule which forbids certain African kings, after the coronation ceremonies have been completed, ever to see their own mothers again. This restriction was imposed on the kings of Benin and Uganda. Yet the queen-mothers lived in regal state with a court and lands of their own. In Uganda it was thought that if the king were to see his mother again, some evil and probably death would surely befall him.[1]

A man's health and strength supposed to vary with the length of his shadow.

Where the shadow is regarded as so intimately bound up with the life of the man that its loss entails debility or death, it is natural to expect that its diminution should be regarded with solicitude and apprehension, as betokening a corresponding decrease in the vital energy of its owner. An elegant Greek rhetorician has compared the man who lives only for fame to one who should set all his heart on his shadow, puffed up and boastful when it lengthened, sad and dejected when it shortened, wasting and pining away when it dwindled to nothing. The spirits of such an one, he goes on, would necessarily be volatile, since they must rise or fall with every passing hour of the day. In the morning, when the level sun, just risen above the eastern horizon, stretched out his shadow to enormous length, rivalling the shadows cast by the cypresses and the towers on the city wall, how blithe and exultant would he be, fancying that in stature he had become a match for the fabled giants of old; with what a lofty port he would then strut and shew himself in the streets and the market-place and wherever men congregated, that he might be seen and admired of all. But as the day wore on, his countenance would change and he would slink back crestfallen to his house. At noon, when his once towering shadow had shrunk to his feet, he would shut himself up and refuse to stir abroad, ashamed to look

---

of incest between them. To the almost universal rule of savage life that a man must avoid his mother-in-law there is a most remarkable exception among the Wahehe of German East Africa. In that tribe a bridegroom must sleep with his mother-in-law before he may cohabit with her daughter. See Rev. H. Cole, "Notes on the Wagogo of German East Africa,"

Journal of the Anthropological Institute, xxxii. (1902) p. 312.

[1] O. Dapper, *Description de l'Afrique,* p. 312; H. Ling Roth, *Great Benin,* p. 119; *Missions Catholiques,* xv. (1883) p. 110; J. Roscoe, "Further Notes on the Manners and Customs of the Baganda," *Journal of the Anthropological Institute,* xxxii. (1902) p. 67.

his fellow-townsmen in the face ; but in the afternoon his
drooping spirits would revive, and as the day declined his
joy and pride would swell again with the length of the evening shadows.[1]   The rhetorician who thus sought to expose
the vanity of fame as an object of human ambition by liken-
ing it to an ever-changing shadow, little dreamed that in
real life there were men who set almost as much store by
their shadows as the fool whom he had conjured up in his
imagination to point a moral.   So hard is it for the strain-
ing wings of fancy to outstrip the folly of mankind.   In
Amboyna and Uliase, two islands near the equator, where
necessarily there is little or no shadow cast at noon, the
people make it a rule not to go out of the house at mid-day,
because they fancy that by doing so a man may lose the
shadow of his soul.[2]   The Mangaians tell of a mighty
warrior, Tukaitawa, whose strength waxed and waned with
the length of his shadow.   In the morning, when his shadow
fell longest, his strength was greatest ; but as the shadow
shortened towards noon his strength ebbed with it, till exactly
at noon it reached its lowest point ; then, as the shadow
stretched out in the afternoon, his strength returned.   A
certain hero discovered the secret of Tukaitawa's strength
and slew him at noon.[3]   The savage Besisis of the Malay
Peninsula fear to bury their dead at noon, because they
fancy that the shortness of their shadows at that hour would
sympathetically shorten their own lives.[4]   The Baganda of
central Africa used to judge of a man's health by the length of
his shadow.   They said, "So-and-so is going to die, his shadow
is very small " ; or, " He is in good health, his shadow is
large."[5]   Similarly the Caffres of South Africa think that a
man's shadow grows very small or vanishes at death.   When
her husband is away at the wars, a woman hangs up his sleep-
ing-mat ; if the shadow grows less, she says her husband is
killed ; if it remains unchanged, she says he is unscathed.[6]

A man's health and strength supposed to vary with the length of his shadow.

[1] Dio Chrysostom, *Or.* lxvii. vol.
ii. p. 230, ed. L. Dindorf.

[2] J. G. F. Riedel, *De sluik- en
kroesharige rassen tusschen Selebes en
Papua*, p. 61.

[3] W. W. Gill, *Myths and Songs of
the South Pacific*, pp. 284 *sqq.*

[4] W. W. Skeat and C. O. Blagden,

Pagan Races of the Malay Peninsula
(London, 1906), ii. 110.

[5] The Rev. J. Roscoe, in a letter to
me dated Mengo, Uganda, May 26,
1904.

[6] T. Arbousset et F. Daumas, *Voyage
d'exploration* (Paris, 1842), p. 291 ;
Dudley Kidd, *The Essential Kafir*, pp.

It is possible that even in lands outside the tropics the observation of the diminished shadow at noon may have contributed, even if it did not give rise, to the superstitious dread with which that hour has been viewed by many peoples, as by the Greeks, ancient and modern, the Bretons, the Russians, the Roumanians of Transylvania, and the Indians of Santiago Tepehuacan.[1] In this observation, too, we may perhaps detect the reason why noon was chosen by the Greeks as the hour for sacrificing to the shadowless dead.[2] The loss of the shadow, real or apparent, has often been regarded as a cause or precursor of death. Whoever entered the sanctuary of Zeus on Mount Lycaeus in Arcadia was believed to lose his shadow and to die within the year.[3] In Lower Austria on the evening of St. Sylvester's day—the last day of the year—the company seated round the table mark whose shadow is not cast on the wall, and believe that the seemingly shadowless person will die next year. Similar presages are drawn in Germany both on St. Sylvester's day and on Christmas Eve.[4] The Galelareese fancy that if a Fear
of the re-
semblance
of a child
to its
parents. child resembles his father, they will not both live long; for the child has taken away his father's likeness or shadow, and consequently the father must soon die.[5] Similarly among

83, 303 ; *id., Savage Childhood,* p. 69. In the last passage Mr. Kidd tells us that "the mat was *not* held up in the sun, but was placed in the hut at the marked-off portion where the *itongo* or ancestral spirit was supposed to live; and the fate of the man was divined, not by the *length* of the shadow, but by its *strength.*"

[1] Theocritus, i. 15 *sqq.*; Philostratus, *Heroic.* i. 3 ; Porphyry, *De antro nympharum,* 26 ; Lucan, iii. 423 *sqq.* ; Drexler, *s.v.* "Meridianus daemon," in Roscher's *Lexikon der griech. und röm. Mythologie,* ii. 2832 *sqq.* ; Bernard Schmidt, *Das Volksleben der Neugriechen,* pp. 94 *sqq.,* 119 *sq.* ; Georgeakis et Pineau, *Folk-lore de Lesbos,* p. 342 ; A. de Nore, *Coutumes, mythes, et traditions des provinces de France,* pp. 214 *sq.* ; J. Grimm, *Deutsche Mythologie,*[4] ii. 972 ; C. L. Rochholz, *Deutscher Glaube und Brauch,* i. 62 *sqq.* ; E. Gerard, *The Land beyond the Forest,* i. 331 ;

"Lettre du curé de Santiago Tepehuacan," *Bulletin de la Société de Géographie* (Paris), IIme Série, ii. (1834) p. 180 ; N. von Stenin, "Die Permier," *Globus,* lxxi. (1897) p. 374 ; D. Louwerier, "Bijgeloovige gebruiken, die door die Javanen worden in acht genomen," *Mededeelingen van wege het Nederlandsche Zendelinggenootschap,* xlix. (1905) p. 257.

[2] Schol. on Aristophanes, *Frogs,* 293.

[3] Pausanias, viii. 38. 6 ; Polybius, xvi. 12. 7 ; Plutarch, *Quaestiones Graecae,* 39.

[4] Th. Vernaleken, *Mythen und Bräuche des Volkes in Österreich,* p. 341 ; Reinsberg-Düringsfeld, *Das festliche Jahr,* p. 401 ; A. Wuttke, *Der deutsche Volksaberglaube,*[2] p. 207, § 314.

[5] M. J. van Baarda, "Fabelen, Verhalen en Overleveringen der Galelareezen," *Bijdragen tot de Taal- Land- en Volkenkunde van Nederlandsch-Indië,* xlv. (1895) p. 459.

some tribes of the Lower Congo, "if the child is like its mother, father, or uncle, they think it has the spirit of the person it resembles, and that that person will soon die. Hence a parent will resent it if you say that the baby is like him or her." [1]

Nowhere, perhaps, does the equivalence of the shadow to the life or soul come out more clearly than in some customs practised to this day in south-eastern Europe. In modern Greece, when the foundation of a new building is being laid, it is the custom to kill a cock, a ram, or a lamb, and to let its blood flow on the foundation-stone, under which the animal is afterwards buried. The object of the sacrifice is to give strength and stability to the building. But sometimes, instead of killing an animal, the builder entices a man to the foundation-stone, secretly measures his body, or a part of it, or his shadow, and buries the measure under the foundation-stone; or he lays the foundation-stone upon the man's shadow. It is believed that the man will die within the year. [2] In the island of Lesbos it is deemed enough if the builder merely casts a stone at the shadow of a passer-by; the man whose shadow is thus struck will die, but the building will be solid. [3] A Bulgarian mason measures the shadow of a man with a string, places the string in a box, and then builds the box into the wall of the edifice. Within forty days thereafter the man whose shadow was measured will be dead and his soul will be in the box beside the string; but often it will come forth and appear in its former shape to persons who were born on a Saturday. If a Bulgarian builder cannot obtain a human shadow for this purpose, he will content himself with measuring the shadow of the first animal that comes that way. [4] The Roumanians of Transylvania think that he whose shadow is thus immured will die within forty days; so persons passing by a building which is in course of erection may hear a warning cry, "Beware lest they take thy shadow!" Not long ago there

The shadows of people built into foundations to strengthen the edifices.

[1] J. H. Weeks, "Notes on some Customs of the Lower Congo People," *Folk-lore*, xix. (1908) p. 422.

[2] B. Schmidt, *Das Volksleben der Neugriechen* (Leipsic, 1871), pp. 196 *sq.*

[3] Georgeakis et Pineau, *Folk-lore de Lesbos*, pp. 346 *sq.*

[4] A. Strausz, *Die Bulgaren* (Leipsic, 1898), p. 199; W. R. S. Ralston, *Songs of the Russian People*, p. 127.

were still shadow-traders whose business it was to provide architects with the shadows necessary for securing their walls.[1] In these cases the measure of the shadow is looked on as equivalent to the shadow itself, and to bury it is to bury the life or soul of the man, who, deprived of it, must die. Thus the custom is a substitute for the old practice of immuring a living person in the walls, or crushing him under the foundation-stone of a new building, in order to give strength and durability to the structure, or more definitely in order that the angry ghost may haunt the place and guard it against the intrusion of enemies. Thus when a new gate was made or an old gate was repaired in the walls of Bangkok, it used to be customary to crush three men to death under an enormous beam in a pit at the gateway. Before they were led to their doom, they were regaled at a splendid banquet : the whole court came to salute them ; and the king himself charged them straitly to guard well the gate that was to be committed to their care, and to warn him if enemies or rebels came to assault the city. The next moment the ropes were cut and the beam descended on them. The Siamese believed that these unfortunates were transformed into the genii which they called *phi*.[2] It is said that when the massive teak posts of the gateways of Mandalay were set up, a man was bound and placed under each post and crushed to death. The Burmese believe that men who die a violent death turn into *nats* or demons and haunt the spot where they were killed, doing a mischief to such as attempt to molest the place. Thus their spirits become guardians of the gates.[3] This theory would explain why such sacrifices appear to be offered most commonly at thoroughfares, such as gates and bridges, where ghostly warders may be deemed especially serviceable in keeping watch on the multitudes that go to and fro.[4] In Bima, a

Marginal note: Living people built into foundations to serve as guardian spirits.

[1] W. Schmidt, *Das Jahr und seine Tage in Meinung und Brauch der Romänen Siebenbürgens* (Hermannstadt, 1866), p. 27 ; E. Gerard, *The Land beyond the Forest*, ii. 17 *sq.* Compare F. S. Krauss, *Volksglaube und religiöser Brauch der Südslaven*, p. 161.

[2] Mgr. Bruguière, in *Annales de l'Association de la Propagation de la Foi*, v. (1831) pp. 164 *sq.* ; Pallegoix, *Description du royaume Thai ou Siam*, ii. 50-52.

[3] A. Fytche, *Burma, Past and Present* (London, 1878), i. 251 note.

[4] On such practices in general, see E. B. Tylor, *Primitive Culture*,[2] i. 104 *sqq.* ; F. Liebrecht, *Zur Volks-*

district of the East Indian island of Sambawa, the custom is marked by some peculiar features, which deserve to be mentioned. When a new flag-pole is set up at the sultan's palace a woman is crushed to death under it; but she must be pregnant. If the destined victim should be brought to bed before her execution, she goes free. The notion may be that the ghost of such a woman would be more than usually fierce and vigilant. Again, when the wooden doors are set up at the palace, it is customary to bury a child under each of the door-posts. For these purposes officers are sent to scour the country for a pregnant woman or little children, as the case may be, and if they come back empty-handed they must give up their own wives or children to serve as victims. When the gates are set up, the children are killed, their bodies stript of flesh, and their bones laid in the holes in which the door-posts are erected. Then the flesh is boiled with horse's flesh and served up to the officers. Any officer who refuses to eat of it is at once cut down.[1] The intention of this last practice is perhaps to secure the fidelity of the officers by compelling them to enter into a covenant of the most solemn and binding nature with the ghosts of the murdered children who are to guard the gates.

The practice of burying the measure of a man's shadow, as a substitute for the man himself, under the foundation-stone of a building may perhaps throw light on the singular deity whom the people of Kisser, an East Indian island, Deification of a measuring-tape.

---

kunde, pp. 284-296; F. S. Krauss, "Der Bauopfer bei den Südslaven," *Mittheilungen der Anthropologischen Gesellschaft in Wien,* xvii. (1887) pp. 16-24; P. Sartori, "Über das Bauopfer," *Zeitschrift für Ethnologie,* xxx. (1898) pp. 1-54; E. Wester-marck, *Origin and Development of the Moral Ideas* (London, 1906-1908), i. 451 *sqq.* For some special evidence, see H. Oldenberg, *Die Religion des Veda,* pp. 363 *sqq.* (as to ancient India); Sonnerat, *Voyage aux Indes Orientales et à la Chine,* ii. 47 (as to Pegu); Guerlach, "Chez les sauvages Ba-hnars," *Missions Catholiques,* xvi. (1884) p. 82 (as to the Sedans of Cochin-China); W. H. Furness, *Home-life of Borneo Head-hunters,* p. 3 (as to

the Kayans and Kenyahs of Burma); A. C. Kruijt, "Van Paloppo naar Posso," *Mededeelingen van wege het Nederlandsche Zendelinggenootschap,* xlii. (1898) p. 56 note (as to central Celebes); L. Hearn, *Glimpses of Un-familiar Japan* (London, 1894), i. 148 *sq.*; H. Ternaux-Compans, *Essai sur l'ancien Cundinamarca,* p. 70 (as to the Indians of Colombia). These customs are commonly called foundation-sacrifices. But the name is inappropriate, as Prof. H. Oldenberg has rightly observed, since they are not sacrifices but charms.

[1] D. F. van Braam Morris, in *Tijdschrift voor Indische Taal- Land-en Volkenkunde,* xxxiv. (1891) p. 224.

choose to guard their houses and villages. The god in question is nothing more or less than the measuring-tape which was used to measure the foundations of the house or of the village temple. After it has served this useful purpose, the tape is wound about a stick shaped like a paddle, and is then deposited in the thatch of the roof of the house, where food is offered to it on all special occasions. The deified measuring-tape of the whole village is that which was used to measure the foundations of the first house or of the village temple. The handle of the paddle-like stick on which it is wound is carved into the figure of a person squatting in the usual posture; and the whole is kept in a rough wooden box along with one or two figures to act as its guards.[1] It is possible, though perhaps hardly probable, that these tapes may be thought to contain the souls of men whose shadows they measured at the foundation ceremony.

The soul sometimes supposed to be in the reflection. As some peoples believe a man's soul to be in his shadow, so other (or the same) peoples believe it to be in his reflection in water or a mirror. Thus " the Andamanese do not regard their shadows but their reflections (in any mirror) as their souls." [2] According to one account, some of the Fijians thought that man has two souls, a light one and a dark one; the dark one goes to Hades, the light one is his reflection in water or a mirror.[3] When the Motumotu of New Guinea first saw their likenesses in a looking-glass they thought that their reflections were their souls.[4] In New Caledonia the old men are of opinion that a person's reflection in water or a mirror is his soul; but the younger men,

---

[1] J. H. de Vries, "Reis door eenige eilandgroepen der Residentie Amboina," *Tijdschrift van het koninklijk Nederlandsch Aardrijkskundig Genootschap*, Tweedie Serie, xvii. (1900) pp. 612 *sq.*

[2] E. H. Mann, *Aboriginal Inhabitants of the Andaman Islands*, p. 94.

[3] T. Williams, *Fiji and the Fijians*,[2] i. 241. However, the late Mr. Lorimer Fison wrote to me that this reported belief in a bright soul and a dark soul "is one of Williams' absurdities. I inquired into it on the island where he was, and

found that there was no such belief. He took the word for ' shadow,' which is a reduplication of *yalo*, the word for soul, as meaning the dark soul. But *yaloyalo* does not mean the soul at all. It is not part of a man as his soul is. This is made certain by the fact that it does not take the possessive suffix *yalo-na* = his soul; but *nona yaloyalo* = his shadow. This settles the question beyond dispute. If *yaloyalo* were any kind of soul, the possessive form would be *yaloyalona*" (letter dated August 26, 1898).

[4] James Chalmers, *Pioneering in New Guinea* (London, 1887), p. 170.

taught by the Catholic priests, maintain that it is a reflection and nothing more, just like the reflection of palm-trees in the water.[1]   The reflection-soul, being external to the man, is exposed to much the same dangers as the shadow-soul. Among the Galelareese, half-grown lads and girls may not look at themselves in a mirror ; for they say that the mirror takes away their bloom and leaves them ugly.[2]   And as the shadow may be stabbed, so may the reflection.   Hence an Aztec mode of keeping sorcerers from the house was to leave a vessel of water with a knife in it behind the door.   When a sorcerer entered he was so much alarmed at seeing his reflection in the water transfixed by a knife that he turned and fled.[3]   In Corrèze, a district of the Auvergne, a cow's milk had dried up through the maleficent spells of a neighbouring witch, so a sorcerer was called in to help.   He made the woman whose cow was bewitched sit in front of a pail of water with a knife in her hand till she thought she saw the image of the witch in the water, whereupon he made her stab the image with the knife.   They say that if the knife strikes the image fair in the eye, the person whose likeness it is will suffer a corresponding injury in his or her eye.   This procedure, we are informed, has been successful in restoring milk to the udders of a cow when even holy water had been tried in vain.[4]   The Zulus will not look into a dark pool because they think there is a beast in it which will take away their reflections, so that they die.[5]   The Basutos say that crocodiles have the power of thus killing a man by dragging his reflection under water.   When one of them dies suddenly and from no apparent cause, his relatives will allege that a crocodile must have taken his shadow some time when he crossed a stream.[6]   In Saddle Island,

Dangers to which the reflection-soul is exposed.

[1] Father Lambert, *Mœurs et superstitions des Néo-Calédoniens* (Nouméa, 1900), pp. 45 *sq.*

[2] M. J. van Baarda, "Fabelen, Verhalen en Overleveringen der Galelareezen," *Bijdragen tot de Taal- Landen Volkenkunde van Nederlandsch-Indië*, xlv. (1895) p. 462.

[3] B. de Sahagun, *Histoire générale des choses de la Nouvelle-Espagne* (Paris, 1880), p. 314.   The Chinese hang brass mirrors over the idols in their houses, because it is thought that evil spirits entering the house and seeing themselves in the mirrors will be scared away (*China Review*, ii. 164).

[4] G. Vuillier, "Chez les magiciens et les sorciers de la Corrèze," *Tour du monde*, N.S. v. (1899) pp. 522, 524.

[5] H. Callaway, *Nursery Tales, Traditions, and Histories of the Zulus* (Natal and London, 1868), p. 342.

[6] T. Arbousset and F. Daumas, *Voyage d'exploration au nord-est de la colonie*

Melanesia, there is a pool "into which if any one looks he dies ; the malignant spirit takes hold upon his life by means of his reflection on the water." [1]

Dread of looking at one's reflection in water. We can now understand why it was a maxim both in ancient India and ancient Greece not to look at one's reflection in water, and why the Greeks regarded it as an omen of death if a man dreamed of seeing himself so reflected. [2] They feared that the water-spirits would drag the person's reflection or soul under water, leaving him soulless to perish. This was probably the origin of the classical story of the beautiful Narcissus, who languished and died through seeing his reflection in the water. The explanation that he died for love of his own fair image was probably devised later, after the old meaning of the story was forgotten. The same ancient belief lingers, in a faded form, in the English superstition that whoever sees a water fairy must pine and die.

> " *Alas, the moon should ever beam*
> *To show what man should never see !—*
> *I saw a maiden on a stream,*
> *And fair was she !*
>
> *I staid to watch, a little space,*
> *Her parted lips if she would sing ;*
> *The waters closed above her face*
> *With many a ring.*
>
> *I know my life will fade away,*
> *I know that I must vainly pine,*
> *For I am made of mortal clay,*
> *But she's divine !* "

Reason for covering up mirrors or turning them to the wall after a death. Further, we can now explain the widespread custom of covering up mirrors or turning them to the wall after a death has taken place in the house. It is feared that the soul, projected out of the person in the shape of his reflection in the mirror, may be carried off by the ghost of the departed,

---

du Cap de Bonne-Espérance, p. 12 ; T. Lindsay Fairclough, " Notes on the Basuto," *Journal of the African Society,* No. 14 (January 1905), p. 201.

[1] R. H. Codrington, " Religious Beliefs and Practices in Melanesia," *Journ. Anthrop. Inst.* x. (1881) p. 313 ;

id., The Melanesians, p. 186.

[2] *Fragmenta philosophorum Graecorum,* ed. F. G. A. Mullach, i. 510 ; Artemidorus, *Onirocr.* ii. 7 ; *Laws of Manu,* iv. 38 (p. 135, G. Bühler's translation, *Sacred Books of the East,* vol. xxv.).

which is commonly supposed to linger about the house till the burial. The custom is thus exactly parallel to the Aru custom of not sleeping in a house after a death for fear that the soul, projected out of the body in a dream, may meet the ghost and be carried off by it.[1] In Oldenburg it is thought that if a person sees his image in a mirror after a death he will die himself. So all the mirrors in the house are covered up with white cloth.[2] In some parts of Germany and Belgium after a death not only the mirrors but everything that shines or glitters (windows, clocks, etc.) is covered up,[3] doubtless because they might reflect a person's image. The same custom of covering up mirrors or turning them to the wall after a death prevails in England, Scotland, Madagascar,[4] and among the Karaits, a Jewish sect in the Crimea.[5] The Suni Mohammedans of Bombay cover with a cloth the mirror in the room of a dying man and do not remove it until the corpse is carried out for burial. They also cover the looking-glasses in their bedrooms before retiring to rest at night.[6] The reason why sick people should not see themselves in a mirror, and why the mirror in a sick-room is therefore covered up,[7] is also plain ; in time of sickness, when the soul might take flight so easily, it is particularly dangerous to project it out of the body by means of the reflection in a mirror. The rule is therefore precisely parallel to the rule observed by some peoples of not allowing sick people to sleep ;[8] for in sleep the soul is projected out of the body,

---

[1] See above, p. 37.

[2] A. Wuttke, Der deutsche Volksaberglaube,[2] pp. 429 sq., § 726.

[3] A. Wuttke, l.c. ; E. Monseur, Le Folklore Wallon, p. 40.

[4] Folk-lore Journal, iii. (1885) p. 281 ; T. F. Thiselton Dyer, English Folk-lore, p. 109 ; J. Napier, Folk-lore, or Superstitious Beliefs in the West of Scotland, p. 60 ; W. Ellis, History of Madagascar, i. 238.   Compare A. Grandidier, "Des rites funéraires chez les Malgaches," Revue d'Ethnographie, v. (1886) p. 215.

[5] S. Weissenberg, "Die Karäer der Krim," Globus, lxxxiv. (1903) p. 143 ; id. "Krankheit und Tod bei den südrussischen Juden," Globus, xci. (1907) p. 360.

[6] Panjab Notes and Queries, ii. p. 169, § 906.

[7] J. V. Grohmann, Aberglauben und Gebräuche aus Böhmen und Mähren, p. 151, § 1097 ; Folk-lore Journal, vi. (1888) pp. 145 sq. ; Panjab Notes and Queries, ii. p. 61, § 378.

[8] J. G. Frazer, "On certain Burial Customs as illustrative of the Primitive Theory of the Soul," Journal of the Anthropological Institute, xv. (1886) pp. 82 sqq. Among the heathen Arabs, when a man had been stung by a scorpion, he was kept from sleeping for seven days, during which he had to wear a woman's bracelets and earrings (Rasmussen, Additamenta ad historiam Arabum ante Islamismum, p. 65, compare p. 69).   The old Mexican custom of masking and

and there is always a risk that it may not return. "In the opinion of the Raskolniks a mirror is an accursed thing, invented by the devil,"[1] perhaps on account of the mirror's supposed power of drawing out the soul in the reflection and so facilitating its capture.

The soul sometimes supposed to be in the portrait.

As with shadows and reflections, so with portraits ; they are often believed to contain the soul of the person portrayed. People who hold this belief are naturally loth to have their likenesses taken ; for if the portrait is the soul, or at least a vital part of the person portrayed, whoever possesses the portrait will be able to exercise a fatal influence over the original of it. Thus the Esquimaux of Bering Strait

This belief among the Esquimaux and American Indians.

believe that persons dealing in witchcraft have the power of stealing a person's *inua* or shade, so that without it he will pine away and die. Once at a village on the lower Yukon River an explorer had set up his camera to get a picture of the people as they were moving about among their houses. While he was focusing the instrument, the headman of the village came up and insisted on peeping under the cloth. Being allowed to do so, he gazed intently for a minute at the moving figures on the ground glass, then suddenly withdrew his head and bawled at the top of his voice to the people, "He has all of your shades in this box." A panic ensued among the group, and in an instant they disappeared helter-skelter into their houses.[2] The Dacotas hold that every man has several *wanagi* or "apparitions," of which after death one remains at the grave, while another goes to the place of the departed. For many years no Yankton Dacota would consent to have his picture taken lest one of his "apparitions" should remain after death in the picture instead of going to the spirit-land.[3] An Indian whose portrait the Prince of Wied

veiling the images of the gods so long as the king was sick (Brasseur de Bourbourg, *Histoire des nations civilisées du Mexique et de l'Amérique-Centrale*, iii. 571 *sq.*) may perhaps have been intended to prevent the images from drawing away the king's soul.

[1] W. R. S. Ralston, *Songs of the Russian People*, p. 117. The objection, however, may be merely Puritanical. W. Robertson Smith informed me that the peculiarities of the Raskolniks are largely due to exaggerated Puritanism.

[2] E. W. Nelson, "The Eskimo about Bering Strait," *Eighteenth Annual Report of the Bureau of American Ethnology*, Part I. (Washington, 1899) p. 422.

[3] J. Owen Dorsey, "A Study of Siouan Cults," *Eleventh Annual Report of the Bureau of Ethnology* (Washington, 1894), p. 484; *id.* "Teton Folk-lore," *American Anthropologist*, ii. (1889) p. 143.

wished to get, refused to let himself be drawn, because he believed it would cause his death.[1] The Mandan Indians also thought that they would soon die if their portraits were in the hands of another; they wished at least to have the artist's picture as a kind of hostage.[2] The Tepehuanes of Mexico stood in mortal terror of the camera, and five days' persuasion was necessary to induce them to pose for it. When at last they consented, they looked like criminals about to be executed. They believed that by photographing people the artist could carry off their souls and devour them at his leisure moments. They said that when the pictures reached his country they would die or some other evil would befall them.[3] The Canelos Indians of Ecuador think that their soul is carried away in their picture. Two of them, who had been photographed, were so alarmed that they came back next day on purpose to ask if it were really true that their souls had been taken away.[4] Similar notions are entertained by the Aymara Indians of Peru and Bolivia.[5] The Araucanians of Chili are unwilling to have their portraits drawn, for they fancy that he who has their portraits in his possession could, by means of magic, injure or destroy themselves.[6]

The Yaos, a tribe of British Central Africa in the neigh-bourhood of Lake Nyassa, believe that every human being has a *lisoka*, a soul, shade, or spirit, which they appear to associate with the shadow or picture of the person. Some of them have been known to refuse to enter a room where pictures were hung on the walls, " because of the *masoka*, souls, in them." The camera was at first an object of dread to them, and when it was turned on a group of natives they scattered in all directions with shrieks of terror. They said that the European was about to take away their shadows and that they would die; the transference of the shadow or portrait (for the Yao word for the two is the same, to wit

The same belief in Africa.

[1] Maximilian Prinz zu Wied, *Reise in das innere Nord-America*, i. 417.

[2] *Ibid.* ii. 166.

[3] C. Lumholtz, *Unknown Mexico* (London, 1903), i. 459 *sq.*

[4] A. Simson, "Notes on the Jivaros and Canelos Indians," *Journal of the Anthropological Institute*, ix. (1880) p. 392.

[5] D. Forbes, in *Journal of the Ethnological Society of London*, ii. (1870) p. 236.

[6] E. R. Smith, *The Araucanians* (London, 1855), p. 222.

chiwilili) to the photographic plate would involve the disease or death of the shadeless body. A Yao chief, after much difficulty, allowed himself to be photographed on condition that the picture should be shewn to none of his subjects, but sent out of the country as soon as possible. He feared lest some ill-wisher might use it to bewitch him. Some time afterwards he fell ill, and his attendants attributed the illness to some accident which had befallen the photographic plate in England.[1] The Ngoni of the same region entertain a similar belief, and formerly exhibited a similar dread of sitting to a photographer, lest by so doing they should yield up their shades or spirits to him and they should die.[2] When Joseph Thomson attempted to photograph some of the Wa-teita in eastern Africa, they imagined that he was a magician trying to obtain possession of their souls, and that if he got their likenesses they themselves would be entirely at his mercy.[3] When Dr. Catat and some companions were exploring the Bara country on the west coast of Madagascar, the people suddenly became hostile. The day before the travellers, not without difficulty, had photographed the royal family, and now found themselves accused of taking the souls of the natives for the purpose of selling them when they returned to France. Denial was vain; in compliance with the custom of the country they were obliged to catch the souls, which were then put into a basket and ordered by Dr. Catat to return to their respective owners.[4]

The same belief in Asia.

Some villagers in Sikhim betrayed a lively horror and hid away whenever the lens of a camera, or "the evil eye of the box" as they called it, was turned on them. They thought it took away their souls with their pictures, and so put it in the power of the owner of the pictures to cast spells on them, and they alleged that a photograph of the scenery blighted the landscape.[5] Until the reign of the late King of Siam no Siamese coins were ever stamped with the image

---

[1] Rev. A. Hetherwick, "Some Animistic Beliefs among the Yaos of British Central Africa," *Journal of the Anthropological Institute*, xxxii. (1902) pp. 89 *sq.*

[2] W. A. Elmslie, *Among the Wild Ngoni* (Edinburgh and London, 1899), pp. 70 *sq.*

[3] J. Thomson, *Through Masai Land* (London, 1885), p. 86.

[4] E. Clodd, in *Folk-lore*, vi. (1895) pp. 73 *sq.*, referring to *The Times* of March 24, 1891.

[5] L. A. Waddell, *Among the Himalayas* (Westminster, 1899), pp. 85 *sq.*

of the king, "for at that time there was a strong prejudice against the making of portraits in any medium. Europeans who travel into the jungle have, even at the present time, only to point a camera at a crowd to procure its instant dispersion. When a copy of the face of a person is made and taken away from him, a portion of his life goes with the picture. Unless the sovereign had been blessed with the years of a Methusaleh he could scarcely have permitted his life to be distributed in small pieces together with the coins of the realm."[1]   Similarly, in Corea, "the effigy of the king is not struck on the coins; only a few Chinese characters are put on them. They would deem it an insult to the king to put his sacred face on objects which pass into the most vulgar hands and often roll on the ground in the dust or the mud. When the French ships arrived for the first time in Corea, the mandarin who was sent on board to communicate with them was dreadfully shocked to see the levity with which these western barbarians treated the face of their sovereign, reproduced on the coins, and the recklessness with which they put it in the hands of the first comer, without troubling themselves in the least whether or not he would shew it due respect."[2]   In Minahassa, a district of Celebes, many chiefs are reluctant to be photographed, believing that if that were done they would soon die. For they imagine that, were the photograph lost by its owner and found by somebody else, whatever injury the finder chose to do to the portrait would equally affect the person whom it represented.[3] Mortal terror was depicted on the faces of the Battas upon whom von Brenner turned the lens of his camera; they thought he wished to carry off their shadows or spirits in a little box.[4]   When Dr. Nieuwenhuis attempted to photograph the Kayans or Bahaus of central Borneo, they were much alarmed, fearing that their souls would follow their photo-

The same belief in the East Indies.

---

[1] E. Young, *The Kingdom of the Yellow Robe* (Westminster, 1898), p. 140.

[2] Ch. Dallet, *Histoire de l'Église de Corée* (Paris, 1874), i. p. xxv. This account of Corea was written at a time when the country was still almost secluded from European influence. The events of recent years have natur-

ally wrought great changes in the habits and ideas of the people.

[3] "Iets over het bijgeloof in de Minahasa," *Tijdschrift voor Nederlandsch Indië*, III. Série, iv. (1870) pp. 8 *sq.*

[4] J. Freiherr von Brenner, *Besuch bei den Kannibalen Sumatras* (Würzburg, 1894), p. 195.

graphs into the far country and that their deserted bodies would fall sick. Further, they imagined that possessing their likenesses the explorer would be able by magic art to work on the originals at a distance.[1]

The same belief in Europe.

Beliefs of the same sort still linger in various parts of Europe. Not very many years ago some old women in the Greek island of Carpathus were very angry at having their likenesses drawn, thinking that in consequence they would pine and die.[2] It is a German superstition that if you have your portrait painted, you will die.[3] Some people in Russia object to having their silhouettes taken, fearing that if this is done they will die before the year is out.[4] In Albania Miss Durham sketched an old man who boasted of being a hundred and ten years old. When every one recognised the likeness, a look of great anxiety came over the patriarch's face, and most earnestly he besought the artist never to destroy the sketch, for he was certain that the moment the sketch was torn he would drop down dead.[5] An artist in England once vainly attempted to sketch a gypsy girl. " I won't have her drawed out," said the girl's aunt. " I told her I'd make her scrawl the earth before me, if ever she let herself be drawed out again." " Why, what harm can there be ? " " I know there's a fiz (a charm) in it. There was my youngest, that the gorja drawed out on Newmarket Heath, she never held her head up after, but wasted away, and died, and she's buried in March churchyard." [6] There are persons in the West of Scotland " who refuse to have their likenesses taken lest it prove unlucky ; and give as instances the cases of several of their friends who never had a day's health after being photographed." [7]

[1] A. W. Nieuwenhuis, *Quer durch Borneo*, i. 314.

[2] " A Far-off Greek Island," *Blackwood's Magazine*, February 1886, p. 235.

[3] J. A. E. Köhler, *Volksbrauch, Aberglauben, Sagen und andre alte Überlieferungen im Voigtlande* (Leipsic, 1867), p. 423.

[4] W. R. S. Ralston, *Songs of the Russian People*, p. 117.

[5] Miss M. E. Durham, *High Albania* (London, 1909), p. 107.

[6] F. H. Groome, *In Gipsy Tents* (Edinburgh, 1880), pp. 337 *sq.*

[7] James Napier, *Folk - lore, or Superstitious Beliefs in the West of Scotland*, p. 142. For more examples of the same sort, see R. Andree, *Ethnographische Parallelen und Vergleiche*, Neue Folge (Leipsic, 1889), pp. 18 *sqq.*

CHAPTER III

TABOOED ACTS

§ 1. *Taboos on Intercourse with Strangers*

So much for the primitive conceptions of the soul and the dangers to which it is exposed. These conceptions are not limited to one people or country; with variations of detail they are ,found all over the world, and survive, as we have seen, in modern Europe. Beliefs so deep-seated and so widespread must necessarily have contributed to shape the mould in which the early kingship was cast. For if every person was at such pains to save his own soul from the perils which threatened it on so many sides, how much more carefully must *he* have been guarded upon whose life hung the welfare and even the existence of the whole people, and whom therefore it was the common interest of all to preserve? Therefore we should expect to find the king's life protected by a system of precautions or safeguards still more numerous and minute than those which in primitive society every man adopts for the safety of his own soul. Now in point of fact the life of the early kings is regulated, as we have seen and shall see more fully presently, by a very exact code of rules. May we not then conjecture that these rules are in fact the very safeguards which we should expect to find adopted for the protection of the king's life? An examination of the rules themselves confirms this conjecture. For from this it appears that some of the rules observed by the kings are identical with those observed by private persons out of regard for the safety of their souls; and even of those which seem peculiar to the king, many, if not all, are most readily

Primitive conceptions of the soul helped to mould early kingships by dictating rules to be observed by the king for his soul's salvation.

explained on the hypothesis that they are nothing but safe-guards or lifeguards of the king. I will now enumerate some of these royal rules or taboos, offering on each of them such comments and explanations as may serve to set the original intention of the rule in its proper light.

The general effect of these rules is to isolate the king, especially from strangers. The savage fears the magic arts of strangers and hence guards himself against them.

Various modes of disenchant-ing strangers.

As the object of the royal taboos is to isolate the king from all sources of danger, their general effect is to compel him to live in a state of seclusion, more or less complete, according to the number and stringency of the rules he observes. Now of all sources of danger none are more dreaded by the savage than magic and witchcraft, and he suspects all strangers of practising these black arts. To guard against the baneful influence exerted voluntarily or involuntarily by strangers is therefore an elementary dictate of savage prudence. Hence before strangers are allowed to enter a district, or at least before they are permitted to mingle freely with the inhabitants, certain ceremonies are often performed by the natives of the country for the purpose of disarming the strangers of their magical powers, of counteracting the baneful influence which is believed to emanate from them, or of disinfecting, so to speak, the tainted atmosphere by which they are supposed to be surrounded. Thus, when the ambassadors sent by Justin II., Emperor of the East, to conclude a peace with the Turks had reached their destination, they were received by shamans, who subjected them to a ceremonial purification for the purpose of exorcising all harmful influence. Having deposited the goods brought by the ambassadors in an open place, these wizards carried burning branches of incense round them, while they rang a bell and beat on a tambourine, snorting and falling into a state of frenzy in their efforts to dispel the powers of evil. Afterwards they purified the ambassadors themselves by leading them through the flames.[1] In the island of Nanumea (South Pacific) strangers from ships or from other islands were not allowed to communicate with the people until they all, or a few as representatives of the rest, had been taken to each of the four temples in the

---

[1] Menander Protector, in *Fragmenta historicorum Graecorum*, ed. C. Müller, iv. 227. Compare Gibbon, *Decline and Fall of the Roman Empire*, ch. xlii. vol. vii. pp. 294 *sq.* (Edinburgh; 1811).

island, and prayers offered that the god would avert any Various disease or treachery which these strangers might have modes of dis- brought with them. Meat offerings were also laid upon the enchanting altars, accompanied by songs and dances in honour of the strangers. god. While these ceremonies were going on, all the people except the priests and their attendants kept out of sight.[1] On returning from an attempted ascent of the great African mountain Kilimanjaro, which is believed by the neighbouring tribes to be tenanted by dangerous demons, Mr. New and his party, as soon as they reached the border of the inhabited country, were disenchanted by the inhabitants, being sprinkled with "a professionally prepared liquor, supposed to possess the potency of neutralising evil influences, and removing the spell of wicked spirits."[2]   In the interior of Yoruba (West Africa) the sentinels at the gates of towns often oblige European travellers to wait till nightfall before they admit them, fearing that if the strangers were admitted by day the devil would enter behind them.[3]   The whole Mahafaly country in Madagascar used to be tabooed to strangers of the white race, the natives imagining that the intrusion of a white man would immediately cause the death of their king.   The traveller Bastard had the greatest difficulty in overcoming the reluctance of the natives to allow him to enter their land and especially to visit their holy city.[4] Amongst the Ot Danoms of Borneo it is the custom that strangers entering the territory should pay to the natives a certain sum, which is spent in the sacrifice of buffaloes or pigs to the spirits of the land and water, in order to reconcile them to the presence of the strangers, and to induce them not to withdraw their favour from the people of the country, but to bless the rice-harvest, and so forth.[5]   The men of a certain district in Borneo, fearing to look upon a European traveller lest he should make them ill, warned their wives and children not

---

[1] G. Turner, *Samoa*, pp. 291 *sq.*

[2] Charles New, *Life, Wanderings, and Labours in Eastern Africa* (London, 1873), p. 432. Compare *ibid.* pp. 400, 402. For the demons on Mt. Kilimanjaro, see also J. L. Krapf, *Travels, Researches, and Missionary Labours in Eastern Africa* (London,

1860), p. 192.

[3] Pierre Bouche, *La Côte des Esclaves et le Dahomey* (Paris, 1885), p. 133.

[4] A. van Gennep, *Tabou et totémisme à Madagascar* (Paris, 1904), p. 42.

[5] C. A. L. M. Schwaner, *Borneo* (Amsterdam, 1853-54), ii. 77.

Various
modes
of dis-
enchanting
strangers.
to go near him.   Those who could not restrain their
curiosity killed fowls to appease the evil spirits and smeared
themselves with the blood.[1]   "More dreaded," says a
traveller in central Borneo, "than the evil spirits of the
neighbourhood are the evil spirits from a distance which
accompany travellers.   When a company from the middle
Mahakam river visited me among the Blu-u Kayans in the
year 1897, no woman shewed herself outside her house without a burning bundle of *plehiding* bark, the stinking smoke of
which drives away evil spirits."[2]   In Laos, before a stranger
can be accorded hospitality, the master of the house must offer
sacrifice to the ancestral spirits ; otherwise the spirits would
be offended and would send disease on the inmates.[3]   When
Madame Pfeiffer arrived at the village of Hali-Bonar, among
the Battas of Sumatra, a buffalo was killed and the liver
offered to her.   Then a ceremony was performed to propitiate the evil spirits.   Two young men danced, and one of
them in dancing sprinkled water from a buffalo's horn on
the visitor and the spectators.[4]   In the Mentawei Islands,
when a stranger enters a house where there are children, the
father or other member of the family takes the ornament
which the children wear in their hair and hands it to the
stranger, who holds it in his hands for a while and then
gives it back to him.   This is thought to protect the children
from the evil effect which the sight of a stranger might have
upon them.[5]   When a Dutch steamship was approaching
their villages, the people of Biak, an island off the north
coast of New Guinea, shook and knocked their idols about
in order to ward off ill-luck.[6]   At Shepherd's Isle Captain
Moresby had to be disenchanted before he was allowed to
land his boat's crew.   When he leaped ashore, a devil-man
seized his right hand and waved a bunch of palm leaves
over the captain's head.   Then "he placed the leaves in my
left hand, putting a small green twig into his mouth, still

[1] *Ibid.* ii. 167.

[2] A. W. Nieuwenhuis, *Quer durch Borneo*, ii. 102.

[3] E. Aymonier, *Notes sur le Laos* (Saigon, 1885), p. 196.

[4] *Bulletin de la Société de Géographie* (Paris), IVme Série, vi. (1853) pp. 134 *sq.*

[5] H. von Rosenberg, *Der malayische Archipel* (Leipsic, 1878), p. 198.

[6] D. W. Horst, "Rapport van eene reis naar de Noordkust van Nieuw Guinea," *Tijdschrift voor Indische Taal- Land- en Volkenkunde*, xxxii. (1889) p. 229.

holding me fast, and then, as if with great effort, drew the
twig from his mouth—this was extracting the evil spirit—
after which he blew violently, as if to speed it away.   I now
held a twig between my teeth, and he went through the
same process."   Then the two raced round a couple of sticks
fixed in the ground and bent to an angle at the top, which
had leaves tied to it.   After some more ceremonies the
devil-man concluded by leaping to the level of Captain
Moresby's shoulders (his hands resting on the captain's
shoulders) several times, " as if to show that he had
conquered the devil, and was now trampling him into
the earth." [1]   North American Indians " have an idea that
strangers, particularly white strangers, are ofttimes accompanied by evil spirits.   Of these they have great dread, as
creating and delighting in mischief.   One of the duties of
the medicine chief is to exorcise these spirits.   I have sometimes ridden into or through a camp where I was unknown
or unexpected, to be confronted by a tall, half-naked savage,
standing in the middle of the circle of lodges, and yelling in
a sing-song, nasal tone, a string of unintelligible words." [2]

When Crevaux was travelling in South America he
entered a village of the Apalai Indians.   A few moments
after his arrival some of the Indians brought him a number
of large black ants, of a species whose bite is painful,
fastened on palm leaves.   Then all the people of the village,
without distinction of age or sex, presented themselves to
him, and he had to sting them all with the ants on their
faces, thighs, and other parts of their bodies.   Sometimes
when he applied the ants too tenderly they called out
" More ! more ! " and were not satisfied till their skin was
thickly studded with tiny swellings like what might have
been produced by whipping them with nettles. [3]   The object
of this ceremony is made plain by the custom observed in
Amboyna and Uliase of sprinkling sick people with pungent
spices, such as ginger and cloves, chewed fine, in order by
the prickling sensation to drive away the demon of disease

*Disen-
chantment
effected by
means of
stinging
ants and
pungent
spices.*

---

[1] Capt. John Moresby, *Discoveries
and Surveys in New Guinea* (London,
1876), pp. 102 *sq.*
[2] R. I. Dodge, *Our Wild Indians*

(Hartford, Conn., 1886), p. 119.
[3] J.   Crevaux,   *Voyages   dans
l'Amérique du Sud* (Paris, 1883), p.
300.

which may be clinging to their persons.[1]   In Java a popular
cure for gout or rheumatism is to rub Spanish pepper into
the nails of the fingers and toes of the sufferer; the pun-
gency of the pepper is supposed to be too much for the gout
or rheumatism, who accordingly departs in haste.[2]   So on
the Slave Coast of Africa the mother of a sick child sometimes believes that an evil spirit has taken possession of the
child's body, and in order to drive him out, she makes small
cuts in the body of the little sufferer and inserts green
peppers or spices in the wounds, believing that she will
thereby hurt the evil spirit and force him to be gone.   The
poor child naturally screams with pain, but the mother
hardens her heart in the belief that the demon is suffering
equally.[3]   In Hawaii a patient is sometimes pricked with
bamboo needles for the sake of hurting and expelling a re-
fractory demon who is lurking in the sufferer's body and
making him ill.[4]   Dyak sorceresses in south-eastern Borneo
will sometimes slash the body of a sick man with sharp
knives in order, it is said, to allow the demon of disease
to escape through the cuts;[5] but perhaps the notion
rather is to make the present quarters of the spirit too
hot for him.   With a similar intention some of the natives
of Borneo and Celebes sprinkle rice upon the head or body
of a person supposed to be infested by dangerous spirits; a
fowl is then brought, which, by picking up the rice from the
person's head or body, removes along with it the spirit or
ghost which is clinging like a burr to his skin.   This is done,
for example, to persons who have attended a funeral, and
who may therefore be supposed to be infested by the ghost

*Disen-
chantment
effected by
cuts with
knives.*

---

[1] J. G. F. Riedel, *De sluik- en
kroesharige rassen tusschen Selebes en
Papua*, p. 78.

[2] J. Kreemer, "Hoe de Javaan zijne
zieken verzorgt," *Mededeelingen van
wege het Nederlandsche Zendelinggenootschap*, xxxvi. (1892) p. 13. Mr. E.
W. Lewis, of Woodthorpe, Atkins
Road, Clapham Park, London, S.W.,
writes to me (July 2, 1902) that his
grandmother, a native of Cheshire,
used to make bees sting her as a cure for
local rheumatism; she said the remedy
was infallible and had been handed

down to her from her mother.

[3] Father Baudin, "Le Fétichisme,"
Missions Catholiques, xvi. (1884) p.
249; A. B. Ellis, *The Yoruba-speaking Peoples of the Slave Coast* (London,
1894), pp. 113 *sq.*

[4] A. Bastian, *Allerlei aus Volks-
und Menschenkunde* (Berlin, 1888), i.
116.

[5] J. B. de Callone, "Iets over de
geneeswijze en ziekten der Daijakers
ter Zuid Oostkust van Borneo,"
Tijdschrift voor Neêrlands Indië,
1840, dl. i. p. 418.

of the deceased.[1]   Similarly Basutos, who have carried a corpse to the grave, have their hands scratched with a knife from the tip of the thumb to the tip of the forefinger, and magic stuff is rubbed into the wound,[2] for the purpose, no doubt, of removing the ghost which may be adhering to their skin.   Among the Barotse of south-eastern Africa a few days after a funeral the sorcerer makes an incision in the forehead of each surviving member of the family and fills it with medicine, " in order to ward off contagion and the effect of the sorcery which caused the death." [3]   When elephant-hunters in East Africa have killed an elephant they get upon its carcase, make little cuts in their toes, and rub gun-powder into the cuts.   This is done with the double intention of counteracting any evil influence that may emanate from the dead elephant, and of acquiring thereby the fleetness of foot possessed by the animal in its life.[4] The people of Nias carefully scrub and scour the weapons and clothes which they buy, in order to efface all connexion between the things and the persons from whom they bought them.[5]

It is probable that the same dread of strangers, rather than any desire to do them honour, is the motive of certain ceremonies which are sometimes observed at their reception, but of which the intention is not directly stated.   In the Ongtong Java Islands, which are inhabited by Polynesians, and lie a little to the north of the Solomon Islands, the priests or sorcerers seem to wield great influence.   Their main business is to summon or exorcise spirits for the purpose of averting or dispelling sickness, and of procuring favour-able winds, a good catch of fish, and so on.   When strangers land on the islands, they are first of all received by the sorcerers, sprinkled with water, anointed with oil, and girt

Cere-
monies
observed
at the
reception
of strangers
may some-
times be
intended to
counteract
their
enchant-
ments.

---

[1] M. T. H. Perelaer, *Ethno-graphische Beschrijving der Dajaks*, pp. 44, 54, 252; B. F. Matthes, *Bijdragen tot de Ethnologie van Zuid-Celebes* (The Hague, 1875), p. 49.

[2] H. Grützner, " Über die Ge-bräuche der Basutho," in *Verhand-lungen der Berliner Gesellschaft für Anthropologie, Ethnologie, und Ur-geschichte*, 1877, pp. 84 *sq.*

[3] L. Decle, *Three Years in Savage Africa* (London, 1898), p. 81.

[4] P. Reichard, *Deutsch - Ostafrika* (Leipsic, 1892), p. 431.

[5] Nieuwenhuisen en Rosenberg, " Verslag omtrent het eiland Nias," in *Verhandelingen van het Bataviaasch Genootschap van Kunsten en Weten-schappen*, xxx. (Batavia, 1863) p. 26.

Ceremonies
observed
at the
reception
of
strangers
may some-
times be
intended to
counteract
their
enchant-
ments. with dried pandanus leaves. At the same time sand and water are freely thrown about in all directions, and the new-comer and his boat are wiped with green leaves. After this ceremony the strangers are introduced by the sorcerers to the chief.[1] In Afghanistan and in some parts of Persia the traveller, before he enters a village, is frequently received with a sacrifice of animal life or food, or of fire and incense. The Afghan Boundary Mission, in passing by villages in Afghanistan, was often met with fire and incense.[2] Sometimes a tray of lighted embers is thrown under the hoofs of the traveller's horse, with the words, "You are welcome."[3] On entering a village in central Africa Emin Pasha was received with the sacrifice of two goats; their blood was sprinkled on the path and the chief stepped over the blood to greet Emin.[4] Before strangers entered the country or city of Benin, custom compelled them to have their feet washed; sometimes the ceremony was performed in a sacred place.[5] Amongst the Esquimaux of Cumberland Inlet, when a stranger arrives at an encampment, the sorcerer goes out to meet him. The stranger folds his arms and inclines his head to one side, so as to expose his cheek, upon which the magician deals a terrible blow, sometimes felling him to the ground. Next the sorcerer in his turn presents his cheek to the smiter and receives a buffet from the stranger. Then they kiss each other, the ceremony is over, and the stranger is hospitably received by all.[6] Sometimes the dread of strangers and their magic is too great to allow of their reception on any terms. Thus when Speke arrived at a certain village, the natives shut their doors against him, "because they had never before seen a white man nor the tin boxes that the men were carrying:

---

1 R. Parkinson, "Zur Ethnographie der Ontong Java- und Tasman-Inseln," *Internationales Archiv für Ethnographie*, x. (1897) p. 112.

2 T. S. Weir, "Note on Sacrifices in India as a Means of averting Epidemics," *Journal of the Anthropological Society of Bombay*, i. 35.

3 E. O'Donovan, *The Merv Oasis* (London, 1882), ii. 58.

4 *Emin Pasha in Central Africa, being a Collection of his Letters and Journals* (London, 1888), p. 107.

5 H. Ling Roth, *Great Benin* (Halifax, England, 1903), p. 123.

6 *Narrative of the Second Arctic Expedition made by Charles F. Hall*, edited by Prof. J. G. Nourse, U.S.N. (Washington, 1879), p. 269, note. Compare Fr. Boas, "The Central Eskimo," *Sixth Annual Report of the Bureau of Ethnology* (Washington, 1888), p. 609.

'Who knows,' they said, 'but that these very boxes are the plundering Watuta transformed and come to kill us? You cannot be admitted.' No persuasion could avail with them, and the party had to proceed to the next village."[1]

The fear thus entertained of alien visitors is often mutual. Entering a strange land the savage feels that he is treading enchanted ground, and he takes steps to guard against the demons that haunt it and the magical arts of its inhabitants. Thus on going to a strange land the Maoris performed certain ceremonies to make it *noa* (common), lest it might have been previously *tapu* (sacred).[2] When Baron Miklucho-Maclay was approaching a village on the Maclay Coast of New Guinea, one of the natives who accompanied him broke a branch from a tree and going aside whispered to it for a while ; then stepping up to each member of the party, one after another, he spat something upon his back and gave him some blows with the branch. Lastly, he went into the forest and buried the branch under withered leaves in the thickest part of the jungle. This ceremony was believed to protect the party against all treachery and danger in the village they were approaching.[3] The idea probably was that the malignant influences were drawn off from the persons into the branch and buried with it in the depths of the forest. Before Stuhlmann and his companions entered the territory of the Wanyamwesi in central Africa, one of his men killed a white cock and buried it in a pot just at the boundary.[4] In Australia, when a strange tribe has been invited into a district and is approaching the encampment of the tribe which owns the land, " the strangers carry lighted bark or burning sticks in their hands, for the purpose, they say, of clearing and purifying the air." [5] On the coast of Victoria there is a tract of country between the La Trobe River and the Yarra River, which some of the aborigines called the Bad Country. It was supposed to act injuriously

Ceremonies observed at entering a strange land to disenchant it.

[1] J. A. Grant, *A Walk across Africa*, pp. 104 *sq.*
[2] E. Shortland, *Traditions and Superstitions of the New Zealanders* [2] (London, 1856), p. 103.
[3] N. von Miklucho-Maclay, " Ethnologische Bemerkungen über die Papuas der Maclay-Kuste in Neu-

Guinea," *Natuurkundig Tijdschrift voor Nederlandsch Indie*, xxxvi. 317 *sq.*
[4] Fr. Stuhlmann, *Mit Emin Pascha ins Herz von Afrika* (Berlin, 1894), p. 94.
[5] R. Brough Smyth, *Aborigines of Victoria*, i. 134.

Ceremonies
at entering
a strange
land to
disenchant
it or to
propitiate
the local
spirits. on strangers. Hence when a man of another clan entered
it he needed some one of the natives to look after him ;
and if his guardian went away from the camp, he deputed
another to take his place. During his first visit, before he
became as it were acclimatised, the visitor did nothing for
himself as to food, drinking-water, or lodging. He was
painted with a band of white pipe-clay across the face below
the eyes, and had to learn the Nulit language before going
further. He slept on a thick layer of leaves so that he
should not touch the ground ; and he was fed with flesh-
meat from the point of a burnt stick, which he removed with
his teeth, not with his lips. His drinking-water was drawn
from a small hole in the ground by his entertainers, and they
made it muddy by stirring it with a stick. He might only
take three mouthfuls at a time, each of which he had to let
slowly trickle down his throat. If he did otherwise, his
throat would close up.[1] The Kayans and Kenyahs of
Borneo think it well to conciliate the spirit of the land
when they enter a strange country. " The old men, indeed,
trusting to the protection afforded by omens, are in little
need of further aid, but when young boys are brought into a
new river of importance, the hospitality of the local demons
is invoked. The Kayans make an offering of fowls' eggs,
which must not be bought on the spot, but are carried from
the house, sometimes for distances so long that the devotion
of the travellers is more apparent than their presents to the
spirits of the land. Each boy takes an egg and puts it in a
bamboo split at the end into four, while one of the older
men calls upon the hills, rocks, trees, and streams to hear
him and to witness the offering. Careful to disguise the
true nature of the gift, he speaks of it as *ovē*, a yam, using
a form of words fixed by usage. ' Omen bird,' he shouts
into the air, ' we have brought you these boys. It is on
their account only that we have prepared this feast. Harm
them not ; make things go pleasantly ; and they give you
the usual offering of a yam. I give this to the country.'
The little ceremony is performed behind the hut where the
night is spent, and the boys wait about for the charm to
take effect. The custom of the Kenyahs shows the same

[1] A. W. Howitt, *Native Tribes of South-East Australia*, p. 403.

feeling for the unknown and unseen spirits that are supposed to abound.   A fowl's feathers, one for each boy, are held by an old man, while the youngsters touch his arm.   The invocation is quite a powerful example of native rhetoric: 'Smooth away trouble, ye mystic mountains, hills, valleys, soil, rocks, trees.   Shield the lives of the children who have come hither.'"[1]   When the Toradjas of central Celebes are on a head-hunting expedition and have entered the enemy's country, they may not eat any fruits which the foe has planted nor any animal which he has reared until they have first committed an act of hostility, as by burning a house or killing a man.   They think that if they broke this rule they would receive something of the soul or spiritual essence of the enemy into themselves, which would destroy the mystic virtue of their talismans.[2]   It is said that just before Greek armies advanced to the shock of battle, a man bearing a lighted torch stepped out from either side and threw his torch into the space between the hosts.   Then they retired unmolested, for they were thought to be sacred to Ares and inviolable.[3]   Now some peoples fancy that when they advance to battle the spirits of their fathers hover in the van.[4]   Hence fire thrown out in front of the line of battle may be meant to disperse these shadowy combatants, leaving the issue of the fight to be determined by more substantial weapons than ghosts can wield.   Similarly the fire which is sometimes borne at the head of an army[5] is perhaps in some cases intended to dissipate the evil influences, whether magical or spiritual, with which the air of the enemy's country may be conceived to teem.

Again, it is thought that a man who has been on a journey may have contracted some magic evil from the strangers with whom he has been brought into contact. Hence, on returning home, before he is readmitted to the

Purification ceremonies observed on the return from a journey.

---

[1] Ch. Hose, *Notes on the Natives of British Borneo* (in manuscript).

[2] A. C. Kruijt, "Het koppensnellen der Toradja's van Midden-Celebes, en zijne beteekenis," *Verslagen en Mededeelingen der Konikl. Akademie van Wetenschappen*, Afdeeling Letterkunde, iv. Reeks, iii. (1899) p. 204.

[3] Scholiast on Euripides, *Phoenissae*, 1377, ed. E. Schwartz.

[4] Conon, *Narrationes*, 18; Pausanias, iii. 19. 12 ; Francis Fleming, *Southern Africa* (London, 1856), p. 259; Dudley Kidd, *The Essential Kafir*, p. 307.

[5] See *The Magic Art and the Evolution of Kings*, vol. ii. pp. 263 *sq.*

Purifica-
tory cere-
monies
observed
on the
return
from a
journey.

society of his tribe and friends, he has to undergo certain purificatory ceremonies. Thus the Bechuanas "cleanse or purify themselves after journeys by shaving their heads, etc., lest they should have contracted from strangers some evil by witchcraft or sorcery."[1] In some parts of western Africa when a man returns home after a long absence, before he is allowed to visit his wife, he must wash his person with a particular fluid, and receive from the sorcerer a certain mark on his forehead, in order to counteract any magic spell which a stranger woman may have cast on him in his absence, and which might be communicated through him to the women of his village.[2] Every year about one-third of the men of the Wanyamwesi tribe make journeys to the east coast of Africa either as porters or as traffickers. Before he sets out, the husband smears his cheeks with a sort of meal-porridge, and during his absence his wife may eat no flesh and must keep for him the sediment of the porridge in the pot. On their return from the coast the men sprinkle meal every day on all the paths leading to the camp, for the purpose, it is supposed, of keeping evil spirits off; and when they reach their homes the men again smear porridge on their faces, while the women who have stayed at home strew ashes on their heads.[3] In Uganda, when a man returns from a journey, his wife takes some of the bark cloths from the bed of one of his children and lays them on her husband's bed ; and as he enters the house, he jumps over one of his wives who has children by him, or over one of his children. If he neglects to do this, one of his children or one of his wives will die.[4] When Damaras return home after a long absence, they are given a small portion of the fat of particular animals, which is supposed to possess certain virtues.[5] A story is told of a Navajo Indian who, after long wanderings, returned to his own people. When he came within sight of his house, his people

[1] John Campbell, *Travels in South Africa, being a Narrative of a Second Journey in the Interior of that Country* (London, 1822), ii. 205.

[2] Ladislaus Magyar, *Reisen in Süd-Afrika* (Buda-Pesth and Leipsic, 1859), p. 203.

[3] Fr. Stuhlmann, *Mit Emin Pascha ins Herz von Afrika* (Berlin, 1894), p. 89.

[4] J. Roscoe, " Further Notes on the Manners and Customs of the Baganda," *Journal of the Anthropological Institute*, xxxii. (1902) p. 62.

[5] C. J. Andersson, *Lake Ngami* [2] (London, 1856), p. 223.

made him stop and told him not to approach nearer till Purifica-
they had summoned a shaman. When the shaman was come tory cere-
monies
" ceremonies were performed over the returned wanderer, observed
and he was washed from head to foot, and dried with corn- on the
return
meal ; for thus do the Navajo treat all who return to their from a
homes from captivity with another tribe, in order that all journey.
alien substances and influences may be removed from them.
When he had been thus purified he entered the house, and
his people embraced him and wept over him."[1] Two
Hindoo ambassadors, who had been sent to England by a
native prince and had returned to India, were considered to
have so polluted themselves by contact with strangers that
nothing but being born again could restore them to purity.
" For the purpose of regeneration it is directed to make an
image of pure gold of the female power of nature, in the
shape either of a woman or of a cow. In this statue the
person to be regenerated is enclosed, and dragged through
the usual channel. As a statue of pure gold and of proper
dimensions would be too expensive, it is sufficient to make
an image of the sacred *Yoni*, through which the person to be
regenerated is to pass." Such an image of pure gold was
made at the prince's command, and his ambassadors were
born again by being dragged through it.[2] In some of the
Moluccas, when a brother or young blood-relation returns
from a long journey, a young girl awaits him at the door with
a *caladi* leaf in her hand and water in the leaf. She throws
the water over his face and bids him welcome.[3] Among the
Kayans of Borneo, men who have been absent on a long
journey are secluded for four days in a small hut made
specially for the purpose before they are allowed to
enter their own house.[4] The natives of Savage Island
(South Pacific) invariably killed, not only all strangers in
distress who were drifted to their shores, but also any
of their own people who had gone away in a ship and
returned home. This was done out of dread of disease.
Long after they began to venture out to ships they

[1] Washington Matthews, " The
Mountain Chant : a Navajo Ceremony,"
*Fifth Annual Report of the Bureau of
Ethnology* (Washington, 1887), p. 410.
[2] *Asiatick Researches*, vi. 535 *sq.* ed.

4to (p. 537 *sq.* ed. 8vo).
[3] François Valentyn, *Oud en nieuw
Oost-Indiën*, iii. 16.
[4] A. W. Nieuwenhuis, *In Centraal
Borneo*, i. 165.

would not immediately use the things they obtained from them, but hung them up in quarantine for weeks in the bush.[1]

Special precautions taken to guard the king against the magic of strangers. When precautions like these are taken on behalf of the people in general against the malignant influence supposed to be exercised by strangers, it is no wonder that special measures are adopted to protect the king from the same insidious danger. In the middle ages the envoys who visited a Tartar Khan were obliged to pass between two fires before they were admitted to his presence, and the gifts they brought were also carried between the fires. The reason assigned for the custom was that the fire purged away any magic influence which the strangers might mean to exercise over the Khan.[2] When subject chiefs come with their retinues to visit Kalamba (the most powerful chief of the Bashilange in the Congo Basin) for the first time or after being rebellious, they have to bathe, men and women together, in two brooks on two successive days, passing the nights under the open sky in the market-place. After the second bath they proceed, entirely naked, to the house of Kalamba, who makes a long white mark on the breast and forehead of each of them. Then they return to the market-place and dress, after which they undergo the pepper ordeal. Pepper is dropped into the eyes of each of them, and while this is being done the sufferer has to make a confession of all his sins, to answer all questions that may be put to him, and to take certain vows. This ends the ceremony, and the strangers are now free to take up their quarters in the town for as long as they choose to remain.[3] Before strangers were admitted to the presence of Lobengula, king of the Matebeles, they had to be treated with a sticky green medicine, which was profusely sprinkled over them by means of a cow's tail.[4] At Kilema, in

[1] G. Turner, *Samoa*, pp. 305 *sq.*

[2] De Plano Carpini, *Historia Mongolorum quos nos Tartaros appellamus,* ed. D'Avezac (Paris, 1838), cap. iii. § iii. p. 627, cap. ult. § i. x. p. 744, and Appendix, p. 775; "Travels of William de Rubriquis into Tartary and China," in Pinkerton's *Voyages and Travels,* vii. 82 *sq.*

[3] Paul Pogge, "Bericht über die Station Mukenge," *Mittheilungen der Afrikanischen Gesellschaft in Deutschland,* iv. (1883-1885) pp. 182 *sq.*

[4] Coillard, "Voyage au pays des Banyais et au Zambèse," *Bulletin de la Société de Géographie* (Paris), VIme Série, xx. (1880) p. 393.

eastern Africa, when a stranger arrives, a medicine is made out of a certain plant or a tree fetched from a distance, mixed with the blood of a sheep or goat. With this mixture the stranger is besmeared or besprinkled before he is admitted to the presence of the king.[1] The king of Monomotapa, in South-East Africa, might not wear any foreign stuffs for fear of their being poisoned.[2] The king of Cacongo, in West Africa, might not possess or even touch European goods, except metals, arms, and articles made of wood and ivory. Persons wearing foreign stuffs were very careful to keep at a distance from his person, lest they should touch him.[3] The king of Loango might not look upon the house of a white man.[4] We have already seen how the native king of Fernando Po dwells secluded from all contact with the whites in the depths of an extinct volcano, shunning the very sight of a pale face, which, in the belief of his subjects, would be instantly fatal to him.[5] In a wild mountainous district of Java, to the south of Bantam, there exists a small aboriginal race who have been described as a living antiquity. These are the Baduwis, who about the year 1443 fled from Bantam to escape conversion to Islam, and in their mountain fastnesses, holding aloof from their neighbours, still cleave to the quaint and primitive ways of their heathen forefathers. Their villages are perched in spots which deep ravines, lofty precipices, raging torrents, and impenetrable forests combine to render almost inaccessible. Their hereditary ruler bears the title of Girang-Pu-un and unites in his hands the temporal and spiritual power. He must never quit the capital, and none even of his subjects who live outside the town are ever allowed to see him. Were an alien to set foot in his dwelling, the place would be desecrated and abandoned. In former times the representatives of the Dutch Government and the Regent of Java

---

[1] J. L. Krapf, *Travels, Researches, and Missionary Labours during an Eighteen Years' Residence in Eastern Africa* (London, 1860), pp. 252 *sq.*

[2] O. Dapper, *Description de l'Afrique* (Amsterdam, 1686), p. 391.

[3] Proyart, "History of Loango, Kakongo," etc., in Pinkerton's *Voyages and Travels*, xvi. 583; Dapper, *op. cit.* p. 340; J. Ogilby, *Africa* (London, 1670), p. 521. Compare A. Bastian, *Die deutsche Expedition an der Loango-Küste*, i. 288.

[4] A. Bastian, *op. cit.* i. 268 *sq.*

[5] See above, pp. 8 *sq.*

once paid a visit to the capital of the Baduwis. That very night all the people fled the place and never returned.[1]

§ 2. *Taboos on Eating and Drinking*

Spiritual dangers of eating and drinking and precautions taken against them.

In the opinion of savages the acts of eating and drinking are attended with special danger ; for at these times the soul may escape from the mouth, or be extracted by the magic arts of an enemy present. Among the Ewe-speaking peoples of the Slave Coast " the common belief seems to be that the indwelling spirit leaves the body and returns to it through the mouth ; hence, should it have gone out, it behoves a man to be careful about opening his mouth, lest a homeless spirit should take advantage of the opportunity and enter his body. This, it appears, is considered most likely to take place while the man is eating." [2] Precautions are therefore taken to guard against these dangers. Thus of the Battas of Sumatra it is said that " since the soul can leave the body, they always take care to prevent their soul from straying on occasions when they have most need of it. But it is only possible to prevent the soul from straying when one is in the house. At feasts one may find the whole house shut up, in order that the soul (*tondi*) may stay and enjoy the good things set before it." [3] The Zafimanelo in Madagascar lock their doors when they eat, and hardly any one ever sees them eating.[4] In Shoa, one of the southern provinces of Abyssinia, the doors of the house are scrupulously barred at meals to exclude the evil eye, and a fire is invariably lighted, else devils would enter and there would be no blessing on the meat.[5] Every time that an Abyssinian of rank drinks, a servant holds a cloth before his master to

[1] L. von Ende, "Die Baduwis auf Java," *Mittheilungen der anthropologischen Gesellschaft in Wien*, xix. (1889) pp. 7-10. As to the Baduwis (Badoejs) see also G. A. Wilken, *Handleiding voor de vergelijkende Volkenkunde van Nederlandsch - Indië* (Leyden, 1893), pp. 640-643.

[2] A. B. Ellis, *The Ewe-speaking Peoples of the Slave Coast*, p. 107.

[3] J. B. Neumann, "Het Pane- en Bila - Stroomgebied op het eiland

Sumatra," *Tijdschrift van het Nederlandsch Aardrijkskundig Genootschap*, Tweede Serie, dl. iii. (1886) Afdeeling, meer uitgebreide artikelen, No. 2, p. 300.

[4] J. Richardson, "Tanala Customs, Superstitions and Beliefs," *The Antananarivo Annual and Madagascar Magazine, Reprint of the First Four Numbers* (Antananarivo, 1885), p. 219.

[5] W. Cornwallis Harris, *The Highlands of Aethiopia*, iii. 171 *sq.*

guard him from the evil eye.[1]   The Warua will not allow
any one to see them eating and drinking, being doubly
particular that no person of the opposite sex shall see them
doing so.   " I had to pay a man to let me see him drink ;
I could not make a man let a woman see him drink."
When offered a drink of *pombe* they often ask that a cloth
may be held up to hide them whilst drinking.   Further,
every man and woman must cook for themselves ; each
person must have his own fire.[2]   The Tuaregs of the
Sahara never eat or drink in presence of any one else.[3]
The Thompson Indians of British Columbia thought that a
shaman could bewitch them most easily when they were
eating, drinking, or smoking ; hence they avoided doing any
of these things in presence of an unknown shaman.[4]   In
Fiji persons who suspected others of plotting against them
avoided eating in their presence, or were careful to leave no
fragment of food behind.[5]

If these are the ordinary precautions taken by common
people, the precautions taken by kings are extraordinary.
The king of Loango may not be seen eating or drinking by
man or beast under pain of death.   A favourite dog having
broken into the room where the king was dining, the king
ordered it to be killed on the spot.   Once the king's
own son, a boy of twelve years old, inadvertently saw the
king drink.   Immediately the king ordered him to be finely
apparelled and feasted, after which he commanded him to
be cut in quarters, and carried about the city with a proclamation that he had seen the king drink.   " When the
king has a mind to drink, he has a cup of wine brought ; he
that brings it has a bell in his hand, and as soon as he has
delivered the cup to the king, he turns his face from him and
rings the bell, on which all present fall down with their faces
to the ground, and continue so till the king has drank. . . .

Seclusion of kings at their meals.

---

[1] Th. Lefebvre, *Voyage en Abyssinie*, i. p. lxxii.

[2] Lieut. V. L. Cameron, *Across
Africa* (London, 1877), ii. 71 ; *id.*, in
Journal of the Anthropological Institute,
vi. (1877) p. 173.

[3] Ebn-el-Dyn el-Eghouâthy, " Relation d'un voyage dans l'intérieur
de l'Afrique septentrionale," *Bulletin*

de la Société de Géographie (Paris),
IIme Série, i. (1834) p. 290.

[4] J. Teit, " The Thompson Indians
of British Columbia," *Memoir of the
American Museum of Natural History*,
The Jesup North Pacific Expedition,
vol. i. part iv. (April 1900) p. 360.

[5] Th. Williams, *Fiji and the Fijians*,[2]
i. 249.

Seclusion of kings at their meals.

His eating is much in the same style, for which he has a house on purpose, where his victuals are set upon a bensa or table : which he goes to, and shuts the door : when he has done, he knocks and comes out. So that none ever see the king eat or drink. For it is believed that if any one should, the king shall immediately die." The remnants of his food are buried, doubtless to prevent them from falling into the hands of sorcerers, who by means of these fragments might cast a fatal spell over the monarch.[1] The rules observed by the neighbouring king of Cacongo were similar ; it was thought that the king would die if any of his subjects were to see him drink.[2] It is a capital offence to see the king of Dahomey at his meals. When he drinks in public, as he does on extraordinary occasions, he hides himself behind a curtain, or handkerchiefs are held up round his head, and all the people throw themselves with their faces to the earth.[3] Any one who saw the Muata Jamwo (a great potentate in the Congo Basin) eating or drinking would certainly be put to death.[4] When the king (*Muata*) of Cazembe raises his glass to his mouth to drink, all who are present prostrate themselves and avert their faces in such a manner as not to see him drinking.[5] At Asaba, on the Lower Niger, where the kings or chiefs number fully four hundred, no one is allowed to prepare the royal dishes. The chiefs act as their own cooks and eat in the strictest privacy.[6] The king and royal family of Walo, on the Senegal, never take their meals in public ; it is expressly forbidden to see them eating.[7] Among the Monbutto of central Africa the king invariably takes his meals in

[1] "Adventures of Andrew Battel," in Pinkerton's *Voyages and Travels*, xvi. 330 ; O. Dapper, *Description de l'Afrique*, p. 330; A. Bastian, *Die deutsche Expedition an der Loango-Küste*, i. 262 *sq.* ; R. F. Burton, *Abeokuta and the Cameroons Mountains*, i. 147.

[2] Proyart's "History of Loango, Kakongo," etc., in Pinkerton's *Voyages and Travels*, xvi. 584.

[3] J. L. Wilson, *Western Africa*, p. 202; John Duncan, *Travels in Western Africa*, i. 222. Compare W. W.

Reade, *Savage Africa*, p. 543.

[4] Paul Pogge, *Im Reiche des Muata Jamwo* (Berlin, 1880), p. 231.

[5] F. T. Valdez, *Six Years of a Traveller's Life in Western Africa* (London, 1861), ii. 256.

[6] A. F. Mockler-Ferryman, *Up the Niger* (London, 1892), p. 38.

[7] Baron Roger, "Notice sur le gouvernement, les mœurs et les superstitions des Nègres du pays de Walo," *Bulletin de la Société de Géographie* (Paris), viii. (1827) p. 351.

private; no one may see the contents of his dish, and all Seclusion that he leaves is carefully thrown into a pit set apart for of kings at their meals. that purpose. Everything that the king has handled is held sacred and may not be touched.[1] When the king of Unyoro in central Africa went to drink milk in the dairy, every man must leave the royal enclosure and all the women had to cover their heads till the king returned. No one might see him drink. One wife accompanied him to the dairy and handed him the milk-pot, but she turned away her face while he drained it.[2] The king of Susa, a region to the south of Abyssinia, presides daily at the feast in the long banqueting-hall, but is hidden from the gaze of his subjects by a curtain.[3] Among the Ewe-speaking peoples of the Slave Coast the person of the king is sacred, and if he drinks in public every one must turn away the head so as not to see him, while some of the women of the court hold up a cloth before him as a screen. He never eats in public, and the people pretend to believe that he neither eats nor sleeps. It is criminal to say the contrary.[4] When the king of Tonga ate, all the people turned their backs to him.[5] In the palace of the Persian kings there were two dining-rooms opposite each other; in one of them the king dined, in the other his guests. He could see them through a curtain on the door, but they could not see him. Generally the king took his meals alone; but sometimes his wife or some of his sons dined with him.[6]

[1] G. Schweinfurth, *The Heart of Africa*, ii. 45 (third edition, London, 1878) ; G. Casati, *Ten Years in Equatoria* (London and New York, 1891), i. 177. As to the various customs observed by Monbutto chiefs in drinking see G. Burrows, *The Land of the Pigmies* (London, 1898), pp. 88, 91.

[2] J. G. Frazer, *Totemism and Exogamy*, ii. 526, from information furnished by the Rev. John Roscoe.

[3] W. Cornwallis Harris, *The Highlands of Aethiopia*, iii. 78.

[4] A. B. Ellis, *The Ewe-speaking Peoples of the Slave Coast*, pp. 162 *sq.*

[5] Capt. James Cook, *Voyages*, v. 374 (ed. 1809).

[6] Heraclides Cumanus, in Athenaeus, iv. 26, p. 145 B-D. On the other hand, in Kafa no one, not even the king, may eat except in the presence of a legal witness. A slave is appointed to witness the king's meals, and his office is esteemed honourable. See F. G. Massaja, in *Bulletin de la Société de Géographie* (Paris), Vme Série, i. (1861) pp. 330 *sq.* ; Ph. Paulitschke, *Ethnographie Nordost-Afrikas : die geistige Cultur der Danâkil, Galla und Somâl* (Berlin, 1896), pp. 248 *sq.*

§ 3. *Taboos on shewing the Face*

Faces
veiled to
avert evil
influences.

In some of the preceding cases the intention of eating and drinking in strict seclusion may perhaps be to hinder evil influences from entering the body rather than to prevent the escape of the soul. This certainly is the motive of some drinking customs observed by natives of the Congo region. Thus we are told of these people that " there is hardly a native who would dare to swallow a liquid without first conjuring the spirits. One of them rings a bell all the time he is drinking ; another crouches down and places his left hand on the earth ; another veils his head ; another puts a stalk of grass or a leaf in his hair, or marks his forehead with a line of clay. This fetish custom assumes very varied forms. To explain them, the black is satisfied to say that they are an energetic mode of conjuring spirits." In this part of the world a chief will commonly ring a bell at each draught of beer which he swallows, and at the same moment a lad stationed in front of him brandishes a spear " to keep at bay the spirits which might try to sneak into the old chief's body by the same road as the *massanga* (beer)." [1] The same motive of warding off evil spirits probably explains the custom observed by some African sultans of veiling their faces. The Sultan of Darfur wraps up his face with a piece of white muslin, which goes round his head several times, covering his mouth and nose first, and then his forehead, so that only his eyes are visible. The same custom of veiling the face as a mark of sovereignty is said to be observed in other parts of central Africa. [2] The Sultan of Wadai always speaks from behind a curtain ; no one sees his face except his intimates and a few favoured persons. [3] Similarly the Sultan of Bornu never shewed himself to his people and

---

[1] *Notes analytiques sur les collections ethnographiques du Musée du Congo*, I. *Les Arts, Religion* (Brussels, 1902-1906), p. 164.

[2] Mohammed Ibn-Omar el Tounsy, *Voyage au Darfour* (Paris, 1845), p. 203 ; *Travels of an Arab Merchant* [Mohammed Ibn-Omar el Tounsy] *in Soudan*, abridged from the French (of Perron) by Bayle St. John (London, 1854), pp. 91 *sq.*

[3] Mohammed Ibn-Omar el Tounsy, *Voyage au Ouadây* (Paris, 1851), p. 375.

only spoke to them from behind a curtain.[1] The king of Kings not
Chonga, a town on the right bank of the Niger above Egga, to be seen
may not be seen by his subjects nor by strangers. At an subjects.
interview he sits in his palace concealed by a mat which
hangs like a curtain, and from behind it he converses with
his visitor.[2] The Muysca Indians of Colombia had such a
respect for their chiefs that they dared not lift their eyes on
them, but always turned their backs when they had to
address them. If a thief, after repeated punishments, proved
incorrigible, they took him to the chief, and one of the nobles,
turning the culprit round, said to him, " Since you think
yourself so great a lord that you have the right to break the
laws, you have the right to look at the chief." From that
moment the criminal was regarded as infamous. Nobody
would have anything to do with him or even speak to him,
and he died an outcast.[3] Montezuma was revered by his
subjects as a god, and he set so much store on their
reverence that if on going out of the city he saw a man
lift up his eyes on him, he had the rash gazer put to death.
He generally lived in the retirement of his palace, seldom
shewing himself. On the days when he went to visit his
gardens, he was carried in a litter through a street which
was enclosed by walls ; none but his bearers had the right
to pass along that street.[4] It was a law of the Medes that
their king should be seen by nobody.[5] The king of Jebu,
on the Slave Coast of West Africa, is surrounded by a great
deal of mystery. Until lately his face might not be seen
even by his own subjects, and if circumstances compelled
him to communicate with them he did so through a screen
which concealed him from view. Now, though his face may
be seen, it is customary to hide his body ; and at audiences
a cloth is held before him so as to conceal him from the
neck downwards, and it is raised so as to cover him altogether
whenever he coughs, sneezes, spits, or takes snuff. His face

[1] Ibn Batoutah, *Voyages*, ed. C.
Defrémery et B. R. Sanguinetti (Paris,
1853-1858), iv. 441.
[2] Le Commandant Mattei, *Bas-
Niger, Bénoué, Dahomey* (Paris, 1895),
pp. 90 *sq.*
[3] H. Ternaux-Compans, *Essai sur*

l'ancien Cundinamarca, p. 60.
[4] *Manuscrit Ramirez, histoire de
l'origine des Indiens qui habitent la
Nouvelle Espagne selon leurs traditions*,
publié par D. Charnay (Paris, 1903),
pp. 107 *sq.*
[5] Herodotus, i. 99.

Faces, and especially mouths, veiled to avert evil influences. is partially hidden by a conical cap with hanging strings of beads.[1]   Amongst the Tuaregs of the Sahara all the men (but not the women) keep the lower part of their face, especially the mouth, veiled constantly; the veil is never put off, not even in eating or sleeping.[2]   Among the Arabs men remarkable for their good looks have been known to veil their faces, especially at festivals and markets, in order to protect themselves against the evil eye.[3]   The same reason may explain the custom of muffling their faces which has been observed by Arab women from the earliest times[4] and by the women of Boeotian Thebes in antiquity.[5]   In Samoa a man whose family god was the turtle might not eat a turtle, and if he helped a neighbour to cut up and cook one he had to wear a bandage tied over his mouth lest an embryo turtle should slip down his throat, grow up, and be his death.[6]   In West Timor a speaker holds his right hand before his mouth in speaking lest a demon should enter his body, and lest the person with whom he converses should harm the speaker's soul by magic.[7]   In New South Wales for some time after his initiation into the tribal mysteries, a young blackfellow (whose soul at this time is in a critical state) must always cover his mouth with a rug when a woman is present.[8]   We have already seen how common is the notion that the life or soul may escape by the mouth or nostrils.[9]

§ 4. *Taboos on quitting the House*

By an extension of the like precaution kings are sometimes forbidden ever to leave their palaces; or, if they are

---

[1] A. B. Ellis, *The Yoruba-speaking Peoples of the Slave Coast*, p. 170.

[2] Ebn-el-Dyn el-Eghouathy, "Relation d'un voyage," *Bulletin de la Société de Géographie* (Paris), IIme Série, i. (1834) p. 290; H. Duveyrier, *Exploration du Sahara: les Touareg du Nord*, pp. 391 *sq.*; Reclus, *Nouvelle Géographie Universelle*, xi. 838 *sq.*; James Richardson, *Travels in the Great Desert of Sahara*, ii. 208.

[3] J. Wellhausen, *Reste arabischen Heidentums*[2] (Berlin, 1897), p. 196.

[4] Tertullian, *De virginibus velandis*, 17 (Migne's *Patrologia Latina*, ii.

col. 912).

[5] Pseudo - Dicaearchus, *Descriptio Graeciae*, 18, in *Geographi Graeci Minores*, ed. C. Müller, i. 103; *id.*, in *Fragmenta Historicorum Graecorum*, ed. C. Müller, ii. 259.

[6] G. Turner, *Samoa*, pp. 67 *sq.*

[7] J. G. F. Riedel, "Die Landschaft Dawan oder West-Timor," *Deutsche geographische Blätter*, x. 230.

[8] A. W. Howitt, "On some Australian Ceremonies of Initiation," *Journal of the Anthropological Institute*, xiii. (1884) p. 456.

[9] Above, pp. 30 *sqq.*

allowed to do so, their subjects are forbidden to see them abroad. We have seen that the priestly king at Shark Point, West Africa, may never quit his house or even his chair, in which he is obliged to sleep sitting; and that the king of Fernando Po, whom no white man may see, is reported to be confined to his house with shackles on his legs.[1] The fetish king of Benin, who was worshipped as a deity by his subjects, might not quit his palace.[2] After his coronation the king of Loango is confined to his palace, which he may not leave.[3] The king of Onitsha, on the Niger, "does not step out of his house into the town unless a human sacrifice is made to propitiate the gods: on this account he never goes out beyond the precincts of his premises."[4] Indeed we are told that he may not quit his palace under pain of death or of giving up one or more slaves to be executed in his presence. As the wealth of the country is measured in slaves, the king takes good care not to infringe the law. One day the monarch, charmed by some presents which he had received from a French officer, politely attended his visitor to the gate, and in a moment of forgetfulness was about to break bounds, when his chamberlain, seizing his majesty by his legs, and his wives, friends, and servants rushing up, prevented him from taking so fatal a step. Yet once a year at the Feast of Yams the king is allowed, and even required by custom, to dance before his people outside the high mud wall of the palace. In dancing he carries a great weight, generally a sack of earth, on his back to prove that he is still able to support the burden and cares of state. Were he unable to discharge this duty, he would be immediately deposed and perhaps stoned.[5] The

---

[1] See above, pp. 5, 8 *sq.*

[2] This rule was mentioned to me in conversation by Miss Mary H. Kingsley. However, he is said to have shewn himself outside his palace on solemn occasions once or twice a year. See O. Dapper, *Description de l'Afrique*, pp. 311 *sq.*; H. Ling Roth, *Great Benin*, p. 74. As to the worship of the king of Benin, see *The Magic Art and the Evolution of Kings*, vol. i. p. 396.

[3] A. Bastian, *Die deutsche Expedition an der Loango-Küste*, i. 263.

However, a case is recorded in which he marched out to war (*ibid.* i. 268 *sq.*).

[4] S. Crowther and J. C. Taylor, *The Gospel on the Banks of the Niger* (London, 1859), p. 433.

[5] Le Commandant Mattei, *Bas-Niger, Bénoué, Dahomey* (Paris, 1895), pp. 67-72. The annual dance of the king of Onitsha outside of his palace is mentioned also by S. Crowther and J. C. Taylor (*op. cit.* p. 379), and A. F. Mockler-Ferryman (*Up the Niger*, p. 22).

Kings forbidden to leave their palaces or to be seen abroad by their subjects.

Tomas or Habes, a hardy race of mountaineers who inhabit Mount Bandiagara in Nigeria, revere a great fetish doctor called the Ogom, who is not suffered to quit his house on any pretext.[1] Among the natives of the Cross River in Southern Nigeria the sacred chiefs of certain villages are confined to their compounds, that is, to the enclosures in which their houses are built. Such chiefs may be confined for years within these narrow bounds. "Among these primitive people, the head chief is often looked upon as half divine, the human representative of their ancestral god. He regulates their religious rites, and is by some tribes believed to have the power of making rain fall when they require it, and of bringing them good harvests. So, being of such value to the community, he is not permitted, except on very rare occasions, to go outside his compound, lest evil should befall him, and the whole town have to suffer."[2] The kings of Ethiopia were worshipped as gods, but were mostly kept shut up in their palaces.[3] On the mountainous coast of Pontus there dwelt in antiquity a rude and warlike people named the Mosyni or Mosynoeci, through whose rugged country the Ten Thousand marched on their famous retreat from Asia to Europe. These barbarians kept their king in close custody at the top of a high tower, from which after his election he was never more allowed to descend. Here he dispensed justice to his people ; but if he offended them, they punished him by stopping his rations for a whole day, or even starving him to death.[4] The kings of Sabaea or Sheba, the spice country of Arabia, were not allowed to go out of their palaces ; if they did so, the mob stoned them to death.[5] But at the top of

---

[1] "Mission Voulet-Chanoine," *Bulletin de la Société de Géographie* (Paris), VIIIme Série, xx. (1899) p. 223.

[2] C. Partridge, *Cross River Natives* (London, 1905), p. 7 ; compare *id.* pp. 8, 200, 202, 203 *sq.* See also Major A. G. Leonard, *The Lower Niger and its Tribes* (London, 1906), pp. 371 *sq.*

[3] Strabo, xvii. 2. 2 σέβονται δ' ὡς θεοὺς τοὺς βασιλέας, κατακλείστους ὄντας καὶ οἰκουροὺς τὸ πλέον.

[4] Xenophon, *Anabasis*, v. 4. 26 ; Scymnus Chius, *Orbis descriptio*, 900

sqq. (*Geographi Graeci Minores*, ed. C. Müller, i. 234) ; Diodorus Siculus, xiv. 30. 6 *sq.* ; Nicolaus Damascenus, quoted by Stobaeus, *Florilegium*, xliv. 41 (vol. ii. p. 185, ed. Meineke) ; Apollonius Rhodius, *Argon.* ii. 1026, *sqq.*, with the note of the scholiast ; Pomponius Mela, i. 106, p. 29, ed. Parthey. Die Chrysostom refers to the custom without mentioning the name of the people (*Or.* xiv. vol. i. p. 257, ed. L. Dindorf).

[5] Strabo, xvi. 4. 19, p. 778 ; Diodorus

the palace there was a window with a chain attached to it. Kings for-
If any man deemed he had suffered wrong, he pulled the bidden to
chain, and the king perceived him and called him in and palaces or
gave judgment.[1]   So down to recent times the kings of to be seen
Corea, whose persons were sacred and received " honours by their
almost divine," were shut up in their palace from the age of subjects.
twelve or fifteen ; and if a suitor wished to obtain justice of
the king he sometimes lit a great bonfire on a mountain
facing the palace ; the king saw the fire and informed
himself of the case.[2]   The Emperor of China seldom quits
his palace, and when he does so, no one may look at him ;
even the guards who line the road must turn their backs.[3]
The king of Tonquin was permitted to appear abroad twice
or thrice a year for the performance of certain religious
ceremonies ; but the people were not allowed to look at
him.   The day before he came forth notice was given to all
the inhabitants of the city and country to keep from the
way the king was to go ; the women were obliged to remain
in their houses ahd durst not shew themselves under pain of
death, a penalty which was carried out on the spot if any
one disobeyed the order, even through ignorance.   Thus the
king was invisible to all but his troops and the officers of
his suite.[4]   In Mandalay a stout lattice-paling, six feet high
and carefully kept in repair, lined every street in the walled

Siculus, iii. 47.   Inscriptions found in
Sheba (the country about two hundred
miles north of Aden) seem to shew
that the land was at first ruled by a
succession of priestly kings, who were
afterwards followed by kings in the
ordinary sense.   The names of many
of these priestly kings (*makarribs*, literally " blessers ") are preserved in inscriptions.   See Prof. S. R. Driver, in
*Authority and Archaeology Sacred and
Profane*, edited by D. G. Hogarth
(London, 1899), p. 82.   Probably these
" blessers " are the kings referred to by
the Greek writers.   We may suppose
that the blessings they dispensed consisted in a proper regulation of the
weather, abundance of the fruits of the
earth, and so on.

[1] Heraclides Cumanus, in Athenaeus,
xii. 13, p. 517 B.C.

[2] Ch. Dallet, *Histoire de l'Église de
Coreé* (Paris, 1874), i. pp. xxiv-xxvi.
The king sometimes, though rarely,
left his palace.   When he did so, notice
was given beforehand to his people.
All doors must be shut and each house-
holder must kneel before his threshold
with a broom and a dust-pan in his
hand.   All windows, especially the
upper ones, must be sealed with slips
of paper, lest some one should look
down upon the king.   See W. E.
Griffis, *Corea, the Hermit Nation*, p.
222.   These customs are now obsolete
(G. N. Curzon, *Problems of the Far
East*, Westminster, 1896, pp. 154 *sq.*
note).

[3] This I learned from the late Mr.
W. Simpson, formerly artist of the
Illustrated London News.

[4] Richard, " History of Tonquin,"
in Pinkerton's *Voyages and Travels*,
ix. 746.

city and all those streets in the suburbs through which the
king was likely at any time to pass. Behind this paling,
which stood two feet or so from the houses, all the people
had to stay when the king or any of the queens went out.
Any one who was caught outside it by the beadles after the
procession had started was severely handled, and might
think himself lucky if he got off with a beating. Nobody
was supposed to peep through the holes in the lattice-work,
which were besides partly stopped up with flowering shrubs.[1]

§ 5. *Taboos on leaving Food over*

Magical
harm done
a man
through
the remains
of his food
or the
dishes he
has eaten
out of.

Ideas and
customs
of the
Narrinyeri
of South
Australia.

Again, magic mischief may be wrought upon a man
through the remains of the food he has partaken of, or the
dishes out of which he has eaten. On the principles of
sympathetic magic a real connexion continues to subsist
between the food which a man has in his stomach and the
refuse of it which he has left untouched, and hence by
injuring the refuse you can simultaneously injure the eater.
Among the Narrinyeri of South Australia every adult is
constantly on the look-out for bones of beasts, birds, or fish,
of which the flesh has been eaten by somebody, in order to
construct a deadly charm out of them. Every one is therefore careful to burn the bones of the animals which he has
eaten lest they should fall into the hands of a sorcerer. Too
often, however, the sorcerer succeeds in getting hold of such
a bone, and when he does so he believes that he has the
power of life and death over the man, woman, or child who
ate the flesh of the animal. To put the charm in operation
he makes a paste of red ochre and fish oil, inserts in it the
eye of a cod and a small piece of the flesh of a corpse, and
having rolled the compound into a ball sticks it on the top
of the bone. After being left for some time in the bosom of
a dead body, in order that it may derive a deadly potency
by contact with corruption, the magical implement is set up
in the ground near the fire, and as the ball melts, so the
person against whom the charm is directed wastes with
disease ; if the ball is melted quite away, the victim will die.

[1] Shway Yoe, *The Burman* (London, 1882), i. 30 *sq.*; compare *Indian Antiquary*, xx. (1891) p. 49.

When the bewitched man learns of the spell that is being cast upon him, he endeavours to buy the bone from the sorcerer, and if he obtains it he breaks the charm by throwing the bone into a river or lake.[1]   Further, the Narrinyeri think that if a man eats of the totem animal of his tribe, and an enemy obtains a portion of the flesh, the latter can make it grow in the inside of the eater, and so cause his death. Therefore when a man partakes of his totem he is careful either to eat it all or else to conceal or destroy the refuse.[2] In the Encounter Bay tribe of South Australia, when a man cannot get the bone of an animal which his enemy has eaten, he cooks a bird, beast, or fish, and keeping back one of the creature's bones, offers the rest under the guise of friendship to his enemy.   If the man is simple enough to partake of the proffered food, he is at the mercy of his perfidious foe, who can kill him by placing the abstracted bone near the fire.[3]

Ideas and practices of the same sort prevail, or used to prevail, in Melanesia ; all that was needed to injure a man was to bring the leavings of his food into contact with a malignant ghost or spirit.   Hence in the island of Florida when a scrap of an enemy's dinner was secreted and thrown into a haunted place, the man was supposed to fall ill ; and in the New Hebrides if a snake of a certain sort carried away a fragment of food to a spot sacred to a spirit, the man who had eaten the food would sicken as the fragment decayed.   In Aurora the refuse is made up by the wizard with certain leaves ; as these rot and stink, the man dies.   Hence it is, or was, a constant care with the Melanesians to prevent the remains of their meals from falling into the hands of persons who bore them a grudge ; for this reason they regularly gave the refuse of food to the pigs.[4]   In Tana, one of the New Hebrides, people bury

Ideas and customs as to the leavings of food in Melanesia and New Guinea.

---

[1] G. Taplin, "The Narrinyeri," in *Native Tribes of South Australia* (Adelaide, 1879), pp. 24-26 ; *id.*, in E. M. Curr, *The Australian Race*, ii. p. 247.

[2] G. Taplin, "The Narrinyeri," in *Native Tribes of South Australia*, p. 63 ; *id.*, "Notes on the Mixed Races of Australia," *Journal of the Anthropological Institute*, iv. (1875) p.

53 ; *id.*, in E. M. Curr, *The Australian Race*, ii. 245.

[3] H. E. A. Meyer, "Manners and Customs of the Aborigines of the Encounter Bay Tribe," in *Native Tribes of South Australia*, p. 196.

[4] R. H. Codrington, *The Melanesians*, pp. 203 *sq.*, compare pp. 178, 188, 214.

Ideas and
customs
as to the
leavings
of food in
Melanesia
and New
Guinea.
or throw into the sea the leavings of their food, lest these
should fall into the hands of the disease-makers. For if
a disease-maker finds the remnants of a meal, say the skin
of a banana, he picks it up and burns it slowly in the fire.
As it burns, the person who ate the banana falls ill and sends
to the disease-maker, offering him presents if he will stop
burning the banana skin.[1] In German New Guinea the
natives take the utmost care to destroy or conceal the husks
and other remains of their food, lest these should be found
by their enemies and used by them for the injury or destruction of the eaters. Hence they burn their leavings,
throw them into the sea, or otherwise put them out of
harm's way. To such an extent does this fear influence
them that many people dare not stir beyond the territory of
their own village, lest they should leave behind them on the
land of their neighbours something by means of which a
hostile sorcerer might do them a mischief.[2] Similar fears
have led to similar customs in New Britain and the other
islands of what is now called the Bismarck Archipelago, off
the north coast of New Guinea. There also the natives bury,
burn, or throw into the sea the remains of their meals to
prevent them from falling into the hands of magicians;
there also the more superstitious of them will not eat in
another village because they dread the use which a sorcerer
might make of their leavings when their back is turned.
This theory has led to an odd practical result; all the cats
in the islands of the Archipelago go about with stumpy tails.
The reason of the peculiarity is this. The natives sometimes
roast and eat their cats; and unscrupulous persons might
be tempted to steal a neighbour's cat in order to furnish
a meal. Accordingly, in the interests of the higher morality
people remove this stumbling-block from the path of their
weaker brothers by docking their cats of a piece of their
tails and keeping the severed portions in a secret place. If

[1] G. Turner, *Samoa*, pp. 302 *sq.*
See *The Magic Art and the Evolution
of Kings*, i. 341 *sq.*

[2] K. Vetter, *Komm herüber und hilf
uns!* iii. (Barmen, 1898) p. 9; M.
Krieger, *Neu-Guinea*, pp. 185 *sq.*;
R. Parkinson, "Die Berlinhafen

Section, ein Beitrag zur Ethnographie
der Neu-Guinea Küste," *Internationales
Archiv für Ethnographie*, xiii. (1900)
p. 44; M. J. Erdweg, "Die Bewohner
der Insel Tumleo, Berlinhafen, Deutsch-
Neu-Guinea," *Mittheilungen der
Anthropologischen Gesellschaft in Wien*,
xxxii. (1902) p. 287.

now a cat is stolen and eaten, the lawful owner of the animal has it in his power to avenge the crime : he need only bury the piece of tail with certain spells in the ground, and the thief will fall ill.   Hence a man will hardly dare to steal and eat a cat with a stumpy tail, knowing the righteous retribution that would sooner or later over-take him for so doing.[1]

From a like fear, no doubt, of sorcery, no one may touch the food which the king of Loango leaves upon his plate ; it is buried in a hole in the ground.   And no one may drink out of the king's vessel.[2]   Similarly, no man may drink out of the same cup or glass with the king of Fida (Whydah) in Guinea ; " he hath always one kept particularly for himself ; and that which hath but once touched another's lips he never uses more, though it be made of metal that may be cleansed by fire." [3]   Amongst the Alfoors of Celebes there is a priest called the *Leleen*, whose duty appears to be to make the rice grow.   His functions begin about a month before the rice is sown, and end after the crop is housed. During this time he has to observe certain taboos ; amongst others he may not eat or drink with any one else, and he may drink out of no vessel but his own.[4]   An ancient Indian way of injuring an enemy was to offer him a meal of rice and afterwards throw the remains of the rice into a fishpond ; if the fish swam up in large numbers to devour the grains, the man's fate was sealed.[5]   In antiquity the Romans used immediately to break the shells of eggs and of snails which they had eaten in order to prevent enemies from making magic with them.[6]   The common practice,

Ideas and customs as to the leavings of food in Africa, Celebes, India, and ancient Rome.

---

[1] Mgr. Couppé, "En Nouvelle-Poméranie," *Missions Catholiques*, xxiii. (1891) p. 364; J. Graf Pfeil, *Studien und Beobachtungen aus der Südsee* (Brunswick, 1899), pp. 141 *sq.*; P. A. Kleintitschen, *Die Küsten-bewohner der Gazellehalbinsel* (Hiltrup bei Münster, N.D.), pp. 343 *sq.*

[2] O. Dapper, *Description de l'Afrique*, p. 330. We have seen that the food left by the king of the Monbutto, is carefully buried (above, p. 119).

[3] Bosman's "Guinea," in Pinkerton's *Voyages and Travels*, xvi. 487.

[4] P. N. Wilken, "Bijdragen tot de kennis van de zeden en gewoonten der Alfoeren in de Minahassa," *Mededeelingen van wege het Nederlandsche Zendelinggenootschap*, vii. (1863) p. 126.

[5] W. Caland, *Altindisches Zauber-ritual*, pp. 163 *sq.*

[6] Pliny, *Nat. Hist.* xxviii. 19. For other examples of witchcraft wrought by means of the refuse of food, see E. S. Hartland, *The Legend of Perseus*, ii. 83 *sqq.*

still observed among us, of breaking egg-shells after the eggs have been eaten may very well have originated in the same superstition.

The fear of the magical evil which may be done a man through his food has had beneficial effects in fostering habits of cleanliness and in strengthening the ties of hospitality.

The superstitious fear of the magic that may be wrought on a man through the leavings of his food has had the beneficial effect of inducing many savages to destroy refuse which, if left to rot, might through its corruption have proved a real, not a merely imaginary, source of disease and death. Nor is it only the sanitary condition of a tribe which has benefited by this superstition; curiously enough the same baseless dread, the same false notion of causation, has indirectly strengthened the moral bonds of hospitality, honour, and good faith among men who entertain it. For it is obvious that no one who intends to harm a man by working magic on the refuse of his food will himself partake of that food, because if he did so he would, on the principles of sympathetic magic, suffer equally with his enemy from any injury done to the refuse. This is the idea which in primitive society lends sanctity to the bond produced by eating together; by participation in the same food two men give, as it were, hostages for their good behaviour; each guarantees the other that he will devise no mischief against him, since being physically united with him by the common food in their stomachs, any harm he might do to his fellow would recoil on his own head with precisely the same force with which it fell on the head of his victim. In strict logic, however, the sympathetic bond lasts only so long as the food is in the stomach of each of the parties. Hence the covenant formed by eating together is less solemn and durable than the covenant formed by transfusing the blood of the covenanting parties into each other's veins, for this transfusion seems to knit them together for life.[1]

---

[1] On the covenant entered into by eating together see the classical exposition of W. Robertson Smith, *The Religion of the Semites*[2] (London, 1894), pp. 269 *sqq.* For examples of the blood-covenant, see H. C. Trumbull, *The Blood Covenant* (London, 1887). The examples might easily be multiplied.

CHAPTER IV

TABOOED PERSONS

§ 1. *Chiefs and Kings tabooed*

WE have seen that the Mikado's food was cooked every day in new pots and served up in new dishes; both pots and dishes were of common clay, in order that they might be broken or laid aside after they had been once used. They were generally broken, for it was believed that if any one else ate his food out of these sacred dishes, his mouth and throat would become swollen and inflamed. The same ill effect was thought to be experienced by any one who should wear the Mikado's clothes without his leave; he would have swellings and pains all over his body.[1] In Fiji there is a special name (*kana lama*) for the disease supposed to be caused by eating out of a chief's dishes or wearing his clothes. "The throat and body swell, and the impious person dies. I had a fine mat given to me by a man who durst not use it because Thakambau's eldest son had sat upon it. There was always a family or clan of commoners who were exempt from this danger. I was talking about this once to Thakambau. 'Oh yes,' said he. 'Here, So-and-so! come and scratch my back.' The man scratched; he was one of those who could do it with impunity." The name of the men thus highly privileged was *Na nduka ni*, or the dirt of the chief.[2]

In the evil effects thus supposed to follow upon the use

Disastrous results supposed to follow from using the dishes of the Mikado or of a Fijian chief.

---

[1] Kaempfer's "History of Japan," in Pinkerton's *Voyages and Travels*, vii. 717.

[2] Rev. Lorimer Fison, in a letter to me dated August 26, 1898. In Fijian, *kana* is to eat; the meaning of *lama* is unknown.

Sacred persons are a source of danger to others: their divinity burns like a fire what it touches.

African examples.

of the vessels or clothes of the Mikado and a Fijian chief we see that other side of the god-man's character to which attention has been already called. The divine person is a source of danger as well as of blessing; he must not only be guarded, he must also be guarded against. His sacred organism, so delicate that a touch may disorder it, is also, as it were, electrically charged with a powerful magical or spiritual force which may discharge itself with fatal effect on whatever comes in contact with it. Accordingly the isolation of the man-god is quite as necessary for the safety of others as for his own. His magical virtue is in the strictest sense of the word contagious: his divinity is a fire, which, under proper restraints, confers endless blessings, but, if rashly touched or allowed to break bounds, burns and destroys what it touches. Hence the disastrous effects supposed to attend a breach of taboo; the offender has thrust his hand into the divine fire, which shrivels up and consumes him on the spot. The Nubas, for example, who inhabit the wooded and fertile range of Jebel Nuba in eastern Africa, believe that they would die if they entered the house of their priestly king; however they can evade the penalty of their intrusion by baring the left shoulder and getting the king to lay his hand on it. And were any man to sit on a stone which the king has consecrated to his own use, the transgressor would die within the year.[1] The Cazembes, in the interior of Angola, regard their king (the *Muata* or *Mambo*) as so holy that no one can touch him without being killed by the magical power which pervades his sacred person. But since contact with him is sometimes unavoidable, they have devised a means whereby the sinner can escape with his life. Kneeling down before the king he touches the back of the royal hand

---

[1] "Coutumes étranges des indigènes du Djebel-Nouba," *Missions Catholiques*, xiv. (1882) p. 460; Father S. Carceri, "Djebel-Nouba," *ibid.* xv. (1883) p. 450. The title of the priestly king is *cogiour* or *codjour*. "The *codjour* is the pontifical king of each group of villages; it is he who regulates and administers the affairs of the Nubas. He is an absolute monarch, on whom all depend. But he has no princely privileges or immunities; no royal insignia, no badge mark him off from his subjects. He lives like them by the produce of his fields and his industry; he works like them, earns his daily bread, and has no guard of honour, no tribunal, no code of laws, no civil list" (Father S. Carceri, *loc. cit.*).

with the back of his own, then snaps his fingers ; afterwards
he lays the palm of his hand on the palm of the king's
hand, then snaps his fingers again.   This ceremony is
repeated four or five times, and averts the imminent danger
of death.[1]   In Tonga it was believed that if any one fed The taboo
himself with his own hands after touching the sacred person of chiefs
of a superior chief or anything that belonged to him, he in Tonga.
would swell up and die ; the sanctity of the chief, like a
virulent poison, infected the hands of his inferior, and, being
communicated through them to the food, proved fatal to the
eater.   A commoner who had incurred this danger could
disinfect himself by performing a certain ceremony, which
consisted in touching the sole of a chief's foot with the palm
and back of each of his hands, and afterwards rinsing his
hands in water.   If there was no water near, he rubbed his
hands with the juicy stem of a plantain or banana.   After
that he was free to feed himself with his own hands without
danger of being attacked by the malady which would otherwise follow from eating with tabooed or sanctified hands.
But until the ceremony of expiation or disinfection had been
performed, if he wished to eat, he had either to get some
one to feed him, or else to go down on his knees and pick
up the food from the ground with his mouth like a beast.
He might not even use a toothpick himself, but might guide
the hand of another person holding the toothpick.   The
Tongans were subject to induration of the liver and certain
forms of scrofula, which they often attributed to a failure to
perform the requisite expiation after having inadvertently
touched a chief or his belongings.   Hence they often went
through the ceremony as a precaution, without knowing that
they had done anything to call for it.   The king of Tonga
could not refuse to play his part in the rite by presenting
his foot to such as desired to touch it, even when they
applied to him at an inconvenient time.   A fat unwieldy
king, who perceived his subjects approaching with this
intention, while he chanced to be taking his walks abroad,

[1] "Der Muata Cazembe und die
Völkerstämme der Maravis, Chevas,
Muembas, Lundas und andere von
Süd-Afrika," *Zeitschrift für allgemeine*
Erdkunde (Berlin), vi. (1856) pp.
398 *sq.* ; F. T. Valdez, *Six Years of a*
Traveller's Life in Western Africa
(London, 1861), ii. 251 *sq.*

has been sometimes seen to waddle as fast as his legs could carry him out of their way, in order to escape the importunate and not wholly disinterested expression of their homage. If any one fancied he might have already unwittingly eaten with tabooed hands, he sat down before the chief, and, taking the chief's foot, pressed it against his own stomach, that the food in his belly might not injure him, and that he might not swell up and die.[1] Since scrofula was regarded by the Tongans as a result of eating with tabooed hands, we may conjecture that persons who suffered from it among them often resorted to the touch or pressure of the king's foot as a cure for their malady. The analogy of the custom with the old English practice of bringing scrofulous patients to the king to be healed by his touch is sufficiently obvious, and suggests, as I have already pointed out elsewhere, that among our own remote ancestors scrofula may have obtained its name of the King's Evil, from a belief, like that of the Tongans, that it was caused as well as cured by contact with the divine majesty of kings.[2]

The King's Evil cured by the king's touch.

In New Zealand the dread of the sanctity of chiefs was at least as great as in Tonga. Their ghostly power, derived from an ancestral spirit or *atua*, diffused itself by contagion over everything they touched, and could strike dead all who rashly or unwittingly meddled with it.[3] For instance, it once happened that a New Zealand chief of high rank and great sanctity had left the remains of his dinner by the wayside. A slave, a stout, hungry fellow, coming up after the chief had gone, saw the unfinished dinner, and ate it up without asking questions. Hardly had he finished when

Fatal effects of contact with sacred chiefs in New Zealand.

[1] W. Mariner, *The Natives of the Tonga Islands*,[2] i. 141 *sq.* note, 434 note, ii. 82 *sq.*, 221-224; Captain J. Cook, *Voyages* (London, 1809), v. 427 *sq.* Similarly in Fiji any person who had touched the head of a living chief or the body of a dead one was forbidden to handle his food, and must be fed by another (J. E. Erskine, *The Western Pacific*, p. 254).

[2] On the custom of touching for the King's Evil, see *The Magic Art and the Evolution of Kings*, vol. i. pp. 368 *sqq.*

[3] "The idea in which this law [the law of taboo or *tapu*, as it was called in New Zealand] originated appears to have been, that a portion of the spiritual essence of an *atua* or of a sacred person was communicated directly to objects which they touched, and also that the spiritual essence so communicated to any object was afterwards more or less retransmitted to anything else brought into contact with it " (E. Shortland, *Traditions and Superstitions of the New Zealanders*, Second Edition, London, 1856, p. 102). Compare *id.*, *Maori Religion and Mythology*, p. 25.

he was informed by a horror-stricken spectator that the food of which he had eaten was the chief's. " I knew the unfortunate delinquent well. He was remarkable for courage, and had signalised himself in the wars of the tribe," but "no sooner did he hear the fatal news than he was seized by the most extraordinary convulsions and cramp in the stomach, which never ceased till he died, about sundown the same day. He was a strong man, in the prime of life, and if any pakeha [European] freethinker should have said he was not killed by the *tapu* of the chief, which had been communicated to the food by contact, he would have been listened to with feelings of contempt for his ignorance and inability to understand plain and direct evidence." [1] This is not a solitary case. A Maori woman having eaten of some fruit, and being afterwards told that the fruit had been taken from a tabooed place, exclaimed that the spirit of the chief, whose sanctity had been thus profaned, would kill her. This was in the afternoon, and next day by twelve o'clock she was dead.[2] An observer who knows the Maoris well, says, " Tapu [taboo] is an awful weapon. I have seen a strong young man die the same day he was tapued ; the victims die under it as though their strength ran out as water." [3] A Maori chief's tinder-box was once the means of killing several persons ; for, having been lost by him, and found by some men who used it to light their pipes, they died of fright on learning to whom it had belonged. So, too, the garments of a high New Zealand chief will kill any one else who wears them. A chief was observed by a missionary to throw down a precipice a blanket which he found too heavy to carry. Being asked by the missionary why he did not leave it on a tree for the use of a future traveller, the chief replied that " it was the fear of its being taken by another which caused him to throw it where he did, for if it were worn, his tapu " (that is, his spiritual power communicated by contact to the blanket and through the blanket to the man) " would

[1] *Old New Zealand*, by a Pakeha Maori (London, 1884), pp. 96 *sq.*

[2] W. Brown, *New Zealand and its Aborigines* (London, 1845), p. 76. For more examples of the same kind see *ibid.* pp. 177 *sq.*

[3] E. Tregear, "The Maoris of New Zealand," *Journal of the Anthropological Institute*, xix. (1890) p. 100.

kill the person." [1] For a similar reason a Maori chief would not blow a fire with his mouth; for his sacred breath would communicate its sanctity to the fire, which would pass it on to the pot on the fire, which would pass it on to the meat in the pot, which would pass it on to the man who ate the meat, which was in the pot, which stood on the fire, which was breathed on by the chief; so that the eater, infected by the chief's breath conveyed through these intermediaries, would surely die. [2]

Examples of the fatal effects of imagination in other parts of the world. Thus in the Polynesian race, to which the Maoris belong, superstition erected round the persons of sacred chiefs a real, though at the same time purely imaginary barrier, to transgress which actually entailed the death of the transgressor whenever he became aware of what he had done. This fatal power of the imagination working through superstitious terrors is by no means confined to one race; it appears to be common among savages. For example, among the aborigines of Australia a native will die after the infliction of even the most superficial wound if only he believes that the weapon which inflicted the wound had been sung over and thus endowed with magical virtue. He simply lies down, refuses food, and pines away. [3] Similarly among some of the Indian tribes of Brazil, if the medicine-man predicted the death of any one who had offended him, " the wretch took to his hammock instantly in such full expectation of dying, that he would neither eat nor drink, and the prediction was a sentence which faith effectually executed." [4] Speaking of certain African races Major Leonard observes: " I have seen more than one hardened old Haussa soldier dying steadily and by inches, because he believed himself to be bewitched; so that no nourishment or medicines that were given to him had the slightest effect either to check the mischief or to improve his condition in any way, and nothing was able to divert him from a fate which he considered inevitable. In the same way, and under very similar conditions, I have seen Kru-men and others die, in spite of every effort that was made to save them, simply because they had made

[1] R. Taylor, *Te Ika a Maui, or, New Zealand and its Inhabitants,*[2] p. 164.

[2] R. Taylor, *op. cit.* p. 165.

[3] Spencer and Gillen, *Native Tribes of Central Australia,* pp. 537 *sq.*

[4] R. Southey, *History of Brazil,* i.[2] (London, 1822), p. 238.

up their minds, not (as we thought at the time) to die, but
that being in the clutch of malignant demons they were
bound to die."[1]   The Capuchin missionary Merolla da
Sorrento, who travelled in the West African kingdom of
Congo in the latter part of the seventeenth century, has
described a remarkable case of death wrought purely by
superstitious fear.   He says: "It is a custom that either
the parents or the wizards give certain rules to be inviolably
observed by the young people, and which they call *chegilla*:
these are to abstain from eating either some sorts of poultry,
the flesh of some kinds of wild beasts, such and such fruits,
roots either raw or boiled after this or another manner, with
several other ridiculous injunctions of the like nature, too
many to be enumerated here.   You would wonder with what
religious observance these commands are obeyed.   These
young people would sooner chuse to fast several days together, than to taste the least bit of what has been forbidden
them ; and if it sometimes happen that the *chegilla* has been
neglected to have been given them by their parents, they
think they shall presently die unless they go immediately to
receive it from the wizards.   A certain young negro, being
upon a journey, lodged in a friend's house by the way: his
friend, before he went out the next morning, had got a wild
hen ready for his breakfast, they being much better than the
tame ones.   The negro hereupon demanded, 'If it were a
wild hen?'   His host answered, 'No': then he fell on
heartily, and afterwards proceeded on his journey.   About
four years after these two met together again, and the afore-
said negro being not yet married, his old friend asked him,
'If he would eat a wild hen?'   To which he answered,
'That he had received the *chegilla*, and therefore could not.'
Hereat the host began immediately to laugh, enquiring of
him, 'What made him refuse it now, when he had eaten one
at his table about four years ago?'   At the hearing of this
the negro immediately fell a trembling, and suffered himself
to be so far possessed with the effects of imagination, that
he died in less than twenty-four hours after."[2]

[1] Major A. G. Leonard, *The Lower
Niger and its Tribes* (London, 1906),
pp. 257 *sq.*

[2] Merolla's "Voyage to Congo," in
Pinkerton's *Voyages and Travels*, xvi.
237 *sq.* As to these *chegilla* or taboos on

§ 2. *Mourners tabooed*

The taboos observed by sacred kings resemble those imposed on persons who are commonly regarded as unclean, such as menstruous women, homicides, and so forth.

Thus regarding his sacred chiefs and kings as charged with a mysterious spiritual force which so to say explodes at contact, the savage naturally ranks them among the dangerous classes of society, and imposes upon them the same sort of restraints that he lays on manslayers, menstruous women, and other persons whom he looks upon with a certain fear and horror. For example, sacred kings and priests in Polynesia were not allowed to touch food with their hands, and had therefore to be fed by others;[1] and as we have just seen, their vessels, garments, and other property might not be used by others on pain of disease and death. Now precisely the same observances are exacted by some savages from girls at their first menstruation, women after childbirth, homicides, mourners, and all persons who have come into contact with the dead. Thus, for example, to begin with the last class of persons, among the Maoris any one who had handled a corpse, helped to convey it to the grave, or touched a dead man's bones, was cut off from all intercourse and almost all communication with mankind. He could not enter any house, or come into contact with any person or thing, without utterly bedevilling them. He might not even touch food with his hands, which had become so frightfully tabooed or unclean as to be quite useless. Food would be set for him on the ground, and he

Taboos laid on persons who have been in contact with the dead in New Zealand.

food, which are commonly observed by the natives of this part of Africa, see further my *Totemism and Exogamy*, ii. 614 *sqq.*

[1] W. Ellis, *Polynesian Researches* (Second Edition, London, 1832-1836), iv. 388. Ellis appears to imply that the rule was universal in Polynesia, but perhaps he refers only to Hawaii, of which in this part of his work he is specially treating. We are told that in Hawaii the priest who carried the principal idol about the country was tabooed during the performance of this sacred office; he might not touch anything with his hands, and the morsels of food which he ate had to be put into his mouth by the chiefs of the villages through which he passed or even by the king himself, who accompanied the priest on his rounds (L. de Freycinet, *Voyage autour du monde*, Historique, ii. Première Partie, Paris, 1829, p. 596). In Tonga the rule applied to chiefs only when their hands had become tabooed by touching a superior chief (W. Mariner, *Tonga Islands*, i. 82 *sq.*). In New Zealand chiefs were fed by slaves (A. S. Thomson, *The Story of New Zealand*, i. 102); or they may, like tabooed people in general, have taken up their food from little stages with their mouths or by means of fern-stalks (R. Taylor, *Te Ika a Maui, or New Zealand and its Inhabitants*,[2] p. 162).

would then sit or kneel down, and, with his hands carefully
held behind his back, would gnaw at it as best he could. In
some cases he would be fed by another person, who with
outstretched arm contrived to do it without touching the
tabooed man ; but the feeder was himself subjected to many
severe restrictions, little less onerous than those which were
imposed upon the other. In almost every populous village
there lived a degraded wretch, the lowest of the low, who
earned a sorry pittance by thus waiting upon the defiled.
Clad in rags, daubed from head to foot with red ochre and
stinking shark oil, always solitary and silent, generally old,
haggard, and wizened, often half crazed, he might be seen
sitting motionless all day apart from the common path or
thoroughfare of the village, gazing with lack-lustre eyes on
the busy doings in which he might never take a part. Twice
a day a dole of food would be thrown on the ground before
him to munch as well as he could without the use of his
hands ; and at night, huddling his greasy tatters about him,
he would crawl into some miserable lair of leaves and refuse,
where, dirty, cold, and hungry, he passed, in broken ghost-
haunted slumbers, a wretched night as a prelude to another
wretched day. Such was the only human being deemed fit
to associate at arm's length with one who had paid the last
offices of respect and friendship to the dead. And when, the
dismal term of his seclusion being over, the mourner was
about to mix with his fellows once more, all the dishes he
had used in his seclusion were diligently smashed, and all the
garments he had worn were carefully thrown away, lest they
should spread the contagion of his defilement among others,[1]
just as the vessels and clothes of sacred kings and chiefs are
destroyed or cast away for a similar reason. So complete
in these respects is the analogy which the savage traces
between the spiritual influences that emanate from divinities
and from the dead, between the odour of sanctity and the
stench of corruption.

---

[1] *Old New Zealand*, by a Pakeha
Maori (London, 1884), pp. 104-114.
For more evidence see W. Yate, *New
Zealand*, p. 85 ; G. F. Angas, *Savage
Life and Scenes in Australia and New
Zealand*, ii. 90 ; E. Dieffenbach, *Tra-*
vels in New Zealand, ii. 104 *sq.* ; J.
Dumont D'Urville, *Voyage autour du
monde et à la recherche de La Pérouse*,
ii. 530 ; Father Servant, " Notice sur la
Nouvelle Zélande," *Annales de la Pro
pagation de la Foi*, xv. (1843) p. 22.

The rule which for- bids per- sons who have been in contact with a corpse to touch food with their hands seems to have been universal in Polynesia.

The rule which forbids persons who have been in contact with the dead to touch food with their hands would seem to have been universal in Polynesia. Thus in Samoa "those who attended the deceased were most careful not to handle food, and for days were fed by others as if they were helpless infants. Baldness and the loss of teeth were supposed to be the punishment inflicted by the household god if they violated the rule." [1] Again, in Tonga, "no person can touch a dead chief without being taboo'd for ten lunar months, except chiefs, who are only taboo'd for three, four, or five months, according to the superiority of the dead chief; except again it be the body of Tooitonga [the great divine chief], and then even the greatest chief would be taboo'd ten months, as was the case with Finow's wife above mentioned. During the time a man is taboo'd he must not feed himself with his own hands, but must be fed by somebody else: he must not even use a toothpick himself, but must guide another person's hand holding the toothpick. If he is hungry and there is no one to feed him, he must go down upon his hands and knees, and pick up his victuals with his mouth: and if he infringes upon any of these rules, it is firmly expected that he will swell up and die: and this belief is so strong that Mr. Mariner thinks no native ever made an experiment to prove the contrary. They often saw him feed himself with his hands after having touched dead chiefs, and not observing his health to decline, they attributed it to his being a foreigner, and being governed by different gods." [2] Again, in Wallis Island "contact with a corpse subjects the hands to the law of taboo till they are washed, which is not done for several weeks. Until that purification has taken place, the tabooed persons may not themselves put food to their mouths; other people render them that service." [3] A rule

---

[1] G. Turner, *Samoa*, p. 145. Compare G. Brown, D.D., *Melanesians and Polynesians* (London, 1910), p. 402: "The men who took hold of the body were *paia* (sacred) for the time, were forbidden to touch their own food, and were fed by others. No food was eaten in the same house with the dead body."

[2] W. Mariner, *The Natives of the Tonga Islands* [2] (London, 1818), i. 141 *sq.*, note.

[3] Father Bataillon, in *Annales de la Propagation de la Foi*, xiii. (1841) p. 19. For more evidence of the practice of this custom in Polynesia, see Captain J. Cook, *Voyages* (London, 1809), vii. 147; James Wilson, *Missionary Voyage to the Southern Pacific Ocean* (London, 1799), p. 363.

of the same sort is or was observed in various parts of Melanesia. Thus in Fiji the taboo for handling a dead chief lasted from one to ten months according to his rank ; for a commoner it lasted not more than four days. It was commonly resorted to by the lazy and idle ; for during the time of their seclusion they were not only provided with food, but were actually fed by attendants or ate their food from the ground.[1] Similarly in the Motu tribe of New Guinea a man is tabooed, generally for three days, after handling a corpse, and while the taboo lasts he may not touch food with his hands. At the end of the time he bathes and the taboo is over.[2] So in New Caledonia the two men who are charged with the duty of burying and guarding a corpse have to remain in seclusion and observe a number of rules of abstinence. They live apart from their wives. They may not shave or cut their hair. Their food is laid for them on leaves and they take it up with their mouth or a stick ; but oftener an attendant feeds them, just as he might feed a man whose limbs were palsied.[3] So among the Nandi of British East Africa persons who have handled a corpse bathe in a river, anoint their bodies with fat, partially shave their heads, and live in the hut of the deceased for four days. All these days they may not be seen by boys or women : they may not drink milk ; and they may not touch food with their hands, but must eat it with the help of a potsherd or chip of a gourd.[4] Similarly in the Ba-Pedi and Ba-Thonga tribes of South Africa men who have dug a grave may not touch food with their fingers till the rites of their purification are accomplished ; meantime they eat with the help of special spoons. If they broke this rule, it is thought that they would be consumptive.[5] So in the Ngarigo tribe of New South Wales a novice who has just passed through the ceremony

[1] Ch. Wilkes, *Narrative of the United States Exploring Expedition,* New Edition (New York, 1851), iii. 99 *sq.*

[2] W. G. Lawes, " Ethnological Notes on the Motu, Koitapu, and Koiari Tribes of New Guinea," *Journal. of the Anthropological Institute,* viii. (1879) p. 370.

[3] Father Lambert, in *Missions Catholiques,* xii. (1880) p. 365 ; *id., Mœurs et superstitions des Néo-Calédoniens* (Nouméa, 1900), pp. 238 *sq.*

[4] A. C. Hollis, *The Nandi* (Oxford, 1909), p. 70.

[5] H. A. Junod, "Les Conceptions physiologiques des Bantou sud-africains et leurs tabous," *Revue d'Ethnographie et de Sociologie,* i. (1910) p. 153.

of initiation has to go away to the mountains and stay there for a while, sometimes for more than six months, under the charge of one or more old men ; and all the time of his absence among the mountains he may not touch cooked food with his hands ; the food is put into his mouth by the man who looks after him.[1]

Taboos laid on mourners among the Indian tribes of North America. Among the Shuswap of British Columbia widows and widowers in mourning are secluded and forbidden to touch their own head or body ; the cups and cooking-vessels which they use may be used by no one else. They must build a sweat-house beside a creek, sweat there all night and bathe regularly, after which they must rub their bodies with branches of spruce. The branches may not be used more than once, and when they have served their purpose they are stuck into the ground all round the hut. No hunter would come near such mourners, for their presence is unlucky. If their shadow were to fall on any one, he would be taken ill at once. They employ thorn bushes for bed and pillow, in order to keep away the ghost of the deceased ; and thorn bushes are also laid all around their beds.[2] This last precaution shews clearly what the spiritual danger is which leads to the exclusion of such persons from ordinary society ; it is simply a fear of the ghost who is supposed to be hovering near them. Among the Thompson Indians of British Columbia the persons who handled a corpse and dug the grave were secluded for four days. They fasted until the body was buried, after which they were given food apart from the other people. They would not touch the food with their hands, but must put it into their mouths with sharp-pointed sticks. They ate off a small mat, and drank out of birch-bark cups, which, together with the mat, were thrown away at the end of the four days. The first four mouthfuls of food, as well as of water, had to be spit into the fire. During their seclusion they bathed in a stream and might not sleep with their wives. Widows and widowers were obliged to observe rules of a similar kind. Immediately after the death they went out and passed through a patch of

[1] A. W. Howitt, *Native Tribes of South-East Australia*, p. 563.
[2] Fr. Boas, in *Sixth Report on the North-Western Tribes of Canada*, pp. 91 *sq.* (separate Reprint from the *Report of the British Association for 1890*).

rose-bushes four times, probably in order to rid themselves Taboos
of the ghost, who might be supposed to stick on a thorn. laid on
mourners
For a year they had to sleep on a bed of fir-boughs, on among the
which sticks of rose-bushes were laid ; many wore twigs of Indian
tribes of
rose-bush and juniper in a piece of buckskin on their persons. North
The first four days they might not touch their food, but ate America.
with sharp-pointed sticks and spat out the first four mouthfuls
of each meal, and the first four of water, into the fire.   A
widower might not fish at another man's fishing-place or
with another man's net ; if he did, it would make the place
and the net useless for the season.   If he transplanted a
trout into another lake, before releasing it he blew on the
head of the fish, and after chewing deer-fat, he spat some of
the grease on its head in order to remove the baneful effect
of his touch.   Then he let the trout go, bidding it farewell,
and asking it to propagate its kind in plenty.   Any grass
or branches that a widow or widower sat or lay down on
withered up.   If a widow should break sticks or boughs, her
hands or arms would also break.   She might not pick berries
for a year, else the whole crop of berries would fall off the
bushes or wither up.   She might not cook food or fetch
water for her children, nor let them lie down on her bed, nor
should she lie or sit where they slept.   Sometimes a widow
would wear a breech-cloth made of dry bunch-grass for
several days to prevent her husband's ghost from having
intercourse with her.[1]   Among the Tinneh or Déné Indians
of North-West America all who have handled a corpse are
subject to many restrictions and taboos.   They are debarred
for a certain period from eating any fresh meat : they may
never use a knife to cut their food but must tear it with
their teeth : they may not drink out of a vessel in common
use, but must employ a gourd which they carry about for
the purpose ; and they wear peeled willow wands about
their arms and necks or carry them in their hands as
disinfectants to annul the evil consequences which are
supposed to follow from handling the dead.[2]   Among the

[1] J. Teit, "The Thompson Indians of British Columbia," *Memoir of the American Museum of Natural History, The Jesup North Pacific Expedition*, vol. i. part iv. (April 1900) pp. 331, 332 *sq.*

[2] C. Hill-Tout, *The Far West, the Home of the Salish and Déné* (London, 1907), pp. 193 *sq.*

Indian tribes of Queen Charlotte Sound a widow or widower goes into special mourning for a month ; among the Koskimos the period of mourning is four months. During this time he or she lives apart in a very small hut behind the house, eating and drinking alone, and using for that purpose dishes which are not employed by other members of the tribe.[1]

Seclusion of widows and widowers in the Philippines and New Guinea.

Among the Agutainos, who inhabit Palawan, one of the Philippine Islands, a widow may not leave her hut for seven or eight days after the death ; and even then she may only go out at an hour when she is not likely to meet anybody, for whoever looks upon her dies a sudden death. To prevent this fatal catastrophe, the widow knocks with a wooden peg on the trees as she goes along, thus warning people of her dangerous proximity ; and the very trees on which she knocks soon die.[2] So poisonous is the atmosphere of death that surrounds those to whom the ghost of the departed may be thought to cleave. In the Mekeo district of British New Guinea a widower loses all his civil rights and becomes a social outcast, an object of fear and horror, shunned by all. He may not cultivate a garden, nor shew himself in public, nor traverse the village, nor walk on the roads and paths. Like a wild beast he must skulk in the long grass and the bushes ; and if he sees or hears any one coming, especially a woman, he must hide behind a tree or a thicket. If he wishes to fish or hunt, he must do it alone and at night. If he would consult any one, even the missionary, he does so by stealth and at night ; he seems to have lost his voice and speaks only in whispers. Were he to join a party of fishers or hunters, his presence would bring misfortune on them ; the ghost of his dead wife would frighten away the fish or the game. He goes about everywhere and at all times armed with a tomahawk to defend himself, not only against wild boars in the jungle, but against the dreaded spirit of his departed spouse, who would do him an ill turn if she

[1] G. M. Dawson, " Notes and Observations on the Kwakiool People of the Northern part of Vancouver Island and adjacent Coasts," *Proceedings and Transactions of the Royal Society of Canada for the Year 1887*, vol. v.

(Montreal, 1888) Trans. Section ii. pp. 78 *sq.*

[2] F. Blumentritt, " Über die Eingeborenen der Insel Palawan und der Inselgruppe der Talamlanen," *Globus*, lix. (1891) p. 182.

could ; for all the souls of the dead are malignant and their only delight is to harm the living.[1]

§ 3. *Women tabooed at Menstruation and Childbirth*

In general, we may say that the prohibition to use the vessels, garments, and so on of certain persons, and the effects supposed to follow an infraction of the rule, are exactly the same whether the persons to whom the things belong are sacred or what we might call unclean and polluted. As the garments which have been touched by a sacred chief kill those who handle them, so do the things which have been touched by a menstruous woman. An Australian black-fellow, who discovered that his wife had lain on his blanket at her menstrual period, killed her and died of terror himself within a fortnight.[2] Hence Australian women at these times are forbidden under pain of death to touch anything that men use, or even to walk on a path that any man frequents. They are also secluded at childbirth, and all vessels used by them during their seclusion are burned.[3] In Uganda the pots which a woman touches while the impurity of childbirth or of menstruation is on her should be destroyed ; spears and shields defiled by her touch are not destroyed but only purified.[4] No Esquimaux of Alaska will willingly drink out of the same cup or eat out of the same dish that has been used by a woman at her confinement until it has been purified by certain incantations.[5] Amongst some of the Indians of North America, women at menstruation are forbidden to touch men's utensils, which would be so defiled by their touch that their subsequent use would be attended by certain mischief or misfortune.[6] For instance, in some of the Tinneh

---

[1] Father Guis, "Les Canaques, Mort-Deuil," *Missions Catholiques*, xxxiv. (1902) pp. 208 *sq.*

[2] Capt. W. E. Armit, "Customs of the Australian Aborigines," *Journal of the Anthropological Institute*, ix. (1880) p. 459.

[3] W. Ridley, "Report on Australian Languages and Traditions," *Journal of the Anthropological Institute*, ii. (1873) p. 268.

[4] From information given me by Messrs. Roscoe and Miller, missionaries to Uganda (June 24, 1897), and afterwards corrected by the *Katikiro* (Prime Minister) of Uganda in conversation with Mr. Roscoe (June 20, 1902).

[5] *Report of the International Polar Expedition to Point Barrow, Alaska* (Washington, 1885), p. 46.

[6] Alexander Mackenzie, *Voyages from Montreal through the Continent of North America* (London, 1801), p. cxxiii.

Taboos
imposed on
women at
menstrua-
tion.
or Déné tribes girls verging on maturity take care that the
dishes out of which they eat are used by no one else. When
their first periodical sickness comes on, they are fed by their
mothers or nearest kinswomen, and will on no account touch
their food with their own hands. At the same time they
abstain from touching their heads with their hands, and keep
a small stick to scratch their heads with when they itch.
They remain outside the house in a hut built for the purpose,
and wear a skull-cap made of skin to fit very tight, which
they never lay aside till the first monthly infirmity is over.
A fringe of shells, bones, and so on hangs down from their
forehead so as to cover their eyes, lest any malicious sorcerer
should harm them during this critical period.[1] " Among all
the Déné and most other American tribes, hardly any other
being was the object of so much dread as a menstruating
woman. As soon as signs of that condition made themselves apparent in a young girl she was carefully segregated
from all but female company, and had to live by herself in a
small hut away from the gaze of the villagers or of the male
members of the roving band. While in that awful state, she
had to abstain from touching anything belonging to man, or
the spoils of any venison or other animal, lest she would
thereby pollute the same, and condemn the hunters to
failure, owing to the anger of the game thus slighted. Dried
fish formed her diet, and cold water, absorbed through a
drinking tube, was her only beverage. Moreover, as the
very sight of her was dangerous to society, a special skin
bonnet, with fringes falling over her face down to her
breast, hid her from the public gaze, even some time

[1] Gavin Hamilton, "Customs of the
New Caledonian Women," *Journal of
the Anthropological Institute*, vii. (1878)
p. 206. Among the Nootkas of British
Columbia a girl at puberty is hidden
from the sight of men for several days
behind a partition of mats ; during her
seclusion she may not scratch her head
or her body with her hands, but she
may do so with a comb or a piece of
bone, which is provided for the purpose.
See Fr. Boas, in *Sixth Report on the
North-Western Tribes of Canada*, p. 41
(separate reprint from the *Report of
the British Association for 1890*).

Again, among the Shuswap of British
Columbia a girl at puberty lives alone
in a little hut on the mountains and is
forbidden to touch her head or scratch
her body ; but she may scratch her
head with a three-toothed comb and her
body with the painted bone of a deer.
See Fr. Boas, *op. cit.* pp. 89 *sq.* In the
East Indian island of Ceram a girl may
not scratch herself with her fingers the
night before her teeth are filed, but she
may do it with a piece of bamboo. See
J. G. F. Riedel, *De sluik- en kroesharige
rassen tusschen Selebes en Papua*,
p. 137.

after she had recovered her normal state." [1]   Among the Bribri Indians of Costa Rica a menstruous woman is regarded as unclean (*bukuru*). The only plates she may use for her food are banana leaves, which, when she has done with them, she throws away in some sequestered spot ; for were a cow to find them and eat them, the animal would waste away and perish.   And she drinks out of a special vessel for a like reason ; because if any one drank out of the same cup after her, he would surely die. [2]   In the islands of Mabuiag and Saibai, in Torres Straits, girls at their first menstruation are strictly secluded from the sight of men.   In Mabuiag the seclusion lasts three months, in Saibai about a fortnight.   During the time of her separation the girl is forbidden to feed herself or to handle food, which is put into her mouth by women or girls told off to wait on her. [3]

Among many peoples similar restrictions are imposed on women in childbed and apparently for similar reasons ; at such periods women are supposed to be in a dangerous condition which would infect any person or thing they might touch ; hence they are put into quarantine until, with the recovery of their health and strength, the imaginary danger has passed away.   Thus, in Tahiti a woman after childbirth was secluded for a fortnight or three weeks in a temporary hut erected on sacred ground ; during the time of her seclusion she was debarred from touching provisions, and had to be fed by another.   Further, if any one else touched the child at this period, he was subjected to the same restrictions as the mother until the ceremony of her purification had been performed. [4]   Similarly in Manahiki, an island of the Southern Pacific, for ten days after her delivery a woman was not allowed to handle food, and had to be fed by some other person. [5]   In the Sinaugolo tribe of British New Guinea, for about a month after her confinement

Taboos imposed on women in childbed.

---

[1] A. G. Morice, "The Canadian Dénes," *Annual Archaeological Report* (*Toronto*), *1905*, p. 218.

[2] H. Pittier de Fabrega, "Die Sprache der Bribri-Indianer in Costa Rica," *Sitzungsberichte der philoso-phischen-historischen Classe der Kaiser-lichen Akademie der Wissenschaften*

(Vienna), cxxxviii. (1898) p. 20.

[3] C. G. Seligmann, in *Reports of the Cambridge Anthropological Expedi-tion to Torres Straits*, v. (Cambridge, 1904) pp. 201, 203.

[4] James Wilson, *Missionary Voyage to the Southern Pacific Ocean*, p. 354.

[5] G. Turner, *Samoa*, p. 276.

a woman may not prepare or handle food; she may not even cook for herself,· and when she is eating the food made ready for her by her friends she must use a sharpened stick to transfer it to her mouth.[1] Similarly in the Roro and Mekeo districts of British New Guinea a woman after childbirth becomes for a time taboo (*opu*), and any person or thing she may chance to touch becomes taboo also. Accordingly during this time she abstains from cooking; for were she to cook food, not only the victuals themselves but the pot and the fire would be tabooed, so that nobody could eat the victuals, or use the pot, or warm himself at the fire. Further at meals she may not dip her hand into the dish and help herself, as the natives commonly do; she must use for the purpose a long fork, with which she takes up the bananas, sweet potatoes, yams, and so forth, in order not to contaminate the rest of the food in the vessel by the touch of her fingers. If she wishes to drink, a gourd is set before her, and wrapping up her hands in a cloth or coco-nut fibre she pours the water into a small calabash for her use; or she may pour the water directly into her mouth without letting the gourd touch her lips. If anything has to be handed to her, it is not given from hand to hand but reached to her at the end of a long stick.[2] Similarly in the island of Kadiak, off Alaska, a woman about to be delivered retires to a miserable low hovel built of reeds, where she must remain for twenty days after the birth of her child, whatever the season may be, and she is considered so unclean that no one will touch her, and food is reached to her on sticks.[3] In the Ba-Pedi and Ba-Thonga tribes of South Africa a woman in childbed may not touch her food with her hands all the time of her seclusion; she must eat with the help of a wooden spoon.

[1] C. G. Seligmann, "The Medicine, Surgery, and Midwifery of the Sinau-golo," *Journal of the Anthropological Institute*, xxxii. (1902) p. 302. In Uganda a bride is secluded for a month, during which she only receives near relatives; she wears her veil all this time. She may not handle food, but is fed by one of her attendants. A peasant's wife is secluded for two or three days only. See J. Roscoe, "Further Notes on the Manners and Customs of the Baganda," *Journal of the Anthropological Institute*, xxxii. (1902) p. 37.

[2] Father Guis, "Les Canaques, ce qu'ils font, ce qu'ils disent," *Missions Catholiques*, xxx. (1898) p. 119.

[3] V. Lisiansky, *A Voyage Round the World* (London, 1814), p. 201.

They think that if she touched her victuals she might infect them with her bloody flux, and that having partaken of such tainted food she would fall into a consumption.[1] The Bribri Indians regard the pollution of childbed as much more dangerous even than that of menstruation.   When a woman feels her time approaching, she informs her husband, who makes haste to build a hut for her in a lonely spot.   There she must live alone, holding no converse with anybody save her mother or another woman.   After her delivery the medicine-man purifies her by breathing on her and laying an animal, it matters not what, upon her.   But even this ceremony only mitigates her uncleanness into a state considered to be equivalent to that of a menstruous woman ; and for a full lunar month she must live apart from her housemates, observing the same rules with regard to eating and drinking as at her monthly periods.   The case is still worse, the pollution is still more deadly, if she has had a miscarriage or has been delivered of a stillborn child.   In that case she may not go near a living soul : the mere contact with things she has used is exceedingly dangerous : her food is handed to her at the end of a long stick.   This lasts generally for three weeks, after which she may go home subject only to the restrictions incident to an ordinary confinement.[2] Among the Adivi or forest Gollas of Southern India, when a woman feels the first pains of labour, she is turned clean out of the village and must take up her quarters in a little hut made of leaves or mats about two hundred yards away.   In this hut she must bring forth her offspring unaided, unless a midwife can be fetched in time to be with her before the child is born ; if the midwife arrives after the birth has taken place she may not go near the woman.   For ninety days the mother lives in the hut by herself.   If any one touches her, he or she becomes, like the mother herself, an outcast and is expelled from the village for three months. The woman's husband generally makes a little hut about fifty yards from hers and stays in it sometimes to watch over her, but he may not go near her on pain of being an

(marginal note:) Taboos imposed on women in childbed.

---

[1] H. A. Junod, " Les Conceptions physiologiques des Bantou sud-africains et leurs tabous," *Revue d'Ethnographie* *et de Sociologie*, i. (1910) p. 153.

[2] H. Pittier de Fábrega, *op. cit.* pp. 20 *sq.*

outcast for three months. Food is placed on the ground
near the woman's hut and she takes it.   On the fourth day
after the birth a woman of the village goes to her and pours
water on her, but may not come into contact with her.
On the fifth day the villagers clear away the stones and
thorny bushes from a patch of ground about ten yards on
the village side of the hut, and to this clearing the woman
removes her hut unaided ; no one may help her to do so.
On the ninth, fifteenth, and thirtieth days she again shifts
her hut nearer and nearer to the village ; and again once in
each of the two following months she brings her hut still
nearer.   On the ninetieth day of her seclusion the woman
is called out from her hut, washed, clad in clean clothes, and
after being taken to the village temple is conducted to her own
house by a man of the caste, who performs purificatory
ceremonies.[1]

Dangers appre-hended from women in childbed.

These customs shew that in the opinion of some primitive
peoples a woman at and after childbirth is pervaded by a
certain dangerous influence which can infect anything and
anybody she touches; so that in the interest of the community it becomes necessary to seclude her from society
for a while until the virulence of the infection has passed
away, when, after submitting to certain rites of purification,
she is again free to mingle with her fellows.   This dread of
lying-in women appears to be widespread, for the practice
of shutting them up at such times in lonely huts away from
the rest of the people is very common.   Sometimes the
nature of the danger which is apprehended from them is
explicitly stated.   Thus in the island of Tumleo, off German
New Guinea, after the birth of her first child a woman is
shut up with her infant for five to eight days, during which
no man, not even her husband, may see her ; for the men
think that were they to see her, their bodies would swell up
and they would die.[2]   Apparently their notion is that the
sight of a woman who has just been big with child will, on

[1] F. Fawcett, "Note on a Custom
of the Mysore 'Gollaválu' or Shepherd
Caste People," *Journal of the Anthro-
pological Society of Bombay*, i. 536 *sq.*;
E. Thurston, *Castes and Tribes of
Southern India* (Madras, 1909), ii.

287 *sq.*
[2] M. J. Erdweg, "Die Bewohner
der Insel Tumleo, Berlinhafen, Deutsch
Neu-Guinea," *Mittheilungen der Anthropologischen Gesellschaft in Wien*,
xxxii. (1902) p. 280.

the principles of homoeopathic magic, make their bodies big Dangers
also to bursting.   The Sulka of New Britain imagine that, apprehended
when a woman has been delivered of a child, the men from
become cowardly, weapons lose their force, and the slips women in
childbed.
which are to be planted out are deprived of their power of
germinating.   Hence they perform a ceremony which is
intended to counteract this mysterious influence on men and
plants.   As soon as it is known that a woman has been
brought to bed, all the male population of the village
assembles in the men's clubhouse.   Branches of a strong-
smelling tree are fetched, the twigs are broken off, the leaves
stripped off and put on the fire.   All the men present then
seize branches with young buds.   One of them holds ginger
in his hand, which, after reciting a spell over it, he distributes
to the others.   They chew it and spit it out on the twigs,
and these twigs are afterwards laid on the shields and other
weapons in the house, and also on the slips which are to be
planted ; moreover they are fastened on the roofs and over
the doorways of the houses.   In this way they seek to annul
the noxious infection of childbirth.[1]   Among the Yabim of
German New Guinea, when a birth has taken place in the
village, all the inhabitants remain at home next morning
"in order that the fruits of the field may not be spoiled." [2]
Apparently they fear that if they went out to their fields
and gardens immediately after a woman had been brought
to bed, they would carry with them a dangerous contagion
which might blight the crops.   When a Herero woman has
given birth to a child, her female companions hastily construct a special hut for her to which she is transferred.   Both
the hut and the woman are sacred and "for this reason, the
men are not allowed to see the lying-in woman until the
navel string has separated from the child, otherwise they
would become weaklings, and when later they *yumbana*, that
is, go to war with spear and bow, they would be shot." [3]
Thus the Herero like the Sulka appear to imagine that the

[1] P. Rascher, "Die Sulka," *Archiv*
für Anthropologie, xxix. (1904) p.
212 ; R. Parkinson, *Dreissig Jahre*
in der Südsee (Stuttgart, 1907), p.
180.
[2] K. Vetter, in *Nachrichten über*

Kaiser Wilhelms-Land und den Bis-
marck-Archipel, 1897, p. 87.
[3] Rev. E. Dannert, "Customs of
the Ovaherero at the Birth of a Child,"
(*South African*) *Folk-lore Journal*, ii.
(1880) p. 63.

weakness of a lying-in woman can, on the principles of homoeopathic magic, infect any men who may chance to see her.

Dangers apprehended from women in childbed by Indians and Esquimaux.

Among the Saragacos Indians of eastern Ecuador, as soon as a woman feels the travail-pangs beginning, she retires into the forest to a distance of three or four leagues from her home, where she takes up her abode in a hut of leaves which has been already prepared for her. "This banishment," we are told, "is the fruit of the superstition of these Indians, who are persuaded that the spirit of evil would attach himself to their house if the women were brought to bed in it."[1] The Esquimaux of Baffin Land think that the body of a lying-in woman exhales a vapour which would adhere to the souls of seals if she ate the flesh of any seals except such as have been caught by her husband, by a boy, or by an aged man. "Cases of premature birth require particularly careful treatment. The event must be announced publicly, else dire results will follow. If a woman should conceal from the other people that she has had a premature birth, they might come near her, or even eat in her hut of the seals procured by her husband. The vapor arising from her would thus affect them, and they would be avoided by the seals. The transgression would also become attached to the soul of the seal, which would take it down to Sedna," the mythical mother of the sea-mammals, who lives in the lower world and controls the destinies of mankind.[2]

Dangers apprehended from women in childbed by Bantu tribes of South Africa.

Some Bantu tribes of South Africa entertain even more exaggerated notions of the virulent infection spread by a woman who has had a miscarriage and has concealed it. An experienced observer of these people tells us that the blood of childbirth "appears to the eyes of the South Africans to be tainted with a pollution still more dangerous than that of the menstrual fluid. The husband is excluded from the hut for eight days of the lying-in period, chiefly from fear that he might be contaminated by this secretion.

[1] Levrault, "Rapport sur les provinces de Canélos et du Napo," *Bulletin de la Société de Géographie* (Paris), Deuxième Série, xi. (1839) p. 74.

[2] Franz Boas, "The Eskimo of Baffin Land and Hudson Bay," *Bulletin of the American Museum of Natural History*, xv. part i. (New York, 1901) pp. 125 *sq.* As to Sedna, see *id.* pp. 119 *sqq.*

He dare not take his child in his arms for the three first
months after the birth.   But the secretion of childbed is Dangers
particularly terrible when it is the product of a miscarriage, appre-
hended
especially *a concealed miscarriage.*   In this case it is not from a
merely the man who is threatened or killed, it is the whole concealed
mis-
country, it is the sky itself which suffers.   By a curious carriage.
association of ideas a physiological fact causes cosmic
troubles ! " [1]   Thus, for example, the Ba-Pedi believe that a
woman who has procured abortion can kill a man merely by
lying with him ; her victim is poisoned, shrivels up, and
dies within a week.   As for the disastrous effect which a
miscarriage may have on the whole country I will quote the
words of a medicine-man and rain-maker of the Ba-Pedi
tribe : " When a woman has had a miscarriage, when she
has allowed her blood to flow, and has hidden the child, it
is enough to cause the burning winds to blow and to parch
the country with heat.   The rain no longer falls, for the
country is no longer in order.   When the rain approaches
the place where the blood is, it will not dare to approach.
It will fear and remain at a distance.   That woman has
committed a great fault.   She has spoiled the country of
the chief, for she has hidden blood which had not yet been
well congealed to fashion a man.   That blood is taboo
(*yila*).   It should never drip on the road !   The chief will
assemble his men and say to them, ' Are you in order in your
villages ? '   Some one will answer, ' Such and such a woman
was pregnant and we have not yet seen the child which she
has given birth to.'   Then they go and arrest the woman.
They say to her, ' Shew us where you have hidden it.'   They
go and dig at the spot, they sprinkle the hole with a
decoction of *mbendoula* and *nyangale* (two sorts of roots)
prepared in a special pot.   They take a little of the earth
of this grave, they throw it into the river, then they bring
back water from the river and sprinkle it where she shed her
blood.   She herself must wash every day with the medicine.
Then the country will be moistened again (by rain).
Further, we (medicine-men) summon the women of the
country ; we tell them to prepare a ball of the earth which

[1] H. A. Junod, "Les Conceptions
physiologiques des Bantou sud-africains
et leurs tabous," *Revue d'Ethnographie
et de Sociologie,* i. (1910) p. 139.

contains the blood. They bring it to us one morning. If
we wish to prepare medicine with which to sprinkle the
whole country, we crumble this earth to powder; at the end
of five days we send little boys and little girls, girls that yet
know nothing of women's affairs and have not yet had
relations with men. We put the medicine in the horns of
oxen, and these children go to all the fords, to all the
entrances of the country. A little girl turns up the soil
with her mattock, the others dip a branch in the horn and
sprinkle the inside of the hole saying, 'Rain! rain!' So
we remove the misfortune which the women have brought
on the roads; the rain will be able to come. The country
is purified!"[1]

Belief of
the Ba-
Thonga
that severe
droughts
result from
the con-
cealment
of mis-
carriages
by women.

Similarly the Ba-Thonga, another Bantu tribe of South
Africa in the valley of the Limpopo river, attribute severe
droughts to the concealment of miscarriages by women,
and they perform the following rites to remove the pollution and procure rain. A small clearing is made in a
thick and thorny wood, and here a pot is buried in the
ground so that its mouth is flush with the surface. From
the pot four channels run in the form of a cross to the four
cardinal points of the horizon. Then a black ox or a
black ram, without a speck of white on it, is killed and the
pot is stuffed with the half-digested grass found in the
animal's stomach. Next, little girls, still in the age of
innocence, are sent to draw water, which they pour into the
pot till it overflows into the four channels. After that the
women assemble, strip off their clothes, and covering their
nakedness only with a scanty petticoat of grass they dance,
leap, and sing, "Rain, fall!" Then they go and dig up the
remains of the prematurely born infants and of twins buried
in dry ground on a hill. These they collect in one place.
No man may approach the spot. The women would beat
any male who might be so indiscreet as to intrude on their
privacy, and they would put riddles to him which he would
have to answer in the most filthy language borrowed from
the circumcision ceremonies; for obscene words, which are
usually forbidden, are customary and legitimate on these
occasions. The women pour water on the graves of the

[1] H. A. Junod, *op. cit.* pp. 139 *sq.*

infants and of twins in order to "extinguish" (*timula*) them, as the natives phrase it; which seems to imply that the graves are thought to be the source of the scorching heat which is blasting the country.   At the fall of evening they bury all the remains they have discovered, poking them away in the mud near a stream.   Then the rain will be free to fall.[1]   In these ceremonies the pouring of water into channels which run in the direction of the four quarters of the heaven is clearly a charm based on the principles of homoeopathic magic to procure rain.   The supposed influence of twins over the waters of heaven and the use of foul language at rain-making ceremonies have been illustrated in another part of this work.[2]

Among the natives of the Nguôn So'n valley in Annam, during the first month after a woman has been delivered of a child, all the persons of the house are supposed to be affected with an evil destiny or ill luck called *phong long*. If a member of such a household enters another house, the inmates never fail to say to him, "You bring me the *phong long*!"   Should a member of a family in which somebody is seriously ill have to enter a house infected by the *phong long*, on returning home he always fumigates himself with tea leaves or some other plant in order to rid himself of the infection which he has contracted; for they fear that the blood of the woman who has been brought to bed may harm the patient.   All the time a house is tainted with the *phong long*, a branch of cactus (*Euphorbia antiquorum*) or pandanus is hung at the door.   The same thing is done to a house infected by small-pox: it is a danger signal to warn people off.   The *phong long* only disappears when the woman has gone to market for the first time after her delivery.[3]   A trace of a similar belief in the dangerous infection of childbirth may be seen in the rule of ancient Greek religion, which forbade persons who had handled a corpse or been in contact with a lying-in woman to enter a temple or approach an altar for a certain time, sometimes for two days.[4]

Dangers apprehended from women in childbed by some tribes of Annam.

---

[1] H. A. Junod, *op. cit.* pp. 140 *sq.*
[2] See *The Magic Art and the Evolution of Kings*, vol. i. pp. 262 *sqq.*, 278.
[3] Le R. P. Cadière, "Coutumes populaires de la vallée du Nguôn-So'n," *Bulletin de l'École Française d'Extrême-Orient*, ii. (Hanoi, 1902) pp. 353 *sq.*
[4] Dittenberger, *Sylloge inscriptionum Graecarum*,[2] No. 566; Ch. Michel,

Restrictions and taboos like those laid on menstruous and lying-in women are imposed by some savages on lads at the initiatory rites which celebrate the attainment of puberty; hence we may infer that at such times young men are supposed to be in a state like that of women at menstruation and in childbed. Thus, among the Creek Indians a lad at initiation had to abstain for twelve moons from picking his ears or scratching his head with his fingers; he had to use a small stick for these purposes. For four moons he must have a fire of his own to cook his food at; and a little girl, a virgin, might cook for him. During the fifth moon any person might cook for him, but he must serve himself first, and use one spoon and pan. On the fifth day of the twelfth moon he gathered corn cobs, burned them to ashes, and with the ashes rubbed his body all over. At the end of the twelfth moon he sweated under blankets, and then bathed in water, which ended the ceremony. While the ceremonies lasted, he might touch no one but lads who were undergoing a like course of initiation.[1] Caffre boys at circumcision live secluded in a special hut; they are smeared from head to foot with white clay; they wear tall head-dresses with horn-like projections and short skirts like those of ballet-dancers. When their wounds are healed, all the vessels which they had used during their seclusion and the boyish mantles which they had hitherto worn are burned,

Recueil d'inscriptions grecques, No. 730 ἀγνευέτωσαν δὲ καὶ εἰσίτωσαν εἰς τὸν τῆς θεο[ῦ ναὸν] . . . ὡσαύτως δὲ καὶ ἀπὸ κήδους καὶ τεκούσης γυναικὸς δευτεραῖος: Euripides, *Iphigenia in Tauris*, 380 *sqq.*:

τὰ τῆς θεοῦ δὲ μέμφομαι σοφίσματα,
ἥτις, βροτῶν μὲν ἤν τις ἅψηται φόνου
ἢ καὶ λοχείας ἢ νεκροῦ θιγῇ χεροῖν,
βωμῶν ἀπείργει, μυσαρὸν ὡς ἡγουμένη.

Compare also a mutilated Greek inscription found in Egypt (*Revue archéologique*, IIIme Série, ii. 182 *sqq.*). In the passage of Euripides which I have just quoted an acute verbal scholar, the late Dr. Badham, proposed to omit the line ἢ καὶ λοχείας ἢ νεκροῦ θιγῇ χεροῖν with the comment: "*Nihil facit ad argumentum puerperae mentio; patet versum a sciolo additum.*" To do Dr. Badham justice, the inscription which furnishes so close a parallel to the line of Euripides had not yet been discovered among the ruins of Pergamum, when he proposed to mutilate the text of the poet.

[1] B. Hawkins, "The Creek Confederacy," *Collections of the Georgia Historical Society*, iii. pt. i. (Savannah, 1848) pp. 78 *sq.* Hawkins's account is reproduced by A. S. Gatschett, in his *Migration Legend of the Creek Indians*, i. 185 *sq.* (Philadelphia, 1884). In the Turrbal tribe of southern Queensland boys at initiation were not allowed to scratch themselves with their fingers, but they might do it with a stick. See A. W. Howitt, *Native Tribes of South-East Australia*, p. 596.

together with the hut, and the boys rush away from the burning hut without looking back, " lest a fearful curse should cling to them." After that they are bathed, anointed, and clad in new garments.[1]

§ 4. *Warriors tabooed*

Once more, warriors are conceived by the savage to move, so to say, in an atmosphere of spiritual danger which constrains them to practise a variety of superstitious observances quite different in their nature from those rational precautions which, as a matter of course, they adopt against foes of flesh and blood. The general effect of these observances is to place the warrior, both before and after victory, in the same state of seclusion or spiritual quarantine in which, for his own safety, primitive man puts his human gods and other dangerous characters. Thus when the Maoris went out on the war-path they were sacred or taboo in the highest degree, and they and their friends at home had to observe strictly many curious customs over and above the numerous taboos of ordinary life. They became, in the irreverent language of Europeans who knew them in the old fighting days, " tabooed an inch thick "; and as for the leader of the expedition, he was quite unapproachable.[2] Similarly, when the Israelites marched forth to war they were bound by certain rules of ceremonial purity identical with rules observed by Maoris and Australian black-fellows on the war-path. The vessels they used were sacred, and they had to practise continence and a custom of personal cleanliness of which the original motive, if we may judge from the avowed motive of savages who conform to the same custom, was a fear lest the enemy should obtain

Marginal note: Taboos laid on warriors when they go forth to fight.

[1] L. Alberti, *De Kaffers* (Amsterdam, 1810), pp. 76 *sq.* ; H. Lichtenstein, *Reisen im südlichen Afrika* (Berlin, 1811-12), i. 427 ; S. Kay, *Travels and Researches in Caffraria* (London, 1833), pp. 273 *sq.*; Dudley Kidd, *The Essential Kafir*, p. 208 ; J. Stewart, D.D., *Lovedale, South Africa* (Edinburgh, 1894), pp. 105 *sq.*, with illustrations.

[2] *Old New Zealand*, by a Pakeha Maori (London, 1884), pp. 96, 114 *sq.* One of the customs mentioned by the writer was that all the people left in the camp had to fast strictly while the warriors were out in the field. This rule is obviously based on the sympathetic connexion supposed to exist between friends at a distance, especially at critical times. See *The Magic Art and the Evolution of Kings*, vol. i. pp. 126 *sqq.*

Taboos
laid on
warriors
when they
go forth
to fight.
the refuse of their persons, and thus be enabled to work their destruction by magic.[1]   Among some Indian tribes of North America a young warrior in his first campaign had to conform to certain customs, of which two were identical with the observances imposed by the same Indians on girls at their first menstruation : the vessels he ate and drank out of might be touched by no other person, and he was forbidden to scratch his head or any other part of his body with his fingers ; if he could not help scratching himself, he had to do it with a stick.[2]   The latter rule, like the one which forbids a tabooed person to feed himself with his own fingers, seems to rest on the supposed sanctity or pollution, whichever we choose to call it, of the tabooed hands.[3]   Moreover

---

[1] Deuteronomy xxiii. 9 - 14 ; I Samuel xxi. 5. The rule laid down in Deuteronomy xxiii. 10, 11, suffices to prove that the custom of continence observed in time of war by the Israelites, as by a multitude of savage and barbarous peoples, was based on a superstitious, not a rational motive. To convince us of this it is enough to remark that the rule is often observed by warriors for some time after their victorious return, and also by the persons left at home during the absence of the fighting men. In these cases the observance of the rule evidently does not admit of a rational explanation, which could hardly, indeed, be entertained by any one conversant with savage modes of thought. For examples, see *The Magic Art and the Evolution of Kings*, vol. i. pp. 125, 128, 131, 133, and below, pp. 161, 163, 165, 166, 167, 168, 169, 175 *sq.*, 178, 179, 181.

The other rule of personal cleanliness referred to in the text is exactly observed, for the reason I have indicated, by the aborigines in various parts of Australia. See (Sir) George Grey, *Journals*, ii. 344 ; R. Brough Smyth, *Aborigines of Victoria*, i. 165 ; J. Dawson, *Australian Aborigines*, p. 12 ; P. Beveridge, in *Journal and Proceedings of the Royal Society of New South Wales*, xvii. (1883) pp. 69 *sq.* Compare W. Stanbridge, "On the Aborigines of Victoria," *Transactions of the Ethnological Society of London*, N.S. i. (1861) p. 299 ; Fison and

Howitt, *Kamilaroi and Kurnai*, p. 251; E. M. Curr, *The Australian Race*, iii. 178 *sq.*, 547 ; W. E. Roth, *North Queensland Ethnography, Bulletin No.* 5 (Brisbane, 1903), p. 22, § 80. The same dread has resulted in a similar custom of cleanliness in Melanesia and Africa.   See R. Parkinson, *Im Bismarck-Archipel*, pp. 143 *sq.* ; R. H. Codrington, *The Melanesians*, p. 203 note ; F. von Luschan, "Einiges über Sitten und Gebräuche der Eingeborenen Neu - Guineas," *Verhandlungen der Berliner Gesellschaft für Anthropologie, Ethnologie, und Urgeschichte* (1900), p. 416 ; J. Macdonald, "Manners, Customs, Superstitions, and Religions of South African Tribes," *Journal of the Anthropological Institute*, xx. (1891) p. 131. Mr. Lorimer Fison sent me some notes on the Fijian practice, which agrees with the one described by Dr. Codrington. The same rule is observed, probably from the same motives, by the Miranha Indians of Brazil.   See Spix and Martius, *Reise in Brasilien*, iii. 1251 note.   On this subject compare F. Schwally, *Semitische Kriegsaltertümer*, i. (Leipsic, 1901) pp. 67 *sq.*

[2] *Narrative of the Captivity and Adventures of John Tanner* (London, 1830), p. 122.

[3] We have seen (pp. 146, 156) that the same rule is observed by girls at puberty among some Indian tribes of British Columbia and by Creek lads at

among these Indian tribes the men on the war-path had always to sleep at night with their faces turned towards their own country ; however uneasy the posture they might not change it. They might not sit upon the bare ground, nor wet their feet, nor walk on a beaten path if they could help it ; when they had no choice but to walk on a path, they sought to counteract the ill effect of doing so by doctoring their legs with certain medicines or charms which they carried with them for the purpose. No member of the party was permitted to step over the legs, hands, or body of any other member who chanced to be sitting or lying on the

initiation. It is also observed by Kwakiutl Indians who have eaten human flesh (see below, p. 189). Among the Blackfoot Indians the man who was appointed every four years to take charge of the sacred pipe and other emblems of their religion might not scratch his body with his finger-nails, but carried a sharp stick in his hair which he used for this purpose. During the term of his priesthood he had to fast and practise strict continence. None but he dare handle the sacred pipe and emblems (W. W. Warren, "History of the Ojibways," *Collections of the Minnesota Historical Society*, v. (1885) pp. 68 *sq.*). In Vedic India the man who was about to offer the solemn sacrifice of soma prepared himself for his duties by a ceremony of consecration, during which he carried the horn of a black deer or antelope wherewith to scratch himself if necessary (*Satapatha-Brāhmana*, bk. iii. 31, vol. ii. pp. 33 *sq.* trans. by J. Eggeling ; H. Oldenberg, *Die Religion des Veda*, p. 399). Some of the Peruvian Indians used to prepare themselves for an important office by fasting, continence, and refusing to wash themselves, to comb their hair, and to put their hands to their heads ; if they wished to scratch themselves, they must do it with a stick. See P. J. de Arriaga, *Extirpacion de la idolatria del Piru* (Lima, 1621), p. 20. Among the Isistines Indians of Paraguay mourners refrained from scratching their heads with their fingers, believing that to break the rule would make them bald, no hair grow-

ing on the part of the head which their fingers had touched. See Guevara, "Historia del Paraguay," in P. de Angelis's *Coleccion de obras y documentos relativos a la historia antigua y moderna de las provincias del Rio de la Plata*, ii. (Buenos-Aires, 1836) p. 30. Amongst the Macusis of British Guiana, when a woman has given birth to a child, the father hangs up his hammock beside that of his wife and stays there till the navel-string drops off the child. During this time the parents have to observe certain rules, of which one is that they may not scratch their heads or bodies with their nails, but must use for this purpose a piece of palm-leaf. If they broke this rule, they think the child would die or be an invalid all its life. See R. Schomburgk, *Reisen in Britisch-Guiana*, ii. 314. Some aborigines of Queensland believe that if they scratched themselves with their fingers during a rain-making ceremony, no rain would fall. See *The Magic Art and the Evolution of Kings*, vol. i. p. 254. In all these cases, plainly, the hands are conceived to be so strongly infected with the venom of taboo that it is dangerous even for the owner of the hands to touch himself with them. The cowboy who herded the cows of the king of Unyoro had to live strictly chaste, no one might touch him, and he might not scratch or wound himself so as to draw blood. But it is not said that he was forbidden to touch himself with his own hands. See my *Totemism and Exogamy*, ii. 527.

Taboos
laid on
warriors
when they
go forth
to fight. ground; and it was equally forbidden to step over his blanket, gun, tomahawk, or anything that belonged to him. If this rule was inadvertently broken, it became the duty of the member whose person or property had been stepped over to knock the other member down, and it was similarly the duty of that other to be knocked down peaceably and without resistance. The vessels out of which the warriors ate their food were commonly small bowls of wood or birch bark, with marks to distinguish the two sides; in marching from home the Indians invariably drank out of one side of the bowl, and in returning they drank out of the other. When on their way home they came within a day's march of the village, they hung up all their bowls on trees, or threw them away on the prairie,[1] doubtless to prevent their sanctity or defilement from being communicated with disastrous effects to their friends, just as we have seen that the vessels and clothes of the sacred Mikado, of women at childbirth and menstruation, of boys at circumcision, and of persons defiled by contact with the dead are destroyed or laid aside for a similar reason. The first four times that an Apache Indian goes out on the war-path, he is bound to refrain from scratching his head with his fingers and from letting water touch his lips. Hence he scratches his head with a stick, and drinks through a hollow reed or cane. Stick and reed are attached to the warrior's belt and to each other by a leathern thong.[2] The rule not to scratch their heads with their fingers, but to use a stick for the purpose instead, was regularly observed by Ojebways on the war-path.[3]

Cere-
monies ob-
served by
American
Indians
before they
went out
on the war-
path. For three or four weeks before they went on a warlike expedition, the Nootka Indians made it an invariable rule to go into the water five or six times a day, when they washed and scrubbed themselves from head to foot with bushes intermixed with briars, so that their bodies and faces were often entirely covered with blood. During this severe exercise they continually exclaimed, "Good or great God, let me live,

---

[1] *Narrative of the Captivity and Adventures of John Tanner* (London, 1830), p. 123. As to the custom of not stepping over a person or his weapons, see the note at the end of the volume.

[2] J. G. Bourke, *On the Border with Crook* (New York, 1891), p. 133; *id.*, in *Folk-lore*, ii. (1891) p. 453; *id.*, in *Ninth Annual Report of the Bureau of Ethnology* (Washington, 1892), p. 490.

[3] J. G. Kohl, *Kitschi-Gami*, ii. 168.

not be sick, find the enemy, not fear him, find him asleep, and kill a great many of them." All this time they had no intercourse with their women, and for a week before setting out abstained from feasting and every kind of merriment. For the last three days they were almost constantly in the water, scrubbing and lacerating themselves in a terrible manner. They believed that this hardened their skin, so that the weapons of the enemy could not pierce them.[1] Before they went out on the war-path the Arikaras and the Big Belly Indians ("*Gros Ventres*") "observe a rigorous fast, or rather abstain from every kind of food for four days. In this interval their imagination is exalted to delirium ; whether it be through bodily weakness or the natural effect of the warlike plans they cherish, they pretend to have strange visions. The elders and sages of the tribe, being called upon to interpret these dreams, draw from them omens more or less favourable to the success of the enterprise ; and their explanations are received as oracles by which the expedition will be faithfully regulated. So long as the preparatory fast continues, the warriors make incisions in their bodies, insert pieces of wood in the flesh, and having fastened leather thongs to them cause themselves to be hung from a beam which is fixed horizontally above an abyss a hundred and fifty feet deep. Often indeed they cut off one or two fingers which they offer in sacrifice to the Great Spirit in order that they may come back laden with scalps."[2] It is hard to conceive any course of training which could more effectually incapacitate men for the business of war than that which these foolish Indians actually adopted. With regard to the Creek Indians and kindred tribes we are told they "will not cohabit with women while they are out at war ; they religiously abstain from every kind of intercourse even with their own wives, for the space of three days and nights before they go to war, and so after they return home, because they are to sanctify themselves."[3] And as a

---

[1] *Narrative of the Adventures and Sufferings of John R. Jewitt* (Middletown, 1820), pp. 148 *sq.*

[2] J. de Smet, in *Annales de la Propagation de la Foi*, xiv. (1842) pp. 67 *sq.* These customs have doubtless long passed away, and the Indians who practised them may well have suffered the extinction which they did their best to incur.

[3] J. Adair, *History of the American Indians* (London, 1775), p. 163.

preparation for attacking the enemy they "go to the afore-
said winter house, and there drink a warm decoction of their
supposed holy consecrated herbs and roots for three days and
nights, sometimes without any other refreshment.   This is to
induce the deity to guard and prosper them, amidst their
impending dangers.   In the most promising appearance of
things, they are not to take the least nourishment of food,
nor so much as to sit down, during that time of sanctifying

Rules
observed
by Indians
on a war-
expedition.

themselves, till after sunset.   While on their expedition, they
are not allowed to lean themselves against a tree, though
they may be exceedingly fatigued, after a sharp day's march ;
nor must they lie by, a whole day to refresh themselves, or
kill and barbicue deer and bear for their war journey.   The
more virtuous they are, they reckon the greater will be their
success against the enemy, by the bountiful smiles of the
deity.   To gain that favourite point, some of the aged
warriors narrowly watch the young men who are newly
initiated, lest they should prove irreligious, and prophane the
holy fast, and bring misfortunes on the out-standing camp.
A gentleman of my acquaintance, in his youthful days observed one of their religious fasts, but under the greatest
suspicion of his virtue in this respect, though he had often
headed them against the common enemy : during their three
days' purification, he was not allowed to go out of the
sanctified ground, without a trusty guard, lest hunger should
have tempted him to violate their old martial law, and by
that means have raised the burning wrath of the holy fire
against the whole camp."   "Every war captain chuses a
noted warrior, to attend on him and the company.   He is
called *Etissû*, or 'the waiter.'   Everything they eat or drink
during their journey, he gives them out of his hand,
by a rigid abstemious rule,—though each carries on his
back all his travelling conveniencies, wrapt in a deer
skin, yet they are so bigoted in their religious customs
in war that none, though prompted by sharp hunger or
burning thirst, dares relieve himself.   They are contented
with such trifling allowance as the religious waiter distributes
to them, even with a scanty hand.   Such a regimen would
be too mortifying to any of the white people, let their opinion
of its violation be ever so dangerous.   When I roved the

woods in a war party with the Indians, though I carried no scrip, nor bottle, nor staff, I kept a large hollow cane well corked at each end, and used to sheer off now and then to drink, while they suffered greatly by thirst. The constancy of the savages in mortifying their bodies, to gain the divine favour, is astonishing, from the very time they beat to arms, till they return from their campaign. All the while they are out, they are prohibited by ancient custom, the leaning against a tree, either sitting or standing ; nor are they allowed to sit in the day-time, under the shade of trees, if it can be avoided ; nor on the ground, during the whole journey, but on such rocks, stones, or fallen wood, as their ark of war rests upon. By the attention they invariably pay to those severe rules of living, they weaken themselves much more than by the unavoidable fatigues of war ; but it is fruitless to endeavour to dissuade them from those things which they have by tradition, as the appointed means to move the deity, to grant them success against the enemy, and a safe return home."[1] "An Indian, intending to go to war, will commence by blacking his face, permitting his hair to grow long, and neglecting his personal appearance, and also will frequently fast, sometimes for two or three days together, and refrain from all intercourse with the other sex. If his dreams are favorable, he thinks that the Great Spirit will give him success."[2] Among the Ba-Pedi and Ba-Thonga tribes of south Africa not only have the warriors to abstain from women, but the people left behind in the villages are also bound to continence ; they think that any incontinence on their part would cause thorns to grow on the ground traversed by the warriors, and that success would not attend the expedition.[3]

When we observe what pains these misguided savages took to unfit themselves for the business of war by abstaining from food, denying themselves rest, and lacerating

The rule of continence observed by savage

---

[1] J. Adair, *History of the American Indians*, pp. 380-382.

[2] Maj. M. Marston, in Rev. Jedidiah Morse's *Report to the Secretary of War of the United States on Indian Affairs* (New-haven, 1822), Appendix, p. 130. The account in the text refers especially to the Sauk, Fox, and Kickapoo Indians, at the junction of the Rock and Mississippi rivers.

[3] H. A. Junod, "Les Conceptions physiologiques des Bantou sud-africains et leurs tabous," *Revue d'Ethnographie et de Sociologie*, i. (1910) p. 149.

warriors is
perhaps
based on a
fear of
infecting
themselves
sympa-
thetically
with
feminine
weakness
and
cowardice.
their bodies, we shall probably not be disposed to attribute their practice of continence in war to a rational fear of dissipating their bodily energies by indulgence in the lusts of the flesh. On the contrary, we can scarcely doubt that the motive which impelled them to observe chastity on a campaign was just as frivolous as the motive which led them simultaneously to fritter away their strength by severe fasts, gratuitous fatigue, and voluntary wounds at the very moment when prudence called most loudly for a precisely opposite regimen. Why exactly so many savages have made it a rule to refrain from women in time of war,[1] we cannot say for certain, but we may conjecture that their motive was a superstitious fear lest, on the principles of sympathetic magic, close contact with women should infect them with feminine weakness and cowardice. Similarly some savages imagine that contact with a woman in childbed enervates warriors and enfeebles their weapons.[2] Indeed the Kayans of central Borneo go so far as to hold that to touch a loom or women's clothes would so weaken a man that he

---

[1] For more evidence of the practice of continence by warriors, see R. Taylor, *Te Ika A Maui, or New Zealand and its Inhabitants*,[2] p. 189; E. Dieffenbach, *Travels in New Zealand*, ii. 85 *sq.* ; Ch. Wilkes, *Narrative of the United States Exploring Expedition*, iii. 78; J. Chalmers, "Toaripi," *Journal of the Anthropological Institute*, xxvii. (1898) p. 332; *id., Pioneering in New Guinea*, p. 65; Van Schmidt, "Aanteekeningen nopens de zeden, etc., der bevolking van de eilanden Saparoea, Haroekoe, Noessa Laut, etc.," *Tijdschrift voor Nederlands Indie*, 1843, deel ii. p. 507; J. G. F. Riedel, *De sluiken kroesharige rassen tusschen Selebes en Papua*, p. 223; *id.*, "Galela und Tobeloresen," *Zeitschrift für Ethnologie*, xvii. (1885) p. 68; W. W. Skeat, *Malay Magic*, p. 524; E. Reclus, *Nouvelle Géographie universelle*, viii. 126 (compare J. Biddulph, *Tribes of the Hindoo Koosh*, p. 18); N. Isaacs, *Travels and Adventures in Eastern Africa*, i. 120; H. Callaway, *Religious System of the Amazulu*, iv. 437 *sq.*; Dudley Kidd, *The Essential Kafir*, p.

306; A. Bastian, *Die deutsche Expedition an der Loango-Küste*, i. 203; H. Cole, "Notes on the Wagogo of German East Africa," *Journal of the Anthropological Institute*, xxxii. (1902) p. 317; R. H. Nassau, *Fetichism in West Africa*, p. 177; H. R. Schoolcraft, *Indian Tribes*, iv. 63; J. Morse, *Report to the Secretary of War of the U.S. on Indian Affairs* (New-haven, 1822), pp. 130, 131; H. H. Bancroft, *Native Races of the Pacific States*, i. 189. On the other hand in Uganda, before an army set out, the general and all the chiefs had either to lie with their wives or to jump over them. This was supposed to ensure victory and plenty of booty. See J. Roscoe, in *Journal of the Anthropological Institute*, xxxii. (1902) p. 59. And in Kiwai Island, off British New Guinea, men had intercourse with their wives before they went to war, and they drew omens from it. See J. Chalmers, "Notes on the Natives of Kiwai," *Journal of the Anthropological Institute*, xxxiii. (1903) p. 123.

[2] See above, pp. 151 *sq.*

would have no success in hunting, fishing, and war.[1]   Hence
it is not merely sexual intercourse with women that the
savage warrior sometimes shuns ; he is careful to avoid the
sex altogether.   Thus among the hill tribes of Assam, not
only are men forbidden to cohabit with their wives during
or after a raid, but they may not eat food cooked by
a woman ; nay they should not address a word even to
their own wives.   Once a woman, who unwittingly broke the
rule by speaking to her husband while he was under the
war taboo, sickened and died when she learned the awful
crime she had committed.[2]

§ 5. *Manslayers tabooed*

If the reader still doubts whether the rules of conduct
which we have just been considering are based on superstitious fears or dictated by a rational prudence, his doubts
will probably be dissipated when he learns that rules of the
same sort are often imposed even more stringently on
warriors after the victory has been won and when all fear
of the living corporeal foe is at an end.   In such cases one
motive for the inconvenient restrictions laid on the victors in
their hour of triumph is probably a dread of the angry ghosts
of the slain ; and that the fear of the vengeful ghosts does
influence the behaviour of the slayers is often expressly
affirmed.   The general effect of the taboos laid on sacred
chiefs, mourners, women at childbirth, men on the war-path,
and so on, is to seclude or isolate the tabooed persons from
ordinary society, this effect being attained by a variety of rules,
which oblige the men or women to live in separate huts or
in the open air, to shun the commerce of the sexes, to avoid
the use of vessels employed by others, and so forth.   Now
the same effect is produced by similar means in the case of
victorious warriors, particularly such as have actually shed
the blood of their enemies.   In the island of Timor, when a
warlike expedition has returned in triumph bringing the
heads of the vanquished foe, the leader of the expedition is

Taboos laid on warriors after slaying their foes.

The effect of the taboos is to seclude the tabooed person from ordinary society.

Seclusion of man-slayers in the East Indies.

---

[1] A. W. Nieuwenhuis, *Quer durch Borneo*, i. 350.
[2] T. C. Hodson, " The *genna* amongst the Tribes of Assam," *Journal of the Anthropological Institute*, xxxvi. (1906) p. 100.

forbidden by religion and custom to return at once to his own house. A special hut is prepared for him, in which he has to reside for two months, undergoing bodily and spiritual purification. During this time he may not go to his wife nor feed himself; the food must be put into his mouth by another person.[1] That these observances are dictated by fear of the ghosts of the slain seems certain; for from another account of the ceremonies performed on the return of a successful head-hunter in the same island we learn that sacrifices are offered on this occasion to appease the soul of the man whose head has been taken; the people think that some misfortune would befall the victor were such offerings omitted. Moreover, a part of the ceremony consists of a dance accompanied by a song, in which the death of the slain man is lamented and his forgiveness is entreated. "Be not angry," they say, "because your head is here with us; had we been less lucky, our heads might now have been exposed in your village. We have offered the sacrifice to appease you. Your spirit may now rest and leave us at peace. Why were you our enemy? Would it not have been better that we should remain friends? Then your blood would not have been spilt and your head would not have been cut off."[2] The people of Paloo, in central Celebes, take the heads of their enemies in war and afterwards propitiate the souls of the slain in the temple.[3] In some Dyak tribes men on returning from an expedition in which they have taken human heads are obliged to keep by themselves and abstain from a variety

[1] S. Müller, *Reizen en Onderzoekingen in den Indischen Archipel* (Amsterdam, 1857), ii. 252.

[2] J. S. G. Gramberg, "Eene maand in de binnenlanden van Timor," *Verhandelingen van het Bataviaasch Genootschap van Kunsten en Wetenschappen*, xxxvi. (1872) pp. 208, 216 *sq.* Compare H. Zondervan, "Timor en de Timoreezen," *Tijdschrift van het Nederlandsch Aardrijkskundig Genootschap*, Tweede Serie, v. (1888) Afdeeling, meer uitgebreide artikelen, pp. 399, 413. Similarly Gallas returning from war sacrifice to the jinn or guardian spirits of their slain foes

before they will re-enter their own houses (Ph. Paulitschke, *Ethnographie Nordost-Afrikas, die geistige Cultur der Danâkil, Galla und Somâl*, pp. 50, 136). Sometimes perhaps the sacrifice consists of the slayers' own blood. See below, pp. 174, 176, 180. Orestes is said to have appeased the Furies of his murdered mother by biting off one of his fingers (Pausanias, viii. 34. 3).

[3] N. Adriani en A. C. Kruijt, "Van Posso naar Parigi, Sigi en Lindoe," *Mededeelingen van wege het Nederlandsche Zendelinggenootschap*, xlii. (1898) p. 451.

of things for several days; they may not touch iron ŋor eat salt or fish with bones, and they may have no intercourse with women.[1]

In Logea, an island off the south-eastern extremity of New Guinea, men who have killed or assisted in killing enemies shut themselves up for about a week in their houses. They must avoid all intercourse with their wives and friends, and they may not touch food with their hands. They may eat vegetable food only, which is brought to them cooked in special pots. The intention of these restrictions is to guard the men against the smell of the blood of the slain; for it is believed that if they smelt the blood, they would fall ill and die.[2] In the Toaripi or Motumotu tribe of south-eastern New Guinea a man who has killed another may not go near his wife, and may not touch food with his fingers. He is fed by others, and only with certain kinds of food. These observances last till the new moon.[3] Among the tribes at the mouth of the Wanigela River, in New Guinea, "a man who has taken life is considered to be impure until he has undergone certain ceremonies: as soon as possible after the deed he cleanses himself and his weapon. This satisfactorily accomplished, he repairs to his village and seats himself on the logs of sacrificial staging. No one approaches him or takes any notice whatever of him. A house is prepared for him which is put in charge of two or three small boys as servants. He may eat only toasted bananas, and only the centre portion of them—the ends being thrown away. On the third day of his seclusion a small feast is prepared by his friends, who also fashion some new perineal bands for him. This is called *ivi poro*. The next day the man dons all his best ornaments and badges for taking life, and sallies forth fully armed and parades the village. The next day a hunt is organised, and a kangaroo selected from the game captured. It is cut open and the spleen and liver rubbed

Seclusion of man-slayers in New Guinea.

[1] S. W. Tromp, "Uit de Salasila van Koetei," *Bijdragen tot de Taal-Land- en Volkenkunde van Neder-landsch-Indië*, xxxvii. (1888) p. 74.

[2] Dr. L. Loria, "Notes on the Ancient War Customs of the Natives of Logea and Neighbourhood," *British New Guinea, Annual Report for 1894-1895* (London, 1896), p. 52.

[3] Rev. J. Chalmers, "Toaripi," *Journal of the Anthropological Institute*, xxvii. (1898) p. 333.

over the back of the man. He then walks solemnly down to the nearest water, and standing straddle-legs in it washes himself. All the young untried warriors swim between his legs. This is supposed to impart courage and strength to them. The following day, at early dawn, he dashes out of his house, fully armed, and calls aloud the name of his victim. Having satisfied himself that he has thoroughly scared the ghost of the dead man, he returns to his house. The beating of flooring-boards and the lighting of fires is also a certain method of scaring the ghost. A day later his purification is finished. He can then enter his wife's house."[1] Among the Roro-speaking tribes of British New Guinea homicides were secluded in the warriors' clubhouse. They had to pass the night in the building, but during the day they might paint and decorate themselves and dance in front of it. For some time they might not eat much food nor touch it with their hands, but were obliged to pick it up on a bone fork, the heft of which was wrapped in a banana leaf. After a while they bathed in the sea and thenceforward for a period of about a month, though they had still to sleep in the warriors' clubhouse, they were free to eat as much food as they pleased and to pick it up with their bare hands. Finally, those warriors who had never killed a man before assumed a beautiful ornament made of fretted turtle shell, which none but homicides were allowed to flaunt in their head-dresses. Then came a dance, and that same night the men who wore the honourable badge of homicide for the first time were chased about the village ; embers were thrown at them and firebrands waved in order, apparently, to drive away the souls of the dead enemies, who seem to be conceived as immanent in some way in the headgear of their slayers.[2] Again, among the Koita of British New Guinea, when a man had killed another, whether the victim were male or female, he did not wash the blood off the spear or club, but carefully allowed it to dry on the weapon. On his way home he bathed in fresh or salt water, and

[1] R. E. Guise, "On the Tribes inhabiting the Mouth of the Wanigela River, New Guinea," *Journal of the Anthropological Institute*, xxviii. (1899) pp. 213 *sq.*

[2] C. G. Seligmann, *The Melanesians of British New Guinea* (Cambridge, 1910), p. 298.

on reaching his village went straight to his own house, where he remained in seclusion for about a week. He was taboo (*aina*): he might not approach women, and he lifted his food to his mouth with a bone fork. His women-folk were not obliged to leave the house, but they might not come near him. At the end of a week he built a rough shelter in the forest, where he lived for a few days. During this time he made a new waist-band, which he wore on his return to the village. A man who has slain another is supposed to grow thin and emaciated, because he had been splashed with the blood of his victim, and as the corpse rotted he wasted away.[1] Among the Southern Massim of British New Guinea a warrior who has taken a prisoner or slain a man remains secluded in his house for six days. During the first three days he may eat only roasted food and must cook it for himself. Then he bathes and blackens his face for the remaining three days.[2]

Among the Monumbos of German New Guinea any one who has slain a foe in war becomes thereby "unclean" (*bolobolo*), and they apply the same term "unclean" to menstruous and lying-in women and also to everything that has come into contact with a corpse, which shews that all these classes of persons and things are closely associated in their minds. The "unclean" man who has killed an enemy in battle must remain a long time in the men's club-house, while the villagers gather round him and celebrate his victory with dance and song. He may touch nobody, not even his own wife and children; if he were to touch them it is believed that they would be covered with sores. He becomes clean again by washing and using other modes of purification.[3] In Windessi, Dutch New Guinea, when a party of head-hunters has been successful, and they are nearing home, they announce their approach and success by blowing on triton shells. Their canoes are also decked with branches. The faces of the men who have taken a head are blackened with charcoal. If several have taken part in

The man-slayer unclean.

Driving away the ghosts of the slain.

---

[1] C. G. Seligmann, *op. cit.* pp. 129 *sq.*

[2] C. G. Seligmann, *op. cit.* pp. 563 *sq.*

[3] P. Franz Vormann, "Zur Psychologie, Religion, Soziologie und Geschichte der Monumbo-Papua, Deutsch-Neuguinea," *Anthropos,* v. (1910) pp. 410 *sq.*

killing the same victim, his head is divided among them. They always time their arrival so as to reach home in the early morning. They come rowing to the village with a great noise, and the women stand ready to dance in the verandahs of the houses. The canoes row past the *room sram* or house where the young men live ; and as they pass, the murderers throw as many pointed sticks or bamboos at the wall or the roof as there were enemies killed. The day is spent very quietly. Now and then they drum or blow on the conch ; at other times they beat the walls of the houses with loud shouts to drive away the ghosts of the slain.[1] Similarly in the Doreh district of Dutch New Guinea, if a murder has taken place in the village, the inhabitants assemble for several evenings in succession and utter frightful yells to drive away the ghost of the victim in case he should be minded to hang about the village.[2] So the Yabim of German New Guinea believe that the spirit of a murdered man pursues his murderer and seeks to do him a mischief. Hence they drive away the spirit with shouts and the beating of drums.[3] When the Fijians had buried a man alive, as they often did, they used at nightfall to make a great uproar by means of bamboos, trumpet-shells, and so forth, for the purpose of frightening away his ghost, lest he should attempt to return to his old home. And to render his house unattractive to him they dismantled it and clothed it with everything that to their ideas seemed most repulsive.[4] On the evening of the day on which they had tortured a prisoner to death, the American Indians were wont to run through the village with hideous yells, beating with sticks on the furniture, the walls, and the roofs of the huts to prevent the angry ghost of their victim from settling there and taking vengeance for the torments that his body had endured at their hands.[5] " Once," says a traveller, " on

---

[1] J. L. D. van der Roest, "Uit het leven der Bevolking van Windessi," *Tijdschrift voor Indische Taal- Landen Volkenkunde,* xl. (1898) pp. 157 *sq.*

[2] H. von Rosenberg, *Der malayische Archipel,* p. 461.

[3] K. Vetter, in *Nachrichten über Kaiser Wilhelms-Land und den Bis-marck-Archipel,* 1897, p. 94.

[4] J. E. Erskine, *The Western Pacific* (London, 1853), p. 477.

[5] Charlevoix, *Histoire de la Nouvelle France,* vi. pp. 77, 122 *sq.* ; J. F. Lafitau, *Mœurs des sauvages ameriquains,* ii. 279. In many places it is customary to drive away the ghosts even of persons who have died a

approaching in the night a village of Ottawas, I found all the
inhabitants in confusion : they were all busily engaged in
raising noises of the loudest and most inharmonious kind.
Upon inquiry, I found that a battle had been lately fought
between the Ottawas and the Kickapoos, and that the object
of all this noise was to prevent the ghosts of the departed
combatants from entering the village." [1]

The executioner at Porto Novo, on the coast of Guinea, Precautions
used to decorate his walls with the jawbones of the persons taken by
on whom he had operated in the course of business. But against the
for this simple precaution their ghosts would unquestionably ghosts of
have come at night to knock with sobs and groans, in victims.
an insufferable manner, at the door of the room where
he slept the sleep of the just.[2]   The temper of a man
who has just been executed is naturally somewhat short,
and in a burst of vexation his ghost is apt to fall foul
of the first person he comes across, without discriminating
between the objects of his wrath with that nicety of judgment which in calmer moments he may be expected to
display.   Hence in China it is, or used to be, customary
for the spectators of an execution to shew a clean pair
of heels to the ghosts as soon as the last head was off.[3]
The same fear of the spirits of his victims leads the
executioner sometimes to live in seclusion for some time
after he has discharged his office.   Thus an old writer,
speaking of Issini on the Gold Coast of West Africa, tells
us that the " executioners, being reckoned impure for three
days, they build them a separate hut at a distance from
the village.   Meantime these fellows run like madmen
through the place, seizing all they can lay hands on ;
poultry, sheep, bread, and oil ; everything they can touch
is theirs ; being deemed so polluted that the owners
willingly give it up.   They continue three days confined
to their hut, their friends bringing them victuals.   This
time expired, they take their hut in pieces, which they

natural death.   An account of these
customs is reserved for another work.

[1] W. H. Keating, *Narrative of an
Expedition to the Source of St. Peter's
River* (London, 1825), i. 109.

[2] Father Baudin, "Féticheurs, ou

ministres religieux des Nègres de la
Guinée," *Missions Catholiques*, xvi.
(1884) p. 332.

[3] Juan de la Concepcion, *Historia
general de Philipinas*, xi. (Manilla,
1791) p. 387.

bundle up, not leaving so much as the ashes of their fire. The first executioner, having a pot on his head, leads them to the place where the criminal suffered. There they all call him thrice by his name. The first executioner breaks his pot, and leaving their old rags and bundles they all scamper home."[1] Here the thrice-repeated invocation of the victim by name gives the clue to the rest of the observances; all of them are probably intended to ward off the angry ghost of the slain man or to give him the slip.

Purification of man-slayers among the Basutos and Bechuanas.

Among the Basutos "ablution is specially performed on return from battle. It is absolutely necessary that the warriors should rid themselves, as soon as possible, of the blood they have shed, or the shades of their victims would pursue them incessantly, and disturb their slumbers. They go in a procession, and in full armour, to the nearest stream. At the moment they enter the water a diviner, placed higher up, throws some purifying substances into the current. This is, however, not strictly necessary. The javelins and battle-axes also undergo the process of washing."[2] According to another account of the Basuto custom, "warriors who have killed an enemy are purified. The chief has to wash them, sacrificing an ox in presence of the whole army. They are also anointed with the gall of the animal, which prevents the ghost of the enemy from pursuing them any further."[3] Among the Bechuanas a man who has killed another, whether in war or in single combat, is not allowed to enter the village until he has been purified.

---

[1] G. Loyer, "Voyage to Issini on the Gold Coast," in T. Astley's *New General Collection of Voyages and Travels*, ii. (London, 1745) p. 444. Among the tribes of the Lower Niger it is customary for the executioner to remain in the house for three days after the execution; during this time he sleeps on the bare floor, eats off broken platters, and drinks out of calabashes or mugs, which are also damaged. See Major A. G. Leonard, *The Lower Niger and its Tribes* (London, 1906), p. 180.

[2] E. Casalis, *The Basutos*, p. 258. So Caffres returning from battle are

unclean and must wash before they enter their houses (L. Alberti, *De Kaffers*, p. 104). It would seem that after the slaughter of a foe the Greeks or Romans had also to bathe in running water before they might touch holy things (Virgil, *Aen.* ii. 719 *sqq.*).

[3] Father Porte, "Les Réminiscences d'un missionnaire du Basutoland," *Missions Catholiques*, xxviii. (1896) p. 371. For a fuller description of a ceremony of this sort see T. Arbousset et F. Daumas, *Voyage d'exploration au nord-est de la colonie du Cap de Bonne-Espérance* (Paris, 1842), pp. 561-563.

The ceremony takes place in the evening. An ox is slaughtered, and a hole having been made through the middle of the carcase with a spear, the manslayer has to force himself through the animal, while two men hold its stomach open.[1] Sometimes instead of being obliged to squeeze through the carcase of an ox the manslayer is merely smeared with the contents of its stomach. The ceremony has been described as follows: "In the purification of warriors, too, the ox takes a conspicuous part. The warrior who has slain a man in the battle is unclean, and must on no account enter his own courtyard, for it would be a serious thing if even his shadow were to fall upon his children. He studiously keeps himself apart from the civil life of the town until he is purified. The purification ceremony is significant. Having bathed himself in running water, or, if that is not convenient, in water that has been appropriately medicated, he is smeared by the doctor with the contents of the stomach of an ox, into which certain powdered roots have been already mixed, and then the doctor strikes him on the back, sides, and belly with the large bowel of an ox. . . . A doctor takes a piece of roasted beef and cuts it into small lumps of about the size of a walnut, laying them carefully on a large wooden trencher. He has already prepared charcoal, by roasting the root of certain trees in an old cracked pot, and this he grinds down and sprinkles on the lumps of meat on the trencher. Then the army surrounds the trencher, and every one who has slain a foe in the battle steps forth, kneels down before the trencher, and takes out a piece of meat with his mouth, taking care not to touch it or the trencher with his hands. As he takes the meat, the doctor gives him a smart cut with a switch. And when he has eaten that lump of meat his purification is complete. This ceremony is called *Go alafsha dintèè*, or 'the purification of the strikers.'" The writer to whom we owe this description adds: "This taking of meat from the trencher without using the hands is evidently a matter of ritual."[2] The

---

[1] "Extrait du journal des missions évangeliques," *Bulletin de la Société de Géographie* (Paris), IIme Série, ii.

(1834) pp. 199 *sq.*

[2] Rev. W. C. Willoughby, "Notes on the Totemism of the Becwana,"

observation is correct.   Here as in so many cases persons ceremonially unclean are forbidden to touch food with defiled hands until their uncleanness has been purged away.

Purification of manslayers among the Bageshu.

The same taboo is laid on the manslayer by the Bageshu of British East Africa.   Among them a man who has killed another may not return to his own house on the same day, though he may enter the village and spend the night in a friend's house.   He kills a sheep and smears his chest, his right arm, and his head with the contents of the animal's stomach.   His children are brought to him and he smears them in like manner.   Then he smears each side of the doorway with the tripe and entrails, and finally throws the rest of the stomach on the roof of his house. For a whole day he may not touch food with his hands, but picks it up with two sticks and so conveys it to his mouth.   His wife is not under any such restrictions.   She may even go to mourn for the man whom her husband has killed, if she wishes to do so.[1]   In some Bechuana tribes the victorious warrior is obliged to eat a piece of the skin of the man he killed ; the skin is taken from about the navel of his victim, and without it he may not enter the cattle pen.   Moreover, the medicine-man makes a gash with a spear in the warrior's

Expulsion of the ghosts of the slain by the Angoni.

thigh for every man he has killed.[2]   Among the Angoni, a Zulu tribe settled to the north of the Zambesi, warriors who have slain foes on an expedition smear their bodies and faces with ashes, hang garments of their victims on their persons, and tie bark ropes round their necks, so that the ends hang down over their shoulders or breasts.   This costume they wear for three days after their return, and rising at break of day they run through the village uttering frightful yells to drive away the ghosts of the slain, which, if they were not thus banished from the houses, might bring sickness and misfortune on the inmates.[3]   In some Caffre tribes of South Africa men who have been wounded or killed an enemy in fight may not see the king nor drink

Journal of the Anthropological Institute, xxxv. (1905) pp. 305 *sq.*

[1] Rev. J. Roscoe, "Notes on the Bageshu," *Journal of the Royal Anthropological Institute*, xxxix. (1909) p. 190.

[2] Dudley Kidd, *The Essential Kafir*, p. 310.

[3] C. Wiese, "Beiträge zur Geschichte der Zulu im Norden des Zambesi," *Zeitschrift für Ethnologie*, xxxii. (1900) pp. 197 *sq.*

milk till they have been purified.   An ox is killed, and its
gall, intestines, and other parts are boiled with roots.   Of
this decoction the men have to take three gulps, and the
rest is sprinkled on their bodies.   The wounded man has
then to take a stick, spit on it thrice, point it thrice at the
enemy, and then throw it in his direction.   After that he
takes an emetic and is declared clean.[1]

In some of these accounts nothing is said of an
enforced seclusion, at least after the ceremonial cleansing,
but some South African tribes certainly require the slayer
of a very gallant foe in war to keep apart from his wife
and family for ten days after he has washed his body in
running water.   He also receives from the tribal doctor a
medicine which he chews with his food.[2]   When a Nandi
of British East Africa has killed a member of another tribe,
he paints one side of his body, spear, and sword red, and the
other side white.   For four days after the slaughter he is
considered unclean and may not go home.   He has to build
a small shelter by a river and live there ; he may not
associate with his wife or sweetheart, and he may eat
nothing but porridge, beef, and goat's flesh.   At the end of
the fourth day he must purify himself by taking a strong
purge made from the bark of the *segetet* tree and by
drinking goat's milk mixed with blood.[3]   Among the
Akikuya of British East Africa all who have shed human
blood must be purified.   The elders assemble and one of
them cuts a strip of hair from above both ears of each manslayer.   After that the warriors rub themselves with the
dung taken from the stomach of a sheep which has been
slaughtered for the occasion.   Finally their bodies are
cleansed with water.   All the hair remaining on their heads
is subsequently shaved off by their wives.   For a month
after the shedding of blood they may have no contact with

Seclusion and purification of man-slayers in Africa.

---

[1] Dudley Kidd, *The Essential Kafir*,
pp. 309 *sq.*

[2] Rev. J. Macdonald, "Manners,
Customs, Superstitions, and Religions
of South African Tribes," *Journal of the
Anthropological Institute*, xx. (1891)
p. 138; *id.*, *Light in Africa*, p.
220.

[3] A. C. Hollis, *The Nandi* (Oxford,
1909), p. 74.   As to the painting of
the body red on one side and white on
the other see also C. W. Hobley,
Eastern Uganda, pp. 38, 42 ; Sir H.
Johnston, *The Uganda Protectorate*,
ii. 868.   As to the custom of painting
the bodies of homicides, see below,
p. 178 note [1] and p. 186 note [1].

women.[1] On the contrary, when a Ketosh warrior of British East Africa, who has killed a foe in battle, returns home, "it is considered essential that he should have connection with his wife as soon as convenient; this is believed to prevent the spirit of his dead enemy from haunting and bewitching him."[2] An Angoni who has killed a man in battle is obliged to perform certain purificatory ceremonies before he may return to ordinary life. Amongst other things, he must be sure to make an incision in the corpse of his slain foe, in order to let the gases escape and so prevent the body from swelling. If he fails to do so, his own body will swell in proportion as the corpse becomes inflated.[3] Among the Ovambos of southern Africa, when the warriors return to their villages, those who have killed an enemy pass the first night in the open fields, and may not enter their houses until they have been cleansed of the guilt of blood by an older man, who smears them for this purpose with a kind of porridge.[4] Herero warriors on their return from battle may not approach the sacred hearth until they have been purified from the guilt of bloodshed. They crouch in a circle round the hearth, but at some distance from it, while the chief besprinkles their brows and temples with water in which branches of a holy bush have been placed.[5] Again, ancient Herero custom requires that he who has killed a man or a lion should have blood drawn from his breast and upper arm so as to trickle on the ground: a special name (outoni) is given to the cuts thus made; they must be made with a flint, not with an iron tool.[6] Among the Bantu tribes of Kavirondo, in eastern Africa, when a man has

[1] H. R. Tate, "Further Notes on the Kikuyu Tribe of British East Africa," *Journal of the Anthropological Institute*, xxxiv. (1904) p. 264.

[2] C. W. Hobley, "British East Africa," *Journal of the Anthropological Institute*, xxxiii. (1903) p. 353.

[3] Miss Alice Werner, *Natives of British Central Africa* (London, 1906), pp. 67 sq.

[4] H. Schinz, *Deutsch - Südwest-Afrika*, p. 321.

[5] P. H. Brincker, "Heidnisch-religiöse Sitten der Bantu, speciell der Ovaherero und Ovambo," *Globus*, lxvii. (1895) p. 289; id., "Charakter, Sitten und Gebräuche speciell der Bantu Deutsch-Südwestafrikas," *Mittheilungen des Seminars für orientalische Sprachen zu Berlin*, iii. (1900) Dritte Abtheilung, p. 76.

[6] *Id.*, "Beobachtungen über die Deisidämonie der Eingeborenen Deutsch - Südwest - Afrikas," *Globus*, lviii. (1890) p. 324; id., in *Globus*, lxvii. (1895) p. 289; id., in *Mittheilungen des Seminars für orientalische Sprachen zu Berlin*, iii. (1900) Dritte Abtheilung, p. 83.

killed an enemy in warfare he shaves his head on his return Purifica-
home, and his friends rub a medicine, which generally tion of
consists of goat's dung, over his body to prevent the spirit manslayers in Africa.
of the slain man from troubling him.[1] Exactly the same
custom is practised for the same reason by the Wageia
of German East Africa.[2] With the Ja-Luo of Kavirondo
the custom is somewhat different. Three days after his
return from the fight the warrior shaves his head. But
before he may enter his village he has to hang a live
fowl, head uppermost, round his neck ; then the bird is
decapitated and its head left hanging round his neck. Soon
after his return a feast is made for the slain man, in order
that his ghost may not haunt his slayer.[3] After the
slaughter of the Midianites the Israelitish warriors were
obliged to remain outside the camp for seven days : whoever had killed a man or touched the slain had to purify
himself and his captive. The spoil taken from the enemy
had also to be purified, according to its nature, either by fire
or water.[4] Similarly among the Basutos cattle taken from
the enemy are fumigated with bundles of lighted branches
before they are allowed to mingle with the herds of the
tribe.[5]

The Arunta of central Australia believe that when a Man-
party of men has been out against the enemy and taken a slayers in Australia
life, the spirit of the slain man follows the party on its guard
return and is constantly on the watch to do a mischief themselves
to those of the band who actually shed the blood. It against the
takes the form of a little bird called the *chichurkna*, and ghosts of the slain.
may be heard crying like a child in the distance as it
flies. If any of the slayers should fail to hear its cry,
he would become paralysed in his right arm and shoulder.
At night-time especially, when the bird is flying over
the camp, the slayers have to lie awake and keep the
right arm and shoulder carefully hidden, lest the bird should
look down upon and harm them. When once they have

---

[1] Sir H. Johnston, *The Uganda Protectorate* (London, 1902), ii. 743 *sq.* ; C. W. Hobley, *Eastern Uganda* (London, 1902), p. 20.

[2] M. Weiss, *Die Völkerstämme im Norden Deutsch - Ostafrikas* (Berlin,

1910), p. 198.

[3] Sir H. Johnston, *op. cit.* ii. 794 ; C. W. Hobley, *op. cit.* p. 31.

[4] Numbers xxxi. 19-24.

[5] E. Casalis, *The Basutos*, pp. 258 *sq.*

Manslayers in Australia guard themselves against the ghosts of the slain. heard its cry their minds are at ease, because the spirit of the dead then recognises that he has been detected, and can therefore do no mischief. On their return to their friends, as soon as they come in sight of the main camp, they begin to perform an excited war-dance, approaching in the form of a square and moving their shields as if to ward off something which was being thrown at them. This action is intended to repel the angry spirit of the dead man, who is striving to attack them. Next the men who did the deed of blood separate themselves from the others, and forming a line, with spears at rest and shields held out in front, stand silent and motionless like statues. A number of old women now approach with a sort of exulting skip and strike the shields of the manslayers with fighting-clubs till they ring again. They are followed by men who smite the shields with boomerangs. This striking of the shields is supposed to be a very effective way of frightening away the spirit of the dead man. The natives listen anxiously to the sounds emitted by the shields when they are struck; for if any man's shield gives forth a hollow sound under the blow, that man will not live long, but if it rings sharp and clear, he is safe. For some days after their return the slayers will not speak of what they have done, and continue to paint themselves all over with powdered charcoal, and to decorate their foreheads and noses with green twigs. Finally, they paint their bodies and faces with bright colours, and become free to talk about the affair; but still of nights they must lie awake listening for the plaintive cry of the bird in which they fancy they hear the voice of their victim.[1]

Seclusion of man-slayers in Polynesia. In the Washington group of the Marquesas Islands, the man who has slain an enemy in battle becomes tabooed for ten days, during which he may hold no intercourse with his wife, and may not meddle with fire. Hence another has to make fire and to cook for him. Nevertheless he is treated with marked distinction and receives presents of pigs.[2] In

---

[1] Spencer and Gillen, *Native Tribes of Central Australia*, pp. 493-495; *id.*, *Northern Tribes of Central Australia*, pp. 563-568. The writers suggest that the practice of painting the slayers black is meant to render them invisible to the ghost. A widow, on the contrary, must paint her body white, in order that her husband's spirit may see that she is mourning for him.

[2] G. H. von Langsdorff, *Reise um die Welt* (Frankfort, 1812), i. 114 *sq.*

Fiji any one who had clubbed a human being to death in war was consecrated or tabooed. He was smeared red by the king with turmeric from the roots of his hair to his heels. A hut was built, and in it he had to pass the next three nights, during which he might not lie down, but must sleep as he sat. Till the three nights had elapsed he might not change his garment, nor remove the turmeric, nor enter a house in which there was a woman.[1] In the Pelew Islands, when the men return from a warlike expedition in which they have taken a life, the young warriors who have been out fighting for the first time, and all who handled the slain, are shut up in the large council-house and become tabooed. They may not quit the edifice, nor bathe, nor touch a woman, nor eat fish ; their food is limited to coco-nuts and syrup. They rub themselves with charmed leaves and chew charmed betel. After three days they go together to bathe as near as possible to the spot where the man was killed.[2]

When the Tupi Indians of Brazil had made a prisoner in war, they used to bring him home amid great rejoicings, decked with the gorgeous plumage of tropical birds. In the village he was well treated : he received a house and furniture and was married to a wife. When he was thus comfortably installed, the relations and friends of his captor, who had the first pick, came and examined him and decided which of his limbs and joints they proposed to eat ; and according to their choice they were bound to provide him with victuals. Thus he might live for months or years, treated like a king, supplied with all the delicacies of the country, and rearing a family of children who, when they were big, might or might not be eaten with their father. While he was thus being fattened like a capon for the slaughter, he wore a necklace of fruit or of fish-bones strung on a cotton thread. This was the measure of his life. For every fruit or every bone on the string he had a month to live ; and as each moon waned and vanished they took a fruit or a bone from the necklace.

Seclusion and purification of man-slayers among the Tupi Indians of Brazil.

---

[1] T. Williams, *Fiji and the Fijians,*[2] i. 55 *sq.*

[2] J. Kubary, *Die socialen Einrich-* *tungen der Pelauer* (Berlin, 1885), pp. 126 *sq.*, 130.

Seclusion
and purifi-
cation of
manslayers
among
the Tupi
Indians
of Brazil.When only one remained, they sent out invitations to
friends and neighbours far and near, who flocked in, sometimes to the number of ten or twelve thousand, to witness
the spectacle and partake of the feast ; for often a number
of prisoners were to die the same day, father, mother, and
children all together.   As a rule they shewed a remarkable
stolidity and indifference to death.   The club with which
they were to be despatched was elaborately prepared by the
women, who adorned it with tassels of feathers, smeared it
with the pounded shells of a macaw's eggs, and traced lines
on the egg-shell powder.   Then they hung it to a pole,
above the ground, in an empty hut, and sang around it all
night.   The executioner, who was painted grey with ashes
and his whole body covered with the beautiful feathers of
parrots and other birds of gay plumage, performed his office
by striking the victim on the head from behind and dashing
out his brains.   No sooner had he despatched the prisoner
than he retired to his house, where he had to stay all that
day without eating or drinking, while the rest of the people
feasted on the body of the victim or victims.   And for
three days he was obliged to fast and remain in seclusion.
All this time he lay in his hammock and might not set foot
on the ground ; if he had to go anywhere, he was carried
by bearers.   They thought that, were he to break this rule,
some disaster would befall him or he would die.   Meantime
he was given a small bow and passed his time in shooting
arrows into wax.   This he did in order to keep his hand
and aim steady.   In some of the tribes they rubbed the
pulse of the executioner with one of the eyes of his victim,
and hung the mouth of the murdered man like a bracelet
on his arm.   Afterwards he made incisions in his breast,
arms, and legs, and other parts of his body with a saw
made of the teeth of an animal.   An ointment and a black
powder were then rubbed into the wounds, which left
ineffaceable scars so artistically arranged that they presented the appearance of a tightly-fitting garment.   It was
believed that he would die if he did not thus draw blood
from his own body after slaughtering the captive.[1]   We

---

[1] F. A. Thevet, *Les Singularitez de
la France Antarctique, autrement*   *nommée Amerique* (Antwerp, 1558),
pp. 74-76 ; *id., Cosmographie univer-*

may conjecture that the original intention of these customs was to guard the executioner against the angry and dangerous ghosts of his victims.

Among the Natchez of North America young braves who had taken their first scalps were obliged to observe certain rules of abstinence for six months. They might not sleep with their wives nor eat flesh; their only food was fish and hasty-pudding. If they broke these rules, they believed that the soul of the man they had killed would work their death by magic, that they would gain no more successes over the enemy, and that the least wound inflicted on them would prove mortal.[1]   When a Choctaw had killed an enemy and taken his scalp, he went into mourning for a month, during which he might not comb his hair, and if his head itched he might not scratch it except with a little stick which he wore fastened to his wrist for the purpose.[2]   This ceremonial mourning for the enemies they had slain was not uncommon among the North American Indians.   Thus the Dacotas, when they had killed a foe, unbraided their hair, blackened themselves all over, and wore a small knot of swan's down on the top of the head. " They dress as mourners yet rejoice." [3]   A Thompson River Indian of British Columbia, who had slain an enemy, used to blacken his own face, lest his victim's ghost should blind him.[4]   When the Osages have mourned over their own dead, " they will mourn for the foe just as if he was a friend." [5]   From observing the great respect paid by

Seclusion and purification of man-slayers among the North American Indians.

selle (Paris, 1575), pp. 944 [978] sq. ; Pero de Magalhanes de Gandavo, Histoire de la province de Sancta-Cruz (Paris, 1837), pp. 134-141 (H. Ternaux-Compans, Voyages, relations, et mémoires originaux pour servir à l'histoire de la découverte de l'Amérique ; the original of Gandavo's work was published in Portuguese at Lisbon in 1576) ; J. Lery, Historia navigationis in Brasiliam, quae et America dicitur (1586), pp. 183-194 ; The Captivity of Hans Stade of Hesse, in A.D. 1547-1555, among the Wild Tribes of Eastern Brazil, translated by A. Tootal (London, 1874), pp. 155-159 ; J. F. Lafitau, Mœurs des sauvages amériquains, ii. 292 sqq. ; R.

Southey, History of Brazil, i.[2] 227- 232.
[1] " Relation des Natchez," Voyages au nord, ix. 24 (Amsterdam, 1737) ; Lettres édifiantes et curieuses, vii. 26 ; Charlevoix, Histoire de la Nouvelle France, vi. 186 sq.
[2] Bossu, Nouveaux Voyages aux Indes occidentales (Paris, 1768), ii. 94.
[3] H. R. Schoolcraft, Indian Tribes, iv. 63.
[4] J. Teit, " The Thompson Indians of British Columbia," Memoir of the American Museum of Natural History, The Jesup North Pacific Expedition, vol. i. part iv. (April 1900) p. 357.
[5] J. O. Dorsey, " An Account of the War Customs of the Osages," American Naturalist, xviii. (1884) p. 126.

the Indians to the scalps they had taken, and listening to the mournful songs which they howled to the shades of their victims, Catlin was convinced that "they have a superstitious dread of the spirits of their slain enemies, and many conciliatory offices to perform, to ensure their own peace."[1]   When a Pima Indian has killed an Apache, he must undergo purication. Sixteen days he fasts, and only after the fourth day is he allowed to drink a little pinole. During the whole time he may not touch meat nor salt, nor look on a blazing fire, nor speak to a human being. He lives alone in the woods, waited on by an old woman, who brings him his scanty dole of food. He bathes often in a river, and keeps his head covered almost the whole time with a plaster of mud. On the seventeenth day a large space is cleared near the village and a fire lit in the middle of it. The men of the tribe form a circle round the fire, and outside of it sit all the warriors who have just been purified, each in a small excavation. Some of the old men then take the weapons of the purified and dance with them in the circle, after which both the slayer and his weapon are considered clean ; but not until four days later is the man allowed to return to his family.[2]   No doubt the peace enforced by the

Seclusion and purification of manslayers among the Pima Indians.

[1] G. Catlin, *North American Indians*, i. 246.

[2] H. H. Bancroft, *Native Races of the Pacific States*, i. 553; Capt. Grossman, cited in *Ninth Annual Report of the Bureau of Ethnology* (Washington, 1892), pp. 475 *sq.* The custom of plastering the head with mud was observed by Egyptian women in mourning (Herodotus, ii. 85 ; Diodorus Siculus, i. 91). Among some of the aboriginal tribes of Victoria and New South Wales widows wore a thick skullcap of clay or burned gypsum, forming a cast of the head, for some months after the death ; when the period of mourning was over, the cap was removed, baked in the fire, and laid on the husband's grave. One of these widows' caps is exhibited in the British Museum. See T. L. Mitchell, *Three Expeditions into the Interior of Eastern Australia* (London, 1838), i. 251 *sq.* ; E. J. Eyre, *Journals of Expeditions of Discovery into Central Australia*, ii. 354 ; G. F. Angas, *Savage Life and Scenes in Australia and New Zealand* (London, 1847), i. 86 ; G. Krefft, "On the Manners and Customs of the Aborigines of the Lower Murray and Darling," *Transactions of the Philosophical Society of New South Wales, 1862-1865* (Sydney, 1866), pp. 373 *sq.* ; J. Dawson, *Australian Aborigines*, p. 66 ; R. Brough Smyth, *The Aborigines of Victoria*, i. p. xxx. ; W. Stanbridge, "On the Aborigines of Victoria," *Transactions of the Ethnological Society of London*, N.S., i. (1861) p. 298 ; A. Oldfield, "The Aborigines of Australia," *ibid.* iii. (1865) p. 248 ; F. Bonney, "On some Customs of the Aborigines of the River Darling, New South Wales," *Journal of the Anthropological Institute*, xiii. (1884) p. 135 ; E. M. Curr, *The Australian Race*, i. 88, ii. 238 *sq.*, iii. 21 ; A. W. Howitt, *Native Tribes of South-East Australia*, pp. 248, 452 ; R. Etheridge, jun., "The 'Widow's Cap' of the Australian

government of the United States has, along with tribal warfare, abolished also these quaint customs. A fuller account of them has been given by a recent writer, and it deserves to be quoted at length. " There was no law among the Pimas," he says, " observed with greater strictness than that which required purification and expiation for the deed that was at the same time the most lauded——the killing of an enemy. For sixteen days the warrior fasted in seclusion and observed meanwhile a number of tabus. . . . Attended by an old man, the warrior who had to expiate the crime of blood guilt retired to the groves along the river bottom at some distance from the villages or wandered about the adjoining hills. During the period of sixteen days he was not allowed to touch his head with his fingers or his hair would turn white. If he touched his face it would become wrinkled. He kept a stick to scratch his head with, and at the end of every four days this stick was buried at the root and on the west side of a cat's claw tree and a new stick was made of greasewood, arrow bush, or any other convenient shrub. He then bathed in the river, no matter how cold the temperature. The feast of victory which his friends were observing in the meantime at the village lasted eight days. At the end of that time, or when his period of retirement was half-completed, the warrior might go to his home to get a fetish made from the hair of the Apache whom he had killed. The hair was wrapped in eagle down and tied with a cotton string and kept in a long medicine basket. He drank no water for the first two days and fasted for the first four. After that time he was supplied with pinole by his attendant, who also instructed him as to his future conduct, telling him that he must henceforth stand back until

Aborigines," *Proceedings of the Linnaean Society of New South Wales for the Year 1899*, xxiv. (Sydney, 1900) pp. 333-345 (with illustrations). In the Andaman Islands mourners coat their heads with a thick mass of white clay (Jagor, in *Verhandlungen der Berliner Gesellschaft für Anthropologie*, 1876, p. (57); M. V. Portman, "Disposal of the Dead among the Andamanese," *Indian Antiquary*, xxv. (1896) p. 57; compare E. H. Man, *Aboriginal In-* habitants of the Andaman Islands, pp. 73, 75). Among the Bahima of the Uganda Protectorate, when herdsmen water their cattle in the evening, they plaster their faces and bodies with white clay, at the same time stiffening their hair with mud into separate lumps. This mud is left on the head for days till it crumbles into dust (Sir H. Johnston, *The Uganda Protectorate*, ii. 626, compare 620).

Seclusion
and purifi-
cation of
manslayers
among the
Pimas and
Apaches. all others were served when partaking of food and drink. If he was a married man his wife was not allowed to eat salt during his retirement, else she would suffer from the owl disease which causes stiff limbs. The explanation offered for the observance of this law of lustration is that if it is not obeyed the warrior's limbs will become stiffened or paralyzed."[1] The Apaches, the enemies of the Pimas, purify themselves for the slaughter of their foes by means of baths in the sweat-house, singing, and other rites. These ceremonies they perform for all the dead simultaneously after their return home; but the Pimas, more punctilious on this point, resort to their elaborate ceremonies of purification the moment a single one of their own band or of the enemy has been laid low.[2] How heavily these religious scruples must have told against the Pimas in their wars with their ferocious enemies is obvious enough. "This long period of retirement immediately after a battle," says an American writer, "greatly diminished the value of the Pimas as scouts and allies for the United States troops operating against the Apaches. The bravery of the Pimas was praised by all army officers having any experience with them, but Captain Bourke and others have complained of their unreliability, due solely to their rigid observance of this religious law."[3] In nothing, perhaps, is the penalty which superstition sooner or later entails on its devotees more prompt and crushing than in the operations of war.

Taboos
observed
by Indians
who had
slain Es-
quimaux. Far away from the torrid home of the Pima and Apaches, an old traveller witnessed ceremonies of the same sort practised near the Arctic Circle by some Indians who had surprised and brutally massacred an unoffending and helpless party of Esquimaux. His description is so interesting that I will quote it in full. "Among the various superstitious customs of those people, it is worth remarking, and ought to have been mentioned in its proper place, that immediately after my companions had killed the Esquimaux at the Copper River, they considered themselves in a state of uncleanness, which induced

---

[1] F. Russell, "The Pima Indians," *Twenty-Sixth Annual Report of the Bureau of American Ethnology* (Washington, 1908), pp. 204 *sq.*

[2] J. G. Bourke, *On the Border with*

Crook, p. 203.

[3] F. Russell, "The Pima Indians," *Twenty-Sixth Annual Report of the Bureau of American Ethnology* (Washington, 1908), p. 204.

them to practise some very curious and unusual ceremonies. In the first place, all who were absolutely concerned in the murder were prohibited from cooking any kind of victuals, either for themselves or others.   As luckily there were two in company who had not shed blood, they were employed always as cooks till we joined the women.   This circumstance was exceedingly favourable on my side; for had there been no persons of the above description in company, that task, I was told, would have fallen on me; which would have been no less fatiguing and troublesome, than humiliating and vexatious.   When the victuals were cooked, all the murderers took a kind of red earth, or oker, and painted all the space between the nose and chin, as well as the greater part of their cheeks, almost to the ears, before they would taste a bit, and would not drink out of any other dish, or smoke out of any other pipe, but their own; and none of the others seemed willing to drink or smoke out of theirs. We had no sooner joined the women, at our return from the expedition, than there seemed to be an universal spirit of emulation among them, vying who should first make a suit of ornaments for their husbands, which consisted of bracelets for the wrists, and a band for the forehead, composed of porcupine quills and moose-hair, curiously wrought on leather.   The custom of painting the mouth and part of the cheeks before each meal, and drinking and smoking out of their own utensils, was strictly and invariably observed, till the winter began to set in; and during the whole of that time they would never kiss any of their wives or children. They refrained also from eating many parts of the deer and other animals, particularly the head, entrails, and blood; and during their uncleanness, their victuals were never sodden in water, but dried in the sun, eaten quite raw, or broiled, when a fire fit for the purpose could be procured.   When the time arrived that was to put an end to these ceremonies, the men, without a female being present, made a fire at some distance from the tents, into which they threw all their ornaments, pipe-stems, and dishes, which were soon consumed to ashes; after which a feast was prepared, consisting of such articles as they had long been prohibited from eating; and when all was over, each man was at liberty to eat, drink, and smoke as he pleased; and also to kiss his wives and children at discretion, which they seemed to do with more raptures than I had ever known them do it either before or since."[1]

The purification of murderers, like that of warriors who have slain enemies, was probably intended to avert or

Thus we see that warriors who have taken the life of a foe in battle are temporarily cut off from free intercourse with their fellows, and especially with their wives, and must undergo certain rites of purification before they are readmitted to society. Now if the purpose of their seclusion and of the expiatory rites which they have to perform is, as we have been led to believe, no other than to shake off, frighten, or appease the angry spirit of the slain man,

[1] S. Hearne, *Journey from Prince of Wales's Fort in Hudson's Bay to the Northern Ocean* (London, 1795), pp. 204-206. The custom of painting the face or the body of the manslayer, which may perhaps be intended to disguise him from the vengeful spirit of the slain, is practised by other peoples, as by the Nandi (see above, p. 175). Among the Ba-Yaka of the Congo Free State a man who has been slain in battle is supposed to send his soul to avenge his death on his slayer; but the slayer can protect himself against the ghost by wearing the red tail-feathers of a parrot in his hair and painting his forehead red (E. Torday and T. A. Joyce, "Notes on the Ethnography of the Ba-Yaka," *Journal of the Anthropological Institute*, xxxvi. (1906) pp. 50 *sq.*). Among the Borâna Gallas, when a war-party has returned to the village, the victors who have slain a foe are washed by the women with a mixture of fat and butter, and their faces are painted with red and white (Ph. Paulitschke, *Ethnographie Nord-ost-Afrikas: die materielle Cultur der Danâkil, Galla und Somâl* (Berlin, 1893), p. 258). When Masai warriors kill enemies in fight they paint the right half of their own bodies red and the left half white (A. C. Hollis, *The Masai*, p. 353). Among the Wagogo of German East Africa, a man who has killed an enemy in battle paints a red circle round his right eye and a black circle round his left eye (Rev. H. Cole, "Notes on the Wagogo of German East Africa," *Journal of the Anthropological Institute*, xxxii. (1902) p. 314). Among the Angoni of central Africa, after a successful raid, the leader calls together all who have killed an enemy and paints their faces and heads white; also he paints a white band round the body under the arms and across the chest (*British Central Africa Gazette*, No. 86, vol. v. No. 6 (April 30, 1898), p. 2). A Koossa Caffre who has slain a man is accounted unclean. He must roast some flesh on a fire kindled with wood of a special sort which imparts a bitter flavour to the meat. This flesh he eats, and afterwards blackens his face with the ashes of the fire. After a time he may wash himself, rinse his mouth with fresh milk, and paint himself brown again. From that moment he is clean (H. Lichtenstein, *Reisen im südlichen Africa*, i. 418). Among the Yabim of German New Guinea, when the relations of a murdered man have accepted a bloodwit instead of avenging his death, they must allow the family of the murderer to mark them with chalk on the brow. If this is not done, the ghost of their murdered kinsman may come and trouble them for not doing their duty by him; for example, he may drive away their swine or loosen their teeth (K. Vetter, in *Nachrichten über Kaiser Wilhelms-Land und den Bismarck-Archipel*, 1897, p. 99). In this last case the marking the face with chalk seems to be clearly a disguise to outwit the ghost.

we may safely conjecture that the similar purification of appease the ghosts of the slain.
homicides and murderers, who have imbrued their hands in
the blood of a fellow-tribesman, had at first the same significance, and that the idea of a moral or spiritual regeneration
symbolised by the washing, the fasting, and so on, was merely
a later interpretation put upon the old custom by men who
had outgrown the primitive modes of thought in which the
custom originated. The conjecture will be confirmed if we
can shew that savages have actually imposed certain restrictions on the murderer of a fellow-tribesman from a definite
fear that he is haunted by the ghost of his victim. This
we can do with regard to the Omahas, a tribe of the
Siouan stock in North America. Among these Indians the
kinsmen of a murdered man had the right to put the
murderer to death, but sometimes they waived their right in
consideration of presents which they consented to accept.
When the life of the murderer was spared, he had to observe
certain stringent rules for a period which varied from two to
four years. He must walk barefoot, and he might eat no warm
food, nor raise his voice, nor look around. He was compelled to pull his robe about him and to have it tied at the
neck even in hot weather ; he might not let it hang loose or
fly open. He might not move his hands about, but had to
keep them close to his body. He might not comb his hair,
and it might not be blown about by the wind. When the
tribe went out hunting, he was obliged to pitch his tent
about a quarter of a mile from the rest of the people " lest
the ghost of his victim should raise a high wind, which might
cause damage." Only one of his kindred was allowed to
remain with him at his tent. No one wished to eat with him,
for they said, " If we eat with him whom Wakanda hates,
Wakanda will hate us." Sometimes he wandered at night
crying and lamenting his offence. At the end of his long
isolation the kinsmen of the murdered man heard his crying
and said, " It is enough. Begone, and walk among the crowd.
Put on moccasins and wear a good robe." [1] Here the reason
alleged for keeping the murderer at a considerable distance
from the hunters gives the clue to all the other restrictions

[1] J. Owen Dorsey, "Omaha Soci-
ology," *Third Annual Report of the*
Bureau of Ethnology (Washington,
1884), p. 369.

Ancient
Greek
dread of
the ghosts
of the
slain.

laid on him : he was haunted and therefore dangerous. The
ancient Greeks believed that the soul of a man who had just
been killed was wroth with his slayer and troubled him ;
wherefore it was needful even for the involuntary homicide
to depart from his country for a year until the anger of the
dead man had cooled down ; nor might the slayer return
until sacrifice had been offered and ceremonies of purification
performed. If his victim chanced to be a foreigner, the
homicide had to shun the native country of the dead man as
well as his own.[1]   The legend of the matricide Orestes, how
he roamed from place to place pursued by the Furies of his
murdered mother, and none would sit at meat with him, or take
him in, till he had been purified,[2] reflects faithfully the real
Greek dread of such as were still haunted by an angry ghost.
When the turbulent people of Cynaetha, after perpetrating
an atrocious massacre, sent an embassy to Sparta, every
Arcadian town through which the envoys passed on their
journey ordered them out of its walls at once ; and the
Mantineans, after the embassy had departed, even instituted
a solemn purification of the city and its territory by carrying
sacrificial victims round them both.[3]

Taboos
imposed on
men who
have par-
taken of
human
flesh.

Among the Kwakiutl Indians of British Columbia, men
who have partaken of human flesh as a ceremonial rite
are subject for a long time afterwards to many restrictions
or taboos of the sort we have been dealing with. They
may not touch their wives for a whole year ; and during the
same time they are forbidden to work or gamble. For four
months they must live alone in their bedrooms, and when
they are obliged to quit the house for a necessary purpose,
they may not go out at the ordinary door, but must use
only the secret door in the rear of the house. On such
occasions each of them is attended by all the rest, carrying
small sticks. They must all sit down together on a long
log, then get up, then sit down again, repeating this three

---

[1] Plato, *Laws*, ix. pp. 865 D-866 A ;
Demosthenes, *Contra Aristocr.* pp. 643
sq. ; Hesychius, *s.v.* ἀπενιαυτισμός.

[2] Euripides, *Iphig. in Taur.* 940
sqq. ; Pausanias, ii. 31. 8. We may
compare the wanderings of the other
matricide Alcmaeon, who could find no

rest till he came to a new land on
which the sun had not yet shone when
he murdered his mother (Thucydides,
ii. 102 ; Apollodorus, iii. 7. 5 ; Pausanias, viii. 24. 8).

[3] Polybius, iv. 21.

times before they are allowed to remain seated. Before they rise they must turn round four times. Then they go back to the house. Before entering they must raise their feet four times; with the fourth step they really pass the door, taking care to enter with the right foot foremost. In the doorway they turn four times and walk slowly into the house. They are not permitted to look back. During the four months of their seclusion each man in eating must use a spoon, dish, and kettle of his own, which are thrown away at the end of the period. Before he draws water from a bucket or a brook, he must dip his cup into it thrice; and he may not take more than four mouthfuls at one time. He must carry a wing-bone of an eagle and drink through it, for his lips may not touch the brim of his cup. Also he keeps a copper nail to scratch his head with, for were his own nails to touch his own skin they would drop off. For sixteen days after he has partaken of human flesh he may not eat any warm food, and for the whole of the four months he is forbidden to cool hot food by blowing on it with his breath. At the end of winter, when the season of ceremonies is over, he feigns to have forgotten the ordinary ways of men, and has to learn everything anew. The reason for these remarkable restrictions imposed on men who have eaten human flesh is not stated; but we may surmise that fear of the ghost of the man whose body was eaten has at least a good deal to do with them. We are confirmed in our conjecture by observing that though these cannibals sometimes content themselves with taking bites out of living people, the rules in question are especially obligatory on them after they have devoured a corpse. Moreover, the careful treatment of the bones of the victim points to the same conclusion; for during the four months of seclusion observed by the cannibals, the bones of the person on whom they feasted are kept alternately for four days at a time under rocks in the sea and in their bedrooms on the north side of the house, where the sun cannot shine on them. Finally the bones are taken out of the house, tied up, weighted with a stone, and thrown into deep water, "because it is believed that if they were buried they would come back and take their master's soul." [1]   This seems to mean that if the bones of the victim were buried, his ghost would come back and fetch away the souls of the men who had eaten his body. The Gebars, a cannibal tribe in the north of New Guinea, are much afraid of the spirit of a slain man or woman. Among them persons who have partaken of human flesh for the first time reside for a month afterwards in a small hut and may not enter the dwelling-house. [2]

§ 6. *Hunters and Fishers tabooed*

Hunters and fishers have to observe taboos and undergo rites of purification, which are probably dictated by a fear of the spirits of the animals or fish which they have killed or intended to kill.
In savage society the hunter and the fisherman have often to observe rules of abstinence and to submit to ceremonies of purification of the same sort as those which are obligatory on the warrior and the manslayer; and though we cannot in all cases perceive the exact purpose which these rules and ceremonies are supposed to serve, we may with some probability assume that, just as the dread of the spirits of his enemies is the main motive for the seclusion and purification of the warrior who hopes to take or has already taken their lives, so the huntsman or fisherman who complies with similar customs is principally actuated by a fear of the spirits of the beasts, birds, or fish which he has killed or intends to kill. For the savage commonly conceives animals to be endowed with souls and intelligences like his own, and hence he naturally treats them with similar respect. Just as he attempts to appease the ghosts of the men he has slain, so he essays to propitiate the spirits of the animals he has killed. These ceremonies of propitiation will be described later on in this work; [3] here we have to deal, first, with the taboos observed by the hunter and the

---

[1] Fr. Boas, "The Social Organization and the Secret Societies of the Kwakiutl Indians," *Report of the U.S. National Museum for 1895*, pp. 440, 537 *sq.*

[2] Th. H. Ruys, "Bezoek an den Kannibalenstam van Noord Nieuw-Guinea," *Tijdschrift van het koninklijk Nederlandsch Aardrijkskundig Genootschap*, Tweede Serie, xxiii. (1906) p. 328. Among these savages the genitals of a murdered man are eaten by

an old woman, and the genitals of a murdered woman are eaten by an old man. What the object of this curious practice may be is not apparent. Perhaps the intention is to unsex and disarm the dangerous ghost. On the dread of ghosts, especially the ghosts of those who have died a violent death, see further *Psyche's Task*, pp. 52 *sqq.*

[3] Meantime I may refer the reader to *The Golden Bough*, Second Edition, vol. ii. pp. 389 *sqq.*

fisherman before or during the hunting and fishing seasons, and, second, with the ceremonies of purification which have to be practised by these men on returning with their booty from a successful chase.

While the savage respects, more or less, the souls of all animals, he treats with particular deference the spirits of such as are either especially useful to him or formidable on account of their size, strength, or ferocity. Accordingly the hunting and killing of these valuable or dangerous beasts are subject to more elaborate rules and ceremonies than the slaughter of comparatively useless and insignificant creatures. Thus the Indians of Nootka Sound prepared themselves for catching whales by observing a fast for a week, during which they ate very little, bathed in the water several times a day, sang, and rubbed their bodies, limbs, and faces with shells and bushes till they looked as if they had been severely torn with briars. They were likewise required to abstain from any commerce with their women for the like period, this last condition being considered indispensable to their success. A chief who failed to catch a whale has been known to attribute his failure to a breach of chastity on the part of his men.[1] It should be remarked that the conduct thus prescribed as a preparation for whaling is precisely that which in the same tribe of Indians was required of men about to go on the war-path.[2] Rules of the same sort are, or were formerly, observed by Malagasy whalers. For eight days before they went to sea the crew of a whaler used to fast, abstaining from women and liquor, and confessing their most secret faults to each other ; and if any man was found to have sinned deeply he was forbidden to share in the expedition.[3] In the island of Kadiak, off the south coast of Alaska, whalers were reckoned unclean during the fishing season, and nobody would eat out of the same dish with them or even come near them. Yet we are told that great respect was paid to them, and that they were regarded as

Taboos and cere- monies observed before catching whales.

[1] *Narrative of the Adventures and Sufferings of John R. Jewitt* (Middletown, 1820), pp. 133, 136.

[2] See above, pp. 160 *sq.*

[3] Baron d'Unienville, *Statistique de l'Île Maurice* (Paris, 1838), iii. 271. Compare A. van Gennep, *Tabou et Totémisme à Madagascar* (Paris, 1904), p. 253, who refers to Le Gentil, *Voyage dans les Mers de l'Inde* (Paris, 1781), ii. 562.

the purveyors of their country.[1]   Though it is not expressly said it seems to be implied, and on the strength of analogy we may assume, that these Kadiak whalers had to remain chaste so long as the whaling season lasted.   In the island of Mabuiag continence was imposed on the people both before they went to hunt the dugong and while the turtles were pairing.   The turtle - season lasts during parts of October and November ; and if at that time unmarried persons had sexual intercourse with each other, it was believed that when the canoe approached the floating turtle, the male would separate from the female and both would dive down in different directions.[2]   So at Mowat in New Guinea men have no relation with women when the turtle are coupling, though there is considerable laxity of morals at other times.[3]   Among the Motu of Port Moresby, in New Guinea, chastity is enjoined before fishing and wallaby-hunting ; they believe that men who have been unchaste will be unable to catch the fish and the wallabies, which will turn round and jeer at their pursuers.[4]   Among the tribes about the mouth of the Wanigela River in New Guinea the preparations for fishing turtle and dugong are most elaborate. They begin two months before the fishing.   A headman is appointed who becomes holy.   On his strict observance of the laws of the dugong net depends the success of the season.   While the men of the village are making the nets, this sanctified leader lives entirely secluded from his family, and may only eat a roasted banana or two after the sun has gone down.   Every evening at sundown he goes ashore and, stripping himself of all his ornaments, which he is never allowed to doff at other times, bathes near where the dugongs feed ; as he does so he throws scraped coco-nut and scented herbs and gums into the water to charm the dugong.[5]

Taboos observed as a preparation for catching dugong and turtle.

[1] U. Lisiansky, *Voyage Round the World* (London, 1814), pp. 174, 209.

[2] A. C. Haddon, "The Ethnography of the Western Tribe of Torres Straits," *Journal of the Anthropological Institute,* xix. (1890) p. 397 ; *Reports of the Cambridge Anthropological Expedition to Torres Straits,* v. 271.

[3] A. C. Haddon, in *Journal of the Anthropological Institute,* xix. (1890)

p. 467.

[4] *Reports of the Cambridge Anthropological Expedition to Torres Straits,* v. 271 note.

[5] R. E. Guise, "On the Tribes inhabiting the Mouth of the Wanigela River," *Journal of the Anthropological Institute,* xxviii. (1899) p. 218.   The account refers specially to Bulaa, which the author describes (pp. 205, 217) as

Among the Roro-speaking tribes of British New Guinea the Taboos observed as a pre- paration for hunting and fishing. magician who performs ceremonies for the success of a wallaby hunt must abstain from intercourse with his wife for a month before the hunt takes place ; and he may not eat food cooked by his wife or by any other woman.[1] In the island of Uap, one of the Caroline group, every fisherman plying his craft lies under a most strict taboo during the whole of the fishing season, which lasts for six or eight weeks. Whenever he is on shore he must spend all his time in the men's clubhouse (*failu*), and under no pretext whatever may he visit his own house or so much as look upon the faces of his wife and womenkind. Were he but to steal a glance at them, they think that flying fish must inevitably bore out his eyes at night. If his wife, mother, or daughter brings any gift for him or wishes to talk with him, she must stand down towards the shore with her back turned to the men's clubhouse. Then the fisherman may go out and speak to her, or with his back turned to her he may receive what she has brought him ; after which he must return at once to his rigorous confinement. Indeed the fishermen may not even join in dance and song with the other men of the clubhouse in the evening ; they must keep to themselves and be silent.[2] In the Pelew Islands, also, which belong to the Caroline group, fisher- men are likewise debarred from intercourse with women, since it is believed that any such intercourse would infallibly have a prejudicial effect on the fishing. The same taboo is said to be observed in all the other islands of the South Sea.[3] In

"a marine village" and "the greatest fishing village in New Guinea." Prob- ably it is built out over the water. This would explain the allusion to the sanctified headman going ashore daily at sundown.

[1] Captain F. R. Barton and Dr. Strong, in C. G. Seligmann's *The Melanesians of British New Guinea* (Cambridge, 1910), pp. 292, 293 *sq.*

[2] W. H. Furness, *The Island of Stone Money, Uap of the Carolines* (Philadelphia and London, 1910), pp. 38 *sq.*, 44 *sq.* Though the fisherman may have nothing to do with his wife and family, he is not wholly debarred from female society ; for each of the

men's clubhouses has one young woman, or sometimes two young women, who have been captured from another dis- trict, and who cohabit promiscuously with all the men of the clubhouse. The name for one of these concubines is *mispil.* See W. H. Furness, *op. cit.* pp. 46 *sqq.* There is a similar practice of polyandry in the men's clubhouses of the Pelew Islands. See J. Kubary, *Die socialen Einrichtungen der Pelauer* (Berlin, 1885), pp. 50 *sqq.* Compare *Adonis, Attis, Osiris*, Second Edition, pp. 435 *sq.*

[3] J. S. Kubary, *Ethnographische Beiträge zur Kenntnis des Karolinen Archipels* (Leyden, 1895), p. 127.

Taboos and ceremonies observed at the hatching and pairing of silkworms.

Mirzapur, when the seed of the silkworm is brought into the house, the Kol or Bhuiyar puts it in a place which has been carefully plastered with holy cow-dung to bring good luck. From that time the owner must be careful to avoid ceremonial impurity. He must give up cohabitation with his wife; he may not sleep on a bed, nor shave himself, nor cut his nails, nor anoint himself with oil, nor eat food cooked with butter, nor tell lies, nor do anything else that he deems wrong. He vows to Singarmati Devi that if the worms are duly born he will make her an offering. When the cocoons open and the worms appear, he assembles the women of the house and they sing the same song as at the birth of a baby, and red lead is smeared on the parting of the hair of all the married women of the neighbourhood. When the worms pair, rejoicings are made as at a marriage.[1] Thus the silk-worms are treated as far as possible like human beings. Hence the custom which prohibits the commerce of the sexes while the worms are hatching may be only an extension, by analogy, of the rule which is observed by many races, that the husband may not cohabit with his wife during pregnancy and lactation.

Taboos observed by fishermen in Uganda.

On Lake Victoria Nyanza the Baganda fishermen use a long stout line which is supported on the surface of the water by wooden floats, while short lines with baited hooks attached to them depend from it at frequent intervals. The place where the fisherman makes his line, whether in his hut or his garden, is tabooed. People may not step over his cords or tools, and he himself has to observe a number of restrictions. He may not go near his wife or any other woman. He eats alone, works alone, sleeps alone. He may not wash, except in the lake. He may not eat salt or meat or butter. He may not smear any fat on his body. When the line is ready he goes to the god, asks his blessing on it, and offers him a pot of beer. In return he receives from

---

[1] W. Crooke, *Popular Religion and Folk - lore of Northern India* (Westminster, 1896), ii. 257. In Chota Nagpur and the Central Provinces of India the rearers of silk-worms "carefully watch over and protect the worms, and while the rearing is going on, live with great cleanliness and self-denial, abstaining from alcohol and all intercourse with women, and adhering very strictly to certain ceremonial observances. The business is a very precarious one, much depending on favourable weather" (*Indian Museum Notes, issued by the Trustees*, vol. i. No. 3 (Calcutta, 1890), p. 160).

the deity a stick or bit of wood to fasten to the line, and also some medicine of herbs to smoke and blow over the water in order that the fish may come to the line and be caught.   Then he carries the line to the lake.   If in going thither he should stumble over a stone or a tree-root, he takes it with him, and he does the same with any grass-seeds that may stick to his clothes.   These stones, roots, and seeds he puts on the line, believing that just as he stumbled over them and they stuck to him, so the fish will also stumble over them and stick to the line.   The taboo lasts till he has caught his first fish.   If his wife has kept the taboo, he eats the fish with her ; but if she has broken it, she may not partake of the fish.   After that if he wishes to go in to his wife, he must take his line out of the water and place it in a tree or some other place of safety ; he is then free to be with her.   But so long as the line is in the water, he must keep apart from women, or the fish would at once leave the shore.   Any breach of this taboo renders the line useless to him.   He must sell it and make a new one and offer an expiatory offering to the god.[1]   Again, in Uganda the fisherman offers fish to his canoe, believing that if he neglected to make this offering more than twice, his net would catch nothing.   The fish thus offered to the canoe is eaten by the fishermen.   But if at the time of emptying the traps there is any man in the canoe who has committed adultery, eaten flesh or salt, or rubbed his body with butter or fat, that man is not allowed to partake of the fish offered to the canoe.   And if the sinner has not confessed his fault to the priest and been purified, the catch will be small. When the adulterer has confessed his sin, the priest calls the husband of the guilty woman and tells him of her crime. Her paramour has to wear a sign to shew that he is doing penance, and he makes a feast for the injured husband, which the latter is obliged to accept in token of reconcilia- tion.   After that the husband may not punish either of the erring couple ; the sin is atoned for and they are able to catch fish again.[2]   Among the Bangala of the Upper Congo,

[1] The Rev. J. Roscoe in letters to me dated Mengo, Uganda, April 23 and June 6, 1903.

[2] Rev. J. Roscoe, "Further Notes on the Manners and Customs of the Baganda," *Journal of the Anthro- pological Institute,* xxxii. (1902) p. 56.

Continence observed by Bangala fishermen and hunters.

while fishermen are making their traps, they must observe strict continence, and the restriction lasts until the traps have caught fish and the fish have been eaten. Similarly Bangala hunters may have no sexual intercourse from the time they made their traps till they have caught game and eaten it ; it is believed that any hunter who broke this rule of chastity would have bad luck in the chase.[1]

Taboos observed by hunters in Nias.

In the island of Nias the hunters sometimes dig pits, cover them lightly over with twigs, grass, and leaves, and then drive the game into them. While they are engaged in digging the pits, they have to observe a number of taboos. They may not spit, or the game would turn back in disgust from the pits. They may not laugh, or the sides of the pit would fall in. They may eat no salt, prepare no fodder for swine, and in the pit they may not scratch themselves, for if they did, the earth would be loosened and would collapse. And the night after digging the pit they may have no intercourse with a woman, or all their labour would be in vain.[2]

The practice of continence by fishers and hunters seems to be based on a notion that incontinence offends the fish and the animals.

This practice of observing strict chastity as a condition of success in hunting and fishing is very common among rude races ; and the instances of it which have been cited render it probable that the rule is always based on a superstition rather than on a consideration of the temporary weakness which a breach of the custom may entail on the hunter or fisherman. In general it appears to be supposed that the evil effect of incontinence is not so much that it weakens him, as that, for some reason or other, it offends the animals, who in consequence will not suffer themselves to be caught. In the Motumotu tribe of New Guinea a man will not see his wife the night before he starts on a great fishing or hunting expedition ; if he did, he would have no luck. In the Motu tribe he is regarded as holy that night, and in the morning no one may speak to him or call out his name.[3] In German East Africa elephant hunters must refrain from women for several days before they set out

---

[1] Rev. J. H. Weeks, "Anthropological Notes on the Bangala of the Upper Congo," *Journal of the Anthropological Institute*, xxxix. (1909) pp. 458, 459.

[2] J. W. Thomas, "De jacht op het eiland Nias," *Tijdschrift voor Indische Taal- Land- en Volkenkunde*, xxvi. (1880) pp. 276 *sq.*

[3] J. Chalmers, *Pioneering in New Guinea* (London, 1887), p. 186.

for the chase.[1]   We have seen that in the same region a
wife's infidelity during the hunter's absence is believed to
give the elephant power over him so as to kill or wound
him.[2]   As this belief is clearly a superstition, based on
sympathetic magic, so doubtless is the practice of chastity
before the hunt.   The pygmies of the great African forest
are also reported to observe strict continence the night
before an important hunt.   It is said that at this time they
propitiate their ancestors by rubbing their skulls, which they
keep in boxes, with palm oil and with water in which the
ashes of the bark and leaves of a certain tree (*moduma*) have
been mixed.[3]

The Huichol Indians of Mexico think that only the pure
of heart should hunt the deer.   The deer would never enter
a snare put up by a man in love ; it would only look at it,
snort " Pooh, pooh," and go back the way it came.   Good
luck in love means bad luck in deer-hunting.   But even
those who have been abstinent must invoke the aid of the
fire to burn the last taint or blemish out of them.   So the
night before they set out for the chase they gather round the
fire and pray aloud, all trying to get as near as they can to
the flaming god, and turning every side of their bodies to
his blessed influence.   They hold out their open hands to it,
warm the palms, spit on them, and then rub them quickly
over their joints, legs, and shoulders, as the shamans do in
curing a sick man, in order that their limbs and sinews may
be as strong as their hearts are pure for the task of the
morrow.[4]   A Carrier Indian of British Columbia used to
separate from his wife for a full month before he set traps
for bears, and during this time he might not drink from
the same vessel as his wife, but had to use a special cup
made of birch bark.   The neglect of these precautions
would cause the game to escape after it had been
snared.   But when he was about to snare martens, the
period of continence was cut down to ten days.[5]   The Sia,

Chastity observed by American Indians before hunting.

[1] P. Reichard, *Deutsch - Ostafrika*
(Leipsic, 1892), p. 427.
  [2] See *The Magic Art and the Evolution of Kings*, vol. i. p. 123.
  [3] Mgr. Le Roy, "Les Pygmées,"
Missions Catholiques, xxix. (1897) p.

269.
  [4] C. Lumholtz, *Unknown Mexico*,
ii. 40 *sq.*
  [5] Father A. G. Morice, "Notes,
Archaeological, Industrial, and Sociological on the Western Denés," *Trans-*

Chastity observed by American Indians before hunting.

a tribe of Pueblo Indians, observe chastity for four days before a hunt as well as the whole time that it lasts, even if the game be only rabbits.[1] Among the Tsetsaut Indians of British Columbia hunters who desire to secure good luck fast and wash their bodies with ginger-root for three or four days, and do not touch a woman for two or three months.[2] A Shuswap Indian, who intends to go out hunting must also keep away from his wife, or he would have no luck.[3] Among the Thompson Indians the grisly-bear hunter must abstain from sexual intercourse for some time before he went forth to hunt. These Indians believe that bears always hear what is said of them. Hence a man who intends to go bear-hunting must be very careful what he says about the beasts or about his preparations for killing them, or they will get wind of it and keep out of his way.[4] In the same tribe of Indians some trappers and hunters, who were very particular, would not eat with other people when they were engaged, or about to be engaged, in hunting or trapping; neither would they eat food cooked by any woman, unless she were old. They drank cold water in which mountain juniper or wild rhubarb had been soaked, using a cup of their own, which no one else might touch. Hunters seldom combed their hair when they were on an expedition, but waited to do so till their return.[5] The reason for this last rule is certainly not that at such seasons they have no time to attend to their persons; the custom is probably based on that superstitious objection to touch the heads of tabooed persons of which some examples have already been given, and of which more will be adduced shortly.

Taboos observed by Hidatsa Indians at catching eagles.

In the late autumn or early winter a few families of the Hidatsa Indians seek some quiet spot in the forest and pitch their camp there to catch eagles. After setting up their

actions of the Canadian Institute, iv. (1892-93) pp. 107, 108.

[1] M. C. Stevenson, "The Sia," *Eleventh Annual Report of the Bureau of Ethnology* (Washington, 1894), p. 118.

[2] Fr. Boas, in *Tenth Report on the North-Western Tribes of Canada,* p. 47 (separate reprint from the *Report of the British Association for 1895*).

[3] *Id.,* in *Sixth Report on the North-Western Tribes of Canada,* p. 90 (separate reprint from the *Report of the British Association for 1890*).

[4] J. Teit, "The Thompson Indians of British Columbia," *Memoir of the American Museum of Natural History, The Jesup North Pacific Expedition,* vol. i. part iv. (April 1900) p. 347.

[5] J. Teit, *op. cit.* p. 348.

tents they build a small medicine-lodge, where the ceremonies supposed to be indispensable for trapping the eagles are performed. No woman may enter it. The traps are set on high places among the neighbouring hills. When some of the men wish to take part in the trapping, they fast and then go by day to the medicine-lodge. There they continue without food until about midnight, when they partake of a little nourishment and fall asleep. They get up just before dawn, or when the morning-star has risen, and go to their traps. There they sit all day without food or drink, watching for their prey, and struggling, it may be, from time to time with a captive eagle, for they always take the birds alive. They return to the camp at sunset. As they approach, every one rushes into his tent; for the hunter may neither see nor be seen by any of his fellow-hunters until he enters the medicine-lodge. They spend the night in the lodge, and about midnight eat and drink for the first time since the previous midnight; then they lie down to sleep, only to rise again before dawn and repair anew to the traps. If any one of them has caught nothing during the day, he may not sleep at night, but must spend his time in loud lamentation and prayer. This routine has to be observed by each hunter for four days and four nights, after which he returns to his own tent, hungry, thirsty, and tired, and follows his ordinary pursuits till he feels able to go again to the eagle-traps. During the four days of the trapping he sees none of his family, and speaks to none of his friends except those who are engaged in the trapping at the same time. They believe that if any hunter fails to perform all these rites, the captive eagle will get one of his claws loose and tear his captor's hands. There are men in the tribe who have had their hands crippled for life in that way.[1] It is obvious that the severe fasting coupled with the short sleep, or even the total sleeplessness, of these eagle-hunters can only impair their physical vigour and so far tend to incapacitate them for capturing the eagles. The motive of their behaviour in

---

[1] Washington Matthews, *Ethnography and Philology of the Hidatsa Indians* (Washington, 1877), pp. 58-60. Other Indian tribes also observe elaborate superstitious ceremonies in hunting eagles. See *Totemism and Exogamy*, iii. 182, 187 *sq.*

these respects is purely superstitious, not rational, and so, we may safely conclude, is the custom which simultaneously cuts them off from all intercourse with their wives and families.

Miscellaneous examples of chastity practised from superstitious motives.

An examination of all the many cases in which the savage bridles his passions and remains chaste from motives of superstition, would be instructive, but I cannot attempt it now. I will only add a few miscellaneous examples of the custom before passing to the ceremonies of purification which are observed by the hunter and fisherman after the chase and the fishing are over. The workers in the salt-pans near Siphoum, in Laos, must abstain from all sexual relations at the place where they are at work ; and they may not cover their heads nor shelter themselves under an umbrella from the burning rays of the sun.[1] Among the Kachins of Burma the ferment used in making beer is prepared by two women, chosen by lot, who during the three days that the process lasts may eat nothing acid and may have no conjugal relations with their husbands ; otherwise it is supposed that the beer would be sour.[2] Among the Masai honey-wine is brewed by a man and a woman who live in a hut set apart for them till the wine is ready for drinking. But they are strictly forbidden to have sexual intercourse with each other during this time ; it is deemed essential that they should be chaste for two days before they begin to brew and for the whole of the six days that the brewing lasts. The Masai believe that were the couple to commit a breach of chastity, not only would the wine be undrinkable but the bees which made the honey would fly away. Similarly they require that a man who is making poison should sleep alone and observe other taboos which render him almost an outcast.[3] The Wandorobbo, a tribe of the same region as the Masai, believe that the mere presence of a woman in the neighbourhood of a man who is brewing poison would deprive the poison of its venom, and

[1] E. Aymonier, *Notes sur le Laos* (Saigon, 1885), p. 141.

[2] P. Ch. Gilhodes, "La Culture matérielle des Katchins (Birmanie)," *Anthropos*, v. (1910) p. 622. Compare J. Anderson, *From Mandalay to Momien* (London, 1876), p. 198, who observes that among the Kakhyens (Kachins) the brewing of beer "is regarded as a serious, almost sacred, task, the women, while engaged in it, having to live in almost vestal seclusion."

[3] J. G. Frazer, *Totemism and Exogamy*, ii. 410 *sq.*, on Mr. A. C. Hollis's authority.

that the same thing would happen if the wife of the poison-
maker were to commit adultery while her husband was
brewing the poison.[1]   In this last case it is obvious that a
rationalistic explanation of the taboo is impossible.   How
could the loss of virtue in the poison be a physical consequence of the loss of virtue in the poison-maker's wife ?
Clearly the effect which the wife's adultery is supposed
to have on the poison is a case of sympathetic magic ; her
misconduct sympathetically affects her husband and his
work at a distance.   We may, accordingly, infer with some
confidence that the rule of continence imposed on the poison-
maker himself is also a simple case of sympathetic magic,
and not, as a civilised reader might be disposed to
conjecture, a wise precaution designed to prevent him
from accidentally poisoning his wife.   Again, to take
other instances, in the East Indian island of Buru people
smear their bodies with coco-nut oil as a protection
against demons.   But in order that the charm may be
effective, the oil must have been made by young unmarried
girls.[2]   In the Seranglao and Gorong archipelagoes
the same oil is regarded as an antidote to poison ;
but it only possesses this virtue if the nuts have been
gathered on a Friday by a youth who has never known
a woman, and if the oil has been extracted by a pure
maiden, while a priest recited the appropriate spells.[3]   So in
the Marquesas Islands, when a woman was making coco-
nut oil, she was tabooed for four or five or more days,
during which she might have no intercourse with her husband.
If she broke this rule, it was believed that she would obtain
no oil.[4]   In the same islands when a man had placed a dish of
bananas and coco-nuts in an oven of hot stones to bake over
night, he might not go in to his wife, or the food would not
be found baked in the morning.[5]   In ancient Mexico
the men who distilled the wine known as *pulque* from the

[1] M. Weiss, *Die Völker-Stämme im Norden Deutsch-Ostafrikas* (Berlin, 1910), p. 396.

[2] G. A. Wilken, "Bijdrage tot de Kennis der Alfoeren van het eiland Boeroe," p. 30 (*Verhandelingen van het Bataviaasch Genootschap van Kunsten en Wetenschappen*, xxxvi.).

[3] J. G. F. Riedel, *De sluik- en kroesharige rassen tusschen Selebes en Papua*, p. 179.

[4] G. H. von Langsdorff, *Reise um die Welt* (Frankfort, 1812), i. 118 sq.

[5] G. H. von. Langsdorff, *op. cit.* i. 117.

sap of the great aloe, might not touch a woman for four days ; if they were unchaste, they thought the wine would be sour and putrid.[1]

Miscellaneous examples of continence observed from superstitious motives. Among the Ba-Pedi and Ba-thonga tribes of South Africa, when the site of a new village has been chosen and the houses are building, all the married people are forbidden to have conjugal relations with each other. If it were discovered that any couple had broken this rule, the work of building would immediately be stopped, and another site chosen for the village. For they think that a breach of chastity would spoil the village which was growing up, that the chief would grow lean and perhaps die, and that the guilty woman would never bear another child.[2] Among the Chams of Cochin-China, when a dam is made or repaired on a river for the sake of irrigation, the chief who offers the traditional sacrifices and implores the protection of the deities on the work, has to stay all the time in a wretched hovel of straw, taking no part in the labour, and observing the strictest continence ; for the people believe that a breach of his chastity would entail a breach of the dam.[3] Here, it is plain, there can be no idea of maintaining the mere bodily vigour of the chief for the accomplishment of a task in which he does not even bear a hand. In New Caledonia the wizard who performs certain superstitious ceremonies at the building and launching of a large canoe is bound to the most rigorous chastity the whole time that the vessel is on the stocks.[4] Among the natives of the Gazelle Peninsula in New Britain men who are engaged in making fish-traps avoid women and observe strict continence. They believe that if a woman were even to touch a fish-trap, it would catch nothing.[5] Here, therefore, the rule of continence probably springs from a fear of infecting sympathetically the traps

---

[1] B. de Sahagun, *Histoire générale des choses de la Nouvelle Espagne*, traduite par D. Jourdanet et R. Simeon, p. 45.

[2] H. A. Junod, "Les Conceptions physiologiques des Bantou sud-africains et leurs tabous," *Revue d'Ethnographie et de Sociologie*, i. (1910) p. 148.

[3] Dameon Grangeon, "Les Chams et leurs superstitions," *Missions Catholiques*, xxviii. (1896) p. 70.

[4] Father Lambert, "Mœurs et superstitions de la tribu Bélep," *Missions Catholiques*, xii. (1880) p. 215 ; *id.*, *Mœurs et superstitions des Néo-Calédoniens* (Nouméa, 1900), pp. 191 *sq.*

[5] R. Parkinson, *Dreissig Jahre in der Südsee* (Stuttgart, 1907), p. 99.

with feminine weakness or perhaps with menstrual pollution.
Every year at the end of September or the beginning of
October, when the north-east monsoon is near an end, a fleet
of large sailing canoes leaves Port Moresby and the neighbouring Motu villages of New Guinea on a trading voyage to
the deltas of the rivers which flow into the Papuan Gulf. The
canoes are laden with a cargo of earthenware pots, and
after about three months they return, sailing before the north-
west monsoon and bringing back a cargo of sago which they
have obtained by barter for their crockery.   It is about the
beginning of the south-east monsoon, that is, in April or May,
that the skippers, who are leading men in the villages, make
up their minds to go on these trading voyages.   When their
resolution is taken they communicate it to their wives, and
from about that time husband and wife cease to cohabit.
The same custom of conjugal separation is observed by what
we may call the mate or second in command of each vessel.
But it is not till the month of August that the work of
preparing the canoes for sea by overhauling and caulking
them is taken seriously in hand.   From that time both
skipper and mate become particularly sacred or taboo
(*helaga*), and consequently they keep apart from their wives
more than ever.   Husband and wife, indeed, sleep in the
same house but on opposite sides of it.   In speaking of his
wife he calls her "maiden," and she calls him "youth."
They have no direct conversation or dealings with each
other.   If he wishes to communicate with her, he does so
through a third person, usually a relative of one of them.
Both refrain from washing themselves, and he from combing
his hair.   "The wife's position indeed becomes very much
like that of a widow."   When the canoe has been launched,
skipper, mate, and crew are all forbidden to touch their food
with their fingers ; they must always handle it and convey
it to their mouths with a bone fork.[1]   A briefer account of
the custom and superstition had previously been given by a
native pastor settled in the neighbourhood of Port Moresby.

Continence observed by the Motu of New Guinea before and during a trading voyage.

---

[1] Captain F. R. Barton, in C. G.
Seligmann's *The Melanesians of British
New Guinea* (Cambridge, 1910), pp.
100-102.   The native words which I
have translated respectively "skipper"
and "mate" are *baditauna* and *dori-
tauna*.   The exact meaning of the
words is doubtful.

He says : " Here is a custom of trading-voyage parties :—
If it is arranged to go westward, to procure arrowroot, the
leader of the party sleeps apart from his wife for the time
being, and on until the return from the expedition, which is
sometimes a term of five months.   They say if this is not
done the canoe of the chief will be sunk on the return
voyage, all the arrowroot lost in the sea, and he himself
covered with shame.   He, however, who observes the rule of
self-denial, returns laden with arrowroot, has not a drop
of salt water to injure his cargo, and so is praised by his

Continence
observed
by the
Akamba
and
Akikuyu
on a
journey
and other
occasions.

companions and crew." [1]   The Akamba and Akikuyu of
eastern Africa refrain from the commerce of the sexes on a
journey, even if their wives are with them in the caravan ;
and they observe the same rule of chastity so long as the
cattle are at pasture, that is, from the time the herds are
driven out to graze in the morning till they come back in the
evening. [2]   Why the rule should be in force just while the
cattle are at pasture is not said, but we may conjecture that
any act of incontinence at that time is somehow supposed,
on the principles of sympathetic magic, to affect the animals
injuriously.   The conjecture is confirmed by the observation
that among the Akikuyu for eight days after the quarterly
festivals, which they hold for the sake of securing God's
blessing on their flocks and herds, no commerce is permitted
between the sexes.   They think that any breach of continence in these eight days would be followed by a mortality
among the flocks. [3]

The taboos
observed
by hunters
and fishers
are often
continued
and even
increased
in strin-
gency after

If the taboos or abstinences observed by hunters and
fishermen before and during the chase are dictated, as we
have seen reason to believe, by superstitious motives, and
chiefly by a dread of offending or frightening the spirits of
the creatures whom it is proposed to kill, we may expect
that the restraints imposed after the slaughter has been
perpetrated will be at least as stringent, the slayer and his

---

[1] Quoted by Dr. George Turner,
Samoa (London, 1884), pp. 349
sq.

[2] J. M. Hildebrandt, "Ethnographische Notizen über Wakamba und ihre
Nachbarn," *Zeitschrift für Ethnologie,*
x. (1878) p. 401.

[3] H. R. Tate, "Further Notes on
the Kikuyu Tribe of British East Africa,"
Journal of the Anthropological Institute,
xxxiv. (1904) pp. 260 *sq.*   At the
festivals sheep and goats are sacrificed
to God (*Ngai*), and the people feast on
the roast flesh.

friends having now the added fear of the angry ghosts of his victims before their eyes. Whereas on the hypothesis that the abstinences in question, including those from food, drink, and sleep, are merely salutary precautions for maintaining the men in health and strength to do their work, it is obvious that the observance of these abstinences or taboos after the work is done, that is, when the game is killed and the fish caught, must be wholly superfluous, absurd, and inexplicable. But as I shall now shew, these taboos often continue to be enforced or even increased in stringency after the death of the animals, in other words, after the hunter or fisher has accomplished his object by making his bag or landing his fish. The rationalistic theory of them therefore breaks down entirely; the hypothesis of superstition is clearly the only one open to us.

the game has been killed and the fish caught. The motive for this conduct can only be superstitious.

Among the Inuit or Esquimaux of Bering Strait "the dead bodies of various animals must be treated very carefully by the hunter who obtains them, so that their shades may not be offended and bring bad luck or even death upon him or his people." Hence the Unalit hunter who has had a hand in the killing of a white whale, or even has helped to take one from the net, is not allowed to do any work for the next four days, that being the time during which the shade or ghost of the whale is supposed to stay with its body. At the same time no one in the village may use any sharp or pointed instrument for fear of wounding the whale's shade, which is believed to be hovering invisible in the neighbourhood; and no loud noise may be made lest it should frighten or offend the ghost. Whoever cuts a whale's body with an iron axe will die. Indeed the use of all iron instruments is forbidden in the village during these four days. These Inuit have a special name (*nu - na hlukh-tuk*) "for a spot of ground where certain things are tabooed, or where there is to be feared any evil influence caused by the presence of offended shades of men or animals, or through the influence of other supernatural means. This ground is sometimes considered unclean, and to go upon it would bring misfortune to the offender, producing sickness, death, or lack of success in hunting or fishing. The same term is also applied to ground where certain animals have been killed or have died." In

Taboos observed by the Bering Strait Esquimaux after catching whales or salmon.

Taboos
observed
by the
Esquimaux
after
catching
whales or
salmon.
the latter case the ground is thought to be dangerous only to him who there performs some forbidden act. For example, the shore where a dead white whale has been beached is so regarded. At such a place and time to chop wood with an iron axe is supposed to be fatal to the imprudent person who chops. Death, too, is supposed to result from cutting wood with an iron axe where salmon are being dressed. An old man at St. Michael told Mr. Nelson of a melancholy case of this kind which had fallen within the scope of his own observation. A man began to chop a log near a woman who was splitting salmon : both of them died soon afterwards. The reason of this disaster, as the old man explained, was that the shade or ghost (*inua*) of the salmon and the spirit or mystery (*yu-a*) of the ground were incensed at the proceeding. Such offences are indeed fatal to every person who may be present at the desecrated spot. Dogs are regarded as very unclean and offensive to the shades of game animals, and great care is taken that no dog shall get at the bones of a white whale. Should a dog touch one of them, the hunter might lose his luck ; his nets would break or be shunned by the whales, and his spears would not strike. But in addition to the state of uncleanness or taboo which arises from the presence of the shades of men or animals, these Esquimaux believe in uncleanness of another sort which, though not so serious, nevertheless produces sickness or bad luck in hunting. It consists, we are told, of a kind of invisible, impalpable vapour, which may attach itself to a person from some contamination. A hunter infected by such a vapour is much more than usually visible to game, so that his luck in the chase is gone until he succeeds in cleansing himself once more. That is why hunters must avoid menstruous women ; if they do not, they will be unable to catch game.[1]

Taboos
observed
by the
Bering
Strait
Esquimaux
These same Esquimaux of Bering Strait celebrate a great annual festival in December, when the bladders of all the seals, whales, walrus, and white bears that have been killed in the year are taken into the assembly-house of the village.

[1] E. W. Nelson, "The Eskimo about Bering Strait," *Eighteenth Annual Report of the Bureau of* *American Ethnology*, part i. (Washington, 1899) pp. 438, 440.

They remain there for several days, and so long as they do and the so the hunters avoid all intercourse with women, saying that Aleuts of if they failed in that respect the shades of the dead animals of regard would be offended.[1]   Similarly among the Aleuts of Alaska for the the hunter who had struck a whale with a charmed spear they have would not throw again, but returned at once to his home and killed. separated himself from his people in a hut specially constructed for the purpose, where he stayed for three days without food or drink, and without touching or looking upon a woman.   During this time of seclusion he snorted occasionally in imitation of the wounded and dying whale, in order to prevent the whale which he had struck from leaving the coast.   On the fourth day he emerged from his seclusion and bathed in the sea, shrieking in a hoarse voice and beating the water with his hands.   Then, taking with him a companion, he repaired to that part of the shore where he expected to find the whale stranded.   If the beast was dead he at once cut out the place where the death-wound had been inflicted.   If the whale was not dead, he again returned to his home and continued washing himself until the whale died.[2]   Here the hunter's imitation of the wounded whale is probably intended by means of homoeopathic magic to make the beast die in earnest.   Among the Kaniagmuts of Alaska the men who attacked the whale were considered by their countrymen as unclean during the fishing season, though otherwise they were held in high honour.[3]

The central Esquimaux of Baffin Land and Hudson Bay Taboos think that whales, ground seals, and common seals originated observed in the severed fingers of the goddess Sedna.   Hence an central Esquimau of these regions must make atonement for each Esquimaux of these animals that he kills, and must observe strictly sea-beasts. certain taboos after their slaughter.   Some of the rules of conduct thus enjoined are identical with those which are in force after the death of a human being.   Thus after the killing of one of these sea-mammals, as after the decease of a person, it is forbidden to scrape the frost from the window,

---

[1] E. W. Nelson, *op. cit.* p. 440, compare pp. 380 *sq.* The bladder festival of these Esquimaux will be described in a later part of this work.

[2] I. Petroff, *Report on the Popula-*tion, *Industries, and Resources of Alaska* (preface dated August 7, 1882), pp. 154 *sq.*

[3] W. H. Dall, *Alaska and its Resources* (London, 1870), p. 404.

Taboos
observed
by the
central
Esquimaux
after killing
sea-beasts. to shake the bed or to disturb the shrubs under the bed, to remove the drippings of oil from under the lamp, to scrape hair from skins, to cut snow for the purpose of melting it, to work on iron, wood, stone, or ivory. Furthermore, women are forbidden to comb their hair, to wash their faces, and to dry their boots and stockings. All these regulations must be kept with the greatest care after a ground seal has been killed, because the transgression of taboos that refer to this animal makes the hands of Sedna very sore. When a seal is brought into the hut, the women must stop working until it is cut up. After the capture of a ground seal, walrus, or whale, they must rest for three days. Not all kinds of work, however, are forbidden; they may mend articles made of sealskin, but they may not make anything new. Working on the new skins of caribou, the American reindeer, is strictly prohibited; for a series of rules forbids all contact between
The sea-
mammals
may not be
brought
into con-
tact with
reindeer. that animal and the sea-mammals. Thus reindeer-skins obtained in summer may not be prepared before the ice has formed and the first seal is caught with the harpoon. Later, as soon as the first walrus has been killed, the work must stop again until the next autumn. Hence everybody is eager to have his reindeer-skins ready as quickly as possible, for until that is done the walrus season will not begin. When the first walrus has been killed a messenger goes from village to village and announces the news, whereupon all work on reindeer-skins immediately ceases. On the other hand, when the season for hunting the reindeer begins, all the winter clothing and the winter tents that had been in use during the walrus hunting season become tabooed and are buried under stones; they may not be used again till the next walrus hunting season comes round. No walrus-hide or thongs made of such hide may be taken inland, where the reindeer live. Venison may not be put in the same boat with walrus-meat, nor yet with salmon. If venison or the antlers of the reindeer were in a boat which goes walrus-hunting, the boat would be liable to be broken by the walrus. The Esquimaux are not allowed to eat venison and walrus on the same day, unless they first strip naked or put on clothing of reindeer-skin that has never been worn in hunting walrus. The transgression of these taboos gives umbrage to the souls of walrus; and a

myth is told to account for the mutual aversion of the walrus and the reindeer. And in general the Esquimaux say that Sedna dislikes the reindeer, wherefore they may not bring the beast into contact with her favourites, the sea-mammals. Hence the meat of the whale and the seal, as well as of the walrus, may not be eaten on the same day with venison. It is not permitted that both sorts of meat lie on the floor of the hut or behind the lamps at the same time. If a man who has eaten venison in the morning happens to enter a hut in which seal meat is being cooked, he is allowed to eat venison on the bed, but it must be wrapped up before it is carried into the hut, and he must take care to keep clear of the floor. Before they change from one food to the other the Esquimaux must wash themselves.

But even among the sea-beasts themselves there are rules of mutual avoidance which these central Esquimaux must observe. Thus a person who has been eating or hunting walrus must strip naked or change his clothes before he eats seal; otherwise the transgression will become fastened to the soul of the walrus in a manner which will be explained presently. Again, the soul of a salmon is very powerful, and its body may not be eaten on the same day with walrus or venison. Salmon may not be cooked in a pot that has been used to boil any other kind of meat; and it must always be cooked at some distance from the hut. The salmon-fisher is not allowed to wear boots that have been used in hunting walrus; and no work may be done on boot-legs till the first salmon has been caught and put on a boot-leg. Once more the soul of the grim polar bear is offended if the taboos which concern him are not observed. His soul tarries for three days near the spot where it left his body, and during these days the Esquimaux are particularly careful to conform rigidly to the laws of taboo, because they believe that punishment overtakes the transgressor who sins against the soul of a bear far more speedily than him who sins against the souls of the sea-beasts.[1]

The native explanation of the taboos thus enjoined on

Even among the sea-beasts themselves there are rules of mutual avoidance which the central Esquimaux must observe.

[1] Fr. Boas, "The Central Eskimo," *Sixth Annual Report of the Bureau of Ethnology* (Washington, 1888), pp. 584 *sq.*, 595; *id.* "The Eskimo of Baffin Land and Hudson Bay," *Bulletin of the American Museum of Natural History*, xv. part i. (1901) pp. 121-124. See also *id.* "Die Sagen der

Native explanation of these Esquimau taboos.

hunters among the central Esquimaux has been given us by the eminent American ethnologist Dr. Franz Boas. As it sets what may be called the spiritual basis of taboo in the clearest light, it deserves to be studied with attention.

The object of the taboos observed after killing sea-beasts is to prevent the souls of the slain animals from contracting certain attachments, which would hurt not only them, but also the great goddess Sedna, in whose house the disembodied souls of the sea-beasts reside.

The goddess Sedna, he tells us, the mother of the sea-mammals, may be considered to be the chief deity of the central Esquimaux. She is supposed to bear supreme sway over the destinies of mankind, and almost all the observances of these tribes have for their object to retain her good will or appease her anger. Her home is in the lower world, where she dwells in a house built of stone and whale-ribs. " The souls of seals, ground seals, and whales are believed to proceed from her house. After one of these animals has been killed, its soul stays with the body for three days. Then it goes back to Sedna's abode, to be sent forth again by her. If, during the three days that the soul stays with the body, any taboo or proscribed custom is violated, the violation (*pitssēte*) becomes attached to the animal's soul, and causes it pain. The soul strives in vain to free itself of these attachments, but is compelled to take them down to Sedna. The attachments, in some manner not explained, make her hands sore, and she punishes the people who are the cause of her pains by sending to them sickness, bad weather, and starvation. If, on the other hand, all taboos have been observed, the sea-animals will allow themselves to be caught; they will even come to meet the hunter. The object of the innumerable taboos that are in force after the killing of these sea-animals, therefore, is to keep their souls free from attachments that would hurt their souls as well as Sedna.

The souls of the sea-beasts have a great aversion to the dark colour of death and to the

" The souls of the sea-animals are endowed with greater powers than those of ordinary human beings. They can see the effect of contact with a corpse, which causes objects touched by it to appear dark in colour; and they can see the effect of flowing human blood, from which a vapour rises that surrounds the bleeding person and is communicated to

Baffin-land Eskimo," *Verhandlungen der Berliner Gesellschaft für Anthropologie, Ethnologie, und Urgeschichte* (1885), pp. 162 *sq.* ; *id.*, in *Proceedings and Transactions of the Royal Society of Canada*, v. (Montreal, 1888) section ii. pp. 35 *sq.* ; C. F. Hall, *Life with the Esquimaux* (London, 1864), ii. 321 *sq.* ; *id.*, *Narrative of the Second Arctic Expedition made by Charles F. Hall*, edited by Professor J. E. Nourse (Washington, 1879), pp. 191 *sq.*

every one and every thing that comes in contact with such a person. This vapour and the dark colour of death are exceedingly unpleasant to the souls of the sea-animals, that will not come near a hunter thus affected. The hunter must therefore avoid contact with people who have touched a body, or with those who are bleeding, more particularly with men-struating women or with those who have recently given birth. The hands of menstruating women appear red to the sea-animals. If any one who has touched a body or who is bleeding should allow others to come in contact with him, he would cause them to become distasteful to the seals, and therefore to Sedna as well. For this reason custom demands that every person must at once announce if he has touched a body, and that women must make known when they are menstruating or when they have had a miscarriage. If they do not do so, they will bring ill-luck to all the hunters. *[vapour that arises from flowing blood, and they avoid persons who are affected by these things.]*

" These ideas have given rise to the belief that it is neces-sary to announce the transgression of any taboo. The trans-gressor of a custom is distasteful to Sedna and to the animals, and those who abide with him will become equally distasteful through contact with him. For this reason it has come to be an act required by custom and morals to confess any and every transgression of a taboo, in order to protect the com-munity from the evil influence of contact with the evil-doer. The descriptions of Eskimo life given by many observers contain records of starvation, which, according to the belief of the natives, was brought about by some one transgressing a law, and not announcing what he had done. *[The trans-gressor of a taboo must announce his trans-gression, in order that other people may shun him]*

" I presume the importance of the confession of a trans-gression, with a view to warning others to keep at a distance from the transgressor, has gradually led to the idea that a transgression, or, we might say, a sin can be atoned for by confession. This is one of the most remarkable traits among the religious beliefs of the central Eskimo. There are innumerable tales of starvation brought about by the transgression of a taboo. In vain the hunters try to supply their families with food ; gales and drifting snow make their endeavours fruitless. Finally the help of the *angakok*[1] is invoked, and he discovers that the cause of the *[Hence the central Esquimaux have come to think that sin can be atoned for by con-fession.]*

---

[1] That is, the wizard or sorcerer.

misfortune of the people is due to the transgression of a taboo. Then the guilty one is searched for. If he confesses, all is well ; the weather moderates, and the seals allow themselves to be caught ; but if he obstinately maintains his innocence, his death alone will soothe the wrath of the offended deity. . . .

The transgression of taboos affects the soul of the transgressor, becoming attached to it and making him sick. If the attachment is not removed by the wizard, the man will die.

" The transgressions of taboos do not affect the souls of game alone. It has already been stated that the sea-mammals see their effect upon man also, who appears to them of a dark colour, or surrounded by a vapour which is invisible to ordinary man. This means, of course, that the transgression also affects the soul of the evil-doer. It becomes attached to it, and makes him sick. The *angakok*[1] is able to see these attachments with the help of his guardian spirit, and is able to free the soul from them. If this is not done, the person must die. In many cases the transgressions become fastened also to persons who come in contact with the evil-doer. This is especially true of children, to whose souls the sins of their parents, and particularly of their mothers, become readily attached. Therefore, when a child is sick, the *angakok*,[1] first of all, asks its mother if she has transgressed any taboos. The attachment seems to have a different appearance, according to the taboo that has been violated. A black attachment is due to removing oil-drippings from under the lamp, a piece of caribou-skin represents the scrapings removed from a caribou-skin at a time when such work was forbidden. As soon as the mother acknowledges the transgression of a taboo, the attachment leaves the child's soul, and the child recovers.

The Esquimaux try to keep the sea-beasts free from contaminating influences, especially from contact with corpses and with women who have

" A number of customs may be explained by the endeavours of the natives to keep the sea-mammals free from contaminating influences. All the clothing of a dead person, the tent in which he died, and the skins obtained by him, must be discarded ; for if a hunter should wear clothing made of skins that had been in contact with the deceased, these would appear dark, and the seal would avoid him. Neither would a seal allow itself to be taken into a hut darkened by a dead body ; and all those who entered such a hut would appear dark to it, and would be avoided.

[1] That is, the wizard or sorcerer.

" While it is customary for a successful hunter to invite all the men of the village to eat of the seal that he has caught, they must not take any of the seal-meat out of the hut, because it might come in contact with persons who are under taboo, and thus the hunter might incur the displeasure of the seal and of Sedna. This is particularly strictly forbidden in the case of the first seal of the season.

" A woman who has a new-born child, and who has not quite recovered, must eat only of seals caught by her husband, by a boy, or by an aged man ; else the vapour arising from her body would become attached to the souls of other seals, which would take the transgression down to Sedna, thus making her hands sore.

" Cases of premature birth require particularly careful treatment. The event must be announced publicly, else dire results will follow. If a woman should conceal from the other people that she has had a premature birth, they might come near her, or even eat in her hut of the seals procured by her husband. The vapour arising from her would thus affect them, and they would be avoided by the seals. The transgression would also become attached to the soul of the seal, which would take it down to Sedna." [1]

In these elaborate taboos so well described by Dr. Boas we seem to see a system of animism in the act of passing into religion. The rules themselves bear the clearest traces of having originated in a doctrine of souls, and of being determined by the supposed likes and dislikes, sympathies and antipathies of the various classes of spirits toward each other. But above and behind the souls of men and animals has grown up the overshadowing conception of a powerful goddess who rules them all, so that the taboos come more and more to be viewed as a means of propitiating her rather than as merely adapted to suit the tastes of the souls themselves. Thus the standard of conduct is shifted from a natural to a supernatural basis : the supposed wish of the deity or, as we commonly put it, the will of God, tends to super-

marginal notes:
recently been brought to bed.

In the system of taboos of the central Esquimaux we see animism passing into religion ; morality is coming to rest on a supernatural basis, namely the will of the goddess Sedna.

---

[1] Fr. Boas, "The Eskimo of Baffin Land and Hudson Bay," *Bulletin of the American Museum of Natural History*, xv., pt. i. (1901) pp. 119- 121, 124 - 126. In quoting these passages I have changed the spelling of a few words in accordance with English orthography.

sede the wishes, real or imaginative, of purely natural beings
as the measure of right and wrong. The old savage taboos,
resting on a theory of the direct relations of living creatures
to each other, remain in substance unchanged, but they are
outwardly transformed into ethical precepts with a religious
or supernatural sanction. In this gradual passage of a rude
philosophy into an elementary religion the place occupied by
confession as a moral purgative is particularly interesting.
I can hardly agree with Dr. Boas that among these
Esquimaux the confession of sins was in its origin no more
than a means of warning others against the dangerous
contagion of the sinner; in other words, that its saving
efficacy consisted merely in preventing the innocent
from suffering with the guilty, and that it had no healing
virtue, no purifying influence, for the evil-doer himself.
It seems more probable that originally the violation of
taboo, in other words, the sin, was conceived as something
almost physical, a sort of morbid substance lurking in the
sinner's body, from which it could be expelled by confession
as by a sort of spiritual purge or emetic. This is confirmed
by the form of auricular confession which is practised by
the Akikuyu of British East Africa. Amongst them, we
are told, " sin is essentially remissable ; it suffices to confess
it. Usually this is done to the sorcerer, who expels the sin
by a ceremony of which the principal rite is a pretended
emetic : *kotahikio*, derived from *tahika*, ' to vomit.' " [1] Thus
among these savages the confession and absolution of sins is,
so to say, a purely physical process of relieving a sufferer of
a burden which sits heavy on his stomach rather than on his
conscience. This view of the matter is again confirmed by
the observation that these same Akikuyu resort to another
physical mode of expelling sin from a sinner, and that is by
the employment of a scapegoat, which by them, as by the
Jews and many other people, has been employed as a vehicle
for carting away moral rubbish and dumping it somewhere
else. For example, if a Kikuyu man has committed incest,
which would naturally entail his death, he produces a substitute in the shape of a he-goat, to which by an ignoble cere-

In this evolution of religion the practice of confession has played a part. It seems to have been regarded as a spiritual purge or emetic, by which sin, conceived as a sort of morbid substance, was expelled from the body of the sinner.

[1] Le P. P. Cayzac, "La Religion des Kikuyu," *Anthropos*, v. (1905) p.
311.

mony he transfers his guilt. Then the throat of the animal is cut, and the human culprit is thereby purged of his sin.[1]

Hence we may suspect that the primary motive of the confession of sins among savages was self-regarding ; in other words, the intention was rather to benefit the sinner himself than to safeguard others by warning them of the danger they would incur by coming into contact with him. This view is borne out by the observation that confession is sometimes used as a means of healing the sick transgressor himself, who is supposed to recover as soon as he has made a clean breast of his transgression. Thus " when the Carriers are severely sick, they often think that they shall not recover, unless they divulge to a priest or magician every crime which they may have committed, which has hitherto been kept secret. In such a case they will make a full confession, and then they expect that their lives will be spared for a time longer. But should they keep back a single crime, they as firmly believe that they shall suffer almost instant death." [2] Again, the Aurohuaca Indians, who, under the tropical sun of South America, inhabit a chilly region bordering on the perpetual snows of the Sierra Nevada in Colombia, believe that all sickness is a punishment for sin. So when one of their medicine-men is summoned to a sick bed, he does not enquire after the patient's symptoms but makes strange passes over him and asks in a sepulchral voice whether he will confess his sins. If the sick man persists in drawing a veil of silence over his frailties, the doctor will not attempt to treat him, but will turn on his heel and leave the house. On the other hand if a satisfactory confession has been made, the leech directs the patient's friends to procure certain odd-looking bits of stone or shell to which the sins of the sufferer may be transferred, for when that is done he will be made whole. For this purpose the sin-laden stones or shells are carried high up into the mountains and laid in some spot

Hence the confession of sins is employed as a sort of medicine for the recovery of the sick.

---

[1] Le P. P. Cayzac, *loc. cit.* The nature of the " ignoble ceremony " of transferring sin to a he-goat is not mentioned by the missionary. It can hardly have been the simple Jewish one of laying hands on the animal's head.

[2] D. W. Harmon, in Rev. Jedidiah Morse's *Report to the Secretary of War of the United States on Indian Affairs* (New-haven, 1822), p. 345. The Carriers are an Indian tribe of North-West America who call themselves *Ta-cul-lies,* "a people who go upon water " (*ibid.* p. 343).

where the first beams of the sun, rising in clear or clouded majesty above the long white slopes or the towering crags of the Sierra Nevada, will strike down on them, driving sin and sickness far away by their radiant influence.[1] Here, again, we see that sin is regarded as something almost material which by confession can be removed from the body of the patient and laid on stones or shells. Further, the confession of sins has been resorted to by some people as a means of accelerating the birth of a child when the mother was in hard labour. Thus, "among the Indians of Guatemala, in the time of their idolatry when a woman was in labour, the midwife ordered her to confess her sins ; and if she was not delivered, the husband was to confess his ; and if that did not do they took off his clouts and put them about his wife's loins ; if still she could not be delivered, the midwife drew blood from herself and sprinkled it towards the four quarters of heaven with some invocations and ceremonies."[2] In these attempts of the Indians to accelerate the birth of the child it seems clear that the confession of sins on the part first of the wife and afterwards of the husband is nothing but a magical ceremony like the putting of the husband's clothes on the suffering woman[3] or the sprinkling of the midwife's blood towards the four quarters of the heaven. Amongst the Antambahoaka, a savage tribe of Madagascar, when a woman is in hard labour, a sorcerer is called in to her aid. After

Similarly the confession of sins is sometimes resorted to by women in hard labour as a means of accelerating their delivery.

---

[1] Francis C. Nicholas, "The Aborigines of Santa Maria, Colombia," *American Anthropologist*, N.S. iii. (1901) pp. 639-641.

[2] A. de Herrera, *The General History of the Vast Continent and Islands of America*, translated by Capt. J. Stevens (London, 1725-26), iv. 148. The confession of sins appears to have held an important place in the native religion of the American Indians, particularly the Mexicans and Peruvians. There is no sufficient reason to suppose that they learned the practice from Catholic priests. For more evidence of the custom among the aborigines of America see L. H. Morgan, *League of the Iroquois* (Rochester, U.S. America, 1851), pp. 170 *sq.*, 187 *sq.* ; B. de Sahagun, *Histoire*

générale des choses de la Nouvelle Espagne, bk. i. ch. 12, bk. vi. ch. 7, pp. 22-27, 339-344 (Jourdanet and Simeon's French translation); A. de Herrera, *op. cit.* iv. 173, 190 ; Diego de Landa, *Relation des choses de Yucatan* (Paris, 1864), pp. 154 *sqq.* ; Brasseur de Bourbourg, *Histoire des nations civilisées du Mexique et de l'Amérique Centrale*, ii. 114 *sq.*, 567, iii. 567-569 ; P. J. de Arriaga, *Extirpacion de la idolatria del Piru* (Lima, 1621), pp. 18, 28 *sq.*

[3] As to this means of hastening the delivery see *Totemism and Exogamy*, iv. 248 *sqq.* The intention of the exchange of clothes at childbirth between husband and wife seems to be to relieve the woman by transferring the travail pangs to the man.

making some magical signs and uttering some incantations, he generally declares that the patient cannot be delivered until she has publicly confessed a secret fault which she has committed.   In such a case a woman has been known to confess to incest with her brother ; and immediately after her confession the child was born.[1]   In these cases the confession of sins is clearly not a mode of warning people to keep clear of the sinner ; it is a magical ceremony primarily intended to benefit the sinner himself or herself and no other.   The same thing may perhaps be said of a confession which was prescribed in a certain case by ancient Hindoo ritual.   At a great festival of Varuna, which fell at the beginning of the rainy season, the priest asked the wife of the sacrificer to name her paramour or paramours, and she had to mention their names or at least to take up as many grass-stalks as she had lovers.[2]   " Now when a woman who belongs to one man carries on intercourse with another, she undoubtedly commits a sin against Varuna.   He therefore thus asks her, lest she should sacrifice with a secret pang in her mind ; for when confessed the sin becomes less, since it becomes truth ; this is why he thus asks her.   And whatever connection she confesses not, that indeed will turn out injurious to her relatives." [3]   In this passage of the *Satapatha Brahmana* confession of sin is said to diminish the sin, just as if the mere utterance of the words ejected or expelled some morbid matter from the person of the sinner, thereby relieving her of its burden and benefiting also her relatives, who would suffer through any sin which she might not have confessed.

In these cases confession is a magical ceremony designed to relieve the sinner.

Thus at an early stage of culture the confession of sins wears the aspect of a bodily rather than of a moral and spiritual purgation ; it is a magical rather than a religious rite, and as such it resembles the ceremonies of washing, scouring, fumigation, and so forth, which in like manner are applied by many primitive peoples to the purification of what we should regard as moral guilt, but what they

Thus the confession of sins is at first rather a bodily than a moral purgation, resembling the cere-

[1] G. Ferrand, *Les Musulmans à Madagascar*, Deuxième Partie (Paris, 1893), pp. 20 *sq.*
[2] H. Oldenberg, *Die Religion des*

Veda (Berlin, 1894), pp. 319 *sq.*
[3] *Satapatha Brahmana*, translated by J. Eggeling, pt. i. p. 397 (*Sacred Books of the East*, vol. xii.).

monies of
washing,
fumigation,
and so on,
which are
observed
by many
primitive
peoples
for the
removal
of sin.

consider rather as a corporeal pollution or infection, which
can be removed by the physical agencies of fire, water,
fasts, purgatives, abrasion, scarification, and so forth.   But
when the guilt of sin ceases to be regarded as something.
material, a sort of clinging vapour of death, and is conceived.
as the transgression of the will of a wise and good God, it
is obvious that the observance of these outward rites of
purification becomes superfluous and absurd, a vain show
which cannot appease the anger of the offended deity.   The
only means of turning away his wrath and averting the fatal
consequences of sin is now believed to be the humble confession and true repentance of the sinner.   At this stage of
ethical evolution the practice of confession loses its old
magical character as a bodily purge and assumes the new
aspect of a purely religious rite, the propitiation of a great
supernatural and moral being, who by a simple fiat can
cancel the transgression and restore the transgressor to
a state of pristine innocence.   This comfortable doctrine
teaches us that in order to blot out the effects of our
misdeeds we have only to acknowledge and confess them
with a lowly and penitent heart, whereupon a merciful
God will graciously pardon our sin and absolve us and ours
from its consequences.   It might indeed be well for the
world if we could thus easily undo the past, if we could
recall the words that have been spoken amiss, if we could
arrest the long train that follows, like a flight of avenging
Furies, on every evil action.   But this we cannot do.
Our words and acts, good and bad, have their natural,
their inevitable consequences.   God may pardon sin, but
Nature cannot.

It is
possible
that some
savage
taboos may
still lurk,
under
various
disguises,
in the
morality of
civilised
peoples.

It seems not improbable that in our own rules of conduct,
in what we call the common decencies of life as well as in
the weightier matters of morality, there may survive not a
few old savage taboos which, masquerading as an expression
of the divine will or draped in the flowing robes of a false
philosophy, have maintained their credit long after the crude
ideas out of which they sprang have been discarded by the
progress of thought and knowledge ; while on the other hand
many ethical precepts and social laws, which now rest firmly
on a solid basis of utility, may at first have drawn some

portion of their sanctity from the same ancient system of superstition. For example, we can hardly doubt that in primitive society the crime of murder derived much of its horror from a fear of the angry ghost of the murdered man. Thus superstition may serve as a convenient crutch to morality till she is strong enough to throw away the crutch and walk alone. To judge by the legislation of the Pentateuch the ancient Semites appear to have passed through a course of moral evolution not unlike that which we can still detect in process among the Esquimaux of Baffin Land. Some of the old laws of Israel are clearly savage taboos of a familiar type thinly disguised as commands of the deity. This disguise is indeed a good deal more perfect in Palestine than in Baffin Land, but in substance it is the same. Among the Esquimaux it is the will of Sedna; among the Israelites it is the will of Jehovah.[1]

But it is time to return to our immediate subject, to wit, the rules of conduct observed by hunters after the slaughter of the game.

When the Kayans or Bahaus of central Borneo have shot one of the dreaded Bornean panthers, they are very anxious about the safety of their souls, for they think that the soul of a panther is almost more powerful than their own. Hence they step eight times over the carcase of the dead beast reciting the spell, "Panther, thy soul under my soul." On returning home they smear themselves, their dogs, and their weapons with the blood of fowls in order to calm their souls and hinder them from fleeing away; for being themselves fond of the flesh of fowls they ascribe the same taste to their souls. For eight days afterwards they must bathe by day and by night before going out again to the chase.[2]

Ceremonies observed by the Kayans after killing a panther.

---

[1] The similarity of some of the Mosaic laws to savage customs has struck most Europeans who have acquired an intimate knowledge of the savage and his ways. They have often explained the coincidences as due to a primitive revelation or to the dispersion of the Jews into all parts of the earth. Some examples of these coincidences were cited in my article "Taboo," *Encyclopaedia Britannica*,[9] xxiii. 17.

The subject has since been handled, with consummate ability and learning, by my lamented friend W. Robertson Smith in his *Religion of the Semites* (New Edition, London, 1894). In *Psyche's Task* I have illustrated by examples the influence of superstition on the growth of morality.

[2] A. W. Nieuwenhuis, *Quer durch Borneo*, i. 106 *sq.*

After killing an animal some Indian hunters used to purify themselves in water as a religious rite.[1] When a Damara hunter returns from a successful chase he takes water in his mouth and ejects it three times over his feet, and also into the fire on his own hearth.[2] Amongst the Caffres of South Africa "the slaughter of a lion, however honourable it is esteemed, is nevertheless associated with an idea of moral uncleanness, and is followed by a very strange ceremony. When the hunters approach the village on their return, the man who gave the lion the first wound is hidden from every eye by the shields which his comrades hold up before him. One of the hunters steps forward and, leaping and bounding in a strange manner, praises the courage of the lion-killer. Then he rejoins the band, and the same performance is repeated by another. All the rest meanwhile keep up a ceaseless shouting, rattling with their clubs on their shields. This goes on till they have reached the village. Then a mean hut is run up not far from the village ; and in this hut the lion-killer, because he is unclean, must remain four days, cut off from all association with the tribe. There he dyes his body all over with white paint ; and lads who have not yet been circumcised, and are therefore, in respect to uncleanness, in the same state as himself, bring him a calf to eat, and wait upon him. When the four days are over, the unclean man washes himself, paints himself with red paint in the usual manner, and is escorted back to the village by the head chief, attended with a guard of honour. Lastly, a second calf is killed ; and, the uncleanness being now at an end, every one is free to eat of the calf with him."[3] Among the Hottentots, when a man has killed a lion, leopard, elephant, or rhinoceros he is esteemed a great hero, but he is deluged with urine by the medicine-man and has to remain at home quite idle for three days, during which his wife may not come near him ; she is also enjoined to restrict herself

Ceremonies of purification observed by African hunters after killing dangerous beasts.

---

[1] J. Adair, *History of the American Indians*, p. 118.

[2] C. J. Andersson, *Lake Ngami*, p. 224.

[3] L. Alberti, *De Kaffers aan de Zuidkust van Afrika* (Amsterdam, 1810), pp. 158 *sq.* Compare H. Lichtenstein, *Reisen im südlichen Africa* (Berlin, 1811-12), i. 419. These accounts were written about a century ago. The custom may since have become obsolete. A similar remark applies to other customs described in this and the following paragraph.

to a poor diet and to eat no more than is barely necessary
to keep her in health.[1]   Similarly the Lapps deem it the
height of glory to kill a bear, which they consider the king
of beasts.   Nevertheless, all the men who take part in the
slaughter are regarded as unclean, and must live by themselves for three days in a hut or tent made specially for
them, where they cut up and cook the bear's carcase.   The
reindeer which brought in the carcase on a sledge may not
be driven by a woman for a whole year ; indeed, according
to one account, it may not be used by anybody for that
period.   Before the men go into the tent where they are to
be secluded, they strip themselves of the garments they had
worn in killing the bear, and their wives spit the red juice of
alder bark in their faces.   They enter the tent not by the
ordinary door but by an opening at the back.   When the
bear's flesh has been cooked, a portion of it is sent by the
hands of two men to the women, who may not approach the
men's tent while the cooking is going on.   The men who
convey the flesh to the women pretend to be strangers
bringing presents from a foreign land ; the women keep up
the pretence and promise to tie red threads round the legs
of the strangers.   The bear's flesh may not be passed in to
the women through the door of their tent, but must be thrust
in at a special opening made by lifting up the hem of the
tent-cover.   When the three days' seclusion is over and the
men are at liberty to return to their wives, they run, one
after the other, round the fire, holding the chain by which
pots are suspended over it.   This is regarded as a form of
purification ; they may now leave the tent by the ordinary
door and rejoin the women.   But the leader of the party
must still abstain from cohabitation with his wife for two
days more.[2]

Again, the Caffres are said to dread greatly the boa-
constrictor or an enormous serpent resembling it ; " and being

Cere-
monies ob-
served by
Lapp
hunters
after killing
a bear.

---

[1] P. Kolbe, *Present State of the Cape
of Good Hope*, I.[2] (London, 1738) pp.
251-255.   The reason alleged for the
custom is to allow the slayer to recruit
his strength.   But the reason is clearly
inadequate as an explanation of this and
similar practices.

J. Scheffer, *Lapponia* (Frankfort,

1673), pp. 234-243 ; C. Leemius, *De
Lapponibus Finmarchiae eorumque
lingua, vita et religione pristina commentatio* (Copenhagen, 1767), pp.
502 *sq.* ; E. J. Jessen, *De Finnorum
Lapponumque Nouvegicorum religione
pagana tractatus singularis*, pp. 64 *sq.*
(bound up with Leemius's work).

Expiatory
ceremonies
performed
for the
slaughter
of serpents. influenced by certain superstitious notions they even fear to kill it.   The man who happened to put it to death, whether in self-defence or otherwise, was formerly required to lie in a running stream of water during the day for several weeks together ; and no beast whatever was allowed to be slaughtered at the hamlet to which he belonged, until this duty had been fully performed.   The body of the snake was then taken and carefully buried in a trench, dug close to the cattle-fold, where its remains, like those of a chief, were henceforward kept perfectly undisturbed.   The period of penance, as in the case of mourning for the dead, is now happily reduced to a few days." [1]   Amongst the Ewe-speaking peoples of the Slave Coast, who worship the python, a native who killed one of these serpents used to be burned alive. But for some time past, though a semblance of carrying out the old penalty is preserved, the culprit is allowed to escape with his life, but he has to pay a heavy fine.   A small hut of dry faggots and grass is set up, generally near the lagoon at Whydah, if the crime has been perpetrated there ; the guilty man is thrust inside, the door of plaited grass is shut on him, and the hut is set on fire.   Sometimes a dog, a kid, and two fowls are enclosed along with him, and he is drenched with palm-oil and yeast, probably to render him the more combustible.   As he is unbound, he easily breaks out of the frail hut before the flames consume him ; but he has to run the gauntlet of the angry serpent-worshippers, who belabour the murderer of their god with sticks and pelt him with clods until he reaches water and plunges into it, which is supposed to wash away his sin.   Thirteen days later a commemoration service is held in honour of the deceased python.[2]   In Madras it is considered a great sin to kill a cobra.   When this has happened, the people generally burn the body of the serpent just as they burn the bodies of human beings.   The murderer deems himself polluted for three days.   On the second day milk is poured on the remains of the cobra.   On the third

---

[1] S. Kay, *Travels and Researches in Caffraria* (London, 1833), pp. 341 *sq.*
[2] J. Duncan, *Travels in Western Africa* (London, 1847), i. 195 *sq.* ; F. E. Forbes *Dahomey and the* *Dahomans* (London, 1851), i. 107 ; P. Bouche, *La Côte des Esclaves* (Paris, 1885), p. 397 ; A. B. Ellis, *The Ewe-speaking Peoples of the Slave Coast*, pp. 58 *sq.*

HUNTERS AND FISHERS TABOOED

day the guilty wretch is free from pollution.[1]   Under native
rule, we may suspect, he would not get off so lightly.

In these last cases the animal whose slaughter has to be All such
atoned for is sacred, that is, it is one whose life is commonly expiatory
spared from motives of superstition.   Yet the treatment of based on
the sacrilegious slayer seems to resemble so closely the treat- the respect
ment of hunters and fishermen who have killed animals for savage
food in the ordinary course of business, that the ideas on the souls of
which both sets of customs are based may be assumed to animals.
be substantially the same.   Those ideas, if I am right,
are the respect which the savage feels for the souls
of beasts, especially valuable or formidable beasts, and
the dread which he entertains of their vengeful ghosts.
Some confirmation of this view may be drawn from the
ceremonies observed by fishermen of Annam when the carcase
of a whale is washed ashore.   These fisherfolk, we are told,
worship the whale on account of the benefits they derive from
it.   There is hardly a village on the sea-shore which has not
its small pagoda, containing the bones, more or less authentic,
of a whale.   When a dead whale is washed ashore, the people
accord it a solemn burial.   The man who first caught sight
of it acts as chief mourner, performing the rites which as
chief mourner and heir he would perform for a human kinsman.   He puts on all the garb of woe, the straw hat, the
white robe with long sleeves turned inside out, and the other
paraphernalia of full mourning.   As next of kin to the
deceased he presides over the funeral rites.   Perfumes are
burned, sticks of incense kindled, leaves of gold and silver
scattered, crackers let off.   When the flesh has been cut off
and the oil extracted, the remains of the carcase are buried
in the sand.   Afterwards a shed is set up and offerings are
made in it.   Usually some time after the burial the spirit of
the dead whale takes possession of some person in the village
and declares by his mouth whether he is a male or a female.[2]

[1] *Indian Antiquary*, xxi. (1892) p.
224.   Many of the above examples of
expiation exacted for the slaughter of
animals have already been cited by me
in a note on Pausanias, ii. 7. 7, where
I suggested that the legendary purification of Apollo for the slaughter of the
python at Delphi (Plutarch, *Quaest.*

Graec., 12; *id.*, *De defectu oraculorum*,
15; Aelian, *Var. Hist.* iii. 1) may be
a reminiscence of a custom of this sort.
[2] Le R. P. Cadière, " Croyances et
dictons populaires de la Vallée du
Nguôn-son, Province de Quang-binh
(Annam),"*Bulletin de l'École Française
d'Extrême Orient*, i. (1901) pp. 183 *sq.*

CHAPTER V

TABOOED THINGS

§ 1. *The Meaning of Taboo*

Taboos of holiness agree with taboos of pollution, because in the savage mind the ideas of holiness and pollution are not yet differentiated. THUS in primitive society the rules of ceremonial purity observed by divine kings, chiefs, and priests agree in many respects with the rules observed by homicides, mourners, women in childbed, girls at puberty, hunters and fishermen, and so on. To us these various classes of persons appear to differ totally in character and condition; some of them we should call holy, others we might pronounce unclean and polluted. But the savage makes no such moral distinction between them; the conceptions of holiness and pollution are not yet differentiated in his mind. To him the common feature of all these persons is that they are dangerous and in danger, and the danger in which they stand and to which they expose others is what we should call spiritual or ghostly, and therefore imaginary. The danger, however, is not less real because it is imaginary; imagination acts upon man as really as does gravitation, and may kill him as certainly as a dose of prussic acid. To seclude these persons from the rest of the world so that the dreaded spiritual danger shall neither reach them, nor spread from them, is the object of the taboos which they have to observe. These taboos act, so to say, as electrical insulators to preserve the spiritual force with which these persons are charged from suffering or inflicting harm by contact with the outer world.[1]

[1] On the nature of taboo see my article "Taboo" in the *Encyclopaedia Britannica*, 9th edition, vol. xxiii. (1888) pp. 15 *sqq.*; W. Robertson Smith, *Religion of the Semites*[2] (London, 1894), pp. 148 *sqq.*, 446 *sqq.* Some languages have retained a word for that general idea which includes under it the notions

To the illustrations of these general principles which have been already given I shall now add some more, drawing my examples, first, from the class of tabooed things, and, second, from the class of tabooed words ; for in the opinion of the savage both things and words may, like persons, be charged or electrified, either temporarily or permanently, with the mysterious virtue of taboo, and may therefore require to be banished for a longer or shorter time from the familiar usage of common life. And the examples will be chosen with special reference to those sacred chiefs, kings and priests, who, more than anybody else, live fenced about by taboo as by a wall. Tabooed things will be illustrated in the present chapter, and tabooed words in the next.

§ 2. *Iron tabooed*

In the first place we may observe that the awful sanctity of kings naturally leads to a prohibition to

which we now distinguish as sanctity and pollution. The word in Latin is *sacer*, in Greek, ἅγιος. In Polynesian it is *tabu* (Tongan), *tapu* (Samoan, Tahitian, Marquesan, Maori, etc.), or *kapu* (Hawaiian). See E. Tregear, *Maori-Polynesian Comparative Dictionary* (Wellington, N.Z., 1891), *s.v. tapu.* In Dacotan the word is *wakan,* which in Riggs's *Dakota-English Dictionary* (*Contributions to North American Ethnology,* vol. vii., Washington, 1890, pp. 507 *sq.*) is defined as "*spiritual, sacred, consecrated; wonderful, incomprehensible;* said also of women at the menstrual period." Another writer in the same dictionary defines *wakan* more fully as follows : "*Mysterious; incomprehensible; in a peculiar state, which, from not being understood, it is dangerous to meddle with;* hence the application of this word to women at the *menstrual period,* and from hence, too, arises the feeling among the wilder Indians, that if the Bible, the church, the missionary, etc., are 'wakan,' they are to be *avoided,* or *shunned,* not as being *bad* or *dangerous,* but as wakan. The word seems to be the only one suitable for *holy, sacred,* etc., but the common acceptation of it,

given above, makes it quite misleading to the *heathen.*" On the notion designated by *wakan,* see also G. H. Pond, "Dakota Superstitions," *Collections of the Minnesota Historical Society for the year 1867* (Saint Paul, 1867), p. 33 ; J. Owen Dorsey, in *Eleventh Annual Report of the Bureau of Ethnology* (Washington, 1894), pp. 366 *sq.* It is characteristic of the equivocal notion denoted by these terms that, whereas the condition of women in childbed is commonly regarded by the savage as what we should call unclean, among the Herero the same condition is described as holy; for some time after the birth of her child, the woman is secluded in a hut made specially for her, and every morning the milk of all the cows is brought to her that she may consecrate it by touching it with her mouth. See H. Schinz, *Deutsch-Südwest-Afrika,* p. 167. . Again, whereas a girl at puberty is commonly secluded as dangerous, among the Warundi of eastern Africa she is led by her grandmother all over the house and obliged to touch everything (O. Baumann, *Durch Massailand zur Nilquelle* (Berlin, 1894), p. 221), as if her touch imparted a blessing instead of a curse.

Kings may not be touched.

touch their sacred persons. Thus it was unlawful to lay hands on the person of a Spartan king;[1] no one might touch the body of the king or queen of Tahiti;[2] it is forbidden to touch the person of the king of Siam under pain of death;[3] and no one may touch the king of Cambodia, for any purpose whatever, without his express command. In July 1874 the king was thrown from his carriage and lay insensible on the ground, but not one of his suite dared to touch him; a European coming to the spot carried the injured monarch to his palace.[4] Formerly no one might touch the king of Corea; and if he deigned to touch a subject, the spot touched became sacred, and the person thus honoured had to wear a visible mark (generally

The use of iron forbidden to kings and priests.

a cord of red silk) for the rest of his life. Above all, no iron might touch the king's body. In 1800 King Tieng-tsong-tai-oang died of a tumour in the back, no one dreaming of employing the lancet, which would probably have saved his life. It is said that one king suffered terribly from an abscess in the lip, till his physician called in a jester, whose pranks made the king laugh heartily, and so the abscess burst.[5] Roman and Sabine priests might not be shaved with iron but only with bronze razors or shears;[6] and whenever an iron graving-tool was brought into the sacred grove of the Arval Brothers at Rome for the purpose of cutting an inscription in stone, an expiatory sacrifice of a lamb and a pig must be offered, which was repeated when the graving-tool was removed from the grove.[7] As a general rule iron might not be brought into Greek sanctuaries.[8] In Crete sacrifices

[1] Plutarch, *Agis*, 19.

[2] W. Ellis, *Polynesian Researches*,[2] iii. 102.

[3] E. Aymonier, *Le Cambodge*, ii. (Paris, 1901) p. 25.

[4] J. Moura, *Le Royaume du Cambodge* (Paris, 1883), i. 226.

[5] Ch. Dallet, *Histoire de l'Église de Corée* (Paris, 1874), i. pp. xxiv. *sq.*; W. E. Griffis, *Corea, the Hermit Nation* (London, 1882), p. 219. These customs are now obsolete (G. N. Curzon, *Problems of the Far East* (Westminster, 1896), pp. 154 *sq.* note).

[6] Macrobius, *Sat.* v. 19. 13; Servius

on Virgil, *Aen.* i. 448; Joannes Lydus, *De mensibus*, i. 31. We have already seen (p. 16) that the hair of the Flamen Dialis might only be cut with a bronze knife. The Greeks attributed a certain cleansing virtue to bronze; hence they employed it in expiatory rites, at eclipses, etc. See the Scholiast on Theocritus, ii. 36.

[7] *Acta Fratrum Arvalium*, ed. G. Henzen (Berlin, 1874), pp. 128-135; J. Marquardt, *Römische Staatsverwaltung*, iii.[2] (*Das Sacralwesen*) pp. 459 *sq.*

[8] Plutarch, *Praecepta gerendae reipublicae*, xxvi. 7. Plutarch here mentions that gold was also excluded from

were offered to Menedemus without the use of iron, because
the legend ran that Menedemus had been killed by an iron
weapon in the Trojan war.[1] The Archon of Plataea might
not touch iron ; but once a year, at the annual commemoration of the men who fell at the battle of Plataea, he was
allowed to carry a sword wherewith to sacrifice a bull.[2] To
this day a Hottentot priest never uses an iron knife, but
always a sharp splint of quartz, in sacrificing an animal or
circumcising a lad.[3] Among the Ovambo of south-west Use of iron
Africa custom requires that lads should be circumcised with forbidden
a sharp flint ; if none is to hand, the operation may be per- at circumcision,
formed with iron, but the iron must afterwards be buried.[4] childbirth,
and so
The Antandroy and Tanala of Madagascar cut the navel- forth.
strings of their children with sharp wood or with a thread,
but never with an iron knife.[5] In Uap, one of the Caroline
Islands, wood of the hibiscus tree, which was used to make
the fire - drill, must be cut with shell knives or shell

some temples. At first sight this is
surprising, for in general neither the
gods nor their ministers have displayed
any marked aversion to gold. But a
little enquiry suffices to clear up the
mystery and set the scruple in its proper
light. From a Greek inscription discovered some years ago we learn that no
person might enter the sanctuary of the
Mistress at Lycosura wearing golden
trinkets, unless for the purpose of dedi-
cating them to the goddess ; and if any
one did enter the holy place with such
ornaments on his body but no such
pious intention in his mind, the trinkets
were forfeited to the use of religion.
See Ἐφημερὶς ἀρχαιολογική (Athens,
1898), col. 249 ; Dittenberger, *Sylloge
inscriptionum Graecarum*,[2] No. 939.
The similar rule, that in the procession
at the mysteries of Andania no woman
might wear golden ornaments (Dittenberger, *op. cit.* No. 653), was probably
subject to a similar exception and enforced by a similar penalty. Once
more, if the maidens who served Athena
on the Acropolis at Athens put on gold
ornaments, the ornaments became
sacred, in other words, the property
of the goddess (Harpocration, *s.v.*
ἀρρηφορεῖν, vol. i. p. 59, ed. Dindorf).
Thus it appears that the pious scruple

about gold was concerned rather with
its exit from, than with its entrance
into, the sacred edifice. At the sacrifice to the Sun in ancient Egypt
worshippers were forbidden to wear
golden trinkets and to give hay to
an ass (Plutarch, *Isis et Osiris*, 30)—a
singular combination of religious precepts. In India gold and silver are
common totems, and members of such
clans are forbidden to wear gold and
silver trinkets respectively. See
Totemism and Exogamy, iv. 24.

[1] Callimachus, referred to by the
Old Scholiast on Ovid, *Ibis*. See
Callimachea, ed. O. Schneider, ii. p.
282, Frag. 100ᵃ E. ; Chr. A. Lobeck,
Aglaophamus, p. 686.

[2] Plutarch, *Aristides*, 21. This
passage was pointed out to me by my
friend Mr. W. Wyse.

[3] Theophilus Hahn, *Tsuni-‖Goam,
the Supreme Being of the Khoi-Khoi*
(London, 1881), p. 22.

[4] Dr. P. H. Brincker, "Charakter,
Sitten und Gebräuche speciell der
Bantu Deutsch-Südwestafrikas," *Mit-
theilungen des Seminars für orienta-
lische Sprachen zu Berlin*, iii. (1900)
Dritte Abtheilung, p. 80.

[5] A. van Gennep, *Tabou et totémisme
à Madagascar* (Paris, 1904), p. 38.

axes, never with iron or steel.[1]   Amongst the Moquis
of Arizona stone knives, hatchets, and so on have passed
out of common use, but are retained in religious ceremonies.[2]   After the Pawnees had ceased to use stone
arrow-heads for ordinary purposes, they still employed
them to slay the sacrifices, whether human captives or
Use of iron forbidden at certain times and places among the Esquimaux. buffalo and deer.[3]   We have seen that among the Esquimaux of Bering Strait the use of iron implements is for-
bidden for four days after the slaughter of a white whale, and
that the use of an iron axe at a place where salmon are being
dressed is believed by these people to be a fatal imprudence.[4]
They hold a festival in the assembly-house of the village,
while the bladders of the slain beasts are hanging there,
and during its celebration no wood may be cut with an iron
axe.   If it is necessary to split firewood, this may be done
with wedges of bone.[5]   At Kushunuk, near Cape Vancouver,
it happened that Mr. Nelson and his party entered an
assembly-house of these Esquimaux while the festival of
the bladders was in progress.   "When our camping outfit
was brought in from the sledges, two men took drums, and
as the clothing and goods of the traders who were with me
were brought in, the drums were beaten softly and a song
was sung in a low, humming tone, but when our guns and
some steel traps were brought in, with other articles of iron,
the drums were beaten loudly and the songs raised in proportion.   This was done that the shades of the animals
present in the bladders might not be frightened."[6]   The
Esquimaux on the western coast of Hudson Bay may not
work on iron during the season for hunting musk-oxen,
which falls in March.   And no such work may be done by
them until the seals have their pups.[7]   Negroes of the Gold
Coast remove all iron or steel from their person when they

[1] W. H. Furness, *The Island of Stone Money, Uap of the Carolines* (Philadelphia and London, 1910), p. 151.

[2] J. G. Bourke, *The Snake Dance of the Moquis of Arizona* (New York, 1891), pp. 178 *sq.*

[3] G. B. Grinnell, *Pawnee Hero Stories and Folk-tales* (New York, 1889), p. 253.

[4] See above, pp. 205 *sq.*

[5] E. W. Nelson, "The Eskimo about Bering Strait," *Eighteenth Annual Report of the Bureau of American Ethnology*, Part I. (Washington, 1899) p. 392.

[6] E. W. Nelson, *op. cit.* p. 383.

[7] Fr. Boas, "The Eskimo of Baffin Land and Hudson Bay," *Bulletin of the American Museum of Natural History*, xv. Part I. (1901) p. 149.

consult their fetish.[1] The men who made the need-fire in
Scotland had to divest themselves of all metal.[2] There was
hardly any belief, we are told, that had a stronger hold on
the mind of a Scottish Highlander than that on no account
whatever should iron be put in the ground on Good Friday.
Hence no grave was dug and no field ploughed on that day.
It has been suggested that the belief was based on that
rooted aversion to iron which fairies are known to feel.
These touchy beings live underground, and might resent
having the roof pulled from over their heads on the hallowed
day.[3] Again, in the Highlands of Scotland the shoulder-
blades of sheep are employed in divination, being consulted
as to future marriages, births, deaths, and funerals ; but the
forecasts thus made will not be accurate unless the flesh has
been removed from the bones without the use of any iron.[4]
In making the *clavie* (a kind of Yule-tide fire-wheel) at

[1] C. F. Gordon Cumming, *In the
Hebrides* (ed. 1883), p. 195.

[2] James Logan, *The Scottish Gael*
(ed. Alex. Stewart), ii. 68 *sq.*

[3] J. G. Campbell, *Witchcraft and
Second Sight in the Highlands and
Islands of Scotland* (Glasgow, 1902),
pp. 262, 298, 299.

[4] R. C. Maclagan, M.D., "Notes
on Folklore Objects from Argyleshire,"
Folk-lore, vi. (1895) p. 157 ; J. G.
Campbell, *Superstitions of the High-
lands and Islands of Scotland* (Glasgow,
1900), pp. 263-266. The shoulder-
blades of sheep have been used in
divination by many peoples, for ex-
ample by the Corsicans, South Slavs,
Tartars, Kirghiz, Calmucks, Chukchees,
and Lolos, as well as by the Scotch.
See J. Brand, *Popular Antiquities*,
iii. 339 *sq.* (Bohn's ed.); Sir John
Lubbock (Lord Avebury), *Origin of
Civilisation*,[4] pp. 237 *sq.*; Ch. Rogers,
Social Life in Scotland, iii. 224 ;
Camden, *Britannia*, translated by
E. Gibson (London, 1695), col. 1046 ;
M. MacPhail, "Traditions, Customs,
and Superstitions of the Lewis," *Folk-
lore*, vi. (1895) p. 167 ; J. G. Dalyell,
Darker Superstitions of Scotland, pp.
515 *sqq.*; F. Gregorovius, *Corsica*,
(London, 1855), p. 187 ; F. S. Krauss,

*Volksglaube und religiöser Brauch der
Südslaven*, pp. 166-170 ; M. E. Dur-
ham, *High Albania* (London, 1909),
pp. 104 *sqq.* ; E. Doutté, *Magie et
religion dans l'Afrique du Nord*
(Algiers, 1908), p. 371 ; W. Radloff,
*Proben der Volksliteratur der tür-
kischen Stämme Süd-Sibiriens*, iii. 115,
note 1, compare p. 132 ; J. Grimm,
Deutsche Mythologie,[4] ii. 932 ; W. W.
Rockhill, *The Land of the Lamas*
(London, 1891), pp. 176, 341-344 ;
P. S. Pallas, *Reise durch verschiedene
Provinzen des russischen Reichs*, i.
393 ; J. G. Georgi, *Beschreibung aller
Nationen des russischen Reichs*, p.
223 ; T. de Pauly, *Description ethno-
graphique des peuples de la Russie,
peuples de la Sibérie orientale* (St.
Petersburg, 1862), p. 7 ; Krahmer,
"Der Anadyr-Bezirk nach A. W.
Olssufjew," *Petermann's Mittheilungen*,
xlv. (1899) pp. 230 *sq.*; W. Bogoras,
"The Chuckchee Religion," *Memoir
of the American Museum of Natural
History, The Jesup North Pacific
Expedition*, vol. vii. part ii. (Leyden and
New York) pp. 487 *sqq.* ; Crabouillet,
"Les Lolos," *Missions Catholiques*, v.
(1873) p. 72 ; W. G. Aston, *Shinto*,
p. 339 ; R. Andree, "Scapulimantia,"
in *Boas Anniversary Volume* (New
York; 1906), pp. 143-165.

Iron not used in building sacred edifices. Burghead, no hammer may be used; the hammering must be done with a stone.[1]   Amongst the Jews no iron tool was used in building the Temple at Jerusalem or in making an altar.[2]   The old wooden bridge (*Pons Sublicius*) at Rome, which was considered sacred, was made and had to be kept in repair without the use of iron or bronze.[3]   It was expressly provided by law that the temple of Jupiter Liber at Furfo might be repaired with iron tools.[4]   The council chamber at Cyzicus was constructed of wood without any iron nails, the beams being so arranged that they could be taken out and replaced.[5]   The late Rajah Vijyanagram, a member of the Viceroy's Council, and described as one of the most enlightened and estimable of Hindoo princes, would not allow iron to be used in the construction of buildings within his territory, believing that its use would inevitably be followed by small-pox and other epidemics.[6]

Everything new excites the awe and fear of the savage. This superstitious objection to iron perhaps dates from that early time in the history of society when iron was still a novelty, and as such was viewed by many with suspicion and dislike.[7]   For everything new is apt to excite the awe and dread of the savage.   "It is a curious superstition," says a pioneer in Borneo, "this of the Dusuns, to attribute anything—whether good or bad, lucky or unlucky—that happens to them to something novel which has arrived in their country.   For instance, my living in Kindram has caused the intensely hot weather we have experienced of late."[8]   Some years ago a harmless naturalist was collecting plants among the high forest-clad mountains on the borders of China and Tibet.   From the summit of a pass he gazed with delight down a long valley which, stretching away as far as eye could reach to the south, resembled a sea of bloom, for everywhere the forest was ablaze with the

[1] C. F. Gordon Cumming, *In the Hebrides*, p. 226 ; E. J. Guthrie, *Old Scottish Customs* (London and Glasgow, 1885), p. 223.
[2] 1 Kings vi. 7; Exodus xx. 25.
[3] Dionysius Halicarnasensis, *Antiquit. Roman.* iii. 45, v. 24 ; Plutarch, *Numa*, 9 ; Pliny, *Nat. Hist.* xxxvi. 100.
[4] *Acta Fratrum Arvalium*, ed. G. Henzen, p. 132; *Corpus Inscriptionum Latinarum*, i. No. 603.
[5] Pliny, *Nat. Hist.* xxxvi. 100.
[6] *Indian Antiquary*, x. (1881) p. 364.
[7] Prof. W. Ridgeway ingeniously suggests that the magical virtue of iron may be based on an observation of its magnetic power, which would lead savages to imagine that it was possessed of a spirit. See *Report of the British Association for 1903*, p. 816.
[8] Frank Hatton, *North Borneo* (1886), p. 233.

gorgeous hues of the rhodcdendron and azalea in flower. In this earthly paradise the votary of science hastened to install himself beside a lake. But hardly had he done so when, alas! the weather changed. Though the season was early June, the cold became intense, snow fell heavily, and the bloom of the rhododendrons was cut off. The inhabitants of a neighbouring village at once set down the unusual severity of the weather to the presence of a stranger in the forest; and a round-robin, signed by them unanimously, was forwarded to the nearest mandarin, setting forth that the snow which had blocked the road, and the hail which was blasting their crops, were alike caused by the intruder, and that all sorts of disturbances would follow if he were allowed to remain. In these circumstances the naturalist, who had intended to spend most of the summer among the mountains, was forced to decamp. "Collecting in this country," he adds pathetically, "is not an easy matter."[1] The unusually heavy rains which happened to follow the English survey of the Nicobar Islands in the winter of 1886-1887 were imputed by the alarmed natives to the wrath of the spirits at the theodolites, dumpy-levellers, and other strange instruments which had been set up in so many of their favourite haunts; and some of them proposed to soothe the anger of the spirits by sacrificing a pig.[2] When the German Hans Stade was a captive in a cannibal tribe of Brazilian Indians, it happened that, shortly before a prisoner was to be eaten, a great wind arose and blew away part of the roofs of the huts. The savages were angry with Stade, and said he had made the wind to come by looking into his thunder-skins, by which they meant a book he had been reading, in order to save the prisoner, who was a friend of his, from their stomachs. So the pious German prayed tó God, and God mercifully heard his prayer; for next morning the weather was beautifully fine, and his friend was butchered, carved, and eaten in the most perfect comfort.[3] According to the

---

[1] A. E. Pratt, "Two Journeys to Ta-tsien-lu on the eastern Borders of Tibet," *Proceedings of the R. Geographical Society*, xiii. (1891) p. 341.

[2] W. Svoboda, "Die Bewohner des Nikobaren-Archipels," *Internationales Archiv für Ethnographie*, vi. (1893) p. 13.

[3] *The Captivity of Hans Stade of Hesse, in A.D. 1547-1555*, translated by A. Tootal (London, 1874), pp. 85 *sq.*

Orotchis of eastern Siberia, misfortunes have multiplied on them with the coming of Europeans ; "they even go so far as to lay the appearance of *new* phenomena like thunder at the door of the Russians."[1]   In the seventeenth century a succession of bad seasons excited a revolt among the Esthonian peasantry, who traced the origin of the evil to a water-mill, which put a stream to some inconvenience by checking its flow.[2]   The first introduction of iron ploughshares into Poland having been followed by a succession of bad harvests, the farmers attributed the badness of the crops to the iron ploughshares, and discarded them for the old wooden ones.[3] To this day the primitive Baduwis of Java, who live chiefly by husbandry, will use no iron tools in tilling their fields.[4]

The dislike of spirits to iron allows men to use the metal as a weapon against them.   The general dislike of innovation, which always makes itself strongly felt in the sphere of religion, is sufficient by itself to account for the superstitious aversion to iron entertained by kings and priests and attributed by them to the gods ; possibly this aversion may have been intensified in places by some such accidental cause as the series of bad seasons which cast discredit on iron ploughshares in Poland. But the disfavour in which iron is held by the gods and their ministers has another side.   Their antipathy to the metal furnishes men with a weapon which may be turned against the spirits when occasion serves.   As their dislike of iron is supposed to be so great that they will not approach persons and things protected by the obnoxious metal, iron may obviously be employed as a charm for banning ghosts *Iron used as a charm against fairies in the Highlands of Scotland.* and other dangerous spirits.   And often it is so used.   Thus in the Highlands of Scotland the great safeguard against the elfin race is iron, or, better yet, steel.   The metal in any form, whether as a sword, a knife, a gun-barrel, or what not, is all-powerful for this purpose.   Whenever you enter a fairy

[1] E. H. Fraser, "The Fish-skin Tartars," *Journal of the China Branch of the R. Asiatic Society for the Year 1891-92,* N.S. xxvi. p. 15.

[2] Fr. Kreutzwald und H. Neus, *Mythische und magische Lieder der Ehsten* (St. Petersburg, 1854), p. 113.

[3] Alexand. Guagninus, "De ducatu Samogitiae," in *Respublica sive status regni Poloniae, Lituaniae, Prussiae,* *Livoniae,* etc. (Elzevir, 1627) p. 276; Johan. Lasicius, "De diis Samogitarum caeterorumque Sarmatum," in *Respublica,* etc. (*ut supra*), p. 294 (p. 84, ed. W. Mannhardt, in *Magazin herausgegeben von der Lettisch - Literärischen Gesellschaft,* vol. xiv.).

[4] L. von Ende, "Die Baduwis von Java," *Mittheilungen der anthropologischen Gesellschaft in Wien,* xix. (1889) p. 10.

dwelling you should always remember to stick a piece of
steel, such as a knife, a needle, or a fish-hook, in the door ;
for then the elves will not be able to shut the door till you
come out again.   So too when you have shot a deer and
are bringing it home at night, be sure to thrust a knife into
the carcase, for that keeps the fairies from laying their weight
on it.   A knife or a nail in your pocket is quite enough to
prevent the fairies from lifting you up at night.   Nails in
the front of a bed ward off elves from women "in the straw"
and from their babes ; but to make quite sure it is better to
put the smoothing-iron under the bed, and the reaping-hook
in the window.   If a bull has fallen over a rock and been
killed, a nail stuck into it will preserve the flesh from the
fairies.   Music discoursed on that melodious instrument, a
Jew's harp, keeps the elfin women away from the hunter,
because the tongue of the instrument is of steel.[1]   Again,
when Scotch fishermen were at sea, and one of them
happened to take the name of God in vain, the first man
who heard him called out " Cauld airn," at which every
man of the crew grasped the nearest bit of iron and held
it between his hands for a while.[2]   So too when he hears
the unlucky word " pig " mentioned, a Scotch fisherman
will feel for the nails in his boots and mutter " Cauld
airn." [3]   The same magic words are even whispered in
the churches of Scotch fishing-villages when the clergy-
man reads the passage about the Gadarene swine.[4]   In
Morocco iron is considered a great protection against demons ;
hence it is usual to place a knife or dagger under a sick
man's pillow.[5]   The Singhalese believe that they are constantly surrounded by evil spirits, who lie in wait to do them
harm.   A peasant would not dare to carry good food, such
as cakes or roast meat, from one place to another without
putting an iron nail on it to prevent a demon from taking
possession of the viands and so making the eater ill.   No

*Iron used
as a
protective
charm by
Scotch
fishermen
and others.*

[1] J. G. Campbell, *Superstitions of
the Highlands and Islands of Scotland*
(Glasgow, 1900), pp. 46 *sq.*

[2] E. J. Guthrie, *Old Scottish Customs*,
p. 149 ; Ch. Rogers, *Social Life in Scotland* (Edinburgh, 1884-1886), iii. 218.

[3] J. Macdonald, *Religion and Myth*,
p. 91.

[4] W. Gregor, *Folk-lore of the North-
East of Scotland* (London, 1881), p.
201.   The fishermen think that if the
word "pig," "sow," or "swine" be
uttered while the lines are being baited,
the line will certainly be lost.

[5] A. Leared, *Morocco and the Moors*
(London, 1876), p. 273.

Iron used as a protective charm against devils and ghosts in India.

sick person, whether man or woman, would venture out of the house without a bunch of keys or a knife in his hand, for without such a talisman he would fear that some devil might take advantage of his weak state to slip into his body. And if a man has a large sore on his body he tries to keep a morsel of iron on it as a protection against demons.[1] The inhabitants of Salsette, an island near Bombay, dread a spirit called *gîrâ*, which plays many pranks with a solitary traveller, leading him astray, lowering him into an empty well, and so on. But a *gîrâ* dare not touch a person who has on him anything made of iron or steel, particularly a knife or a nail, of which the spirit stands in great fear. Nor will he meddle with a woman, especially a married woman, because he is afraid of her bangles.[2] Among the Majhwâr, an aboriginal tribe in the hill country of South Mirzapur, an iron implement such as a sickle or a betel-cutter is constantly kept near an infant's head during its first year for the purpose of warding off the attacks of ghosts.[3] Among the Maravars, an aboriginal race of southern India, a knife or other iron object lies beside a woman after childbirth to keep off the devil.[4] When a Mala woman is in labour, a sickle and some *nīm* leaves are always kept on the cot. In Malabar people who have to pass by burning-grounds or other haunted places commonly carry with them iron in some form, such as a knife or an iron rod used as a walking-stick. When pregnant women go on a journey, they carry with them a few twigs or leaves of the *nīm* tree, or iron in some shape, to scare evil spirits lurking in groves or burial-grounds which they may pass.[5] In Bilaspore people attribute cholera to a goddess who visits the afflicted family. But they think that she may be kept off by iron ; hence during an epidemic of cholera people go about with axes or sickles in their hands. "Their horses are not shod, otherwise they might possibly nail horse-shoes to the door,

---

[1] Wickremasinghe, in *Am Urquell*, v. (1894) p. 7.

[2] G. F. D'Penha, "Superstitions and Customs in Salsette," *Indian Antiquary*, xxviii. (1899) p. 114.

[3] W. Crooke, *Tribes and Castes of the North-Western Provinces and Oudh*, iii. 431.

[4] F. Jagor, "Bericht über verschiedene Volksstämme in Vorderindien," *Zeitschrift für Ethnologie*, xxvi. (1894) p. 70.

[5] E. Thurston, *Ethnographic Notes in Southern India* (Madras, 1906), p. 341.

but their belief is more primitive ; for with them iron does not *bring* good luck, but it *scares away* the evil spirits, so when a man has had an epileptic fit he will wear an iron bracelet to keep away the evil spirit which was supposed to have possessed him." [1]   The Annamites imagine that a new-born child is exposed to the attacks of evil spirits. To protect the infant from these malignant beings the parents sometimes sell the child to the village smith, who makes a small ring or circlet of iron and puts it on the child's foot, commonly adding a little chain of iron.   When the infant has been sold to the smith and firmly attached to him by the chain, the demons no longer have any power over him.   After the child has grown big and the danger is over, the parents ask the smith to break the iron ring and thank him for his services.   No metal but iron will serve the purpose. [2]   On the Slave Coast of Africa when a mother sees her child gradually wasting away, she concludes that a demon has entered into the child and takes her measures accordingly.   To lure the demon out of the body of her offspring, she offers a sacrifice of food ; and while the devil is bolting it, she attaches iron rings and small bells to her child's ankles and hangs iron chains round his neck. The jingling of the·iron and the tinkling of the bells are supposed to prevent the demon, when he has concluded his repast, from entering again into the body of the little sufferer. Hence many children may be seen in this part of Africa weighed down with iron ornaments. [3]   The use of iron as a means to exorcise demons was forbidden by the Coptic church. [4]   In India " the mourner who performs the ceremony of putting fire into the dead person's mouth carries with him a piece of iron : it may be a key or a knife, or a simple piece of iron, and during the whole time of his separation (for he is unclean for a certain time, and no one will either touch him or eat or drink with him, neither can he change his

Iron used as a protective charm in Annam, Africa, and India.

[1] E. M. Gordon, *Indian Folk Tales* (London, 1908), p. 31.

[2] L. R. P. Cadière, "Coutumes populaires de la vallée du Nguôn-So'n," *Bulletin de l'École Française d'Extrême-Orient*, ii. (1902) pp. 354 *sq.*

[3] Baudin, "Le Fétichisme," *Missions Catholiques*, xvi. (1884) p. 249 ; A. B. Ellis, *The Yoruba-speaking Peoples of the Slave Coast*, p. 113.

[4] *Il Fetha Nagast o legislazione dei re, codice ecclesiastico e civile d. Abissinia*, tradotto e annotato da Ignazio Guidi (Rome, 1899), p. 140.

Iron used as a protective charm in India and Scotland.

clothes[1]) he carries the piece of iron about with him to keep off the evil spirit. In Calcutta the Bengali clerks in the Government Offices used to wear a small key on one of their fingers when they had been chief mourners."[2]　When a woman dies in childbed in the island of Salsette, they put a nail or other piece of iron in the folds of her dress; this is done especially if the child survives her. The intention plainly is to prevent her spirit from coming back; for they believe that a dead mother haunts the house and seeks to carry away her child.[3]　In the north-east of Scotland immediately after a death had taken place, a piece of iron, such as a nail or a knitting-wire, used to be stuck into all the meal, butter, cheese, flesh, and whisky in the house, "to prevent death from entering them." The neglect of this salutary precaution is said to have been closely followed by the corruption of the food and drink; the whisky has been known to become as white as milk.[4]　When iron is used as a protective charm after a death, as in these Hindoo and Scotch customs, the spirit against which it is directed is the ghost of the deceased.[5]

[1] The reader may observe how closely the taboos laid upon mourners resemble those laid upon kings. From what has gone before, the reason of the resemblance is obvious.

[2] *Panjab Notes and Queries*, iii. p. 61, § 282.

[3] G. F. D'Penha, "Superstitions and Customs in Salsette," *Indian Antiquary*, xxviii. (1899) p. 115.

[4] W. Gregor, *Folk-lore of the North-East of Scotland*, p. 206.

[5] This is expressly said in *Panjab Notes and Queries*, iii. p. 202, § 846. On iron as a protective charm see also F. Liebrecht, *Gervasius von Tilbury*, pp. 99 *sqq.*; *id.*, *Zur Volkskunde*, p. 311; L. Strackerjan, *Aberglaube und Sagen aus dem Herzogthum Oldenburg*, i. pp. 354 *sq.* § 233; A. Wuttke, *Der deutsche Volksaberglaube*,[2] § 414 *sq.*; E. B. Tylor, *Primitive Culture*,[2] i. 140; W. Mannhardt, *Baumkultus*, p. 132 note. Many peoples, especially in Africa, regard the smith's craft with awe or fear as something uncanny and savouring of magic. Hence smiths are sometimes held in high honour, sometimes looked down upon with great contempt. These feelings probably spring in large measure from the superstitions which cluster round iron. See R. Andree, *Ethnographische Parallelen und Vergleiche*, pp. 153-159; G. McCall Theal, *Records of South-Eastern Africa*, vii. 447; O. Lenz, *Skizzen aus West-Afrika* (Berlin, 1878), p. 184; A. Bastian, *Die deutsche Expedition an der Loango-Küste*, ii. 217; M. Merkel, *Die Masai* (Berlin, 1904), pp. 110 *sq.*; A. C. Hollis, *The Masai* (Oxford, 1905), pp. 330 *sq.*; *id.*, *The Nandi* (Oxford, 1909), pp. 36 *sq.*; J. Spieth, *Die Ewe-Stämme* (Berlin, 1906), p. 776; E. Doutté, *Magie et religion dans l'Afrique du Nord*, pp. 40 *sqq.*; Ph. Paulitschke, *Ethnographie Nordost-Afrikas, die geistige Cultur der Danâkil, Galla und Somâl* (Berlin, 1896), p. 30; *id.*, *Ethnographie Nordost-Afrikas, die materielle Cultur der Danâkil, Galla und Somâl* (Berlin, 1893), p. 202; Th. Levebvre, *Voyage en Abyssinie*, i. p. lxi.; A. Cecchi, *Da Zeila alle frontiere del Caffa*, i. (Rome, 1886) p. 45; M.

§ 3. *Sharp Weapons tabooed*

There is a priestly king to the north of Zengwih in
Burma, revered by the Sotih as the highest spiritual and
temporal authority, into whose house no weapon or cutting
instrument may be brought.[1]   This rule may perhaps be
explained by a custom observed by various peoples after a
death; they refrain from the use of sharp instruments so
long as the ghost of the deceased is supposed to be near,
lest they should wound it.   Thus among the Esquimaux of
Bering Strait "during the day on which a person dies in the
village no one is permitted to work, and the relatives must
perform no labour during the three following days.   It is
especially forbidden during this period to cut with any
edged instrument, such as a knife or an axe ; and the use of
pointed instruments, like needles or bodkins, is also forbidden.   This is said to be done to avoid cutting or injuring
the shade, which may be present at any time during this
period, and, if accidentally injured by any of these things, it
would become very angry and bring sickness or death to the
people.   The relatives must also be very careful at this time
not to make any loud or harsh noises that may startle or
anger the shade."[2]   We have seen that in like manner after
killing a white whale these Esquimaux abstain from the use
of cutting or pointed instruments for four days, lest they
should unwittingly cut or stab the whale's ghost.[3]   The
same taboo is sometimes observed by them when there is a
sick person in the village, probably from a fear of injuring

The use of sharp-edged weapons is sometimes forbidden lest they should wound spirits.

Parkyns, *Life in Abyssinia*[2] (London,
1868), pp. 300 *sq.* ; J. T. Bent, *Sacred
City of the Ethiopians* (London, 1893),
p. 212; G. Rohlf, "Reise durch
Nord-Afrika," *Petermann's Mittheilungen, Ergänzungsheft*, No. 25
(Gotha, 1868), pp. 30, 54; G.
Nachtigal, "Die Tibbu," *Zeitschrift
für Erdkunde zu Berlin*, v. (1870)
pp. 312 *sq.* ; *id.*, *Sahara und Sudan*,
i. 443 *sq.*, ii. 145, 178, 371, iii. 189,
234 *sq.*   The Kayans of Borneo think
that a smith is inspired by a special
spirit, the smith's spirit, and that
without this inspiration he could do no

good work.   See A. W. Nieuwenhuis,
Quer durch Borneo, ii. 198.
[1] A. Bastian, *Die Völker des östlichen
Asien*, i. (Leipsic, 1866) p. 136.
[2] E. W. Nelson, "The Eskimo
about Bering Strait," *Eighteenth
Annual Report of the Bureau of
American Ethnology*, part i. (Washington, 1899) p. 312.   Compare *ibid.*
pp. 315, 364; W. H. Dall, *Alaska
and its Resources*, p. 146; *id.*, in
American Naturalist, xii. 7; *id.*, in
The Yukon Territory (London, 1898),
p. 146.
[3] See above, p. 205.

his shade which may be hovering outside of his body.[1] After a death the Roumanians of Transylvania are careful not to leave a knife lying with the sharp edge uppermost as long as the corpse remains in the house, "or else the soul will be forced to ride on the blade."[2] For seven days after a death, the corpse being still in the house, the Chinese abstain from the use of knives and needles, and even of chopsticks, eating their food with their fingers.[3] On the third, sixth, ninth, and fortieth days after the funeral the old Prussians and Lithuanians used to prepare a meal, to which, standing at the door, they invited the soul of the deceased. At these meals they sat silent round the table and used no knives, and the women who served up the food were also without knives. If any morsels fell from the table they were left lying there for the lonely souls that had no living relations or friends to feed them. When the meal was over the priest took a broom and swept the souls out of the house, saying, "Dear souls, ye have eaten and drunk. Go forth, go forth."[4] In cutting the nails and combing the hair of a dead prince in South Celebes only the back of the knife and of the comb may be used.[5] The Germans say that a knife should not be left edge upwards, because God and the spirits dwell there, or because it will cut the face of God and the angels.[6] Among the Monumbos of New Guinea a pregnant woman may not use sharp instruments; for example, she may not sew. If she used such instruments, they think that she would thereby stab the child in her womb.[7] Among

[1] A. Woldt, Captain Jacobsen's Reise an der Nordwestküste Americas 1881-1883 (Leipsic, 1884), p. 243.

[2] W. Schmidt, Das Jahr und seine Tage in Meinung und Brauch der Romänen Siebenbürgens (Hermannstadt, 1866), p. 40; E. Gerard, The Land beyond the Forest, i. 312.

[3] J. H. Gray, China (London, 1878), i. 288.

[4] Jo. Meletius (Maeletius, Menecius), "De religione et sacrificiis veterum Borussorum," in De Russorum Muscovitarum et Tartarorum religione, sacrificiis, nuptiarum, funerum ritu (Spires, 1582), p. 263; id., reprinted in Scriptores rerum Livonicarum, vol. ii. (Riga and Leipsic, 1848) pp.

391 sq., and in Mitteilungen der Litterarischen Gesellschaft Masovia, viii. (Lötzen, 1902) pp. 194 sq. Compare Chr. Hartknoch, Alt und neues Preussen (Frankfort and Leipsic, 1684), pp. 187 sq.

[5] B. F. Matthes, Bijdragen tot de Ethnologie van Zuid-Celebes, p. 136.

[6] Tettau und Temme, Die Volkssagen Ostpreussens, Litthauens und Westpreussens, p. 285; J. Grimm, Deutsche Mythologie,[4] iii. 454, compare pp. 441, 469; J. V. Grohmann, Aberglauben und Gebräuche aus Böhmen und Mähren, p. 198, § 1387.

[7] Franz Vormann, "Zur Psychologie, Soziologie und Geschichte der

the Kayans of Borneo, when the birth-pangs begín, all
men leave the room, and all cutting weapons and iron
are also removed, "perhaps in order not to frighten the
child," says the writer who reports the custom.[1]   The
reason may rather be a fear of injuring the flitting soul of
mother or babe.   In Uganda, when the hour of a woman's
delivery is at hand, her husband carries all spears and
weapons out of the house,[2] doubtless in order that they
may not hurt the tender soul of the new-born child.
Early in the period of the Ming dynasty a professor of
geomancy made the alarming discovery that the spiritual
atmosphere of Kü-yung, a city near Nanking, was in a truly
deplorable condition through the intrusion of an evil spirit.
The Chinese emperor, with paternal solicitude, directed that
the north gate, by which the devil had effected his entrance,
should be built up solid, and that for the future the population of the city should devote their energies to the pursuits
of hair-dressing, corn-cutting, and the shaving of bamboo-
roots, because, as he sagaciously perceived, all these professions
call for the use of sharp-edged instruments, which could not
fail to keep the demon at bay.[3]   We can now understand
why no cutting instrument may be taken into the house
of the Burmese pontiff.   Like so many priestly kings, he is
probably regarded as divine, and it is therefore right that
his sacred spirit should not be exposed to the risk of being
cut or wounded whenever it quits his body to hover invisible
in the air or to fly on some distant mission.

Sharp-edged weapons removed from a room where there is a lying-in woman.

§ 4. *Blood tabooed*

We have seen that the Flamen Dialis was forbidden to
touch or even name raw flesh.[4]   At certain times a Brahman
teacher is enjoined not to look on raw flesh, blood, or persons
whose hands have been cut off.[5]   In Uganda the father of

Raw meat tabooed because the life or spirit is in the blood.

Monumbo-Papua, Deutsch-Neuginea,"
Anthropos, v. (1910) p. 410.
   [1] A. W. Nieuwenhuis, *In Centraal
Borneo* (Leyden, 1900), i. 61 ; *id.*,
Quer durch Borneo, i. 69.
   [2] Fr. Stuhlmann, *Mit Emin Pascha
ins Herz von Afrika* (Berlin, 1894), p.
184.

   [3] J. J. M. de Groot, *The Religious
System of China*, iii. 1045 (Leyden,
1897).
   [4] Plutarch, *Quaest. Rom.* 110; Aulus
Gellius, x. 15. 12.   See above, p. 13.
   [5] *Grihya-Sutras*, translated by H.
Oldenberg, part i. pp. 81, 141 (*Sacred
Books of the East*, vol. xxix.).

Raw meat
tabooed
because
the life or
spirit is in
the blood. twins is in a state of taboo for some time after the birth; among other rules he is forbidden to kill anything or to see blood.[1] In the Pelew Islands when a raid has been made on a village and a head carried off, the relations of the slain man are tabooed and have to submit to certain observances in order to escape the wrath of his ghost. They are shut up in the house, touch no raw flesh, and chew betel over which an incantation has been uttered by the exorcist. After this the ghost of the slaughtered man goes away to the enemy's country in pursuit of his murderer.[2] The taboo is probably based on the common belief that the soul or spirit of the animal is in the blood. As tabooed persons are believed to be in a perilous state—for example, the relations of the slain man are liable to the attacks of his indignant ghost—it is especially necessary to isolate them from contact with spirits ; hence the prohibition to touch raw meat. But as usual the taboo is only the special enforcement of a general precept; in other words, its observance is particularly enjoined in circumstances which seem urgently to call for its application, but apart from such circumstances the prohibition is also observed, though less strictly, as a common rule of life. Thus some of the Esthonians will not taste blood because they believe that it contains the animal's soul, which would enter the body of the person who tasted the blood.[3] Some Indian tribes of North America, "through a strong principle of religion, abstain in the strictest manner from eating the blood of any animal, as it contains the life and spirit of the beast." These Indians "commonly pull their new-killed venison (before they dress it) several times through the smoke and flame of the fire, both by the way of a sacrifice and to consume the blood, life, or animal spirits of the beast, which with them would be a most horrid abomination to eat."[4] Among the western Dénés or Tinneh Indians of British Columbia until lately no woman

[1] J. Roscoe, "Further Notes on the Manners and Customs of the Baganda," *Journal of the Anthropological Institute*, xxxii. (1902) p. 53.

[2] J. Kubary, *Die socialen Einrichtungen der Pelauer* (Berlin, 1885), pp. 126 *sq.*

[3] F. J. Wiedemann, *Aus dem inneren und äussern Leben der Ehsten* (St. Petersburg, 1876), pp. 448, 478.

[4] James Adair, *History of the American Indians* (London, 1775), pp. 134, 117. The Indians described by Adair are the Creek, Cherokee, and other tribes in the south-east of the United States.

would partake of blood, "and both men and women abhorred the flesh of a beaver which had been caught and died in a trap, and of a bear strangled to death in a snare, because the blood remained in the carcase."[1] Many of the Slave, Hare, and Dogrib Indians scruple to taste the blood of game; hunters of the former tribes collect the blood in the animal's paunch and bury it in the snow.[2] The Malepa, a Bantu tribe in the north of the Transvaal, will taste no blood. Hence they cut the throats of the cattle they slaughter and let the blood drain out of the carcase before they will eat it. And they do the same with game.[3] Jewish hunters poured out the blood of the game they had killed and covered it up with dust. They would not taste the blood, believing that the soul or life of the animal was in the blood, or actually was the blood.[4] The same belief was held by the Romans,[5] and is shared by the Arabs,[6] by Chinese medical writers,[7] and by some of the Papuan tribes of New Guinea.[8]

It is a common rule that royal blood may not be shed upon the ground. Hence when a king or one of his family is to be put to death a mode of execution is devised by which the royal blood shall not be spilt upon the earth. About the year 1688 the generalissimo of the army rebelled against the king of Siam and put him to death "after the manner of royal criminals, or as princes of the blood are treated when convicted of capital crimes, which is by putting them into a large iron caldron, and pounding them to pieces with wooden pestles, because none of their royal blood must be spilt on the ground, it being, by their religion, thought great impiety to contaminate the divine blood by mixing it with earth."[9]

Royal blood may not be spilt on the ground; hence kings and princes are put to death by methods which do not involve bloodshed.

---

[1] A. G. Morice, "The Western Dénés, their Manners and Customs," *Proceedings of the Canadian Institute*, Third Series, vii. (1888-89) p. 164.

[2] E. Petitot, *Monographie des Dènè-Dindjié* (Paris, 1876), p. 76.

[3] Schlömann, "Die Malepa in Transvaal," *Verhandlungen der Berliner Gesellschaft für Anthropologie, Ethnologie und Urgeschichte*, 1894, p. (67).

[4] Leviticus xvii. 10-14. The Hebrew word (נֶפֶשׁ) translated "life" in the English version of verse 11 means also

"soul" (marginal note in the Revised Version). Compare Deuteronomy xii. 23-25.

[5] Servius on Virgil, *Aen.* v. 79; compare *id.* on *Aen.* iii. 67.

[6] J. Wellhausen, *Reste arabischen Heidentumes* (Berlin, 1887), p. 217.

[7] J. J. M. de Groot, *Religious System of China*, iv. 80-82.

[8] A. Goudswaard, *De Papoewa's van de Geelvinksbaai* (Schiedam, 1863), p. 77.

[9] Hamilton's "Account of the East

Royal
blood may
not be spilt
on the
ground ;
hence
kings and
princes
are put
to death
in ways
which do
not involve
bloodshed.

Other Siamese modes of executing a royal person are
starvation, suffocation, stretching him on a scarlet cloth and
thrusting a billet of fragrant sandal-wood into his stomach,[1]
or lastly, sewing him up in a leather sack with a large stone
and throwing him into the river; sometimes the sufferer's
neck is broken with sandal-wood clubs before he is thrown
into the water.[2] When Kublai Khan defeated and took his
uncle Nayan, who had rebelled against him, he caused Nayan
to be put to death by being wrapt in a carpet and tossed to
and fro till he died, " because he would not have the blood
of his Line Imperial spilt upon the ground or exposed in the
eye of Heaven and before the Sun."[3] " Friar Ricold mentions
the Tartar maxim : ' One Khan will put another to death to
get possession of the throne, but he takes great care that the
blood be not spilt. For they say that it is highly improper
that the blood of the Great Khan should be spilt upon the
ground ; so they cause the victim to be smothered somehow
or other.' The like feeling prevails at the court of Burma,
where a peculiar mode of execution without bloodshed is
reserved for princes of the blood."[4] Another writer on
Burma observes that "according to Mongolian tradition, it
is considered improper to spill the blood of any member of
the royal race. Princes of the Blood are executed by a
blow, or blows, of a bludgeon, inflicted on the back of the
neck. The corpse is placed in a red velvet sack, which is
fixed between two large perforated jars, and then sunk in
the river Irawadi. Princesses are executed in a similar
manner, with the exception that they are put to death by a
blow in front, instead of the back of the neck."[5] In 1878
the relations of Theebaw, king of Burma, were despatched
by being beaten across the throat with a bamboo.[6] In
Tonquin the ordinary mode of execution is beheading, but
persons of the blood royal are strangled.[7] In Ashantee the

Indies," in Pinkerton's *Voyages and
Travels*, viii. 469. Compare W.
Robertson Smith, *Religion of the
Semites*,[2] i. 369, note 1.

[1] De la Loubere, *Du royaume de
Siam* (Amsterdam, 1691), i. 317.

[2] Pallegoix, *Description du royaume
Thai ou Siam*, i. 271, 365 sq.

[3] Marco Polo, translated by Col. H.

Yule (Second Edition, 1875), i. 335.

[4] Col. H. Yule on Marco Polo, *l.c.*

[5] A. Fytche, *Burma, Past and
Present* (London, 1878), i. 217 note.
Compare *Indian Antiquary*, xxix.
(1900) p. 199.

[6] *Indian Antiquary*, xx. (1891)
p. 49.

[7] Baron's " Description of the King-

blood of none of the royal family may be shed ; if one of
them is guilty of a great crime he is drowned in the river
Dah.[1] As the blood royal of Dahomey may not be spilled,
offenders of the royal family are drowned or strangled.
Commonly they are bound hand and foot, carried out to sea
in a canoe, and thrown overboard.[2] When a king of Benin
came to the throne he used to put his brothers to death ;
but as no one might lay hands on a prince of the blood, the
king commanded his brothers to hang themselves, after
which he buried their bodies with great pomp.[3] In Madagascar the blood of nobles might not be shed ; hence when
four Christians of that class were to be executed they were
burned alive.[4] In Uganda " no one may shed royal blood
on any account, not even when ordered by the king to slay
one of the royal house ; royalty may only be starved or
burned to death." [5] Formerly when a young king of
Uganda came of age all his brothers were burnt except two
or three, who were preserved to keep up the succession.[6]
Or a space of ground having been fenced in with a high
paling and a deep ditch, the doomed men were led into the
enclosure and left there till they died, while guards kept
watch outside to prevent their escape.[7] Among the Bawenda
of southern Africa dangerous princes are strangled, for their
blood may not be shed.[8]

The reluctance to spill royal blood seems to be only a
particular case of a general unwillingness to shed blood or at
least to allow it to fall on the ground. Marco Polo tells us
that in his day persons caught in the streets of Cambaluc

Reluctance to shed any human blood on the ground.

dom of Tonqueen," in Pinkerton's
Voyages and Travels, ix. 691.

[1] T. E. Bowdich, *Mission from
Cape Coast Castle to Ashantee* (London,
1873), p. 207.

[2] A. B. Ellis, *Ewe-speaking Peoples of
the Slave Coast*, p. 224, compare p. 89.

[3] O. Dapper, *Description de l'Afrique*
(Amsterdam, 1686), p. 313.

[4] J. Sibree, *Madagascar and its
People*, p. 430.

[5] J. Roscoe, " Further Notes on the
Manners and Customs of the Baganda,"
Journal of the Anthropological Institute,
xxxii. (1902) p. 50.

[6] C. T. Wilson and R. W. Felkin,

Uganda and the Egyptian Soudan
(London, 1882), i. 200.

[7] J. Roscoe, *op. cit.* p. 67. There
is an Arab legend of a king who was
slain by opening the veins of his arms
and letting the blood drain into a bowl ;
not a drop might fall on the ground,
otherwise there would be blood revenge
for it. Robertson Smith conjectured
that the legend was based on an old
form of sacrifice regularly applied to
captive chiefs (*Religion of the Semites*,[2]
p. 369 note, compare p. 418 note).

[8] Rev. E. Gottschling, " The Bawenda," *Journal of the Anthropological
Institute*, xxxv. (1905) p. 366.

(Peking) at unseasonable hours were arrested, and if found guilty of a misdemeanour were beaten with a stick. "Under this punishment people sometimes die, but they adopt it in order to eschew bloodshed, for their *Bacsis* say that it is an evil thing to shed man's blood."[1] When Captain Christian was shot by the Manx Government at the Restoration in 1660, the spot on which he stood was covered with white blankets, that his blood might not fall on the ground.[2] In West Sussex people believe that the ground on which human blood has been shed is accursed and will remain barren for ever.[3] Among some primitive peoples, when the blood of a tribesman has to be spilt it is not suffered to fall upon the ground, but is received upon the bodies of his fellow-tribesmen. Thus in some Australian tribes boys who are being circumcised are laid on a platform, formed by the living bodies of the tribesmen;[4] and when a boy's tooth is knocked out as an initiatory ceremony, he is seated on the shoulders of a man, on whose breast the blood flows and may not be wiped away.[5] When Australian blacks bleed each other as a cure for headache and other ailments, they are very careful not to spill any of the blood on the ground, but sprinkle it on each other.[6] We have already seen that in the Australian ceremony for making rain the blood which is supposed to imitate the rain is received upon the bodies of the tribesmen.[7] "Also the Gauls used to drink their enemies' blood and paint themselves therewith. So also they write that the old Irish were wont; and so have I seen some of the Irish do, but not their enemies' but friends' blood, as, namely, at the execution of a notable traitor at Limerick, called Murrogh O'Brien, I saw an old woman, which was his foster-mother, take up his head whilst he was quartered and suck

---

[1] Marco Polo, i. 399, Yule's translation, Second Edition.

[2] Sir Walter Scott, note 2 to *Peveril of the Peak*, ch. v.

[3] Charlotte Latham, "Some West Sussex Superstitions," *Folk-lore Record*, i. (1878) p. 17.

[4] *Native Tribes of South Australia*, p. 230; E. J. Eyre, *Journals of Expeditions of Discovery into Central Australia*, ii. 335; R. Brough Smyth,

Aborigines of Victoria, i. 75 note.

[5] D. Collins, *Account of the English Colony of New South Wales* (London, 1798), p. 580.

[6] *Native Tribes of South Australia*, pp. 224 *sq.*; G. F. Angas, *Savage Life and Scenes in Australia and New Zealand* (London, 1847), i. 110 *sq.*

[7] *The Magic Art and the Evolution of Kings*, vol. i. p. 256.

up all the blood that ran thereout, saying that the earth was Reluctance
not worthy to drink it, and therewith also steeped her face to allow
and breast and tore her hair, crying out and shrieking most human
terribly." [1]   After a battle in Horne Island, South Pacific, it fall on the
was found that the brother of the vanquished king was ground.
among the wounded.   " It was sad to see his wife collect in
her hands the blood which had flowed from his wounds, and
throw it on to her head, while she uttered piercing cries.
All the relatives of the wounded collected in the same
manner the blood which had flowed from them, down even
to the last drop, and they even applied their lips to the
leaves of the shrubs and licked it all up to the last drop." [2]
In the Marquesas Islands the persons who helped a woman
at childbirth received on their heads the blood which flowed
at the cutting of the navel-string ; for the blood might not
touch anything but a sacred object, and in Polynesia the
head is sacred in a high degree.[3]   In South Celebes at
childbirth a female slave stands under the house (the houses
being raised on posts above the ground) and receives in a
basin on her head the blood which trickles through the
bamboo floor.[4]   Among the Latuka of central Africa the
earth on which a drop of blood has fallen at childbirth is
carefully scraped up with an iron shovel, put into a pot along
with the water used in washing the mother, and buried
tolerably deep outside the house on the left-hand side.[5]   In
West Africa, if a drop of your blood has fallen on the ground,
you must carefully cover it up, rub and stamp it into the
soil ; if it has fallen on the side of a canoe or a tree, the
place is cut out and the chip destroyed.[6]   The Caffres, we
are told, have a great horror of blood, and must purify
themselves from the pollution if they have shed it and been
bespattered by it.   Hence warriors on the return from
battle purge themselves with emetics, and that so violently
that some of them give up the ghost.   A Caffre would

---

[1] Edmund Spenser, *View of the State of Ireland*, p. 101 (reprinted in H. Morley's *Ireland under Elizabeth and James the First*, London, 1890).

[2] " Futuna, or Horne Island and its People," *Journal of the Polynesian Society*, vol. i. No. 1 (April 1892), p. 43.

[3] Max Radiguet, *Les Derniers Sauvages* (Paris, 1882), p. 175.

[4] B. F. Matthes, *Bijdragen tot de Ethnologie van Zuid-Celebes*, p. 53.

[5] Fr. Stuhlmann, *Mit Emin Pascha ins Herz von Afrika*, p. 795.

[6] Miss Mary H. Kingsley, *Travels in West Africa*, pp. 440, 447.

Reluctance
to allow
human
blood to
fall on the
ground.
never allow even a drop of blood from his nose or a wound to lie uncovered, but huddles it over with earth, that his feet may not be defiled by it.[1]   One motive of these African customs may be a wish to prevent the blood from falling into the hands of magicians, who might make an evil use of it.   That is admittedly the reason why people in West Africa stamp out any blood of theirs which has fallen on the ground or cut out any wood that has been soaked with it.[2]   From a like dread of sorcery natives of New Guinea are careful to burn any sticks, leaves, or rags which are stained with their blood ; and if the blood has dripped on the ground they turn up the soil and if possible light a fire on the spot.[3]   The same fear explains the curious duties discharged by a class of men called *ramanga* or " blue blood" among the Betsileo of Madagascar.   It is their business to eat all the nail-parings and to lick up all the spilt blood of the nobles.   When the nobles pare their nails, the parings are collected to the last scrap and swallowed by these *ramanga*.   If the parings are too large, they are minced small and so gulped down.   Again, should a nobleman wound himself, say in cutting his nails or treading on something, the *ramanga* lick it up as fast as possible.   Nobles of high rank hardly go anywhere without these humble attendants ; but if it should happen that there are none of them present, the cut nails and the spilt blood are carefully collected to be afterwards swallowed by the *ramanga*.   There is scarcely a nobleman of any pretensions who does not strictly observe this custom,[4] the intention of which probably is to prevent these parts of his person from falling into the hands of sorcerers, who on the principles of contagious magic could work him harm thereby.   The tribes of the White Nile are said never to shed human blood in their villages because they think the

[1] A. Kropf, "Die religiösen Anschauungen der Kaffern," *Verhandlungen der Berliner Gesellschaft für Anthropologie, Ethnologie und Urgeschichte*, 1888, p. (46).

[2] R. H. Nassau, *Fetichism in West Africa* (London, 1904), p. 83.

[3] Le R. P. Guis, " Les *Nepu* ou Sorciers," *Missions Catholiques*, xxxvi.

(1904) p. 370. See also *The Magic Art and the Evolution of Kings*, vol. i. p. 205.

[4] A. van Gennep, *Tabou et totémisme à Madagascar*, p. 338, quoting J. Sibree, " Remarkable Ceremonial at the Decease and Burial of a Betsileo Prince," *Antananarivo Annual*, No. xxii. (1898) pp. 195 *sq.*

sight of it would render women barren or bring misfortune on their children. Hence executions and murders commonly take place on the roads or in the forest.[1]

The unwillingness to shed blood is extended by some Unwilling-peoples to the blood of animals. Thus, when the Caffres ness to shed the offer an ox to the spirits, the blood of the beast must be blood of carefully caught in a calabash, and none of it may fall on animals. the ground.[2] When the Wanika in eastern Africa kill their cattle for food, "they either stone or beat the animal to death, so as not to shed the blood."[3] Amongst the Damaras cattle killed for food are suffocated, but when sacrificed they are speared to death.[4] But like most pastoral tribes in Africa, both the Wanika and Damaras very seldom kill their cattle, which are indeed commonly invested with a kind of sanctity.[5] Some of the Ewe-speaking negroes of Togoland, in West Africa, celebrate a festival in honour of the Earth at which it is unlawful to shed blood on the ground. Hence the fowls which are sacrificed on these occasions have their necks wrung, not their throats cut.[6] In killing an animal for food the Easter Islanders do not shed its blood, but stun it or suffocate it in smoke.[7] When the natives of San Cristoval, one of the Solomon Islands, sacrifice a pig to a ghost in a sacred place, they take great care that the blood shall not fall on the ground ; so they place the animal in a large bowl and cut it up there.[8] It is said that in ancient India the sacrificial victims were not slaughtered but strangled.[9]

The general explanation of the reluctance to shed blood Anything on the ground is probably to be found in the belief that the on which soul is in the blood, and that therefore any ground on which it a Maori chief's

[1] Brun-Rollet, *Le Nil Blanc et le Soudan* (Paris, 1855), pp. 239 *sq.*

[2] Dudley Kidd, *The Essential Kafir*, p. 169.

[3] Lieut. Emery, in *Journal of the R. Geographical Society*, iii. 282.

[4] Ch. Andersson, *Lake Ngami* (London, 1856), p. 224.

[5] Ch. New, *Life, Wanderings, and Labours in Eastern Africa*, p. 124 ; Francis Galton, "Domestication of Animals," *Transactions of the Ethnological Society of London*, N.S., iii. (1865)

p. 135. On the original sanctity of domestic animals see, above all, W. Robertson Smith, *The Religion of the Semites*,[2] pp. 280 *sqq.*, 295 *sqq.*

[6] J. Spieth, *Die Ewe-Stämme*, p. 796.

[7] L. Linton Palmer, "A Visit to Easter Island," *Journal of the R. Geographical Society*, xl. (1870) p. 171.

[8] R. H. Codrington, *The Melanesians*, p. 129.

[9] Strabo, xv. 1. 54, p. 710.

blood falls
becomes
sacred to
him.

may fall necessarily becomes taboo or sacred. In New Zealand anything upon which even a drop of a high chief's blood chances to fall becomes taboo or sacred to him. For instance, a party of natives having come to visit a chief in a fine new canoe, the chief got into it, but in doing so a splinter entered his foot, and the blood trickled on the canoe, which at once became sacred to him. The owner jumped out, dragged the canoe ashore opposite the chief's house, and left it there. Again, a chief in entering a missionary's house knocked his head against a beam, and the blood flowed. The natives said that in former times the house would have belonged to the chief.[1] As usually happens with taboos of universal application, the prohibition to spill the blood of a tribesman on the ground applies with peculiar stringency to chiefs and kings, and is observed in their case long after it has ceased to be observed in the case of others.

The pro-
hibition to
pass under
a trellised
vine is
probably
based on
the idea
that the
juice of the
grape is the
blood or
spirit of the
vine. This
notion is
confirmed
by the in-
toxicating
or inspiring
effect of
wine.

We have seen that the Flamen Dialis was not allowed to walk under a trellised vine.[2] The reason for this prohibition was perhaps as follows. It has been shewn that plants are considered as animate beings which bleed when cut, the red juice which exudes from some of them being regarded as the blood of the plant.[3] The juice of the grape is therefore naturally conceived as the blood of the vine.[4] And since, as we have just seen, the soul is often believed to be in the blood, the juice of the grape is regarded as the soul, or as containing the soul, of the vine. This belief is strengthened by the intoxicating effects of wine. For, according to primitive notions, all abnormal mental states, such as intoxication or madness, are caused by the entrance of a spirit into the person ; such mental states, in other words, are accounted forms of possession or inspiration. Wine, therefore, is considered on two distinct grounds as a spirit, or containing a spirit ; first because, as a red juice, it is identified with the blood of the plant, and second because it intoxicates or inspires. Therefore if the Flamen Dialis had walked under a trellised vine, the spirit of the vine, embodied in the

---

[1] R. Taylor, *Te Ika a Maui, or New Zealand and its Inhabitants*,[2] pp. 194 *sq.*

[2] Plutarch, *Quaest. Rom.* 112 ; Aulus Gellius, x. 15. 13. See above,

p. 14.

[3] *The Magic Art and the Evolution of Kings*, vol. ii. pp. 18, 20.

[4] Compare W. Robertson Smith, *Religion of the Semites*,[2] p. 230.

clusters of grapes, would have been immediately over his head and might have touched it, which for a person like him in a state of permanent taboo[1] would have been highly dangerous. This interpretation of the prohibition will be made probable if we can shew, first, that wine has been actually viewed by some peoples as blood, and intoxication as inspiration produced by drinking the blood ; and, second, that it is often considered dangerous, especially for tabooed persons, to have either blood or a living person over their heads.

With regard to the first point, we are informed by Plutarch that of old the Egyptian kings neither drank wine nor offered it in libations to the gods, because they held it to be the blood of beings who had once fought against the gods, the vine having sprung from their rotting bodies ; and the frenzy of intoxication was explained by the supposition that the drunken man was filled with the blood of the enemies of the gods.[2] The Aztecs regarded *pulque* or the wine of the country as bad, on account of the wild deeds which men did under its influence. But these wild deeds were believed to be the acts, not of the drunken man, but of the wine-god by whom he was possessed and inspired ; and so seriously was this theory of inspiration held that if any one spoke ill of or insulted a tipsy man, he was liable to be punished for disrespect to the wine-god incarnate in his votary. Hence, says Sahagun, it was believed, not without ground, that the Indians intoxicated themselves on purpose to commit with impunity crimes for which they would certainly have been punished if they had committed them

Marginal note: Wine treated as blood, and intoxication as inspiration.

---

[1] " *Dialis cotidie feriatus est,*" Aulus Gellius, x. 15. 16.

[2] Plutarch, *Isis et Osiris*, 6. A myth apparently akin to this has been preserved in some native Egyptian writings. See Ad. Erman, *Ägypten und ägyptisches Leben im Altertum*, p. 364. Wine might not be taken into the temple at Heliopolis (Plutarch, *Isis et Osiris*, 6). It was apparently forbidden to enter the temple at Delos after drinking wine (Dittenberger, *Sylloge Inscriptionum Graecarum*,[2] No.

564). When wine was offered to the Good Goddess at Rome it was not called wine but milk (Macrobius, *Saturn*, i. 12. 5 ; Plutarch, *Quaest. Rom.* 20). It was a rule of Roman religion that wine might not be poured out in libations to the gods which had been made either from grapes trodden with bleeding feet or from the clusters of a vine beside which a human body had hung in a noose (Pliny, *Nat. Hist.* xiv. 119). This rule shews that wine was supposed to be defiled by blood or death.

sober.[1]   Thus it appears that on the primitive view intoxication or the inspiration produced by wine is exactly parallel
to the inspiration produced by drinking the blood of animals.[2]
The soul or life is in the blood, and wine is the blood of the
vine.   Hence whoever drinks the blood of an animal is
inspired with the soul of the animal or of the god, who, as
we have seen,[3] is often supposed to enter into the animal
before it is slain ; and whoever drinks wine drinks the blood,
and so receives into himself the soul or spirit, of the god of
the vine.

Fear of
passing
under.
women's
blood.

With regard to the second point, the fear of passing
under blood or under a living person, we are told that some
of the Australian blacks have a dread of passing under a
leaning tree or even under the rails of a fence.   The reason
they give is that a woman may have been upon the tree or
fence, and some blood from her may have fallen on it and
might fall from it on them.[4]   In Ugi, one of the Solomon
Islands, a man will never, if he can help it, pass under a tree
which has fallen across the path, for the reason that a woman
may have stepped over it before him.[5]   Amongst the Karens
of Burma "going under a house, especially if there are
females within, is avoided ; as is also the passing under
trees of which the branches extend downwards in a particular
direction, and the butt-end of fallen trees, etc."[6]   The
Siamese think it unlucky to pass under a rope on which
women's clothes are hung, and to avert evil consequences
the person who has done so must build a chapel to the
earth-spirit.[7]

[1] Bernardino de Sahagun, *Histoire
générale des choses de la Nouvelle-
Espagne*, traduite par Jourdanet et
Siméon (Paris, 1880), pp. 46 *sq.* The
native Mexican wine (*pulque*) is made
from the sap of the great American
aloe.   See the note of the French
translators of Sahagun, *op. cit.* pp.
858 *sqq.* ; E. J. Payne, *History of the
New World called America*, i. 374 *sqq.*
The Chiquites Indians of Paraguay
believed that the spirit of *chica*, or
beer made from maize, could punish
with sickness the person who was so
irreverent or careless as to upset a
vessel of the liquor.   See Charlevoix,

Histoire du Paraguay (Paris, 1756),
ii. 234.

[2] See *The Magic Art and the Evolution of Kings*, vol. i. pp. 381 *sqq.*

[3] *Op. cit.* vol. i. pp. 384 *sq.*

[4] E. M. Curr, *The Australian Race*
(Melbourne and London, 1887), iii.
179.

[5] H. B. Guppy, *The Solomon
Islands and their Natives* (London,
1887), p. 41.

[6] E. B. Cross, "On the Karens,"
*Journal of the American Oriental
Society*, iv. (1854) p. 312.

[7] A. Bastian, *Die Völker des östlichen
Asien*, iii. 230.

Probably in all such cases the rule is based on a fear of being brought into contact with blood, especially the blood of women. From a like fear a Maori will never lean his back against the wall of a native house.[1] For the blood of women is supposed to have disastrous effects upon males. The Arunta of central Australia believe that a draught of woman's blood would kill the strongest man.[2] In the Encounter Bay tribe of South Australia boys are warned that if they see the blood of women they will early become grey-headed and their strength will fail prematurely.[3] Men of the Booandik tribe in South Australia think that if they see the blood of their women they will not be able to fight against their enemies and will be killed ; if the sun dazzles their eyes at a fight, the first woman they afterwards meet is sure to get a blow from their club.[4] In the island of Wetar it is thought that if a man or a lad comes upon a woman's blood he will be unfortunate in war and other undertakings, and that any precautions he may take to avoid the misfortune will be vain.[5] The people of Ceram also believe that men who see women's blood will be wounded in battle.[6] It is an Esthonian belief that men who see women's blood will suffer from an eruption on the skin.[7] A Fan negro told Miss Kingsley that a young man in his village, who was so weak that he could hardly crawl about, had fallen into this state through seeing the blood of a woman who had been killed by a falling tree. " The underlying idea regarding blood is of course the old one that the blood is the life. The life in Africa means a spirit, hence the liberated blood is the liberated spirit, and liberated spirits are always whipping into people who do not want them. In the case of the young Fan, the opinion held was that the weak spirit of the woman had got into him."[8]

(margin note: Disastrous effect of women's blood on men.)

[1] For the reason, see E. Shortland, *Traditions and Superstitions of the New Zealanders*, pp. 112 *sq.*, 292 ; E. Tregear, "The Maoris of New Zealand," *Journal of the Anthropological Institute*, xix. (1890) p. 118.

[2] F. J. Gillen, in *Report of the Horn Scientific Expedition to Central Australia*, pt. iv. p. 182.

[3] *Native Tribes of South Australia*, p. 186.

[4] Mrs. James Smith, *The Booandik Tribe*, p. 5.

[5] J. G. F. Riedel, *De sluik- en kroesharige rassen tusschen Selebes en Papua*, p. 450.

[6] J. G. F. Riedel, *op. cit.* p. 139, compare p. 209.

[7] F. J. Wiedemann, *Aus dem innern und äussern Leben der Ehsten*, p. 475.

[8] Miss Mary H. Kingsley, *Travels in West Africa*, p. 447. Conversely

§ 5. *The Head tabooed*

The head
sacred
because a
spirit
resides
in it.

Again, the reason for not passing under dangerous objects, like a vine or women's blood, is a fear that they may come in contact with the head ; for among many peoples the head is peculiarly sacred. The special sanctity attributed to it is sometimes explained by a belief that it is the seat of a spirit which is very sensitive to injury or disrespect. Thus the Yorubas of the Slave Coast hold that every man has three spiritual inmates, of whom the first, called Olori, dwells in the head and is the man's protector, guardian, and guide. Offerings are made to this spirit, chiefly of fowls, and some of the blood mixed with palm-oil is rubbed on the forehead.[1] The Karens of Burma suppose that a being called the *tso* resides in the upper part of the head, and while it retains its seat no harm can befall the person from the efforts of the seven *Kelahs*, or personified passions. " But if the *tso* becomes heedless or weak certain evil to the person is the result. Hence the head is carefully attended to, and all possible pains are taken to provide such dress and attire as will be pleasing to the *tso*." [2] The Siamese think that a spirit called *khuan* or *kwun* dwells in the human head, of which it is the guardian spirit. The spirit must be carefully protected from injury of every kind ; hence the act of shaving or cutting the hair is accompanied with many ceremonies. The *kwun* is very sensitive on points of honour, and would feel mortally insulted if the head in which he resides were touched by the hand of a stranger. When Dr. Bastian, in conversation with a brother of the king of Siam, raised his hand to touch the prince's skull in order to illustrate some medical remarks he was making, a sullen and threatening murmur bursting from the lips of the crouching

among the central Australian tribes women are never allowed to witness the drawing of blood from men, which is often done for purposes of decoration ; and when a quarrel has taken place and men's blood has been spilt in the presence of women, it is usual for the man whose blood has been shed to perform a ceremony connected with his own or his father or mother's totem. See Spencer and Gillen, *Native Tribes of Central Australia*, p. 463.

[1] A. B. Ellis, *The Yoruba-speaking Peoples of the Slave Coast*, pp. 125 *sq.*

[2] E. B. Cross, "On the Karens," *Journal of the American Oriental Society*, iv. (1854) pp. 311 *sq.*

courtiers warned him of the breach of etiquette he had committed, for in Siam there is no greater insult to a man of rank than to touch his head. If a Siamese touch the head of another with his foot, both of them must build chapels to the earth-spirit to avert the omen. Nor does the guardian spirit of the head like to have the hair washed too often ; it might injure or incommode him. It was a grand solemnity when the king of Burma's head was washed with water drawn from the middle of the river. Whenever the native professor, from whom Dr. Bastian took lessons in Burmese at Mandalay, had his head washed, which took place as a rule once a month, he was generally absent for three days together, that time being consumed in preparing for, and recovering from, the operation of head - washing. Dr. Bastian's custom of washing his head daily gave rise to much remark.[1] The head of the king of Persia was cleaned only once a year, on his birthday.[2] Roman women washed their heads annually on the thirteenth of August, Diana's day.[3] The Indians of Peru fancied they could rid themselves of their sins by scrubbing their heads with a small stone and then washing them in a stream.[4]

Again, the Burmese think it an indignity to have any one, especially a woman, over their heads, and for this reason Burmese houses have never more than one story. The houses are raised on posts above the ground, and whenever anything fell through the floor Dr. Bastian had always difficulty in persuading a servant to fetch it from under the house. In Rangoon a priest, summoned to the bedside of a sick man, climbed up a ladder and got in at the window rather than ascend the staircase, to reach which he must have passed under a gallery. A pious Burman of Rangoon, finding some images of Buddha in a ship's cabin, offered a high price for them, that they might not be degraded

Objection to have any one over-head.

---

[1] A. Bastian, *Die Völker des östlichen Asien*, ii. 256, iii. 71, 230, 235 *sq.* The spirit is called *kwun* by E. Young (*The Kingdom of the Yellow Robe*, pp. 75 *sqq.*). See below, pp. 266 *sq.*

[2] Herodotus, ix. 110. This passage was pointed out to me by the late Mr. E. S. Shuckburgh of Emmanuel College, Cambridge.

[3] Plutarch, *Quaestiones Romanae*, 100. Plutarch's words (μάλιστα ῥύπτεσθαι τὰς κεφαλὰς καὶ καθαίρειν ἐπιτηδεύουσι) leave room to hope that the ladies did not strictly confine their ablutions to one day in the year.

[4] P. J. de Arriaga, *Extirpacion de la Idolatria del Piru* (Lima, 1621), pp. 28, 29.

Objection
to have
any one
overhead.

by sailors walking over them on the deck.[1] Formerly in
Siam no person might cross a bridge while his superior in
rank was passing underneath, nor might he walk in a room
above one in which his superior was sitting or lying.[2] The
Cambodians esteem it a grave offence to touch a man's
head ; some of them will not enter a place where anything
whatever is suspended over their heads ; and the meanest
Cambodian would never consent to live under an inhabited
room. Hence the houses are built of one story only ; and
even the Government respects the prejudice by never placing
a prisoner in the stocks under the floor of a house, though
the houses are raised high above the ground.[3] The same
superstition exists amongst the Malays ; for an early
traveller reports that in Java people " wear nothing on their
heads, and say that nothing must be on their heads . . .
and if any person were to put his hand upon their head they
would kill him ; and they do not build houses with storeys,
in order that they may not walk over each other's heads." [4]
In Uganda no person belonging to the king's totem clan
was allowed to get on the top of the palace to roof it, for
that would have been regarded as equivalent to getting on
the top of the king. Hence the palace had to be roofed by
men of a different clan from the king.[5]

Sanctity of
the head,
especially
of a chief's
head, in
Polynesia.

The same superstition as to the head is found in full
force throughout Polynesia. Thus of Gattanewa, a Marquesan
chief, it is said that " to touch the top of his head, or anything which had been on his head, was sacrilege. To pass
over his head was an indignity never to be forgotten.
Gattanewa, nay, all his family, scorned to pass a gateway
which is ever closed, or a house with a door ; all must be

---

[1] A. Bastian, *op. cit.* ii. 150 ; Sanger-
mano, *Description of the Burmese Empire* (Rangoon, 1885), p. 131; C. F. S.
Forbes, *British Burma,* p. 334; Shway
Yoe, *The Burman* (London, 1882),
i. 91.

[2] E. Young, *The Kingdom of the
Yellow Robe* (Westminster, 1898), p.
131.

J. Moura, *Le Royaume du Cambodge,* i. 178, 388.

[4] Duarte Barbosa, *Description of the
Coasts of East Africa and Malabar in*

the beginning of the Sixteenth Century
(Hakluyt Society, 1866), p. 197.

[5] This I learned in conversation
with Messrs. Roscoe and Miller, missionaries to Uganda. The system of
totemism exists in full force in Uganda.
No man will eat his totem animal
or marry a woman of his own totem
clan. Among the totems of the clans
are the lion, leopard, elephant, antelope,
mushroom, buffalo, sheep, grasshopper,
crocodile, otter, beaver, and lizard. See
Totemism and Exogamy, ii. 472 *sqq.*

as open and free as their unrestrained manners. He would
pass under nothing that had been raised by the hand of
man, if there was a possibility of getting round or over it.
Often have I seen him walk the whole length of our barrier,
in preference to passing between our water-casks ; and at
the risk of his life scramble over the loose stones of a wall,
rather than go through the gateway." [1]   Marquesan women
have been known to refuse to go on the decks of ships for
fear of passing over the heads of chiefs who might be below.[2]
The son of a Marquesan high priest has been seen to roll
on the ground in an agony of rage and despair, begging for
death, because some one had desecrated his head and
deprived him of his divinity by sprinkling a few drops of
water on his hair.[3]   But it was not the Marquesan chiefs
only whose heads were sacred.   The head of every Marquesan was taboo, and might neither be touched nor stepped
over by another ; even a father might not step over the
head of his sleeping child ;[4] women were forbidden to carry
or touch anything that had been in contact with, or had
merely hung over, the head of their husband or father.[5]   No
one was allowed to be over the head of the king of Tonga.[6]
In Hawaii (the Sandwich Islands) if a man climbed upon a
chief's house or upon the wall of his yard, he was put to
death ; if his shadow fell on a chief, he was put to death ;
if he walked in the shadow of a chief's house with his head
painted white or decked with a garland or wetted with
water, he was put to death.[7]   In Tahiti any one who
stood over the king or queen, or passed his hand over
their heads, might be put to death.[8]   Until certain rites
were performed over it, a Tahitian infant was especially
taboo ; whatever touched the child's head, while it was
in this state, became sacred and was deposited in a conse-

[1] David Porter, *Journal of a Cruise
made to the Pacific Ocean in the U.S.
Frigate "Essex"* (New York, 1822),
ii. 65.
[2] Vincendon-Dumoulin et C. Desgraz
Îles Marquises (Paris, 1843), p. 262.
[3] Le P. Matthias G * * *, *Lettres sur
les Îles Marquises* (Paris, 1843), p. 50.
[4] G. H. von Langsdorff, *Reise um
die Welt* (London, 1812), i. 115 sq.

[5] Max Radiguet, *Les Derniers Sauvages* (Paris, 1882), p. 156.
[6] Capt. James Cook, *Voyages*, v. 427
(London, 1809).
[7] Jules Remy, *Ka Mooolelo Hawaii,
Histoire de l'Archipel Havaiien* (Paris
and Leipsic, 1862), p. 159.
[8] W. Ellis, *Polynesian Researches*[2]
(London, 1832-36), iii. 102.

Sanctity of
the head,
especially
of a chief's
head, in
Polynesia. crated place railed in for the purpose at the child's house.
If a branch of a tree touched the child's head, the tree
was cut down ; and if in its fall it injured another tree
so as to penetrate the bark, that tree also was cut down as
unclean and unfit for use.   After the rites were performed
these special taboos ceased ; but the head of a Tahitian was
always sacred, he never carried anything on it, and to touch
it was an offence.[1]   In New Zealand "the heads of the
chiefs were always tabooed (*tapu*), hence they could not
pass, or sit, under food hung up ; or carry food, as others,
on their backs ; neither would they eat a meal in a house,
nor touch a calabash of water in drinking.   No one could
touch their head, nor, indeed, commonly speak of it, or
allude to it ; to do so offensively was one of their heaviest
curses, and grossest insults, only to be wiped out with
blood."[2]   So sacred was the head of a Maori chief that
"if he only touched it with his fingers, he was obliged
immediately to apply them to his nose, and snuff up the
sanctity which they had acquired by the touch, and thus
restore it to the part from whence it was taken."[3]   On account
of the sacredness of his head a Maori chief "could not blow
the fire with his mouth, for the breath being sacred, communicated his sanctity to it, and a brand might be taken by
a slave, or a man of another tribe, or the fire might be used
for other purposes, such as cooking, and so cause his death."[4]
It is a crime for a sacred person in New Zealand to leave
his comb, or anything else which has touched his head, in
a place where food has been cooked, or to suffer another
person to drink out of any vessel which has touched his
lips.   Hence when a chief wishes to drink he never puts his
lips to the vessel, but holds his hands close to his mouth so
as to form a hollow, into which water is poured by another
person, and thence is allowed to flow into his mouth.   If a
light is needed for his pipe, the burning ember taken from

---

[1] James Wilson, *A Missionary
Voyage to the Southern Pacific Ocean*
(London, 1799), pp. 354 *sq.*

[2] W. Colenso, "The Maori Races
of New Zealand," p. 43, in *Transactions and Proceedings of the New
Zealand Institute*, 1868, vol. i. (separately paged).

[3] R. Taylor, *To Ika a Maui, or
New Zealand and its Inhabitants,*[2] p.
165.   We have seen that under certain
special circumstances common persons
also are temporarily forbidden to touch
their heads with their hands. See above,
pp. 146, 156, 158, 160, 183.

[4] R. Taylor, *l.c.*

the fire must be thrown away as soon as it is used; for the pipe becomes sacred because it has touched his mouth; the coal becomes sacred because it has touched the pipe; and if a particle of the sacred cinder were replaced on the common fire, the fire would also become sacred and could no longer be used for cooking.[1] Some Maori chiefs, like other Polynesians, object to go down into a ship's cabin from fear of people passing over their heads.[2] Dire misfortune was thought by the Maoris to await those who entered a house where any article of animal food was suspended over their heads. "A dead pigeon, or a piece of pork hung from the roof, was a better protection from molestation than a sentinel."[3] If I am right, the reason for the special objection to having animal food over the head is the fear of bringing the sacred head into contact with the spirit of the animal; just as the reason why the Flamen Dialis might not walk under a vine was the fear of bringing his sacred head into contact with the spirit of the vine. Similarly King Darius would not pass through a gate over which there was a tomb, because in doing so he would have had a corpse above his head.[4] Among the Awuna tribes of the Gold Coast, West Africa, the worshippers of Hebesio, the god of thunder, believe that their heads are sacred, being associated in some mysterious way with the presence of the protective spirit of their god, which has passed into them through this channel at baptism. Hence they carefully guard their heads against injury, especially against any wound that might draw blood, for they think that such a wound would entail the loss of reason on the sufferer, and that it would bring down the wrath of the thundering god and of his mouth-piece the fetish priest on the impious smiter.[5]

[1] E. Shortland, *The Southern Districts of New Zealand* (London, 1851), p. 293; *id.*, *Traditions and Superstitions of the New Zealanders*, pp. 107 *sq.*

[2] J. Dumont D'Urville, *Voyage autour du monde et à la recherche de La Pérouse, exécuté sous son commandement sur la corvette "Austrolabe"*: *histoire du voyage*, ii. 534.

[3] R. A. Cruise, *Journal of a Ten Months' Residence in New Zealand* (London, 1823), p. 187; J. Dumont D'Urville, *op. cit.* ii. 533; E. Shortland, *The Southern Districts of New Zealand*, p. 30.

[4] Herodotus, i. 187.

[5] H. France, "Customs of the Awuna Tribes," *Journal of the African Society*, No. 17 (October, 1905), p. 39.

§ 6. *Hair tabooed*

When the head is sacred, the cutting of the hair becomes a difficult and dangerous operation.

When the head was considered so sacred that it might not even be touched without grave offence, it is obvious that the cutting of the hair must have been a delicate and difficult operation. The difficulties and dangers which, on the primitive view, beset the operation are of two kinds. There is first the danger of disturbing the spirit of the head, which may be injured in the process and may revenge itself upon the person who molests him. Secondly, there is the difficulty of disposing of the shorn locks. For the savage believes that the sympathetic connexion which exists between himself and every part of his body continues to exist even after the physical connexion has been broken, and that therefore he will suffer from any harm that may befall the severed parts of his body, such as the clippings of his hair or the parings of his nails. Accordingly he takes care that these severed portions of himself shall not be left in places where they might either be exposed to accidental injury or fall into the hands of malicious persons who might work magic on them to his detriment or death. Such dangers are common to all, but sacred persons have more to fear from them than ordinary people, so the precautions taken by them are proportionately stringent.

The hair of kings, priests, and other tabooed persons is sometimes kept unshorn.

The simplest way of evading the peril is not to cut the hair at all; and this is the expedient adopted where the risk is thought to be more than usually great. The Frankish kings were never allowed to crop their hair; from their childhood upwards they had to keep it unshorn.[1] To poll the long locks that floated

---

[1] Agathias, *Hist.* i. 3; J. Grimm, *Deutsche Rechtsalterthümer*,[3] pp. 239 *sqq.* Compare F. Kauffmann, *Balder* (Strasburg, 1902), pp. 209 *sq.* The story of the Phrygian king Midas, who concealed the ears of an ass under his long hair (Aristophanes, *Plutus*, 287; Ovid, *Metam.* xi. 146-193) may perhaps be a distorted reminiscence of a similar custom in Phrygia. Parallels to the story are recorded in modern Greece, Ireland, Brittany, Servia, India, and among the Mongols. See B. Schmidt, *Griechische Märchen, Sagen und Volkslieder*, pp. 70 *sq.*, 224 *sq.*; Grimm's *Household Tales*, ii. 498, trans. by M. Hunt; Patrick Kennedy, *Legendary Fictions of the Irish Celts*, pp. 248 *sqq.* (ed. 1866); A. de Nore, *Coutumes, mythes, et traditions des provinces de la France*, pp. 219 *sq.*; W. S. Karadschitsch, *Volksmärchen der Serben*, No. 39, pp. 225 *sqq.*; *North Indian Notes and Queries*, iii. p. 104, § 218; B. Jülg, *Mongolische Märchen-Sammlung*, No. 22, pp. 182 *sqq.*; *Sagas from the Far East*, No. 21, pp. 206 *sqq.*

on their shoulders would have been to renounce their right to the throne. When the wicked brothers Clotaire and Childebert coveted the kingdom of their dead brother Clodomir, they inveigled into their power their little nephews, the two sons of Clodomir; and having done so, they sent a messenger bearing scissors and a naked sword to the children's grandmother, Queen Clotilde, at Paris. The envoy shewed the scissors and the sword to Clotilde, and bade her choose whether the children should be shorn and live or remain unshorn and die. The proud queen replied that if her grandchildren were not to come to the throne she would rather see them dead than shorn. And murdered they were by their ruthless uncle Clotaire with his own hand.[1] The king of Ponape, one of the Caroline Islands, must wear his hair long, and so must his grandees.[2] The hair of the Aztec priests hung down to their hams, so that the weight of it became very troublesome; for they might never poll it so long as they lived, or at least until they had been relieved of their office on the score of old age. They wore it braided in great tresses, six fingers broad, and tied with cotton.[3] A Haida medicine-man may neither clip nor comb his tresses, so they are always long and tangled.[4] Among the Hos, a negro tribe of Togoland in West Africa, "there are priests on whose head no razor may come during the whole of their lives. The god who dwells in the man forbids the cutting of his hair on pain of death. If the hair is at last too long, the owner must pray to his god to allow him at least to clip the tips of it. The hair is in fact conceived as the seat and lodging-place of his god, so that were it shorn the god would lose his abode in the priest."[5] A rain-maker at Boroma, on the lower Zambesi, used to give out that he was

[1] Gregory of Tours, *Histoire ecclésiastique des Francs*, iii. 18, compare vi. 24 (Guizot's translation).

[2] Dr. Hahl, "Mitteilungen über Sitten und rechtliche Verhältnisse auf Ponape," *Ethnologisches Notizblatt*, ii. Heft 2 (Berlin, 1901), p. 6.

[3] *Manuscrit Ramirez, Histoire de l'origine des Indiens qui habitent la Nouvelle Espagne* (Paris, 1903), p. 171; J. de Acosta, *Natural and Moral History of the Indies*, ii. 365 (Hakluyt Society); A. de Herrera, *General History of the vast Continent and Islands of America*, iii. 216 (Stevens's translation). The author of the *Manuscrit Ramirez* speaks as if the rule applied only to the priests of the god Tezcatlipoca.

[4] G. M. Dawson, "On the Haida Indians of Queen Charlotte Islands," in *Geological Survey of Canada, Report of Progress for 1878-79*, p. 123 B.

[5] J. Spieth, *Die Ewe-Stämme*, p. 229.

Hair of priests, chiefs, sorcerers, and others kept unshorn.

possessed by two spirits, one of a lion, the other of a leopard, and in the assemblies of the people he mimicked the roaring of these beasts. In order that their spirits might not leave him, he never cut his hair nor drank alcohol.[1] The Masai clan of the El Kiboron, who are believed to possess the art of making rain, may not pluck out their beards, because the loss of their beards would, it is supposed, entail the loss of their rain-making powers. The head chief and the sorcerers of the Masai observe the same rule for a like reason : they think that were they to pull out their beards, their supernatural gifts would desert them.[2] In central Borneo the chiefs of a particular Kayan family never allow their hair to be shorn.[3] Ancient Indian law required that when a new king had performed the ceremony of consecration he might not shave his hair for a year, though he was allowed to crop it. According to one account none of his subjects, except a Brahman, might have his hair cut during this period, and even horses were left unclipped.[4] Amongst the Alfoors of Celebes the *Leleen* or priest who looks after the rice-fields may not shear his hair during the time that he exercises his special functions, that is from a month before the rice is sown until it is housed.[5] In Usukuma, a district to the south of Lake Victoria Nyanza, the people are forbidden to shave their heads till the corn has been sown.[6] Men of the Tsetsaut tribe in British Columbia do not cut their hair, believing that if they cut it they would quickly grow old.[7] In Ceram men do not crop their hair : if married men did so, they would lose their wives ; if young men did so, they would grow weak and enervated.[8] In Timorlaut married men may not poll their hair for the same reason as in Ceram, but widowers and men on a

[1] *Missions Catholiques*, xxv. (1893) p. 266.

[2] M. Merker, *Die Masai* (Berlin, 1904), pp. 21, 22, 143.

[3] A. W. Nieuwenhuis, *Quer durch Borneo*, i. 68.

[4] *Satapatha Brahmana*, translated by J. Eggeling, part iii. pp. 126, 128, with the translator's note on p. 126 (*Sacred Books of the East*, vol. xli.).

[5] P. N. Wilken, "Bijdragen tot de kennis van de zeden en gewoonten der Alfoeren in de Minahassa," *Mededeelingen van wege het Nederlandsche Zendelinggenootschap*, vii. (1863) p. 126.

[6] R. P. Ashe, *Two Kings of Uganda* (London, 1889), p. 109.

[7] Fr. Boas, in *Tenth Report on the North-Western Tribes of Canada*, p. 45 (separate reprint from the *Report of the British Association for 1895*).

[8] J. G. F. Riedel, *De sluik- en kroesharige rassen tusschen Selebes en Papua*, p. 137.

journey may do so after offering a fowl or a pig in sacrifice.[1] Hair kept
Malays of the Peninsula are forbidden to clip their hair unshorn
during their wife's pregnancy and for forty days after the occasions,
child has been born; and a similar abstention is said to such as
have been formerly incumbent on all persons prosecuting pregnancy,
a journey or engaged in war.[2] Elsewhere men travelling and war.
abroad have been in the habit of leaving their hair unshorn
until their return. The reason for this custom is probably
the danger to which, as we have seen, a traveller is believed
to be exposed from the magic arts of the strangers amongst
whom he sojourns; if they got possession of his shorn hair,
they might work his destruction through it. The Egyptians
on a journey kept their hair uncut till they returned home.[3]
" At Tâif when a man returned from a journey his first duty
was to visit the Rabba and poll his hair." [4] Achilles kept
unshorn his yellow hair, because his father had vowed to
offer it to the River Sperchius if ever his son came home
from the wars beyond the sea.[5] Formerly when Dyak
warriors returned with the heads of their enemies, each man
cut off a lock from the front of his head and threw it into
the river as a mode of ending the taboo to which they had
been subjected during the expedition.[6] Bechuanas after a
battle had their hair shorn by their mothers " in order that
new hair might grow, and that all which was old and polluted
might disappear and be no more." [7]

Again, men who have taken a vow of vengeance some- Hair
times keep their hair unshorn till they have fulfilled their unshorn
vow. Thus of the Marquesans we are told that " occasionally vow.
they have their head entirely shaved, except one lock on the
crown, which is worn loose or put up in a knot. But the
latter mode of wearing the hair is only adopted by them

---

[1] J. G. F. Riedel, *op. cit.* pp. 292 *sq.*

[2] W. W. Skeat, *Malay Magic*, p. 44.

[3] Diodorus Siculus, i. 18.

[4] W. Robertson Smith, *Kinship and Marriage in Early Arabia* (Cambridge, 1885), pp. 152 *sq.*

[5] Homer, *Iliad*, xxiii. 141 *sqq.* This Homeric passage has been imitated by Valerius Flaccus (*Argonaut.* i. 378). The Greeks often dedicated a lock of their hair to rivers. See Aeschylus, *Choephori*, 5 *sq.*; Philostratus, *Heroica*, xiii. 4; Pausanias, i. 37. 3, viii. 20. 3, viii. 41. 3. The lock might be at the side or the back of the head or over the brow; it received a special name (Pollux, ii. 30).

[6] S. W. Tromp, "Een Dajaksch Feest," *Bijdragen tot de Taal- Land- en Volkenkunde van Nederlandsch-Indië*, xxxix. (1890) p. 38.

[7] T. Arbousset et F. Daumas, *Relation d'un voyage d'exploration*, p. 565.

Hair
unshorn
during
a vow. when they have a solemn vow, as to revenge the death of some near relation, etc. In such case the lock is never cut off until they have fulfilled their promise."[1] A similar custom was sometimes observed by the ancient Germans; among the Chatti the young warriors never clipped their hair or their beard till they had slain an enemy.[2] Six thousand Saxons once swore that they would not poll their hair nor shave their beards until they had taken vengeance on their foes.[3] On one occasion a Hawaiian taboo is said to have lasted thirty years, "during which the men were not allowed to trim their beards, etc."[4] While his vow lasted, a Nazarite might not have his hair cut: "All the days of the vow of his separation there shall no razor come upon his head."[5] Possibly in this case there was a special objection to touching the tabooed man's head with iron. The Roman priests, as we have seen, were shorn with

The nails
of infants
should not
be pared. bronze knives. The same feeling perhaps gave rise to the European rule that a child's nails should not be pared during the first year, but that if it is absolutely necessary to shorten them they should be bitten off by the mother or nurse.[6] For in all parts of the world a young child is believed to be especially exposed to supernatural dangers, and particular precautions are taken to guard it against them; in other words, the child is under a number of taboos, of which the rule just mentioned is one. "Among Hindus the usual custom seems to be that the nails of a first-born child are cut at the age of six months. With other children a year

[1] D. Porter, *Journal of a Cruise made to the Pacific Ocean*, ii. 120.

[2] Tacitus, *Germania*, 31. Vows of the same sort were occasionally made by the Romans (Suetonius, *Julius*, 67; Tacitus, *Hist.* iv. 61).

[3] Paulus Diaconus, *Hist. Langobard.* iii. 7; Gregory of Tours, *Histoire ecclésiastique des Francs*, v. 15, vol. i. p. 268 (Guizot's translation, Nouvelle Edition, Paris, 1874).

[4] W. Ellis, *Polynesian Researches*,[2] iv. 387.

[5] Numbers vi. 5.

[6] J. A. E. Köhler, *Volksbrauch*, etc., *im Voigtlande*, p. 424; W. Henderson,

Folk-lore of the Northern Counties, pp. 16 sq.; F. Panzer, *Beitrag zur deutschen Mythologie*, i. p. 258, § 23; I. V. Zingerle, *Sitten, Bräuche und Meinungen des Tiroler Volkes*,[2] §§ 46, 72; J. W. Wolf, *Beiträge zur deutschen Mythologie*, i. p. 208 § 45, p. 209 § 53; O. Knoop, *Volkssagen, Erzählungen*, etc., *aus dem östlichen Hinterpommern*, p. 157 § 23; E. Veckenstedt, *Wendische Sagen, Märchen und abergläubische Gebräuche*, p. 445; J. Haltrich, *Zur Volkskunde der Siebenbürger Sachsen*, p. 313; E. Krause, "Abergläubische Kuren und sonstiger Aberglaube in Berlin," *Zeitschrift für Ethnologie*, xv. (1883) p. 84.

or two is allowed to elapse."[1]   The Slave, Hare, and Dogrib Indians of North-West America do not pare the nails of female children till they are four years of age.[2]   In Uganda a child's hair may not be cut until the child has received a name. Should any of it be rubbed or plucked off accidentally, it is refastened to the child's head with string or by being knotted to the other hair.[3]   Amongst the Ewe negroes of the Slave Coast, a mother sometimes vows a sacrifice to the fetish if her infant should live.   She then leaves the child unshorn till its fourth or sixth year, when she fulfils her vow and has the child's hair cut by a priest.[4]   To this day a Syrian mother will sometimes, like Hannah, devote her little one to God.   When the child reaches a certain age, its hair is cut and weighed, and money is paid in proportion to the weight. If the boy thus dedicated is a Moslem, he becomes in time a dervish ; if he is a Christian, he becomes a monk.[5]   Among the Toradjas of central Celebes, when a child's hair is cut to rid it of vermin, some locks are allowed to remain on the crown of the head as a refuge for one of the child's souls. Otherwise the soul would have no place in which to settle, and the child would sicken.[6]   The Karo-Bataks of Sumatra are much afraid of frightening away the soul (*těndi*) of a child ; hence when they cut its hair, they always leave a patch unshorn, to which the soul can retreat before the shears.   Usually this lock remains unshorn all through life, or at least up till manhood.[7]   In some parts of Germany it

Child's hair left unshorn as a refuge for its soul.

---

[1] *Panjab Notes and Queries*, ii. p. 205, § 1092.

[2] G. Gibbs, "Notes on the Tinneh or Chepewyan Indians of British and Russian America," in *Annual Report of the Smithsonian Institution*, 1866, p. 305; W. Dall, *Alaska and its Resources*, p. 202.   The reason alleged by the Indians is that if the girls' nails were cut sooner the girls would be lazy and unable to embroider in porcupine quill-work.   But this is probably a late invention like the reasons assigned in Europe for the similar custom, of which the commonest is that the child would become a thief if its nails were cut.

[3] J. Roscoe, "Further Notes on the Manners and Customs of the Baganda,"

Journal of the Anthropological Institute, xxxii. (1902) p. 30.

[4] Lieut. Herold, "Religiöse Anschauungen und Gebräuche der deutschen Ewe-Neger," *Mittheilungen aus den Deutschen Schutzgebieten*, v. 148 *sq.*

[5] S. J. Curtiss, *Primitive Semitic Religion To-day* (Chicago, etc., 1902), p. 153.

[6] A. C. Kruyt, "Het koppensnellen der Toradja's," *Verslagen en Mededeelingen der konink. Akademie van Wetenschapen*, Afdeeling Letterkunde, iv. Reeks, iii. 198 n[2] (Amsterdam, 1899).

[7] R. Römer, "Bijdrage tot de Geneeskunst der Karo-Batak's," *Tijdschrift voor Indische Taal- Land- en Volkenkunde*, l. (1908) p. 216.

is thought that if a child's hair is combed in its first year the child will be unlucky;[1] or that if a boy's hair is cut before his seventh year he will have no courage.[2]

§ 7. *Ceremonies at Hair-cutting*

Solemn ceremonies observed at hair-cutting.
But when it becomes necessary to crop the hair, measures are taken to lessen the dangers which are supposed to attend the operation. The chief of Namosi in Fiji always ate a man by way of precaution when he had had his hair cut. " There was a certain clan that had to provide the victim, and they used to sit in solemn council among themselves to choose him. It was a sacrificial feast to avert evil from the chief." [3] This remarkable custom has been described more fully by another observer. The old heathen temple at Namosi is called Rukunitambua, "and round about it are hundreds of stones, each of which tells a fearful tale. A subject tribe, whose town was some little distance from Namosi, had committed an unpardonable offence, and were condemned to a frightful doom. The earth-mound on which their temple had stood was planted with the mountain *ndalo* (arum), and when the crop was ripe, the poor wretches had to carry it down to Namosi, and give at least one of their number to be killed and eaten by the chief. He used to take advantage of these occasions to have his hair cut, for the human sacrifice was supposed to avert all danger of witchcraft if any ill-wisher got hold of the cuttings of his hair, human hair being the most dangerous channel for the deadliest spells of the sorcerers. The stones round Rukunitambua represented these and other' victims who had been killed and eaten at Namosi. Each stone was the record of a murder succeeded by a cannibal feast." [4] Amongst the Maoris many spells were uttered at hair-cutting ; one, for

[1] O. Knoop, *Volkssagen, Erzählungen*, etc., *aus dem östlichen Hinterpommern* (Posen, 1885), p. 157, § 23.
[2] J. W. Wolf, *Beiträge zur deutschen Mythologie*, i. p. 209, § 57.
[3] Rev. Lorimer Fison, in a letter to the author, dated August 26, 1898.
[4] From the report of a lecture delivered in Melbourne, December 9, 1898, by the Rev. H. Worrall, of Fiji, missionary. The newspaper cutting from which the above extract is quoted was sent to me by the Rev. Lorimer Fison in a letter, dated Melbourne, January 9, 1899. Mr. Fison omitted to give the name and date of the newspaper.

example, was spoken to consecrate the obsidian knife with Solemn ceremonies observed at hair-cutting. which the hair was cut; another was pronounced to avert the thunder and lightning which hair-cutting was believed to cause.[1] "He who has had his hair cut is in immediate charge of the Atua (spirit); he is removed from the contact and society of his family and his tribe; he dare not touch his food himself; it is put into his mouth by another person; nor can he for some days resume his accustomed occupations or associate with his fellow-men."[2] The person who cuts the hair is also tabooed; his hands having been in contact with a sacred head, he may not touch food with them or engage in any other employment; he is fed by another person with food cooked over a sacred fire. He cannot be released from the taboo before the following day, when he rubs his hands with potato or fern root which has been cooked on a sacred fire; and this food having been taken to the head of the family in the female line and eaten by her, his hands are freed from the taboo. In some parts of New Zealand the most sacred day of the year was that appointed for hair-cutting; the people assembled in large numbers on that day from all the neighbourhood.[3] Sometimes a Maori chief's hair was shorn by his wife, who was then tabooed for a week as a consequence of having touched his sacred locks.[4] It is an affair of state when the king of Cambodia's hair is cropped. The priests place on the barber's fingers certain old rings set with large stones, which are supposed to contain spirits favourable to the kings, and during the operation the Brahmans keep up a noisy music to drive away the evil spirits.[5] The hair and nails of the Mikado could only be cut while he was asleep,[6] perhaps because his soul being then absent from his body, there was less chance of injuring it with the shears.

From their earliest days little Siamese children have the

---

[1] R. Taylor, *Te Ika a Maui, or New Zealand and its Inhabitants* [2] (London, 1870), pp. 206 *sqq.*

[2] Richard A. Cruise, *Journal of a Ten Months' Residence in New Zealand* (London, 1823), pp. 283 *sq.* Compare J. Dumont D'Urville, *Voyage autour du monde et à la recherche de La Pérouse: histoire du voyage* (Paris, 1832), ii. 533.

[3] E. Shortland, *Traditions and Superstitions of the New Zealanders*, pp. 108 *sqq.*; R. Taylor, *l.c.*

[4] G. F. Angas, *Savage Life and Scenes in Australia and New Zealand* (London, 1847), ii. 90 *sq.*

[5] J. Moura, *Le Royaume du Cambodge*, i. 226 *sq.*

[6] See above, p. 3.

Cere-
monies at
cutting the
hair of
Siamese
children.

crown of the head clean shorn with the exception of a single small tuft of hair, which is daily combed, twisted, oiled, and tied in a little knot until the day when it is finally removed with great pomp and ceremony. The ceremony of shaving the top-knot takes place before the child has reached puberty, and great anxiety is felt at this time lest the *kwun*, or guardian - spirit who commonly resides in the body and especially the head of every Siamese,[1] should be so disturbed by the tonsure as to depart and leave the child a hopeless wreck for life. Great pains are therefore taken to recall this mysterious being in case he should have fled, and to fix him securely in the child. This is the object of an elaborate ceremony performed on the afternoon of the day when the top-knot has been cut. A miniature pagoda is erected, and on it are placed several kinds of food known to be favourites of the spirit. When the *kwun* has arrived and is feasting on these dainties, he is caught and held fast under a cloth thrown over the food. The child is now placed near the pagoda, and all the family and friends form a circle, with the child, the captured spirit, and the Brahman priests in the middle. Hereupon the priests address the spirit, earnestly entreating him to enter into the child. They amuse him with tales, and coax and wheedle him with flattery, jest, and song ; the gongs ring out their loudest; the people cheer, and only a *kwun* of the sourest and most obdurate disposition could resist the combined appeal. The last sentences of the formal invocation run as follows : " Benignant *kwun !* Thou fickle being who art wont to wander and dally about ! From the moment that the child was conceived in the womb, thou hast enjoyed every pleasure, until ten (lunar) months having elapsed and the time of delivery arrived, thou hast suffered and run the risk of perishing by being born alive into the world. Gracious *kwun !* thou wast at that time so tender, delicate, and wavering as to cause great anxiety concerning thy fate ; thou was exactly like a child, youthful, innocent, and inexperienced. The least trifle frightened thee and made thee shudder. In thy infantile playfulness thou wast wont to frolic and wander to no purpose. As thou didst commence to learn to sit, and,

---

[1] See above, p. 252.

unassisted, to crawl totteringly on all fours, thou wast ever
falling flat on thy face or on thy back. As thou didst grow
up in years and couldst move thy steps firmly, thou didst
begin to run and sport thoughtlessly and rashly all round
the rooms, the terrace, and bridging planks of travelling boat
or floating house, and at times thou didst fall into the
stream, creek, or pond, among the floating water-weeds, to
the utter dismay of those to whom thy existence was most
dear.   O gentle *kwun*, come into thy corporeal abode ; do
not delay this auspicious rite.   Thou art now full-grown and
dost form everybody's delight and admiration.   Let all the
tiny particles of *kwun* that have fallen on land or water
assemble and take permanent abode in this darling little
child.   Let them all hurry to the site of this auspicious
ceremony and admire the magnificent preparations made for
them in this hall."   The brocaded cloth from the pagoda,
under which lurks the captive spirit, is now rolled up tightly
and handed to the child, who is told to clasp it firmly to
his breast and not let the *kwun* escape.   Further, the child
drinks the milk of the coco-nuts which had been offered to
the spirit, and by thus absorbing the food of the *kwun*
ensures the presence of that precious spirit in his body.   A
magic cord is tied round his wrist to keep off the wicked
spirits who would lure the *kwun* away from home ; and for
three nights he sleeps with the embroidered cloth from the
pagoda fast clasped in his arms.[1]

§ 8. *Disposal of Cut Hair and Nails*

But even when the hair and nails have been safely cut,
there remains the difficulty of disposing of them, for their
owner believes himself liable to suffer from any harm that
may befall them.   The notion that a man may be
bewitched by means of the clippings of his hair, the parings
of his nails, or any other severed portion of his person is

[1] E. Young, *The Kingdom of the Yellow Robe* (Westminster, 1898), pp. 64 *sq.*, 67-84. I have abridged the account of the ceremonies by omitting some details.   For an account of the ceremonies observed at cutting the hair of a young Siamese prince, at the age of thirteen or fourteen, see Mgr. Bruguière, in *Annales de l'Association de la Propagation de la Foi*, v. (1831) pp. 197 *sq.*

of their
nails, and
other
severed
parts
of their
persons.

almost world-wide,[1] and attested by evidence too ample,
too familiar, and too tedious in its uniformity to be here
analysed at length. The general idea on which the
superstition rests is that of the sympathetic connexion
supposed to persist between a person and everything that
has once been part of his body or in any way closely related
to him. A very few examples must suffice. They belong
to that branch of sympathetic magic which may be called
contagious.[2] Thus, when the Chilote Indians, inhabiting the
wild, deeply indented coasts and dark rain-beaten forests
of southern Chili, get possession of the hair of an enemy,
they drop it from a high tree or tie it to a piece of
seaweed and fling it into the surf; for they think that the
shock of the fall, or the blows of the waves as the tress is
tossed to and fro on the heaving billows, will be transmitted
through the hair to the person from whose head it was cut.[3]
Dread of sorcery, we are told, formed one of the most salient
characteristics of the Marquesan islanders in the old days.
The sorcerer took some of the hair, spittle, or other bodily
refuse of the man he wished to injure, wrapped it up in a leaf,
and placed the packet in a bag woven of threads or fibres,
which were knotted in an intricate way. The whole was then
buried with certain rites, and thereupon the victim wasted away
of a languishing sickness which lasted twenty days. His life,
however, might be saved by discovering and digging up the
buried hair, spittle, or what not; for as soon as this was
done the power of the charm ceased.[4] A Marquesan chief
told Lieutenant Gamble that he was extremely ill, the
Happah tribe having stolen a lock of his hair and buried it
in a plantain leaf for the purpose of taking his life.
Lieutenant Gamble argued with him, but in vain; die he
must unless the hair and the plantain leaf were brought back
to him; and to obtain them he had offered the Happahs the
greater part of his property. He complained of excessive

---

[1] The aboriginal tribes of Central
Australia form an exception to this
rule; for among them no attempt is
made to injure a person by performing
magical ceremonies over his shorn hair.
See Spencer and Gillen, *Northern
Tribes of Central Australia*, p. 478.

[2] See *The Magic Art and the Evolu-*

tion of Kings, vol. i. pp. 52-54, 174
sqq.

[3] C. Martin, "Über die Eingeborenen von Chiloe," *Zeitschrift für
Ethnologie*, ix. (1877) p. 177.

[4] Vincendon-Dumoulin et C. Desgraz, *Îles Marquises* (Paris, 1843), pp.
247 *sq.*

pain in the head, breast, and sides.[1]   A Maori sorcerer
intent on bewitching somebody sought to get a tress
of his victim's hair, the parings of his nails, some of his
spittle, or a shred of his garment.   Having obtained the
object, whatever it was, he chanted certain spells and curses
over it in a falsetto voice and buried it in the ground.   As
the thing decayed, the person to whom it had belonged was
supposed to waste away.[2]   Again, an Australian girl, sick of
a fever, laid the blame of her illness on a young man who
had come behind her and cut off a lock of her hair ; she was
sure he had buried it and that it was rotting.   " Her hair,"
she said, " was rotting somewhere, and her *Marm-bu-la*
(kidney fat) was wasting away, and when her hair had
completely rotted, she would die." [3]   When an Australian
blackfellow wishes to get rid of his wife, he cuts off a lock of
her hair in her sleep, ties it to his spear-thrower, and goes with
it to a neighbouring tribe, where he gives it to a friend.   His
friend sticks the spear-thrower up every night before the
camp fire, and when it falls down it is a sign that the wife
is dead.[4]   The way in which the charm operates was
explained to Dr. Howitt by a Wirajuri man.   " You see,"
he said, " when a blackfellow doctor gets hold of something
belonging to a man and roasts it with things, and sings over
it, the fire catches hold of the smell of the man, and that
settles the poor fellow." [5]   A slightly different form of the
charm as practised in Australia is to fasten the enemy's hair
with wax to the pinion bone of a hawk, and set the bone in
a small circle of fire.   According as the sorcerer desires the
death or only the sickness of his victim he leaves the bone
in the midst of the fire or removes it and lays it in the sun.
When he thinks he has done his enemy enough harm, he
places the bone in water, which ends the enchantment.[6]

[1] D. Porter, *Journal of a Cruise
made to the Pacific Ocean* [2] (New York,
1882), ii. 188.
[2] R. Taylor, *Te Ika a Maui, or
New Zealand and its Inhabitants,*[2] pp.
203 *sq.* ; A. S. Thomson, *The Story
of New Zealand* (London, 1859), i.
116 *sq.*
[3] R. Brough Smyth, *Aborigines of
Victoria*, i. 468 *sq.*

[4] J. Dawson, *Australian Aborigines*,
p. 36.
[5] A. W. Howitt, " On Australian
Medicine-men," *Journal of the Anthropological Institute*, xvi. (1887) p. 27.
Compare *id.*, *Native Tribes of South-
East Australia*, pp. 360 *sq.*
[6] E. Palmer, " Notes on some Australian Tribes," *Journal of the Anthropological Institute*, xiii. (1884) p. 293.

Belief that
people
may be
bewitched
through the
clippings of
their hair.

Lucian describes how a Syrian witch professed to bring back a faithless lover to his forsaken fair one by means of a lock of his hair, his shoes, his garments, or something of that sort. She hung the hair, or whatever it was, on a peg and fumigated it with brimstone, sprinkling salt on the fire and mentioning the names of the lover and his lass. Then she drew a magic wheel from her bosom and set it spinning, while she gabbled a spell full of barbarous and fearsome words. This soon brought the false lover back to the feet of his charmer.[1] Apuleius tells how an amorous Thessalian witch essayed to win the affections of a handsome Boeotian youth by similar means. As darkness fell she mounted the roof, and there, surrounded by a hellish array of dead men's bones, she knotted the severed tresses of auburn hair and threw them on the glowing embers of a perfumed fire. But her cunning hand-maid had outwitted her; the hair was only goat's hair; and all her enchantments ended in dismal and ludicrous failure.[2]

Clipped
hair may
cause head-
ache.

The Huzuls of the Carpathians imagine that if mice get a person's shorn hair and make a nest of it, the person will suffer from headache or even become idiotic.[3] Similarly in Germany it is a common notion that if birds find a person's cut hair, and build their nests with it, the person will suffer from headache;[4] sometimes it is thought that he will have an eruption on the head.[5] The same superstition prevails,

---

[1] Lucian, *Dial. meretr.* iv. 4 *sq.*

[2] Apuleius, *Metamorph.* iii. 16 *sqq.* For more evidence of the same sort, see Th. Williams, *Fiji and the Fijians,*[2] i. 248 ; James Bonwick, *Daily Life of the Tasmanians,* p. 178 ; James Chalmers, *Pioneering in New Guinea,* p. 187 ; J. S. Polack, *Manners and Customs of the New Zealanders,* i. 282 ; A. Bastian, *Die Völker des östlichen Asien,* iii. 270 ; G. H. von Langsdorff, *Reise um die Welt,* i. 134 *sq.* ; W. Ellis, *Polynesian Researches,*[2] i. 364 ; A. B. Ellis, *Ewe-speaking peoples of the Slave Coast,* p. 99 ; R. H. Codrington, *The Melanesians,* p. 203 ; K. von den Steinen, *Unter den Naturvölkern Zentral-Brasiliens,* p. 343 ; Miss Mary H. Kingsley, *Travels in West Africa,* p. 447 ; I. V. Zingerle, *Sitten, Bräuche und Meinungen des Tiroler Volkes,*[2] § 178 ; R. Andree, *Ethnographische*

Parallelen und Vergleiche, Neue Folge, pp. 12 *sqq.* ; E. S. Hartland, *Legend of Perseus,* ii. 64-74, 132-139.

[3] R. F. Kaindl, "Neue Beiträge zur Ethnologie und Volkeskunde der Huzulen," *Globus,* lxix. (1896) p. 94.

[4] E. Meier, *Deutsche Sagen, Sitten und Gebräuche aus Schwaben,* p. 509 ; A. Birlinger, *Volksthümliches aus Schwaben,* i. 493 ; F. Panzer, *Beitrag zur deutschen Mythologie,* i. 258 ; J. A. E. Köhler, *Volksbrauch,* etc., *im Voigtlande,* p. 425 ; A. Witzschel, *Sagen, Sitten und Gebräuche aus Thüringen,* p. 282 ; I. V. Zingerle, *op. cit.* § 180 ; J. W. Wolf, *Beiträge zur deutschen Mythologie,* i. p. 224, § 273. A similar belief prevails among the gypsies of Eastern Europe (H. von Wlislocki, *Volksglaube und religiöser Brauch der Zigeuner,* p. 81).

[5] I. V. Zingerle, *op. cit.* § 181.

or used to prevail, in West Sussex. " I knew how it would
be," exclaimed a maidservant one day, " when I saw that
bird fly off with a bit of my hair in its beak that blew out
of the window this morning when I was dressing ; I knew I
should have a clapping headache, and so I have." [1]   In like
manner the Scottish Highlanders believe that if cut or loose
hair is allowed to blow away with the wind and it passes
over an empty nest, or a bird takes it to its nest, the head
from which it came will ache.[2]   The Todas of southern India
hide their clipped hair in bushes or hollows in the rocks, in
order that it may not be found by crows, and they bury the
parings of their nails lest they should be eaten by buffaloes,
with whom, it is believed, they would disagree.[3]

Again it is thought that cut or combed-out hair may
disturb the weather by producing rain and hail, thunder and
lightning.   We have seen that in New Zealand a spell was
uttered at hair-cutting to avert thunder and lightning.   In the
Tyrol, witches are supposed to use cut or combed-out hair to
make hailstones or thunderstorms with.[4]   Thlinkeet Indians
have been known to attribute stormy weather to the rash
act of a girl who had combed her hair outside of the house.[5]
The Romans seem to have held similar views, for it was a
maxim with them that no one on shipboard should cut his
hair or nails except in a storm,[6] that is, when the mischief
was already done.   In the Highlands of Scotland it is said
that no sister should comb her hair at night if she have a
brother at sea.[7]   In West Africa, when the Mani of Chitombe
or Jumba died, the people used to run in crowds to the
corpse and tear out his hair, teeth, and nails, which they
kept as a rain-charm, believing that otherwise no rain would
fall.   The Makoko of the Anzikos begged the missionaries
to give him half their beards as a rain-charm.[8]   When
Du Chaillu had his hair cut among the Ashira of West

Cut hair may cause rain, hail, thunder and lightning.

---

[1] Charlotte Latham, " Some West
Sussex Superstitions," *Folk-lore Record*,
i. (1878) p. 40.
[2] J. G. Campbell, *Superstitions of
the Highlands and Islands of Scotland*
(Glasgow, 1900), p. 237.
[3] W. H. R. Rivers, *The Todas*
(London, 1906), pp. 268 *sq.*
[4] I. V. Zingerle, *op. cit.* §§ 176, 179.

[5] A. Krause, *Die Tlinkit-Indianer*
(Jena, 1885), p. 300.
[6] Petronius, *Sat.* 104.
[7] J. G. Campbell, *op. cit.* pp. 236
sq.
[8] A. Bastian, *Die deutsche Expedition
an der Loango-Küste*, i. 231 *sq.* ; *id.*,
Ein Besuch in San Salvador, pp. 117
sq.

Magical uses of cut hair.

Africa, the people scuffled and fought for the clippings of his hair, even the aged king himself taking part in the scrimmage.   Every one who succeeded in getting some of the hairs wrapped them up carefully and went off in triumph.   When the traveller, who was regarded as a spirit by these simple-minded folk, asked the king what use the clippings could be to him, his sable majesty replied, " Oh, spirit ! these hairs are very precious ; we shall make *mondas* (fetiches) of them, and they will bring other white men to us, and bring us great good luck and riches.   Since you have come to us, oh spirit ! we have wished to have some of your hair, but did not dare to ask for it, not knowing that it could be cut." [1]   The Wabondei of eastern Africa preserve the hair and nails of their dead chiefs and use them both for the making of rain and the healing of the sick.[2]   The hair, beard, and nails of their deceased chiefs are the most sacred possession, the most precious treasure of the Baronga of south-eastern Africa.   Preserved in pellets of cow-dung wrapt round with leathern thongs, they are kept in a special hut under the charge of a high priest, who offers sacrifices and prayers at certain seasons, and has to observe strict continence for a month before he handles these holy relics in the offices of religion.   A terrible drought was once the result of this palladium falling into the hands of the enemy.[3]   In some Victorian tribes the sorcerer used to burn human hair in time of drought ; it was never burned at other times for fear of causing a deluge of rain.   Also when the river was low, the sorcerer would place human hair in the stream to increase the supply of water.[4]

Cut hair and nails may be used as hostages for good behaviour

If cut hair and nails remain in sympathetic connexion with the person from whose body they have been severed, it is clear that they can be used as hostages for his good behaviour by any one who may chance to possess them ; for on the principles of contagious magic he has only to

---

[1] P. B. du Chaillu, *Explorations and Adventures in Equatorial Africa* (London, 1861), pp. 426 *sq.*

[2] O. Baumann, *Usambara und seine Nachbargebiete* (Berlin, 1891), p. 141.

[3] A. Junod, *Les Ba-Ronga* (Neuchâtel, 1898), pp. 398-400.

[4] W. Stanbridge, "On the Aborigines of Victoria," *Transactions of the Ethnological Society of London*, N.S., i. (1861) p. 300.

injure the hair or nails in order to hurt simultaneously _{of the}
their original owner.   Hence when the Nandi have taken _{persons} _{from whose}
a prisoner they shave his head and keep the shorn hair as _{bodies they}
a surety that he will not attempt to escape ; but when the _{have been} _{taken.}
captive is ransomed, they return his shorn hair with him
to his own people.[1]   For a similar reason, perhaps, when the
Tiaha, an Arab tribe of Moab, have taken a prisoner whom
they do not wish to put to death, they shave one corner of
his head above his temples and let him go.   So, too, an
Arab of Moab who pardons a murderer will sometimes
cut off the man's hair and shave his chin before releasing
him.   Again, when two Moabite Arabs had got hold of a
traitor who had revealed their plan of campaign to the
enemy, they contented themselves with shaving completely
one side of his head and his moustache on the other,
after which they set him at liberty.[2]   We can now, perhaps,
understand why Hanun King of Ammon shaved off one-
half of the beards of King David's messengers and cut
off half their garments before he sent them back to their
master.[3]   His intention, we may conjecture, was not simply
to put a gross affront on the envoys.   He distrusted the
ambitious designs of King David and wished to have some
guarantee of the maintenance of peace and friendly relations
between the two countries.   That guarantee he may have
imagined that he possessed in half of the beards and
garments of the ambassadors ; and if that was so, we may
suppose that when the indignant David set the army of
Israel in motion against Ammon, and the fords of Jordan
were alive with the passage of his troops, the wizards of
Ammon were busy in the strong keep of Rabbah muttering
their weird spells and performing their quaint enchantments
over the shorn hair and severed skirts in order to dispel the
thundercloud of war that was gathering black about their
country.   Vain hopes !   The city fell, and from the gates
the sad inhabitants trooped forth in thousands to be laid
in long lines on the ground and sawed asunder or ripped
up with harrows or to walk into the red glow of the

---

[1] A. C. Hollis, *The Nandi* (Oxford, 1909), pp. 30, 74 *sq.*

[2] Le P. A. Jaussen, *Coutumes des*

Arabes au pays de Moab (Paris, 1908),
pp. 94 *sq.*

[3] 2 Samuel, x. 4.

burning brick kilns.[1]   Again, the parings of nails may serve
the same purpose as the clippings of hair ; they too may
be treated as bail for the good behaviour of the persons
from whose fingers they have been cut.   It is apparently
on this principle that when the Ba-yaka of the Congo
valley cement a peace, the chiefs of the two tribes meet
and eat a cake which contains some of their nail-parings
as a pledge of the maintenance of the treaty.   They believe
that he who breaks an engagement contracted in this solemn
manner will die.[2]   Each of the high contracting parties has
in fact given hostages to fortune in the shape of the nail-
parings which are lodged in the other man's stomach.

Cut hair
and nails
are de-
posited in
sacred
places,
such as
temples
and ceme-
teries, to
preserve
them from
injury.

To preserve the cut hair and nails from injury and from
the dangerous uses to which they may be put by sorcerers,
it is necessary to deposit them in some safe place.   Hence
the natives of the Maldives carefully keep the cuttings of
their hair and nails and bury them, with a little water, in
the cemeteries ; " for they would not for the world tread
upon them nor cast them in the fire, for they say that they
are part of their body, and demand burial as it does ; and,
indeed, they fold them neatly in cotton ; and most of them
like to be shaved at the gates of temples and mosques." [3]
In New Zealand the severed hair was deposited on some
sacred spot of ground " to protect it from being touched
accidentally or designedly by any one." [4]   The shorn locks
of a chief were gathered with much care and placed in an
adjoining cemetery.[5]   The Tahitians buried the cuttings of
their hair at the temples.[6]   In the streets of Soku, West
Africa, a modern traveller observed cairns of large stones
piled against walls with tufts of human hair inserted in the
crevices.   On asking the meaning of this, he was told that
when any native of the place polled his hair he carefully

---

[1] 2 Samuel, x., xii. 26-31.

[2] R. Torday and T. A. Joyce,
" Notes on the Ethnography of the
Ba-Yaka," *Journal of the Anthropo-
logical Institute*, xxxvi. (1906) p. 49.

[3] François Pyrard, *Voyages to the
East Indies, the Maldives, the Moluccas,
and Brazil*, translated by Albert Gray
(Hakluyt Society, 1887), i. 110 *sq.*

[4] E. Shortland, *Traditions and
Superstitions of the New Zealanders*,
p. 110.

[5] J. S. Polack, *Manners and Customs of the New Zealanders*, i. 38 *sq.*
Compare G. F. Angas, *Savage Life
and Scenes in Australia and New
Zealand* (London, 1847), ii. 108 *sq.*

[6] James Wilson, *A Missionary Voyage to the Southern Pacific Ocean*
(London, 1799), p. 355.

gathered up the clippings and deposited them in one of these cairns, all of which were sacred to the fetish and therefore inviolable. These cairns of sacred stones, he further learned, were simply a precaution against witchcraft, for if a man were not thus careful in disposing of his hair, some of it might fall into the hands of his enemies, who would, by means of it, be able to cast spells over him and so compass his destruction.[1] When the top-knot of a Siamese child has been cut with great ceremony, the short hairs are put into a little vessel made of plantain leaves and set adrift on the nearest river or canal. As they float away, all that was wrong or harmful in the child's disposition is believed to depart with them. The long hairs are kept till the child makes a pilgrimage to the holy Footprint of Buddha on the sacred hill at Prabat. They are then presented to the priests, who are supposed to make them into brushes with which they sweep the Footprint; but in fact so much hair is thus offered every year that the priests cannot use it all, so they quietly burn the superfluity as soon as the pilgrims' backs are turned.[2] The cut hair and nails of the Flamen Dialis were buried under a lucky tree.[3] The shorn tresses of the Vestal virgins were hung on an ancient lotus-tree.[4] In Morocco women often hang their cut hair on a tree that grows on or near the grave of a wonder-working saint; for they think thus to rid themselves of headache or to guard against it.[5] In Germany the clippings of hair used often to be buried under an elder-bush.[6] In Oldenburg cut hair and nails are wrapt in a cloth which is deposited in a hole in an

Cut hair and nails buried under certain trees or deposited among the branches.

[1] R. A. Freeman, *Travels and Life in Ashanti and Jaman* (Westminster, 1898), pp. 171 *sq.*

[2] E. Young, *The Kingdom of the Yellow Robe*, p. 79.

[3] Aulus Gellius, x. 15. 15. The ancients were not agreed as to the distinction between lucky and unlucky trees. According to Cato and Pliny, trees that bore fruit were lucky, and trees which did not were unlucky (Festus, ed. C. O. Müller, p. 29, *s.v. Felices*; Pliny, *Nat. Hist.* xvi. 108); but according to Tarquitius Priscus those trees were unlucky which were sacred to the infernal gods and bore

black berries or black fruit (Macrobius, *Saturn.* ii. 16, but iii. 20 in L. Jan's edition, Quedlinburg and Leipsic, 1852).

[4] Pliny, *Nat. Hist.* xvi. 235 ; Festu , p. 57 ed. C. O. Müller, *s.v. Capillatam vel capillarem arborem.*

[5] M. Quedenfelt, "Aberglaube und halbreligiöse Bruderschaft bei den Marokkanern," *Verhandlungen der Berliner Gesellschaft für Anthropologie, Ethnologie und Urgeschichte*, 1886, p. (680).

[6] A. Wuttke, *Der deutsche Volksaberglaube*,[2] pp. 294 *sq.*, § 464.

Cut hair and nails buried under certain trees or deposited among the branches.

elder-tree three days before the new moon ; the hole is then plugged up.[1] In the West of Northumberland it is thought that if the first parings of a child's nails are buried under an ash-tree, the child will turn out a fine singer.[2] In Amboyna, before a child may taste sago-pap for the first time, the father cuts off a lock of the infant's hair, which he buries under a sago-palm.[3] In the Aru Islands, when a child is able to run alone, a female relation shears a lock of its hair and deposits it on a banana-tree.[4] In the island of Rotti it is thought that the first hair which a child gets is not his own, and that, if it is not cut off, it will make him weak and ill. Hence, when the child is about a month old, his hair is polled with much ceremony. As each of the friends who are invited to the ceremony enters the house he goes up to the child, snips off a little of its hair and drops it into a coco-nut shell full of water. Afterwards the father or another relation takes the hair and packs it into a little bag made of leaves, which he fastens to the top of a palm-tree. Then he gives the leaves of the palm a good shaking, climbs down, and goes home without speaking to any one.[5] Indians of the Yukon territory, Alaska, do not throw away their cut hair and nails, but tie them up in little bundles and place them in the crotches of trees or wherever they are not likely to be disturbed by beasts. For " they have a superstition that disease will follow the disturbance of such remains by animals." [6]

Cut hair and nails may be stowed away for safety in any secret place.

Often the clipped hair and nails are stowed away in any secret place, not necessarily in a temple or cemetery or at a tree, as in the cases already mentioned. Thus in Swabia you are recommended to deposit your clipped hair in some spot where neither sun nor moon can shine on it, for example in the earth or under a stone.[7] In Danzig it is buried in a

[1] W. Mannhardt, *Germanische Mythen* (Berlin, 1858), p. 630.

[2] W. Henderson, *Folk-lore of the Northern Counties* (London, 1879), p. 17.

[3] J. G. F. Riedel, *De sluik- en kroesharige rassen tusschen Selebes en Papua*, p. 74.

[4] J. G. F. Riedel, *op. cit.* p. 265.

[5] G. Heijmering, "Zeden en gewoon-ten op het eiland Rottie," *Tijdschrift voor Neêrlands Indië*, 1843, dl. ii. pp. 634-637.

[6] W. Dall, *Alaska and its Resources* (London, 1870), p. 54 ; F. Whymper, "The Natives of the Youkon River," *Transactions of the Ethnological Society of London*, N.S., vii. (1869) p. 174.

[7] E. Meier, *Deutsche Sagen, Sitten*

bag under the threshold.[1] In Ugi, one of the Solomon Islands, men bury their hair lest it should fall into the hands of an enemy who would make magic with it and so bring sickness or calamity on them.[2] The same fear seems to be general in Melanesia, and has led to a regular practice of hiding cut hair and nails.[3] In Fiji, the shorn hair is concealed in the thatch of the house.[4] Most Burmese and Shans tie the combings of their hair and the parings of their nails to a stone and sink them in deep water or bury them in the ground.[5] The Zend-Avesta directs that the clippings of hair and the parings of nails shall be placed in separate holes, and that three, six, or nine furrows shall be drawn round each hole with a metal knife.[6] In the Grihya-Sûtras it is provided that the hair cut from a child's head at the end of the first, third, fifth, or seventh year shall be buried in the earth at a place covered with grass or in the neighbourhood of water.[7] At the end of the period of his studentship a Brahman has his hair shaved and his nails cut ; and a person who is kindly disposed to him gathers the shorn hair and the clipped nails, puts them in a lump of bull's dung, and buries them in a cow-stable or near an *adumbara* tree or in a clump of *darbha* grass, with the words, " Thus I hide the sins of So-and-so." [8] The Madi or Moru tribe of central Africa bury the parings of their nails in the ground.[9] In Uganda grown people throw away the clippings of their hair, but carefully bury the parings of their nails.[10] The A-lur

und Gebräuche aus Schwaben, p. 509 ; A. Birlinger, *Volksthümliches aus Schwaben*, i. 493.

[1] W. Mannhardt, *Germanische Mythen*, p. 630.

[2] H. B. Guppy, *The Solomon Islands and their Natives* (London, 1887), p. 54.

[3] R. H. Codrington, *The Melanesians*, p. 203.

[4] Th. Williams, *Fiji and the Fijians*,[2] i. 249.

[5] J. G. Scott and J. P. Hardiman, *Gazetteer of Upper Burma and the Shan States*, part i. vol. ii. p. 37.

[6] *The Zend-Avesta*, *Vendîdâd*, Fargaard, xvii. (vol. i. pp. 186 *sqq.*, translated by J. Darmesteter, *Sacred Books of the East*, vol. iv.).

[7] *Grihya-Sûtras*, translated by H. Oldenberg, part i. p. 57 ; compare *id.*, pp. 303, 399, part ii. p. 62 (*Sacred Books of the East*, vols. xxix., xxx.). Compare H. Oldenberg, *Die Religion des Veda*, p. 487.

[8] *Grihya-Sûtras*, translated by H. Oldenberg, part ii. pp. 165 *sq.*, 218.

[9] R. W. Felkin, "Notes on the Madi or Moru Tribe of Central Africa," *Proceedings of the Royal Society of Edinburgh*, xii. (1882-84) p. 332.

[10] Fr. Stuhlmann, *Mit Emin Pascha ins Herz von Afrika*, p. 185 note. The same thing was told me in conversation by the Rev. J. Roscoe, missionary to Uganda ; but I understood him to mean that the hair was

Cut hair and nails deposited in safe places.

are careful to collect and bury both their hair and nails in safe places.[1] The same practice prevails among many tribes of South Africa, from a fear lest wizards should get hold of the severed particles and work evil with them.[2] The Caffres carry still further this dread of allowing any portion of themselves to fall into the hands of an enemy ; for not only do they bury their cut hair and nails in a secret spot, but when one of them cleans the head of another he preserves the vermin which he catches, "carefully delivering them to the person to whom they originally appertained, supposing, according to their theory, that as they derived their support from the blood of the man from whom they were taken, should they be killed by another, the blood of his neighbour would be in his possession, thus placing in his hands the power of some superhuman influence."[3] Amongst the Wanyoro of central Africa all cuttings of the hair and nails are carefully stored under the bed and afterwards strewed about among the tall grass.[4] Similarly the Wahoko of central Africa take pains to collect their cut hair and nails and scatter them in the forest.[5] The Asa, a branch of the Masai, hide the clippings of their hair and the parings of their nails or throw them away far from the kraal, lest a sorcerer should get hold of them and make their original owners ill by his magic.[6] In North Guinea the parings of the finger-nails and the shorn locks of the head are scrupulously concealed, lest they be converted into a charm for the destruction of the person to whom they belong.[7] For the same reason the clipped hair and nail-parings of chiefs in Southern Nigeria are secretly buried.[8] Among the Thompson Indians of British Columbia loose hair was buried, hidden, or thrown into the water, because, if an

not carelessly disposed of, but thrown away in some place where it would not easily be found.

[1] Fr. Stuhlmann, *op. cit.* pp. 516 *sq.*

[2] J. Macdonald, *Light in Africa,* p. 209 ; *id.,* "Manners, Customs, Superstitions and Religions of South African Tribes," *Journal of the Anthropological Institute,* xx. (1891) p. 131.

[3] A. Steedman, *Wanderings and Adventures in the Interior of Southern*

Africa (London, 1835), i. 266.

[4] *Emin Pasha in Central Africa, being a Collection of his Letters and Journals* (London, 1888), p. 74.

[5] Fr. Stuhlmann, *Mit Emin Pascha ins Herz von Afrika,* p. 625.

[6] M. Merkel, *Die Masai* (Berlin, 1904), p. 243.

[7] J. L. Wilson, *Western Africa,* p. 215.

[8] Ch. Partridge, *Cross River Natives* (London, 1905), pp. 8, 203 *sq.*

enemy got hold of it, he might bewitch the owner.[1] In
Bolang Mongondo, a district of western Celebes, the first
hair cut from a child's head is kept in a young coco-nut,
which is commonly hung on the front of the house, under
the roof.[2] To spit upon the hair before throwing it away is
thought in some parts of Europe to be a sufficient safeguard
against its use by witches.[3] Spitting as a protective charm
is well known.[4]

Sometimes the severed hair and nails are preserved, not *Cut hair*
to prevent them from falling into the hands of a magician, *and nails kept*
but that the owner may have them at the resurrection of the *against the*
body, to which some races look forward. Thus the Incas *resurrection.*
of Peru "took extreme care to preserve the nail-parings and
the hairs that were shorn off or torn out with a comb;
placing them in holes or niches in the walls; and if they fell
out, any other Indian that saw them picked them up and
put them in their places again. I very often asked different
Indians, at various times, why they did this, in order to see
what they would say, and they all replied in the same words
saying, 'Know that all persons who are born must return to
life' (they have no word to express resuscitation), 'and the
souls must rise out of their tombs with all that belonged to
their bodies. We, therefore, in order that we may not have
to search for our hair and nails at a time when there will be
much hurry and confusion, place them in one place, that

---

[1] James Teit, "The Thompson River
Indians of British Columbia," *Memoir
of the American Museum of Natural
History, The Jesup North Pacific
Expedition*, vol. i. part iv. (April
1900) p. 360.

[2] N. P. Wilken en J. A. Schwarz,
"Allerlei over het land en volk van
Bolaang Mongondou," *Mededeelingen
van wege het Nederlandsche Zendelinggenootschap*, xi. (1867) p. 322.

[3] I. V. Zingerle, *Sitten, Bräuche
und Meinungen des Tiroler Volkes*[2]
(Innsbruck, 1871), §§ 176, 580;
Mélusine, 1878, col. 79; E. Monseur,
Le Folklore Wallon, p. 91.

[4] Pliny, *Nat. Hist.* xxviii. 35;
Theophrastus, *Characters*, "The Superstitious Man"; Theocritus, *id.* vi. 39,
vii. 127 : Persius, *Sat.* ii. 31 *sqq.* At

the siege of Danzig in 1734, when the
old wives saw a bomb coming, they
used to spit thrice and cry, "Fi, fi, fi,
there comes the dragon!" in the persuasion that this secured them against
being hit (Tettau und Temme, *Die
Volkssagen Ostpreussens, Litthauens
und Westpreussens* (Berlin, 1837), p.
284). For more examples, see J. E. B.
Mayor on Juvenal, *Sat.* vii. 112; J. E.
Crombie, "The Saliva Superstition,"
International Folk-lore Congress, 1891,
Papers and Transactions, pp. 249 *sq.* ;
C. de Mensignac, *Recherches ethnographiques sur la salive et le crachat*
(Bordeaux, 1892), pp. 50 *sqq.* ; F. W.
Nicolson, "The Saliva Superstition in
Classical Literature," *Harvard Studies
in Classical Philology*, viii. (1897) pp.
35 *sqq.*

Cut hair
and nails
kept
against the
resurrec-
tion.

they may be brought together more conveniently, and, whenever it is possible, we are also careful to spit in one place.'"[1] In Chili this custom of stuffing the shorn hair into holes in the wall is still observed, it being thought the height of imprudence to throw the hair away.[2] Similarly the Turks never throw away the parings of their nails, but carefully stow them in cracks of the walls or of the boards, in the belief that they will be needed at the resurrection.[3] The Armenians do not throw away their cut hair and nails and extracted teeth, but hide them in places that are esteemed holy, such as a crack in the church wall, a pillar of the house, or a hollow tree. They think that all these severed portions of themselves will be wanted at the resurrection, and that he who has not stowed them away in a safe place will have to hunt about for them on the great day.[4] With the same intention the Macedonians bury the parings of their nails in a hole,[5] and devout Moslems in Morocco hide them in a secret place.[6] Similarly the Arabs of Moab bestow the parings of their nails in the crannies of walls, where they are sanguine enough to expect to find them when they appear before their Maker.[7] Some of the Esthonians keep the parings of their finger and toe nails in their bosom, in order to have them at hand when they are asked for them at the day of judgment.[8] In a like spirit peasants of the Vosges will sometimes bury their extracted teeth secretly, marking the spot well so that they may be able to walk straight to it on the resurrection day.[9] In the village of Drumconrath, near Abbeyleix, in Ireland, there used to be some old women who, having ascertained from Scripture that the hairs of their heads were all

[1] Garcilasso de la Vega, *First Part of the Royal Commentaries of the Yncas*, bk. ii. ch. 7 (vol. i. p. 127, Markham's translation).

[2] *Mélusine*, 1878, coll. 583 *sq.*

[3] *The People of Turkey*, by a Consul's daughter and wife, ii. 250.

[4] M. Abeghian, *Der armenische Volksglaube*, p. 68.

[5] G. F. Abbott, *Macedonian Folklore* (Cambridge, 1903), p. 214.

[6] M. Quedenfelt, "Aberglaube und halbreligiöse Bruderschaft bei den Marokkanern," *Verhandlungen der*

Berliner Gesellschaft für Anthropologie, Ethnologie und Urgeschichte, 1886, p. (680).

[7] Le P. A. Jaussen, *Coutumes des Arabes au pays de Moab* (Paris, 1908), p. 94 note [1].

[8] Boecler-Kreutzwald, *Der Ehsten abergläubische Gebräuche, Weisen und Gewohnheiten*, p. 139; F. J. Wiedemann, *Aus dem innern und äussern Leben der Ehsten*, p. 491.

[9] L. F. Sauvé, *Le Folk-lore des Hautes-Vosges* (Paris, 1889), p. 41.

numbered by the Almighty, expected to have to account for them at the day of judgment. In order to be able to do so they stuffed the severed hair away in the thatch of their cottages.[1]   In Abyssinia men who have had their hands or feet cut off are careful to dry the severed limbs over a fire and preserve them in butter for the purpose of being buried with them in the grave. Thus they expect to get up with all their limbs complete at the general rising.[2] The pains taken by the Chinese to preserve corpses entire and free from decay seems to rest on a firm belief in the resurrection of the dead ; hence it is natural to find their ancient books laying down a rule that the hair, nails, and teeth which have fallen out during life should be buried with the dead in the coffin, or at least in the grave.[3]   The Fors of central Africa object to cut any one else's nails, for should the part cut off be lost and not delivered into its owner's hands, it will have to be made up to him somehow or other after death. The parings are buried in the ground.[4]

Some people burn their loose hair to save it from falling into the hands of sorcerers. This is done by the Patagonians and some of the Victorian tribes.[5]   In the Upper Vosges they say that you should never leave the clippings of your hair and nails lying about, but burn them to hinder the sorcerers from using them against you.[6]   For the same reason Italian women either burn their loose hairs or throw them into a place where no one is likely to look for them.[7] The almost universal dread of witchcraft induces the West African negroes, the Makololo of South Africa, and the Tahitians to burn or bury their shorn hair.[8]   For the

Cut hair and nails burnt to prevent them from falling into the hands of sorcerers.

---

[1] Miss A. H. Singleton, in a letter to me, dated Rathmagle House, Abbeyleix, Ireland, 24th February 1904.

[2] Dr. Antoine Petit, in Th. Lefebvre, *Voyage en Abyssinie*, i. 373.

[3] J. J. M. de Groot, *The Religious System of China*, i. 342 *sq.* (Leyden, 1892).

[4] R. W. Felkin, "Notes on the For Tribe of Central Africa," *Proceedings of the Royal Society of Edinburgh*, xiii. (1884-86) p. 230.

[5] A. D'Orbigny, *Voyage dans l'Amérique méridionale*, ii. 93; Lieut. Musters,

"On the Races of Patagonia," *Journal of the Anthropological Institute*, i. (1872) p. 197 ; J. Dawson, *Australian Aborigines*, p. 36. The Patagonians sometimes throw their hair into a river instead of burning it.

[6] L. F. Sauvé, *Le Folk-lore des Hautes-Vosges*, p. 170.

[7] Z. Zanetti, *La Medicina delle nostre donne* (Città di Castello, 1892), pp. 234 *sq.*

[8] A. B. Ellis, *The Ewe-speaking Peoples of the Slave Coast*, p. 99 ; Miss Mary H. Kingsley, *Travels in West Africa*, p. 447 ; R. H. Nassau, *Fetich-*

same reason the natives of Uap, one of the Caroline
Islands, either burn or throw into the sea the clippings
of their hair and the parings of their nails.[1] One of the
pygmies who roam through the gloomy depths of the vast
central African forests has been seen to collect carefully the
clippings of his hair in a packet of banana leaves and keep
them till next morning, when, the camp breaking up for the
day's march, he threw them into the hot ashes of the abandoned fire.[2] Australian aborigines of the Proserpine River,
in Queensland, burn a woman's cut hair to prevent it from
getting into a man's bag ; for if it did, the woman would
fall ill.[3] When an English officer had cut off a lock of hair
of a Fuegian woman, the men of her party were angry, and
one of them, taking the lock away, threw half of it into the
fire and swallowed the rest. " Immediately afterwards,
placing his hands to the fire, as if to warm them, and
looking upwards, he uttered a few words, apparently of
invocation : then, looking at us, pointed upwards, and exclaimed, with a tone and gesture of explanation, ' *Pecheray,
Pecheray.*' After which they cut off some hair from several
of the officers who were present, and repeated a similar
ceremony."[4] The Thompson Indians used to burn the
parings of their nails, because if an enemy got possession
of the parings he might bewitch the person to whom they
belonged.[5] In the Tyrol many people burn their hair
lest the witches should use it to raise thunderstorms ; others
burn or bury it to prevent the birds from lining their nests
with it, which would cause the heads from which the hair
came to ache.[6] Cut and combed-out hair is burned in

ism in *West Africa* (London, 1904),
p. 83 ; A. F. Mockler - Ferryman,
British Nigeria (London, 1902),
p. 286 ; David Livingstone, *Narrative
of Expedition to the Zambesi*, pp. 46
sq. ; W. Ellis, *Polynesian Researches*,[2]
i. 365. In some parts of New Guinea
cut hair is destroyed for the same
reason (H. H. Romilly, *From my
Verandah in New Guinea*, London,
1889, p. 83).
　　[1] W. H. Furness, *The Island of
Stone Money, Uap of the Carolines*
(Philadelphia and London, 1910),
p. 137.

[2] Fr. Stuhlmann, *Mit Emin Pascha
ins Herz von Afrika*, p. 451.
　　[3] W. E. Roth, *North Queensland
Ethnography, Bulletin No.* 5 (Brisbane, 1903), p. 21.
　　[4] Captain R. Fitzroy, *Narrative of
the Surveying Voyages of His Majesty's
Ships Adventure and Beagle*, i. (London,
1839), pp. 313 *sq.*
　　[5] J. Teit, " The Thompson Indians
of British Columbia," *Memoir of the
American Museum of Natural History,
The Jesup North Pacific Expedition*,
vol. i. part iv. (April 1900) p. 360.
　　[6] I. V. Zingerle, *Sitten, Bräuche*

Pomerania and sometimes in Belgium.[1] In Norway the Cut hair and nails burnt. parings of nails are either burned or buried, lest the elves or the Finns should find them and make them into bullets wherewith to shoot the cattle.[2] In Corea all the clippings and combings of the hair of a whole family are carefully preserved throughout the year and then burned in potsherds outside the house on the evening of New Year's Day. At such seasons the streets of Seoul, the capital, present a weird spectacle. They are for the most part silent and deserted, sometimes muffled deep in snow ; but through the dusk of twilight red lights glimmer at every door, where little groups are busy tending tiny fires whose flickering flames cast a ruddy fitful glow on the moving figures. The burning of the hair in these fires is thought to exclude demons from the house for a year ; but coupled with this belief may well be, or once have been, a wish to put these relics out of the reach of witches and wizards.[3]

This destruction of the hair and nails plainly involves Inconsistency in burning cut hair and nails. an inconsistency of thought. The object of the destruction is avowedly to prevent these severed portions of the body from being used by sorcerers. But the possibility of their being so used depends upon the supposed sympathetic connexion between them and the man from whom they were severed. And if this sympathetic connexion still exists, clearly these severed portions cannot be destroyed without injury to the man.

Before leaving this subject, on which I have perhaps Hair is sometimes cut because it is infected with the virus of taboo. In these cases hair-cutting is a form of purification. dwelt too long, it may be well to call attention to the motive assigned for cutting a young child's hair in Rotti.[4] In that island the first hair is regarded as a danger to the child, and its removal is intended to avert the danger. The reason of this may be that as a young child is almost universally supposed to be in a tabooed or dangerous state, it is neces- sary, in removing the taboo, to remove also the separable

und Meinungen des Tiroler Volkes[2] (Innsbruck, 1871), p. 28, §§ 177, 179, 180.

[1] U. Jahn, *Hexenwesen und Zauberei in Pommern* (Breslau, 1886), p. 15 ; *Mélusine*, 1878, col. 79 ; E. Monseur, *Le Folklore Wallon*, p. 91.

[2] E. H. Meyer, *Indogermanische*

Mythen, ii. *Achilleis* (Berlin, 1877), p. 523.

[3] P. Lowell, *Chosön, the Land of the Morning Calm, a Sketch of Korea* (London, Preface dated 1885), pp. 199-201 ; Mrs. Bishop, *Korea and her Neighbours* (London, 1898), ii. 55 *sq.*

[4] Above, p. 276.

Hair some-
times cut
because it
is infected
with the
virus of
taboo.
In these
cases hair-
cutting is
a form of
purification. parts of the child's body because they are infected, so to say, by the virus of taboo and as such are dangerous. The cutting of the child's hair would thus be exactly parallel to the destruction of the vessels which have been used by a tabooed person.[1] This view is borne out by a practice, observed by some Australians, of burning off part of a woman's hair after childbirth as well as burning every vessel which has been used by her during her seclusion.[2] Here the burning of the woman's hair seems plainly intended to serve the same purpose as the burning of the vessels used by her ; and as the vessels are burned because they are believed to be tainted with a dangerous infection, so, we must suppose, is also the hair. Similarly among the Latuka of central Africa, a woman is secluded for fourteen days after the birth of her child, and at the end of her seclusion her hair is shaved off and burnt.[3] Again, we have seen that girls at puberty are strongly infected with taboo ; hence it is not surprising to find that the Ticunas of Brazil tear out all the hair of girls at that period.[4] Once more, the father of twins in Uganda is tabooed for some time after the birth of the children, and during that time he may not dress his hair nor cut his finger nails. This state of taboo lasts until the next war breaks out. When the army is under orders to march, the father of twins has the whole of his body shaved and his nails cut. The shorn hair and the cut nails are then tied up in a ball, which the man takes with him to the war, together with the bark cloth he wore at the ceremonial dances after the birth of the twins. When he has killed a foe, he crams the ball into the dead man's mouth, ties the bark cloth round the neck of the corpse, and leaves them there on the battlefield.[5] The ceremony appears to be intended to rid the man of the taint of taboo which may be supposed to adhere to his hair, nails, and the garment he wore. Hence we can understand the importance attached by many

---

[1] Above, pp. 4, 131, 139, 145, 156.

[2] W. Ridley, " Report on Australian Languages and Traditions," *Journal of the Anthropological Institute*, ii. (1873) p. 268.

[3] Fr. Stuhlmann, *Mit Emin Pascha ins Herz von Afrika*, p. 795.

[4] F. de Castelnau, *Expédition dans les parties centrales de l'Amérique du Sud*, v. (Paris, 1851) p. 46.

[5] J. Roscoe, " Further Notes on the Manners and Customs of the Baganda," *Journal of the Anthropological Institute*, xxxii. (1902) p. 34.

peoples to the first cutting of a child's hair and the elaborate
ceremonies by which the operation is accompanied.[1]   Again,
we can understand why a man should poll his head
after a journey.[2]   For we have seen that a traveller is
often believed to contract a dangerous infection from
strangers, and that, therefore, on his return home he is
obliged to submit to various purificatory ceremonies before
he is allowed to mingle freely with his own people.[3]   On
my hypothesis the polling of the hair is simply one of
these purificatory or disinfectant ceremonies.   Certainly
this explanation applies to the custom as practised by the
Bechuanas, for we are expressly told that "they cleanse or
purify themselves after journeys by shaving their heads, etc.,
lest they should have contracted from strangers some evil
by witchcraft or sorcery."[4]   The cutting of the hair after a
vow may have the same meaning.   It is a way of ridding
the man of what has been infected by the dangerous state,
whether we call it taboo, sanctity, or uncleanness (for all
these are only different expressions for the same primitive
conception), under which he laboured during the continuance
of the vow.   Still more clearly does the meaning of the
practice come out in the case of mourners, who cut their
hair and nails and use new vessels when the period of their
mourning is at an end.   This was done in ancient India,
obviously for the purpose of purifying such persons from the
dangerous influence of death and the ghost to which for a
time they had been exposed.[5]   Among the Bodos and
Dhimals of Assam, when a death has occurred, the family of
the deceased is reckoned unclean for three days.   At the end
of that time they bathe, shave, and are sprinkled with holy
water, after which they hold the funeral feast.[6]   Here the act

Hair sometimes cut because it is infected with the virus of taboo. In these cases haircutting is a form of purification.

Hair of mourners cut to rid them of the pollution of death.

---

[1] See G. A. Wilken, *Über das Haaropfer und einige andere Trauergebräuche bei den Völkern Indonesiens,* pp. 94 *sqq.* (reprinted from the *Revue Coloniale Internationale,* Amsterdam, 1886-87) ; H. Ploss, *Das Kind in Brauch und Sitte der Völker,*[2] i. 289 *sqq.* ; K. Potkanski, "Die Ceremonie der Haarschur bei den Slaven und Germanen," *Anzeiger der Akademie der Wissenschaften in Krakau,* May 1896, pp. 232-251.

[2] Above, p. 261.

[3] Above, pp. 111 *sqq.*

[4] J. Campbell, *Travels in South Africa, Second Journey* (London, 1822), ii. 205.

[5] H. Oldenberg, *Die Religion des Veda,* pp. 426 *sq.*

[6] L. F. Alfred Maury, "Les Populations primitives du nord de l'Hindoustan," *Bulletin de la Société de Géographie* (Paris), IVme Série, vii. (1854) p. 197.

Hair of
mourners
cut to rid
them of the
pollution
of death.
of shaving must clearly be regarded as a purificatory rite, like
the bathing and sprinkling with holy water.   At Hierapolis
no man might enter the great temple of Astarte on the same
day on which he had seen a corpse ; next day he might
enter, provided he had first purified himself.   But the kinsmen
of the deceased were not allowed to set foot in the sanctuary
for thirty days after the death, and before doing so they had
to shave their heads.[1]   At Agweh, on the Slave Coast of
West Africa, widows and widowers at the end of their
period of mourning wash themselves, shave their heads, pare
their nails, and put on new cloths ; and the old cloths,
the shorn hair, and the nail-parings are all burnt.[2]   The
Kayans of Borneo are not allowed to cut their hair or shave
their temples during the period of mourning ; but as soon
as the mourning is ended by the ceremony of bringing home
a newly severed human head, the barber's knife is kept busy
enough.   As each man leaves the barber's hands, he gathers
up the shorn locks and spitting on them murmurs a prayer
to the evil spirits not to harm him.   He then blows the
hair out of the verandah of the house.[3]   Among the
Wajagga of East Africa mourners shear their hair under a
fruit-bearing banana-tree and lay their shorn locks at the
foot of the tree.   When the fruit of the tree is ripe, they
brew beer with it and invite all the mourners to partake of
it, saying, " Come and drink the beer of those hair-bananas." [4]
The tribes of British Central Africa destroy the house in
which a man has died, and on the day when this is done the
mourners have their heads shaved and bury the shorn hair on
the site of the house ; the Atonga burn it in a new fire made
by the rubbing of two sticks.[5]   When an Akikuyu woman has,
in accordance with custom, exposed her misshapen or prematurely born infant in the wood for the hyaenas to devour,
she is shaved on her return by an old woman and given a
magic potion to drink ; after which she is regarded as clean.[6]

[1] Lucian, *De dea Syria*, 53.

[2] A. B. Ellis, *The Ewe-speaking
Peoples of the Slave Coast*, p. 160.

[3] W. H. Furness, *Folk-lore in Borneo* (Wallingford, Pennsylvania, 1899 ;
privately printed), p. 28.

[4] B. Gutmann, " Trauer und Begräbnissitten der Wadschagga," *Globus*,

lxxxix. (1906) p. 198.

[5] Miss A. Werner, *The Natives of
British Central Africa* (London, 1906),
pp. 165, 166, 167.

[6] J. M. Hildebrandt, "Ethnographische Notizen über Wakamba und
ihre Nachbarn," *Zeitschrift für Ethnologie*, x. (1878) p. 395.   Children who

Similarly at some Hindoo places of pilgrimage on the banks of rivers men who have committed great crimes or are troubled by uneasy consciences have every hair shaved off by professional barbers before they plunge into the sacred stream, from which " they emerge new creatures, with all the accumulated guilt of a long life effaced." [1]   The matricide Orestes is said to have polled his hair after appeasing the angry Furies of his murdered mother.[2]

§ 9. Spittle tabooed

The same fear of witchcraft which has led so many people to hide or destroy their loose hair and nails has induced other or the same people to treat their spittle in a like fashion.   For on the principles of sympathetic magic the spittle is part of the man, and whatever is done to it will have a corresponding effect on him.   A Chilote Indian, who has gathered up the spittle of an enemy, will put it in a potato, and hang the potato in the smoke, uttering certain spells as he does so in the belief that his foe will waste away as the potato dries in the smoke.   Or he will put the spittle in a frog and throw the animal into an inaccessible, un-navigable river, which will make the victim quake and shake with ague.[3]   When a Cherokee sorcerer desires to destroy a man, he gathers up his victim's spittle on a stick and puts it in a joint of wild parsnip, together with seven earthworms beaten to a paste and several splinters from a tree which has been struck by lightning.   He then goes into the forest, digs a hole at the foot of a tree which has been struck by lightning, and deposits in the hole the joint of wild parsnip

People may be bewitched by means of their spittle.

---

are born in an unusual position, the second born of twins, and children whose upper teeth appear before the lower, are similarly exposed by the Akikuyu.   The mother is regarded as unclean, not so much because she has exposed, as because she has given birth to such a child.

[1] Monier   Williams,   *Religious Thought and Life in India*, p. 375.

[2] Strabo, xii. 2. 3, p. 535; Pausanias, viii. 34. 3.   In two paintings on Greek vases we see Apollo in his character

of the purifier preparing to cut off the hair of Orestes.   See *Monumenti inediti*, 1847, pl. 48 ; *Annali dell' Instituto di Corrispondenza Archeologica*, 1847, pl. x. ; *Archaeologische Zeitung*, 1860, pll. cxxxvii. cxxxviii. ; L. Stephani, in *Compte rendu de la Commission archéologique* (St. Petersburg), 1863, pp. 271 *sq.*

[3] C. Martin, " Über die Eingeborenen von Chiloe," *Zeitschrift für Ethnologie*, ix. (1877) pp. 177 *sq.*

People may be bewitched by means of their spittle.

with its contents. Further, he lays seven yellow stones in the hole, then fills in the earth, and makes a fire over the spot to destroy all traces of his work. If the ceremony has been properly carried out, the man whose spittle has thus been treated begins to feel ill at once; his soul shrivels up and dwindles; and within seven days he is a dead man.[1] In the East Indian island of Siaoo or Siauw, one of the Sangi group, there are witches who by means of hellish charms compounded from the roots of plants can change their shape and bring sickness and misfortune on other folk. These hags also crawl under the houses, which are raised above the ground on posts, and there gathering up the spittle of the inmates cause them to fall ill.[2] If a Wotjobaluk sorcerer cannot get the hair of his foe, a shred of his rug, or something else that belongs to the man, he will watch till he sees him spit, when he will carefully pick up the spittle with a stick and use it for the destruction of the careless spitter.[3] The natives of Urewera, a district in the north island of New Zealand, enjoyed a high reputation for their skill in magic. It was said that they made use of people's spittle to bewitch them. Hence visitors were careful to conceal their spittle, lest they should furnish these wizards with a handle for working them harm.[4] Similarly among some tribes of South Africa no man will spit when an enemy is near, lest his foe should find the spittle and give it to a wizard, who would then mix it with magical ingredients so as to injure the person from whom it fell. Even in a man's own house his saliva is carefully swept away and obliterated for a similar reason.[5] For a like reason, no doubt, the natives of the Marianne Islands use great precautions in spitting and take care never to expectorate near somebody else's house.[6]

Hence people take care of their spittle to prevent it from falling into the hands of sorcerers.

[1] J. Mooney, "Sacred Formulas of the Cherokees," *Seventh Annual Report of the Bureau of Ethnology* (Washington, 1891), pp. 392 *sq.*

[2] B. C. A. J. van Dinter, "Eenige geographische en ethnographische aanteekeningen betreffende het eiland Siaoe," *Tijdschrift voor Indische Taal- Land- en Volkenkunde*, xli. (1899) p. 381.

[3] A. W. Howitt, "On Australian Medicine-men," *Journal of the Anthropological Institute*, xvi. (1887) p. 27; id., *Native Tribes of South-east Australia*, p. 365.

[4] E. Dieffenbach, *Travels in New Zealand* (London, 1843), ii. 59.

[5] Rev. J. Macdonald, *Light in Africa*, p. 209; id., in *Journal of the Anthropological Institute*, xx. (1891) p. 131.

[6] C. le Gobin, *Histoire des Isles Marianes* (Paris, 1700), p. 52. The writer confesses his ignorance of the reason of the custom.

Negroes of Senegal, the Bissagos Archipelago, and some of the West Indian Islands, such as Guadeloupe and Martinique, are also careful to efface their spittle by pressing it into the ground with their feet, lest a sorcerer should use it to their hurt.[1]   Natives of Astrolabe Bay, in German New Guinea, wipe out their spittle for the same reason ;[2] and a like dread of sorcery prevents some natives of German New Guinea from spitting on the ground in presence of others.[3] The Telugus say that if a man, rinsing his teeth with charcoal in the mornings, spits on the road and somebody else treads on his spittle, the spitter will be laid up with a sharp attack of fever for two or three days.   Hence all who wish to avoid the ailment should at once efface their spittle by sprinkling water on it.[4]

If common folk are thus cautious, it is natural that kings and chiefs should be doubly so.   In the Sandwich Islands chiefs were attended by a confidential servant bearing a portable spittoon, and the deposit was carefully buried every morning to put it out of the reach of sorcerers.[5]   On the Slave Coast of Africa, for the same reason, whenever a king or chief expectorates, the saliva is scrupulously gathered up and hidden or buried.[6]   The same precautions are taken for the same reason with the spittle of the chief of Tabali in Southern Nigeria.[7]   At Bulebane, in Senegambia, a French traveller observed a captive engaged, with an air of great importance, in covering over with sand all the spittle that fell from the lips of a native dignitary ; the man used a small stick for the purpose.[8] Page-boys, who carry tails of elephants, hasten to sweep up or cover with sand the spittle of the king of Ashantee ;[9] an attendant used to perform a similar service for the king

Precautions taken by chiefs and kings to guard their spittle from being put to evil uses by magicians.

---

[1] C. de Mensignac, *Recherches ethnographiques sur la salive et le crachat* (Bordeaux, 1892), pp. 48 sq.

[2] Vahness, reported by F. von Luschan, in *Verhandlungen der Berliner Gesellschaft für Anthropologie, Ethnologie und Urgeschichte*, 1900, p. (416).

[3] K. Vetter, *Komm herüber und hilf uns!* iii. (Barmen, 1898) pp. 9 sq.

[4] *Indian Antiquary*, xxviii. (1899) pp. 83 sq.

[5] W. Ellis, *Polynesian Researches*,[2] i. 365.

[6] A. B. Ellis, *The Ewe - speaking Peoples of the Slave Coast*, p. 99.

[7] C. Partridge, *Cross River Natives* (London, 1905), p. 8.

[8] A. Raffenel, *Voyage dans l'Afrique occidentale* (Paris, 1846), p. 338.

[9] C. de Mensignac, *op. cit.* p. 48.

Spittle of chiefs and wizards guarded against enchanters.

of Congo ;[1] and a custom of the same sort prevails or used to prevail at the court of the Muata Jamwo in the interior of Angola.[2]　In Yap, one of the Caroline Islands, there are two great wizards, the head of all the magicians, whose exalted dignity compels them to lead a very strict life. They may eat fruit only from plants or trees which are grown specially for them.　When one of them goes abroad the other must stay at home, for if they were to meet each other on the road, some direful calamity would surely follow. Though they may not smoke tobacco, they are allowed to chew a quid of betel ; but that which they expectorate is carefully gathered up, carried away, and burned in a special manner, lest any evil-disposed person should get possession of the spittle and do their reverences a mischief by uttering a curse over it.[3]　Among the Guaycurus and Payaguas of Brazil, when a chief spat, the persons about him received his saliva on their hands,[4] probably in order to prevent it from being misused by magicians.

Use of spittle in making a covenant.

The magical use to which spittle may be put marks it out, like blood or nail-parings, as a suitable material basis for a covenant, since by exchanging their saliva the covenanting parties give each other a guarantee of good faith.　If either of them afterwards forswears himself, the other can punish his perfidy by a magical treatment of the perjurer's spittle which he has in his custody.　Thus when the Wajagga of East Africa desire to make a covenant, the two parties will sometimes sit down with a bowl of milk or beer between them, and after uttering an incantation over the beverage they each take a mouthful of the milk or beer and spit it into the other's mouth.　In urgent cases, when there is no time to stand on ceremony, the two will simply spit into each other's mouth, which seals the covenant just as well.[5]

[1] *Mission Evangelica al reyno de Congo por la serafica religion de los Capuchinos* (Madrid, 1649), p. 70 verso.

[2] R. Andree, *Ethnographische Parallelen und Vergleiche*, Neue Folge (Leipsic, 1889), p. 13.

[3] F. W. Christian, *The Caroline Islands* (London, 1899), pp. 289 sq.

[4] R. Southey, *History of Brazil*, i.[2] (London, 1822) pp. 127, 138.

[5] J. Raum, "Blut und Speichelbünde bei den Wadschagga," *Archiv für Religionswissenschaft*, x. (1907) pp. 290 sq.

§ 10. *Foods tabooed*

As might have been expected, the superstitions of the savage cluster thick about the subject of food; and he abstains from eating many animals and plants, wholesome enough in themselves, which for one reason or another he fancies would prove dangerous or fatal to the eater. Examples of such abstinence are too familiar and far too numerous to quote. But if the ordinary man is thus deterred by superstitious fear from partaking of various foods, the restraints of this kind which are laid upon sacred or tabooed persons, such as kings and priests, are still more numerous and stringent. We have already seen that the Flamen Dialis was forbidden to eat or even name several plants and animals, and that the flesh diet of Egyptian kings was restricted to veal and goose.[1] In antiquity many priests and many kings of barbarous peoples abstained wholly from a flesh diet.[2] The *Gangas* or fetish priests of the Loango Coast are forbidden to eat or even see a variety of animals and fish, in consequence of which their flesh diet is extremely limited; often they live only on herbs and roots, though they may drink fresh blood.[3] The heir to the throne of Loango is forbidden from infancy to eat pork; from early childhood he is interdicted the use of the *cola* fruit in company; at puberty he is taught by a priest not to partake of fowls except such as he has himself killed and cooked; and so the number of taboos goes on increasing with his years.[4] In Fernando Po the king after installation is forbidden to eat *cocco* (*arum acaule*), deer, and porcupine, which are the ordinary foods of the people.[5] The head chief of the Masai may eat nothing but milk, honey, and the roasted livers of goats; for if he partook of any other food he would lose his power of soothsaying and of compounding charms.[6] The diet of the king of Unyoro

Certain foods are tabooed to sacred persons, such as kings and priests.

---

[1] Above, pp. 13 *sq.*

[2] Porphyry, *De abstinentia*, iii. 18.

[3] A. Bastian, *Die deutsche Expedition an der Loango-Küste*, ii. 170. The blood may perhaps be drunk by them as a medium of inspiration. See *The Magic Art and the Evolution of*

Kings, vol. i. pp. 381 *sqq.*

[4] O. Dapper, *Description de l'Afrique*, p. 336.

[5] T. J. Hutchinson, *Impressions of Western Africa* (London, 1858), p. 198.

[6] M. Merker, *Die Masai* (Berlin, 1904), p. 21.

in Central Africa was strictly regulated by immemorial custom. He might never eat vegetables, but must live on milk and beef. Mutton he might not touch. The beef he ate must be that of young animals not more than one year old, and it must be spitted and roasted before a wood fire. But he might not drink milk and eat beef at the same meal. He drank milk thrice a day in the dairy, and the milk was always drawn from a sacred herd which was kept for his exclusive use. Nine cows, neither more nor less, were daily brought from pasture to the royal enclosure to be milked for the king. The herding and the milking of the sacred animals were performed according to certain rules prescribed by ancient custom.[1] Amongst the Murrams of Manipur (a district of eastern India, on the border of Burma) "there are many prohibitions in regard to the food, both animal and vegetable, which the chief should eat, and the Murrams say the chief's post must be a very uncomfortable one."[2] Among the hill tribes of Manipur the scale of diet allowed by custom to the *ghennabura* or religious head of a village is always extremely limited. The savoury dog, the tomato, the *murghi*, are forbidden to him. If a man in one of these tribes is wealthy enough to feast his whole village and to erect a memorial stone, he is entitled to become subject to the same self-denying ordinances as the *ghennabura*. He wears the same special clothes, and for the space of a year at least he may not use a drinking horn, but must drink from a bamboo cup.[3] Among the Karennis or Red Karens of Burma a chief attains his position not by hereditary right but in virtue of the observance of taboo. He must abstain from rice and liquor. His mother too must have eschewed these things and lived only on yams and potatoes while she was with child. During that time she might neither eat meat nor drink water from a common well ; and in order to be duly qualified for a chiefship her son must continue these habits.[4] Among the Pshaws and Chewsurs of the Caucasus,

[1] J. G. Frazer, *Totemism and Exogamy*, ii. 526 *sqq.*, from information furnished by the Rev. J. Roscoe.

[2] G. Watt (quoting Col. W. J. M'Culloch), "The Aboriginal Tribes of Manipur," in *Journal of the Anthro-* pological Institute, xvi. (1887) p. 360.

[3] T. C. Hodson, "The Native Tribes of Manipur," *Journal of the Anthropological Institute*, xxxi. (1901) p. 306.

[4] *Indian Antiquary*, xxi. (1892) pp. 317 *sq.* ; (Sir) J. G. Scott and J. P.

whose nominal Christianity has degenerated into superstition and polytheism, there is an annual office which entails a number of taboos on the holder or *dasturi*, as he is called. He must live the whole year in the temple, without going to his house or visiting his wife ; indeed he may not speak to any one, except the priests, for fear of defiling himself. Once a week he must bathe in the river, whatever the weather· may be, using for the purpose a ladder on which no one else may set foot. His only nourishment is bread and water. In the temple he superintends the brewing of the beer for the festivals.[1]   In the village of Tomil, in Yap, one of the Caroline Islands, the year consists of twenty-four months, and there are five men who for a hundred days of the year may eat only fish and taro, may not chew betel, and must observe strict continence. The reason assigned by them for submitting to these restraints is that if they did not act thus the immature girls would attain to puberty too soon.[2]

To explain the ultimate reason why any particular food is prohibited to a whole tribe or to certain of its members would commonly require a far more intimate knowledge of the history and beliefs of the tribe than we possess. The general motive of such prohibitions is doubtless the same which underlies the whole taboo system, namely, the conservation of the tribe and the individual.

margin note: Certain foods tabooed to sacred persons.

§ 11. *Knots and Rings tabooed*

We have seen that among the many taboos which the Flamen Dialis at Rome had to observe, there was one that forbade him to have a knot on any part of his garments, and another that obliged him to wear no ring unless it were broken.[8]   In like manner Moslem pilgrims to Mecca are in a state of sanctity or taboo and may wear on their persons

margin note: Knots and rings not worn by certain sacred persons.

Hardiman, *Gazetteer of Upper Burma and the Shan States*, part ii. vol. i. p. 308.

[1] " Die Pschawen und Chewsuren im Kaukasus," *Zeitschrift für allge-meine Erdkunde*, ii. (1857) p. 76.

[2] A. Senfft, " Ethnographische Bei-träge über die Karolineninsel Yap,"

Petermanns Mitteilungen, xlix. (1903) p. 54.   In Gall, another village of the same island, the people grow bananas for sale, but will not eat them themselves, fearing that if they did so the women of the village would be barren (*ibid.*).

[3] Aulus Gellius, x. 15. 6 and 9. See above, p. 13.

neither knots nor rings.[1] These rules are probably of kindred significance, and may conveniently be considered together. To begin with knots, many people in different parts of the world entertain a strong objection to having any knot about their person at certain critical seasons, particularly childbirth,

Knots loosed and locks unlocked at childbirth to facilitate delivery.

marriage, and death. Thus among the Saxons of Transylvania, when a woman is in travail all knots on her garments are untied, because it is believed that this will facilitate her delivery, and with the same intention all the locks in the house, whether on doors or boxes, are unlocked.[2] The Lapps think that a lying-in woman should have no knot on her garments, because a knot would have the effect of making the delivery difficult and painful.[3] In ancient India it was a rule to untie all knots in a house at the moment of childbirth.[4] Roman religion required that women who took part in the rites of Juno Lucina, the goddess of childbirth, should have no knot tied on their persons.[5] In the East Indies this superstition is extended to the whole time of pregnancy ; the people believe that if a pregnant woman were to tie knots, or braid, or make anything fast, the child would thereby be constricted or the woman would herself be " tied up " when her time came.[6] Nay, some of them enforce the observance of the rule on the father as well as the mother of the unborn child. Among the Sea Dyaks neither of the parents may bind up anything with string or make anything fast during the wife's pregnancy.[7] Among the Land Dyaks the husband of the expectant mother is bound to refrain from tying things together with rattans until after her delivery.[8]

---

[1] E. Doutté, *Magie et religion dans l'Afrique du Nord*, pp. 87 *sq.*

[2] J. Hillner, *Volksthümlicher Brauch und Glaube bei Geburt und Taufe im Siebenbürger Sachsenlande*, p. 15. This tractate (of which I possess a copy) appears to be a programme of the High School (*Gymnasium*) at Schässburg in Transylvania for the school year 1876-1877.

[3] C. Leemius, *De Lapponibus Finmarchiae eorumque lingua, vita, et religione pristina commentatio* (Copenhagen, 1767), p. 494.

[4] W. Caland, *Altindisches Zauberritual* (Amsterdam, 1900), p. 108.

[5] Servius on Virgil, *Aen.* iii. 518.

[6] J. Kreemer, " Hoe de Javaan zijne zieken verzorgt," *Mededeelingen van wege het Nederlandsche Zendelinggenootschap*, xxxvi. (1892) p. 114; C. M. Pleyte, " Plechtigheden en gebruiken uit den cyclus van het familienleven der volken van den Indischen Archipel," *Bijdragen tot de Taal- Land- en Volkenkunde van Nederlandsch-Indië*, xli. (1892) p. 586.

[7] H. Ling Roth, *The Natives of Sarawak and British North Borneo*, i. 98.

[8] Spenser St. John, *Life in the Forests of the Far East*,[2] i. 170.

In the Toumbuluh tribe of North Celebes a ceremony is performed in the fourth or fifth month of a woman's pregnancy, and after it her husband is forbidden, among many other things, to tie any fast knots and to sit with his legs crossed over each other.[1] In the Kaitish tribe of central Australia the father of a newborn child goes out into the scrub for three days, away from his camp, leaving his girdle and arm-bands behind him, so that he has nothing tied tightly round any part of his body. This freedom from constriction is supposed to benefit his wife.[2]

In all these cases the idea seems to be that the tying of a knot would, as they say in the East Indies, "tie up" the woman, in other words, impede and perhaps prevent her delivery, or delay her convalescence after the birth. On the principles of homoeopathic or imitative magic the physical obstacle or impediment of a knot on a cord would create a corresponding obstacle or impediment in the body of the woman. That this is really the explanation of the rule appears from a custom observed by the Hos of Togoland in West Africa at a difficult birth. When a woman is in hard labour and cannot bring forth, they call in a magician to her aid. He looks at her and says, "The child is bound in the womb, that is why she cannot be delivered." On the entreaties of her female relations he then promises to loose the bond so that she may bring forth. For that purpose he orders them to fetch a tough creeper from the forest, and with it he binds the hands and feet of the sufferer on her back. Then he takes a knife and calls out the woman's name, and when she answers he cuts through the creeper with a knife, saying, "I cut through to-day thy bonds and thy child's bonds." After that he chops up the creeper small, puts the bits in a vessel of water, and bathes the woman with the water.[3] Here the cutting of the creeper with which the woman's hands and feet are bound is a simple piece of homoeopathic or imitative magic: by releasing her

On the principles of homoeopathic magic knots are impediments which tie up the mother and prevent her from bringing the child to the birth.

[1] J. G. F. Riedel, "Alte Gebräuche bei Heirathen, Geburt und Sterbefällen bei dem Toumbuluh - Stamm in der Minahasa (Nord Selebes)," *Internationales Archiv für Ethnographie*, viii. (1895) pp. 95 *sq.*

[2] Spencer and Gillen, *Northern Tribes of Central Australia*, pp. 606 *sq.*

[3] J. Spieth, *Die Ewe-Stämme*, p. 692.

limbs from their bonds the magician imagines that he simultaneously releases the child in her womb from the trammels which impede its birth. For a similar reason, no doubt, among the same people a priest ties up the limbs of a pregnant woman with grass and then unties the knots, saying, "I will now open you." After that the woman has to partake of some maize-porridge in which a ring made of a magic cord had been previously placed by the priest.[1] The intention of this ceremony is probably, on the principles of homoeopathic magic, to ensure for the woman an easy delivery by releasing her from the bonds of grass. The same train of thought underlies a practice observed by some peoples of opening all locks, doors, and so on, while a birth is taking place in the house. We have seen that at such a time the Germans of Transylvania open all the locks, and the same thing is done also in Voigtland and Mecklenburg.[2] In north-western Argyllshire superstitious people used to open every lock in the house at childbirth.[3] The old Roman custom of presenting women with a key as a symbol of an easy delivery[4] perhaps points to the observance of a similar custom. In the island of Salsette near Bombay, when a woman is in hard labour, all locks of doors or drawers are opened with a key to facilitate her delivery.[5] Among the Mandelings of Sumatra the lids of all chests, boxes, pans and so forth are opened; and if this does not produce the desired effect, the anxious husband has to strike the projecting ends of some of the house-beams in order to loosen them; for they think that "everything must be open and loose to facilitate the delivery."[6] At a difficult birth the Battas of Sumatra make a search through the possessions of husband and wife and untie everything that is tied up in a

All locks, doors, drawers, windows, etc. opened in order to facilitate childbirth.

---

[1] J. Spieth, *Die Ewe-Stämme*, pp. 433 *sq.*

[2] J. A. E. Köhler, *Volksbrauch, Aberglauben, Sagen und andre alte Überlieferungen im Voigtlande*, pp. 435 *sq.*; A. Wuttke, *Der deutsche Volksaberglaube*,[2] p. 355, § 574.

[3] J. G. Campbell, *Superstitions of the Highlands and Islands of Scotland*, p. 37, note 1.

[4] Festus, p. 56, ed. C. O. Müller.

[5] G. F. D'Penha, "Superstitions and Customs in Salsette," *Indian Antiquary*, xxviii. (1899) p. 115.

[6] H. Ris, "De onderafdeeling Klein Mandailing Oeloe en Pahantan en hare Bevolking," *Bijdragen tot de Taal- Land- en Volkenkunde van Nederlandsch-Indië*, xlvi. (1896) p. 503. Compare A. L. van Hasselt, *Volksbeschrijving van Midden Sumatra*, p. 266.

bundle.[1]   In some parts of Java, when a woman is in travail, everything in the house that was shut is opened, in order that the birth may not be impeded ; not only are doors opened and the lids of chests, boxes, rice-pots, and water-buts lifted up, but even swords are unsheathed and spears drawn out of their cases.[2]   Customs of the same sort are practised with the same intention in other parts of the East Indies.[3]   In Chittagong, when a woman cannot bring her child to the birth, the midwife gives orders to throw all doors and windows wide open, to uncork all bottles, to remove the bungs from all casks, to unloose the cows in the stall, the horses in the stable, the watchdog in his kennel, to set free sheep, fowls, ducks, and so forth.   This universal liberty accorded to the animals and even to inanimate things is, according to the people, an infallible means of ensuring the woman's delivery and allowing the babe to be born.[4]   At the moment of childbirth the Chams of Cochin-China hasten to open the stall of the buffaloes and to unyoke the plough, doubtless with the intention of aiding the woman in travail, though the writer who reports the custom is unable to explain it.[5]   Among the Singhalese, a few hours before a birth is expected to take place, all the cupboards in the house are unlocked with the express purpose of facilitating the delivery.[6]   In the island of Saghalien, when a woman is in labour, her husband undoes everything that can be undone.   He loosens the plaits of his

[1] J. H. Meerwaldt, "Gebruiken der Bataks in het maatschappelijk leven," *Mededeelingen van wege het Nederlandsche Zendinggenootschap*, xlix. (1905) p. 117.

[2] H. K[ern], "Bijgeloof onder de inlanders in den Oosthoek van Java," *Tijdschrift voor Indische Taal- Land- en Volkenkunde*, xxvi. (1880) 310 ; J. Kreemer, "Hoe de Javaan zijne zieken verzorgt," *Mededeelingen van wege het Nederlandsche Zendinggenootschap*, xxxvi. (1892) pp. 120, 124 ; D. Louwerier, "Bijgeloovige gebruiken, die door de Javanen worden in acht genomen bij de verzorging en opvoeding hunner kinderen," *Mededeelingen van wege het Nederlandsche Zendeling-genootschap*, xlix. (1905) p. 253.

[3] A. W. P. V. Pistorius, *Studien over de inlandsche huishouding in de PadangscheBovenlanden* (Zalt-Bommel, 1871), pp. 55 *sq.*; A. L. van Hasselt, *Volksbeschrijving van Midden-Sumatra* (Leyden, 1882), p. 266; J. G. F. Riedel, *De sluik- en kroesharige rassen tusschen Selebes en Papua* (the Hague, 1886), pp. 135, 207, 325.

[4] Th. Bérengier, "Croyances super-stitieuses dans le pays de Chittagong," *Missions Catholiques*, xiii. (1881) p. 515.

[5] Damien Grangeon, "Les Chams et leurs superstitions," *Missions Catholiques*, xxviii. (1896) p. 93.

[6] A. A. Perera, "Glimpses of Sing-halese Social Life," *Indian Antiquary*, xxxi. (1902) p. 378.

hair and the laces of his shoes. Then he unties whatever is
tied in the house or its vicinity. In the courtyard he takes
the axe out of the log in which it is stuck ; he unfastens
the boat, if it is moored to a tree, he withdraws the
cartridges from his gun, and the arrows from his crossbow.[1]
In Bilaspore a woman's hair is never allowed to remain
knotted while she is in the act of giving birth to a child.[2]
Among some modern Jews of Roumania it is customary for
the unmarried girls of a household to unbraid their hair and
let it hang loose on their shoulders while a woman is in hard
labour in the house.[3]

On the principles of homoeopathic magic the crossing of the legs is also thought to impede childbirth and other things.

Again, we have seen that a Toumbuluh man abstains
not only from tying knots, but also from sitting with
crossed legs during his wife's pregnancy. The train of
thought is the same in both cases. Whether you cross
threads in tying a knot, or only cross your legs in sitting
at your ease, you are equally, on the principles of homoeopathic magic, crossing or thwarting the free course of
things, and your action cannot but check and impede
whatever may be going forward in your neighbourhood.
Of this important truth the Romans were fully aware. To
sit beside a pregnant woman or a patient under medical
treatment with clasped hands, says the grave Pliny, is
to cast a malignant spell over the person, and it is worse
still if you nurse your leg or legs with your clasped hands,
or lay one leg over the other. Such postures were regarded
by the old Romans as a let and hindrance to business of
every sort, and at a council of war or a meeting of magis-
trates, at prayers and sacrifices, no man was suffered to
cross his legs or clasp his hands.[4] The stock instance of
the dreadful consequences that might flow from doing one
or the other was that of Alcmena, who travailed with
Hercules for seven days and seven nights, because the
goddess Lucina sat in front of the house with clasped hands

---

[1] B. Pilsudski, "Schwangerschaft,
Entbindung und Fehlgeburt bei den
Bewohnern der Insel Sachalin," *An-
thropos*, v. (1910) p. 759.

[2] E. M. Gordon, *Indian Folk Tales*
(London, 1908), p. 39.

[3] R. Campbell Thompson, *Semitic*

Magic (London, 1908), p. 169.

[4] Pliny, *Nat. Hist.* xxviii. 59.
Compare Hippocrates, *De morbo sacro*,
μηδὲ πόδα ἐπὶ ποδὶ ἔχειν, μηδὲ χεῖρα ἐπὶ
χειρί· ταῦτα γὰρ πάντα κωλύματα εἶναι
(vol. i. p. 589, ed. Kühn, Leipsic,
1825, quoted by E. Rohde, *Psyche*,[3]
ii. 76 note [1]).

and crossed legs, and the child could not be born until the
goddess had been beguiled into changing her attitude.[1]   It
is a Bulgarian superstition that if a pregnant woman is in
the habit of sitting with crossed legs, she will suffer much
in childbed.[2]   In some parts of Bavaria, when conversation
comes to a standstill and silence ensues, they say, " Surely
somebody has crossed his legs." [3]

The magical effect of knots in trammelling and obstruct-
ing human activity was believed to be manifested at
marriage not less than at birth.   During the Middle Ages,
and down to the eighteenth century, it seems to have been
commonly held in Europe that the consummation of
marriage could be prevented by any one who, while the
wedding ceremony was taking place, either locked a lock or
tied a knot in a cord, and then threw the lock or the cord
away.   The lock or the knotted cord had to be flung into
water ; and until it had been found and unlocked, or untied,
no real union of the married pair was possible.[4]   Hence it
was a grave offence, not only to cast such a spell, but also
to steal or make away with the material instrument of it,
whether lock or knotted cord.   In the year 1718 the par-
liament of Bordeaux sentenced some one to be burned alive
for having spread desolation through a whole family by means
of knotted cords ; and in 1705 two persons were condemned
to death in Scotland for stealing certain charmed knots which
a woman had made, in order thereby to mar the wedded
happiness of Spalding of Ashintilly.[5]   The belief in the efficacy of these charms appears to have lingered in the Highlands
of Perthshire down to the end of the eighteenth century, for
at that time it was still customary in the beautiful parish of
Logierait, between the river Tummel and the river Tay, to
unloose carefully every knot in the clothes of the bride and

Knots are supposed to prevent the consummation of marriage.

---

[1] Ovid, *Metam.* ix. 285 *sqq.* An-
toninus Liberalis, quoting Nicander,
says it was the Fates and Ilithyia who
impeded the birth of Hercules, but
though he says they clasped their
hands, he does not say that they
crossed their legs (*Transform.* 29).
Compare Pausanias, ix. 11. 3.

[2] A. Strausz, *Die Bulgaren* (Leipsic,
1898), p. 293.

[3] F. Panzer, *Beitrag zur deutschen*

Mythologie, ii. 303.

[4] J. Grimm, *Deutsche Mythologie*,[4]
ii. 897, 983 ; J. Brand, *Popular Antiquities*, iii. 299 ; J. G. Dalyell, *Darker
Superstitions of Scotland*, pp. 302,
306 *sq.* ; B. Souché, *Croyances, pré-
sages et traditions diverses*, p. 16 ;
J. G. Bourke, in *Ninth Annual Report
of the Bureau of Ethnology* (Washington, 1892), p. 567.

[5] J. G. Dalyell, *ll.cc.*

Knots loosed in the costume of bride and bridegroom in order to ensure the consummation of the marriage.

bridegroom before the celebration of the marriage ceremony. When the ceremony was over, and the bridal party had left the church, the bridegroom immediately retired one way with some young men to tie the knots that had been loosed a little before; and the bride in like manner withdrew somewhere else to adjust the disorder of her dress.[1] In some parts of the Highlands it was deemed enough that the bridegroom's left shoe should be without buckle or atchet, "to prevent witches from depriving him, on the nuptial night, of the power of loosening the virgin zone."[2] We meet with the same superstition and the same custom at the present day in Syria. The persons who help a Syrian bridegroom to don his wedding garments take care that no knot is tied on them and no button buttoned, for they believe that a button buttoned or a knot tied would put it within the power of his enemies to deprive him of his nuptial rights by magical means.[3] In Lesbos the malignant person who would thus injure a bridegroom on his wedding day ties a thread to a bush, while he utters imprecations; but the bridegroom can defeat the spell by wearing at his girdle a piece of an old net or of an old mantilla belonging to the bride in which knots have been tied.[4]

Knots tied by enchanters to render the bridegroom impotent.

The fear of such charms is diffused all over North Africa at the present day. To render a bridegroom impotent the enchanter has only to tie a knot in a handkerchief which he had previously placed quietly on some part of the bridegroom's body when he was mounted on horseback ready to fetch his bride: so long as the knot in the handkerchief

---

[1] Rev. Dr. Th. Bisset, in Sir John Sinclair's *Statistical Account of Scotland*, v. (Edinburgh, 1793) p. 83. In his account of the second tour which he made in Scotland in the summer of 1772, Pennant says that "the precaution of loosening every knot about the new-joined pair is strictly observed" (Pinkerton's *Voyages and Travels*, iii. 382). He is here speaking particularly of the Perthshire Highlands.

[2] Pennant, "Tour in Scotland," Pinkerton's *Voyages and Travels*, iii. 91. However, at a marriage in the island of Skye, the same traveller observed that "the bridegroom put all

the powers of magic to defiance, for he was married with both shoes tied with their latchet" (Pennant, "Second Tour in Scotland," Pinkerton's *Voyages and Travels*, iii. 325). According to another writer the shoe-tie of the bridegroom's *right* foot was unloosed at the church-door (Ch. Rogers, *Social Life in Scotland*, iii. 232).

[3] Eijūb Abéla, "Beiträge zur Kenntniss abergläubischer Gebräuche in Syrien," *Zeitschrift des deutschen Palaestina-Vereins*, vii. (1884) pp. 91 *sq.*

[4] Georgeakis et Pineau, *Folk-lore de Lesbos*, pp. 344 *sq.*

remains tied, so long will the bridegroom remain powerless to consummate the marriage. Another way of effecting the same object is to stand behind the bridegroom when he is on horseback, with an open clasp-knife or pair of scissors in your hand and to call out his name; if he imprudently answers, you at once shut the clasp-knife or the pair of scissors with a snap, and that makes him impotent. To guard against this malignant spell the bridegroom's mother will sometimes buy a penknife on the eve of the marriage, shut it up, and then open it just at the moment when her son is about to enter the bridal chamber.[1]

A curious use is made of knots at marriage in the little East Indian island of Rotti. When a man has paid the price of his bride, a cord is fastened round her waist, if she is a maid, but not otherwise. Nine knots are tied in the cord, and in order to make them harder to unloose, they are smeared with wax. Bride and bridegroom are then secluded in a chamber, where he has to untie the knots with the thumb and forefinger of his left hand only. It may be from one to twelve months before he succeeds in undoing them all. Until he has done so he may not look on the woman as his wife. In no case may the cord be broken, or the bridegroom would render himself liable to any fine that the bride's father might choose to impose. When all the knots are loosed, the woman is his wife, and he shews the cord to her father, and generally presents his wife with a golden or silver necklace instead of the cord.[2] The meaning of this custom is not clear, but we may conjecture that the nine knots refer to the nine months of pregnancy, and that miscarriage would be the supposed result of leaving a single knot untied.

Use of knots at marriage in the island of Rotti.

The maleficent power of knots may also be manifested in the infliction of sickness, disease, and all kinds of misfortune. Thus among the Hos of Togoland a sorcerer will sometimes curse his enemy and tie a knot in a stalk of grass, saying, "I have tied up So-and-So in this knot.

Knots may be used to inflict disease.

[1] E. Doutté, *Magie et religion dans l'Afrique du Nord*, pp. 288-292.

[2] "Eenige mededeelingen betreffende Rote door een inlandischen Schoolmeester," *Tijdschrift voor Indische Taal-Land-en Volkenkunde*, xxvii. (1882) p. 554; N. Graafland, "Eenige aanteekeningen op ethnographisch gebied ten aanzien van het eiland Rote," *Mededeelingen van wege het Nederlandsche Zendelinggenootschap*, xxxiii. (1889) pp. 373 *sq.*

May all evil light upon him! When he goes into the field, may a snake sting him! When he goes to the chase, may a ravening beast attack him! And when he steps into a river, may the water sweep him away! When it rains, may the lightning strike him! May evil nights be his!"

It is believed that in the knot the sorcerer has bound up the life of his enemy.[1] Babylonian witches and wizards of old used to strangle their victim, seal his mouth, wrack his limbs, and tear his entrails by merely tying knots in a cord, while at each knot they muttered a spell. But happily the evil could be undone by simply undoing the knots.[2] We hear of a man in one of the Orkney Islands who was utterly ruined by nine knots cast on a blue thread; and it would seem that sick people in Scotland sometimes prayed to the devil to restore them to health by loosing the secret knot that was doing all the mischief.[3] In the Koran there is an allusion to the mischief of "those who puff into the knots," and an Arab commentator on the passage explains that the words refer to women who practise magic by tying knots in cords, and then blowing and spitting upon them. He goes on to relate how, once upon a time, a wicked Jew bewitched the prophet Mohammed himself by tying nine knots on a string, which he then hid in a well. So the prophet fell ill, and nobody knows what might have happened if the archangel Gabriel had not opportunely revealed to the holy man the place where the knotted cord was concealed. The trusty Ali soon fetched the baleful thing from the well; and the prophet recited over it certain charms, which were specially revealed to him for the purpose. At every verse of the charms a knot untied itself, and the prophet experienced a certain relief.[4] It will hardly be disputed that by tying knots on the string the pestilent Hebrew contrived, if I may say so, to constrict or astringe or, in short, to tie up some vital organ or organs in the prophet's stomach. At least we are informed that something of this sort is done by

Knots used by witches and wizards to inflict disease.

---

[1] J. Spieth, *Die Ewe-Stämme*, p. 533.
[2] M. Jastrow, *The Religion of Babylonia and Assyria*, pp. 268, 270.
[3] J. G. Dalyell, *Darker Superstitions of Scotland*, p. 307.

[4] *Al Baidawī's Commentary on the Koran*, chap. 113, verse 4. I have to thank my friend Prof. A. A. Bevan for indicating this passage to me, and furnishing me with a translation of it.

Australian blackfellows at the present day, and if so, why should it not have been done by Arabs in the time of Mohammed? The Australian mode of operation is as follows. When a blackfellow wishes to settle old scores with another blackfellow, he ties a rope of fibre or bark so tightly round the neck of his slumbering friend as partially to choke him. Having done this he takes out the man's caul-fat from under his short rib, ties up his inside carefully with string, replaces the skin, and having effaced all external marks of the wound, makes off with the stolen fat. The victim on awakening feels no inconvenience, but sooner or later, sometimes months afterwards, while he is hunting or exerting himself violently in some other way, he will feel the string snap in his inside. " Hallo," says he, " somebody has tied me up inside with string!" and he goes home to the camp and dies on the spot.[1] Who can doubt but that in this lucid diagnosis we have the true key to the prophet's malady, and that he too might have succumbed to the wiles of his insidious foe if it had not been for the timely intervention of the archangel Gabriel?

If knots are supposed to kill, they are also supposed to cure. This follows from the belief that to undo the knots which are causing sickness will bring the sufferer relief. But apart from this negative virtue of maleficent knots, there are certain beneficent knots to which a positive power of healing is ascribed. Pliny tells us that some folk cured diseases of the groin by taking a thread from a web, tying seven or nine knots on it, and then fastening it to the patient's groin; but to make the cure effectual it was necessary to name some widow as each knot was tied.[2] The ancient Assyrians seem to have made much use of knotted cords as a remedy for ailments and disease. The cord with its knots, which were sometimes twice seven in number, was tied round the head, neck, or limbs of the patient, and then after a time cut off and thrown away, carrying with it, as was apparently supposed, the aches and

Knots may be used to cure disease.

---

[1] E. Palmer, "Notes on some Australian Tribes," *Journal of the Anthropological Institute*, xiii. (1884) p. 293. The Tahitians ascribed certain painful illnesses to the twisting and knotting of their insides by demons (W. Ellis, *Polynesian Researches*,[2] i. 363).

[2] Pliny, *Nat. Hist.* xxviii. 48.

pains of the sufferer. Sometimes the magic cord which was used for this beneficent purpose consisted of a double strand of black and white wool; sometimes it was woven of the hair of a virgin kid.[1] A modern Arab cure for fever reported from the ruins of Nineveh is to tie a cotton thread with seven knots on it round the wrist of the patient, who must wear it for seven or eight days or till such time as the fever passes, after which he may throw it away.[2] O'Donovan describes a similar remedy for fever employed among the Turcomans. The enchanter takes some camel hair and spins it into a stout thread, droning a spell the while. Next he ties seven knots on the thread, blowing on each knot before he pulls it tight. This knotted thread is then worn as a bracelet on his wrist by the patient. Every day one of the knots is untied and blown upon, and when the seventh knot is undone the whole thread is rolled up into a ball and thrown into a river, bearing away (as they imagine) the fever with it.[3] The Hos of Togoland in like manner tie strings round a sick man's neck, arms, or legs, according to the nature of the malady; some of the strings are intended to guard him against the influence of "the evil mouth"; others are a protection against the ghosts of the dead.[4] In Argyllshire, threads with three knots on them are still used to cure the internal ailments of man and beast. The witch rubs the sick person or cow with the knotted thread, burns two of the knots in the fire, saying, "I put the disease and the sickness on the top of the fire," and ties the rest of the thread with the single knot round the neck of the person or the tail of the cow, but always so that it may not be seen.[5] A Scotch cure for a sprained leg or arm is to cast nine knots in a black thread and then tie the thread round the suffering limb, while you say :

[1] C. Fossey, *La Magie assyrienne* (Paris, 1902), pp. 83 *sq.*; R. Campbell Thompson, *Semitic Magic* (London, 1908), pp. 164 *sqq.*

[2] R. Campbell Thompson, *Semitic Magic*, pp. 168 *sq.*

[3] E. O'Donovan, *The Merv Oasis* (London, 1882), ii. 319.

[4] J. Spieth, *Die Ewe-Stämme*, p. 531.

[5] R. C. Maclagan, M.D., "Notes on Folklore Objects collected in Argyleshire," *Folk-lore*, vi. (1895) pp. 154-156. In the north-west of Ireland divination by means of a knotted thread is practised in order to discover whether a sick beast will recover or die. See E. B. Tylor, in *International Folk-lore Congress*, 1891, *Papers and Transactions*, pp. 391 *sq.*

" *The Lord rade,*
And the foal slade;
He lighted
And he righted,
Set joint to joint,
Bone to bone,
And sinew to sinew.
Heal, in the Holy Ghost's name!" [1]

In Gujarat, if a man takes seven cotton threads, goes to a place where an owl is hooting, strips naked, ties a knot at each hoot, and fastens the knotted thread round the right arm of a man sick of the fever, the malady will leave him.[2]

Again, knots may be used by an enchantress to win a lover and attach him firmly to herself. Thus the love-sick maid in Virgil seeks to draw Daphnis to her from the city by spells and by tying three knots on each of three strings of different colours.[3] So an Arab maiden, who had lost her heart to a certain man, tried to gain his love and bind him to herself by tying knots in his whip ; but her jealous rival undid the knots.[4] On the same principle magic knots may be employed to stop a runaway. In Swazieland you may often see grass tied in knots at the side of the footpaths. Every one of these knots tells of a domestic tragedy. A wife has run away from her husband, and he and his friends have gone in pursuit, binding up the paths, as they call it, in this fashion to prevent the fugitive from doubling back over them.[5] When a Swaheli wishes to capture a runaway slave he will sometimes take a string of coco-nut fibre to a wise man and get him to recite a passage of the Koran seven

Knots may be used to win a lover or capture a runaway slave.

---

[1] R. Chambers, *Popular Rhymes of Scotland*, New Edition, p. 349. Grimm has shewn that the words of this charm are a very ancient spell for curing a lame horse, a spell based on an incident in the myth of the old Norse god Balder, whose foal put its foot out of joint and was healed by the great master of spells, the god Woden. See J. Grimm, *Deutsche Mythologie*,[4] i. 185, ii. 1030 *sq.* Christ has been substituted for Balder in the more modern forms of the charm both in Scotland and Germany.

[2] W. Crooke, *Popular Religion and Folk-lore of Northern India* (Westminster, 1896), i. 279.

[3] Virgil, *Ecl.* viii. 78-80. Highland sorcerers also used three threads of different colours with three knots tied on each thread. See J. G. Dalyell, *Darker Superstitions of Scotland*, p. 306.

[4] J. Wellhausen, *Reste arabischen Heidentums* [2] (Berlin, 1897), p. 163.

[5] Dudley Kidd, *The Essential Kafir*, p. 263.

X

times over it, while at each reading the wizard ties a knot in the string. Then the slave-owner, armed with the knotted string, takes his stand in the door of the house and calls on his slave seven times by name, after which he hangs the string over the door.[1]

Knots tied by hunters and travellers.

The obstructive power of knots and locks as means of barring out evil manifests itself in many ways. Thus on the principle that prevention is better than cure, Zulu hunters immediately tie a knot in the tail of any animal they have killed, because they believe that this will hinder the meat from giving them pains in their stomachs.[2] An ancient Hindoo book recommends that travellers on a dangerous road should tie knots in the skirts of their garments, for this will cause their journey to prosper.[3] Similarly among some Caffre tribes, when a man is going on a doubtful journey, he knots a few blades of grass together that the journey may turn out well.[4] In Laos hunters fancy that they can throw a spell over a forest so as to prevent any one else from hunting there successfully. Having killed game of any kind, they utter certain magical words, while they knot together some stalks of grass, adding, " As I knot this grass, so let no hunter be lucky here." The virtue of this spell will last, as usually happens in such cases, so long as the stalks remain knotted together.[5] The Yabims of German New Guinea lay a knot in a fishing-boat that is not ready for sea, in order that a certain being called Balum may not embark in it ; for he has the power of taking away the fish and weighing down the boat.[6]

Knots used as protective amulets in Russia and elsewhere.

In Russia amulets often derive their protective virtue in great measure from knots. Here, for example, is a spell which will warrant its employer against all risk of being shot : " I attach five knots to each hostile, infidel shooter, over arquebuses, bows, and all manner of warlike weapons.

[1] C. Velten, *Sitten und Gebräuche der Suaheli* (Göttingen, 1903), p. 317.

[2] David Leslie, *Among the Zulus and Amatongas* (Edinburgh, 1875), p. 147.

[3] *Grihya-Sûtras*, translated by H. Oldenberg, part i. p. 432, part ii. p. 127 (Sacred Books of the East,

vols. xxix., xxx.).

[4] J. Shooter, *The Kafirs of Natal and the Zulu Country* (London, 1857), pp. 217 *sq.*

[5] E. Aymonier, *Notes sur le Laos* (Saigon, 1885), pp. 23 *sq.*

[6] Vetter, in *Mitteilungen der geographischen Gesellschaft zu Jena*, xii. (1893) p. 95.

Do ye, O knots, bar the shooter from every road and way, lock fast every arquebuse, entangle every bow, involve all warlike weapons, so that the shooters may not reach me with their arquebuses, nor may their arrows attain to me, nor their warlike weapons do me hurt. In my knots lies hid the mighty strength of snakes—from the twelve-headed snake." A net, from its affluence of knots, has always been considered in Russia very efficacious against sorcerers ; hence in some places, when a bride is being dressed in her wedding attire, a fishing-net is flung over her to keep her out of harm's way. For a similar purpose the bridegroom and his companions are often girt with pieces of net, or at least with tight-drawn girdles, for before a wizard can begin to injure them he must undo all the knots in the net, or take off the girdles. But often a Russian amulet is merely a knotted thread. A skein of red wool wound about the arms and legs is thought to ward off agues and fevers ; and nine skeins, fastened round a child's neck, are deemed a preservative against scarlatina. In the Tver Government a bag of a special kind is tied to the neck of the cow which walks before the rest of a herd, in order to keep off wolves ; its force binds the maw of the ravening beast. On the same principle, a padlock is carried thrice round a herd of horses before they go afield in the spring, and the bearer locks and unlocks it as he goes, saying, " I lock from my herd the mouths of the grey wolves with this steel lock." After the third round the padlock is finally locked, and then, when the horses have gone off, it is hidden away somewhere till late in the autumn, when the time comes for the drove to return to winter quarters. In this case the "firm word" of the spell is supposed to lock up the mouths of the wolves. The Bulgarians have a similar mode of guarding their cattle against wild beasts. A woman takes a needle and thread after dark, and sews together the skirt of her dress. A child asks her what she is doing, and she tells him that she is sewing up the ears, eyes, and jaws of the wolves so that they may not hear, see, or bite the sheep, goats, calves, and pigs.[1] Similarly in antiquity a witch fancied that she could shut the mouths of her enemies by sewing up the mouth of a fish

[1] W. R. S. Ralston, *Songs of the Russian People*, pp. 388-390.

with a bronze needle,[1] and farmers attempted to ward off
hail from their crops by tying keys to ropes all round the
fields.[2]   The Armenians essay to lock the jaws of wolves
by uttering a spell, tying seven knots in a shoe-lace, and
placing the string between the teeth of a wool-comber, which
are probably taken to represent the fangs of a wolf.[3]   And
an Armenian bride and bridegroom will carry a locked lock
on their persons at and after marriage to guard them
against those evil influences to which at this crisis of life
they are especially exposed.[4]   The following mode of
keeping an epidemic from a village is known to have been
practised among the Balkan Slavs.   Two old women
proceed to a spot outside the village, the one with a copper
kettle full of water, the other with a house-lock and key.
The old dame with the kettle asks the other, "Whither
away?"   The one with the lock answers, "I came to lock
the village against mishap," and suiting the action to the
words she locks the lock and throws it, together with the
key, into the kettle of water.   Then she strides thrice round
the village, each time repeating the performance with the
lock and kettle.[5]   To this day a Transylvanian sower thinks
he can keep birds from the corn by carrying a lock in the
seed-bag.[6]   Such magical uses of locks and keys are clearly
parallel to the magical use of knots, with which we are here
concerned.   In Ceylon the Singhalese observe "a curious
custom of the threshing-floor called 'Goigote'—the tying of
the cultivator's knot.   When a sheaf of corn has been
threshed out, before it is removed the grain is heaped up
and the threshers, generally six in number, sit round it, and
taking a few stalks, with the ears of corn attached, jointly
tie a knot and bury it in the heap.   It is left there until all
the sheaves have been threshed, and the corn winnowed
and measured.   The object of this ceremony is to prevent
the devils from diminishing the quantity of corn in the

---

[1] Ovid, *Fasti*, ii. 577 *sqq.*; compare W. Warde Fowler, *Roman Festivals of the Period of the Republic*,
pp. 309 *sq.*

[2] *Geoponica*, i. 14.

[3] M. Abeghian, *Der armenische
Volksglaube*, p. 115.

[4] M. Abeghian, *op. cit.* p. 91.

[5] V. Titelbach, "Das heilige Feuer
bei den Balkanslaven," *Internationales
Archiv für Ethnographie*, xiii. (1900)
p. 3.

[6] A. Heinrich, *Agrarische Sitten
und Gebräuche unter den Sachsen
Siebenbürgens* (Hermannstadt, 1880),
p. 9.

heap." [1]   Knots and locks may serve to avert not only devils Knots and
but death itself.   When they brought a woman to the stake locks as protective
at St. Andrews in 1572 to burn her alive for a witch, they amulets.
found on her a white cloth like a collar, with strings and
many knots on the strings.   They took it from her, sorely
against her will, for she seemed to think that she could not
die in the fire, if only the cloth with the knotted strings
was on her.   When it was taken away, she said, "Now I
have no hope of myself." [2]   In many parts of England it is
thought that a person cannot die so long as any locks are
locked or bolts shot in the house.   It is therefore a very
common practice to undo all locks and bolts when the
sufferer is plainly near his end, in order that his agony
may not be unduly prolonged.[3]   For example, in the
year 1863, at Taunton, a child lay sick of scarlatina
and death seemed inevitable.   "A jury of matrons was,
as it were, empanelled, and to prevent the child 'dying
hard' all the doors in the house, all the drawers, all the
boxes, all the cupboards were thrown wide open, the keys
taken out, and the body of the child placed under a beam,
whereby a sure, certain, and easy passage into eternity could
be secured."   Strange to say, the child declined to avail
itself of the facilities for dying so obligingly placed at its
disposal by the sagacity and experience of the British matrons
of Taunton ; it preferred to live rather than give up the
ghost just then.[4]   A Masai man whose sons have gone out to
war will take a hair and tie a knot in it for each of his absent
sons, praying God to keep their bodies and souls as firmly
fastened together as these knots.[5]

The precise mode in which the virtue of the knot is

[1] C. J. R. Le Mesurier, "Customs and Superstitions connected with the Cultivation of Rice in the Southern Province of Ceylon," *Journal of the Royal Asiatic Society*, N.S., xvii. (1885) p. 371.

[2] J. G. Dalyell, *Darker Superstitions of Scotland*, p. 307.

[3] J. Brand, *Popular Antiquities*, ii. 231 (Bohn's edition) ; R. Hunt, *Popular Romances of the West of England*, p. 379 ; T. F. Thiselton Dyer, *English Folk-lore*, pp. 229 *sq.*

On the other hand the Karaits, a Jewish sect in the Crimea, lock all cupboards when a person is in the last agony, lest their contents should be polluted by the contagion of death. See S. Weissenberg, "Die Karäer der Krim," *Globus*, lxxxiv. (1903) p. 143.

[4] Extract from *The Times* of 4th September 1863, quoted in *Folk-lore*, xix. (1908) p. 336.

[5] M. Merker, *Die Masai* (Berlin, 1904), p. 98.

The
magical
virtue of
a knot is
always
that of an
impedi-
ment or
hindrance
whether
for good
or evil.

supposed to take effect in some of these instances does not clearly appear. But in general we may say that in all the cases we have been considering the leading characteristic of the magic knot or lock is that, in strict accordance with its physical nature, it always acts as an impediment, hindrance, or obstacle, and that its influence is maleficent or beneficent according as the thing which it impedes or hinders is good or evil. The obstructive tendency attributed to the knot in spiritual matters appears in a Swiss superstition that if, in sewing a corpse into its shroud, you make a knot on the thread, it will hinder the soul of the deceased on its passage to eternity.[1] In coffining a corpse the Highlanders of Scotland used to untie or cut every string in the shroud ; else the spirit could not rest.[2] The Germans of Transylvania place a little pillow with the dead in the coffin ; but in sewing it they take great care not to make any knot on the thread, for they say that to do so would hinder the dead man from resting in the grave and his widow from marrying again.[3] Among the Pidhireanes, a Ruthenian people on the hem of the Carpathians, when a widow wishes to marry again soon, she unties the knots on her dead husband's grave-clothes before the coffin is shut down on him. This removes all impediments to her future marriage.[4] A Nandi who is starting on a journey will tie a knot in grass by the wayside, as he believes that by so doing he will prevent the people whom he is going to visit from taking their meal till he arrives, or at all events he will ensure that they leave enough food over for him.[5]

The rule which prescribes that at certain magical and religious ceremonies the hair should hang loose and the feet

---

[1] H. Runge, " Volksglaube in der Schweiz," *Zeitschrift für deutsche Mythologie und Sittenkunde*, iv. (1859) p. 178, § 25. The belief is reported from Zurich.

[2] J. G. Campbell, *Witchcraft and Second Sight in the Highlands and Islands of Scotland*, p. 174 ; *id.*, *Superstitions of the Highlands and Islands of Scotland*, p. 241.

[3] E. Gerard, *The Land beyond the Forest*, i. 208.

[4] R. F. Kaindl, " Volksüberlieferungen der Pidhireane," *Globus*, lxxiii. (1898) p. 251.

[5] A. C. Hollis, *The Nandi* (Oxford, 1909), pp. 89 *sq.* The tying and untying of magic knots was forbidden by the Coptic church, but we are not told the purposes for which the knots were used. See *Il Fetha Nagast o legislazione dei re, codice ecclesiastico e civile di Abissinia*, tradotto e annotato da Ignazio Guidi (Rome, 1899), p. 140.

should be bare[1] is probably based on the same fear of
trammelling and impeding the action in hand, whatever it
may be, by the presence of any knot or constriction,
whether on the head or on the feet of the performer. This
connexion of ideas comes out clearly in a passage of Ovid, who
bids a pregnant woman loosen her hair before she prays to the
goddess of childbirth, in order that the goddess may gently
loose her teeming womb.[2] It is less easy to say why on
certain solemn occasions it appears to have been customary
with some people to go with one shoe off and one shoe on.
The forlorn hope of two hundred men who, on a dark and
stormy night, stole out of Plataea, broke through the lines
of the besieging Spartans, and escaped from the doomed
city, were shod on the left foot only. The historian who
records the fact assumes that the intention was to prevent
their feet from slipping in the mud.[3] But if so, why were
not both feet unshod or shod? What is good for the one
foot is surely good for the other. The peculiar attire of the
Plataeans on this occasion had probably nothing to do with
the particular state of the ground and the weather at the time
when they made their desperate sally, but was an old custom,
a form of consecration or devotion, observed by men in any
great hazard or grave emergency. Certainly the costume
appears to have been regularly worn by some fighting
races in antiquity, at least when they went forth to battle.
Thus we are told that all the Aetolians were shod only on
one foot, " because they were so warlike," [4] and Virgil
represents some of the rustic militia of ancient Latium as
marching to war, their right feet shod in boots of raw hide,
while their left feet were bare.[5] An oracle warned Pelias,
king of Iolcus, to beware of the man with one sandal, and
when Jason arrived with a sandal on his right foot but with
his left foot bare, the king recognised the hand of fate. The

The rule that at certain magical and religious rites the hair should be loose and the feet bare is probably based on a fear of the impediment which is thought to be caused by any knot or constriction.

Custom of going on certain solemn occasions with one shoe on and one shoe off.

---

[1] For examples see Horace, *Sat.* i. 8, 23 *sq.* ; Virgil, *Aen.* iii. 370, iv. 509 ; Ovid, *Metam.* vii. 182 *sq.* ; Tibullus, i. 3. 29-32 ; Petronius, *Sat.* 44 ; Aulus Gellius, iv. 3. 3 ; Columella, *De re rustica*, x. 357-362 ; Athenaeus, v. 28, p. 198 E ; Dittenberger, *Sylloge inscriptionum Graecarum*,[2] Nos. 653 (lines 23 *sq.*) and 939 ; Ch. Michel,

Recueil d'inscriptions grecques, No. 694. Compare Servius on Virgil, *Aen.* iv. 518, " *In sacris nihil solet esse religatum.*"

[2] Ovid, *Fasti*, iii. 257 *sq.*

[3] Thucydides, iii. 22.

[4] Schol. on Pindar, *Pyth.* iv. 133.

[5] Virgil, *Aen.* vii. 689 *sq.*

Custom of going on certain solemn occasions with one shoe on and one shoe off.

common story that Jason had lost one of his sandals in fording a river was probably invented when the real motive of the costume was forgotten.[1]　Again, according to one legend Perseus seems to have worn only one shoe when he went on his perilous enterprise to cut off the Gorgon's head.[2] In certain forms of purification Greek ritual appears to have required that the person to be cleansed should wear a rough shoe on one foot, while the other was unshod.　The rule is not mentioned by ancient writers, but may be inferred from a scene painted on a Greek vase, where a man, naked except for a fillet round his head, is seen crouching on the skin of a sacrificial victim, his bare right foot resting on the skin, while his left foot, shod in a rough boot, is planted on the ground in front of him. Round about women with torches and vessels are engaged in performing ceremonies of purification over him.[3]　When Dido in Virgil, deserted by Aeneas, has resolved to die, she feigns to perform certain magical rites which will either win back her false lover or bring relief to her wounded heart. In appealing to the gods and the stars, she stands by the altar with her dress loosened and with one foot bare.[4] Among the heathen Arabs the cursing of an enemy was a public act.　The maledictions were often couched in the form of a satirical poem, which the poet himself recited with certain solemn formalities.　Thus when the young Lebid appeared at the Court of Norman to denounce the Absites, he anointed the hair of his head on one side only, let his garment hang down loosely, and wore but one shoe.　This, we are told, was the costume regularly adopted by certain poets on such occasions.[5]

[1] Pindar, *Pyth.* iv. 129 *sqq.* ; Apollonius Rhodius, *Argonaut.* i. 5 *sqq.* ; Apollodorus, i. 9. 16.

[2] Artemidorus, *Onirocrit.* iv. 63. At Chemmis in Upper Egypt there was a temple of Perseus, and the people said that from time to time Perseus appeared to them and they found his great sandal, two cubits long, which was a sign of prosperity for the whole land of Egypt. See Herodotus, ii. 91.

[3] *Gazette archéologique,* 1884, plates 44, 45, 46 with the remarks of

De Witte and F. Lenormant, pp. 352 *sq.* The skin on which the man is crouching is probably the so-called "fleece of Zeus" (Διὸς κῴδιον), as to which see Hesychius and Suidas, *s.v.* ; Polemo, ed. Preller, pp. 140-142 ; C. A. Lobeck, *Aglaophamus,* pp. 183 *sqq.* Compare my note on Pausanias, ii. 31. 8.

[4] Virgil, *Aen.* iv. 517 *sqq.*

[5] I. Goldziher, "Der Dîwân des Garwal b. Aus Al-Ḥuṭej' a," *Zeitschrift der Deutschen Morgenländischen Gesellschaft,* xlvi. (1892) p. 5.

Thus various peoples seem to be of opinion that it stands a man in good stead to go with one foot shod and one foot bare on certain momentous occasions. But why? The explanation must apparently be sought in the magical virtue attributed to knots; for down to recent times, we may take it, shoes have been universally tied to the feet by latchets. Now the magical action of a knot, as we have seen, is supposed to be to bind and restrain not merely the body but the soul,[1] and this action is beneficial or harmful according as the thing which is bound and restrained is evil or good. It is a necessary corollary of this doctrine that to be without knots is to be free and untrammelled, which, by the way, may be the reason why the augur's staff at Rome had to be made from a piece of wood in which there was no knot;[2] it would never do for a divining rod to be spell-bound. Hence we may suppose that the intention of going with one shoe on and one shoe off is both to restrain and to set at liberty, to bind and to unbind. But to bind or unbind whom or what? Perhaps the notion is to rid the man himself of magical restraint, but to lay it on his foe, or at all events on his foe's magic; in short, to bind his enemy by a spell while he himself goes free. This is substantially the explanation which the acute and learned Servius gives of Dido's costume. He says that she went with one shoe on and one shoe off in order that Aeneas might be entangled and herself released.[3] An analogous explanation would obviously apply to all the other cases we have considered, for in all of them the man who wears this peculiar costume is confronted with hostile powers, whether human or supernatural, which it must be his object to lay under a ban.

A similar power to bind and hamper spiritual as well as bodily activities is ascribed by some people to rings. Thus in the Greek island of Carpathus, people never button the clothes they put upon a dead body and they are careful to

---

[1] See Servius, on Virgil, *Aen.* iii. 370: "*In ratione sacrorum par est et animae et corporis causa : nam plerumque quae non possunt circa animam fieri fiunt circa corpus, ut solvere vel ligare, quo possit anima, quod per se non potest, ex cognatione sentire.*"

[2] Livy, i. 18. 7.

[3] "*UNUM EXUTA PEDEM quia id agitur, ut et ista solvatur et implicetur Aeneas,*" Servius, on Virgil, *Aen.* iv. 518.

vent the
egress or
ingress of
spirits.

remove all rings from it ; "for the spirit, they say, can even
be detained in the little finger, and cannot rest."[1]   Here it
is plain that even if the soul is not definitely supposed to
issue at death from the finger-tips, yet the ring is conceived
to exercise a certain constrictive influence which detains and
imprisons the immortal spirit in spite of its efforts to escape
from the tabernacle of clay ; in short the ring, like the knot,
acts as a spiritual fetter.   This may have been the reason of
an ancient Greek maxim, attributed to Pythagoras, which
forbade people to wear rings.[2]   Nobody might enter the
ancient Arcadian sanctuary of the Mistress at Lycosura with
a ring on his or her finger.[3]   Persons who consulted the
oracle of Faunus had to be chaste, to eat no flesh, and
to wear no rings.[4]

Rings
worn as
amulets
against
demons,
witches,
and ghosts.

On the other hand, the same constriction which
hinders the egress of the soul may prevent the entrance of
evil spirits ; hence we find rings used as amulets against
demons, witches, and ghosts.   In the Tyrol it is said that
a woman in childbed should never take off her wedding-
ring, or spirits and witches will have power over her.[5]
Among the Lapps, the person who is about to place a
corpse in the coffin receives from the husband, wife, or
children of the deceased a brass ring, which he must wear
fastened to his right arm until the corpse is safely deposited
in the grave.   The ring is believed to serve the person as
an amulet against any harm which the ghost might do to
him.[6]   The Huzuls of the Carpathians sometimes milk a
cow through a wedding-ring to prevent witches from stealing

---

[1] "On a Far-off Island," *Blackwood's Magazine*, February 1886,
p. 238.

[2] Clement of Alexandria, *Strom.* v.
5. 28, p. 662, ed. Potter ; Jamblichus,
Adhortatio ad philosophiam, 23 ;
Plutarch, *De educatione puerorum*, 17.
According to others, all that Pythagoras forbade was the wearing of a
ring on which the likeness of a god
was engraved (Diogenes Laertius, viii.
1. 17 ; Porphyry, *Vit. Pythag.* 42 ;
Suidas, *s.v.* Πυθαγόρας) ; according to
Julian a ring was only forbidden if it
bore the names of the gods (Julian, *Or.*
vii. p. 236 D, p. 306 ed. Dindorf).   I

have shewn elsewhere that the maxims
or symbols of Pythagoras, as they were
called, are in great measure merely
popular superstitions (*Folk-lore*, i.
(1890) pp. 147 *sqq.*).

[3] This we learn from an inscription
found on the site.   See Ἐφημερὶς
ἀρχαιολογική, Athens, 1898, col. 249 ;
Dittenberger, *Sylloge inscriptionum
Graecarum*,[2] No. 939.

[4] Ovid, *Fasti*, iv. 657 *sq.*

[5] I. V. Zingerle, *Sitten, Bräuche
und Meinungen des Tiroler Volkes*,[2]
p. 3.

[6] J. Scheffer, *Lapponia* (Frankfort,
1673), p. 313.

its milk.[1]   In India iron rings are often worn as an amulet Rings worn as amulets.
against disease or to counteract the malignant influence of
the planet Saturn.   A coral ring is used in Gujarat to ward
off the baleful influence of the sun, and in Bengal mourners
touch it as a form of purification.[2]   A Masai mother who
has lost one or more children at an early age will put a
copper ring on the second toe of her next infant's right foot
to guard it against sickness.[3]   Masai men also wear on the
middle finger of the right hand a ring made out of the hide
of a sacrificial victim ; it is supposed to protect the wearer
from witchcraft and disease of every kind.[4]   We have seen
that magic cords are fastened round the wrists of Siamese
children to keep off evil spirits ;[5] that some people tie strings
round the wrists of women in childbed, of convalescents after
sickness, and of mourners after a funeral in order to prevent
the escape of their souls at these critical seasons ;[6] and that
with the same intention the Bagobos put brass rings on
the wrists or ankles of the sick.[7]   This use of wrist-bands,
bracelets, and anklets as amulets to keep the soul in the
body is exactly parallel to the use of finger-rings which we
are here considering.   The placing of these spiritual fetters
on the wrists is especially appropriate, because some people
fancy that a soul resides wherever a pulse is felt beating.[8]
How far the custom of wearing finger-rings, bracelets, and
anklets may have been influenced by, or even have sprung
from, a belief in their efficacy as amulets to keep the soul in
the body, or demons out of it, is a question which seems worth
considering.[9]   Here we are only concerned with the belief
in so far as it seems to throw light on the rule that the
Flamen Dialis might not wear a ring unless it were broken.
Taken in conjunction with the rule which forbade him to

---

[1] R. F. Kaindl, *Die Huzulen*
(Vienna, 1894), p. 89 ; *id.*, "Viehzucht und Viehzauber in den Ostkarpaten," *Globus*, lxix. (1896) p. 386.
[2] W. Crooke, *Popular Religion and
Folk-lore of Northern India* (Westminster, 1896), ii. 13, 16.
[3] M. Merker, *Die Masai* (Berlin,
1904), p. 143.
[4] M. Merker, *op. cit.* pp. 200 *sq.*,
202 ; compare, *id.* p. 250.
[5] Above, p. 267.

[6] Above, pp. 32, 51.
[7] Above, p. 31.
[8] De la Borde, "Relation de l'origine, etc., des Caraibes sauvages," p.
15, in *Recueil de divers voyages faits en
Afrique et en l'Amérique* (Paris, 1684).
[9] A considerable body of evidence
as to rings and the virtues attributed
to them has been collected by Mr. W.
Jones in his work *Finger-ring Lore*
(London, 1877).   See also W. G.
Black, *Folk-medicine*, pp. 172-177.

Reason why the Flamen Dialis might not wear knots and rings.

have a knot on his garments, it points to a fear that the powerful spirit embodied in him might be trammelled and hampered in its goings-out and comings-in by such corporeal and spiritual fetters as rings and knots. The same fear probably dictated the rule that if a man in bonds were taken into the house of the Flamen Dialis, the captive was to be unbound and the cords to be drawn up through a hole in the roof and so let down into the street.[1] Further, we may conjecture that the custom of releasing prisoners at a festival may have originated in the same train of thought ; it might be imagined that their fetters would impede the flow of the divine grace. The custom was observed at the Greek festival of the Thesmophoria,[2] and at the Athenian festival of Dionysus in the city.[3] At the great festival of the Dassera, celebrated in October by the Goorkhas of Nepaul, all the law courts are closed, and all prisoners in gaol are removed from the precincts of the city ; but those who are imprisoned outside the city do not have to change their place of confinement at the time of the Dassera.[4] This Nepaulese custom appears strongly to support the explanation here suggested of such gaol-deliveries. For observe that the prisoners are not released, but merely removed from the city. The intention is therefore not to allow them to share the general happiness, but merely to rid the city of their inopportune presence at the festival.

The Gordian knot was perhaps a royal talisman.

Before quitting the subject of knots I may be allowed to hazard a conjecture as to the meaning of the famous Gordian knot, which Alexander the Great, failing in his efforts to untie it, cut through with his sword. In Gordium, the ancient capital of the kings of Phrygia, there was preserved a waggon of which the yoke was fastened to the pole by a strip of cornel-bark or a vine-shoot twisted and tied in an intricate knot. Tradition ran that the waggon had been dedicated by Midas, the first king of the dynasty, and that whoever untied the knot would be ruler of Asia.[5] Perhaps

---

[1] Aulus Gellius, x. 15. 8. See above, p. 14.

[2] Marcellinus on Hermogenes, in *Rhetores Graeci*, ed. Walz, iv. 462 ; Sopater, *ibid.* viii. 67.

[3] Demosthenes, *Contra Androt.* 68, p. 614 ; P. Foucart, *Le Culte de*

Dionysos en Attique (Paris, 1904), p. 168.

[4] H. A. Oldfield, *Sketches from Nipal* (London, 1880), ii. 342 *sq.*

[5] Arrian, *Anabasis*, ii. 3 ; Quintus Curtius, iii. 1 ; Justin, xi. 7 ; Schol. on Euripides, *Hippolytus*, 671.

the knot was a talisman with which the fate of the dynasty
was believed to be bound up in such a way that whenever
the knot was loosed the reign of the dynasty would come
to an end.   We have seen that the magic virtue ascribed
to knots is naturally enough supposed to last only so long
as they remain untied.   If the Gordian knot was the talisman of the Phrygian kings, the local fame it enjoyed, as
guaranteeing to them the rule of Phrygia, might easily be
exaggerated by distant-rumour into a report that the sceptre
of Asia itself would fall to him who should undo the wondrous
knot.[1]

[1] Public talismans, on which the
safety of the state was supposed to
depend, were common in antiquity.
See C. A. Lobeck, *Aglaophamus*, pp.
278 *sqq.*, and my note on Pausanias,
viii. 47. 5.

CHAPTER VI

TABOOED WORDS

§ 1. *Personal Names tabooed*

The savage confuses words and things, and hence regards his name as a vital part of himself, and fancies that he can be magically injured through it. UNABLE to discriminate clearly between words and things, the savage commonly fancies that the link between a name and the person or thing denominated by it is not a mere arbitrary and ideal association, but a real and substantial bond which unites the two in such a way that magic may be wrought on a man just as easily through his name as through his hair, his nails, or any other material part of his person.[1] In fact, primitive man regards his name as a vital portion of himself and takes care of it accordingly. Thus, for example, the North American Indian "regards his name, not as a mere label, but as a distinct part of his personality, just as much as are his eyes or his teeth, and believes that injury will result as surely from the malicious handling of his name as from a wound inflicted on any part of his physical organism. This belief was found among the various tribes from the Atlantic to the Pacific, and has occasioned a number of curious regulations in regard to the concealment and change of names. It may be on this account that both Powhatan and Pocahontas are known in history under assumed appellations, their true names having been concealed from the whites until the pseudonyms were too firmly established to be supplanted. Should his prayers

---

[1] On the primitive conception of the relation of names to persons and things, see E. B. Tylor, *Early History of Mankind*,[3] pp. 123 *sqq.*; R. Andree, *Ethnographische Parallelen und Vergleiche* (Stuttgart, 1878), pp. 165 *sqq.*; E. Clodd, *Tom-tit-tot* (London, 1898), pp. 53 *sqq.*, 79 *sqq.* In what follows I have used with advantage the works of all these writers.

have no apparent effect when treating a patient for some Savage
serious illness, the shaman sometimes concludes that the confusion of the name
name is affected, and accordingly goes to water, with with the
appropriate ceremonies, and christens the patient with a person.
new name, by which he is henceforth to be known. He
then begins afresh, repeating the formulas with the new
name selected for the patient, in the confident hope that his
efforts will be crowned with success."[1] Some Esquimaux
take new names when they are old, hoping thereby to get a
new lease of life.[2] The Tolampoos of central Celebes
believe that if you write a man's name down you can carry
off his soul along with it. On that account the headman of
a village appeared uneasy when Mr. A. C. Kruijt wrote
down his name. He entreated the missionary to erase it,
and was only reassured on being told that it was not his
real name but merely his second name that had been put on
paper. Again, when the same missionary took down the
names of villages from the lips of a woman, she asked him
anxiously if he would not thereby take away the soul of the
villages and so cause the inhabitants to fall sick.[3] If we
may judge from the evidence of language, this crude
conception of the relation of names to persons was widely
prevalent, if not universal, among the forefathers of the
Aryan race. For an analysis of the words for " name " in
the various languages of that great family of speech points
to the conclusion that " the Celts, and certain other widely
separated Aryans, unless we should rather say the whole
Aryan family, believed at one time not only that the name
was a part of the man, but that it was that part of him
which is termed the soul, the breath of life, or whatever you
may choose to define it as being."[4] However this may
have been among the primitive Aryans, it is quite certain
that many savages at the present day regard their names as
vital parts of themselves, and therefore take great pains to

[1] J. Mooney, " Sacred Formulas of
the Cherokees," *Seventh Annual Report
of the Bureau of Ethnology* (Washington, 1891), p. 343.
[2] E. W. Nelson, " The Eskimo
about Bering Strait," *Eighteenth
Annual Report of the Bureau of
American Ethnology*, part i. (Washington, 1899) p. 289.
[3] A. C. Kruijt, " Van Paloppo naar
Posso," *Mededeelingen van wege het
Nederlandsche Zendelinggenootschap*,
xlii. (1898) pp. 61 *sq.*
[4] Professor (Sir) J. Rhys, " Welsh
Fairies," *The Nineteenth Century*, xxx.
(July-December 1891) pp. 566 *sq.*

conceal their real names, lest these should give to evil-disposed persons a handle by which to injure their owners.

The Australian savages keep their names secret lest sorcerers should injure them by means of their names.

Thus, to begin with the savages who rank at the bottom of the social scale, we are told that the secrecy with which among the Australian aborigines personal names are often kept from general knowledge " arises in great measure from the belief that an enemy, who knows your name, has in it something which he can use magically to your detriment." [1] " An Australian black," says another writer, " is always very unwilling to tell his real name, and there is no doubt that this reluctance is due to the fear that through his name he may be injured by sorcerers." [2]   On Herbert River in Queensland the wizards, in order to practise their arts against some one, " need only to know the name of the person in question, and for this reason they rarely use their proper names in addressing or speaking of each other, but simply their class names." [3]   In the tribes of south-eastern Australia " when the new name is given at initiation, the child's name becomes secret, not to be revealed to strangers, or to be mentioned by friends. The reason appears to be that a name is part of a person, and therefore can be made use of to that person's detriment by any who wish to ' catch ' him by evil magic." [4]   Thus among the Yuin of New South Wales the totem name is said to have been something magical rather than a mere name in our sense, and it was kept secret lest an enemy should injure its bearer by sorcery. The name was revealed to a youth by his father at initiation, but very few other people knew it. [5]   Another writer, who knew the Australians well, observes that in many tribes the belief prevails " that the life of an enemy may be taken by the use of his name in incantations. The consequence of this idea is, that in the tribes in which it obtains, the name of the male is given up for ever at the time when he undergoes the first of a series of ceremonies which end in conferring the rights of manhood. In such tribes a man has no name, and when a man desires to attract the attention of

[1] A. W. Howitt, *Native Tribes of South-East Australia*, p. 377 ; compare *id.* p. 440.

[2] R. Brough Smyth, *Aborigines of Victoria*, i. 469, note.

[3] C. Lumholtz, *Among Cannibals* (London, 1889), p. 280.

[4] A. W. Howitt, *op. cit.* p. 736.

[5] A. W. Howitt, *op. cit.* p. 133.

any male of his tribe who is out of his boyhood, instead of
calling him by name, he addresses him as brother, nephew,
or cousin, as the case may be, or by the name of the class
to which he belongs. I used to notice, when I lived amongst
the Bangerang, that the names which the males bore in
infancy were soon almost forgotten by the tribe."[1] It may
be questioned, however, whether the writer whom I have just
quoted was not deceived in thinking that among these tribes
men gave up their individual names on passing through the
ceremony of initiation into manhood. It is more in harmony
with savage beliefs and practices to suppose either that the
old names were retained but dropped out of use in daily life,
or that new names were given at initiation and sedulously
concealed from fear of sorcery. A missionary who resided
among the aborigines at Lake Tyers, in Victoria, informs us
that "the blacks have great objections to speak of a person
by name. In speaking to each other they address the
person spoken to as brother, cousin, friend, or whatever
relation the person spoken to bears. Sometimes a black
bears a name which we would term merely a nickname, as
the left-handed, or the bad-handed, or the little man. They
would speak of a person by this name while living, but they
would never mention the proper name. I found great difficulty in collecting the native names of the blacks here. I
found afterwards that they had given me wrong names; and,
on asking the reason why, was informed they had two or
three names, but they never mentioned their right name for
fear any one got it, when they would die."[2] Amongst the
tribes of central Australia every man, woman, and child has,
besides a personal name which is in common use, a secret or
sacred name which is bestowed by the older men upon him
or her soon after birth, and which is known to none but the
fully initiated members of the group. This secret name is
never mentioned except upon the most solemn occasions; to
utter it in the hearing of women or of men of another group
would be a most serious breach of tribal custom, as serious as

---

[1] E. M. Curr, *The Australian Race*, i. 46.
[2] J. Bulmer, in Brough Smyth's *Aborigines of Victoria*, ii. 94. The writer appears to mean that the natives feared they would die if any one, or at any rate, an enemy, learned their real names.

the most flagrant case of sacrilege among ourselves. When mentioned at all, the name is spoken only in a whisper, and not until the most elaborate precautions have been taken that it shall be heard by no one but members of the group. "The native thinks that a stranger knowing his secret name would have special power to work him ill by means of magic." [1]

The same fear seems to have led to a custom of the same sort amongst the ancient Egyptians, whose comparatively high civilisation was strangely dashed and chequered with relics of the lowest savagery. Every Egyptian received two names, which were known respectively as the true name and the good name, or the great name and the little name; and while the good or little name was made public, the true or great name appears to have been carefully concealed.[2] Similarly in Abyssinia at the present day it is customary to conceal the real name which a person receives at baptism and to call him only by a sort of nickname which his mother gives him on leaving the church. The reason for this concealment is that a sorcerer cannot act upon a person whose real name he does not know. But if he has ascertained his victim's real name, the magician takes a particular kind of straw, and muttering something over it bends it into a circle and places it under a stone. The person aimed at is taken ill at the very moment of the bending of the straw; and if the straw snaps, he dies.[3] A Brahman child receives two names, one for common use, the other a secret name which none but his father and mother should know. The latter is. only used at ceremonies such as marriage. The custom is intended to protect the person against · magic, since a charm only becomes effectual in combination with the real name.[4] Amongst the Kru

The same fear of sorcery has led people to conceal their names in Egypt, Africa, Asia, and the East Indies.

[1] Spencer and Gillen, *Native Tribes of Central Australia*, p. 139; compare *ibid.* p. 637; *id.*, *Northern Tribes of Central Australia*, pp. 584 *sq.*

[2] E. Lefébure, "La Vertu et la vie du nom en Égypte," *Mélusine*, viii. (1897) coll. 226 *sq.*

[3] Mansfield Parkyns, *Life in Abyssinia* (London, 1868), pp. 301 *sq.*

[4] *Grihya Sûtras*, translated by H. Oldenberg, part i. pp. 50, 183, 395, part ii. pp. 55, 215, 281; A. Hillebrandt, *Vedische Opfer und Zauber*, pp. 46, 170 *sq.*; W. Caland, *Altindisches Zauberritual*, p. 162, note [20]; D. C. J. Ibbetson, *Outlines of Punjáb Ethnography* (Calcutta, 1883), p. 118; W. Crooke, *Popular Religion and Folklore of Northern India* (Westminster, 1896), i. 24, ii. 5; *id.*, *Natives of Northern India* (London, 1907), p. 199

negroes of West Africa a man's real name is always concealed from all but his nearest relations; to other people he is known only under an assumed name.[1] The Ewe-speaking people of the Slave Coast "believe that there is a real and material connexion between a man and his name, and that by means of the name injury may be done to the man. An illustration of this has been given in the case of the tree-stump that is beaten with a stone to compass the death of an enemy; for the name of that enemy is not pronounced solely with the object of informing the animating principle of the stump who it is whose death is desired, but through a belief that, by pronouncing the name, the personality of the man who bears it is in some way brought to the stump."[2]   The Wolofs of Senegambia are very much annoyed if any one calls them in a loud voice, even by day; for they say that their name will be remembered by an evil spirit and made use of by him to do them a mischief at night.[3]   Similarly, the natives of Nias believe that harm may be done to a person by the demons who hear his name pronounced. Hence the names of infants, who are especially exposed to the assaults of evil spirits, are never spoken; and often in haunted spots, such as the gloomy depths of the forest, the banks of a river, or beside a bubbling spring, men will abstain from calling each other by their names for a like reason.[4]   Among the hill tribes of Assam each individual has a private name which may not be revealed. Should any one imprudently allow his private name to be known, the whole village is tabooed for two days and a feast is provided at the expense of the culprit.[5]   A Manegre of the upper valley of the Amoor, will never mention his own name nor that of one of his fellows. Only the names of children are an exception to this rule.[6]   A Bagobo man of Mindanao, one of the Philippine Islands, never

[1] A. B. Ellis, *The Tshi-speaking Peoples of the Gold Coast*, p. 109.

[2] A. B. Ellis, *The Ewe-speaking Peoples of the Slave Coast*, p. 98.

[3] L. J. B. Bérenger-Féraud, *Les Peuples de la Sénégambie* (Paris, 1879), p. 28.

[4] E. Modigliani, *Un Viaggio a Nías* (Milan, 1890), p. 465.

[5] T. C. Hodson, "The *genna* amongst the Tribes of Assam," *Journa of the Anthropological Institute*, xxxvi. (1906) p. 97.

[6] C. de Sabir, "Quelques notes sur les Manègres," *Bulletin de la Société de Géographie* (Paris), Vme Série, i. (1861) p. 51.

utters. his own name from fear of being turned into a raven, because the raven croaks out its own name.[1] The natives of the East Indian island of Buru, and the Manggarais of West Flores are forbidden by custom to mention their own names.[2]   When Fafnir had received his death-wound from Sigurd, he asked his slayer what his name was ; but the cunning Sigurd concealed his real name and mentioned a false one, because he well knew how potent are the words of a dying man when he curses his enemy by name.[3]

The South and Central American Indians also keep their names secret from fear of sorcery.

The Indians of Chiloe, a large island off the southern coast of Chili, keep their names secret and do not like to have them uttered aloud ; for they say that there are fairies or imps on the mainland or neighbouring islands who, if they knew folk's names, would do them an injury ; but so long as they do not know the names, these mischievous sprites are powerless.[4]   The Araucanians, who inhabit the mainland of Chili to the north of Chiloe, will hardly ever tell a stranger their names because they fear that he would thereby acquire some supernatural power over themselves. Asked his name by a stranger, who is ignorant of their superstitions, an Araucanian will answer, "I have none."[5] Names taken from plants, birds, or other natural objects are bestowed on the Indians of Guiana at their birth by their parents or the medicine-man, "but these names seem of little use, in that owners have a very strong objection to telling or using them, apparently on the ground that the name is part of the man, and that he who knows the name has part of the owner of that name in his power.   To avoid any danger of spreading knowledge of their names, one Indian, therefore, generally addresses another only according to the relationship of the caller and the called, as brother,

---

[1] A. Schadenburg, "Die Bewohner von Süd-Mindanao und der Insel Samal," *Zeitschrift für Ethnologie*, xvii. (1885) p. 30.

[2] J. H. W. van der Miesen, "Een en ander over Boeroe," *Mededeelingen van wege het Nederlandsche Zendeling-genootschap*, xlvi. (1902) p. 455 ; J. W. Meerburg, "Proeve einer beschrijving van land en volk van Midden-Manggarai (West-Flores), Afdeeling

Bima," *Tijdschrift voor Indische Taal-Land- en Volkenkunde*, xxxiv. (1891) p. 465.

[3] F. Kauffmann, *Balder* (Strasburg, 1902), p. 198.

[4] This I learned from my wife, who spent some years in Chili and visited the island of Chiloe.

[5] E. R. Smith, *The Araucanians* (London, 1855), p. 222.

sister, father, mother, and so on ; or, when there is no relationship, as boy, girl, companion, and so on. These terms, therefore, practically form the names actually used by Indians amongst themselves."[1] Amongst the Indians of the Goajira peninsula in Colombia it is a punishable offence to mention a man's name ; in aggravated cases heavy compensation is demanded.[2] The Indians of Darien never tell their names, and when one of them is asked, "What is your name?" he answers, "I have none."[3] For example, the Guami of Panama, "like the greater part of the American Indians, has several names, but that under which he is known to his relations and friends is never mentioned to a stranger ; according to their ideas a stranger who should learn a man's name would obtain a secret power over him. As to the girls, they generally have no name of their own up to the age of puberty."[4] Among the Tepehuanes of Mexico a name is a sacred thing, and they never tell their real native names.[5]

In North America superstitions of the same sort are current. "Names bestowed with ceremony in childhood," says Schoolcraft, "are deemed sacred, and are seldom pronounced, out of respect, it would seem, to the spirits under whose favour they are supposed to have been selected. Children are usually called in the family by some name which can be familiarly used."[6] The Navajoes of New Mexico are most unwilling to reveal their own Indian names or those of their friends ; they generally go by some Mexican names which they have received from the whites.[7] "No Apache will give his name to a stranger, fearing some hidden power may thus be placed in the stranger's hand to his detriment."[8] The Tonkawe Indians of Texas will give

Similar superstition as to personal names among the Indians of North America.

---

[1] E. F. im Thurn, *Among the Indians of Guiana* (London, 1883), p. 220.

[2] F. A. Simons, "An Exploration of the Goajira Peninsula, U.S. of Colombia," *Proceedings of the Royal Geographical Society*, N.S., vii. (1885) p. 790.

[3] Dr. Cullen, "The Darien Indians," *Transactions of the Ethnological Society of London*, N.S., iv. (1866) p. 265.

[4] A. Pinart, "Les Indiens de l'Etat de Panama," *Revue d'Ethnographie*, vi. (1887) p. 44.

[5] C. Lumholtz, *Unknown Mexico*, i. 462.

[6] H. R. Schoolcraft, *The American Indians, their History, Condition, and Prospects* (Buffalo, 1851), p. 213. Compare *id.*, *Oneóta, or Characteristics of the Red Race of America* (New York and London, 1845), p. 456.

[7] H. R. Schoolcraft, *Indian Tribes*, iv. 217.

[8] J. G. Bourke, "Notes upon the Religion of the Apache Indians," *Folklore*, ii. (1891) p. 423.

Personal
names kept
secret
among the
North
American
Indians. their children Comanche and English names in addition to their native names, which they are unwilling to communicate to others; for they believe that when somebody calls a person by his or her native name after death the spirit of the deceased may hear it, and may be prompted to take revenge on such as disturbed his rest; whereas if the spirit be called by a name drawn from another language, it will pay no heed.[1] Speaking of the Californian Indians, and especially of the Nishinam tribe, a well-informed writer observes: "One can very seldom learn an Indian's and never a squaw's Indian name, though they will tell their American titles readily enough. . . . No squaw will reveal her own name, but she will tell all her neighbors' that she can think of. For the reason above given many people believe that half the squaws have no names at all. So far is this from the truth that every one possesses at least one and sometimes two or three."[2] Blackfoot Indians believe that they would be unfortunate in all their undertakings if they were to speak their names.[3] When the Canadian Indians were asked their names, they used to hang their heads in silence or answer that they did not know.[4] When an Ojebway is asked his name, he will look at some bystander and ask him to answer. "This reluctance arises from an impression they receive when young, that if they repeat their own names it will prevent their growth, and they will be small in stature. On account of this unwillingness to tell their names, many strangers have fancied that they either have no names or have forgotten them."[5]

Sometimes
savages,
though
they will
not utter
their own
names, In this last case no scruple seems to be felt about communicating a man's name to strangers, and no ill effects appear to be dreaded as a consequence of divulging it; harm is only done when a name is spoken by its owner. Why is this? and why in particular should a man be thought to

---

[1] A. S. Gatschet, *The Karankawa Indians, the Coast People of Texas* (*Archaeological and Ethnological Papers of the Peabody Museum, Harvard University*, vol. i. No. 2), p. 69.

[2] S. Powers, *Tribes of California* Washington, 1877), p. 315.

[3] G. B. Grinnell, *Blackfoot Lodge*

[4] *Relations des Jésuites*, 1633, p. 3 (Canadian reprint, Quebec, 1858).

[5] Peter Jones, *History of the Ojebway Indians*, p. 162. Compare A. P. Reid, "Religious Beliefs of the Ojibois or Sauteux Indians," *Journal of the Anthropological Institute*, iii. (1874) p. 107.

stunt his growth by uttering his own name? We may con-^{do not} jecture that to savages who act and think thus a person's object to other name only seems to be a part of himself when it is uttered people's with his own breath; uttered by the breath of others it has doing so. no vital connexion with him, and no harm can come to him through it. Whereas, so these primitive philosophers may have argued, when a man lets his own name pass his lips, he is parting with a living piece of himself, and if he persists in so reckless a course he must certainly end by dissipating his energy and shattering his constitution. Many a broken-down debauchee, many a feeble frame wasted with disease, may have been pointed out by these simple moralists to their awe-struck disciples as a fearful example of the fate that must sooner or later overtake the profligate who in-dulges immoderately in the seductive habit of mentioning his own name.

However we may explain it, the fact is certain that Men who many a savage evinces the strongest reluctance to pronounce will not mention his own name, while at the same time he makes no objection their own at all to other people pronouncing it, and will even invite names will yet invite them to do so for him in order to satisfy the curiosity of other people to an inquisitive stranger. Thus in some parts of Madagascar do so for it is *fàdy* or taboo for a person to tell his own name, but a them. slave or attendant will answer for him.[1] "Chatting with an old Sakalava while the men were packing up, we happened to ask him his name; whereupon he politely requested us to ask one of his servants standing by. On expressing our astonishment that he should have forgotten this, he told us that it was *fàdy* (tabooed) for one of his tribe to pronounce his own name. We found this was perfectly true in that district, but it is not the case with the Sakalava a few days farther down the river."[2] The same curious inconsistency, as it may seem to us, is recorded of some tribes of American Indians. Thus we are told that "the name of an American Indian is a sacred thing, not to be divulged by the owner himself without due consideration. One may ask a warrior

---

[1] J. Sibree, *The Great African Island* (London, 1880), p. 289.

[2] H. W. Grainge, "Journal of a Visit to Mojanga on the North-West Coast," *Antananarivo Annual and Madagascar Magazine*, No. i. p. 25 (reprint of the first four numbers, Antananarivo and London, 1885).

Men who
will not
mention
their own
names will
yet invite
other
people to
do so for
them.

of any tribe to give his name, and the question will be met
with either a point-blank refusal or the more diplomatic
evasion that he cannot understand what is wanted of him.
The moment a friend approaches, the warrior first interrog-
ated will whisper what is wanted, and the friend can tell
the name, receiving a reciprocation of the courtesy from
the other." [1] This general statement applies, for example,
to the Indian tribes of British Columbia, as to whom it is
said that " one of their strangest prejudices, which appears
to pervade all tribes alike, is a dislike to telling their names
—thus you never get a man's right name from himself;
but they will tell each other's names without hesitation." [2]
Though it is considered very rude for a stranger to ask an
Apache his name, and the Apache will never mention it himself, he will allow his friend at his side to mention it for him.[3]
The Abipones of South America thought it a sin in a man to
utter his own name, but they would tell each other's names
freely ; when Father Dobrizhoffer asked a stranger Indian his
name, the man would nudge his neighbour with his elbow
as a sign that his companion should answer the question.[4]
Some of the Malemut Esquimaux of Bering Strait dislike
very much to pronounce their own names; if a man be
asked his name he will appear confused and will generally
turn to a bystander, and request him to mention it for him.[5]
In the whole of the East Indian Archipelago the etiquette
is the same. As a general rule no one will utter his own
name. To enquire, " What is your name ? " is a very in-
delicate question in native society. When in the course of
administrative or judicial business a native is asked his name,
instead of replying he will look at his comrade to indicate
that he is to answer for him, or he will say straight out,
" Ask him." The superstition is current all over the East
Indies without exception,[6] and it is found also among the

[1] J. G. Bourke, " Medicine-men of
the Apaches," *Ninth Annual Report of
the Bureau of Ethnology* (Washington,
1892), p. 461.

[2] R. C. Mayne, *Four Years in
British Columbia and Vancouver
Island* (London, 1862), pp. 278 *sq.*

[3] J. G. Bourke, *On the Border with
Crook*, pp. 131 *sq.*

[4] M. Dobrizhoffer, *Historia de Abiponibus* (Vienna, 1784), ii. 498.

[5] E. W. Nelson, " The Eskimo
about Bering Strait," *Eighteenth Annual Report of the Bureau of American
Ethnology*, part i. (Washington, 1899)
p. 289.

[6] G. A. Wilken, *Handleiding voor de
vergelijkende Volkenkunde van Neder-*

Motu and Motumotu tribes of British New Guinea,[1] the Papuans of Finsch Haven in German New Guinea,[2] the Nufoors of Dutch New Guinea,[3] and the Melanesians of the Bismarck Archipelago.[4] Among many tribes of South Africa men and women never mention their names if they can get any one else to do it for them, but they do not absolutely refuse when it cannot be avoided.[5] No Warua will tell his name, but he does not object to being addressed by it.[6] Among the Masai, "when a man is called or spoken to, he is addressed by his father's name, and his own name is only used when speaking to his mother. It is considered unlucky for a man to be addressed by name. The methods employed in finding out what an individual is called seem apt to lead to confusion. If a man is asked his name, he replies by giving that of his father, and to arrive at his own

landsch-Indië, p. 221. Compare J. H. F. Kohlbrugge, "Naamgeving in Insulinde," *Bijdragen tot de Taal-Land- en Volkenkunde van Neder-landsch-Indië*, lii. (1901) pp. 172 *sq.* The custom is reported for the British settlements in the Straits of Malacca by T. J. Newbold (*Political and Statistical Account of the British Settlements in the Straits of Malacca*, London, 1839, ii. 176); for Sumatra in general by W. Marsden (*History of Sumatra*, pp. 286 *sq.*), and A. L. van Hasselt (*Volksbeschrijving van Midden-Sumatra*, p. 271); for the Battas by Baron van Hoëvell ("Iets over 't oorlogvoeren der Batta's," *Tijdschrift voor Nederlandsch Indië*, N.S., vii. (1878) p. 436, note); for the Dyaks by C. Hupe ("Korte Verhandeling over de Godsdienst, Zeden, enz. der Dajakkers," *Tijdschrift voor Neêrlands Indië*, 1846, dl. iii. p. 250), and W. H. Furness (*Home-life of Borneo Head-hunters*, Philadelphia, 1902, p. 16); for the island of Sumba by S. Roos ("Bijdrage tot de Kennis van Taal, Land en Volk op het Eiland Soemba," p. 70, *Verhandelingen van het Bataviaasch Genootschap van Kunsten en Wetenschappen*, xxxvi.); and for Bolang Mongondo, in the west of Celebes, by N. P. Wilken and J. A. Schwarz ("Allerlei over het land en volk van Bolaang Mongondou," *Mededeelingen van wege*

het Nederlandsche Zendelinggenootschap, xi. (1867) p. 356).

[1] J. Chalmers, *Pioneering in New Guinea*, p. 187. If a Motumotu man is hard pressed for his name and there is nobody near to help him, he will at last in a very stupid way mention it himself.

[2] O. Schellong, "Über Familienleben und Gebräuche der Papuas der Umgebung von Finschhafen," *Zeitschrift für Ethnologie*, xxi. (1889) p. 12. Compare M. Krieger, *Neu Guinea* (Berlin, 1899), p. 172.

[3] Th. J. F. van Hasselt, "Gebruik van vermomde Taal door de Nufooren," *Tijdschrift voor Indische Taal- Landen Volkenkunde*, xlv. (1902) p. 279. The Nufoors are a Papuan tribe on Doreh Bay, in Dutch New Guinea. See *id.*, in *Tijdschrift voor Indische Taal- Land- en Volkenkunde*, xlvi. (1903) p. 287.

[4] J. Graf Pfeil, *Studien und Beobachtungen aus der Südsee* (Brunswick, 1899), p. 78; P. A. Kleintitschen, *Die Küstenbewohner der Gazellehalbinsel* (Hiltrup bei Münster, preface dated Christmas, 1906), pp. 237 *sq.*

[5] J. Macdonald, "Manners, Customs, Superstitions, and Religions of South African Tribes," *Journal of the Anthropological Institute*, xx. (1891) p. 131.

[6] V. L. Cameron, *Across Africa* (London, 1877), ii. 61.

name it is necessary to ask a third person, or to ask him what is the name of his mother. There is no objection to another person mentioning his name even in his presence."[1] We are told that the Wanyamwesi almost always address each other as "Mate" or "Friend," and a man sometimes quite forgets his own name and has to be reminded of it by another.[2] The writer who makes this statement was probably unaware of the reluctance of many savages to utter their own names, and hence he mistook that reluctance for forgetfulness. In Uganda no one will mention his totem. If it is necessary that it should be known, he will ask a bystander to mention it for him.[3] The Ba-Lua in the Congo region are unwilling to pronounce the name of their tribe; if they are pressed on the subject, they will call on some foreigner to give the required information.[4]

Sometimes the prohibition to mention personal names is not permanent but temporary and contingent.

Sometimes the embargo laid on personal names is not permanent; it is conditional on circumstances, and when these change it ceases to operate. Thus when the Nandi men are away on a foray, nobody at home may pronounce the names of the absent warriors; they must be referred to as birds. Should a child so far forget itself as ·to mention one of the distant ones by name, the mother would rebuke it, saying, "Don't talk of the birds who are in the heavens."[5] Among the Bangala of the Upper Congo, while a man is fishing and when he returns with his catch, his proper name is in abeyance and nobody may mention it. Whatever the fisherman's real name may be, he is called *mwele* without distinction. The reason is that the river is full of spirits, who, if they heard the fisherman's real name, might so work against him that he would catch little or nothing. Even when he has caught his fish and landed with them, the buyer must still not address him by his proper name, but must only call him *mwele*; for even then, if the spirits were to

[1] S. L. Hinde and H. Hinde, *The Last of the Masai* (London, 1901), pp. 48 *sq.* Compare Sir H. Johnston, *The Uganda Protectorate* (London, 1902), ii. 826 *sq.*; M. Merker, *Die Masai* (Berlin, 1904), p. 56.

[2] P. Reichard, "Die Wanjamuesi," *Zeitschrift der Gesellschaft für Erdkunde zu Berlin*, xxiv. (1889) p. 258.

[3] J. Roscoe, "Further Notes on the Manners and Customs of the Baganda," *Journal of the Anthropological Institute*, xxxii. (1902) p. 29.

[4] E. Torday and T. A. Joyce, "Note on the Southern Ba-Mbala," *Man*, vii. (1907) p. 81.

[5] A. C. Hollis, *The Nandi*, p. 43.

hear his proper name, they would either bear it in mind and serve him out another day, or they might so mar the fish he had caught that he would get very little for them. Hence the fisherman can extract heavy damages from anybody who mentions his name, or can compel the thoughtless speaker to relieve him of the fish at a good price so as to restore his luck.[1] When the Sulka of New Britain are near the territory of their enemies the Gaktei, they take care not to mention them by their proper name, believing that were they to do so, their foes would attack and slay them. Hence in these circumstances they speak of the Gaktei as *o lapsiek*, that is, "the rotten tree-trunks," and they imagine that by calling them that they make the limbs of their dreaded enemies ponderous and clumsy like logs.[2] This example illustrates the extremely materialistic view which these savages take of the nature of words; they suppose that the mere utterance of an expression signifying clumsiness will homoeopathically affect with clumsiness the limbs of their distant foemen. Another illustration of this curious misconception is furnished by a Caffre superstition that the character of a young thief can be reformed by shouting his name over a boiling kettle of medicated water, then clapping a lid on the kettle and leaving the name to steep in the water for several days. It is not in the least necessary that the thief should be aware of the use that is being made of his name behind his back; the moral reformation will be effected without his knowledge.[3]

When it is deemed necessary that a man's real name should be kept secret, it is often customary, as we have seen, to call him by a surname or nickname. As distinguished from the real or primary names, these secondary names are apparently held to be no part of the man himself, so that they may be freely used and divulged to everybody without endangering his safety thereby. Sometimes in order to avoid the use of his own name a man will be called after his child. Thus we are informed that "the Gippsland

In order to avoid the use of people's own names, parents are sometimes named after their children, uncles and aunts after

---

[1] Rev. J. H. Weeks, "Anthropological Notes on the Bangala of the Upper Congo River," *Journal of the Anthropological Institute*, xxxix. (1909) pp. 128, 459.

[2] R. Parkinson, *Dreissig Jahre in der Südsee*, p. 198.

[3] Dudley Kidd, *Savage Childhood*, p. 73

their
nephews
and nieces,
and so
forth.
blacks objected strongly to let any one outside the tribe
know their names, lest their enemies, learning them, should
make them vehicles of incantation, and so charm their lives
away. As children were not thought to have enemies, they
used to speak of a man as 'the father, uncle, or cousin of
So-and-so,' naming a child; but on all occasions abstained from
mentioning the name of a grown-up person."[1]   Similarly
among the Nufoors of Dutch New Guinea, grown-up persons
who are related by marriage may not mention each other's
names, but it is lawful to mention the names of children;
hence in order to designate a person whose name they may
not pronounce they will speak of him or her as the father or
mother of So-and-so.[2]   The Alfoors of Poso, in Celebes,
will not pronounce their own names.   Among them, accordingly, if you wish to ascertain a person's name, you ought
not to ask the man himself, but should enquire of others.
But if this is impossible, for example, when there is no one
else near, you should ask him his child's name, and then
address him as the "Father of So-and-so."   Nay, these Alfoors
are shy of uttering the names even of children; so when a
boy or girl has a nephew or niece, he or she is addressed
as " Uncle of So-and-so," or " Aunt of So-and-so."[3]   In pure
Malay society, we are told, a man is never asked his name,
and the custom of naming parents after their children is
adopted only as a means of avoiding the use of the parents'
own names.   The writer who makes this statement adds
in confirmation of it that childless persons are named after
their younger brothers.[4]   Among the land Dyaks of
northern Borneo children as they grow up are called,
according to their sex, the father or mother of a child of
their father's or mother's younger brother or sister,[5] that is,

[1] E. M. Curr, *The Australian Race*,
iii. 545.   Similarly among the Dacotas " there is no secrecy in children's
names, but when they grow up there
is a secrecy in men's names " (H. R.
Schoolcraft, *Indian Tribes*, iii. 240).

[2] Th. J. F. van Hasselt, " Gebruik
van vermomde Taal door de Nufooren,"
*Tijdschrift voor Indische Taal- Land-
en Volkenkunde*, xlv. (1902) p. 278.

[3] A. C. Kruijt, " Een en ander aangaande het geestelijk en maatschappelijk

leven van den Poso-Alfoer," *Mededeelingen van wege het Nederlandsche Zendelinggenootschap*, xl. (1896) pp. 273 *sqq.*

[4] G. Mansveld (Kontroleur van
Nias), " Iets over de namen en Galars
onder de Maleijers in de Padangsche
Bovenlanden, bepaaldelijk in noorde-
lijk Agam," *Tijdschrift voor Indische
Taal- Land- en Volkenkunde*, xxiii.
(1876) pp. 443, 449.

[5] Spenser St. John, *Life in the Forests of the Far East*,[2] i. 208

they are called the father or mother of what we should call their first cousin. The Caffres used to think it discourteous to call a bride by her own name, so they would call her "the Mother of So-and-so," even when she was only betrothed, far less a wife and a mother.[1] Among the Kukis and Zemis or Kacha Nagas of Assam parents drop their own names after the birth of a child and are named Father and Mother of So-and-so. Childless couples go by the names of "the childless father," "the childless mother," "the father of no child," "the mother of no child."[2] A Zulu woman may not utter her husband's name; if she speaks to or of him she says, "Father of So-and-so," mentioning the name of one of his children.[3] A Hindoo woman will not name her husband. If she has to refer to him she will designate him as the father of her child or by some other periphrasis.[4] The widespread custom of naming a father after his child has sometimes been supposed to spring from a desire on the father's part to assert his paternity, apparently as a means of obtaining those rights over his children which had previously, under a system of mother-kin, been possessed by the mother.[5] But this explanation does not account for the parallel custom of naming the mother after her child, which seems commonly to co-exist with the practice of naming the father after the child. Still less, if possible, does it apply to the customs of calling childless couples the father and mother of children which do not exist, of naming people after their younger brothers, and of

The common custom of naming parents after their children seems to arise from a reluctance to mention the real names of persons addressed or directly referred to.

---

[1] Dudley Kidd, _The Essential Kafir_, p. 202.

[2] L. A. Waddell, "The Tribes of the Brahmapootra Valley," _Journal of the Asiatic Society of Bengal_, lxix. part iii. (1901) pp. 52, 69, compare 46.

[3] H. Callaway, _Religious System of the Amazulu_, part iii. p. 316, note.

[4] W. Crooke, _Popular Religion and Folk-lore of Northern India_ (Westminster, 1896), ii. 5 _sq._ Compare _id._, _Tribes and Castes of the North-Western Provinces and Oudh_, ii. 251.

[5] G. A. Wilken, _Handleiding voor de vergelijkende Volkenkunde van Nederlandsch-Indië_, pp. 216-219; E. B. Tylor, "On a Method of Investigating the Developement of Institutions,"

Journal of the Anthropological Institute, xviii. (1889) pp. 248-250 (who refers to a series of papers by G. A. Wilken, "Over de primitieve vormen van het huwelijk," published in _Indische Gids_, 1880, etc., which I have not seen). Wilken's theory is rejected by Mr. A. C. Kruijt (_l.c._), who explains the custom by the fear of attracting the attention of evil spirits to the person named. Other explanations are suggested by Mr. J. H. F. Kohlbrugge ("Naamgeving in Insulinde," _Bijdragen tot de Taal- Land- en Volkenkunde van Nederlandsch-Indië_, lii. (1901) pp. 160-170), and by Mr. E. Crawley (_The Mystic Rose_, London, 1902, pp. 428-433).

designating children as the uncles and aunts of So-and-so, or as the fathers and mothers of their first cousins. But all these practices are explained in a simple and natural way if we suppose that they originate in a reluctance to utter the real names of persons addressed or directly referred to. That reluctance is probably based partly on a fear of attracting the notice of evil spirits, partly on a dread of revealing the name to sorcerers, who would thereby obtain a handle for injuring the owner of the name.[1]

[1] For evidence of the custom of naming parents after their children in Australia, see E. J. Eyre, *Journals of Expeditions of Discovery into Central Australia* (London, 1845), ii. 325 *sq.*: in Sumatra, see W. Marsden, *History of Sumatra*, p. 286; Baron van Hoëvell, "Iets over 't oorlogvoeren der Batta's," *Tijdschrift voor Nederlandsch-Indië*, N.S. vii. (1878) p. 436, note; A. L. van Hasselt, *Volksbeschrijving van Midden-Sumatra*, p. 274: in Nias, see J. T. Nieuwenhuisen en H. C. B. von Rosenberg, *Verslag omtrent het eiland Nias*, p. 28 (*Verhandelingen van het Bataviaasch Genootschap van Kunsten en Wetenschappen*, xxx. Batavia, 1863): in Java, see P. J. Veth, *Java*, i. (Haarlem, 1875) p. 642; J. H. F. Kohlbrugge, "Die Tenggeresen, ein alter Javanischen Volksstamm," *Bijdragen tot de Taal- Land- en Volkenkunde van Nederlandsch-Indië*, liii. (1901) p. 121: in Borneo, see C. Hupe, "Korte Verhandeling over de Godsdienst, Zeden, enz. der Dajakkers," *Tijdschrift voor Neêrlands Indië*, 1846, dl. iii. p. 249; H. Low, *Sarawak*, p. 249; Spenser St. John, *Life in the Forests of the Far East*,[2] i. 208; M. T. H. Perelaer, *Ethnographische Beschrijving der Dajaks*, p. 42; C. Hose, "The Natives of Borneo," *Journal of the Anthropological Institute*, xxiii. (1894) p. 170; W. H. Furness, *Folk-lore in Borneo* (Wallingford, Pennsylvania, 1899, privately printed), p. 26; *id.*, *Home-life of Borneo Head-hunters*, pp. 17 *sq.*, 55; A. W. Nieuwenhuis, *Quer durch Borneo*, i. 75: among the Mantras of Malacca, see W. W. Skeat and C. O. Blagden, *Pagan Races of the Malay Peninsula*, ii. 16 *sq.*: among the Negritos of Zambales in the Philippines, see W. A. Reed, *Negritos of Zambales* (Manilla, 1904), p. 55: in the islands between Celebes and New Guinea, see J. G. F. Riedel, *De sluik- en kroesharige rassen tusschen Selebes en Papua*, pp. 5, 137, 152 *sq.*, 238, 260, 353, 392, 418, 450; J. H. W. van der Miesen, "Een en ander over Boeroe," *Mededeelingen van wege het Nederlandsche Zendelinggenootschap*, xlvi. (1902) p. 444: in Celebes and other parts of the Indian Archipelago, see J. H. F. Kohlbrugge, "Naamgeving in Insulinde," *Bijdragen tot de Taal- Land- en Volkenkunde van Nederlandsch-Indië*, lii. (1901) pp. 160-170; G. A. Wilken, *Handleiding voor de vergelijkende Volkenkunde van Nederlandsch-Indië*, pp. 216 *sqq.*: in New Guinea, see P. W. Schmidt, "Ethnographisches von Berlinhafen, Deutsch- Neu- Guinea," *Mittheilungen der Anthropologischen Gesellschaft in Wien*, xxx. (1899) p. 28: among the Kasias of North-eastern India, see Col. H. Yule, in *Journal of the Anthropological Institute*, ix. (1880) p. 298; L. A. Waddell, "The Tribes of the Brahmaputra Valley," *Journal of the Asiatic Society of Bengal*, lxix. part iii. (Calcutta, 1901) p. 46: among some of the indigenous races of southern China, see P. Vial, "Les Gni ou Gnipa, tribu Lolote du Yun-Nan," *Missions Catholiques*, xxv. (1893) p. 270; *La Mission lyonnaise d'exploration commerciale en Chine* (Lyons, 1898), p. 369: in Corea, see Mrs. Bishop, *Korea and her Neighbours* (London, 1898), i. 136: among the Yukagirs of north-eastern Asia, see W. Jochelson, "Die Jukagiren im äussersten Nordosten

§ 2. *Names of Relations tabooed*

It might naturally be expected that the reserve so commonly maintained with regard to personal names would be dropped or at least relaxed among relations and friends. But the reverse of this is often the case. It is precisely the persons most intimately connected by blood and especially by marriage to whom the rule applies with the greatest stringency. Such people are often forbidden, not only to pronounce each other's names, but even to utter ordinary words which resemble or have a single syllable in common with these names. The persons who are thus mutually debarred from mentioning each other's names are especially husbands and wives, a man and his wife's parents, and a woman and her husband's father. For example, among the Caffres of South Africa a woman may not publicly pronounce the birth-name of her husband or of any of his brothers, nor may she use the interdicted word in its ordinary sense. If her husband, for instance, be called u-Mpaka, from *impaka*, a small feline animal, she must speak of that beast by some other name.[1] Further, a Caffre wife is forbidden to pro-

The names of persons related to the speaker by blood and especially by marriage may often not be mentioned.

Women's speech among the Caffres.

Asiens," xvii. *Jahresbericht der Geographischen Gesellschaft von Bern* (Bern, 1900), pp. 26 *sq.*; P. von Stenin, "Jochelson's Forschungen unter den Jukagiren," *Globus*, lxxvi. (1899) p. 169: among the Masai, see M. Merker, *Die Masai* (Berlin, 1904), pp. 59, 235: among the Bechuanas, Basutos, and other Caffre tribes of South Africa, see D. Livingston, *Missionary Travels and Researches in South Africa* (London, 1857), p. 126; J. Shooter, *The Kafirs of Natal* (London, 1857), pp. 220 *sq.*; D. Leslie, *Among the Zulus and Amatongas* [2] (Edinburgh, 1875), pp. 171 *sq.*; G. M'Call Theal, *Kaffir Folk-lore* [2] (London, 1886), p. 225; Father Porte, "Les reminiscences d'un missionaire du Basutoland," *Missions Catholiques*, xxviii. (1896) p. 300: among the Hos of Togoland in West Africa, see J. Spieth, *Die Ewe-Stämme*, p. 217: among the Patagonians, see G. C. Musters, *At Home with the Patagonians*

(London, 1871), p. 177: among the Lengua Indians of the Gran Chaco, see G. Kurze, "Sitten und Gebräuche der Lengua-Indianer," *Mittheilungen der Geographischen Gesellschaft zu Jena*, xxiii. (1905) p. 28: among the Mayas of Guatemala, see H. H. Bancroft, *Native Races of the Pacific States*, ii. 680: among the Haida Indians of Queen Charlotte Islands, see J. R. Swanton, "Contributions to the Ethnology of the Haida," *Memoir of the American Museum of Natural History, The Jesup North Pacific Expedition*, vol. v. part i. (Leyden and New York, 1905) p. 118: and among the Tinneh and occasionally the Thlinkeet Indians of northwest America, see E. Petitot, *Monographie des Dènè-Dindjié* (Paris, 1876), p. 61; H. J. Holmberg, "Ethnographische Skizzen über die Völker des russischen Amerika," *Acta Societatis Scientiarum Fennicae*, iv. (1856) p. 319.

[1] J. Shooter, *The Kafirs of Natal* (London, 1857), p. 221.

nounce even mentally the names of her father-in-law and of all her husband's male relations in the ascending line ; and whenever the emphatic syllable of any of their names occurs in another word, she must avoid it by substituting either an entirely new word, or, at least, another syllable in its place. Hence this custom has given rise to an almost distinct language among the women, which the Caffres call *Ukuteta Kwabafazi* or "women's speech."[1] The interpretation of this "women's speech" is naturally very difficult, "for no definite rules can be given for the formation of these substituted words, nor is it possible to form a dictionary of them, their number being so great — since there may be many women, even in the same tribe, who would be no more at liberty to use the substitutes employed by some others, than they are to use the original words themselves."[2] A Caffre man, on his side, may not mention the name of his mother-in-law, nor may she pronounce his ; but he is free to utter words in which the emphatic syllable of her name occurs.[3] In Northern Nyassaland no woman will speak the name of her husband or even use a word that may be synonymous with it. If she were to call him by his proper name, she believes it would be unlucky and would affect her powers of conception. In like manner women abstain, for superstitious reasons, from using the common names of articles of food, which they designate by terms peculiar to themselves.[4] Among the Kondes, at the north-western end of Lake

[1] Maclean, *Compendium of Kafir Laws and Customs* (Cape Town, 1866), pp. 92 *sq.* ; D. Leslie, *Among the Zulus and Amatongas,*[2] pp. 141 *sq.*, 172 ; M. Kranz, *Natur- und Kulturleben der Zulus* (Wiesbaden, 1880), pp. 114 *sq.* ; G. M'Call Theal, *Kaffir Folk-lore*[2] (London, 1886), p. 214 ; *id., Records of South-Eastern Africa*, vii. 435 ; Dudley Kidd, *The Essential Kafir*, pp. 236-243 ; Father Porte, "Les reminiscences d'un missionaire du Basutoland," *Missions Catholiques*, xxviii. (1896) p. 233.

[2] Rev. Francis Fleming, *Kaffraria and its Inhabitants* (London, 1853), p. 97; *id., Southern Africa* (London, 1856), pp. 238 *sq.* This writer states that the women are forbidden to pronounce "any word which may happen to contain a sound similar to any one in the names of their nearest male relatives."

[3] Maclean, *op. cit.* p. 93; D. Leslie, *Among the Zulus and Amatongas,*[2] pp. 46, 102, 172. The extensive system of taboos on personal names among the Caffres is known as *Ukuhlonipa*, or simply *hlonipa*. The fullest account of it with which I am acquainted is given by Leslie, *op. cit.* pp. 141 *sq.*, 172-180. See further Miss A. Werner, "The Custom of *Hlonipa* in its Influence on Language," *Journal of the African Society*, No. 15 (April, 1905), pp. 346-356.

[4] Sir H. H. Johnston, *British Central Africa* (London, 1897), p. 452.

Nyassa, a woman may not mention the name of her father-in-law ; indeed she may not even speak to him nor see him.[1] Among the Barea and Bogos of Eastern Africa a woman never mentions her husband's name ; a Bogo wife would rather be unfaithful to him than commit the monstrous sin of allowing his name to pass her lips.[2]   Among the Haussas "the first-born son is never called by his parents by his name ; indeed they will not even speak with him if other people are present.   The same rule holds good of the first husband and the first wife." [3]   In antiquity Ionian women would not call their husbands by their names.[4]   While the rites of Ceres were being performed in Rome, no one might name a father or a daughter.[5]   Among the South Slavs at the present day husbands and wives will not mention each other's names, and a young wife may not call any of her housemates by their true names ; she must invent or at least adopt other names for them.[6]   A Kirghiz woman dares not pronounce the names of the older relations of her husband, nor even use words which resemble them in sound.   For example, if one of these relations is called Shepherd, she may not speak of sheep, but must call them "the bleating ones" ; if his name is Lamb, she must refer to lambs as "the young of the bleating ones." [7]   After marriage an Aino wife may not mention her husband's name ; to do so would be deemed equivalent to killing him.[8]   Among the Sgaus, a Karen tribe of Burma, children never mention their parents' names.[9]   A Toda man may not utter the names of his mother's brother, his grandfather and grandmother, his wife's mother, and of the man from whom he has received

[1] A. Merensky, "Das Konde-volk im deutschen Gebiet am Nyassa-See," *Verhandlungen der Berliner Gesellschaft für Anthropologie, Ethnologie, und Urgeschichte*, 1893, p. (296).

[2] W. Munzinger, *Ostafrikanische Studien* (Schaffhausen, 1864), p. 526 ; *id., Sitten und Recht der Bogos* (Winterthur, 1859), p. 95.

[3] G. A. Krause, "Merkwürdige Sitten der Haussa,' *Globus*, lxix. (1896) p. 375.

[4] Herodotus, i. 146.

[5] Servius, on Virgil, *Aen.* iv. 58.

[6] K. Rhamm, "Der Verkehr der Geschlecter unter den Slaven in seinen gegensätzlichen Erscheinungen," *Globus*, lxxxii. (1902) p. 192.

[7] W. Radloff, *Proben der Volkslitteratur der türkischen Stämme Süd-Sibiriens*, iii. (St. Petersburg, 1870) p. 13, note 3.

[8] J. Batchelor, *The Ainu and their Folk-lore* (London, 1901), pp. 226, 249 *sq.*, 252.

[9] Bringaud, "Les Karins de la Birmanie," *Missions Catholiques*, xx. (1888) p. 308.

Names of relations by marriage tabooed.

his wife, who is usually the wife's father. All these names are tabooed to him in the lifetime of the persons who bear them, and after death the prohibitions are not only maintained but extended.[1] In southern India wives believe that to tell their husband's name or to pronounce it even in a dream would bring him to an untimely end. Further, they may not mention the names of their parents, their parents-in-law, and their brothers-in-law and sisters-in-law.[2] Among the Ojebways husbands and wives never mention each other's names;[3] among the Omahas a man and his father-in-law and mother-in-law will on no account utter each other's names in company.[4] A Dacota "is not allowed to address or to look towards his wife's mother, especially, and the woman is shut off from familiar intercourse with her husband's father and others, and etiquette prohibits them from speaking the names of their relatives by marriage." "None of their customs," adds the same writer, "is more tenacious of life than this; and no family law is more binding."[5] In the Nishinam tribe of California "a husband never calls his wife by name on any account, and it is said that divorces have been produced by no other provocation than that."[6]

Names of relations, especially of persons related to the speaker by marriage, may not be mentioned in the East Indies.

The Battas or Bataks of Sumatra display a great aversion to mentioning their own names and a still greater aversion to mentioning the names of their parents, grandparents, or elder blood-relations. Politeness forbids the putting of direct questions on this subject, so that the investigation of personal identity becomes difficult and laborious. When a Batta expects to be questioned as to his relations, he will usually provide himself with a friend to answer for him.[7] A Batak man may never mention the names of his wife, his daughter-in-law and of his son-in-law; a woman is most particularly forbidden to mention the name of the man who

---

[1] W. H. R. Rivers, *The Todas*, p. 626.

[2] E. Thurston, *Ethnographic Notes in Southern India*, p. 533.

[3] Peter Jones, *History of the Ojebway Indians*, p. 162.

[4] E. James, *Expedition from Pittsburgh to the Rocky Mountains* (London, 1823), i. 232.

[5] S. R. Riggs, *Dakota Grammar, Texts, and Ethnography* (Washington, 1893), p. 204.

[6] S. Powers, *Tribes of California*, p. 315.

[7] Willer, "Verzameling der Battasche Wetten en Instellingen in Mandheling en Pertibie," *Tijdschrift voor Nederlandsch-Indië*, 1846, dl. ii. 337 *sq.*

has married her daughter.[1] Among the Karo-Bataks the forbidden names are those of parents, uncles, aunts, parents-
in-law, brothers and sisters, and especially grandparents.[2]
Among the Dyaks a child never pronounces the names of
his parents, and is angry if any one else does so in his presence.
A husband never calls his wife by her name, and she never
calls him by his. If they have children, they name each other
after them, "Father of So-and-so" and "Mother of So-and-so";
if they have no children they use the pronouns "he" and "she,"
or an expression such as "he or she whom I love"; and in
general, members of a Dyak family do not mention each other's
names.[3] Moreover, when the personal names happen also, as
they often do, to be names of common objects, the Dyak is
debarred from designating these objects by their ordinary
names. For instance, if a man or one of his family is called
Bintang, which means "star," he must not call a star a star
(*bintang*); he must call it a *pariama*. If he or a member of
his domestic circle bears the name of Bulan, which means
"moon," he may not speak of the moon as the moon
(*bulan*); he must call it *penala*. Hence it comes about that
in the Dyak language there are two sets of distinct names
for many objects.[4] Among the sea Dyaks of Sarawak a
man may not pronounce the name of his father-in-law or
mother-in-law without incurring the wrath of the spirits.
And since he reckons as his father-in-law and mother-in-law
not only the father and mother of his own wife, but also the
fathers and mothers of his brothers' wives and sisters'
husbands, and likewise the fathers and mothers of all his
cousins, the number of tabooed names may be very considerable and the opportunities of error correspondingly numerous.
To make confusion worse confounded, the names of persons
are often the names of common things, such as moon, bridge,

[1] J. H. Meerwaldt, "Gebruiken der
Bataks in het maatschappelijk leven,"
*Mededeelingen van wege het Neder-
landsche Zendelinggenootschap*, xlix.
(1905) pp. 123, 125.
[2] J. E. Neumann, "*Kemali, Pantang* en *Rěboe* bij de Karo-Bataks,"
*Tijdschrift voor Indische Taal- Land-
en Volkenkunde*, xlviii. (1906) p.
510.

[3] C. Hupe, "Korte Verhandeling
over de Godsdienst, Zeden, enz. der
Dajakkers," *Tijdschrift voor Neêrlands
Indië*, 1846, dl. iii. pp. 249 *sq.*
[4] "De Dajaks op Borneo,"*Mededeelingen van wege het Nederlandsche Zendelinggenootschap*, xiii. (1869) p. 78;
G. A. Wilken, *Handleiding voor de
vergelijkende Volkenkunde van Nederlandsch-Indië*, p. 599.

Names of relations, especially of persons related to the speaker by marriage, may not be mentioned in the East Indies.

barley, cobra, leopard ; so that when any of a man's many fathers-in-law and mothers-in-law are called by such names, these common words may not pass his lips.[1] Among the Dyaks of Landak and Tajan it is forbidden to mention the names of parents and grandparents, sometimes also of great-grandparents, whether they are alive or dead.[2] Among the Alfoors or Toradjas of Poso, in central Celebes, you may not pronounce the names of your father, mother, grand-parents, and other near relations. But the strictest taboo is on the names of parents-in-law. A son-in-law and a daughter-in-law may not only never mention the names of their parents-in-law, but if the names happen to be ordinary words of the language, they may never allow the words in their common significance to pass their lips. For example, if my father is called Njara ("horse"), I may not speak of him by that name ; but in speaking of the animal I am free to use the word horse (*njara*). But if my father-in-law is called Njara, the case is different, for then not only may I not refer to him by his name, but I may not even call a horse a horse ; in speaking of the animal I must use some other word. The missionary who reports the custom is acquainted with a man whose mother-in-law rejoices in the name of Ringgi ("rixdollar"). When this man has occasion to refer to real rixdollars, he alludes to them delicately as "large guilders" (*roepia bose*). Another man may not use the ordinary word for water (*oewe*) ; in speaking of water he employs a word (*owai*) taken from a different dialect. Indeed, among these Alfoors it is the common practice in such cases to replace the forbidden word by a kindred word of the same significance borrowed from another dialect. In this way many fresh terms or new forms of an old word pass into general circulation.[3] Among the Alfoors of Minahassa,

[1] R. Shelford, "Two Medicine-baskets from Sarawak," *Journal of the Anthropological Institute*, xxxiii. (1903) pp. 78 *sq.*

[2] M. C. Schadee, "Bijdrage tot de kennis van den godsdienst der Dajaks van Landak en Tajan," *Bijdragen tot de Taal- Land- en Volkenkunde van Neder-landsche-Indië*, lvi. (1904) p. 536.

[3] A. C. Kruijt, "Een en ander aan-gaande het geestelijk en maatschappelijk leven van den Poso-Alfoer," *Mededeelin-gen van wege het Nederlandsche Zende-linggenootschap*, xl. (1896) pp. 273 *sq.* The word for taboo among these people is *kapali*. See further A. C. Kruijt, "Eenige ethnographische aanteeken-ingen omtrent de Toboengkoe en Tomori," *op. cit.* xliv. (1900) pp. 219, 237.

in northern Celebes, the custom is carried still further so as to forbid the use even of words which merely resemble the personal names in sound. It is especially the name of a father-in-law which is thus laid under an interdict. If he, for example, is called Kalala, his son-in-law may not speak of a horse by its common name *kawalo*; he must call it a "riding-beast" (*sasakajan*).[1] So among the Alfoors of the island of Buru it is taboo to mention the names of parents and parents-in-law, or even to speak of common objects by words which resemble these names in sound. Thus, if your mother-in-law is called Dalu, which means "betel," you may not ask for betel by its ordinary name, you must ask for "red mouth" (*mue miha*); if you want betel-leaf, you may not say betel-leaf (*dalu 'mun*), you must say *karon fenna*. In the same island it is also taboo to mention the name of an elder brother in his presence.[2] Transgressions of these rules are punished with fines.[3] In Bolang Mongondo, a district in the west of Celebes, the unmentionable names are those of parents, parents-in-law, uncles and aunts.[4] Among the Alfoors of Halmahera a son-in-law may never use his father-in-law's name in speaking to him; he must simply address him as "Father-in-law."[5] In Sunda it is thought that a particular crop would be spoilt if a man were to mention the names of his father and mother.[6]

Among the Nufoors, as we have seen,[7] persons who are related to each other by marriage are forbidden to mention

[1] G. A. Wilken, *Handleiding voor de vergelijkende Volkenkunde van Nederlandsch-Indië*, pp. 599 *sq.*

[2] G. A. Wilken, "Bijdrage tot de Kennis der Alfoeren van het Eiland Boeroe," p. 26 (*Verhandelingen van het Bataviaasch Genootschap van Kunsten en Wetenschappen*, xxxvi.). The words for taboo among these Alfoors are *poto* and *koin*; *poto* applies to actions, *koin* to things and places. The literal meaning of *poto* is "warm," "hot" (Wilken, *op. cit.* p. 25).

[3] J. H. W. van der Miesen, "Een en ander over Boeroe," *Mededeelingen van wege het Nederlandsche Zendelinggenootschap*, xlvi. (1902) p. 455.

[4] N. P. Wilken and J. A. Schwarz, "Allerlei over het Land en Volk van Bolaang Mongondou," *Mededeelingen van wege het Nederlandsche Zendelinggenootschap*, xi. (1867) p. 356.

[5] C. F. H. Campen, "De godsdienstbegrippen der Halmaherasche Alfoeren," *Tijdschrift voor Indische Taal- Land- en Volkenkunde*, xxvii. (1882) p. 450.

[6] K. F. Holle, "Snippers van den Regent van Galoeh," *Tijdschrift voor Indische Taal- Land- en Volkenkunde*, xxvii. (1882) pp. 101 *sq.* The precise consequence supposed to follow is that the *oebi* (?) plantations would have no bulbs (*geen knollen*). The names of several animals are also tabooed in Sunda. See below, p. 415.

[7] Above, p. 332.

Names of
persons
related by
marriage
to the
speaker are
tabooed in
New
Guinea.

each other's names. Among the connexions whose names
are thus tabooed are wife, mother-in-law, father-in-law, your
wife's uncles and aunts and also her grand-uncles and grand-
aunts, and the whole of your wife's or your husband's family
in the same generation as yourself, except that men may
mention the names of their brothers-in-law, though women
may not. The taboo comes into operation as soon as the
betrothal has taken place and before the marriage has been
celebrated. Families thus connected by the betrothal of two
of their members are not only forbidden to pronounce each
other's names ; they may not even look at each other, and
the rule gives rise to the most comical scenes when they
happen to meet unexpectedly. And not merely the names
themselves, but any words that sound like them are scrupulously avoided and other words used in their place. If it
should chance that a person has inadvertently uttered a
forbidden name, he must at once throw himself on the floor
and say, " I have mentioned a wrong name. I throw it
through the chinks of the floor in order that I may
eat well." [1]   In German New Guinea near relations by
marriage, particularly father-in-law and daughter-in-law,
mother-in-law and son-in-law, as well as brothers-in-law
and sisters-in-law, must see as little of each other as possible;
they may not converse together and they may not mention
each other's names, not even when these names have passed
to younger members of the family. Thus if a child is called
after its deceased paternal grandfather, the mother may not
call her child by its name but must employ another name
for the purpose.[2]   Among the Yabim, for example, on the
south-east coast of German New Guinea, parents-in-law may
neither be touched nor named. Even when their names are
borne by other people or are the ordinary names of common
objects, they may not pass the lips of their sons-in-law and
daughters-in-law.[3]   Among the western tribes of British New

[1] Th. J. F. van Hasselt, "Gebruik
van vermomde Taal door de Nufooren;"
*Tijdschrift voor Indische Taal- Land-
en Volkenkunde*, xlv. (1902) pp. 278 *sq.*
The writer explains that "to eat well"
is a phrase used in the sense of "to be
decent, well-behaved," "to know what
is customary."

[2] M. Krieger, *Neu - Guinea*, pp.
171 *sq.*
[3] K. Vetter, in *Nachrichten über
Kaiser Wilhelms - Land und den
Bismarck-Archipel*, 1897, p. 92. For
more evidence of the observance of this
custom in German New Guinea see
O. Schellong, "Über Familienleben

Guinea the principal taboo or *sabi*, as it is there called, concerns the names of relatives by marriage. A man may not mention the name of his wife's father, mother, elder sister, or elder brother, nor the name of any male or female relative of her father or mother, so long as the relative in question is a member of the same tribe as the speaker. The names of his wife's younger brothers and sisters are not tabooed to him. The same law applies to a woman with reference to the names of her husband's relatives. As a general rule, this taboo does not extend outside the tribal boundaries. Hence when a man or woman marries out of his or her tribe, the taboo is usually not applied. And when members of one tribe, who may not pronounce each other's names at home, are away from their own territory, they are no longer strictly bound to observe the prohibition. A breach of the taboo has to be atoned for by the offender paying a fine to the person whose name he has taken in vain. Until that has been done, neither of the parties concerned, if they are males, may enter the men's club-house. In the old times the offended party might recover his social standing by cutting off somebody else's head.[1]

In the western islands of Torres Straits a man never mentioned the personal names of his father-in-law, mother-in-law, brother-in-law, and sister-in-law; and a woman was subject to the same restrictions. A brother-in-law might be spoken of as the husband or brother of some one whose name it was lawful to mention; and similarly a sister-in-law might be called the wife of So-and-so. If a man by chance used the personal name of his brother-in-law, he was ashamed and hung his head. His shame was only relieved when he had made a present as compensation to the man whose name he had taken in vain. The same compensation was made to a sister-in-law, a father-in-law, and a mother-in-law for the accidental mention of their names. This

Names of persons related by marriage to the speaker are tabooed in Melanesia.

---

und Gebräuche der Papuas der Umgebung von Finschhafen," *Zeitschrift für Ethnologie*, xxi. (1889) p. 12; M. J. Erdweg, "Die Bewohner der Insel Tumleo, Berlinhafen, Deutsch - Neu-Guinea," *Mittheilungen der Anthropologischen Gesellschaft in Wien*, xxxii.

(1902) pp. 379 *sq.*

[1] B. A. Hely, "Notes on Totemism, etc., among the Western Tribes," *British New Guinea, Annual Report for 1894-95*, pp. 54 *sq.* Compare M. Krieger, *Neu - Guinea*, pp. 313 *sq.*

Names of persons related by marriage to the speaker are tabooed in Melanesia.

disability to use the personal names of relatives by marriage was associated with the custom, so common throughout the world, that a man or woman is not allowed to speak to these relatives. If a man wished to communicate with his father-in-law or mother-in-law, he spoke to his wife and she spoke to her parent. When direct communication became absolutely necessary, it was said that a man might talk to his father-in-law or mother-in-law a very little in a low voice. The behaviour towards a brother-in-law was the same.[1] Similar taboos on the names of persons connected by marriage are in force in New Britain and New Ireland.[2] Among the natives who inhabit the coast of the Gazelle Peninsula in New Britain to mention the name of a brother-in-law is the grossest possible affront you can offer to him ; it is a crime punishable with death.[3] In the Santa Cruz and Reef Islands a man is forbidden to pronounce the name of his mother-in-law, and he may never see her face so long as he lives. She on her side lies under similar restrictions in regard to him. Further, a man is prohibited from mentioning the name of his son-in-law, though he is allowed to look at him. And if a husband has paid money for his wife to several men, none of these men may ever utter his name or look him in the face. If one of them did by chance look at him, the offended husband would destroy some of the offender's property.[4] In New Caledonia a brother may not mention his sister's name, and she may not mention his. The same rule is observed by male and female cousins in regard to each other's names.[5] In the Banks' Islands, Melanesia, the taboos laid on the names of persons connected by marriage are very strict. A man will not mention the name of his father-in-law, much less

[1] *Reports of the Cambridge Anthropological Expedition to Torres Straits,* v. 142 *sq.*

[2] Dr. Hahl, "Über die Rechtsanschauungen der Eingeborenen eines Teiles der Blanchebucht und des Innern der Gazelle Halbinsel," *Nachrichten über Kaiser Wilhelms - Land und den Bismarck - Archipel,* 1897, p. 80 ; O. Schellong, in *Zeitschrift für Ethnologie,* xxi. (1889) p. 12.

[3] P. A. Kleintitschen, *Die Küsten-*

bewohner der Gazellehalbinsel, pp. 190, 238.

[4] Rev. W. O'Ferrall, "Native Stories from Santa Cruz and Reef Islands," *Journal of the Anthropological Institute,* xxxiv. (1904) pp. 223 *sq.*

[5] Father Lambert, "Mœurs et superstitions de la tribu Belep," *Missions Catholiques,* xii. (1880) pp. 30, 68 ; *id., Mœurs et superstitions des Néo-Calédoniens* (Nouméa, 1900), pp. 94 *sq.*

the name of his mother-in-law, nor may he name his wife's brother; but he may name his wife's sister—she is nothing to him.   A woman may not name her father-in-law, nor on any account her son-in-law.   Two people whose children have intermarried are also debarred from mentioning each other's names.   And not only are all these persons forbidden to utter each other's names; they may not even pronounce ordinary words which chance to be either identical with these names or to have any syllables in common with them.   "A man on one occasion spoke to me of his house as a shed, and when that was not understood, went and touched it with his hand to shew what he meant; a difficulty being still made, he looked round to be sure that no one was near and whispered, not the name of his son's wife, but the respectful substitute for her name, *amen Mulegona,* she who was with his son, and whose name was Tuwarina, Hind-house."   Again, we hear of a native of these islands who might not use the common words for "pig" and "to die," because these words occurred in the polysyllabic name of his son-in-law; and we are told of another unfortunate who might not pronounce the everyday words for "hand" and "hot" on account of his wife's brother's name, and who was even debarred from mentioning the number "one," because the word for "one" formed part of the name of his wife's cousin.[1]

It might be expected that similar taboos on the names of relations and on words resembling them would commonly occur among the aborigines of Australia, and that some light might be thrown on their origin and meaning by the primitive modes of thought and forms of society prevalent among these savages.   Yet this expectation can scarcely be said to be fulfilled; for the evidence of the observance of such customs in Australia is scanty and hardly of a nature to explain their origin.   We are told that there are instances "in which the names of natives are never allowed to be spoken, as those of a father or mother-in-law, of a son-in-law, and some cases arising from a connection with each other's wives."[2]   Among some Victorian tribes, a man never at

---

[1] R. H. Codrington, *The Melanesians,* pp. 43 *sq.*

[2] E. J. Eyre, *Journals of Expeditions,* ii. 339.

any time mentioned the name of his mother-in-law, and from the time of his betrothal to his death neither she nor her sisters might ever look at or speak to him. He might not go within fifty yards of their habitation, and when he met them on a path they immediately left it, clapped their hands, and covering up their heads with their rugs, walked in a stooping posture and spoke in whispers until he had gone by. They might not talk with him, and when he and they spoke to other people in each other's presence, they used a special form of speech which went by the name of "turn tongue." This was not done with any intention of concealing their meaning, for "turn tongue" was understood by everybody.[1] A writer, who enjoyed unusually favourable opportunities of learning the language and customs of the Victorian aborigines, informs us that "A stupid custom existed among them, which they called *knal-oyne*. Whenever a female child was promised in marriage to any man, from that very hour neither he nor the child's mother were permitted to look upon or hear each other speak nor hear their names mentioned by others; for, if they did, they would immediately grow prematurely old and die."[2] Among the Gudangs of Cape York, in Queensland, and the Kowraregas of the Prince of Wales Islands, a man carefully avoids speaking to or even mentioning the name of his mother-in-law, and his wife acts similarly with regard to her father-in-law. "Thus the mother of a person called Nuki—which means water—is obliged to call water by another name."[3] In the Booandik tribe of South Australia persons connected by marriage, except husbands and wives, spoke to each other in a low whining voice, and employed words different from those in common use.[4] Another writer, speaking of

---

[1] J. Dawson, *Australian Aborigines*, p. 29. Specimens of this peculiar form of speech are given by Mr. Dawson. For example, "It will be very warm by and by" was expressed in the ordinary language *Baawan kulluun*; in "turn tongue" it was *Gnullewa gnatnæn tirambuul*.

[2] Joseph Parker, in Brough Smyth's *Aborigines of Victoria*, ii. 156.

[3] J. Macgillivray, *Narrative of the*

Voyage of H.M.S. Rattlesnake (London, 1852), ii. 10 *sq.* It is obvious that the example given by the writer does not illustrate his general statement. Apparently he means to say that Nuki is the son-in-law, not the son, of the woman in question, and that the prohibition to mention the names of persons standing in that relationship is mutual.

[4] Mrs. James Smith, *The Booandik Tribe*, p. 5.

the same tribe, says : " Mothers-in-law and sons-in-law studiously avoid each other.   A father-in-law converses with his son-in-law in a low tone of voice, and in a phraseology differing somewhat from the ordinary one." [1]

It will perhaps occur to the reader that customs of this latter sort may possibly have originated in the intermarriage of tribes speaking different languages ; and there are some Australian facts which seem at first sight to favour this supposition.   Thus with regard to the natives of South Australia we are told that " the principal mark of distinction between the tribes is difference of language or dialect ; where the tribes intermix greatly no inconvenience is experienced on this account, as every person understands, in addition to his own dialect, that of the neighbouring tribe ; the consequence is that two persons commonly converse in two languages, just as an Englishman and German would hold a conversation, each person speaking his own language, but understanding that of the other as well as his own.   This peculiarity will often occur in one family through inter-marriages, neither party ever thinking of changing his or her dialect for that of the other.   Children do not always adopt the language of the mother, but that of the tribe among whom they live." [2]   Among some tribes of western Victoria a man was actually forbidden to marry a wife who spoke the same dialect as himself; and during the preliminary visit, which each paid to the tribe of the other, neither was permitted to speak the language of the tribe which he or she was visiting.   The children spoke the language of their father and might never mix it with any other.   To her children the mother spoke in their father's language, but to her husband she spoke in her own, and he answered her in his ; " so that all conversation is carried on between husband and wife in the same way as between an Englishman and a Frenchwoman, each speaking his or her own language. This very remarkable law explains the preservation of so many distinct dialects within so limited a space, even where there are no physical obstacles to ready and frequent

These taboos can hardly be accounted for by the inter-marriage of tribes speaking different languages.

---

[1] D. Stewart, in E. M. Curr's *Australian Race*, iii. 461.

[2] C. W. Schürmann, in *Native*

Tribes of South Australia (Adelaide, 1879), p. 249.

communication between the tribes."[1]   So amongst the
Sakais, an aboriginal race of the Malay Peninsula, a man goes
to a considerable distance for a wife, generally to a tribe
who speak quite a different dialect.[2]   The Indian tribes of
French Guiana have each their own dialect and would hardly
be able to understand each other, were it not that almost
every person marries a wife or a husband of a different tribe,
and thus the newcomers serve as interpreters between the
tribe in which they live and that in which they were born
and brought up.[3]   It is well known that the Carib women
spoke a language which differed in some respects from that
of the men, and the explanation generally given of the
difference is that the women preserved the language of a
race of whom the men had been exterminated and the
women married by the Caribs.   This explanation is not, as
some seem to suppose, a mere hypothesis of the learned,
devised to clear up a curious discrepancy ; it was a tradition
current among the Caribs themselves in the seventeenth
century,[4] and as such it deserves serious attention.   But
there are other facts which seem to point to a different
explanation.[5]   Among the Carayahis, a tribe of Brazilian
Indians on the Rio Grande or Araguaya River, the dialect
of the women differs from that of the men.   For the most
part the differences are limited to the form and sound of the

[1] J. Dawson, *Australian Aborigines*,
pp. 27, 30 *sq.*, 40. So among the
Gowmditch - mara tribe of western
Victoria the child spoke his father's
language, and not his mother's, when
she happened to be of another tribe
(Fison and Howitt, *Kamilaroi and
Kurnai*, p. 276). Compare A. W.
Howitt, *Native Tribes of South-East
Australia*, pp. 250 *sq.*

[2] A. Hale, "On the Sakais," *Journal
of the Anthropological Institute*, xv.
(1886) p. 291.

[3] H. A. Coudreau, *La France
équinoxiale* (Paris, 1887), ii. 178.

[4] De Rochefort, *Histoire naturelle
et morale des Iles Antilles de l'Amerique*[2] (Rotterdam, 1665), pp. 349 *sq.* ;
De la Borde, " Relation de l'origine,
etc., des Caraibs sauvages des Isles
Antilles de l'Amerique," pp. 4, 39
(*Recueil de divers voyages faits en*

*Afrique et en Amerique, qui n'ont point
esté encore publiez*, Paris, 1684) ;
Lafitau, *Mœurs des sauvages ameriquains*, i. 55. On the language of
the Carib women see also Jean Bap-
tiste du Tertre, *Histoire generale des
Isles de S. Christophe, de la Guadeloupe, de la Martinique et autres dans
l'Amerique* (Paris, 1654), p. 462 ;
Labat, *Nouveau Voyage aux isles de
l'Amerique* (Paris, 1713), vi. 127 *sq.* ;
J. N. Rat, " The Carib Language,"
Journal of the Anthropological Institute,
xxvii. (1898) pp. 311 *sq.*

[5] See C. Sapper, " Mittelamericani-
sche Caraiben," *Internationales Archiv
für Ethnographie*, x. (1897) pp. 56 *sqq.* ;
and my article, " A Suggestion as to the
Origin of Gender in Language," *Fort-
nightly Review*, January 1900, pp.
79-90 ; also *Totemism and Exogamy*,
iv. 237 *sq.*

words ; only a few words seem to be quite distinct in the
two dialects.   The speech of the women appears to preserve
older and fuller forms than that of the men : for instance,
" girl " is *yadokoma* in the female speech but *yadôma* in the
male ; " nail " is *desika* in the mouth of a woman but *desia*
in the mouth of a man.[1]   However such remarkable differ- Inter-
ences are to be explained, a little reflection will probably mixture of
convince us that a mere intermixture of races speaking speaking
different tongues could scarcely account for the phenomena different
of language under consideration.   For the reluctance to would
mention the names or even syllables of the names of persons account for
connected with the speaker by marriage can hardly be the taboos
separated from the reluctance evinced by so many people names of
to utter their own names or the names of the dead or of relations.
chiefs and kings ; and if the reticence as to these latter
names springs mainly from superstition, we may infer that
the reticence as to the former has no better foundation.
That the savage's unwillingness to mention his own name is
based, at least in part, on a superstitious fear of the ill use
that might be made of it by his foes, whether human or
spiritual, has already been shewn.   It remains to examine
the similar usage in regard to the names of the dead and of
royal personages.

§ 3. *Names of the Dead tabooed*

The custom of abstaining from all mention of the names The names
of the dead was observed in antiquity by the Albanians of of the
the Caucasus,[2] and at the present day it is in full force general not
among many savage tribes.   Thus we are told that one of mentioned
the customs most rigidly observed and enforced amongst the Australian
Australian aborigines is never to mention the name of a aborigines.
deceased person, whether male or female ; to name aloud
one who has departed this life would be a gross violation of
their most sacred prejudices, and they carefully abstain from
it.[3]   The chief motive for this abstinence appears to be a

[1] P. Ehrenreich, " Materialien zur
Sprachenkunde Brasiliens," *Zeitschrift
für Ethnologie,* xxvi. (1894) pp. 23-35.
[2] Strabo, xi. 4. 8, p. 503.
[3] G. Grey, *Journals of Two Expedi-*
*tions of Discovery in North-West and
Western Australia* (London, 1841), ii.
232, 257.   The writer is here speaking
especially of western Australia, but his
statement applies, with certain restric-

The
names of
the dead
are not
generally
mentioned
by the
Australian
aborigines.

fear of evoking the ghost, although the natural unwillingness
to revive past sorrows undoubtedly operates also to draw the
veil of oblivion over the names of the dead.[1]   Once Mr.
Oldfield so terrified a native by shouting out the name of a
deceased person, that the man fairly took to his heels and
did not venture to shew himself again for several days.   At
their next meeting he bitterly reproached the rash white man
for his indiscretion ; " nor could I," adds Mr. Oldfield, " induce
him by any means to utter the awful sound of a dead man's
name, for by so doing he would have placed himself in the
power of the malign spirits." [2]   On another occasion, a
Watchandie woman having mentioned the name of a certain
man, was informed that he had long been dead.   At that she
became greatly excited and spat thrice to counteract the
evil effect of having taken a dead man's name into her lips.
This custom of spitting thrice, as Mr. Oldfield afterwards
learned, was the regular charm whereby the natives freed
themselves from the power of the dangerous spirits whom
they had provoked by such a rash act.[3]   Among the
aborigines of Victoria the dead were very rarely spoken of,
and then never by their names ; they were referred to in a
subdued voice as " the lost one " or " the poor fellow that is
no more."   To speak of them by name would, it was supposed, excite the malignity of Couit-gil, the spirit of the
departed, which hovers on earth for a time before it departs
for ever towards the setting sun.[4]   Once when a Kurnai

tions which will be mentioned presently,
to all parts of the continent. For evidence see D. Collins, *Account of the
English Colony in New South Wales*
(London, 1804), p. 390 ; Hueber,
" À travers l'Australie," *Bulletin de
la Société de Géographie* (Paris), Vme
Série, ix. (1865) p. 429 ; S. Gason,
in *Native Tribes of South Australia*, p.
275 ; R. Brough Smyth, *Aborigines of
Victoria*, i. 120, ii. 297 ; A. L. P.
Cameron, in *Journal of the Anthropological Institute*, xiv. (1885) p. 363 ;
E. M. Curr, *The Australian Race*, i.
88, 338, ii. 195, iii. 22, 29, 139, 166,
596 ; J. D. Lang, *Queensland* (London,
1861), pp. 367, 387, 388 ; C. Lumholtz,
Among Cannibals (London, 1889), p.
279 ; *Report on the Work of the Horn*

*Scientific Expedition to Central Aus-
tralia* (London and Melbourne, 1896),
pp. 137, 168.   More evidence is
adduced below.

[1] On this latter motive see especially
the remarks of A. W. Howitt, in
Kamilaroi and Kurnai, p. 249.   Compare also C. W. Schürmann, in *Native
Tribes of South Australia*, p. 247 ;
F. Bonney, in *Journal of the Anthropological Institute*, xiii. (1884) p.
127.

[2] A. Oldfield, "The Aborigines of
Australia," *Transactions of the Ethnological Society of London*, N.S., iii.
(1865) p. 238.

[3] A. Oldfield, *op. cit.* p. 240.

[4] W. Stanbridge, "On the Aborigines of Victoria," *Transactions of the*

man was spoken to about a dead friend, soon after the decease, he looked round uneasily and said, " Do not do that, he might hear you and kill me ! "[1]   If a Kaiabara black dies, his tribes-people never mention his name, but call him *Wurponum,* " the dead," and in order to explain who it is that has died, they speak of his father, mother, brothers, and so forth.[2]   Of the tribes on the Lower Murray River we are told that when a person dies " they carefully avoid mentioning his name ; but if compelled to do so, they pronounce it in a very low whisper, so faint that they imagine the spirit cannot hear their voice."[3]   Amongst the tribes of Central Australia no one may utter the name of the deceased during the period of mourning, unless it is absolutely necessary to do so, and then it is only done in a whisper for fear of disturbing and annoying the man's spirit which is walking about in ghostly form.   If the ghost hears his name mentioned he concludes that his kinsfolk are not mourning for him properly ; if their grief were genuine they could not bear to bandy his name about.   Touched to the quick by their hard-hearted indifference, the indignant ghost will come and trouble them in dreams.[4]   In these tribes no woman may ever again mention the name of a dead person, but the restriction on the male sex is not so absolute, for the name may be mentioned by men of the two subclasses to which the wife's father and wife's brother of the deceased belong.[5]   Among some tribes of north-western Australia a dead man's name is never mentioned after his burial and he is only spoken of as " that one " ; otherwise they think that he would return and frighten them at night in camp.[6]

The same reluctance to utter the names of the dead appears to prevail among all the Indian tribes of America from Hudson's Bay Territory to Patagonia.   Among the *The names of the dead are not uttered*

Ethnological Society of London, N.S., i. (1861) p. 299.

[1] A. W. Howitt, " On some Australian Beliefs," *Journal of the Anthropological Institute,* xiii. (1884) p. 191 ; *id., Native Tribes of South-East Australia,* p. 440.

[2] *Id., Native Tribes of South-East Australia,* p. 469.

[3] G. F. Angas, *Savage Life and*

Scenes in Australia and New Zealand (London, 1847), i. 94.

[4] Spencer and Gillen, *Native Tribes of Central Australia,* p. 498.

[5] Spencer and Gillen, *Northern Tribes of Central Australia,* p. 526.

[6] E. Clement, " Ethnographical Notes on the Western Australian Aborigines," *Internationales Archiv für Ethnographie,* xvi. (1904) p. 9.

by the
American
Indians.

Iroquois, for example, the name of the deceased was never mentioned after the period of mourning had expired.[1] The same rule was rigidly observed by the Indians of California and Oregon ; its transgression might be punished with a heavy fine or even with death.[2] Thus among the Karok of California we are told that "the highest crime one can commit is the *pet-chi-é-ri*, the mere mention of the dead relative's name. It is a deadly insult to the survivors, and can be atoned for only by the same amount of blood-money paid for wilful murder. In default of that they will have the villain's blood."[3] Amongst the Wintun, also of California, if some one in a group of merry talkers inadvertently mentions the name of a deceased person, "straightway there falls upon all an awful silence. No words can describe the shuddering and heart-sickening terror which seizes upon them at the utterance of that fearful word."[4] Among the Goajiros of Colombia to mention the dead before his kinsmen is a dreadful offence, which is often punished with death ; for if it happen on the *rancho* of the deceased, in presence of his nephew or uncle, they will assuredly kill the offender on the spot if they can. But if he escapes, the penalty resolves itself into a heavy fine, usually of two or more oxen.[5] So among the Abipones of Paraguay to mention the departed by name was a serious crime, which often led to blows and bloodshed. When it was needful to refer to such an one, it was done by means of a general phrase such as "he who is no more," eked out with particulars which served to identify the person meant.[6]

[1] L. H. Morgan, *League of the Iroquois* (Rochester, U.S., 1851), p. 175.

[2] A. S. Gatschett, *The Klamath Indians of South-Western Oregon* (Washington, 1890) (*Contributions to North American Ethnology*, vol. ii. pt. 1), p. xli ; Chase, quoted by H. H. Bancroft, *Native Races of the Pacific States*, i. 357, note 76.

[3] S. Powers, *Tribes of California*, p. 33 ; compare p. 68.

[4] S. Powers, *op. cit.* p. 240.

[5] F. A. Simons, "An Exploration of the Goajira Peninsula, U.S. of Colombia," *Proceedings of the Royal Geographical Society*, vii. (1885) p. 791.

[6] M. Dobrizhoffer, *Historia de Abiponibus*, ii. 301, 498. For more evidence of the observance of this taboo among the American Indians see A. Woldt, *Captain Jacobsen's Reise an der Nordwestküste Americas* (Leipsic, 1884), p. 57 (as to the Indians of the north-west coast) ; W. Colquhoun Grant, "Description of Vancouver's Island," *Journal of the Royal Geographical Society*, xxvii. (1857) p. 303 (as to Vancouver Island) ; Capt. Wilson, "Report on the Indian Tribes," *Transactions of the Ethnological Society of London*, N.S., iv. (1866) p. 286 (as to Vancouver Island and neighbour-

A similar reluctance to mention the names of the dead is reported of peoples so widely separated from each other as the Samoyeds of Siberia and the Todas of southern India ; the Mongols of Tartary and the Tuaregs of the Sahara ; the Ainos of Japan and the Akamba and Nandi of central Africa ; the Tinguianes of the Philippines and the inhabitants of the Nicobar Islands, of Borneo, of Madagascar, and of Tasmania.[1] In all cases, even where it is not expressly stated, the fundamental reason for this avoidance is probably the fear of the ghost. That this is the real motive with the Tuaregs of the Sahara we are positively informed. They dread the return of the dead man's spirit, and do all they can to avoid it by shifting their camp after a death, ceasing for ever to pronounce the name of the departed, and eschewing everything that might be regarded as an evocation or recall of his soul. Hence they do not, like the Arabs, designate individuals by adding to their personal names the names of their fathers ; they never speak of So-and-so, son of So-and-so ; they give to every man a name which will live and die with him.[2] So among some of the Victorian tribes in

[margin note] Many other peoples are reluctant to mention the names of the dead.

[margin note] This reluctance seems to be based on a fear of the ghosts, whose attention might be attracted by the mention of their names.

hood) ; C. Hill Tout, in *Journal of the Anthropological Institute*, xxxv. (1905) p. 138 ; *id.*, *The Far West, the Land of the Salish and Déné*, p. 201 ; A. Ross, *Adventures on the Oregon or Columbia River*, p. 322 ; H. R. Schoolcraft, *Indian Tribes*, iv. 226 (as to the Bonaks of California) ; Ch. N. Bell, "The Mosquito Territory," *Journal of the Royal Geographical Society*, xxxii. (1862) p. 255 ; A. Pinart, "Les Indiens de l'Etat de Panama," *Revue d'Ethnographie*, vi. (1887) p. 56 ; G. C. Musters, in *Journal of the Royal Geographical Society*, xli. (1871) p. 68 (as to Patagonia). More evidence is adduced below.

[1] See P. S. Pallas, *Reise durch verschiedene Provinzen des russischen Reichs*, iii. 76 (Samoyeds) ; J. W. Breeks, *Account of the Primitive Tribes and Monuments of the Nīlagiris* (London, 1873), p. 19 ; W. E. Marshall, *Travels amongst the Todas*, p. 177 ; W. H. R. Rivers, *The Todas*, pp. 462, 496, 626 ; Plan de Carpin (de Plano Carpini), *Relation des Mongols ou Tartares*, ed. D'Avezac, cap. iii. § iii. ; H. Duveyrier,

Exploration du Sahara, les Touareg du nord (Paris, 1864), p. 415 ; Lieut. S. C. Holland, "The Ainos," *Journal of the Anthropological Institute*, iii. (1874) p. 238 ; J. Batchelor, *The Ainu and their Folk-lore* (London, 1901), pp. 252, 564 ; J. M. Hildebrandt, "Ethnographische Notizen über Wakamba und ihre Nachbarn," *Zeitschrift für Ethnologie*, x. (1878) p. 405 ; A. C. Hollis, *The Nandi*, p. 71 ; F. Blumentritt, *Versuch einer Ethnographie der Philippinen* (Gotha, 1882), p. 38 (*Petermann's Mittheilungen*, *Ergänzungsheft*, No. 67) ; N. Fontana, "On the Nicobar Isles," *Asiatick Researches*, iii. (London, 1799) p. 154 ; W. H. Furness, *Folk-lore in Borneo* (Wallingford, Pennsylvania, 1899), p. 26 ; A. van Gennep, *Tabou et totémisme à Madagascar*, pp. 70 *sq.* ; J. E. Calder, "Native Tribes of Tasmania," *Journal of the Anthropological Institute*, iii. (1874) p. 23 ; J. Bonwick, *Daily Life of the Tasmanians*, pp. 97, 145, 183.

[2] H. Duveyrier, *Exploration du Sahara, les Touareg du nord*, p. 431.

Australia personal names were rarely perpetuated, because the natives believed that any one who adopted the name of a deceased person would not live long;[1] probably his ghostly namesake was supposed to come and fetch him away to the spirit-land. The Yabims of German New Guinea, who believe that the spirits of the dead pass their time in the forest eating unpalatable fruits, are unwilling to mention the names of the deceased lest their ghosts should suspend their habitual occupation to come and trouble the living.[2] In Logea, one of the Samarai Archipelago, off the south-eastern end of New Guinea, no custom is observed so strictly as the one which forbids the naming of the dead in presence of their relations. To say to a person "Your fathers are dead," is considered a direct challenge to fight; it is an insult which must be avenged either by the death of the man who pronounced these awful words, or by the death of one of his relatives or friends. The uttering of the names of the dead is, along with homicide, one of the chief causes of war in the island. When it is necessary to refer to a dead man they designate him by such a phrase as "the father of So-and-so," or "the brother of So-and-so."[3] Thus the fear of mentioning the names of the dead gives rise to circumlocutions of precisely the same sort as those which originate in a reluctance to name living people. Among the Klallam Indians of Washington State no person may bear the name of his deceased father, grandfather, or any other direct ancestor in the paternal line.[4] The Masai of eastern Africa are said to resort to a simple device which enables them to speak of the dead freely without risk of the inopportune appearance of the ghost. As soon as a man or woman dies, they change his or her name, and henceforth always speak of him or her by the new name, while the old name falls into oblivion, and

---

[1] J. Dawson, *Australian Aborigines*, p. 42.

[2] K. Vetter, *Komm herüber und hilf uns!* iii. (Barmen, 1898) p. 24; *id.*, in *Nachrichten über Kaiser Wilhelms-Land und den Bismarck-Archipel*, 1897, p. 92.

[3] Dr. L. Loria, "Notes on the ancient War Customs of the Natives of Logea," *British New Guinea, Annual Report for 1894-95*, pp. 45, 46 *sq.* Compare M. Krieger, *Neu-Guinea*, p. 322.

[4] Myron Eels, "The Twana, Chemakum, and Klallam Indians of Washington Territory," *Annual Report of the Smithsonian Institute for 1887*, part i. p. 656.

to utter it in the presence of a kinsman of the deceased is
an insult which calls for vengeance. They assume that the
dead man will not know his new name, and so will not
answer to it when he hears it pronounced.[1] Ghosts are
notoriously dull-witted; nothing is easier than to dupe
them. However, according to another and more probable
account, the name of a Masai is not changed after his
death; it is merely suppressed, and he or she is referred to
by a descriptive phrase, such as "my brother," "my uncle,"
"my sister." To call a dead man by his name is deemed
most unlucky, and is never done except with the intention
of doing harm to his surviving family, who make great
lamentations on such an occasion.[2]

The same fear of the ghost, which moves people to
suppress his old name, naturally leads all persons who bear
a similar name to exchange it for another, lest its utterance
should attract the attention of the ghost, who cannot
reasonably be expected to discriminate between all the
different applications of the same name. Thus we are told
that in the Adelaide and Encounter Bay tribes of South
Australia the repugnance to mentioning the names of
those who have died lately is carried so far, that persons
who bear the same name as the deceased abandon it, and
either adopt temporary names or are known by any others
that happen to belong to them.[3] The same practice was
observed by the aborigines of New South Wales,[4] and is
said to be observed by the tribes of the Lower Murray
River,[5] and of King George's Sound in western Australia.[6]
A similar custom prevails among some of the Queensland
tribes; but the prohibition to use the names of the dead is
not permanent, though it may last for many years. On the

The like
fear leads
people who
bear the
same name
as the dead
to change
it for
another.

---

[1] Baron C. C. von der Decken,
Reisen in Ost-Afrika (Leipsic, 1869-
1871), ii. 25; R. Andree, *Ethnographische Parallelen und Vergleiche*,
pp. 182 *sq.*
[2] S. L. Hinde and H. Hinde, *The
last of the Masai* (London, 1901), p.
50; Sir H. Johnston, *The Uganda
Protectorate*, ii. 826.
[3] W. Wyatt, in *Native Tribes of
South Australia*, p. 165.
[4] D. Collins, *Account of the English

Colony in New South Wales (London,
1804), p. 392.
[5] P. Beveridge, "Notes on the
Dialects, Habits, and Mythology of the
Lower Murray Aborigines," *Transactions of the Royal Society of Victoria*,
vi. 20 *sq.*
[6] "Description of the Natives of
King George's Sound (Swan River) and
adjoining Country," *Journal of the R.
Geographical Society*, i. (1832) pp. 46
sq.

People
bearing the
same
name as
the dead
change it
from fear
of the
ghost. Bloomfield River, when a namesake dies, the survivor is
called Tanyu, a word whose meaning is unknown; or else
he or she receives a name which refers to the corpse, with
the syllable Wau prefixed to it.   For example, he may be
called Wau-batcha, with reference to the place where the
man was buried; or Wau-wotchinyu ("burnt"), with reference to the cremation of the body.   And if there should be
several people in camp all bearing one of these allusive
designations, they are distinguished from each other by the
mention of the names of their mothers or other relatives,
even though these last have long been dead and gone.
Whenever Mr. W. E. Roth, to whom we owe this information, could obtain an explanation of the custom, the reason
invariably assigned was a fear that the ghost, hearing himself
called by name, might return and cause mischief.[1]   In some
Australian tribes the change of name thus brought about is
permanent; the old name is laid aside for ever, and the
man is known by his new name for the rest of his life, or at
least until he is obliged to change it again for a like reason.[2]
Among the North American Indians all persons, whether
men or women, who bore the name of one who had just died
were obliged to abandon it and to adopt other names, which
was formally done at the first ceremony of mourning for
the dead.[3]   In some tribes to the east of the Rocky
Mountains this change of name lasted only during the
season of mourning,[4] but in other tribes on the Pacific
Coast of North America it seems to have been permanent.[5]
Amongst the Masai also, when two men of the same tribe
bear the same name, and one of them dies, the survivor
changes his name.[6]

Sometimes by an extension of the same reasoning all
the near relations of the deceased change their names, what-

[1] W. E. Roth, *North Queensland
Ethnography*, Bulletin No. 5 (Brisbane, 1903), § 72, p. 20.
[2] G. F. Angas, *Savage Life and
Scenes in Australia and New Zealand*
(London, 1847), ii. 228.
[3] J. F. Lafitau, *Mœurs des sauvages
ameriquains*, ii. 434; R. Southey,
History of Brazil, iii. 894 (referring
to Roger Williams).

[4] Charlevoix, *Histoire de la Nouvelle
France*, vi. 109.
[5] S. Powers, *Tribes of California*,
p. 349; Myron Eels, "The Twana,
Chemakum, and Klallam Indians of
Washington Territory," *Annual Report
of the Smithsonian Institute for 1887*,
p. 656.
[6] S. L. Hinde and H. Hinde, *The
Last of the Masai*, p. 50.

ever they may happen to be, doubtless from a fear that the
sound of the familiar names might lure back the vagrant
spirit to its old home.   Thus in some Victorian tribes the
ordinary names of all the next of kin were disused during
the period of mourning, and certain general terms, prescribed
by custom, were substituted for them.   To call a mourner
by his own name was considered an insult to the departed,
and often led to fighting and bloodshed.[1]   Among Indian
tribes of north-western America near relations of the deceased
often change their names " under an impression that spirits
will be attracted back to earth if they hear familiar names
often repeated." [2]   Among the Kiowa Indians the name of
the dead is never spoken in the presence of the relatives, and
on the death of any member of a family all the others take
new names.   This custom was noted by Raleigh's colonists
on Roanoke Island more than three centuries ago.[3]   Among
the Lengua Indians of the Gran Chaco in South America not
only is a dead man's name never mentioned, but all the
survivors change their names also.   They say that Death has
been among them and has carried off a list of the living, and
that he will soon come back for more victims ; hence in order
to defeat his fell purpose they change their names, believing
that on his return Death, though he has got them all on his
list, will not be able to identify them under their new names,
and will depart to pursue the search elsewhere.[4]   So among
the Guaycurus of the Gran Chaco, when a death had taken
place, the chief used to change the names of every person in
the tribe, man and woman, young and old, and it is said to
have been wonderful to observe how from that moment
everybody remembered his new name just as if he had borne
it all his life.[5]   Nicobarese mourners take new names in
order to escape the unwelcome attentions of the ghost ; and

Sometimes all the near relations of the deceased change their names.

---

[1] J. Dawson, *Australian Aborigines,*
p. 42.

[2] H. H. Bancroft, *Native Races of
the Pacific States,* i. 248.   Compare
K. F. v. Baer und Gr. v. Helmersen,
*Beiträge zur Kenntniss des russischen
Reiches und der angränzenden Länder
Asiens,* i. (St. Petersburg, 1839), p.
108 (as to the Kenayens of Cook's
Inlet and the neighbourhood).

[3] J. Mooney, " Calendar History of

the Kiowa Indians," *Seventeenth Annual
Report of the Bureau of American Ethnology,* part i. (Washington, 1898) p.
231.

[4] F. de Azara, *Voyages dans
l'Amérique Méridionale* (Paris, 1808),
ii. 153 *sq.*

[5] P. Lozano, *Descripcion choro-
graphica,* etc., *del Gran Chaco* (Cordova,
1733), p. 70.

for the same purpose they disguise themselves by shaving their heads so that the ghost is unable to recognise them.[1] The Chukchees of Bering Strait believe that the souls of the dead turn into malignant spirits who seek to harm the living. Hence when a mother dies the name of her youngest and dearest child is changed, in order that her ghost may not know the child.[2]

When the name of the deceased is that of a common object, the word is often dropped in ordinary speech and another substituted for it. Further, when the name of the deceased happens to be that of some common object, such as an animal, or plant, or fire, or water, it is sometimes considered necessary to drop that word in ordinary speech and replace it by another. A custom of this sort, it is plain, may easily be a potent agent of change in language; for where it prevails to any considerable extent many words must constantly become obsolete and new ones spring up. And this tendency has been remarked by observers who have recorded the custom in Australia, America, and elsewhere. For example, with regard to the Australian aborigines it has been noted that "the dialects change with almost every tribe. Some tribes name their children after natural objects; and when the person so named dies, the word is never again mentioned; another word has therefore to be invented for the object after which the child was called." The writer gives as an instance the case of a man whose name Karla signified "fire"; when Karla died, a new word for fire had to be introduced. "Hence," adds the writer, "the language is always changing."[3] In the Moorunde tribe the name for "teal" used to be *torpool*; but when a boy called Torpool died, a new name (*tilquaitch*) was given to the bird, and the old name dropped out altogether from the language of the tribe.[4] Sometimes, however, such substitutes for common words were only in vogue for a limited time after the death, and were then discarded in favour of the old words. Thus among the Kowraregas of the Prince of Wales' Islands and

[1] E. H. Man, "Notes on the Nicobarese," *Indian Antiquary*, xxviii. (1899) p. 261. Elsewhere I have suggested that mourning costume in general may have been adopted with this intention. See *Journal of the Anthropological Institute*, xv. (1886) pp. 73, 98 *sqq.*

[2] J. Enderli, "Zwei Jahre bei den Tchuktschen und Korjaken," *Petermanns Mitteilungen*, xlix. (1903) p. 257.

[3] R. Brough Smyth, *Aborigines of Victoria*, ii. 266.

[4] E. J. Eyre, *Journals of Expeditions of Discovery*, ii. 354 *sq.*

the Gudangs of Cape York in Queensland, the names of the
dead are never mentioned without great reluctance, so that,
for example, when a man named Us, or quartz, died, the
name of the stone was changed to *nattam ure*, "the thing
which is a namesake," but the original word would gradually
return to common use.[1]   Again, a missionary, who lived
among the Victorian aborigines, remarks that "it is
customary among these blacks to disuse a word when a
person has died whose name was the same, or even of the
same sound.   I find great difficulty in getting blacks to
repeat such words.   I believe this custom is common to all
the Victorian tribes, though in course of time the word is
resumed again.   I have seen among the Murray blacks the
dead freely spoken of when they have been dead some
time."[2]   Again, in the Encounter Bay tribe of South
Australia, if a man of the name of Ngnke, which means
"water," were to die, the whole tribe would be obliged to
use some other word to express water for a considerable
time after his decease.   The writer who records this custom
surmises that it may explain the presence of a number of
synonyms in the language of the tribe.[3]   This conjecture is
confirmed by what we know of some Victorian tribes whose
speech comprised a regular set of synonyms to be used
instead of the common terms by all members of a tribe in
times of mourning.   For instance, if a man called Waa
("crow") departed this life, during the period of mourning
for him nobody might call a crow a *waa*; everybody had to
speak of the bird as a *narrapart*.   When a person who
rejoiced in the title of Ringtail Opossum (*weearn*) had
gone the way of all flesh, his sorrowing relations and the
tribe at large were bound for a time to refer to ringtail
opossums by the more sonorous name of *manuungkuurt*.
If the community were plunged in grief for the loss of a
respected female who bore the honourable name of Turkey
Bustard, the proper name for turkey bustards, which was
barrim barrim, went out, and *tillit tilliitsh* came in.   And so

---

[1] J. Macgillivray, *Narrative of the Voyage of H.M.S. Rattlesnake* (London, 1852), ii. 10 *sq.*
[2] J. Bulmer, in Brough Smyth's *Aborigines of Victoria*, ii. 94.
[3] H. E. A. Meyer, in *Native Tribes of South Australia*, p. 199, compare p. xxix.

mutatis mutandis with the names of Black Cockatoo, Grey Duck, Gigantic Crane, Kangaroo, Eagle, Dingo, and the rest.[1]

This custom has transformed some of the languages of the American Indians.

A similar custom used to be constantly transforming the language of the Abipones of Paraguay, amongst whom, however, a word once abolished seems never to have been revived. New words, says the missionary Dobrizhoffer, sprang up every year like mushrooms in a night, because all words that resembled the names of the dead were abolished by proclamation and others coined in their place. The mint of words was in the hands of the old women of the tribe, and whatever term they stamped with their approval and put in circulation was immediately accepted without a murmur by high and low alike, and spread like wildfire through every camp and settlement of the tribe. You would be astonished, says the same missionary, to see how meekly the whole nation acquiesces in the decision of a withered old hag, and how completely the old familiar words fall instantly out of use and are never repeated either through force of habit or forgetfulness. In the seven years that Dobrizhoffer spent among these Indians the native word for jaguar was changed thrice, and the words for crocodile, thorn, and the slaughter of cattle underwent similar though less varied vicissitudes. As a result of this habit, the vocabularies of the missionaries teemed with erasures, old words having constantly to be struck out as obsolete and new ones inserted in their place.[2] Similarly, a peculiar feature of the Comanche language is that a portion of the vocabulary is continually changing. If, for example, a person called Eagle or Bison dies, a new name is invented for the bird or beast, because it is forbidden to mention the name of any one who is dead.[3] So amongst the Kiowa Indians all words that suggest the name of a deceased person are dropped for a term of years and other words

[1] J. Dawson, *Australian Aborigines*, p. 43. Mr. Howitt mentions the case of a native who arbitrarily substituted the name *nobler* ("spirituous liquor") for *yan* ("water") because Yan was the name of a man who had recently died (*Kamilaroi and Kurnai*, p. 249).

[2] M. Dobrizhoffer, *Historia de Abiponibus* (Vienna, 1784), ii. 199, 301.

[3] H. Ten Kate, "Notes ethnographiques sur les Comanches," *Revue d'Ethnographie*, iv. (1885) p. 131.

are substituted for them. The old word may after the lapse of years be restored, but it often happens that the new one keeps its place and the original word is entirely forgotten. Old men sometimes remember as many as three different names which have been successively used for the same thing. The new word is commonly a novel combination of existing roots, or a novel use of a current word, rather than a deliberately invented term.[1]

The Basagala, a cattle-breeding people to the west of Uganda, cease to use a word if it was the name of an influential person who has died. For example, after the death of a chief named Mwenda, which means "nine," the name for the numeral was changed.[2] "On the death of a child, or a warrior, or a woman amongst the Masai, the body is thrown away, and the person's name is buried, *i.e.* it is never again mentioned by the family. Should there be anything which is called by that name, it is given another name which is not like that of the deceased. For instance, if an unimportant person called Ol-onana (he who is soft, or weak, or gentle) were to die, gentleness would not be called *enanai* in that kraal, but it would be called by another name, such as *epolpol* (it is smooth). . . . If an elder dies leaving children, his name is not buried for his descendants are named after him."[3] From this statemnet, which is translated from a native account in the Masai language, we may perhaps infer that among the Masai it is as a rule only the childless dead whose names are avoided. In the island of Buru it is unlawful to mention the names of the dead or any words that resemble them in sound.[4] In many tribes of British New Guinea the names of persons are also the names of common things. The people believe that if the name of a deceased person is pronounced, his spirit will return, and as they have no wish to see it back among them the mention of his name is tabooed and a new word

A similar custom has modified languages in Africa, Buru, New Guinea, and the Caroline Islands.

---

[1] J. Mooney, "Calendar History of the Kiowa Indians," *Seventeenth Annual Report of the Bureau of American Ethnology*, part i. (Washington, 1898) p. 231.

[2] Rev. J. Roscoe in a letter to me dated Mengo, Uganda, 17th February 1904.

[3] A. C. Hollis, *The Masai* (Oxford, 1905), pp. 304 *sq.* As to the Masai customs in this respect see also above, pp. 354 *sq.*, 356.

[4] J. H. W. van der Miesen, "Een en ander over Boeroe," *Mededeelingen van wege het Nederlandsche Zendelinggenootschap*, xlvi. (1902) p. 455.

is created to take its place, whenever the name happens to be a common term of the language.[1]　Thus at Waga-waga, near the south-eastern extremity of New Guinea, the names of the dead become taboo immediately after death, and if they are, as generally happens, the names of common objects, new words must be adopted for these things and the old words are dropped from the language, so long at least as the memory of the dead survives.　For example, when a man died whose name Binama meant "hornbill," a new name *ambadina*, literally "the plasterer," was adopted for the bird.　Consequently many words are permanently lost or revived with modified or new meanings.　The frequent changes of vocabulary caused by this custom are very inconvenient, and nowadays the practice of using foreign words as substitutes is coming more and more into vogue.　English profanity now contributes its share to the language of these savages.[2]　In the Caroline Islands the ordinary name for pig is *puik*, but in the Paliker district of Ponape the pig is called not *puik* but *man-teitei*, or "the animal that grubs in the soil," for the word *puik* was there tabooed after the death of a man named Puik. "This is a living instance showing how under our very eyes old words are dropping out of use in these isolated dialects and new ones are taking their place."[3]　In the Nicobar Islands a similar practice has similarly affected the speech of the natives.　"A most singular custom," says Mr. de Roepstorff, "prevails among them which one would suppose must most effectually hinder the 'making of history,' or, at any rate, the transmission of historical narrative.　By a strict rule, which has all the sanction of Nicobar superstition, no man's name may be mentioned after his death !　To such a length is this carried that when, as very frequently happens, the man rejoiced in the name of 'Fowl,' 'Hat,' 'Fire,' 'Road,' etc., in its Nicobarese equivalent, the use of these words is carefully eschewed for the future, not only as being the personal designation of the deceased, but even as the names

A similar practice has altered the speech of the Nico-barese.

---

[1] Sir William Macgregor, *British New Guinea* (London, 1897), p. 79.

[2] C. G. Seligmann, *The Melanesians*

of *British New Guinea* (Cambridge, 1910), pp. 629-631.

[3] F. W. Christian, *The Caroline Islands* (London, 1899), p. 366.

of the common things they represent ; the words die out of
the language, and either new vocables are coined to express
the thing intended, or a substitute for the disused word is
found in other Nicobarese dialects or in some foreign tongue.
This extraordinary custom not only adds an element of
instability to the language, but destroys the continuity of
political life, and renders the record of past events precarious
and vague, if not impossible." [1]

That a superstition which suppresses the names of the
dead must cut at the very root of historical tradition has
been remarked by other workers in this field.   " The
Klamath people," observes Mr. A. S. Gatschet. " possess no
historic traditions going further back in time than a
century, for the simple reason that there was a strict
law prohibiting the mention of the person or acts of a
deceased individual by *using his name.*   This law was
rigidly observed among the Californians no less than among
the Oregonians, and on its transgression the death penalty
could be inflicted.   This is certainly enough to suppress all
historical knowledge within a people.   How can history be
written without names ? " [2]   Among some of the tribes of
New South Wales the simple ditties, never more than two
lines long, to which the natives dance, are never transmitted
from one generation to another, because, when the rude poet
dies, " all the songs of which he was author are, as it were,
buried with him, inasmuch as they, in common with his very
name, are studiously ignored from thenceforward, consequently they are quite forgotten in a very short space of
time indeed.   This custom of endeavouring persistently to
forget everything which had been in any way connected
with the dead entirely precludes the possibility of anything
of an historical nature having existence amongst them ; in

The sup-
pression of
the names
of the dead
cuts at the
root of
a historical
tradition.

---

[1] F. A. de Roepstorff, "Tiom-
berombi, a Nicobar Tale," *Journal of
the Asiatic Society of Bengal,* liii. (1884)
pt. i. pp. 24 *sq.*   In some tribes
apparently the names of the dead are
only tabooed in the presence of their
relations.   See C. Hill-Tout, in " Report of the Committee on the Ethnological Survey of Canada," *Report of
the British Association for the Advancement of Science,* Bradford, 1900,

p. 484 ; G. Brown, *Melanesians and
Polynesians* (London, 1910), p. 399.
But in the great majority of the
accounts which I have consulted no
such limitation of the taboo is mentioned.

[2] A. S. Gatschet, *The Klamath
Indians of South - Western Oregon*
(Washington, 1890), p. xli. (*Contributions to North American Ethnology,*
vol. ii. pt. i).

fact the most vital occurrence, if only dating a single generation back, is quite forgotten, that is to say, if the recounting
thereof should necessitate the mention of a defunct
aboriginal's name."[1]   Thus among these simple savages
even a sacred bard could not avail to rescue an Australian
Agamemnon from the long night of oblivion.

In many tribes, however, the power of this superstition to
blot out the memory of the past is to some extent weakened
and impaired by a natural tendency of the human mind.
Time, which wears out the deepest impressions, inevitably
dulls, if it does not wholly efface, the print left on the savage
mind by the mystery and horror of death.   Sooner or later,
as the memory of his loved ones fades slowly away, he
becomes more willing to speak of them, and thus their rude
names may sometimes be rescued by the philosophic enquirer
before they have vanished, like autumn leaves or winter
snows, into the vast undistinguished limbo of the past.
This was Sir George Grey's experience when he attempted
to trace the intricate system of kinship prevalent among the
natives of western Australia.   He says : " It is impossible
for any person, not well acquainted with the language of the
natives, and who does not possess great personal influence
over them, to pursue an inquiry of this nature ; for one of
the customs most rigidly observed and enforced amongst
them is, never to mention the name of a deceased person,
male or female.   In an inquiry, therefore, which principally
turns upon the names of their ancestors, this prejudice must
be every moment violated, and a very great difficulty
encountered in the outset.   The only circumstance which at
all enabled me to overcome this was, that the longer a
person has been dead the less repugnance do they evince in
uttering his name.   I, therefore, in the first instance,
endeavoured to ascertain only the oldest names on record ;
and on subsequent occasions, when I found a native alone,
and in a loquacious humour, I succeeded in filling up some

Marginal note: Sometimes the names of the dead are revived after a certain time.

---

[1] P. Beveridge, " Of the Aborigines
inhabiting the great Lacustrine and
Riverine Depression of the Lower
Murray," etc., *Journal and Proceedings
of the Royal Society of New South
Wales for 1883*, vol. xvii. p. 65.   The
custom of changing common words on
the death of persons who bore them as
their names seems also to have been
observed by the Tasmanians.   See J.
Bonwick, *Daily Life of the Tasmanians*,
p. 145.

of the blanks. Occasionally, round their fires at night, I managed to involve them in disputes regarding their ancestors, and, on these occasions, gleaned much of the information of which I was in want."¹ In some of the Victorian tribes the prohibition to mention the names of the dead remained in force only during the period of mourning;² in the Port Lincoln tribe of South Australia it lasted many years.³ Among the Chinook Indians of North America " custom forbids the mention of a dead man's name, at least till many years have elapsed after the bereavement."⁴ In the Twana, Chemakum, and Klallam tribes of Washington State the names of deceased members may be mentioned two or three years after their death.⁵ Among the Puyallup Indians the observance of the taboo is relaxed after several years, when the mourners have forgotten their grief; and if the deceased was a famous warrior, one of his descendants, for instance a great-grandson, may be named after him. In this tribe the taboo is not much observed at any time except by the relations of the dead.⁶ Similarly the Jesuit missionary Lafitau tells us that the name of the departed and the similar names of the survivors were, so to say, buried with the corpse until, the poignancy of their grief being abated, it pleased the relations to " lift up the tree and raise the dead." By raising the dead they meant bestowing the name of the departed upon some one else, who thus became to all intents and purposes a reincarnation of the deceased, since on the principles of savage philosophy the name is a vital part, if not the soul, of the man. When Father Lafitau arrived at St. Louis to begin work among the Iroquois, his colleagues decided that in order to make a favourable impression on his flock the new shepherd should assume the native name of his deceased predecessor, Father

The American Indians used to bring the dead to life again by solemnly bestowing their names on living persons, who were thereafter regarded as reincarnations of the dead.

---

¹ G. Grey, *Journals of two Expeditions of Discovery in North-West and Western Australia*, ii. 231 *sq.*

² J. Dawson, *Australian Aborigines*, p. 42.

³ C. W. Schürmann, in *Native Tribes of South Australia*, p. 247.

⁴ H. H. Bancroft, *Native Races of the Pacific States*, iii. 156.

⁵ Myron Eels, "The Twana, Chemakum, and Klallam Indians of Washington Territory," *Annual Report of the Smithsonian Institution for 1887*, p. 656.

⁶ S. R. M'Caw, "Mortuary Customs of the Puyallups," *The American Antiquarian and Oriental Journal*, viii. (1886) p. 235.

Brüyas, "the celebrated missionary," who had lived many years among the Indians and enjoyed their high esteem. But Father Brüyas had been called from his earthly labours to his heavenly rest only four short months before, and it was too soon, in the phraseology of the Iroquois, to "raise up the tree." However, raised up it was in spite of them ; and though some bolder spirits protested that their new pastor had wronged them by taking the name of his predecessor, "nevertheless," says Father Lafitau, "they did not fail to regard me as himself in another form (*un autre lui-même*), since I had entered into all his rights."[1]

Mode of reviving the dead in the persons of their namesakes among the North American Indians.

The same mode of bringing a dead man to life again by bestowing his name upon a living person was practised by the Hurons and other Indian tribes of Canada. An early French traveller in Canada has described the ceremony of resurrection as it was observed by a tribe whom he calls the Attiuoindarons. He says : " The Attiuoindarons practise resurrections of the dead, principally of persons who have deserved well of their country by their remarkable services, so that the memory of illustrious and valiant men revives in a certain way in others. Accordingly they call assemblies for this purpose and hold councils, at which they choose one of them who has the same virtues and qualities, if possible, as he had whom they wish to resuscitate ; or at least he must be of irreproachable life, judged by the standard of a savage people. Wishing, then, to proceed to the resurrection they all stand up, except him who is to be resuscitated, to whom they give the name of the deceased, and all letting their hands down very low they pretend to lift him up from the earth, intending by that to signify that they draw the great personage deceased from the grave and restore him to life in the person of this other, who stands up and, after great acclamations of the people, receives the presents which the bystanders offer him. They further hold several feasts in his honour and regard him thenceforth as the deceased whom he represents; and by this

[1] J. F. Lafitau, *Mœurs des sauvages ameriquains* (Paris, 1724), ii. 434. Charlevoix merely says that the taboo on the names of the dead lasted " a certain time " (*Histoire de la Nouvelle France*, vi. 109). " A good long while " is the phrase used by Captain J. G. Bourke in speaking of the same custom among the Apaches (*On the Border with Crook*, p. 132).

means the memory of virtuous men and of good and valiant captains never dies among them."[1]   Among the Hurons the ceremony took place between the death and the great Festival of the Dead, which was usually celebrated at intervals of twelve years.   When it was resolved to resuscitate a departed warrior, the members of his family met and decided which of them was to be regarded as an incarnation of the deceased.   If the dead man had been a famous chief and leader in war, his living representative and namesake succeeded to his functions.   Presents were made to him, and he entertained the whole tribe at a magnificent banquet.   His old robes were taken from him, and he was clad in richer raiment.   Thereupon a herald proclaimed aloud the mystery of the incarnation.   "Let all the people," he said, "remain silent.   Open your ears and shut your mouths.   That which I am about to say is of importance. Our business is to resuscitate a dead man and to bring a great captain to life again."   With that he named the dead man and all his posterity, and reminded his hearers of the place and manner of his death.   Then turning to him who was to succeed the departed, he lifted up his voice: "Behold him," he cried, "clad in this beautiful robe.   It is not he whom you saw these past days, who was called Nehap.   He has given his name to another, and he himself is now called Etouait" (the name of the defunct).   "Look on him as the true captain of this nation.   It is he whom you are bound to obey; it is he whom you are bound to listen to; it is he whom you are bound to honour."   The new incarnation meanwhile maintained a dignified silence, and afterwards led the young braves out to war in order to prove that he had inherited the courage and virtues as well as the name of the dead chief.[2]   The Carrier Indians of British Columbia firmly believe "that a departed soul can, if it pleases, come back to the earth, in a human shape or body, in order to see his friends, who are still alive.   Therefore, as they are about to set fire to the pile of wood on which a corpse is laid, a

---

[1] Gabriel Sagard, *Le Grand Voyage du pays des Hurons*, Nouvelle Édition (Paris, 1865), p. 202.   The original edition of Sagard's book was published at Paris in 1632.

[2] *Relations des Jésuites*, 1636, p. 131; *id.*, 1642, pp. 53, 85; *id.*, 1644, pp. 66 *sq.* (Canadian reprint, Quebec, 1858).

relation of the deceased person stands at his feet, and asks him if he will ever come back among them. Then the priest or magician, with a grave countenance, stands at the head of the corpse, and looks through both his hands on its naked breast, and then raises them toward heaven, and blows through them, as they say, the soul of the deceased, that it may go and find, and enter into a relative. Or, if any relative is present, the priest will hold both his hands on the head of this person, and blow through them, that the spirit of the deceased may enter into him or her; and then, as they affirm, the first child which this person has will possess the soul of the deceased person."[1] The writer does not say that the infant took the name of the deceased who was born again in it; but probably it did. For sometimes the priest would transfer the soul from a dead to a living person, who in that case took the name of the departed in addition to his own.[2]

The dead revived in their namesakes among the Lapps, Khonds, Yorubas, Baganda, and Makalaka.

Among the Lapps, when a woman was with child and near the time of her delivery, a deceased ancestor or relation (known as a *Jabmek*) used to appear to her in a dream and inform her what dead person was to be born again in her infant, and whose name the child was therefore to bear. If the woman had no such dream, it fell to the father or the relatives to determine the name by divination or by consulting a wizard.[3] Among the Khonds a birth is celebrated on the seventh day after the event by a feast given to the priest and to the whole village. To determine the child's name the priest drops grains of rice into a cup of water, naming with each grain a deceased ancestor. From the movements of the seed in the water, and from observations made on the person of the infant, he pronounces which of his progenitors has reappeared in him, and the child generally, at least

---

[1] Daniel W. Harmon, quoted by Rev. Jedidiah Morse, *Report to the Secretary of War of the United States on Indian Affairs* (New-Haven, 1822), Appendix, p. 345. The custom seems now to be extinct. It is not mentioned by Father A. G. Morice in his accounts of the tribe (in *Proceedings of the Canadian Institute*, Third Series, vol. vii. 1888-89; *Transactions of the Canadian Institute*, vol. iv. 1892-93;

Annual Archaeological Report, Toronto, 1905).

[2] Ch. Wilkes, *Narrative of the United States Exploring Expedition* (New York, 1851), iv. 453.

[3] E. J. Jessen, *De Finnorum Lapponumque Norwegicorum religione pagana*, pp. 33 *sq.* (bound up with C. Leemius, *De Lapponibus Finmarchiae eorumque lingua, vita, et religione pristina commentatio*, Copenhagen, 1767).

among the northern tribes, receives the name of that ancestor.[1] Among the Ewe-speaking peoples of Togo, in West Africa, when a woman is in hard labour, a fetish priest or priestess is called in to disclose the name of the deceased relative who has just been born again into the world in the person of the infant. The name of that relative is bestowed on the child.[2] Among the Yorubas, soon after a child has been born, a priest of Ifa, the god of divination, appears on the scene to ascertain what ancestral soul has been reborn in the infant. As soon as this has been decided, the parents are told that the child must conform in all respects to the manner of life of the ancestor who now animates him or her, and if, as often happens, they profess ignorance, the priest supplies the necessary information. The child usually receives the name of the ancestor who has been born again in him.[3] In Uganda a child is named with much ceremony by its grandfather, who bestows on it the name of one of its ancestors, but never the name of its father. The spirit of the deceased namesake then enters the child and assists him through life.[4] Here the reincarnation of the ancestor appears to be effected by giving his name, and with it his soul, to his descendant. The same idea seems to explain a curious ceremony observed by the Makalaka of South Africa at the naming of a child. The spirit of the ancestor (*motsimo*), whose name the child is to bear, is represented by an elderly kinsman or kinswoman,

Reincarnation of an ancestor effected by giving his name to a child.

[1] Major S. C. Macpherson, *Memorials of Service in India* (London, 1865), pp. 72 *sq.*

[2] C. Spiess, "Einiges über die Bedeutung der Personennamen der Evheer in Togo-Gebiete," *Mittheilungen des Seminars für orientalische Sprachen zu Berlin*, vi. (1903) Dritte Abtheilung, pp. 56 *sq.*

[3] A. B. Ellis, *The Yoruba-speaking Peoples of the Slave Coast*, p. 152; *id.*, *The Ewe-speaking Peoples of the Slave Coast*, pp. 153 *sq.* In the former passage the writer says nothing about the child's name. In the latter he merely says that an ancestor is supposed to have sent the child, who accordingly commonly takes the name of that ancestor. But the analogy of other peoples makes it highly probable that, as Col. Ellis himself states in his later work (*The Yoruba-speaking Peoples*), the ancestor is believed to be incarnate in the child. That the Yoruba child takes the name of the ancestor who has come to life again in him is definitely stated by A. Dieterich in *Archiv für Religionswissenschaft*, viii. (1904) p. 20, referring to *Zeitschrift für Missionskunde und Religionswissenschaft*, xv. (1900) p. 17, a work to which I have not access. Dieterich's account of the subject of rebirth (*op. cit.* pp. 18-21) deserves to be consulted.

[4] J. Roscoe, "Further Notes on the Manners and Customs of the Baganda," *Journal of the Anthropological Institute*, xxxii. (1902) p. 32.

according as the little one is a boy or a girl.   A pretence
is made of catching the representative of the spirit, and
dragging him or her to the hut of the child's parents.   Outside the hut the pretended spirit takes his seat and the skin
of an animal is thrown over him.   He then washes his
hands in a vessel of water, eats some millet-porridge, and
washes it down with beer.   Meantime the women and girls
dance gleefully round him, screaming or singing, and throw
copper rings, beads, and so forth as presents into the vessel
of water.   The men do the same, but without dancing ; after
that they enter the hut to partake of a feast.   The representative of the ancestral spirit now vanishes, and the child
thenceforth bears his or her name.[1]   This ceremony may be
intended to represent the reincarnation of the ancestral spirit
in the child.

Revival of the names of the dead among the Nicobarese and Gilyaks.   In the Nicobar Islands the names of dead relatives are
tabooed for a generation ; but when both their parents are
dead, men and women are bound to assume the names of
their deceased grandfathers or grandmothers respectively.[2]
Perhaps with the names they may be thought to inherit
the spirits of their ancestors.   Among the Tartars in the
Middle Ages the names of the dead might not be uttered till
the third generation.[3]   Among the Gilyaks of Saghalien no
two persons in the same tribe may bear the same name at
the same time ; for they think that if a child were to receive
the name of a living man, either the child or the man would
die within the year.   When a man dies, his name may not
be uttered until after the celebration of the festival at which
they sacrifice a bear for the purpose of procuring plenty of
game and fish.   At that festival they call out the name of
the deceased while they beat the skin of the bear.   Thenceforth the name may be pronounced by every one, and it will
be bestowed on a child who shall afterwards be born.[4]   These
customs suggest that the Gilyaks, like other peoples, suppose

---

[1] C. Mauch, *Reisen im Inneren von Süd-Afrika* (Gotha, 1874), p. 43 (*Petermann's Mittheilungen, Ergänzungsheft*, No. 37).

[2] Sir R. C. Temple, in *Census of India, 1901*, vol. iii. 207, 212.

[3] Plan de Carpin (de Plano Carpini),

Relation des Mongols ou Tartares, ed. D'Avezac, cap. iii. § iii.   The writer's statement ("*nec nomen proprium ejus usque ad tertiam generationem audet aliquis nominare*") is not very clear.

[4] P. Labbé, *Un Bagne russe, l'île de Sakhaline* (Paris, 1903), p. 166.

the namesake of a deceased person to be his or her reincarnation ; for their objection to let two living persons bear the same name seems to imply a belief that the soul goes with the name, and therefore cannot be shared by two people at the same time.

Among the Esquimaux of Bering Strait the first child born in a village after some one has died receives the dead person's name, and must represent him in subsequent festivals which are given in his honour. The day before the great feast of the dead the nearest male relative of the deceased goes to the grave and plants before it a stake bearing the crest or badge of the departed. This is the notice served to the ghost to attend the festival. Accordingly he returns from the spirit-land to the grave. Afterwards a song is sung at the grave inviting the ghost to repair to the assembly-house, where the people are gathered to celebrate the festival. The shade accepts the invitation and takes his place, with the other ghosts, in the fire-pit under the floor of the assembly-house. All the time of the festival, which lasts for several days, lamps filled with seal-oil are kept burning day and night in the assembly-house in order to light up the path to the spirit-land and enable the ghosts to find their way back to their old haunts on earth. When the spirits of the dead are gathered in the pit, and the proper moment has come, they all rise up through the floor and enter the bodies of their living namesakes. Offerings of food, drink, and clothes are now made to these namesakes, who eat and drink and wear the clothes on behalf of the ghosts. Finally, the shades, refreshed and strengthened by the banquet, are sent away back to their graves thinly clad in the spiritual essence of the clothes, while the gross material substance of the garments is retained by their namesakes.[1] Here the reincarnation of the dead in the living is not permanent, but merely occasional and temporary. Still a special connexion may well be thought to subsist at all times between the deceased and the living person who bears his or her name.

Namesakes of the dead treated as the dead in person among the Esquimaux of Bering Strait.

[1] E. W. Nelson, "The Eskimo about Bering Strait," *Eighteenth Annual Report of the Bureau of* *American Ethnology*, part i. (Washington, 1899), pp. 363 *sq.*, 365, 368, 371, 377, 379, 424 *sq.*

The foregoing facts seem to render it probable that even where a belief in the reincarnation of ancestors either is not expressly attested or has long ceased to form part of the popular creed, many of the solemnities which attend the naming of children may have sprung originally from the widespread notion that the souls of the dead come to life again in their namesakes.[1]

In some cases the period during which the name of the deceased may not be pronounced seems to bear a close relation to the time during which his mortal remains may be supposed still to hold together. Thus, of some Indian tribes on the north-west coast of America it is said that they may not speak the name of a dead person "until the bones are finally disposed of."[2] Among the Narrinyeri of South Australia the name might not be uttered until the corpse had decayed.[3] In the Encounter Bay tribe of the same country the dead body is dried over a fire, packed up in mats, and carried about for several months among the scenes which had been familiar to the deceased in his life. Next it is placed on a platform of sticks and left there till it has completely decayed, whereupon the next of kin takes the skull and uses it as a drinking-cup. After that the name of the departed may be uttered without offence. Were it pronounced sooner his kinsmen would be deeply offended, and a war might be the result.[4] The rule that the name of the dead may not be spoken until his body has mouldered away seems to point to a belief that the spirit continues to exist only so long as the body does so, and that, when the material frame is dissolved, the spiritual part of the man perishes with it, or goes away, or at least becomes so feeble and incapable of mischief that his name may be bandied about with impunity.[5] This view is to some extent con-

---

[1] On the doctrine of the reincarnation of ancestors in their descendants see E. B. Tylor, *Primitive Culture*,[2] ii. 3-5, who observes with great probability that "among the lower races generally the renewal of old family names by giving them to new-born children may always be suspected of involving some such thought." See further *Totemism and Exogamy*, iii. 297-299.

[2] II. H. Bancroft, *Native Races of the Pacific States*, i. 248.

[3] G. Taplin, in *Native Tribes of South Australia*, p. 19.

[4] H. E. A. Meyer, in *Native Tribes of South Australia*, p. 199.

[5] Some of the Indians of Guiana bring food and drink to their dead so long as the flesh remains on the bones; when it has mouldered away, they con-

firmed by the practice of the Arunta tribe in central Australia. We have seen that among them no one may mention the name of the deceased during the period of mourning for fear of disturbing and annoying the ghost, who is believed to be walking about at large. Some of the relations of the dead man, it is true, such as his parents, elder brothers and sisters, paternal aunts, mother-in-law, and all his sons-in-law, whether actual or possible, are debarred all their lives from taking his name into their lips; but other people, including his wife, children, grandchildren, grandparents, younger brothers and sisters, and father-in-law, are free to name him so soon as he has ceased to walk the earth and hence to be dangerous. Some twelve or eighteen months after his death the people seem to think that the dead man has enjoyed his liberty long enough, and that it is time to confine his restless spirit within narrower bounds. Accordingly a grand battue or ghost-hunt brings the days of mourning to an end. The favourite haunt of the deceased is believed to be the burnt and deserted camp where he died. Here therefore on a certain day a band of men and women, the men armed with shields and spear-throwers, assemble and begin dancing round the charred and blackened remains of the camp, shouting and beating the air with their weapons and hands in order to drive away the lingering spirit from the spot he loves too well. When the dancing is over, the whole party proceed to the grave at a run, chasing the ghost before them. It is in vain that the unhappy ghost makes a last bid for freedom, and, breaking away from the beaters,

---

clude that the man himself has departed. See A. Biet, *Voyage de la France équinoxiale en l'Isle de Cayenne* (Paris, 1664), p. 392. The Alfoors or Toradjas of central Celebes believe that the souls of the dead cannot enter the spirit-land until all the flesh has been removed from their bones; till that has been done, the gods (*lamoa*) in the other world could not bear the stench of the corpse. Accordingly at a great festival the bodies of all who have died within a certain time are dug up and the decaying flesh scraped from the bones. See A. C. Kruijt, "Een en ander aangaande het geestelijk· en maat-

schappelijk leven van den Poso-Alfoer," *Mededeelingen van wege het Nederlandsche Zendelinggenootschap*, xxxix. (1895) pp. 26, 32 *sqq.*; *id.*, "Het wezen van het Heidendom te Posso," *ibid.* xlvii. (1903) p. 32. The Matacos Indians of the Gran Chaco believe that the soul of a dead man does not pass down into the nether world until his body is decomposed or burnt. See J. Pelleschi, *Los Indios Matacos* (Buenos Ayres, 1897), p. 102. These ideas perhaps explain the widespread custom of disinterring the dead after a certain time and disposing of their bones otherwise.

doubles back towards the camp ; the leader of the party is prepared for this manœuvre, and by making a long circuit adroitly cuts off the retreat of the fugitive. Finally, having run him to earth, they trample him down into the grave, dancing and stamping on the heaped-up soil, while with downward thrusts through the air they beat and force him under ground. There, lying in his narrow house, flattened and prostrate under a load of earth, the poor ghost sees his widow wearing the gay feathers of the ring-neck parrot in her hair, and he knows that the time of her mourning for him is over. The loud shouts of the men and women shew him that they are not to be frightened and bullied by him any more, and that he had better lie quiet. But he may still watch over his friends, and guard them from harm, and visit them in dreams.[1]

§ 4. *Names of Kings and other Sacred Persons tabooed*

The birth-names of kings kept secret or not pronounced.

When we see that in primitive society the names of mere commoners, whether alive or dead, are matters of such anxious care, we need not be surprised that great precautions should be taken to guard from harm the names of sacred kings and priests. Thus the name of the king of Dahomey is always kept secret, lest the knowledge of it should enable some evil-minded person to do him a mischief. The appellations by which the different kings of Dahomey have been known to Europeans are not their true names, but mere titles, or what the natives call "strong names" (*nyi-sese*). As a rule, these "strong names" are the first words of sentences descriptive of certain qualities. Thus Agaja, the name by which the fourth king of the dynasty was known, was part of a sentence meaning, " A spreading tree must be lopped before it can be cast into the fire " ; and Tegbwesun, the name of the fifth king, formed the first word of a sentence which signified, " No one can take the cloth off the neck of a wild bull." The natives seem to think that no harm comes of such titles being known, since they are not, like the birth-names, vitally connected with their owners.[2]

---

[1] Spencer and Gillen, *Native Tribes of Central Australia*, pp. 498-508.

[2] A. B. Ellis, *The Ewe - speaking Peoples of the Slave Coast*, pp. 98 *sq.*

In the Galla kingdom of Ghera the birth-name of the sovereign may not be pronounced by a subject under pain of·death, and common words which resemble it in sound are changed for others.   Thus when a queen named Carre reigned over the kingdom, the word *hara*, which means smoke, was exchanged for *unno*; further, *arre*, "ass," was replaced by *culula*; and *gudare*, "potato," was dropped and *loccio* substituted for it.[1]   Among the Bahima of central Africa, when the king dies, his name is abolished from the language, and if his name was that of an animal, a new appellation must be found for the creature at once.   For example, the king is often called a lion ; hence at the death of a king named Lion a new name for lions in general has to be coined.[2] Thus in the language of the Bahima the word for " lion " some years ago was *mpologoma*.   But when a prominent chief of that name died, the word for lion was changed to *kichunchu*.   Again, in the Bahima language the word for " nine " used to be *mwenda*, a word which occurs with the same meaning but dialectical variations in the languages of other tribes of central and eastern Africa.   But when a chief who bore the name Mwenda died, the old name for " nine " had to be changed, and accordingly the word *isaga* has been substituted for it.[3]   In Siam it used to be difficult to ascertain the king's real name, since it was carefully kept secret from fear of sorcery ; any one who mentioned it was clapped into gaol. The king might only be referred to under certain high-sounding titles, such as " the august," " the perfect," " the supreme," " the great emperor," " descendant of the angels," and so on.[4] In Burma it was accounted an impiety of the deepest dye to mention the name of the reigning sovereign ; Burmese subjects, even when they were far from their country, could not be prevailed upon to do so ;[5] after his accession to the throne the king was known by his royal titles only.[6]   The proper name of the Emperor of China may neither be pronounced

[1] A. Cecchi, *Da Zeila alle frontiere del Caffa*, ii. (Rome, 1885) p. 551.

[2] Rev. J. Roscoe, " The Bahima," *Journal of the Royal Anthropological Institute*, xxxvii. (1907) p. 96.

[3] J. F. Cunningham, *Uganda and its Peoples* (London, 1905), pp. 14, 16.

[4] De la Loubere, *Du royaume de Siam* (Amsterdam, 1691), i. 306 ; Pallegoix, *Royaume Thai ou Siam*, i. 260.

[5] J. S. Polack, *Manners and Customs of the New Zealanders* (London, 1840), ii. 127, note 43.

[6] A. Fytche, *Burma Past and Present* (London, 1878), i. 238.

nor written by any of his subjects.[1]   Coreans were formerly
forbidden, under severe penalties, to utter the king's name,
which, indeed, was seldom known.[2]   When a prince ascends
the throne of Cambodia he ceases to be designated by his
real name ; and if that name happens to be a common word
in the language, the word is often changed.   Thus, for
example, since the reign of King Ang Duong the word
duong, which meant a small coin, has been replaced by *dom*.[3]
In the island of Sunda it is taboo to utter any word which
coincides with the name of a prince or chief.[4]   The name of
the rajah of Bolang Mongondo, a district in the west of
Celebes, is never mentioned except in case of urgent
necessity, and even then his pardon must be asked repeatedly before the liberty is taken.[5]   In the island of Sumba
people do not mention the real name of a prince, but refer to
him by the name of the first slave whom in his youth he
became master of.   This slave is regarded by the chief as
his second self, and he enjoys practical impunity for any
misdeeds he may commit.[6]

The names
of Zulu
kings and
chiefs may
not be pro-
nounced.

Among the Zulus no man will mention the name of the
chief of his tribe or the names of the progenitors of the chief,
so far as he can remember them ; nor will he utter common
words which coincide with or merely resemble in sound
tabooed names.   " As, for instance, the Zungu tribe say *mata*
for *manzi* (water), and *inkosta* for *tshanti* (grass), and *embi-
gatdu* for *umkondo* (assegai), and *inyatugo* for *enhlela* (path),
because their present chief is Umfan-o inhlela, his father was
Manzini, his grandfather Imkondo, and one before him
Tshani."   In the tribe of the Dwandwes there was a chief

---

[1] J. Edkins, *Religion in China* [2]
(London, 1878), p. 35.

[2] Ch. Dallet, *Histoire de l'Église
de Corée*, i. p. xxiv. ; Mrs. Bishop,
Korea and her Neighbours (London,
1898), i. 48. The custom is now
obsolete (G. N. Curzon, *Problems of
the Far East*, Westminster, 1896, p.
155 note).

[3] E. Aymonier, *Notice sur le Cambodge* (Paris, 1875), p. 22 ; *id.*, *Le
Cambodge*, i. {Paris, 1900) p. 58.

[4] K. F. Holle, " Snippers van den
Regent van Galoeh," *Tijdschrift voor
Indische Taal- Land- en Volkenkunde*,

xxvii. (1882) p. 101.

[5] N. P. Wilken en J. A. Schwarz,
" Allerlei over het land en volk van
Bolaang Mongondou," *Mededeelingen
van wege het Nederlandsche Zendelinggenootschap*, xi. (1867) p. 356.

[6] S. Roos, " Bijdrage tot de Kennis
van Taal, Land, en Volk op het eiland
Soemba," p. 70, *Verhandelingen van
het Bataviaasch Genootschap van Kunsten en Wetenschappen*, xxxvi. Compare
J. H. F. Kohlbrugge, " Naamgeving
in Insulinde," *Bijdragen tot de Taal-
Land- en Volkenkunde van Neder-
landsche-Indië*, li. (1900) p. 173.

called Langa, which means the sun ; hence the name of the
sun was changed from *langa* to *gala*, and so remains to this
day, though Langa died more than a hundred years ago.
Once more, in the Xnumayo tribe the word meaning "to
herd cattle" was changed from *alusa* or *ayusa* to *kagesa*,
because u-Mayusi was the name of the chief. Besides these
taboos, which were observed by each tribe separately, all the
Zulu tribes united in tabooing the name of the king who
reigned over the whole nation. Hence, for example, when
Panda was king of Zululand, the word for "a root of a tree,"
which is *impando*, was changed to *nxabo*. Again, the word
for "lies" or "slander" was altered from *amacebo* to *amakwata*,
because *amacebo* contains a syllable of the name of the
famous King Cetchwayo. These substitutions are not, however, carried so far by the men as by the women, who omit
every sound even remotely resembling one that occurs in a
tabooed name. At the king's kraal, indeed, it is sometimes
difficult to understand the speech of the royal wives, as they
treat in this fashion the names not only of the king and his
forefathers, but even of his and their brothers back for generations. When to these tribal and national taboos we add
those family taboos on the names of connexions by marriage
which have been already described,[1] we can easily understand how it comes about that in Zululand every tribe has
words peculiar to itself, and that the women have a considerable vocabulary of their own. Members, too, of one
family may be debarred from using words employed by
those of another. The women of one kraal, for instance,
may call a hyaena by its ordinary name ; those of the next
may use the common substitute ; while in a third the substitute may also be unlawful and another term may have to be
invented to supply its place. Hence the Zulu language at
the present day almost presents the appearance of being a
double one ; indeed, for multitudes of things it possesses
three or four synonyms, which through the blending of tribes
are known all over Zululand.[2]

[1] Above, pp. 335 *sq.*

[2] J. Shooter, *The Kafirs of Natal
and the Zulu Country*, pp. 221 *sq.* ;
David Leslie, *Among the Zulus and*
Amatongas [2] (Edinburgh, 1875), pp.
172-179 ; J. Macdonald, "Manners,
Customs, Superstitions, and Religions of
South African Tribes," *Journal of the*

The names of living kings and chiefs may not be pronounced in Madagascar.

In Madagascar a similar custom everywhere prevails and has resulted, as among the Zulus, in producing certain dialectic differences in the speech of the various tribes. There are no family names in Madagascar, and almost every personal name is drawn from the language of daily life and signifies some common object or action or quality, such as a bird, a beast, a tree, a plant, a colour, and so on. Now, whenever one of these common words forms the name or part of the name of the chief of the tribe, it becomes sacred and may no longer be used in its ordinary signification as the name of a tree, an insect, or what not. Hence a new name for the object must be invented to replace the one which has been discarded. Often the new name consists of a descriptive epithet or a periphrasis. Thus when the princess Rabodo became queen in 1863 she took the name of Rasoherina. Now *soherina* was the word for the silkworm moth, but having been assumed as the name of the sovereign it could no longer be applied to the insect, which ever since has been called *zany-dandy*, "offspring of silk." So, again, if a chief had or took the name of an animal, say of the dog (*amboa*), and was known as Ramboa, the animal would henceforth be called by another name, probably a descriptive one, such as "the barker" (*famovo*) or "the driver away" (*fandroaka*), etc. In the western part of Imerina there was a chief called Andria-mamba; but *mamba* was one of the names of the crocodile, so the chief's subjects might not call the reptile by that name and were always scrupulous to use another. It is easy to conceive what confusion and uncertainty may thus be introduced into a language when it is spoken by many little local tribes each ruled by a petty chief with his own sacred name. Yet there are tribes and people who submit to this tyranny of words as their fathers did before them from time immemorial. The inconvenient results of the custom are especially marked on the western coast of the island, where, on account of the large number of independent chieftains, the names of things, places, and rivers have suffered so many changes that confusion often arises, for when once common words have been banned by

Anthropological Institute, xx. (1891) p. 131. The account in the text is based mainly on Leslie's description, which is by far the fullest.

the chiefs the natives will not acknowledge to have ever known them in their old sense.[1]

But it is not merely the names of living kings and chiefs which are tabooed in Madagascar; the names of dead sovereigns are equally under a ban, at least in some parts of the island. Thus among the Sakalavas, when a king has died, the nobles and people meet in council round the dead body and solemnly choose a new name by which the deceased monarch shall be henceforth known. The new name always begins with *andrian,* " lord," and ends with *arrivou,* " thousand," to signify that the late king ruled over a numerous nation. The body of the name is composed of an epithet or phrase descriptive of the deceased or of his reign. After the new name has been adopted, the old name by which the king was known during his life becomes sacred and may not be pronounced under pain of death. Further, words in the common language which bear any resemblance to the forbidden name also become sacred and have to be replaced by others. For example, after the death of King Makka the word *laka,* which meant a canoe, was abandoned and the word *fiounrâma* substituted for it. When Taoussi died, the word *taoussi,* signifying " beautiful," was replaced by *senga.* For similar reasons the word *ântétsi,* " old," was changed for *matoué,* which properly means " ripe " ; the word *voûssi,* " castrated," was dropped and *manapaka,* " cut," adopted in its place ; and the word for island (*nossi*) was changed into *varioû,* which signifies strictly " a place where there is rice." Again, when a Sakalava king named Marentoetsa died, two words fell into disuse, namely, the word *màry* or *màre* meaning " true," and the word *toetsa* meaning " condition." Persons who uttered these forbidden words were looked on not only as grossly rude, but even as felons ; they had committed a capital crime. However, these changes of vocabulary are confined to the

The names of dead kings and chiefs are also tabooed in Madagascar.

---

[1] D. Tyerman and G. Bennet, *Journal of Voyages and Travels* (London, 1831), ii. 525 *sq.* ; J. Sibree, *The Great African Island* (London, 1880), pp. 150 *sq.* ; *id.,* " Curiosities of Words connected with Royalty and Chieftainship," *Antananarivo Annual and Madagascar Magazine,* No. xi. (Christmas, 1887) pp. 308 *sq.*; *id.,* in *Journal of the Anthropological Institute,* xxi. (1887) pp. 226 *sqq.* On the custom of tabooing royal or chiefly names in Madagascar, see A. van Gennep, *Tabou et totémisme à Madagascar* (Paris, 1904), pp. 104 *sqq.*

district over which the deceased king reigned; in the neighbouring districts the old words continue to be employed in the old sense.[1] Again, among the Bara, another tribe of Madagascar, "the memory of their deceased kings is held in the very highest respect; the name of such kings is considered sacred—too sacred indeed for utterance, and no one is allowed to pronounce it. To such a length is this absurdity carried that the name of any person or thing whatsoever, if it bear a resemblance to the name of the deceased king, is no longer used, but some other designation is given. For instance, there was a king named Andriamasoandro. After his decease the word *masoandro* was no longer employed as the name of the sun, but *mahenika* was substituted for it."[2] An eminent authority on Madagascar has observed: "A curious fact, which has had a very marked influence on the Malagasy language, is the custom of no longer pronouncing the name of a dead person nor even the words which resemble it in their conclusions. The name is replaced by another. King Ramitra, since his decease, has been called Mahatenatenarivou, 'the prince who has conquered a thousand foes,' and a Malagasy who should utter his old name would be regarded as the murderer of the prince, and would therefore be liable to the confiscation of his property, or even to the penalty of death. It is easy accordingly to understand how the Malagasy language, one in its origin, has been corrupted, and how it comes about that at the present day there are discrepancies between the various dialects. In Menabe, since the death of King Vinany, the word *vilany*, meaning a pot, has been replaced by *fiketrehane*, 'cooking vessel,' whereas the old word continues in use in the rest of Madagascar. These changes, it

---

[1] V. Noel, "Île de Madagascar, recherches sur les Sakkalava," *Bulletin de la Société de Géographie* (Paris), IIme Série, xx. (1843) pp. 303-306. Compare A. Grandidier, "Les Rites funéraires chez les Malgaches," *Revue d'Ethnographie*, v. (1886) p. 224; A. Walen, "The Sakalava," *Antananarivo Annual and Madagascar Magazine*, vol. ii., Reprint of the Second Four Numbers (Antananarivo, 1896), p. 242; A. van Gennep, *Tabou*

et totémisme à Madagascar, pp. 110 sq. Amongst the Sakalavas it is forbidden to mention the name of any dead person. See A. Voeltzkow, "Vom Morondava zum Mangoky, Reiseskizzen aus West-Madagascar," *Zeitschrift der Gesellschaft für Erdkunde zu Berlin*, xxxi. (1896) p. 118.

[2] R. Baron, "The Bara," *Antananarivo Annual and Madagascar Magazine*, vol. ii., Reprint of the Second Four Numbers (Antananarivo, 1896), p. 83.

is true, hardly take place except for kings and great chiefs." [1]

The sanctity attributed to the persons of chiefs in Poly- The names of chiefs may not be pronounced in Polynesia.nesia naturally extended also to their names, which on the primitive view are hardly separable from the personality of their owners. Hence in Polynesia we find the same systematic prohibition to utter the names of chiefs or of common words resembling them which we have already met with in Zululand and Madagascar. Thus in New Zealand the name of a chief is held so sacred that, when it happens to be a common word, it may not be used in the language, and another has to be found to replace it. For example, a chief to the southward of East Cape bore the name of Maripi, which signified a knife, hence a new word (*nekra*) for knife was introduced, and the old one became obsolete. Elsewhere the word for water (*wai*) had to be changed, because it chanced to be the name of the chief, and would have been desecrated by being applied to the vulgar fluid as well as to his sacred person. This taboo naturally produced a plentiful crop of synonyms in the Maori language, and travellers newly arrived in the country were sometimes puzzled at finding the same things called by quite different names in neighbouring tribes.[2] When a king comes to the throne in Tahiti, any words in the language that resemble his name in sound must be changed for others. In former times, if any man were so rash as to disregard this custom and to use the forbidden words, not only he but all his relations were immediately put to death.[3] On the accession of King Otoo, which happened before Vancouver's visit to Tahiti, the proper names of all the chiefs were changed, as well as forty or fifty of the commonest words in the language, and every native was obliged to adopt the new terms, for any neglect

---

[1] A. Grandidier, "Madagascar," *Bulletin de la Société de Géographie* (Paris), Vme Série, xvii. (1869) pp. 401 *sq.* The writer is here speaking specially of the Sakalavas, though his remarks appear to be of general application.

[2] J. S. Polack, *Manners and Customs of the New Zealanders*, i. 37 *sq.*, ii. 126 *sq.* Compare E. Tregear,

"The Maoris of New Zealand," *Journal of the Anthropological Institute*, xix. (1890) p. 123.

[3] Captain J. Cook, *Voyages* (London, 1809), vi. 155 (Third Voyage). Compare Captain James Wilson, *Missionary Voyage to the Southern Pacific Ocean* (London, 1799), p. 366 ; W. Ellis, *Polynesian Researches*,[2] iii. 101.

to do so was punished with the greatest severity.[1]   When a certain king named Tu came to the throne of Tahiti the word *tu*, which means "to stand," was changed to *tia*; *fetu*, "a star," became *fetia*; *tui*, "to strike," was turned into *tiai*, and so on.   Sometimes, as in these instances, the new names were formed by merely changing or dropping some letter or letters of the original words; in other cases the substituted terms were entirely different words, whether chosen for their similarity of meaning though not of sound, or adopted from another dialect, or arbitrarily invented.   But the changes thus introduced were only temporary; on the death of the king the new words fell into disuse, and the original ones were revived.[2]   Similarly in Samoa, when the name of a sacred chief was that of an animal or bird, the name of the animal or bird was at once changed for another, and the old one might never again be uttered in that chief's district. For example, a sacred Samoan chief was named Pe'a, which means "flying-fox."   Hence in his district a flying-fox was no longer called a flying-fox but a "bird of heaven" (*manu langi*).[3]

The names of the Eleusinian priests might not be uttered.   In ancient Greece the names of the priests and other high officials who had to do with the performances of the Eleusinian mysteries might not be uttered in their lifetime. To pronounce them was a legal offence.   The pedant in Lucian tells how he fell in with these august personages hailing along to the police court a ribald fellow who had dared to name them, though well he knew that ever since their consecration it was unlawful to do so, because they had become anonymous, having lost their old names and acquired new and sacred titles.[4]   From two inscriptions found at

[1] Vancouver, *Voyage of Discovery to the North Pacific Ocean and round the World* (London, 1798), i. 135.

[2] *United States Exploring Expedition, Ethnography and Philology*, by Horatio Hale (Philadelphia, 1846), pp. 288 *sq.*

[3] G. Brown, D.D., *Melanesians and Polynesians* (London, 1910), p. 280.

[4] Lucian, *Lexiphanes*, 10.   The inscriptional and other evidence of this Greek superstition was first brought to the notice of anthropologists by Mr.

W. R. Paton in an interesting article, "The Holy Names of the Eleusinian Priests," *International Folk-lore Congress, 1891, Papers and Transactions*, pp. 202-214.   Compare E. Maass, *Orpheus* (Munich, 1895), p. 70; Aug. Mommsen, *Feste der Stadt Athen im Altertum* (Leipsic, 1898), pp. 253-255; P. Foucart, *Les Grands Mystères d'Eleusis* (Paris, 1900), pp. 28-31.   The two last writers shew that, contrary to what we might have expected, the custom appears not to have been very ancient.

Eleusis it appears that the names of the priests were committed to the depths of the sea;[1] probably they were engraved on tablets of bronze or lead, which were then thrown into deep water in the Gulf of Salamis. The intention doubtless was to keep the names a profound secret; and how could that be done more surely than by sinking them in the sea? what human vision could spy them glimmering far down in the dim depths of the green water? A clearer illustration of the confusion between the incorporeal and the corporeal, between the name and its material embodiment, could hardly be found than in this practice of civilised Greece.

In Togo, a district of West Africa, a secret religious society flourishes under the name of the Yewe order. Both men and women are admitted to it. The teaching and practice of the order are lewd and licentious. Murderers and debtors join it for the sake of escaping from justice, for the members are not amenable to the laws. On being initiated every one receives a new name, and thenceforth his or her old name may never be mentioned by anybody under penalty of a heavy fine. Should the old name be uttered in a quarrel by an uninitiated person, the aggrieved party, who seems to be oftener a woman than a man, pretends to fall into a frenzy, and in this state rushes into the house of the offender, smashes his pots, destroys the grass roof, and tears down the fence. Then she runs away into the forest, where the simple people believe that she is changed into a leopard. In truth she slinks by night into the conventual buildings of

The old names of members of the Yewe order in Togo may not be uttered.

---

[1] G. Kaibel, *Epigrammata Graeca ex lapidibus conlecta*, No. 863; Ἐφημερὶς ἀρχαιολογική, 1883, col. 79 *sq.* From the latter of these inscriptions we learn that the name might be made public after the priest's death. Further, a reference of Eunapius (*Vitae sophistarum*, p. 475 of the Didot edition) shews that the name was revealed to the initiated. In the essay cited in the preceding note Mr. W. R. Paton assumes that it was the new and sacred name which was kept secret and committed to the sea. The case is not clear, but both the evidence and the probability seem to me in favour of the view that it was rather the old everyday name of the priest. or priestess which was put away at his or her consecration. If, as is not improbable, these sacred personages had to act the parts of gods and goddesses at the mysteries, it might well be deemed indecorous and even blasphemous to recall the vulgar names by which they had been known in the familiar intercourse of daily life. If our clergy, to suppose an analogous case, had to personate the most exalted beings of sacred history, it would surely be grossly irreverent to address them by their ordinary names during the performance of their solemn functions.

the order, and is there secretly kept in comfort till the business is settled. At last she is publicly brought back by the society with great pomp, her body smeared with red earth and adorned with an artificial tail in order to make the ignorant think that she has really been turned into a leopard.[1]

The utterance of the names of gods and spirits is supposed to disturb the course of nature. When the name is held to be a vital part of the person, it is natural to suppose that the mightier the person the more potent must be his name. Hence the names of supernatural beings, such as gods and spirits, are commonly believed to be endowed with marvellous virtues, and the mere utterance of them may work wonders and disturb the course of nature. The Warramunga of central Australia believe in a formidable but mythical snake called the Wollunqua, which lives in a pool. When they speak of it amongst themselves they designate it by another name, because they say that, were they to call the snake too often by its real name, they would lose control over the creature, and it would come out of the water and eat them all up.[2] For this reason, too, the sacred books of the Mongols, which narrate the miraculous deeds of the divinities, are allowed to be read only in spring or summer ; because at other seasons the reading of them would bring on tempests or snow.[3] When Mr. Campbell was travelling with some Bechuanas, he asked them one morning after breakfast to tell him some of their stories, but they informed him that were they to do so before sunset, the clouds would fall from the heavens upon their heads.[4] The Sulka of New Britain believe in a certain hostile spirit named Kot, to whose wrath they attribute earthquakes, thunder, and lightning. Among

[1] H. Seidel, "Der Yew'e Dienst im Togolande," *Zeitschrift für afrikanische und oceanische Sprachen,* iii. (1897) pp. 161-173 ; H. Klose, *Togo unter deutscher Flagge* (Berlin, 1899), pp. 197-205. Compare Lieut. Herold, "Bericht betreffend religiöse Anschauungen und Gebräuche der deutschen Ewe-Neger," *Mittheilungen aus den deutschen Schutzgebieten,* v. (1892) p. 146 ; J. Spieth, "Der Jehve Dienst der Evhe-Neger," *Mittheilungen der Geographischen Gesellschaft zu Jena,*

xii. (1893) pp. 83-88 ; C. Spiess, "Religionsbegriffe der Evheer in Westafrika," *Mittheilungen des Seminars für orientalische Sprachen zu Berlin,* vi. (1903) Dritte Abtheilung, p. 126.

[2] Spencer and Gillen, *Northern Tribes of Central Australia,* p. 227.

[3] G. Timkowski, *Travels of the Russian Mission through Mongolia to China* (London, 1827), ii. 348.

[4] J. Campbell, *Travels in South Africa, Second Journey* (London, 1822), ii. 204 *sq.*

the things which provoke his vengeance is the telling of
tales and legends by day; stories should be told only at
evening or night.[1]   Most of the rites of the Navajo
Indians may be celebrated only in winter, when the thunder
is silent and the rattlesnakes are hibernating.   Were they
to tell of their chief gods or narrate the myths of the
days of old at any other time, the Indians believe that they
would soon be killed by lightning or snake-bites.   When Dr.
Washington Matthews was in New Mexico, he often employed as his guide and informant a liberal-minded member
of the tribe who had lived with Americans and Mexicans
and seemed to be free from the superstitions of his fellows.
"On one occasion," says Dr. Matthews, " during the month
of August, in the height of the rainy season, I had him in my
study conversing with him.   In an unguarded moment, on
his part, I led him into a discussion about the gods of his
people, and neither of us had noticed a heavy storm coming
over the crest of the Zuñi mountains, close by.   We were just
talking of Estsanatlehi, the goddess of the west, when the
house was shaken by a terrific peal of thunder.   He rose at
once, pale and evidently agitated, and, whispering hoarsely,
'Wait till Christmas ; they are angry,' he hurried away.   I
have seen many such evidences of the deep influence of this
superstition on them." [2]   Among the Iroquois the rehearsal
of tales of wonder formed the chief entertainment at the
fireside in winter.   But all the summer long, from the
time when the trees began to bud in spring till the
red leaves of autumn began to fall, these marvellous
stories were hushed and historical traditions took their
place.[3]   Other Indian tribes also will only tell their
mythic tales in winter, when the snow lies like a pall on
the ground, and lakes and rivers are covered with sheets of
ice ; for then the spirits underground cannot hear the stories
in which their names are made free with by merry groups

[1] P. Rascher, "Die Sulka, ein Beitrag
zur Ethnographie Neu - Pommern,"
Archiv für Anthropologie, xxix. (1904)
p. 216.   Compare R. Parkinson,
Dreissig Jahre in der Südsee, p. 198.
[2] Washington   Matthews,   " The
Mountain Chant, a Navajo Ceremony,"
Fifth Annual Report of the Bureau

of Ethnology (Washington, 1887), pp.
386 sq.
[3] L. H. Morgan, League of the Iroquois (Rochester, U.S., 1851), pp.
167 sq.   The writer derives the prohibition to tell tales of wonder in
summer "from a vague and indefinable
dread."

gathered round the fire.[1]　The Yabims of German New Guinea tell their magical tales especially at the time when the yams have been gathered and are stored in the houses. Such tales are told at evening by the light of the fire to a circle of eager listeners, the narrative being broken from time to time with a song in which the hearers join.　The telling of these stories is believed to promote the growth of the crops.　Hence each tale ends with a wish that there may be many yams, that the taro may be big, the sugar-cane thick, and the bananas long.[2]

Winter and summer names of the Kwa-kiutl Indians.

Among the Kwakiutl Indians of British Columbia the superstition about names has affected in a very curious way the social structure of the tribe.　The nobles have two different sets of names, one for use in winter and the other in summer.　Their winter names are those which were given them at initiation by their guardian spirits, and as these spirits appear to their devotees only in winter, the names which they bestowed on the Indians may not be pronounced in summer.　Conversely the summer names may not be used in winter.　The change from summer to winter names takes place from the moment when the spirits are supposed to be present, and it involves a complete transformation of the social system ; for whereas during summer the people are grouped in clans, in winter they are grouped in societies, each society consisting of all persons who have been initiated by the same spirit and have received from him the same magical powers.　Thus among these Indians the fundamental constitution of society changes with the seasons : in summer it is organised on a basis of kin, in winter on a basis of spiritual affinity : for one half the year it is civil, for the other half religious.[3]

---

[1] H. R. Schoolcraft, *Indian Tribes*, iii. 314, 492.

[2] K. Vetter, in *Mittheilungen der Geographischen Gesellschaft zu Jena*, xii. (1893) p. 95 ; *id.*, *Komm herüber und hilf uns !* ii. (Barmen, 1898) p. 26 ; B. Hagen, *Unter den Papuas* (Wiesbaden, 1898), p. 270. On myths or magical tales told as spells to produce the effects which they describe,

compare F. Kauffmann, *Balder* (Strasburg, 1902), pp. 299 *sqq.*; C. Fossey, *La Magie assyrienne* (Paris, 1902), pp. 95-97.

[3] Fr. Boas, "The Social Organization and the Secret Societies of the Kwakiutl Indians," *Report of the U.S. National Museum for 1895*, pp. 396, 418 *sq.*, 503, 504. Compare *Totemism and Exogamy*, iii. 333 *sq.*, 517 *sq.*

§ 5. *Names of Gods tabooed*

Primitive man creates his gods in his own image. Names of gods kept secret. Xenophanes remarked long ago that the complexion of negro gods was black and their noses flat; that Thracian gods were ruddy and blue-eyed; and that if horses, oxen, and lions only believed in gods and had hands wherewith to portray them, they would doubtless fashion their deities in the form of horses, and oxen, and lions.[1] Hence just as the furtive savage conceals his real name because he fears that sorcerers might make an evil use of it, so he fancies that his gods must likewise keep their true names secret, lest other gods or even men should learn the mystic sounds and thus be able to conjure with them. Nowhere was this crude conception of the secrecy and magical virtue of the divine name more firmly held or more fully developed than in ancient Egypt, where the superstitions of a dateless past were embalmed in the hearts of the people hardly less effectually than the bodies of cats and crocodiles and the rest of the divine menagerie in their rock-cut tombs. The conception How Isis discovered the name of Ra, the sun-god. is well illustrated by a story which tells how the subtle Isis wormed his secret name from Ra, the great Egyptian god of the sun. Isis, so runs the tale, was a woman mighty in words, and she was weary of the world of men, and yearned after the world of the gods. And she meditated in her heart, saying, "Cannot I by virtue of the great name of Ra make myself a goddess and reign like him in heaven and earth?" For Ra had many names, but the great name which gave him all power over gods and men was known to none but himself. Now the god was by this time grown old; he slobbered at the mouth and his spittle fell upon the ground. So Isis gathered up the spittle and the earth with it, and kneaded thereof a serpent and laid it in the path where the great god passed every day to his double kingdom after his heart's desire. And when he came forth according to his wont, attended by all his company of gods, the sacred serpent

---

[1] Xenophanes, quoted by Eusebius, *Praeparatio Evangelii*, xiii. 13, pp. 269 *sq.*, ed. Heinichen, and by Clement of Alexandria, *Strom.* vii. 4, pp. 840 *sq.*, ed. Potter; H. Diels, *Die Fragmente der Vorsokratiker*[2] (Berlin, 1906-1910), i. 49.

How Isis
discovered
the name
of Ra, the
sun-god.
stung him, and the god opened his mouth and cried, and
his cry went up to heaven.   And the company of gods cried,
" What aileth thee ? " and the gods shouted, " Lo and behold ! "
But he could not answer ; his jaws rattled, his limbs shook,
the poison ran through his flesh as the Nile floweth over the
land.   When the great god had stilled his heart, he cried to
his followers, " Come to me, O my children, offspring of my
body.   I am a prince, the son of a prince, the divine seed of
a god.   My father devised my name ; my father and my
mother gave me my name, and it remained hidden in my
body since my birth, that no magician might have magic
power over me.   I went out to behold that which I have
made, I walked in the two lands which I have created, and
lo ! something stung me.   What it was, I know not.   Was
it fire ? was it water ?   My heart is on fire, my flesh
trembleth, all my limbs do quake.   Bring me the children
of the gods with healing words and understanding lips, whose
power reacheth to heaven."   Then came to him the children
of the gods, and they were very sorrowful.   And Isis came
with her craft, whose mouth is full of the breath of life,
whose spells chase pain away, whose word maketh the dead
to live.   She said, " What is it, divine Father ? what is it ? "
The holy god opened his mouth, he spake and said, " I went
upon my way, I walked after my heart's desire in the two
regions which I have made to behold that which I have
created, and lo ! a serpent that I saw not stung me.   Is it
fire ? is it water ?   I am colder than water, I am hotter than
fire, all my limbs sweat, I tremble, mine eye is not steadfast,
I behold not the sky, the moisture bedeweth my face as in
summer-time."   Then spake Isis, " Tell me thy name, divine
Father, for the man shall live who is called by his name."
Then answered Ra, " I created the heavens and the earth, I
ordered the mountains, I made the great and wide sea, I
stretched out the two horizons like a curtain.   I am he who
openeth his eyes and it is light, and who shutteth them and
it is dark.   At his command the Nile riseth, but the gods
know not his name.   I am Khepera in the morning, I am
Ra at noon, I am Tum at eve."   But the poison was not
taken away from him ; it pierced deeper, and the great god
could no longer walk.   Then said Isis to him, " That was

not thy name that thou spakest unto me. Oh tell it me, that the poison may depart; for he shall live whose name is named." Now the poison burned like fire, it was hotter than the flame of fire. The god said, " I consent that Isis shall search into me, and that my name shall pass from my breast into hers." Then the god hid himself from the gods, and his place in the ship of eternity was empty. Thus was the name of the great god taken from him, and Isis, the witch, spake, " Flow away poison, depart from Ra. It is I, even I, who overcome the poison and cast it to the earth ; for the name of the great god hath been taken away from him. Let Ra live and let the poison die." Thus spake great Isis, the queen of the gods, she who knows Ra and his true name.[1]

Thus we see that the real name of the god, with which his power was inextricably bound up, was supposed to be lodged, in an almost physical sense, somewhere in his breast, from which it could be extracted by a sort of surgical operation and transferred with all its supernatural powers to the breast of another. In Egypt attempts like that of Isis to appropriate the power of a high god by possessing herself of his name were not mere legends told of the mythical beings of a remote past ; every Egyptian magician aspired to wield like powers by similar means. For it was believed that he who possessed the true name possessed the very being of god or man, and could force even a deity to obey him as a slave obeys his master. Thus the art of the magician consisted in obtaining from the gods a revelation of their sacred names, and he left no stone unturned to accomplish his end. When once a god in a moment of weakness or forgetfulness had imparted to the wizard the wondrous lore, the deity had no choice but to submit humbly to the man or pay the penalty of his contumacy.[2]

Egyptian wizards have worked enchantments by the names of the gods both in ancient and modern times

[1] A. Erman, *Ägypten und ägyptisches Leben im Altertum*, pp. 359-362 ; A. Wiedemann, *Die Religion der alten Ägypter*, pp. 29-32 ; G. Maspero, *Histoire ancienne des peuples de l'Orient classique: les origines*, pp. 162-164 ; R. V. Lanzone, *Dizionario di mitologia egizia* (Turin, 1881-1884), pp. 818-822 ; E. A. Wallis Budge, *The Book of the Dead* (London, 1895), pp. lxxxix.-xci. ; *id.*, *Egyptian Magic*, pp.

136 *sqq.*; *id.*, *The Gods of the Egyptians* (London, 1904), i. 360 *sq.* The abridged form of the story given in the text is based on a comparison of these various versions, of which Erman's is slightly, and Maspero's much curtailed. Mr. Budge's version is reproduced by Mr. E. Clodd (*Tom Tit Tot*, pp. 180 *sqq.*).

[2] G. Maspero, *Études de mythologie et d'archéologie égyptienne* (Paris, 1893), ii. 297 *sq.*

In one papyrus we find the god Typhon thus adjured : " I invoke thee by thy true names, in virtue of which thou canst not refuse to hear me " ; and in another the magician threatens Osiris that if the god does not do his bidding he will name him aloud in the port of Busiris.[1] So in the Lucan the Thessalian witch whom Sextus Pompeius consulted before the battle of Pharsalia threatens to call up the Furies by their real names if they will not do her bidding.[2] In modern Egypt the magician still works his old enchantments by the same ancient means ; only the name of the god by which he conjures is different. The man who knows " the most great name " of God can, we are told, by the mere utterance of it kill the living, raise the dead, transport himself instantly wherever he pleases, and perform any other miracle.[3]

Similarly among the Arabs of North Africa at the present day " the power of the name is such that when one knows the proper names the jinn can scarcely help answering the call and obeying ; they are the servants of the magical names ; in this case the incantation has a constraining quality which is for the most part very strongly marked. When Ibn el Hâdjdj et-Tlemsânî relates how the jinn yielded up their secrets to him, he says, ' I once met the seven kings of the jinn in a cave and I asked them to teach me the way in which they attack men and women, causing them to fall sick, smiting them, paralysing them, and the like. They all answered me : " If it were anybody but you we would teach that to nobody, but you have discovered the bonds, the spells, and the names which compel us ; were it not for the names by which you have constrained us, we would not have answered to your call." ' "[4] So, too, " the Chinese of ancient times were dominated by the notion that beings are intimately associated with their names, so that a man's knowledge of the name of a spectre might enable him to exert power over the latter and to bend it to his will."[5]

---

[1] E. Lefébure, "La Vertu et la vie du nom en Égypte," *Mélusine*, viii. (1897) coll. 227 *sq.* Compare A. Erman, *Ägypten und ägyptisches Leben im Altertum*, pp. 472 *sq.* ; E. A. Wallis Budge, *Egyptian Magic*, pp. 157 *sqq.*

[2] Lucan, *Pharsalia*, vi. 730 *sqq.*

[3] E. W. Lane, *Manners and Customs of the Ancient Egyptians* (Paisley and London, 1895), ch. xii. p. 273.

[4] E. Doutté, *Magie et religion dans l'Afrique du nord*, p. 130.

[5] J. J. M. de Groot, *The Religious System of China*, vi. (Leyden, 1910) p. 1126.

The belief in the magic virtue of divine names was Divine names used by the Romans to conjure with.
shared by the Romans. When they sat down before a city,
the priests addressed the guardian deity of the place in a
set form of prayer or incantation, inviting him to abandon
the beleaguered city and come over to the Romans, who
would treat him as well as or better than he had ever
been treated in his old home. Hence the name of the
guardian deity of Rome was kept a profound secret, lest the
enemies of the republic might lure him away, even as the
Romans themselves had induced many gods to desert, like
rats, the falling fortunes of cities that had sheltered them in
happier days.[1] Nay, the real name, not merely of its
guardian deity, but of the city itself, was wrapt in mystery
and might never be uttered, not even in the sacred rites. A
certain Valerius Soranus, who dared to divulge the priceless
secret, was put to death or came to a bad end.[2] In like manner,
it seems, the ancient Assyrians were forbidden to mention
the mystic names of their cities ;[3] and down to modern
times the Cheremiss of the Caucasus keep the names of their
communal villages secret from motives of superstition.[4]

If the reader has had the patience to follow this long The taboos on names of kings and commoners are alike in origin.
and perhaps tedious examination of the superstitions attaching
to personal names, he will probably agree that the mystery
in which the names of royal personages are so often shrouded
is no isolated phenomenon, no arbitrary expression of courtly
servility and adulation, but merely the particular application
of a general law of primitive thought, which includes within
its scope common folk and gods as well as kings and priests.

---

[1] Pliny, *Nat. Hist.* xxviii. 18 ;
Macrobius, *Saturn.* iii. 9 ; Servius on
Virgil, *Aen.* ii. 351 ; Plutarch, *Quaest.
Rom.* 61. According to Servius (*l.c.*)
it was forbidden by the pontifical law
to mention any Roman god by his
proper name, lest it should be profaned. Compare Festus, p. 106, ed.
C. O. Müller : "*Indigetes dii quorum
nomina vulgari non licet.*" On the
other hand the Romans were careful,
for the sake of good omen, to choose
men with lucky names, like Valerius,
Salvius, Statorius, to open any enterprise
of moment, such as to lead the sacrificial
victims in a religious procession or to

be the first to answer to their names in
a levy or a census. See Cicero, *De
divinatione,* i. 45. 102 *sq.* ; Festus,
s.v. "Lacus Lucrinus," p. 121, ed.
C. O. Müller ; Pliny, *Nat. Hist.*
xxviii. 22 ; Tacitus, *Histor.* iv. 53.

[2] Pliny, *Nat. Hist.* iii. 65 ; Solinus,
i. 4 *sq.* ; Macrobius, *Sat.* iii. 9, 3, and
5 ; Servius, on Virgil, *Aen.* i. 277 ;
Joannes Lydus, *De mensibus,* iv. 50.

[3] F. Fossey, *La Magie assyrienne*
(Paris, 1902), pp. 58, 95.

[4] T. de Pauly, *Description ethnographique des peuples de la Russie* (St.
Petersburg, 1862), *Peuples ouralo-
altaïques,* p. 24.

§ 6. *Common Words tabooed*

Common words as well as personal names are often tabooed from superstitious motives.

But personal names are not the only words which superstitious fears have banished from everyday use.   In many cases similar motives forbid certain persons at certain times to call common things by common names, thus obliging them either to refrain from mentioning these things altogether or to designate them by special terms or phrases reserved for such occasions.   A consideration of these cases follows naturally on an examination of the taboos imposed upon personal names ; for personal names are themselves very often ordinary terms of the language, so that an embargo laid on them necessarily extends to many expressions current in the commerce of daily life.   And though a survey of some of the interdicts on common words is not strictly necessary for our immediate purpose, it may serve usefully to complete our view of the transforming influence which superstition has exercised on language.   I shall make no attempt to subject the examples to a searching analysis or a rigid classification, but will set them down as they come in a rough geographical order.   And since my native land furnishes as apt instances of the superstition as any other, we may start on our round from Scotland.

Common words tabooed by Highland fowlers and fishermen.

In the Atlantic Ocean, about six leagues to the west of Gallon Head in the Lewis, lies a small group of rocky islets known as the Flannan Islands.   Sheep and wild fowl are now their only inhabitants, but remains of what are described as Druidical temples and the title of the Sacred Isles given them by Buchanan suggest that in days gone by piety or superstition may have found a safe retreat from the turmoil of the world in these remote solitudes, where the dashing of the waves and the strident scream of the sea-birds are almost the only sounds that break the silence.   Once a year, in summer-time, the inhabitants of the adjacent lands of the Lewis, who have a right to these islands, cross over to them to fleece their sheep and kill the wild fowl for the sake both of their flesh and their feathers.   They regard the islands as invested with a certain sanctity, and have been heard to say that none ever yet landed in them but found himself more

disposed to devotion there than anywhere else. Accordingly
the fowlers who go thither are bound, during the whole of
the time that they ply their business, to observe very punc-
tiliously certain quaint customs, the transgression of which
would be sure, in their opinion, to entail some serious inconvenience. When they have landed and fastened their boat
to the side of a rock, they clamber up into the island by a
wooden ladder, and no sooner are they got to the top, than
they all uncover their heads and make a turn sun-ways round
about, thanking God for their safety. On the biggest of the
islands are the ruins of a chapel dedicated to St. Flannan.
When the men come within about twenty paces of the altar,
they all strip themselves of their upper garments at once and
betake themselves to their devotions, praying thrice before
they begin fowling. On the first day the first prayer is
offered as they advance towards the chapel on their knees ;
the second is said as they go round the chapel ; and the
third is said in or hard by the ruins. They also pray thrice
every evening, and account it unlawful to kill a fowl after
evening prayers, as also to kill a fowl at any time with a
stone. Another ancient custom forbids the crew to carry
home in the boat any suet of the sheep they slaughter in
the islands, however many they may kill. But what here
chiefly concerns us is that so long as they stay on the islands
they are strictly forbidden to use certain common words, and
are obliged to substitute others for them. Thus it is absolutely unlawful to call the island of St. Kilda, which lies
thirty leagues to the southward, by its proper Gaelic name
of Hirt ; they must call it only " the high country." They
may not so much as once name the islands in which they
are fowling by the ordinary name of Flannan ; they must
speak only of " the country." " There are several other
things that must not be called by their common names : *e.g.*
visk, which in the language of the natives signifies water,
they call burn ; a rock, which in their language is *creg*, must
here be called *cruey*, *i.e.* hard ; shore in their language
expressed by *claddach*, must here be called *vah*, *i.e.* a cave ;
sour in their language is expressed *gort*, but must here be
called *gaire*, *i.e.* sharp ; slippery, which is expressed *bog*,
must be called soft ; and several other things to this

purpose." [1]   When Highlanders were in a boat at sea, whether sailing or fishing, they were forbidden to call things by the names by which they were known on land.   Thus the boat-hook should not be called a *croman*, but a *chliob ;* a knife not *sgian*, but "the sharp one" (*a ghiar*) ; a seal not *ròn*, but "the bald beast" (*béisd mhaol*) ; a fox not *sionnach*, but "the red dog" (*madadh ruadh*) ; the stone for anchoring the boat not *clach*, but "hardness" (*cruaidh*).   This practice now prevails much more on the east coast than on the west, where it may be said to be generally extinct.   It is reported to be carefully observed by the fishermen about the Cromarty Firth.[2] Among the words tabooed by fishermen in the north of Scotland when they are at sea are minister, salmon, hare, rabbit, rat, pig, and porpoise.   At the present day if some of the boats that come to the herring-fishing at Wick should meet a salmon-boat from Reay in Caithness, the herring-men will not speak to, nor even look at, the salmon-fishers.[3]

Common words tabooed by Scotch fishermen and others.   When Shetland fishermen are at sea, they employ a nomenclature peculiar to the occasion, and hardly anything may be mentioned by its usual name.   The substituted terms are mostly of Norwegian origin, for the Norway men were reported to be good fishers.[4]   In setting their lines the Shetland fishermen are bound to refer to certain objects only by some special words or phrases.   Thus a knife is then called a *skunie* or *tullie* ; a church becomes *buanhoos* or *banehoos* ; a minister is *upstanda* or *haydeen* or *prestingolva* ; the devil is *da auld chield, da sorrow, da ill-healt* (health), or *da black tief* ; a cat is *kirser, fitting, vengla*, or *foodin*.[5]   On the north-east coast of Scotland there are some villages, of which the inhabitants never pronounce certain words and family names when they are at sea ; each village has its peculiar aversion to one or more of these words, among which are " minister," " kirk," " swine," " salmon,"

[1] M. Martin, "Description of the Western Islands of Scotland," in Pinkerton's *Voyages and Travels*, iii. 579 *sq.* As to the Flannan Islands see also Sir J. Sinclair's *Statistical Account of Scotland*, xix. (Edinburgh, 1797), p. 283.

[2] J. G. Campbell, *Superstitions of the Highlands and Islands of Scotland*

(Glasgow, 1900), p. 239.

[3] Miss Morag Cameron, "Highland Fisher-folk and their Superstitions," *Folk-lore*, xiv. (1903) p. 304.

[4] A. Edmonston, *Zetland Islands* (Edinburgh, 1809), ii. 74.

[5] Ch. Rogers, *Social Life in Scotland* (Edinburgh, 1884 - 1886), iii. 218.

"trout," and "dog." When a church has to be referred to, as often happens, since some of the churches serve as land-marks to the fishermen at sea, it is spoken of as the "bell-hoose" instead of the "kirk." A minister is called "the man wi' the black quyte." It is particularly unlucky to utter the word "sow" or "swine" or "pig" while the line is being baited; if any one is foolish enough to do so, the line is sure to be lost. In some villages on the coast of Fife a fisherman who hears the ill-omened word spoken will cry out "Cold iron." In the village of Buckie there are some family names, especially Ross, and in a less degree Coull, which no fisherman will pronounce. If one of these names be men-tioned in the hearing of a fisherman, he spits or, as he calls it, "chiffs." Any one who bears the dreaded name is called a "chiffer-oot," and is referred to only by a circumlocution such as "The man it diz so in so," or "the laad it lives at such and such a place." During the herring-season men who are unlucky enough to inherit the tabooed names have little chance of being hired in the fishing-boats; and some-times, if they have been hired before their names were known, they have been refused their wages at the end of the season, because the boat in which they sailed had not been successful, and the bad luck was set down to their presence in it.[1] Although in Scotland superstitions of this kind appear to be specially incident to the callings of fishermen and fowlers, other occupations are not exempt from them. Thus in the Outer Hebrides the fire of a kiln is not called fire (*teine*) but *aingeal*. Such a fire, it is said, is a dangerous thing, and ought not to be referred to except by a euphemism. "Evil be to him who called it fire or who named fire in the kiln. It was considered the next thing to setting it on fire."[2] Again, in some districts of Scotland a brewer would have resented the use of the word "water" in reference to the work in which he was engaged. "Water be your part of it," was the common retort. It was supposed that the use of the word would spoil the brewing.[3] The Highlanders say

[1] W. Gregor, *Folk-lore of the North-East of Scotland*, pp. 199-201.

[2] "Traditions, Customs, and Super-stitions of the Lewis," *Folk-lore*, vi. (1895) p. 170; Miss A. Goodrich-Freer,

"The Powers of Evil in the Outer Hebrides," *Folk-lore*, x. (1899) p. 265.

[3] J. Mackenzie, *Ten Years north of the Orange River* (Edinburgh, 1871), p. 151, note 1.

that when you meet a hobgoblin, and the fiend asks what is the name of your dirk, you should not call it a dirk (*biodag*), but "my father's sister" (*piuthar m'athar*) or "my grandmother's sister" (*piuthar mo sheanamhair*) or by some similar title. If you do not observe this precaution, the goblin will lay such an enchantment on the blade that you will be unable to stab him with it; the dirk will merely make a tinkling noise against the soft impalpable body of the fiend.[1]

Common words, especially the names of dangerous animals, tabooed in various parts of Europe.

Manx fishermen think it unlucky to mention a horse or a mouse on board a fishing-boat.[2] The fishermen of Dieppe on board their boats will not speak of several things, for instance priests and cats.[3] German huntsmen, from motives of superstition, call everything by names different from those in common use.[4] In some parts of Bavaria the farmer will not mention a fox by its proper name, lest his poultry-yard should suffer from the ravages of the animal. So instead of *Fuchs* he calls the beast *Loinl, Henoloinl, Henading*, or *Henabou*.[5] In Prussia and Lithuania they say that in the month of December you should not call a wolf a wolf but "the vermin" (*das Gewürm*), otherwise you will be torn in pieces by the werewolves.[6] In various parts of Germany it is a rule that certain animals may not be mentioned by their proper names in the mystic season between Christmas and Twelfth Night. Thus in Thüringen they say that if you would be spared by the wolves you must not mention their name at this time.[7] In Mecklenburg people think that were they to name a wolf on one of these days the animal would appear. A shepherd would rather mention the devil than the wolf at this season; and we read of a farmer who had a bailiff named Wolf, but did not dare to call the man by his name between Christmas and Twelfth Night, referring to him instead as Herr Undeert (Mr. Monster).

[1] J. G. Campbell, *Witchcraft and Second Sight in the Highlands and Islands of Scotland* (Glasgow, 1902), pp. 184 *sq.*

[2] J. Rhys, "Manx Folk-lore and Superstitions," *Folk-lore*, iii. (1892) p. 84.

[3] A. Bosquet, *La Normandie romanesque et merveilleuse* (Paris and Rouen, 1845), p. 308.

[4] J. G. Gmelin, *Reise durch Sibirien*, ii. (Göttingen, 1752), p. 277.

[5] *Bavaria, Landes- und Volkskunde des Königreichs Bayern*, ii. (Munich, 1863), p. 304.

[6] Tettau und Temme, *Die Volkssagen Ostpreussens, Litthauens und Westpreussens* (Berlin, 1837), p. 281.

[7] W. Witzschel, *Sagen, Sitten, und Gebräuche aus Thüringen*, p. 175, § 30.

In Quatzow, a village of Mecklenburg, there are many
animals whose common names are disused at this season
and replaced by others: thus a fox is called "long-tail,"
and a mouse "leg-runner" (*Boenlöper*). Any person who
disregards the custom has to pay a fine.[1] In the Mark of
Brandenburg they say that between Christmas and Twelfth
Night you should not speak of mice as mice but as
dinger; otherwise the field-mice would multiply excessively.[2]
According to the Swedish popular belief, there are certain
animals which should never be spoken of by their proper
names, but must always be signified by euphemisms and
kind allusions to their character. Thus, if you speak slight-
ingly of the cat or beat her, you must be sure not to mention
her name; for she belongs to the hellish crew, and is a friend
of the mountain troll, whom she often visits. Great caution is
also needed in talking of the cuckoo, the owl, and the magpie,
for they are birds of witchery. The fox must be called
"blue-foot," or "he that goes in the forest"; and rats are
"the long-bodied," mice "the small grey," and the seal
"brother Lars." Swedish herd-girls, again, believe that if
the wolf and the bear be called by other than their proper
and legitimate names, they will not attack the herd. Hence
they give these brutes names which they fancy will not hurt
their feelings. The number of endearing appellations
lavished by them on the wolf is legion; they call him
"golden tooth," "the silent one," "grey legs," and so on;
while the bear is referred to by the respectful titles of "the
old man," "grandfather," "twelve men's strength," "golden
feet," and more of the same sort. Even inanimate things
are not always to be called by their usual names. For
instance, fire is sometimes to be called "heat" (*hetta*) not
eld or *ell*; water for brewing must be called *lag* or *löu*, not
vatn, else the beer would not turn out so well.[3] The Huzuls
of the Carpathians, a pastoral people, who dread the ravages
of wild beasts on their flocks and herds, are unwilling to
mention the bear by his proper name, so they call him

[1] K. Bartsch, *Sagen, Märchen, und
Gebräuche aus Meklenburg*, ii. p. 246,
§§ 1273, 1274.
[2] A. Kuhn, *Märkische Sagen und
Märchen*, p. 378, § 14.
[3] B. Thorpe, *Northern Mythology*,
ii. 83 *sq.*; L. Lloyd, *Peasant Life in
Sweden* (London, 1870), p. 251.

respectfully "the little uncle" or "the big one." In like manner and for similar reasons they name the wolf "the little one" and the serpent "the long one."[1]　They may not say that wool is scalded, or in the heat of summer the sheep would rub themselves till their sides were raw; so they merely say that the wool is warmed.[2]　The Lapps fear to call the bear by his true name, lest he should ravage their herds; so they speak of him as "the old man with the coat of skin," and in cooking his flesh to furnish a meal they may not refer to the work they are engaged in as "cooking," but must designate it by a special term.[3]　The Finns speak of the bear as "the apple of the wood," "beautiful honey-paw," "the pride of the thicket," "the old man," and so on.[4]　And in general a Finnish hunter thinks that he will have poor sport if he calls animals by their real names; the beasts resent it.　The fox and the hare are only spoken of as "game," and the lynx is termed "the forest cat," lest it should devour the sheep.[5]　Esthonian peasants are very loth to mention wild beasts by their proper names, for they believe that the creatures will not do so much harm if only they are called by other names than their own.　Hence they speak of the bear as "broad foot" and the wolf as "grey coat."[6]

The names of various animals tabooed in Siberia, Kamtchatka, and America.　　The natives of Siberia are unwilling to call a bear a bear; they speak of him as "the little old man," "the master of the forest," "the sage," "the respected one."　Some who are more familiar style him "my cousin."[7]　The Kamtchatkans reverence the whale, the bear, and the wolf from fear, and never mention their names when they meet them, believing that they understand human speech.[8]　Further, they

[1] R. F. Kaindl, *Die Huzulen* (Vienna, 1894), p. 103; *id.*, "Viehzucht und Viehzauber in den Ostkarpaten," *Globus*, lxix. (1896) p. 387.

[2] *Id.*, "Neue Beiträge zur Ethnologie und Volkskunde der Huzulen," *Globus*, lxix. (1896) p. 73.

[3] C. Leemius, *De Lapponibus Finmarchiae eorumque lingua, vita, et religione pristina commentatio* (Copenhagen, 1767), pp. 502 *sq.*

[4] M. A. Castren, *Vorlesungen über die finnische Mythologie* (St. Petersburg, 1853), p. 201.

[5] Varonen, reported by Hon. J. Abercromby in *Folk-lore*, .ii. (1891) pp. 245 *sq.*

[6] Boecler - Kreutzwald, *Der Ehsten abergläubische Gebräuche, Weisen und Gewohnheiten*, p. 120.

[7] P. Labbé, *Un Bagne russe, l'île de Sakhaline* (Paris, 1903), p. 231.

[8] G. W. Steller, *Beschreibung von dem Lande Kamtschatka* (Frankfort and Leipsic, 1774), p. 276.

think that mice also understand the Kamtchatkan language ; so in autumn, when they rob the field-mice of the bulbs which these little creatures have laid up in their burrows as a store against winter, they call everything by names different from the ordinary ones, lest the mice should know what they were saying.   Moreover, they leave odds and ends, such as old rags, broken needles, cedar-nuts, and so forth, in the burrows, to make the mice think that the transaction has been not a robbery but a fair exchange.   If they did not do that, they fancy that the mice would go and drown or hang themselves out of pure vexation ; and then what would the Kamtchat-kans do without the mice to gather the bulbs for them ? They also speak kindly to the animals, and beg them not to take it ill, explaining that what they do is done out of pure friendship.[1]   The Cherokee Indians regard the rattlesnake as a superior being and take great pains not to offend him. They never say that a man has been bitten by a snake but that he has been " scratched by a briar."   In like manner, when an eagle has been shot for a ceremonial dance, it is announced that " a snowbird has been killed."   The purpose is to deceive the spirits of rattlesnakes or eagles which might be listening.[2]   The Esquimaux of Bering Strait think that some animals can hear and understand what is said of them at a distance.   Hence, when a hunter is going out to kill bears he will speak of them with the greatest respect and give out that he is going to hunt some other beast.   Thus the bears will be deceived and taken unawares.[3]   Among the Esquimaux of Baffin Land, women in mourning may not mention the names of any animals.[4]   Among the Thompson Indians of British Columbia, children may not name the coyote or prairie wolf in winter, lest he should turn on his back and so bring cold weather.[5]

[1] G. W. Steller, *op. cit.* p. 91 ; compare *ib.* pp. 129, 130.

[2] J. Mooney, " Sacred Formulas of the Cherokees," *Seventh Annual Report of the Bureau of Ethnology* (Washington, 1892), p. 352. Compare *id.*, " Myths of the Cherokee," *Nineteenth Annual Report of the Bureau of American Ethnology*, Part i. (Washington, 1900) p. 295.

[3] E. W. Nelson, " The Eskimo about Bering Strait," *Eighteenth Annual Report of the Bureau of American Ethnology*, Part i. (Washington, 1899) p. 438.

[4] F. Boas, " The Eskimo of Baffin Land and Hudson Bay," *Bulletin of the American Museum of Natural History*, xv. (1901) p. 148.

[5] J. Teit, " The Thompson Indians of British Columbia," *Memoir of the American Museum of Natural History*,

Names of animals and things tabooed by the Arabs, Africans, and Malagasy.

The Arabs call a man who has been bitten by a snake "the sound one"; leprosy or the scab they designate "the blessed disease"; the left side they name "the lucky side"; they will not speak of a lion by his right name, but refer to him as for example "the fox."[1] In Africa the lion is alluded to with the same ceremonious respect as the wolf and the bear in northern Europe and Asia. The Arabs of Algeria, who hunt the lion, speak of him as Mr. John Johnson (Johan·ben-el-Johan), because he has the noblest qualities of man and understands all languages. Hence, too, the first huntsman to catch sight of the beast points at him with his finger and says, "He is not there"; for if he were to say "He is there," the lion would eat him up.[2] Except under dire necessity the Waziguas of eastern Africa never mention the name of the lion from fear of attracting him. They call him "the owner of the land" or "the great beast."[3] The negroes of Angola always use the word *ngana* ("sir") in speaking of the same noble animal, because they think that he is "fetish" and would not fail to punish them for disrespect if they omitted to do so.[4] Bushmen and Bechuanas both deem it unlucky to speak of the lion by his proper name; the Bechuanas call him "the boy with the beard."[5] During an epidemic of smallpox in Mombasa, British East Africa, it was noticed that the people were unwilling to mention the native name (*ndui*) of the disease. They referred to it either as "grains of corn" (*tete*) or simply as "the bad disease."[6] So the Chinese of Amoy are averse to speak of fever by its proper name; they prefer to call it "beggar's disease," hoping thereby to make the demons of fever imagine that they despise it and that therefore it would be useless to attack them.[7] Some of the natives of Nigeria

The Jesup North Pacific Expedition, vol. i. part iv. (April 1900) p. 374.

[1] J. Wellhausen, *Reste arabischen Heidentums* [2] (Berlin, 1897), p. 199.

[2] A. Certeux et E. H. Carnoy, *L'Algérie traditionnelle* (Paris and Algiers, 1884), pp. 172, 175.

[3] Father Picarda, "Autour de Mandéra," *Missions Catholiques*, xviii. (1886) p. 227.

[4] J. J. Monteiro, *Angola and the*

River Congo (London, 1875), ii. 116.

[5] J. Mackenzie, *Ten Years north of the Orange River* (Edinburgh, 1871), p. 151; C. R. Conder, in *Journal of the Anthropological Institute*, xvi. (1887) p. 84.

[6] H. B. Johnstone, "Notes on the Customs of the Tribes occupying Mombasa Sub-district, British East Africa," *Journal of the Anthropological Institute*, xxxii. (1902) p. 268.

[7] J. J. M. de Groot, *The Religious*

dread the owl as a bird of ill omen and are loth to mention its name, preferring to speak of it by means of a circumlocution such as "the bird that makes one afraid."[1] The Herero think that if they see a snake and call it by its name, the reptile will sting them, but that if they call it a strap (*omuvia*) it will lie still.[2] When Nandi warriors are out on an expedition, they may not call a knife a knife (*chepkeswet*); they must call it "an arrow for bleeding cattle" (*loñget*); and none of the party may utter the usual word employed in greeting males.[3] In Madagascar there seems to be an aversion to pronouncing the word for lightning (*vàratra*); the word for mud (*fòtaka*) is sometimes substituted for it.[4] Again, it is strictly forbidden to mention the word for crocodile (*màmba*) near some rivers of Madagascar ; and if clothes should be wetted in certain other rivers of the island, you may not say that they are wet (*lèna*); you must say that they are on fire (*may*) or that they are drinking water (*misòtro ràno*).[5] A certain spirit, who used to inhabit a lake in Madagascar, entertained a rooted aversion to salt, so that whenever the thing was carried past the lake in which he resided it had to be called by another name, or it would all have been dissolved and lost. The persons whom he inspired had to veil their references to the obnoxious article under the disguise of "sweet peppers."[6] In a West African story we read of a man who was told that he would die if ever the word for salt was pronounced in his hearing. The fatal word was pronounced, and die he did sure enough, but he soon came to life again with the help of a magical wooden pestle of which he was the lucky possessor.[7]

In India the animals whose names are most commonly tabooed are the snake and the tiger, but the same tribute of respect is paid to other beasts also. Sayids and Mussul-

Names of animals, especially the snake

System of China, v. (Leyden, 1907) p. 691.

[1] A. F. Mockler-Ferryman, *British Nigeria* (London, 1902), p. 285.

[2] J. Irle, *Die Herero* (Gütersloh, 1906), p. 133.

[3] A. C. Hollis, *The Nandi* (Oxford, 1909), p. 43.

[4] H. F. Standing, "Malagasy *fady*,"

Antananarivo Annual and Madagascar Magazine, vol. ii., *Reprint of the Second Four Numbers* (Antananarivo, 1896), p. 258.

[5] H. F. Standing, *op. cit.* p. 263.

[6] J. Sibree, *The Great African Island*, pp. 307 *sq.*

[7] R. H. Nassau, *Fetichism in West Africa* (London, 1904), pp. 381 *sqq.*

mans of high rank in northern India say that you should
never call a snake by its proper name, but always describe
it either as a tiger (*sher*) or a string (*rassi*).[1]   In Telingana
the euphemistic name for a snake, which should always be
employed, is worm or insect (*purugu*) ; if you call a cobra by
its proper name, the creature will haunt you for seven years
and bite you at the first opportunity.[2]   Ignorant Bengalee
women will not mention a snake or a thief by their proper
names at night, for fear that one or other might appear.
When they have to allude to a serpent, they call it " the
creeping thing " ; when they speak of a thief, they say " the
unwelcome visitor." [3]   Other euphemisms for the snake in
northern India are " maternal uncle " and " rope."   They
say that if a snake bites you, you should not mention its
name, but merely observe " A rope has touched me." [4]
Natives of Travancore are careful not to speak disrespectfully of serpents.   A cobra is called " the good lord " (*nalla
tambiran*) or " the good snake" (*nalla pambu*).   While the
Malayalies of the Shervaray Hills are hunting the tiger, they
speak of the beast only as " the dog." [5]   The Canarese of
southern India call the tiger either "the dog" or " the
jackal"; they think that if they called him by his proper
name, he would be sure to carry off one of them.[6]   The
jungle people of northern India, who meet the tiger in his
native haunts, will not pronounce his name, but speak of him
as " the jackal " (*gídar*), or " the beast " (*janwar*), or use
some other euphemistic term.   In some places they treat
the wolf and the bear in the same fashion.[7]   The Pankas of
South Mirzapur will not name the tiger, bear, camel, or
donkey by their proper names ; the camel they call " long
neck."   Other tribes of the same district only scruple to
mention certain animals in the morning.   Thus, the Khar-
wars, a Dravidian tribe, will not name a pig, squirrel, hare,
jackal, bear, monkey, or donkey in the morning hours ; if

[1] *Panjab Notes and Queries*, i. p. 15,
§ 122.
[2] *North Indian Notes and Queries*,
i. p. 104, § 690.
[3] *Id.* v. p. 133, § 372.
[4] W. Crooke, *Popular Religion
and Folk-lore of Northern India*

(Westminster, 1896), ii. 142 *sq.*
[5] S. Mateer, *Native Life in Travancore*, pp. 320 *sq.*
[6] *North Indian Notes and Queries*,
v. p. 133, § 372.
[7] W. Crooke, *op. cit.* ii. 212.

they have to allude to these animals at that time, they call them by special names. For instance, they call the hare "the four-footed one" or "he that hides in the rocks"; while they speak of the bear as *jigariya*, which being interpreted means "he with the liver of compassion." If the Bhuiyars are absolutely obliged to refer to a monkey or a bear in the morning, they speak of the monkey as "the tree-climber" and the bear as "the eater of white ants." They would not mention a crocodile. Among the Pataris the matutinal title of the bear is "the hairy creature."[1] The Kols, a Dravidian race of northern India, will not speak of death or beasts of prey by their proper names in the morning. Their name for the tiger at that time of day is "he with the claws," and for the elephant "he with the teeth."[2] The forests of the Sundarbans, the district at the mouth of the Ganges, are full of man-eating tigers and the annual loss of life among the woodcutters is heavy. Here accordingly the ferocious animal is not called a tiger but a jackal (*çial*).[3]

In Annam the fear inspired by tigers, elephants, and other wild animals induces the people to address these creatures with the greatest respect as "lord" or "grandfather," lest the beasts should take umbrage and attack them.[4] The tiger reigns supreme in the forests of Tonquin and Cochin-China, and the peasants honour him as a maleficent deity. In talking of him they always call him *ong*, which means monsieur or grandfather. They are convinced that if they dared to speak of him disrespectfully, he would avenge the insult.[5] In Siam there are many people who would never venture to utter the words tiger or crocodile in a spot where these terrible creatures might be in hiding, lest

[marginal note:] Names of animals and things tabooed in Indo-China.

---

[1] W. Crooke in *North Indian Notes and Queries*, i. p. 70, § 579; *id.*, *Tribes and Castes of the North-Western Provinces and Oudh*, iii. 249; *id.*, *Popular Religion and Folk-lore of Northern India* (Westminster, 1896), ii. 54.

[2] W. Crooke, *Tribes and Castes of the North-Western Provinces and Oudh*, iii. 314.

[3] D. Sunder, "Exorcism of Wild Animals in the Sundarbans," *Journal of the Asiatic Society of Bengal*, lxxii. part iii. (Calcutta, 1904) pp. 45 *sqq.*, 51.

[4] H. Mouhot, *Travels in the Central Parts of Indo-China* (London, 1864), i. 263 *sq.*

[5] Mgr Masson, in *Annales de la Propagation de la Foi*, xxiv. (1852) p. 323. Compare Le R. P. Cadière, "Croyances et dictons populaires de la vallée du Nguôn-son," *Bulletin de l'École Française d'Extrême-Orient*, i. (1901) p. 134.

Names of animals and things tabooed in Indo-China.

the sound of their names should attract the attention of the beasts towards the speakers.[1] When the Malays of Patani Bay in Siam are in the jungle and think there is a tiger near, they will either speak of him in complimentary terms as the "grandfather of the woods" or only mention him in a whisper.[2] In Laos, while a man is out hunting elephants he is obliged to give conventional names to all common objects, which creates a sort of special language for elephant-hunters.[3] So when the Chams and Orang-Glaï of Indo-China are searching for the precious eagle-wood in the forest, they must employ an artificial jargon to designate most objects of everyday life ; thus, for example, fire is called "the red," a she-goat becomes "a spider," and so on. Some of the terms which compose the jargon are borrowed from the dialects of neighbouring tribes.[4] When the Mentras or aborigines of Malacca are searching for what they call *gaharu* (*lignum aloes*) they are obliged to use a special language, avoiding the words in ordinary use. At such times they call *gaharu* by the name of *tabak*, and they speak of a snake as "the long animal" and of the elephant as "the great animal." They have also to observe a number of other taboos, particularly in the matter of diet. If a man has found a promising *gaharu* tree, and on going home dreams that the guardian spirit of the tree (*hantu gaharu*) demands a human victim as the price of his property, the dreamer will try next day to catch somebody asleep and to smear his forehead with lime. This is a sign to the guardian spirit of the tree, who accordingly carries away the soul of the sleeper to the land of the dead by means of a fever or other ailment, whereas the original dreamer gets a good supply of aloes wood.[5]

[1] E. Young, *The Kingdom of the Yellow Robe* (Westminster, 1898), p. 61.

[2] N. Annandale, "Primitive Beliefs and Customs of the Patani Fishermen," *Fasciculi Malayenses, Anthropology*, part i. (April 1903) p. 104.

[3] E. Aymonier, *Notes sur le Laos*, p. 113 ; *id.*, *Voyage dans le Laos*, i. (Paris, 1895) p. 311. In the latter passage the writer observes that the custom of giving conventional names

to common objects is very generally observed in Indo-China during the prosecution of long and perilous journeys undertaken periodically.

[4] *Id.*, "Les Tchames et leurs religions," *Revue de l'Histoire des Religions*, xxiv. (1891) p. 278. Compare A. Cabaton, *Nouvelles Recherches sur les Chams* (Paris, 1901), p. 53.

[5] D. F. A. Hervey, in *Indian Notes and Queries* (December 1886), p. 45, § 154.

At certain seasons of the year parties of Jakuns and
Binuas go out to seek for camphor in the luxuriant forests
of their native country, which is the narrow southern
extremity of the Malay Peninsula, the Land's End of Asia.
They are absent for three or four months together, and
during the whole of this time the use of the ordinary Malay
language is forbidden to them, and they have to speak a
special language called by them the *bassa kapor* (camphor
language) or *pantang*[1] *kapur*. Indeed not only have the
searchers to employ this peculiar language, but even the
men and women who stay at home in the villages are
obliged to speak it while the others are away looking for
the camphor. They believe that a spirit presides over the
camphor trees, and that without propitiating him they could
not obtain the precious gum ; the shrill cry of a species of
cicada, heard at night, is supposed to be the voice of the
spirit. If they failed to employ the camphor language, they
think that they would have great difficulty in finding the
camphor trees, and that even when they did find them the
camphor would not yield itself up to the collector. The
camphor language consists in great part of words which are
either Malayan or of Malay origin ; but it also contains
many words which are not Malayan but are presumed to be
remains of the original Jakun dialects now almost extinct in
these districts. The words derived from Malayan are formed
in many cases by merely substituting a descriptive phrase
for the common term. Thus instead of rice they say " grass
fruit " ; instead of gun they say " far sounding " ; the epithet
" short-legged " is substituted for hog ; hair is referred to as
"leaves," and so on.[2] So when the Battas or Bataks of Sumatra
have gone out to search for camphor, they must abandon the
speech of daily life as soon as they reach the camphor

---

[1] *Pantang* is equivalent to taboo. In this sense it is used also by the Dyaks. See S. W. Tromp, " Een Dajaksch Feest," *Bijdragen tot de Taal- Land- en Volkenkunde van Neder-landsch-Indië*, xxxix. (1890) pp. 31 *sq.*

[2] J. R. Logan, " The Orang Binua of Johore," *Journal of the Eastern Archipelago and Eastern Asia*, i. (1847) pp. 249, 263-265 ; A. Bastian,

Die Völker des östlichen Asien, v. 37 ; H. Lake and H. J. Kelsall, " The Camphor Tree and Camphor Language of Johore," *Journal of the Straits Branch of the Royal Asiatic Society*, No. 26 (January 1894), pp. 39 *sq.* ; W. W. Skeat, *Malay Magic*, pp. 212-214 ; W. W. Skeat and C. O. Blagden, *Pagan Races of the Malay Peninsula* (London, 1906), ii. 414-431.

forest. For example, if they wish to speak of the forest they may not use the ordinary word for it (*hoetan*), but must call it *kerrengettetdoeng*. When they have fixed on a spot in which to try their luck, they set up a booth and clear a space in front of it to serve as a place of sacrifice. Here, after summoning the camphor spirit (*berroe ni kapoer*) by playing on a flute, they offer sacrifice to him repeatedly. Then they lie down to dream of the place where camphor is to be found. If this succeeds, the leader goes and chooses the tree. When it has been cut down to the accompaniment of certain spells or incantations, one of the men runs and wraps the top of the fallen tree in a garment to prevent the camphor from escaping from the trunk before they have secured it. Then the tree is cleft and split up in the search for the camphor crystals, which are to be found in the fibres of the wood.[1] Similarly, when the Kayans of Borneo are searching for camphor, they talk a language invented solely for their use at this time. The camphor itself is never mentioned by its proper name, but is always referred to as " the thing that smells " ; and all the tools employed in collecting the drug receive fanciful names. Unless they conform to this rule they suppose that the camphor crystals, which are found only in the crevices of the wood, will elude them.[2] The Malanau tribes of Borneo observe the same custom very strictly, believing that the crystals would immediately dissolve if they spoke anything but the camphor language. For example, the common Malanau word for " return " is *muli*, but in presence of a camphor tree they say *beteku*. Again, " to hide " is *palim* in the Malanau language, but when they are looking for camphor they say *krian*. In like manner, all common names for implements and food are exchanged for others. In some tribes the camphor - seekers may never mention the names of chiefs and influential men ;

---

[1] C. M. Pleyte, "Herinneringen uit Oost-Indië,"*Tijdschrift van het koninklijk Nederlandsch Aardrijkskundig Genootschap*, II Serie, xvii. (1900) pp. 27 *sq.*

[2] W. H. Furness, *Folk-lore in Borneo* (Wallingford, Pennsylvania, 1899 ; privately printed), p. 27 ; *id., Home-life of Borneo Head-hunters* (Philadelphia, 1902), p. 17. A special language is also used in the search for camphor by some of the natives of Sumatra. See Th. A. L. Heyting, " Beschrijving der onder - afdeeling Groot-Mandeling en Batang-Natal," *Tijdschrift van het Nederlandsch Aardrijkskundig Genootschap*, Tweede Serie, xiv. (1897) p. 276.

if they broke this rule, they would find no camphor in the trees.[1]

In the western states of the Malay Peninsula the chief industry is tin-mining, and odd ideas prevail among the natives as to the nature and properties of the ore. They regard it as alive and growing, sometimes in the shape of a buffalo, which makes its way from place to place underground. Ore of inferior quality is excused on the score of its tender years; it will no doubt improve as it grows older. Not only is the tin believed to be under the protection and command of certain spirits who must be propitiated, but it is even supposed to have its own special likes and dislikes for certain persons and things. Hence the Malays deem it advisable to treat tin ore with respect, to consult its convenience, nay, to conduct the business of mining in such a way that the ore may, as it were, be extracted without its own knowledge. When such are their ideas about the mineral it is no wonder that the miners scruple to employ certain words in the mines, and replace them by others which are less likely to give offence to the ore or its guardian spirits. Thus, for example, the elephant must not be called an elephant but "the tall one who turns himself about"; and in like manner special words, different from those in common use, are employed by the miners to designate the cat, the buffalo, the snake, the centipede, tin sand, metallic tin, and lemons. Lemons are particularly distasteful to the spirits; they may not be brought into the mines.[2] Again, the Malay wizard, who is engaged in snaring pigeons with the help of a decoy-bird and a calling-tube, must on no account call things by their common names. The tiny conical hut, in which he sits waiting for the wild pigeons to come fluttering about him, goes by the high-sounding name of the Magic Prince, perhaps with a delicate allusion to its noble inmate. The calling-tube is known as Prince

Special language used by Malay miners.

Special language used by Malay fowlers.

[1] W. H. Furness, *Home-life of Borneo Head-hunters*, pp. 168 *sq.*

[2] W. W. Skeat, *Malay Magic*, pp. 250, 253-260. In like manner the people of Sikhim intensely dread all mining operations, believing that the ores and veins of metals are the stored treasures of the earth-spirits, who are enraged by the removal of these treasures and visit the robbers with sickness, failure of crops, and other calamities. Hence the Sikhimese leave the copper mines to be worked by Nepaulese. See L. A. Waddell, *Among the Himalayas* (Westminster, 1899), p. 101.

Distraction, doubtless on account of the extraordinary fascination it exercises on the birds. The decoy-pigeon receives the name of the Squatting Princess, and the rod with a noose at the end of it, which serves to catch the unwary birds, is disguised under the title of Prince Invitation. Everything, in fact, is on a princely scale, so far at least as words can make it so. The very nooses destined to be slipped over the necks or legs of the little struggling prisoners are dignified by the title of King Solomon's necklaces and armlets; and the trap into which the birds are invited to walk is variously described as King Solomon's Audience Chamber, or a Palace Tower, or an Ivory Hall carpeted with silver and railed with amalgam. What pigeon could resist these manifold attractions, especially when it is addressed by the respectful title of Princess Kapor or Princess Sarap or Princess Puding?[1] Again, the fisher-folk on the east coast of the Malay Peninsula, like their brethren in Scotland, are reluctant to mention the names of birds or beasts while they are at sea. All animals then go by the name of *cheweh*, a meaningless word which is believed not to be understood by the creatures to whom it refers. Particular kinds of animals are distinguished by appropriate epithets; the pig is "the grunting *cheweh*," the buffalo is "the *cheweh* that says *uak*," the snipe is "the *cheweh* that cries *kek-kek*," and so on.[2] In this respect the fishermen of Patani Bay class together sea spirits, Buddhist monks, beasts, and reptiles; these are all *cheweh* and their common names may not be mentioned at sea. But, curiously enough, they lay no such embargo on the names of fish and birds, except the vulture and domestic fowls and ducks. At sea the vulture is named "bald head," the tiger "striped," the snake "weaver's sword," the horse "fast," and a species of monkey "long tail." The human foot is called "tortoise," and a Buddhist monk "yellow" on account of the colour of his robe. These Malay fishermen are at least as unwilling to speak of a Buddhist monk at sea as Scotch fishermen are to mention a minister in similar circumstances. If one of them mentions a monk, his mates will fall on him and beat him; whereas for other slips of the tongue they

Special language used by Malay fishermen.

---

[1] W. W. Skeat, *op. cit.* pp. 139 *sq.*   [2] W. W. Skeat, *op. cit.* pp. 192 *sq.*

think it enough to throw a little bilge-water over the back of the transgressor and to say, " May the ill-luck be dismissed ! " The use of this special language is even more obligatory by night than by day. On shore the fishermen make very merry over those lubberly landsmen who cannot talk correctly at sea.[1] In like manner Achinese fishermen, in northern Sumatra, employ a special vocabulary when they are at sea. Thus they may not call a mountain a mountain, or mountain-high billows would swamp the boat ; they refer to it as " high ground." They may not speak of an elephant by its proper name of *gadjah*, but must call it *pò meurah*. If a man wishes to say that something is clear, he must not use the ordinary word for clear (*lheuëh*) because it bears the meaning also of " free," " loose " ; and the utterance of such a word might enable the fish to get free from the net and escape. Instead of *lheuëh* he must therefore employ the less dangerous synonym *leungka*. In like manner, we are told, among the fishermen of the north coast of Java whole lists of words might be compiled which are tabooed at sea and must be replaced by others.[2]

In Sumatra the spirits of the gold mines are treated with as much deference as the spirits of the tin-mines in the Malay Peninsula. Tin, ivory, and the like may not be brought by the miners to the scene of their operations, for at the scent of such things the spirits of the mine would cause the gold to vanish. For the same reason it is forbidden to refer to certain things by their proper names, and in speaking of them the miners must use other words. In some cases, for example in removing the grains of the gold, a deep silence must be observed ; no commands may be given or questions asked,[3] probably because the removal of the precious metal is regarded as a theft which the spirits would punish if they caught the thieves in the act. Certainly the

Names of things and animals tabooed in Sumatra, Nias, and Java.

[1] N. Annandale, "Primitive Beliefs and Customs of the Patani Fishermen," *Fasciculi Malayenses, Anthropology*, part i. (April 1903) pp. 84-86.

[2] C. Snouck Hurgronje, *De Atjèhers* (Batavia and Leyden, 1893-1894), i. 303.

[3] J. L. van der Toorn, "Het ani-misme bij den Minangkabauer der Padangsche Bovenlanden," *Bijdragen tot de Taal- Land- en Volkenkunde van Nederlandsch-Indië*, xxxix. (1890) p. 100. As to the superstitions of gold-washers among the Gayos of Sumatra, see C. Snouck Hurgronje, *Het Gajoland en zijne Bewoners* (Batavia, 1903), pp. 361 *sq.*

Names of
things and
animals
tabooed in
Sumatra,
Nias, and
Java.
Dyaks believe that gold has a soul which seeks to avenge itself on men who dig the precious metal. But the angry spirit is powerless to harm miners who observe certain precautions, such as never to bathe in a river with their faces turned up stream, never to sit with their legs dangling, and never to tie up their hair.[1] Again, a Sumatran who fancies that there is a tiger or a crocodile in his neighbourhood, will speak of the animal by the honourable title of "grandfather" for the purpose of propitiating the creature.[2] In the forest a Karo-Batak refers to a tiger as "Grandfather to whom the wood belongs," "he with the striped coat," or "the roving trap."[3] Among the Gayos of Sumatra it is forbidden to mention the name of small-pox in the house of a man who is suffering from the disease; and the words for ugly, red, stinking, unlucky, and so forth are forbidden under the same circumstances. The disease is referred to under the title of "prince of the averters of misfortune."[4] So long as the hunting season lasts, the natives of Nias may not name the eye, the hammer, stones, and in some places the sun by their true names; no smith may ply his trade in the village, and no person may go from one village to another to have smith's work done for him. All this, with the exception of the rule about not naming the eye and the sun, is done to prevent the dogs from growing stiff, and so losing the power of running down the game.[5] During the rice-harvest in Nias the reapers seldom speak to each other, and when they do so, it is only in whispers. Outside the field they must speak of everything by names different from those in common use, which gives rise to a special dialect or jargon known as "field speech." It has been observed that some of the words in this jargon

---

[1] M. T. H. Perelaer, *Ethnographische Beschrijving der Dajaks* (Zalt-Bommel, 1870), p. 215.

[2] J. T. Nieuwenhuisen en H. C. B. von Rosenberg, "Verslag omtrent het eiland Nias," *Verhandelingen van het Bataviaasch Genootschap van Kunsten en Wetenschappen*, xxx. (1863) p. 115. Compare W. Marsden, *History of Sumatra*, p. 292; T. J. Newbold, *Account of the British Settlements in the Straits of Malacca*, ii. 192 *sq.*

[3] J. E. Neumann, "*Kemali, Pantang en Rěboe* bij de Karo-Bataks," *Tijdschrift voor Indische Taal- Land- en Volkenkunde*, xlviii. (1906) pp. 511 *sq.*

[4] C. Snouck Hurgronje, *Het Gajoland en zijne Bewoners* (Batavia, 1903), pp. 311 *sq.*

[5] J. W. Thomas, "De jacht op het eiland Nias," *Tijdschrift voor Indische Taal- Land- en Volkenkunde*, xxvi. (1880) p. 275.

resemble words in the language of the Battas of Sumatra.[1] While these rice-reapers of Nias are at work they may not address each other by their names ; they must use only such general terms as " man," " woman," " girl," " old man," and " old woman." The word for " fire " may not pass their lips ; instead of it they must use the word for " cold." Other words tabooed to them during the harvest are the words for " smoke " and " stone." If a reaper wishes to ask another for his whetstone to sharpen his knife, he must speak of it as a " fowl's egg."[2] In Java when people suspect that a tiger or crocodile is near, they avoid the use of the proper name of the beast and refer to him as " the old lord " or " grandfather." Similarly, men who are watching a plantation to protect it from wild boars speak of these animals as " handsome men " (*wong bagus*). When after harvest the unhusked rice is to be brought into the barn, the barn is not called a barn but " the dark store-house." Serious epidemics may not be mentioned by their true names ; thus smallpox is called the " pretty girl " (*lara bagus*). The Javanese are particularly careful to eschew certain common words at evening or night. Thus the snake is then called a " tree-root " ; the venomous centipede is referred to as the " red ant " ; oil is spoken of as " water " ; and so forth. And when leaves and herbs are being gathered for use in medicine they are regularly designated by other than their ordinary names.[3]

The Alfoors or Toradjas of Poso, in Celebes, are for- Names of bidden by custom to speak the ordinary language when they things and animals are at work in the harvest-field. At such times they employ tabooed in a secret language which is said to agree with the ordinary Celebes. one only in this, that in it some things are designated by

[1] L. N. H. A. Chatelin, " Gods-dienst en bijgeloof der Niassers," *Tijd-schrift voor Indische Taal- Land- en Volkenkunde*, xxvi. (1880) p. 165 ; H. Sundermann, " Die Insel Nias und die Mission daselbst," *Allgemeine Mis-sions-Zeitschrift*, xi. (1884) p. 349 ; E. Modigliani, *Un Viaggio a Nías* (Milan, 1890), p. 593.

[2] A. L. van Hasselt, " Nota, betreff-ende de rijstcultuur in de Residentie Tapanoeli," *Tijdschrift voor Indische*

Taal- Land- en Volkenkunde, xxxvi. (1893) pp. 525 *sq*. The Singhalese also call things by strange names when they are in the rice-fields. See A. A. Perera, " Glimpses of Singhalese Social Life," *Indian Antiquary*, xxxii. (1903) p. 437.

[3] G. A. J. Hazeu, " Kleine Bij-dragen tot de Ethnografie en de Folk-lore van Java," *Tijdschrift voor Indische Taal- Land- en Volkenkunde*, xlvii. (1903) pp. 291 *sq*.

words usually applied in a different sense, or by descriptive phrases or circumlocutions.   Thus instead of " run " they say " limp " ;   instead of " hand " they say " that with which one reaches " ;   instead of " foot " they say " that with which one limps " ;   and instead of " ear " they say " that with which one hears."   Again, in the field-speech " to drink " becomes " to thrust forward the mouth " ; " to pass by " is expressed by " to nod with the head " ; a gun is " a fire-producer " ; and wood is " that which is carried on the shoulder."   The writer who reports the custom was formerly of opinion that this secret language was designed to avoid attracting the attention of evil spirits to the ripe rice ; but further enquiry has satisfied him that the real reason for adopting it is a wish not to frighten the soul of the rice by revealing to it the alarming truth that it is about to be cut, carried home, boiled, and eaten.   It is just the words referring to these actions, he tells us, which are especially tabooed and replaced by others.   Beginning with a rule of avoiding a certain number of common words, the custom has grown among people of the Malay stock till it has produced a complete language for use in the fields.   In Minahassa also this secret field-speech consists in part of phrases or circumlocutions, of which many are said to be very poetical.[1]   But it is not only on the harvest field that the Toradja resorts to the use of a secret language from superstitious motives.   In the great primaeval forest he feels ill at ease, for well he knows the choleric temper of the spirits who inhabit the giant trees of the wood, and that were he to excite their wrath they would assuredly pay him out in one way or other, it might be by carrying off his soul and so making him ill, it might be by crushing him flat under a falling tree.   These touchy beings particularly dislike to hear certain words pronounced, and accordingly on his way through the forest the Toradja takes care to avoid the offensive terms and to substitute others for them.   Thus he will not call a dog a dog, but refers to it as " the hairy one " ; a buffalo is spoken of as " thick hide " ; a

---

[1] A. C. Kruijt, " Een en ander aangaande het geestelijk en maatschappelijk leven van den Poso-Alfoer," *Mededeelingen van wege het Nederlandsche Zendelinggenootschap*, xxxix. (1895) pp. 146-148 ; *id.*, " Eenige ethnografische aanteekeningen omtrent de Toboengkoe en de Tomori," *ibid.* xliv. (1900) pp. 228 *sq.*

cooking pot becomes "that which is set down"; the hair of the head is alluded to as "betel"; goats and pigs are "the folk under the house"; a horse is "long nose"; and deer are "denizens of the fell." If he is rash or careless enough to utter a forbidden word in the forest, a short-tempered tree-spirit will fetch him such a bang on the head that the blood will spout from his nose and mouth.[1] Again, when the weather is fine and the Toradja wishes it to continue so, he is careful not to utter the word "rain," for if he did so the rain would fancy he was called for and would obligingly present himself. Indeed, in the district of Pakambia, which is frequently visited by heavy storms, the word "rain" may not be mentioned throughout the year lest it should provoke a tempest; the unmentionable thing is there delicately alluded to as "tree-blossoms."[2]

When a Bugineese or Macassar man is at sea and sailing past a place which he believes to be haunted by evil spirits, he keeps as quiet as he can; but if he is obliged to speak he designates common things and actions, such as water, wind, fire, cooking, eating, the rice-pot, and so forth, by peculiar terms which are neither Bugineese nor Macassar, and therefore cannot be understood by the evil spirits, whose knowledge of languages is limited to these two tongues. However, according to another and later account given by the same authority, it appears that many of the substituted terms are merely figurative expressions or descriptive phrases borrowed from the ordinary language. Thus the word for water is replaced by a rare word meaning "rain"; a rice-pot is called a "black man"; boiled rice is "one who is eaten"; a fish is a "tree-leaf"; a fowl is "one who lives in a poultry hatch"; and an ape is a "tree-dweller."[3] Natives of the island of Saleyer, which lies off the south coast of

Common words tabooed by East Indian mariners at sea.

---

[1] N. Adriani und A. C. Kruijt, "Van Posso naar Mori," *Mededeelingen van wege het Nederlandsche Zendelinggenootschap*, xliv. (1900) pp. 145 *sq.*

[2] A. C. Kruijt, "Regen lokken en regen verdrijven bij de Toradja's van Midden Celebes," *Tijdschrift voor Indische Taal- Land- en Volkenkunde*, xliv. (1901) p. 8; *id.*, "Het rijk Mori," *Tijdschrift van het Koniklijk Nederlandsch Aardrijkskundig Genoot-schap*, II. Serie, xvii. (1900) p. 464, note.

[3] B. F. Matthes, *Bijdragen tot de Ethnologie van Zuid-Celebes* (The Hague, 1875), p. 107; *id.*, "Over de *ådå's* of gewoonten der Makassaren en Boegineezen," *Verslagen en Mededeelingen der Koninklijke Akademie van Wetenschappen*, Afdeeling Letterkunde, III. Reeks, ii. (Amsterdam, 1885) pp. 164 *sq.*

Common
words
tabooed
by East
Indian
mariners
at sea.

Celebes, will not mention the name of their island when they are making a certain sea-passage ; and in sailing they will never speak of a fair wind by its proper name. The reason in both cases is a fear of disturbing the evil spirits.[1] When natives of the Sapoodi Archipelago, to the north-east of Java, are at sea they will never say that they are near the island of Sapoodi, for if they did so they would be carried away from it by a head wind or by some other mishap.[2] When Galelareese sailors are crossing over to a land that is some way off, say one or two days' sail, they do not remark on any vessels that may heave in sight or any birds that may fly past ; for they believe that were they to do so they would be driven out of their course and not reach the land they are making for. Moreover, they may not mention their own ship, or any part of it. If they have to speak of the bow, for example, they say "the beak of the bird " ; starboard is named " sword," and larboard "shield." [3] The inhabitants of Ternate and of the Sangi Islands deem it very dangerous to point at distant objects or to name them while they are at sea. Once while sailing with a crew of Ternate men a European asked one of them the name of certain small islands which they had passed. The man had been talkative before, but the question reduced him to silence. " Sir," he said, " that is a great taboo ; if I told you we should at once have wind and tide against us, and perhaps suffer a great calamity. As soon as we come to anchor I will tell you the name of the islands." The Sangi Islanders have, besides the ordinary language, an ancient one which is only partly understood by some of the people. This old language is often used by them at sea, as well as in popular songs and certain heathen rites.[4] The reason for resorting to it on shipboard is to hinder the evil spirits from overhearing

[1] H. E. D. Engelhard, "Mededeelingen over het eiland Saleijer," *Bijdragen tot de Taal- Land- en Volkenkunde van Neêrlandsch-Indië*, Vierde Volgreeks, viii. (1884) p. 369.

[2] E. F. Jochim, "Beschrijving van den Sapoedi Archipel," *Tijdschrift voor Indische Taal- Land- en Volkenkunde*, xxxvi. (1893) p. 361.

[3] M. J. van Baarda, "Fabelen, Verhalen en Overleveringen der Galelareezen," *Bijdragen tot de Taal- Land- en Volkenkunde van Nederlandsch-Indië*, xlv. (1895) p. 508.

[4] S. D. van de Velde van Cappellan, "Verslag eener Bezoekreis naar de Sangi-eilanden," *Mededeelingen van wege het Nederlandsche Zendelinggenootschap*, i. (1857) pp. 33, 35.

and so frustrating the plans of the voyagers.[1]   The Nufoors
of Dutch New Guinea believe that if they were to mention
the name of an island to which the bow of their vessel was
pointing, they would be met by storm, rain, or mist which
would drive them from their course.[2]

In some parts of Sunda it is taboo or forbidden to call *Common*
a goat a goat; it must be called a "deer under the house." *words*
A tiger may not be spoken of as a tiger; he must be referred *tabooed in Sunda,*
to as "the supple one," "the one there," "the honourable," *Borneo,*
"the whiskered one," and so on.   Neither a wild boar nor a *and the Philippines.*
mouse may be mentioned by its proper name; a boar must
be called "the beautiful one" (masculine) and the mouse
"the beautiful one" (feminine).   When the people are asked
what would be the consequence of breaking a taboo, they
generally say that the person or thing would suffer for it,
either by meeting with a mishap or by falling ill.   But some
say they do not so much fear a misfortune as experience
an indefinite feeling, half fear, half reverence, towards an
institution of their forefathers.   Others can assign no reason
for observing the taboos, and cut enquiry short by saying
that "It is so because it is so."[3]   When the Kenyahs of
Borneo are about to poison the fish of a section of the river
with the *tuba* root, they always speak of the matter as little
as possible and use the most indirect and fanciful modes of
expression.   Thus they will say, "There are many leaves
fallen here," meaning that there are many fish in the river.
And they will not breathe the name of the *tuba* root; if they
must refer to it, they call it *pakat abong*, where *abong* is the
name of a strong-smelling root something like *tuba*, and
pakat means "to agree upon"; so that *pakat abong* signifies
"what we have agreed to call *abong*."   This concealment of
the truth deceives all the bats, birds, and insects, which might
otherwise overhear the talk of the men and inform the fish of
the deep-laid plot against them.[4]   These Kenyahs also fear

[1] A. C. Kruijt, "Een en ander
aangaande het geestelijk en maatschappelijk leven van den Poso-Alfoer,"
*Mededeelingen van wege het Neder-
landsche Zendelinggenootschap*, xxxix.
(1895) p. 148.

[2] Th. J. F. van Hasselt, "Gebruik
van vermomde Taal door de Nufooren,"

*Tijdschrift voor Indische Taal- Land-
en Volkenkunde*, xlv. (1902) pp. 279 *sq.*

[3] K. F. Holle, "Snippers van den
Regent van Galoeh," *Tijdschrift voor
Indische Taal- Land- en Volkenkunde*,
xxvii. (1882) pp. 101 *sq.*

[4] Ch. Hose and W. McDougall,
"The Relations between Men and

the crocodile and do not like to mention it by name, especially
if one be in sight; they refer to the beast as "the old
grandfather."[1] When small-pox invades a village of the
Sakarang Dyaks in Borneo, the people desert the place and
take refuge in the jungle. In the daytime they do not dare
to stir or to speak above a whisper, lest the spirits should see
or hear them. They do not call the small-pox by its proper
name, but speak of it as "jungle leaves" or "fruit" or "the
chief," and ask the sufferer, "Has he left you?" and the
question is put in a whisper lest the spirit should hear.[2]
Natives of the Philippines were formerly prohibited from
speaking of the chase in the house of a fisherman and from
speaking of fishing in the house of a hunter; journeying by
land they might not talk of marine matters, and sailing on
the sea they might not talk of terrestrial matters.[3]

The avoidance of common words seems to be based on a fear of spirits and a wish to deceive them or elude their notice.

When we survey the instances of this superstition which
have now been enumerated, we can hardly fail to be struck
by the number of cases in which a fear of spirits, or of other
beings regarded as spiritual and intelligent, is assigned as the
reason for abstaining in certain circumstances from the use
of certain words.[4] The speaker imagines himself to be over-
heard and understood by spirits, or animals, or other beings

Animals in Sarawak," *Journal of the Anthropological Institute*, xxxi. (1902) p. 205; W. H. Furness, *Home-life of Borneo Head-hunters* (Philadelphia, 1902), pp. 17, 186 *sq.*

[1] Ch. Hose and W. McDougall, *op. cit.* p. 186.

[2] Ch. Brooke, *Ten Years in Sarawak* (London, 1866), i. 208; Spenser St. John, *Life in the Forests of the Far East*,[2] i. 71 *sq.*

[3] Juan de la Concepcion, *Historia general de Philipinas*, i. (Manilla, 1788), p. 20. Compare J. Mallat, *Les Philippines* (Paris, 1846), i. 64.

[4] On this subject Mr. R. J. Wilkinson's account of the Malay's attitude to nature (*Malay Beliefs*, London and Leyden, 1906, pp. 67 *sq.*) deserves to be quoted: "The practice of magic arts enters into every department of Malay life. If (as the people of the Peninsula believe) all nature is teeming with spiritual life, some spiritual weapon is necessary to protect man against possible ghostly foes. Now the chief and most characteristic weapon of the Malay in his fight against the invisible world is courtesy. The peasant will speak no evil of a tiger in the jungle or of an evil spirit within the limits of that spirit's authority. . . . The tiger is the symbol of kingly oppression; still, he is royal and must not be insulted; he is the 'shaggy-haired father' or 'grandfather' of the traveller in the woods. Even the birds, the fish and the fruits that serve as human food are entitled to a certain consideration: the deer is addressed as a 'prince,' the coco-nut tree as a 'princess,' the chevrotin as 'emperor of the jungle' (*shah alam di-rimba*). In all this respect paid to unseen powers—for it is the soul of the animal or plant that is feared—there is no contemptible adulation or cringeing; the Malay believes that courtesy honours the speaker more than the person addressed."

whom his fancy endows with human intelligence; and hence
he avoids certain words and substitutes others in their stead,
either from a desire to soothe and propitiate these beings by
speaking well of them, or from a dread that they may understand his speech and know what he is about, when he happens
to be engaged in that which, if they knew of it, would excite
their anger or their fear. Hence the substituted terms fall into
two classes according as they are complimentary or enigmatic;
and these expressions are employed, according to circumstances, for different and even opposite reasons, the complimentary because they will be understood and appreciated,
and the enigmatic because they will not. We can now see
why persons engaged in occupations like fishing, fowling,
hunting, mining, reaping, and sailing the sea, should abstain
from the use of the common language and veil their meaning in strange words and dark phrases. For they have this
in common that all of them are encroaching on the domain
of the elemental beings, the creatures who, whether visible
or invisible, whether clothed in fur or scales or feathers,
whether manifesting themselves in tree or stone or running
stream or breaking wave, or hovering unseen in the air, may
be thought to have the first right to those regions of earth
and sea and sky into which man intrudes only to plunder
and destroy. Thus deeply imbued with a sense of the all-
pervading life and intelligence of nature, man at a certain
stage of his intellectual development cannot but be visited
with fear or compunction, whether he is killing wild fowl
among the stormy Hebrides, or snaring doves in the sultry
thickets of the Malay Peninsula; whether he is hunting the
bear in Lapland snows, or the tiger in Indian jungles, or
hauling in the dripping net, laden with silvery herring, on
the coast of Scotland; whether he is searching for the
camphor crystals in the shade of the tropical forest, or
extracting the red gold from the darksome mine, or laying
low with a sweep of his sickle the yellow ears on the harvest
field. In all these his depredations on nature, man's first
endeavour apparently is by quietness and silence to escape
the notice of the beings whom he dreads; but if that cannot
be, he puts the best face he can on the matter by dissembling
his foul designs under a fair exterior, by flattering the

Common
words
avoided by
hunters
and fowlers
in order to
deceive the
beasts and
birds.
creatures whom he proposes to betray, and by so guarding his lips, that, though his dark ambiguous words are understood well enough by his fellows, they are wholly unintelligible to his victims.   He pretends to be what he is not, and to be doing something quite different from the real business in hand.   He is not, for example, a fowler catching pigeons in the forest ; he is a Magic Prince or King Solomon himself[1] inviting fair princesses into his palace tower or ivory hall. Such childish pretences suffice to cheat the guileless creatures whom the savage intends to rob or kill, perhaps they even impose to some extent upon himself ; for we can hardly dissever them wholly from those forms of sympathetic magic in which primitive man seeks to effect his purpose by imitating the thing he desires to produce, or even by assimilating himself to it.   It is hard indeed for us to realise the mental state of a Malay wizard masquerading before wild pigeons in the character of King Solomon ; yet perhaps the make-believe of children and of the stage, where we see the players daily forgetting their real selves in their passionate impersonation of the shadowy realm of fancy, may afford us some glimpse into the workings of that instinct of imitation or mimicry which is deeply implanted in the constitution of the human mind.

[1] The character of King Solomon appears to be a favourite one with the Malay sorcerer when he desires to ingratiate himself with or lord it over the powers of nature.   Thus, for example, in addressing silver ore the sage observes :—

" *If you do not come hither at this very moment*

You shall be a rebel unto God,
And a rebel unto God's Prophet Solomon,
For I am God's Prophet Solomon."—

See W. W. Skeat, *Malay Magic*, p. 273. No doubt the fame of his wisdom has earned for the Hebrew monarch this distinction among the dusky wizards of the East.

CHAPTER VII

OUR DEBT TO THE SAVAGE

IT would be easy to extend the list of royal and priestly General conclusion. taboos, but the instances collected in the preceding pages may suffice as specimens. To conclude this part of our subject it only remains to state summarily the general conclusions to which our enquiries have thus far conducted us. We have seen that in savage or barbarous society there are often found men to whom the superstition of their fellows ascribes a controlling influence over the general course of nature. Such men are accordingly adored and treated as gods. Whether these human divinities also hold temporal sway over the lives and fortunes of their adorers, or whether their functions are purely spiritual and supernatural, in other words, whether they are kings as well as gods or only the latter, is a distinction which hardly concerns us here. Their supposed divinity is the essential fact with which we have to deal. In virtue of it they are a pledge and guarantee to their worshippers of the continuance and orderly succession of those physical phenomena upon which mankind depends for subsistence. Naturally, therefore, the life and health of such a god-man are matters of anxious concern to the people whose welfare and even existence are bound up with his ; naturally he is constrained by them to conform to such rules as the wit of early man has devised for averting the ills to which flesh is heir, including the last ill, death. These rules, as an examination of them has shewn, are nothing but the maxims with which, on the primitive view, every man of common prudence must comply if he would live long in the land. But while in the

Human gods, on whom the welfare of the community is believed to depend, are obliged to observe many rules to ensure their own safety and that of their people.

case of ordinary men the observance of the rules is left to
the choice of the individual, in the case of the god-man it
is enforced under penalty of dismissal from his high station,
or even of death. For his worshippers have far too great
a stake in his life to allow him to play fast and loose with
it. Therefore all the quaint superstitions, the old - world
maxims, the venerable saws which the ingenuity of savage
philosophers elaborated long ago, and which old women at
chimney corners still impart as treasures of great price to
their descendants gathered round the cottage fire on winter
evenings—all these antique fancies clustered, all these cob-
webs of the brain were spun about the path of the old king,
the human god, who, immeshed in them like a fly in the
toils of a spider, could hardly stir a limb for the threads of
custom, "light as air but strong as links of iron," that
crossing and recrossing each other in an endless maze bound
him fast within a network of observances from which death
or deposition alone could release him.

A study of
these rules
affords us
an insight
into the
philosophy
of the
savage.
Thus to students of the past the life of the old kings
and priests teems with instruction. In it was summed up
all that passed for wisdom when the world was young. It
was the perfect pattern after which every man strove to
shape his life ; a faultless model constructed with rigorous
accuracy upon the lines laid down by a barbarous philosophy.
Crude and false as that philosophy may seem to us, it would
be unjust to deny it the merit of logical consistency. Starting from a conception of the vital principle as a tiny being
or soul existing in, but ·distinct and separable from, the
living being, it deduces for the practical guidance of life a
system of rules which in general hangs well together and
forms a fairly complete and harmonious whole.[1] The flaw—

[1] " The mind of the savage is not a
blank ; and when one becomes familiar
with his beliefs and superstitions, and
the complicated nature of his laws and
customs, preconceived notions of his
simplicity of thought go to the winds.
I have yet to find that most apocryphal
of beings described as the ' unsophisti-
cated African.' We laugh at and
ridicule his fetishes and superstitions,
but we fail to follow the succession of
ideas and effort of mind which have
created these things. After most careful observations extending over nineteen
years, I have come to the conclusion that
there is nothing in the customs and
fetishes of the African which does not
represent a definite course of reasoning"
(Rev. Thomas Lewis, " The Ancient
Kingdom of Kongo," *The Geographical
Journal*, xix. (1902) p. 554). " The
study of primitive peoples is extremely
curious and full of surprises. It is
twenty years since I undertook it

and it is a fatal one—of the system lies not in its reasoning, but in its premises; in its conception of the nature of life, not in any irrelevancy of the conclusions which it draws from that conception.   But to stigmatise these premises as ridiculous because we can easily detect their falseness, would be ungrateful as well as unphilosophical.   We stand upon Our debt to our savage forefathers. the foundation reared by the generations that have gone before, and we can but dimly realise the painful and prolonged efforts which it has cost humanity to struggle up to the point, no very exalted one after all, which we have reached.   Our gratitude is due to the nameless and forgotten toilers, whose patient thought and active exertions have largely made us what we are.   The amount of new knowledge which one age, certainly which one man, can add to the common store is small, and it argues stupidity or dishonesty, besides ingratitude, to ignore the heap while vaunting the few grains which it may have been our privilege to add to it.   There is indeed little danger at present of undervaluing the contributions which modern times and even classical antiquity have made to the general advancement of our race.   But when we pass these limits, the case is different.   Contempt and ridicule or abhorrence and denunciation are too often the only recognition vouchsafed to the savage and his ways.   Yet of the benefactors whom

among the Thonga and Pedi tribes of South Africa, and the further I advance, the more I am astonished at the great number, the complexity, and the profundity of the rites of these so-called savages.   Only a superficial observer could accuse their individual or tribal life of superficiality.   If we take the trouble to seek the reason of these strange customs, we perceive that at their base there are secret, obscure reasons, principles hard to grasp, even though the most fervent adepts of the rite can give no account of it.   To discover these principles, and so to give a true explanation of the rites, is the supreme task of the ethnographer,—a task in the highest degree delicate, for it is impossible to perform it if we do not lay aside our personal ideas to saturate ourselves with those of primitive peoples" (Rev. H. A. Junod, "Les Conceptions physiologiques des Bantou sud-africains et leurs tabous," *Revue d'Ethnographie et de Sociologie*, i. (1910) p. 126).   These weighty words, the fruit of ripe experience, deserve to be pondered by those who fancy that the elaborate system of savage custom can have grown up instinctively without a correspondingly elaborate process of reasoning in the minds of its founders.   We may not, indeed, always be able to discover the reason for which a particular custom or rite was instituted, for we are only beginning to understand the mind of uncivilised man; but all that we know of him tends to shew that his practice, however absurd it may seem to us, originated in a definite train of thought and for a definite and very practical purpose.

we are bound thankfully to commemorate, many, perhaps most, were savages. For when all is said and done our resemblances to the savage are still far more numerous than our differences from him ; and what we have in common with him, and deliberately retain as true and useful, we owe to our savage forefathers who slowly acquired by experience and transmitted to us by inheritance those seemingly fundamental ideas which we are apt to regard as original and intuitive. We are like heirs to a fortune which has been handed down for so many ages that the memory of those who built it up is lost, and its possessors for the time being regard it as having been an original and unalterable possession of their race since the beginning of the world. But reflection and enquiry should satisfy us that to our predecessors we are indebted for much of what we thought most our own, and that their errors were not wilful extravagances or the ravings of insanity, but simply hypotheses, justifiable as such at the time when they were propounded, but which a fuller experience has proved to be inadequate. It is only by the successive testing of hypotheses and rejection of the false that truth is at last elicited. After all, what we call truth is only the hypothesis which is found to work best. Therefore in reviewing the opinions and practices of ruder ages and races we shall do well to look with leniency upon their errors as inevitable slips made in the search for truth, and to give them the benefit of that indulgence which we ourselves may one day stand in need of: *cum excusatione itaque veteres audiendi sunt.*

NOTE

THE superstition that harm is done to a person or thing by stepping over him or it is very widely spread. Thus the Galelareese think that if a man steps over your fishing-rod or your arrow, the fish will not bite when you fish with that rod, and the game will not be hit by that arrow when you shoot it. They say it is as if the implements merely skimmed past the fish or the game.[2] Similarly, if a Highland sportsman saw a person stepping over his gun or fishing-rod, he presumed but little on that day's diversion.[3] When a Dacota had bad luck in hunting, he would say that a woman had been stepping over some part of the animal which he revered.[4] Amongst many South African tribes it is considered highly improper to step over a sleeper; if a wife steps over her husband he cannot hit his enemy in war; if she steps over his assegais, they are from that time useless, and are given to boys to play with.[5] The Baganda think that if a woman steps over a man's weapons, they will not aim straight and will not kill, unless they have been first purified.[6] The Nandi of British East Africa hold that to step over a snare or trap is to court death and must be avoided at all risks; further, they are of opinion that if a man were to step over a pot, he would fall to pieces whenever the pot were broken.[7] The people of the Lower Congo deem that to step over a person's body or legs will cause ill-luck to that person and they are careful not to do so, especially

[1] See above, pp. 159 sq.

[2] M. J. van Baarda, "Fabelen, Verhalen en Overleveringen der Galelareezen," *Bijdragen tot de Taal- Land- en Volkenkunde van Nederlandsch-Indië*, xlv. (1895) p. 513.

[3] John Ramsay, *Scotland and Scotsmen in the Eighteenth Century* (Edinburgh, 1888), ii. 456.

[4] H. R. Schoolcraft, *Indian Tribes*, ii. 175.

[5] J. Macdonald, *Light in Africa* (London, 1890), p. 209.

[6] Rev. J. Roscoe, in *Journal of the Anthropological Institute*, xxxii. (1902) p. 59.

[7] A. C. Hollis, *The Nandi*, pp. 24 sq., 36. In these cases the harm is thought to fall on the person who steps over, not on the thing which is stepped over.

in passing men who are holding a palaver. At such times a passer-by will shuffle his feet along the ground without lifting them in order that he may not be charged with bringing bad luck on any one.[1] On the other hand among the Wajagga of East Africa grandchildren leap over the corpse of their grandfather, when it is laid out, expressing a wish that they may live to be as old as he.[2] In Laos hunters are careful never to step over their weapons.[3] The Tepehuanes of Mexico believe that if anybody steps over them, they will not be able to kill another deer in their lives.[4] Some of the Australian aborigines are seriously alarmed if a woman steps over them as they lie asleep on the ground.[5] In the tribes about Maryborough in Queensland, if a woman steps over anything that belongs to a man he will throw it away.[6] In New Caledonia it is thought to endanger a canoe if a woman steps over the cable.[7] Everything that a Samoyed woman steps over becomes unclean and must be fumigated.[8] Malagasy porters believe that if a woman strides over their poles, the skin will certainly peel off the shoulders of the bearers when next they take up the burden.[9] The Cherokees fancy that to step over a vine causes it to wither and bear no fruit.[10] The Ba-Pendi and Ba-thonga of South Africa think that if a woman steps over a man's legs, they will swell and he will not be able to run.[11] According to the South Slavonians, the most serious maladies may be communicated to a person by stepping over him, but they can afterwards be cured by stepping over him in the reverse direction.[12] The belief that to step over a child hinders it from growing is found in France, Belgium, Germany, Austria, and Syria ; in Syria, Germany, and Bohemia the mischief can be remedied by stepping over the child in the opposite direction.[13]

[1] Rev. J. H. Weeks, "Customs of the Lower Congo People," *Folk-lore*, xx. (1909) p. 474.

[2] B. Gutmann, "Trauer und Begräbnissitten der Wadschagga," *Globus*, lxxxix. (1906) p. 199.

[3] E. Aymonier, *Voyage dans le Laos*, i. (Paris, 1895) p. 144.

[4] C. Lumholtz, *Unknown Mexico* (London, 1903), i. 435.

[5] E. M. Curr, *The Australian Race*, i. 50.

[6] A. W. Howitt, *Native Tribes of South-East Australia*, p. 402.

[7] Father Lambert, *Mœurs et superstitions des Néo-Calédoniens*, pp. 192 *sq.*

[8] P. von Stenin, "Das Gewohnheitsrecht der Samojeden," *Globus*, lx. (1891) p. 173.

[9] J. Richardson, in *Antananarivo Annual and Madagascar Magazine, Reprint of the First Four Numbers* (Antananarivo, 1885), p. 529; *id.*, *Reprint of the Second Four Numbers* (Antananarivo, 1896), p. 296 ; J. Sibree, *The Great African Island*, p. 288; compare De Flacourt, *Histoire de la grande isle Madagascar* (Paris, 1658), p. 99.

[10] J. Mooney, "Myths of the Cherokee," *Nineteenth Annual Report of the Bureau of American Ethnolgoy*, pt. i. (Washington, 1900) p. 424.

[11] H. A. Junod, "Les Conceptions physiologiques des Bantou sud-africains," *Revue d'Ethnographie et de Sociologie*, i. (1910) p. 138, note [3].

[12] F. S. Krauss, *Volksglaube und religiöser Brauch der Südslaven*, p. 52.

[13] See L. F. Sauvé, *Folk-lore des Hautes-Vosges*, p. 226, compare pp. 219 *sq.* ; E. Monseur, *Le Folk-lore Wallon*, p. 39; A. Wuttke, *Der deutsche Volksaberglaube*,[2] § 603; J. W. Wolf, *Beiträge zur deutschen Mytho-*

logie, i. p. 208, § 42; J. A. E. Köhler, *Volksbrauch,* etc., *im Voigtlande,* p. 423; A. Kuhn und W. Schwartz, *Norddeutsche Sagen, Märchen und Gebräuche,* p. 462, § 461; E. Krause, "Abergläubische Kuren und sonstiger Aberglaube in Berlin," *Zeitschrift für Ethnologie,* xv. (1883) p. 85; R. H. Kaindl, *Die Huzulen,* p. 5; J. V. Grohmann, *Aberglauben und Gebräuche aus Böhmen und Mähren,* p. 109, §§ 798, 799; Eijüb Abëla, "Beiträge zur Kenntniss abergläubischer Gebräuche in Syrien," *Zeitschrift des deutschen Palästina-Vereins,* vii. (1884) p. 81; compare B. Chemali, "Naissance et premier âge au Liban," *Anthropos,* v. (1910) p. 741.

INDEX

THE END

Printed by R. & R. CLARK, LIMITED, *Edinburgh.*